The Afterlife in Akhmim

Exploring El-Salamuni Tombs C1 and C3

WAHID OMRAN

BAR INTERNATIONAL SERIES 3137 | 2023

Published in 2023 by
BAR Publishing, Oxford, UK

BAR International Series 3137

The Afterlife in Akhmim

ISBN 978 1 4073 5999 1 paperback
ISBN 978 1 4073 6000 3 e-format

DOI https://doi.org/10.30861/9781407359991

A catalogue record for this book is available from the British Library

© Wahid Omran 2023

COVER IMAGE *The court of the judgment, the north wall, the antechamber – Tomb C1 (photo: W. Omran).*

The Author's moral rights under the 1988 UK Copyright, Designs and Patents Act, are hereby expressly asserted.

All rights reserved. No part of this work may be copied, reproduced, stored, sold, distributed, scanned, saved in any form of digital format or transmitted in any form digitally, without the written permission of the Publisher.

Links to third party websites are provided by BAR Publishing in good faith and for information only. BAR Publishing disclaims any responsibility for the materials contained in any third party website referenced in this work.

BAR titles are available from:

BAR Publishing
122 Banbury Rd, Oxford, OX2 7BP, UK
info@barpublishing.com
www.barpublishing.com

Of Related Interest

Excavations in Akhmīm, Egypt
Continuity and change in city life from late antiquity to the present. First Report
Sheila McNally and Ivančica Dvoržak Schrunk

BAR International Series **590** | 1993

https://doi.org/10.30861/9780860547600

Tell Timai, (Egypt) 2009-2020
The Ptolemaic–Roman north western temple zone and Roman city excavations
James E. Bennett

BAR International Series **3127** | 2023

https://doi.org/ 10.30861/9781407360737

Africa, Egypt and the Danubian Provinces of the Roman Empire
Military and religious interactions (2nd -3rd centuries AD)
Edited by Ștefana Cristea, Călin Timoc and Eric C. De Sena

BAR International Series **3058** | 2021

https://doi.org/10.30861/9781407359045

Kom Tuman II: Late Period to Graeco-Roman Pottery, Volumes I and II
Sabine A. Laemmel

BAR International Series **3037** | 2021

https://doi.org/10.30861/9781407358000

L'eau dans les espaces et les pratiques funéraires d'Alexandrie aux époques grecque et romaine (IVe siècle av. J.-C. - IIIe siècle ap. J.-C.)
Agnès Tricoche

BAR International Series **1919** | 2009

https://doi.org/10.30861/9781407304021

Corpus of Inscriptions of the Herakleopolitan Period from the Memphite Necropolis
Translation, commentary and analyses
Khaled Abdalla Daoud

BAR International Series **1459** | 2005

https://doi.org/10.30861/9781841718972

The Architectural Decoration of Marina el-Alamein
An analysis and catalogue of the late Hellenistic and Roman decorative architectural features of the town and cemetery
Rafal Czerner

BAR International Series **1942** | 2009

https://doi.org/10.30861/9781407304229

The Afterlife in Akhmim

L'architecture et les pratiques funéraires dans l'Égypte romaine
Volume I Synthèse. Volume II Catalogue
Gael Cartron

BAR International Series 2398 | 2012

https://doi.org/10.30861/9781407309934

Nazlet Tuna
An Archaeological Survey in Middle Egypt
Joyce A. Tyldesley and S. R. Snape

BAR International Series 414 | 1988

https://doi.org/10.30861/9780860545330

For more information, or to purchase these titles, please visit **www.barpublishing.com**

Acknowledgements

This work would not have been possible without the support of many people. I would like to take this chance to express my sincere gratitude and deepest thanks.

First and foremost, praises and thanks to God, the Almighty, for His showers of blessings throughout my research and work. I am also extremely grateful to my family, and especially to my wife, for their continuous care, support, and sacrifices to help me finish this work. I send my love to my sons Omar and Yassin, who are the apples of my eye, and who light up my life.

I would like especially to acknowledge the *Gerda Henkel Foundation (the Patrimiones Program AZ 12/BE/20)* for supporting and funding the project 'The Documentation and Investigation of the Great Heritage Value of ElSalamuni Tombs C1 and C3' (2020/2021). The project includes the study of both tombs at the Lehrstühl für Ägyptologie in Würzburg, Germany with the assistance of Prof. Dr Martin Stadler.

I am grateful to the Ministry of Tourism and Antiquities for their permission to document and study the El-Salamuni necropolis. I am very fortunate that I received such kind cooperation and help from Mr Ashraf Okasha, the Head of the Sohag Antiquities Office, as well as from Mr Abdellah Abou Gebel, the head of east Sohag Antiquities Office and Mr Samir Abdelatif, the head of Akhmim Antiquities Office who spent their precious time and efforts to help me overcome multiple problems during my work. I also take this opportunity to express a deep sense of gratitude to all the project members, and especially to the four professional Egyptian conservators who successfully treated and helped revive tomb C1. Their names are: Mr Mohamed Abou el-Makarem (supervisor), Mr Ramdan Ahmed, Mr Mahmoud el-Sherif, and Mr Hossam Faisal.

I would also like to thank Jacqueline M. Huwyler for her great efforts and time in the editing of this book via BAR Publishing. Many thanks to Prof. Dr Susanne Bickel for providing funding for the publication of this manuscript via the University of Basel, Switzerland.

Contents

List of figures ix
List of tables xvii

Abstract xviii
    a.1: A Historical Overview of the Site xviii
    a.2: An Archaeological Overview of the Site xviii
    a.3: The Documentation of the Site To-Date xix

1. Panopolis: An Overview 1

2. The Necropoleis of Akhmim 15
    2.1: El-Hawawish A (Naga al-Diabat, or 'the Ridge Cemetery') 15
    2.2: El-Hawawish B, or 'Bayt El-Madina' 22
    2.3: El-Salamuni C 23

3. A History of the Investigations and Surveys of El-Salamuni 27
    3.1: Travellers and Visitors to the Site 27
    3.2: Recent Excavations 31
    3.3: Typology and Topography 31
    3.4: The Rock-Cut Temple of El-Salamuni 33
    3.5: The Characteristics of El-Salamuni 41
        3.5.1: Typology 41
        3.5.2: Heritage Significance 45
        3.5.3: Funerary Art 48
        3.5.4: Burial Customs 57
    3.6: A Risk Assessment of El-Salamuni 63
        3.6.1: Heritage Risks 66
        3.6.2: Urban Risks 68
        3.6.3: Environmental Risks 68
        3.6.4: Black Bitumen 69

4. Tomb C1: The So-called 'Tomb of von Bissing' (1897) 71
    4.1 Location and History of Investigations 71
    4.2: Layout of the Tomb 78
        4.2.1: The Antechamber 81
        4.2.2: The Southern A3 Wall: Left Jamb of the Entrance, The Upper Register 81
        4.2.3: The Southern A3 Wall: Left Jamb of the Entrance, The Lower Register 86
        4.2.4: The Southern A3 Wall: Right Jamb of the Entrance 86
        4.2.5: The Western A4 Wall: Overview 86
        4.2.6: The Upper Register of the Western A4 Wall 87
        4.2.7: The Lower Register of the Western A4 Wall 93
        4.2.8: The Northern A1 Wall: Left Jamb of the Doorway 96
        4.2.9: The Inner Right Side of the Doorway Leading Into the Burial Chamber 105
        4.2.10: The Eastern A2 Wall: Overview 105
        4.2.11: The Upper Register of the Eastern A2 Wall 105
        4.2.12: The Lower Register of the Eastern A2 Wall 107
        4.2.13: The Zodiac Ceiling 111
        4.2.14: The Burial Chamber 115
        4.2.15: The Southern B3 Wall 118
        4.2.16: The Eastern Upper Frieze to the Right of the Doorway 118
        4.2.17: The Eastern Lower Frieze to the Right of the Doorway 119
        4.2.18: The Western Left Side the Entrance 119
        4.2.19: The Upper Frieze to the Left of the Entrance 120
        4.2.20: The Lower Frieze to the Left of the Entrance 121

- 4.2.21: The Western B4 Wall: Overview 121
- 4.2.22: The Lower Frieze on the Western B4 Wall 121
- 4.2.23: The Wall B4 Niche 125
- 4.2.24: The B4 Wall to the Left of the Niche 128
- 4.2.25: The Northern B1 Wall: Overview 131
- 4.2.26: The Lower Register of Wall B1 131
- 4.2.27: The Upper Frieze to the Left of the B1 Niche 133
- 4.2.28: The Eastern Burial Niche in Wall B1 133
- 4.2.29: The Eastern B2 Wall 138
- 4.2.30: The Upper Frieze to the Right of the Wall B2 Niche 139
- 4.2.31: The Upper Frieze to the Left of the Wall B2 Niche 141
- 4.2.32: The Wall B2 Niche 141
- 4.2.33: The Lower Register of Wall B2 144
- 4.2.34 The Ceiling of the Burial Chamber 144
- 4.3: The Patron of the Tomb and its Date 146
- 4.4: The Most Recent Conservation Work 148
- 4.5: Previous Documentation and Conservation Efforts 149
- 4.6: An Assessment of the Condition of the Tomb 149
- 4.7: Some General Observations on the Construction and Decay of the Tomb 149
  - 4.7.1: The Superficial Decay of the Walls and Ceilings 149
  - 4.7.2: The Decay of the Paint Layer on the Walls and Ceilings 150
  - 4.7.3: The Decay of the Pictorial and Preparatory Layers of Paint 151
  - 4.7.4: The Decay of the Support Layer of the Walls and Ceilings 152
- 4.8: The Methodology of the Treatment of Tomb C1 152
- 4.9: The Processing of the Tomb To-Date 152
  - 4.9.1: The Documentation of the Tomb 152
  - 4.9.2: The Pre-Consolidation of the Damaged Areas 153
  - 4.9.3: The Mechanical Cleaning of the Tomb 153
  - 4.9.4: The Chemical Cleaning Process 153
  - 4.9.5.: The Consolidation Process 154
  - 4.9.6: The Treatment of the Fragments 154
  - 4.9.7: The Cracks in the Walls and Their Treatment by Injections 155
  - 4.9.8: The Masonry Work Undertaken for the Niches 156
  - 4.9.9: Filling the Gaps in the Tomb Walls 156

5. Tomb C3 159
- 5.1: The Location and Layout 159
  - 5.1.1: The Antechamber 159
  - 5.1.2: The Northern A4 Wall 159
  - 5.1.3: The Eastern A1 Wall: An Overview 161
  - 5.1.4: The Upper Register of the Eastern A1 Wall 161
  - 5.1.5: The Lower Register of the Eastern A1 Wall 163
  - 5.1.6: The Southern A2 Wall 167
  - 5.1.7: The Western A3 Wall 169
  - 5.1.8: The Ceiling 170
  - 5.1.9: The Burial Chamber 170
  - 5.1.10: The Inner Part of the Wall B3 Doorjamb 170
  - 5.1.11: The Lower Frieze on the Northern Part of Wall B3 172
  - 5.1.12: The Eastern Side of Wall B3: The Upper Frieze 173
  - 5.1.13: The Western Side of Wall B3: The Upper Frieze 174
  - 5.1.14: The Eastern B4 Wall 176
  - 5.1.15: The Southern B1 Wall 181
  - 5.1.16: The Western B2 Wall 181
  - 5.1.17: The Lower Registers in the Burial Chamber 185
  - 5.1.18: The Ceiling 185
  - 5.1.19: The Floor 187
- 5.2: The Patron and Date of the Tomb 187

6. Conclusion 191

Bibliography 195

List of figures

Figure 1.1. The *Ptolemagrios* monument, the so-called 'Agrios Pillar' of Panopolis, the Cairo Museum 11

Figure 1.2a. The ruined temple of Min in Akhmim 13

Figure 1.2b. A Roman calcite statue of Venus(?) in the Open-Air Museum............ 13

Figure 1.2c. A Roman Period structure which may be a magazine 14

Figure 2.1. The Akhmim cemeteries, Kuhlmann, *SDAIK* 11, 53............ 16

Figure 2.2. An overview of the cemetery of El-Hawawish A ('el-Tallah')............ 16

Figure 2.3. The location of El-Salamuni Mountain from El-Hawawish A cemetery............ 17

Figure 2.4. Remains of some mudbrick constructions in the cemetery before the rock-cut Ptolemaic tombs 21

Figure 2.5. The entrance of the Ptolemaic rock-cut tomb of Tutu with a mud brick entrance 22

Figure 2.6a. The Coptic remains in the El-Hawawish B tombs............ 23

Figure 2.6b. A Coptic inscription from El-Hawawish B............ 23

Figure 2.7. The tombs along the upper terraces of El-Hawawish B 24

Figure 2.8. El-Salamuni village, to the south of El-Salamuni Mountain............ 24

Figure 2.9. El- Sawâma- sharq village and the Muslim cemetery to the north of El-Salamuni Mountain............ 25

Figure 2.10. El-Salamuni, as approached from Akhmim............ 25

Figure 3.1. An architrave with a zodiac from the temple of Min, Kuhlmann, *SDAIK* 11, 44 after Wilkinson and Burton ... 28

Figure 3.2. The attempts at hiding façade-entrances of certain tombs by the Akhmim Inspectorate............ 31

Figure 3.3a. The Old Kingdom tombs on both sides of the temple of Ay 32

Figure 3.3b. Niches and damaged benches in one of the Old Kingdom tombs 32

Figure 3.4. An underground shaft of an Old Kingdom tomb, located north of the temple of Ay 32

Figure 3.5a. A C2-type tomb of the Late and Ptolemaic Periods, Kuhlmann, *SDAIK* 11, 77, fig. 24 33

Figure 3.5b. Shaft tombs along the upper terraces of the southern section of El-Salamuni Mountain 33

Figure 3.6. The layout of the so-called 'Tomb of von Bissing (1913)', von Bissing, *ASAE* 50, 560, fig.7............ 33

Figure 3.7a. A C3-type tomb of the Roman Period, Kuhlmann, *SDIAK* 11, 79, fig. 27 34

Figure 3.7b. Tombs of the C3-type, which are cut into some tombs of the C2-type, Kuhlmann, *SDAIK* 11, 78, fig. 26.. 34

Figure 3.8. A C4-type tomb of the Late Roman Period, von Bissing, *ASAE* 50, 566, fig.10............ 34

Figure 3.9. The temple of Ay on the uppermost part of the northern section of El-Salamuni Mountain 35

Figure 3.10. The Ptolemaic quarry to the north of the temple of Ay 36

Figure 3.11. The layout of the temple of Ay at El-Salamuni, Kuhlmann., *MDAIK* 35, 167, fig.1............ 37

Figure 3.12. Ay and Tiye in the act of adoring Min, Isis, Horus, and Aperet-Isis. Seen on the left side of the entrance .. 38

Figure 3.13a. The soot that covers the doorway of the *pronaos* (F) into the sanctuary (G)............ 39

Figure 3.13b. Chamber B, to the left of the forecourt............ 39

Figure 3.13c. Hormaacheru shown making libations before six figures of Min on the southern wall of chamber D 40

Figure 3.14. The *anachoretes* crypt in the sanctuary of the temple of Ay 40

Figure 3.15. El-Salamuni Mountain............ 41

The Afterlife in Akhmim

Figure 3.16a. The first slope of El-Salamuni Mountain..42

Figure 3.16b. The second slope of El-Salamuni Mountain..42

Figure 3.16c. The third slope of El-Salamuni Mountain 42

Figure 3.16d. The fourth slope of El-Salamuni Mountain 42

Figure 3.16e. The fifth slope of El-Salamuni Mountain 42

Figure 3.16f. The sixth slope of El-Salamuni Mountain..42

Figure 3.17. The terraces on the southern section of El-Salamuni Mountain..43

Figure 3.18. Shallow trenches on the lower terrace of the northern section of El-Salamuni Mountain..............................43

Figure 3.19. A rock-cut stela of a kneeling pharaoh, located south of the temple of Ay 43

Figure 3.20a. The southern section of El-Salamuni Mountain, which is the location of El-Hawawish Mountain 44

Figure 3.20b. An overview of the southern section of El-Salamuni Mountain 44

Figure 3.21a. The northern section of El-Salamuni Mountain 45

Figure 3.21b. The distribution of the most important tombs on the northern section of El-Salamuni Mountain..............45

Figure 3.22. The so-called 'honeycomb tombs', located on the middle register of the southern section..........................46

Figure 3.23. Landslide Roman tombs on the lower terraces of the southern section of El-Salamuni Mountain 46

Figure 3.24. The layout of Tomb B7, Philippe Soubias, *CEAlex* 2015..47

Figure 3.25. An unregistered tomb that is only decorated with lower *orthostates*, found on the northern section of El-Salamuni Mountain...50

Figure 3.26a. The Roman *orthostates* style, as seen in the antechamber of tomb C4 on the northern section of El-Salamuni Mountain. 51

Figure 3.26b. Another example of the *orthostates* style, this time in an unregistered tomb from the northern section of El-Salamuni Mountain 51

Figure 3.27. Trees flanking a damaged figure of the deceased in tomb C8, which is on the southern section of El-Salamuni Mountain...51

Figure 3.28. A bird that adorns some *orthostates* of an unregistered tomb located north of tomb F5, on the register below it...51

Figure 3.29. Festoons and flowers that decorate the ceiling of tomb C8 on the southern section of El-Salamuni Mountain...52

Figure 3.30. Some geometrical decorations from a New Kingdom tomb(?), just to the south of the temple of Ay..........52

Figure 3.31. A partially faded zodiac on the ceiling of an unregistered tomb on the northern section of El-Salamuni Mountain...56

Figure 3.32. The plastered floor of the burial niche in tomb C6, located on the southern section of El-Salamuni Mountain 58

Figure 3.33a. A hollowed niche in tomb B2, which is located on the southern section of El-Salamuni Mountain 58

Figure 3.33b. A flat and hollowed-out burial niche from tomb B2, on the northern section of El-Salamuni Mountain above Tomb C1..58

Figure 3.34. Two adjacent burial niches placed in the same wall, as seen in an unregistered tomb from the southern section of El-Salamuni Mountain, above register F 59

Figure 3.35. An underground shaft located below the burial niche of an unregistered tomb on the southern section of El-Salamuni Mountain 59

Figure 3.36. The sandal decorations found in the burial niche of an unregistered tomb on the southern section of El-Salamuni Mountain...60

Figure 3.37. The leg of a funerary bed (Greek: *kline*), found in tomb C6 on the southern section of El-Salamuni Mountain 60

List of figures

Figure 3.38. A glass on a table located to the right of a niche in the burial chamber of tomb F2 60

Figure 3.39. A shallow pit in the antechamber of tomb F1, which is located on the southern section of El-Salamuni Mountain 61

Figure 3.40a. The first slope of El-Salamuni Mountain, which is the location of many mummified animal and a bird *hypogeum*, as well as looting activities 62

Figure 3.40b. Some species of mummified birds and animals from the northern section of El-Salamuni Mountain 62

Figure 3.41a. 'Hawsh El-Gemaal', a quarry of the New Kingdom, located south of the temple of Ay in the southern section of El-Salamuni Mountain 64

Figure 3.41b. Some rock-cut shrines from 'Hawsh El-Gemaal' 64

Figure 3.42. The so-called 'Wadi el-Batikh' on the flat roof of the mountain 64

Figure 3.43a. 'El Birba', the main gallery-quarry located opposite El-Salamuni village 65

Figure 3.43b. The damaged *dromos* of 'El Birba' 65

Figure 3.43c. A graffito in 'El Birba' 65

Figure 3.44a. Overview of the western gallery of the 'El Birba' quarry, covered with sand 66

Figure 3.44b. A damaged *dromos* in front of the eastern gallery of the 'El Birba' quarry 66

Figure 3.45. 'Taket el-Diik', which is located on the southern-most part of El-Salamuni Mountain 66

Figure 3.46a. Mummy shrouds inside an unregistered tomb on El-Salamuni Mountain 67

Figure 3.46b. Mummy shrouds on the terraces of the northern section of El-Salamuni Mountain 67

Figure 3.47. The name 'In Gordon', as found in an unregistered tomb above register F on the southern section of El-Salamuni Mountain 68

Figure 3.48. The expansion of the agricultural lands into the archaeological belt of El-Salamuni Mountain 68

Figure 4.1a. The topography of the northern section of the mountain 72

Figure 4.1b. The location of the Ptolemaic quarry on the most northern part of El-Salamuni Mountain 72

Figure 4.1c. The location of tomb C1 72

Figure 4.2a. The location of tomb C1 at the start of the northern section of El-Salamuni Mountain 73

Figure 4.2b. The location of tomb C1 from the start of the southern section of El-Salamuni Mountain 73

Figure 4.3a. The heavy debris in the antechamber of tomb C1, as photographed in 2015 77

Figure 4.3b. The heavy debris in the antechamber of tomb C1, as photographed in 2015 77

Figure 4.3c. The heavy debris in the burial chamber of tomb C1, as photographed in 2015 77

Figure 4.4 The looters' attempts to cut out some of the scenes in the antechamber of tomb C1 78

Figure 4.5a. The state of the tomb C1 burial chamber and the southern burial niche, as photographed in 2019 79

Figure 4.5b. The state of the tomb C1 east burial niche in 2019 79

Figure 4.6. The antechamber of tomb C1 after cleaning 80

Figure 4.7. The burial chamber of tomb C1 after cleaning 80

Figure 4.8. Part of the original floor of tomb C1, showing the southeast corner of the burial chamber 81

Figure 4.9. The tomb C1 entrance, showing the damaged descending staircases 81

Figure 4.10. The level of the antechamber floor, which is lower than the entrance of the tomb 81

Figure 4.11a. The layout of tomb C1 82

Figure 4.11b. The dimensions of tomb C1 82

Figure 4.11c. A 3D model of tomb C1 82

Figure 4.12a. The locations of tombs B1 and B2 83

The Afterlife in Akhmim

Figure 4.12b. Tomb B2, which is located north of tomb C1 83

Figure 4.13. Von Bissing's layout of tomb C1 83

Figure 4.14. The upper frieze on the south A3 wall of the tomb C1 antechamber 84

Figure 4.15. A figure of Min from tomb B7 86

Figure 4.16. The lower frieze on the south wall of the antechamber of tomb C1 86

Figure 4.17a. Photogrammetry of the south A3 wall of the tomb C1 antechamber, before its restoration in 2019 88

Figure 4.17b. Photogrammetry of the south A3 wall of the tomb C1 antechamber after its restoration in 2021 88

Figure 4.17c. A facsimile of the south A3 wall of tomb C1 89

Figure 4.18. The west A4 wall, as photographed by the German Archaeological Institute (DAI) 89

Figure 4.19. The upper frieze of the west A4 wall of the tomb C1 antechamber, showing the judgement court 90

Figure 4.20. The introduction of the deceased to the judgement court by Maat, as shown in the tomb of Psenosiris at Athribis 90

Figure 4.21. The judgment court in the so-called 'von Bissing tomb (1913)' 91

Figure 4.22a. An image of the deceased male adoring the mummified figure of Osiris 93

Figure 4.22b. The same scene as that of fig. 22a, this time recorded in 2019 93

Figure 4.23a. A procession of daemons along the lower frieze of the west A4 wall in the antechamber of tomb C1 94

Figure 4.23b. The procession of daemons along the lower frieze of the west A4 wall in the antechamber of tomb C1 ... 94

Figure 4.24a. Photogrammetry of the whole west A4 wall (including the upper and lower friezes) of tomb C1 94

Figure 4.24b. A facsimile of the whole west A4 wall (including the upper and lower friezes) of tomb C1 95

Figure 4.24c. A facsimile/reconstruction of the whole west A4 wall of tomb C1 95

Figure 4.25a. The daemons with their knives, as seen in an unregistered tomb from the northern section of El-Salamuni Mountain 97

Figure 4.25b. The daemons standing before their gates, as seen in the tomb of Psenosiris at Athribis 97

Figure 4.26a. The north A1 wall, located in the antechamber of tomb C1, Kaplan, *BzÄ* 16, fig. 87a 100

Figure 4.26b. Photogrammetry of the north A1 wall of tomb C1 (after the restoration in 2021) 100

Figure 4.26c. A facsimile of the north A1 wall of tomb C1 101

Figure 4.27. Dumps of pottery sherds beneath the temple of Ay 102

Figure 4.28. The 21 local judges in the afterlife court, as seen on the north A1 wall of tomb C1 106

Figure 4.29. The east A2 wall of tomb C1, as photographed by the German Archaeological Institute (DAI) 107

Figure 4.30a. Osiris flanked by two female deities 108

Figure 4.30b. The damage done to the previous scene (figure 4.30a) in 2019 108

Figure 4.31a. The lower frieze scene on the east A2 wall of tomb C1 (before the restoration in 2019) 109

Figure 4.31b. The lower frieze scene on the east A2 wall of tomb C1 (after the restoration in 2021) 109

Figure 4.32a. The erotic scene from tomb C1, as photographed in 2015 110

Figure 4.32b. The erotic scene from tomb C1, as recorded by the German Archaeological Institute (DAI) 110

Figure 4.33a. Photogrammetry of the east A2 wall of tomb C1 (before the restoration in 2019) 112

Figure 4.33b. Photogrammetry of the east A2 wall of tomb C1 (after the restoration in 2021) 112

Figure 4.33c. A facsimile of the east A2 wall of tomb C1 113

Figure 4.33d. A reconstruction/facsimile of the damaged parts of the east A2 wall of tomb C1 113

Figure 4.34a. The circular zodiac in tomb C1, as recorded by the German Archaeological Institute (DAI) 116

Figure 4.34b. Photogrammetry of the tomb C1 zodiac (before the restoration in 2019) 116

List of figures

Figure 4.34c. Photogrammetry of the tomb C1 zodiac (after the restoration in 2021) 116

Figure 4.34d. A facsimile of the tomb C1 zodiac 117

Figure 4.34e. A reconstruction/facsimile of the damaged parts of the tomb C1 zodiac 117

Figure 4.35. The presence of silverfish in the burial chamber of tomb C1 118

Figure 4.36. The south B3 wall of tomb C1, which is covered with debris and soot 119

Figure 4.37. The upper frieze of the south B3 wall of tomb C1, to the right of the doorway 119

Figure 4.38. The B3 wall of tomb C1 after removing the soot 120

Figure 4.39. The deceased male in a gesture of veneration in tomb C1 120

Figure 4.40. The west side of the south B3 wall of tomb C1 (before the restoration in 2019) 122

Figure 4.41. Photogrammetry of the upper frieze on the west side of the south B3 wall in tomb C1 122

Figure 4.42. The west side of the south B3 wall of tomb C1, Kanawati, *Sohag in Upper Egypt*, pl. 41 123

Figure 4.43a. Photogrammetry of the west side of the south B3 wall of tomb C1 124

Figure 4.43b. A facsimile drawing of the south B3 wall of tomb C1 124

Figure 4.43c. A reconstruction/facsimile of the south B3 wall of tomb C1 125

Figure 4.44a. The heavy debris covering the west B4 wall of tomb C1 125

Figure 4.44b. The west B4 wall of tomb C1 after removing the debris 125

Figure 4.45. The male deities' procession before Osiris-Sokar, as depicted on the lower frieze of the west
B4 wall of tomb C1 126

Figure 4.46. Haryotes(?) shown guiding a deceased male in tomb F3, which is located on the southern
section of El-Salamuni Mountain 126

Figure 4.47. The damaged west burial niche in the B4 wall of tomb C1 126

Figure 4.48a. The back of the west burial niche on wall B4 of tomb C1 (after the restoration in 2021) 127

Figure 4.48b. A facsimile of the west burial niche in tomb C1 127

Figure 4.48c. A reconstruction drawing of the west burial niche in tomb C1 127

Figure 4.49a. The wall left of the niche in tomb C1 (before the restoration in 2019) 128

Figure 4.49b. The wall left of the niche in tomb C1 (after the restoration in 2021) 129

Figure 4.50. A depiction of Shu raising the *pt* sign of the sky in tomb C1 129

Figure 4.51. Vignette 17 of the Book of the Dead, as depicted on the south wall of the antechamber of tomb F2 132

Figure 4.52. Vignette 17 of the Book of the Dead, as seen in the tomb of Tutu at El-Hawawish cemetery A 133

Figure 4.53a. Photogrammetry of the west B4 wall of tomb C1 134

Figure 4.53b. A facsimile of the west B4 wall of tomb C1 135

Figure 4.54a. The north B1 wall of tomb C1 (before the restoration in 2019) 136

Figure 4.54b. The damaged burial niche on the north B1 wall of tomb C1 136

Figure 4.54c. The north B1 wall of tomb C1 (after the restoration in 2021) 136

Figure 4.55a. The wall below the burial niche in tomb C1, as photographed by the German Archaeological
Institute (DAI), Kuhlmann, *SDAIK* 11, fig. 36 c 137

Figure 4.55b. A coloured photo of the damaged north B1 niche in tomb C1, Kaplan, *BzÄ* 16, fig. 88c 137

Figure 4.56. A reconstruction/facsimile of the whole procession scene of the B1 niche, found in tomb C1 138

Figure 4.57a. The soot covering the upper frieze to the left of the B1 niche in tomb C1 (before restoration) 139

Figure 4.57b. The deceased adoring Osiris while Isis stands behind him. The scene is found on the upper
frieze to the left of the B1 niche in tomb C1 (after the restoration in 2021) 139

Figure 4.57c. A facsimile of the B1 wall in tomb C1 139

Figure 4.58. The back wall of the north B1 niche of tomb C1 140

Figure 4.59a. A hieroglyphic column on the north B1 niche of tomb C1 140

Figure 4.59b. A second hieroglyphic column on the north B1 niche in tomb C1 140

Figure 4.60a. The left side of the wall of the B1 niche in tomb C1. 141

Figure 4.60b. A facsimile of the wall to the left of the B1 niche in tomb C1 141

Figure 4.60c. A facsimile of the back and lateral east walls of the burial niche on wall B1 of tomb C1 141

Figure 4.61a. The east B2 wall of tomb C1 (before the restoration in 2019) 142

Figure 4.61b. The east B2 wall of tomb C1 (after removing the debris) 142

Figure 4.62a. The soot covering the upper frieze to the right of the B2 niche in tomb C1 143

Figure 4.62b. The deceased adoring a seated Anubis, with Isis behind the god (after the restoration in 2021) 143

Figure 4.63a. The soot covering the upper frieze of the wall to the right of the B2 niche in tomb C1 143

Figure 4.63b. A recumbent Anubis on the upper frieze of the wall left of the B2 niche in tomb C1 143

Figure 4.64. The back wall of the B1 niche in tomb C1 (before restoration) 144

Figure 4.65. Recumbent jackals and *khekrew* signs, shown adorning the back wall of tomb C1 (after restoration) 145

Figure 4.66a. The dimensions of the damaged part of the B2 niche back wall, found in tomb C1 145

Figure 4.66b. A facsimile of the back wall of the B1 niche, found in a tomb C1 145

Figure 4.66c. A reconstruction drawing of the damaged parts on the back wall of the B1 niche, as seen in tomb C1 ... 145

Figure 4.67. A depiction of a tree goddess pouring water for the *ba* of the deceased 146

Figure 4.68. The deceased adoring a recumbent jackal, as seen on the left lateral wall of the B2 niche 146

Figure 4.69a. Photogrammetry of the whole B2 wall in tomb C1 147

Figure 4.69b. A facsimile of the whole B2 wall of tomb C1 147

Figure 4.70a. The superficial decay and dirt covering the upper frieze of the west A4 wall of the antechamber 150

Figure 4.70b. The soil covering the lower wall of the north B1 niche of the burial chamber 150

Figure 4.71. The presence of surface deposits such as wasp and spider nests on the ceiling of the burial chamber 150

Figure 4.72. The use of ancient mortar on the ceiling of the antechamber, probably during the Coptic hermitage in the tomb 151

Figure 4.73. An image of the decay of the wall's paint layer, showing the patron of the tomb 151

Figure 4.74. The documentation of the damage by the conservators 152

Figure 4.75. The pre-consolidation process in the tomb, as carried out by the conservators 153

Figure 4.76a. The mechanical cleaning carried out in tomb C1 with the help of a *weishab* sponge 154

Figure 4.76b. The chemical cleaning of the soot by use of a suitable poultice on the walls of the tomb 154

Figure 4.76c. Another example of using a poultice for the chemical cleaning process, this time on the ceiling of the burial chamber 154

Figure 4.77. The consolidation of the vulnerable edges of the plaster 154

Figure 4.78. Fixing and re-gluing the small, fallen pieces of wall 154

Figure 4.79. The injection of material into a crack in the tomb C1 wall 155

Figure 4.80a. The damaged north B1 burial niche, as shown in the burial chamber, before the conservation work 156

Figure 4.80b. Masonry work in the north B1 burial niche 156

Figure 4.80c. The north B1 burial niche after the masonry work 156

Figure 4.81a. The addition of a mortar lining to the upper register of the eastern A2 wall of the tomb C1 antechamber .. 157

List of figures

Figure 4.81b. The scratching of the mortar lining on the upper register of the eastern A2 wall of the tomb C1 antechamber 157

Figure 5.1a. The topography of the southern section of El-Salamuni Mountain 160

Figure 5.1b. The location of tomb C3, below the security hut 160

Figure 5.1c. The façade-entrance of tomb C3.. 160

Figure 5.2. The layout of tomb C3... 161

Figure 5.3a. Photogrammetry of the north A4 wall of the antechamber in tomb C3..................................... 162

Figure 5.3b. A facsimile of the north A4 wall of tomb C3... 162

Figure 5.4. The Court of Judgement, as shown on the upper register of the east A1 wall in tomb C3 164

Figure 5.5. The whole scene of the lower register of the east A1 wall in tomb C3 164

Figure 5.6a. Photogrammetry of the whole east A1 wall of tomb C3 165

Figure 5.6b. A facsimile of the east A1 wall of tomb C3... 165

Figure 5.6c. A deterioration map of the east A1 wall of tomb C3 166

Figure 5.7. Photogrammetry of the south A2 wall of tomb C3.. 168

Figure 5.8. Bes in the Court of Judgement scene, as depicted in the burial chamber of tomb F2.................. 170

Figure 5.9a. Photogrammetry of the west A3 wall of tomb C3 171

Figure 5.9b. A deterioration map of the west A3 wall of tomb C3 172

Figure 5.10. The ceiling of the antechamber of tomb C3 173

Figure 5.11a. A female (a mourner) shown welcoming a visitor on the interior right side of the doorway into the burial chamber of tomb C3 173

Figure 5.11b. Another figure of a damaged female (a mourner). The scene comes from the interior left side of the doorway into the tomb C3 burial chamber 173

Figure 5.12. The lower *orthostates* on the north B3 wall of tomb C3 174

Figure 5.13a. Photogrammetry of the north B3 wall of the tomb C3 burial chamber................................... 175

Figure 5.13b. A facsimile of the north B3 wall of the tomb C3 burial chamber.. 175

Figure 5.14a. Photogrammetry of the east B4 wall in the tomb C3 burial chamber 177

Figure 5.14b. A facsimile of the east B4 wall in the tomb C3 burial chamber 177

Figure 5.14c. A deterioration map of the east B4 wall in the tomb C3 burial chamber................................. 178

Figure 5.14d. An image of the deceased shown adoring some *genni* mummiform figures............................. 178

Figure 5.14e. Photogrammetry of the east walls A1 (in the antechamber), and B4 (in the burial chamber) of tomb C3 ... 179

Figure 5.15. A depiction of the reborn tomb owner in a solar barque, flanked by two ladies (Isis and Nephthys)......... 179

Figure 5.16. A scene of the reborn tomb owner in a solar barque, flanked by two ladies (Isis and Nephthys)............... 180

Figure 5.17a. A winged vulture surmounting the ceiling of a burial niche on the south B1 wall of tomb C3 182

Figure 5.17b. Photogrammetry of the south B1 wall of tomb C3... 182

Figure 5.18a. Photogrammetry of the west B2 wall of tomb C3 183

Figure 5.18b. A facsimile of the west B2 wall of tomb C3.. 183

Figure 5.18c. A deterioration map of the west B2 wall of tomb C3 184

Figure 5.18d. Photogrammetry of the west walls A3 (the antechamber), and B2 (the burial chamber) of tomb C3 184

Figure 5.19. The offering of *ṯ3w* breath (first vignette), along with the veneration of the four sons of Horus 185

Figure 5.20. An image of a deceased male venerating a seated damaged deity (either Osiris or Osiris-Sokar) 186

Figure 5.21. A deceased male shown venerating a seated damaged Osiris 186

Figure 5.22. A winged vulture surmounting the ceiling of a burial niche on the west B2 wall of tomb C3 186

Figure 5.23. The lower *orthostates* of the tomb C3 the burial chamber 187

Figure 5.24a. Photogrammetry of the ceiling of the tomb C3 burial chamber 188

Figure 5.24b. A facsimile of the ceiling of tomb C3 burial chamber.. 188

Figure 5.24c. A facsimile of the ceilings of tomb C3 ante and burial chambers 189

Figure 5.25. The geometrical squares which cover the ceiling of the so-called 'Tomb 1913 of von Bissing'................ 189

Figure 5.26. The floor of tomb C3 189

List of tables

Table a.1: Overview of Previous Research at El-Salamuni xix

Table 4.1: Stations Created to Document El-Salamuni (First Step) 79

Table 4.2: More Stations Created to Document El-Salamuni (Second Step) 79

Table 4.3: Examples of the Use of Materials for the Grout Injection Process 155

Abstract

This book describes the first long-term scientific work to have been conducted at the site of El-Salamuni. The work has enabled the author to collect valuable data about the history and archaeology of this little-known cemetery, including the architectural and funerary iconography of its tombs, and the serious threats to their preservation. The work undertaken at El-Salamuni includes the documentation, conservation, and investigation of tombs C1 and C3. This book records the results of these efforts. While the El-Salamuni necropolis was widely used during the Late Ptolemaic Period, and even until the Late Roman Period (the second century BC to third century AD), its tombs are still relatively undocumented and unexplored.

a.1: A Historical Overview of the Site

Panopolis (*Ḫnty-Mnw*, Χεμμισ, Χεμμω, or modern 'Akhmim') was the capital of the ninth Upper Egyptian nome, and played a distinct role in the Graeco-Roman Period. It was a Hellenised metropolis with several ethnicities living there, such as Greeks and Romans, and the indigenous Egyptian population. Thus, it was a centre of both traditional Egyptian and classical Greek culture. Panopolis is paradigmatic of Graeco-Roman Egypt as a complex intersection of Egyptian traditions and Hellenistic culture. As early as the mid-fifth century BC, Herodotus reports a large Greek community settling in Khemmis and describes the city as the largest town in the Thebaid nome. Hellenistic-style games were organised there, such as the so-called *Paneia* for the local Greek god Perseus Ouranios. This event is attested to have taken place since at least the fifth century BC. By the third century BC, Panopolis possessed several Greek civic buildings and was already heavily Hellenised. Septimius Severus finally granted the metropolis a city council (*boule*) through which Panopolis became a Greek *polis* in 201 AD. At this time, it became filled with elite Greek citizens. The Panhellenic festivals were an important part of civic life from the third century onwards.

Panopolis was a centre of both traditional Egyptian and classical Greek culture. This distinctive blend of Hellenistic and Egyptian styles in Panopolis characterises not only the world of the living in this period but also the realms of funerary art and architecture; multi-culturalism and the incorporation of classical features into indigenous architecture and iconography became a prominent feature of religious and funerary art in the Graeco-Roman Panopolite nome. The pantheon of Panopolis was therefore varied and vibrant, having its own gods, saints, and martyrs, as well as its own temples and festivals. Unfortunately, the modern town of Akhmim lies on top of the ancient one. Therefore, the ancient city remains virtually unexplored and difficult to access. Its accessible temples have been dismantled by the local community to use as stones for construction. Meanwhile, the rest of the archaeological remains are almost completely inaccessible.

Since the first half of the 18th century, the cemetery of El-Salamuni has been well-known as a regular stopping point for European travellers and Archaeologists. As early as 1743, R. Pococke describes the already partly-pillaged cemetery in one of his publications. The history of archaeological and epigraphical research and investigations of the site is very extensive, as the overview below illustrates:

Three large cemeteries provide rich data with which to study the culture of the town in the Graeco-Roman Period: El-Hawawish A and B, and El-Salamuni (the latter of which is the location of five tombs). El-Salamuni Mountain C, which is located about 4km. east of Akhmim at a height of 400m., was the main necropolis of Panopolis during the Graeco-Roman Period. The ancient El-Faraoukiya canal, now known as El-Isawiah, passes by the foot of the mountain from the southeast to the northwest. During the reign of Ay, a rock-cut temple for Min, Repit/Triphis or 'Aperet-Isis', and the child-god Kolanthes, who together represent the divine triad of Akhmim, was erected on the uppermost part of the mountain, in the centre of the necropolis. The temple was expanded under Ptolemy II Philadelphus.

a.2: An Archaeological Overview of the Site

The El-Salamuni cliffs are honeycombed with tombs dating from the Old Kingdom to the Roman period. Out of the necropoleis of El-Hawawish A, B, and El-Salamuni, El-Salamuni is the most unknown, with the least amount of information available about its funerary art and burial customs. Unlike El-Hawawish B, the tombs of which have been completely studied and published, published material about El-Salamuni is scarce. The numerous stelae and other funerary objects known from the region were found almost exclusively at El-Hawawish A. They provide valuable information about the local deities and clergy in the Ptolemaic Period.

The local Akhmim Antiquities Inspectorate divided El-Salamuni Mountain into eight terraces (A to H) from the bottom of the hill to the top. The recorded tombs of the Ptolemaic and Roman Periods are mainly located on terraces A–F, while terraces G and H contain tombs of the Old and New Kingdoms and the Late Period. It is here that one can find the unpublished tombs C1 and C3, which are the subject of the author's ongoing investigations.

Abstract

Table a.1: Overview of Previous Research at El-Salamuni

1838–1839	N. L'Hôte	Documentation of the decorated tombs with Egyptian scenes and with two circular zodiacs; first sketch of the temple of Ay.
1843–1845	C. Schmidt	Excavation of a tomb with undecorated walls and multiple burials of mummies without coffins, some including portraits and labels.
1897	F. W. von Bissing	Recording of decorated tombs at the foot of the hill, including the so-called 'von Bissing Tomb of 1897'.
1903	J. Clédat	Mentioning of tombs F2, F3, and F4 in a publication.
1906	O. Rubensohn	Description of a Roman tomb in a publication.
1909	M. Rostovtzeff	Documentation of a decorated tomb with a burial niche.
1913	F. W. von Bissing and H. Kees	Examination of the scenes and inscriptions of the temple of Min.
1952	C. F. Nims	Photography of six zodiacs from tombs 3A, 3B, 6, 7, 8A, and 8B.
1957	DAIK	An expedition to El-Salamuni that remains unpublished.
1979-1982	DAIK (Kuhlmann)	A quick survey of Akhmim and its necropoleis, including the creation of an architectural typology of the El-Salamuni tombs.
End of 1980s	N. Kanawati	Cleaning of the 'von Bissing Tomb of 1897'.
1996–1997 2018–2019	Akhmim Inspectorate Office	Uncovering of new painted tombs such as B7 and B1, and the re-discovery and cleaning of other tombs such as F1-F5 and C1-C5.

Tomb C1 was discovered by von Bissing with the help of *fellahin* during his visit to the area in 1897. It is now registered by the Akhmim Inspectorate Office as tomb C1. It is located on the northern section of the mountain, just below the temple of Ay. Meanwhile, tomb C3 lies on the south section of the mountain. Both tombs consist of two chambers, and are painted with Egyptian and Hellenistic influences. Astronomical zodiacs in a Greek style cover the ceiling of the antechamber of tomb C1. Both tombs are invariably of a Roman date.

Von Bissing published tomb C1 in two articles (ASAE 50, and JDAI 61/62). In his publications, he only describes the funerary scenes in the antechamber, and only includes one part of the Court of the Judgement scene. The walls of the burial chamber are fully covered with heavy bitumen, and therefore the burial chamber is still unexplored. Unfortunately, right before the 25th of January revolution, violent robbers plundered the tomb and destroyed the three niches in the burial chamber. They also attempted to cut off some of the friezes in the tomb.

The documentation and investigation of the El-Salamuni tombs C1 and C3, as well as the conservation process for tomb C1, includes four field campaigns to-date. During the first campaign (November-December 2019), the workers cleaned tomb C3 of rubbish and dust, and removed the debris in the antechamber of tomb C1. The second season (October 2020) included efforts to remove heavy debris from the burial chamber of tomb C1. The restorers also started to document all of the vulnerabilities of and risks to the tomb, determining a suitable method of conservation, as well as the materials required for their ongoing preservation efforts. The mechanical cleaning of the tomb was also started. During the third season (May-June 2021), the chemical conservation process was undertaken. Cleaning the walls and the ceilings of the tomb from such a thick layer of soot was a complicated challenge; in many parts of the tomb, the soot was so heavy, oily, and slick that it was impossible to uncover any details behind it. However, many tomb paintings were completely restored by consolidation efforts and by cleaning. During the most recent campaign (November-December 2021), the workers continued to remove the heavy soot covering the large ceiling of the C1 burial chamber. Unfortunately, after being cleaned, it became clear that the ceiling is unpainted; no astronomical decorations were found. The final phase of the conservation efforts of 2021 was to fill the damaged gaps in the walls and ceiling, and to reconstruct the burial niches which were damaged by robbers. For the first time in centuries, the funerary paintings in the burial chamber were made visible.

a.3: The Documentation of the Site To-Date

The preservation of the El-Salamuni tombs is highly threatened by the vast illicit digging activities taking place in the area, as well as by the environment. The safeguarding and virtual documentation of the tombs is therefore imperative and indispensable. Most of the tombs which are partially painted are still accessible. They are doorless, being full of garbage, dust, bats, and harmful reptiles. Furthermore, the mountain is frequently exposed to torrential rains. Because of all these threats, it is possible to lose these great heritage assets at any time.

With the help of various experts and specialists, the tombs were documented. A topographical survey was conducted,

The Afterlife in Akhmim

and the dimensions of the tombs were measured in order to create architectural 3D layouts. An epigraphic study was also undertaken; drawings and facsimiles were made of the funerary scenes, the geometric and floral decorations, the zodiacs, and the hieroglyphic inscriptions. Furthermore, the team used photogrammetric documentation via Meshlab to create VR models of the tombs.

Panopolis: An Overview

Akhmim is a town-site on the east bank of the Nile, opposite modern Sohag. The town lies about 450km. south of Cairo and 200km. north of Luxor[1]. At Akhmim, the Nile makes a deep bend, flowing northeast to southwest. It lies north of the river at the southern edge of a fertile plain that is roughly 20 km.², which is bordered on the east and northeast by high limestone ridges, stretching from the river to the Arabian Plateau[2]. By the 19th century, Akhmim was situated along one of the pilgrimage routes to Mecca.

Since the Pharaonic Period, ancient Akhmim was the capital of the ninth nome of Upper Egypt, known as *Mnw*, or the Panopolite nome[3]. Akhmim itself was called *ḫntj-Mnw* and *Ipw*[4], while the town and its necropolis were named *Snw-t* or *Snt*[5]. In the Graeco-Roman Period, it was named Χεμμισ, 'Chemmis'[6], or Χεμμω, 'Chemmw'. It was known by the Greeks as Πανῶν πόγις, Πανὸς πόγις, and 'Panopolis', the city of the god Pan. Pan was the god of wilderness, and had a strong phallic aspect, being eventually assimilated with the god Min[7]. Later, ϣⲙⲓⲛ, *shmin*, and *khmin* became the Coptic names for Akhmim[8].

The Panopolite nome extends along both the east and the west banks of a bend in the Nile, and is known for its agricultural productivity. Both sides of the river are dominated by their own distinct cluster of villages, sanctuaries, and cemeteries. The metropolis of Panopolis was the most important city on the east side; it played a distinct historical and cultural role during the Graeco-Roman Period of Egypt. Athribis, which was also known as *Ḥw.t-t3-Rpj.t*, Τριφ(ε)ιov, Τριφ(ε)ιov/ Triphion, *atripe* (in Coptic), Sheikh-Hamad (modern), and Wannina al-Gharbiya (modern) was the most important village in the Phenebythis toparchy on the west bank, lying 7km. southwest of Sohag[9]. Min was the primary god of the district, known from the New Kingdom to the Ptolemaic Period as *ḫnt Snw-t*, and holding the epithet *Nb- Snw-t*, or 'the Lord of *Senwt*'[10]. He was worshipped as part of

---

[1] I. Kaplan, *Grabmalerei und Grabreliefs der Römerzeit, Wedisel Wirkungen Zwischen der Ägyptischen und Griechisch-Alexandrinischen Kunst, BzÄ* 16 (Wien 1999), 166.; S. McNally and I. Schrunk, *Excavations in Akhmim, Egypt, Continuity and Change in City Life from Late Antiquity to the Present, First Report, BAR Publishing* 590 (Oxford 1993), 1.

[2] McNally and Schrunk, *Excavations in Akhmim*, 1. Kuhlmann links the fertility of this plain in part to the directions in which flood waters would spread over it. He indicates how the distinguished geographical position of Akhmim, as a fertilized agricultural land, includes a river bend that creates humidity, K. Kuhlmann, *Materialien zur Archaologie und Geschichte des Raumes von Achmim, SDAIK* 11 (Mainz 1983), 4.

[3] W. Helck, *Die altägyptische Gaue* (Wiesbaden 1974), 93–95.; I. Shawn and P. Nicholson, *British Museum Dictionary of Ancient Egypt* (Cairo 2001), 21.; A. Barakat, *Notes of the Ancient Akhmim, ASAE* 66 (1987), 155.

[4] H. Kees, 'Die Schlangensteine und Ihre Beziehungen zu den Reich Sceiligtumern', *ZÄS* 57)1922(, 128. An inscription in the Temple of Min at El-Salamuni, which dates to the reign of Eje (ca. 1300 BC), still refers to Ipu and Khent-Min as two separate cities, H. Kees, 'Das Felsheiligtum des Min bei Achmim', *Rec.Trav.* 36, (1914)., fig III; K. Kuhlmann, 'Der Felstempel des Eje bei Achmim', *MDAIK* 35 (1979), 178.

[5] Barakat, *ASAE* 66, 155. Akhmim and Coptos, and to a lesser extent, Dendera and Edfu, were the main cult centres of Min. Min was called the 'Lord of *Ipu*, who presides at *Senut*, who resides in Dendera'. He was also known as 'Min, Lord of Koptos, Lord of *Ipu*, Lord of *Senut*, the Great God who resides in Edfu', as seen in C. Bleeker, *Die Geburt eines Gottes, eine Studie über den ägyptischen Gott Min und sein Fest*, Studies in the History of Religions: suppl. to no. 3 (Leiden 1966), 26–33, 34–40.

[6] A. Schweitzer, 'L'évolution stylistique et iconographique des parures de cartonnage d'Akhmim du début de l'époque ptolémaïque à l'époque romaine', *BIFAO* 62 (1964), 325–52. There is another place called 'Chemmis' in the Delta, which is the site of the contest between Horus and Seth, J. Zandee, 'A Site of Conflict between Horus and Seth', in P. Prior (ed.), *Exorbe Religionum Studia Geo widengren* (Leiden 1972), 32–33.

[7] P. Borgeaud, *Recherches sur le dieu Pan, Bibliotheca Helvetica Romana* 17 (Geneva 1979). Pan is usually depicted as a hybrid creature with the upper body of a man, a grotesquely leering face, long horns, pointed ears, and the lower body of a goat. He typically grasps a shepherd's flute and staff as his main attributes. For more information on the combination between Min and Pan, see H. Cuvigny, 'Le Crepuscule d'un Dieu, le Declin du Culte de Pan dans le Desert Oriental', *BIFAO* 97 (1997), 139–48.; S. Emmel, 'Ithyphallic Gods and Undetected Ligatures, Pan is not 'Ours'; he is Min (Rectification of a Misreading in a Work of Shenoute)', *GM* 141 (1994), 43–46. A papyrus from the late second century refers to a priest of Pan who is serving in a temple in Panopolis, *CPR* XVIIB, 3,1.6. Pan nevertheless has a clear Egyptian character; he appears as a guard of the desert in Ptolemaic and early Roman dedications in the quarries of Gebel El-Haridi, Gebel Toukh, Mons Claudianus, and Mons Porphyrites. In a dedication to Pan and Serapis in Mons Porphyrites, Pan is depicted in an ithyphallic style similar to that of the Egyptian god Min, V. Maxfield, 'Stone Quarrying in the Eastern Desert with Particular Reference to Mons Claudianus and Mons Porphyrites', in J. Mattingly and J. Salmon (eds.), *Economies Beyond Agriculture in the Classical World*, Leicester-Nottingham Studies in Ancient Society 9 (London, New York 2001), 143–70. Many dedications that were made for Pan *Aerobates* 'who walks in the mountains', and Pan *euodos* 'of the good road', were discovered in the Wadi bir El-Aïn (the 'Valley of the Magic Spring'), located east of El-Hawawish, *I. Pan* 1a.; A. Bernard, *Pan du désert* (Leiden 1977), 1–11. On Pan's epithets, see Bernand, *Pan du désert*, 276–77.

[8] Kees, *ZÄS* 57, 128.; Kuhlmann, *SDAIK* 11, 9–13.; J. Karig, 'Achmim', *LÄ* I, cols. 54–55.; H. Bonnet, 'Panopolis', *RÄRG* (1952), 580.

[9] The Panopolite nome is bordered by the Antaiopolite nome to the north and the Thinite nome to the south. Its northern borders are El-Khazindariya on the east bank and Tahta (ancient Toeto) on the west bank, while its southern west-bank border is El Manschah (ancient Ptolemais Hermiou), extending along the east bank as far south as Kainopolis (Qena). Beyond this, the nome bordered the Coptite nome, C. Kirby, 'Preliminary Report of the First Season of Work at Gebel El-Haridi 1991–1992', *JEA* 78 (1992), 21.; C. Kirby and S. Orel, 'From Cave to Monastery, Transformations at the Nome Frontier of Gebel El-Haridi in Upper Egypt', in R. Mathisen and H. Sivan (eds.), *Shifting Frontiers in Late Antiquity* (Aldershot 1996), 203. From looking at the Sesostris I chapel at Karnak, it is estimated that the Panopolite nome covered about 44km., and measured about 525 km.², which is somewhat equal to the neighbouring Antaiopolite and Thinite nomes, and a little smaller than the Oxyrhynchite nome. It is twice as small as the Hermopolite nome, R. Bagnall, *Egypt in Late Antiquity* (Princeton 1993), 334.

[10] The god Min is called the 'Lord of *Ipu*, who presides at *Senut*, who resides in Dendera'. He is also called 'Min, Lord of Koptos, Lord of *Ipu*, Lord of *Senut*, the Great God who resides in Edfu', S. Aufrère, 'Religious Aspects of the Mine in the Eastern Desert in Ptolemaic and Roman Times (=Autour de l'Univers minéral VIII)', in O. Kaper (ed.), *Life on the Fringe, Living in the Southern Egyptian Deserts During the*

a triad with his consort *T3-Rpj.t*, ('Repit' or 'Triphis' in Greek)[11], and his child Kolanthes, who was originally a form of Horus Harsiesis ('Horus, son of Isis', Harendotes, or Horus, who Protects his Father')[12]. The cult of Min-Triphis-Kolanthes was concentrated at Panopolis and Athribis and spread to the neighbouring nomes[13]. The goddess Wadjet is also widely depicted in the El-Salamuni tombs, and she had a special local cult centre in Akhmim. For instance, the high priest Hormaacheru was called *Hm-ntr w3Di.t*, and served as a priest of Wadjet in the rock temple of Ay in El-Salamuni[14]. Furthermore, another local deity known as 'Thmesios' ('the midwife')[15], served as one of Min's consorts, as a goddess of birth. Bompae was her main local cult centre.

Four main temples are known in the Panopolite nome from the Graeco-Roman Period and are mainly dedicated to the triad. Two temples were erected on each river bank. The ruined temples of Ptolemy IX (Physkon), and the temple of Ptolemy XII (Auletes) have been excavated in Athribis[16],

while the rock-cut temple of Ay, which was later reused in the Ptolemaic Period, lies on the peak of El-Salamuni Mountain[17]. The second one (it is unclear which one) was the main temple of Min, and was the main building of the city. This temple is repeatedly mentioned in sources dating from ancient to medieval times, but today the only remains are the following: two colossal statues, originally of King Ay and his wife Tey (but later usurped by Ramesses II and his daughter-wife Meritamun), a gate, and some ruins of red brick buildings[18].

The temple was still a centre of cultic and religious life in the Early Roman Period, as suggested by the discovery of blocks from the temple ruins mentioning Ptolemais II, IV, X[19], and XII, Nero, Domitian, Trajan, and possibly Antonius Pius[20]. During the Roman period, this temple may have allowed Panopolis to become more culturally important than places such as Koptos, where Min also had a cult centre[21]. Like most of the major temples in Roman Egypt, this temple could have fulfilled not only a traditional cultic purpose, but also political, social, and economic purposes associated with markets, banks, and guilds[22]. In Late Antiquity, the temple was converted into a Coptic nunnery[23]. Later, the temple was dismantled to be used as building material for new mosques, schools, and houses in the modern city[24]. The temple apparently survived in good condition until the 14th century and its

---

Roman and Early Byzantine Periods, Proceedings of a Colloquium Held on the Occasion of the 25th Anniversary of the Nederlands Institute for Archaeology and Arabic Studies in Cairo, 9–12 December 1996 (Leiden 1998), 7.

[11] On the cult of Triphis, see H. Gauthier, 'La déesse Triphis', *BIFAO* 3 (1903), 165–81. The cult of Triphis continued into the fourth century; the title 'Priestess of Triphion' is mentioned in the private letter P. Fouad. 80, written in 332 AD. Furthermore, the name of a priestess (probably of Triphis) called 'Besous' is mentioned in a lawsuit, J. Beaucamp, *Le statut de la femme à Byzance (4e–7e siècle), II. Les pratiques sociales, Travaux et Mémoires du Centre de Recherche d'Histoire et Civilisation de Byzance, Monographies* 6 (Paris 1992), 6.

[12] H. Kees, *Der Götterglaube im alten Ägypten, Mitteilungen der vorderasiatischaegyptischen Gesellschaft, E.V.* 45 (Leipzig 1941), 199–200.; A. Gardiner, *Ancient Egyptian Onomastica II* (London 1968), 41. A royal inscription in Gebel El-Haridi commemorates the opening of the quarry by Ptolemy XIII (71/70 BC), showing him offering to the Panopolite pantheon of Min, Horus, Isis, Horus the Younger, and Triphis, Kirby and Orel, 'From Cave to Monastery', 203. Kolanthes is usually shown wearing a *pschent*, as well as a mantle and whip. As a child-god, he is often shown seated on a lotus similar to Harpocrates, M. Ryhiner, *L'offrande du Lotus dans les temples égyptiens de l'époque tardive, Rites égyptiens* 6 (Brussels 1986).

[13] Kolanthes is first attested in Panopolis from the second century BC, L. Kákosy, 'Probleme der Religion in römerzeitlichen Ägypten', *ANRW* II, 18.5 (Berlin, New York 1995), 2987. The number of names of Kolanthes in the onomastics of Panopolis is striking, and even more bear the names of Min and Triphis. On the cult of Kolanthes, see C. Leitz, 'Ein Hymnus an den Kindgott Kolanthes in Athribis', in S. Lippert, M. Schentuleit, and M. Stadler (eds.), *Sapientia Felicitas, Festschrift für Günter Vittmann zu seinem 64. Geburtstag am 29. Februar 2016, CENiM* 14 (Montpellier 2016), 325–41. A Demotic inscription in the quarry of Gebel Toukh mentions the triad together with Harnebeschinis, another important god of the Panopolite region, W. Spiegelberg, 'Miszellen, Der Gott Kolanthes', *ZÄS* 58 (1923), 155–56.; F. Bilabel, 'Der Gott Kolanthes', *AfP* 8 (1927), 62. The triad(?) may also be mentioned in a Greek dedication of 138/7 BC from Ptolemais, south of Athribis, *SB* III, 6184, l.9.

[14] Kuhlmann, *MDAIK* 35, 186.

[15] Lüdd, *DNB* XIV, 1066–67.; Geens, *Panopolis, a Nome Capital in Egypt*, 316.; K. Vandorpe, 'Identity', in C. Riggs (ed.), *The Oxford Handbook of Roman Egypt* (Oxford 2012), 273.

[16] Since 2003, Athribis has been the focus of a multi-disciplinary research project entitled 'Investigations Into the Archaeology, Philology, and Material and Conservation Science of the Late Ptolemaic/Early Roman Temple of Athribis in Upper Egypt'. The project is being conducted by a joint German-Egyptian team, directed by Tübingen Egyptologists, *http://www.isprs.org/congresses/beijing2008/proceedings/5_pdf/117.pdf*.; C. Leitz, 'Le temple de Ptolemée XII à Athribis- un temple pour Min(-Re) ou pour Repit', *BSFE* 172 (2008), 32–52.; id., 'Le temple d'Athribis en Haute Egypte', *Annuaire de l'Ecole pratiqu des hautes études, Section des sciences religieuses* 115 (2006–07), 85–91.; R. El-

Sayed, *Zur Erforschung des Oberägyptischen Athribis, Erste Ergebnisse aus der Projektarbeit in den Jahren 2003 bis 2006, SOKAR* 13 (2006), 75.; id., 'The Temple of Min and Repit at Athribis', *EA* 32 (2008), 20–24.; R. El-Sayed and Y. El-Masry, *Athribis I, General Site Survey 2003–2007, Archaeological & Conservation Studies, the Gate of Ptolemy IX, Architecture and Inscriptions, IFAO* (Cairo 2012).; C. Leitz, D. Mendel, and Y. El-Masri, *Athribis 2, Der Tempel Ptolemaios XII, die Inschriften und Reliefs der Opfersäle, des Umgangs und der Sanktuarraüme* (Cairo 2010). Other minor Graeco-Roman temples were known in the Panopolite nome, such as the temple of Pan at Plevit (modern Banawit). The remains of a Ptolemaic temple with scenes of Ptolemy XI Alexander I in Banawit are recorded in *PM* V, 5. In 2012, Rafed El-Sayed began his multi-disciplinary project titled 'The Archaeology of Religious Change: The Cultic Topography of the Akhmim District (Upper Egypt) in Late Antiquity' at the Georg August Universität Göttingen. This served as the basis for the later AIS-Min-Panos project.

[17] For more information about this temple, see Kees, *Rec.Trav.* 36, 54.; Kuhlmann, *MDAIK* 35, 165–88.; id., 'Archäologische Forschungen im Raum von Achmim', *MDAIK* 38 (1982), 347–49.

[18] The temple had already existed in the reign of Thutmose III, K. Baedeker, *Egypte, Manuel du Voyageur* (Leipzig 1891), 56.; Kuhlmann, *SDAIK* 11, 22–23. The statue of Meritamun is about 8m. high, and is the tallest female statue known from ancient Egypt.

[19] Champollion first read the name as 'Ptolemaios Philopator', but later changed the name to 'Ptolemaios Philometor X', or 'Alexander I', Kuhlmann, *SDAIK* 11, 46 no. 223.

[20] The history of the temple of Min between the early second century and the Early Christian Period is very vague, Kuhlmann, *SDAIK* 11, 16, 25, 45. The European travellers of the 18th and 19th centuries confirmed the existence of two ruined field temples in the *Birba* at about a 90m. distance from each other, Kuhlmann, *SDAIK* 11, 39–40, fig. 7. Both temples of Min could be Pharaonic. One is a new Ptolemaic-Roman temple.

[21] J. Baines, 'Temples as Symbols, Guarantors and Participants in Egyptian Civilisation', in S. Quirke (ed.), *The Temple in Ancient Egypt, New Discoveries and Recent Research* (London 1997), 232.

[22] On the various roles of the main temples in the Roman period, see A. Bowman, 'Public Buildings in Roman Egypt', *JRA* 5 (1992), 501–02.

[23] Z. Hawass, 'Recent Discoveries at Akhmim', *KMT* 16.1 (2005), 22.

[24] C. Sonnini, *Voyage dans la Haute et Basse Égypte, fait par ordre de l'ancient gouvernement III* (Paris 1880), 144.

eventual demolition in 1350 AD[25]. Ibn-Gubair states that the sun had to rise and set again before he had finished exploring the ruins[26].

A canal that starts east of the temple at Athribis runs almost directly towards the temple of Min at Akhmim on the east bank[27], connecting the two main temples of the nome. A cult statue on a barge would sometimes be brought along the Nile in a ritual comparable to the valley festival in Thebes[28]. The *dromos* of the Athribis temple led to a quay which connected the temple with Akhmim[29]. Funerary hymns on the gate of the Athribis temple imply a processional event[30]. The hymns in the Athribis temple, located at either side of the gate's front, are addressed to Min[31], while the inner inscriptions are dedicated to Repit alone[32]. Min's focal position on the gate may suggest a topographical connection with the main Akhmim temple[33].

Repit-Triphis, the consort of Min-Re, had a strong connection to the west, as the right eye of Re in her temple. She was called 'the Horus Eye in the West' of Athribis[34]. She was associated with Aperet-Isis[35], who was mainly worshipped as the consort of Min on the east bank of the Panopolite nome alongside their child Harendotes, Harsiesis, or Harmuthes (Horus Iounmoutef, *Ḥr-iwn-mw.t =f*)[36]. Aperet-Isis was more commonly known as the main female companion of Min on the east bank of the Panopolite nome[37]. In Akhmim, there was a special relationship between Min and Isis[38]. Many stelae found in El-Salamuni show Aperet-Isis following Min as his consort, described as 'the Lady of *Ipu*'[39]. Therefore, Depauw notes that the female counterpart of Min in the Panopolite nome can be Isis, Aperet-Isis, or Triphis[40]. A mortuary stela from Esna mentions that Aperet-Isis is the queen of all deities and the 'Lady of Panopolis'[41]. Furthermore, the appearance of the title 'Priest of the Beneficent Gods (*n3 ntr. w mnh. w*)' on an offering table strongly suggests that Akhmim housed the royal family cult of Ptolemy III and Berenike II[42].

The papyrus known as P. Berl. Bork contains a fragmentary topographical survey of the city in the early fourth century AD, as well as a register of houses and residents from

---

[25] G. Fowden, *The Egyptian Hermes, A Historical Approach to the Late Pagan Mind* (Princeton 1986), 124.; B. Rogers and D. Rathbone, *Egypt from Alexander to the Copts* (London 2004), 172. Sauneron describes the temple according to a translation of Ibn Gobair, which dates to the 12th century, S. Sauneron, 'Le Temple d'Akhmim describe par Ibn-Gobair', *BIFAO* 51, 123–35. On the damage of the temple, see M. Gabolde, 'La Fin du Temple d'Akhmim', *Akhmim, un tour d'horizon, Egypte, Afrique & Orient* 96 (2020), 53–64.; id., 'La Fin du Temple d'Akhmim', in M. Chauveau et al. (eds.), *Curiosité d'Égypte, entre quête de soi et découverte de l'autre, de l'Antiquité à l'époque contemporaine* (Geneva 2020), 75–104.
[26] The *Birba* temple of Akhmim was comparable to the temples of Dendera and Philae. It was described by Herodotus, *Hdt.* II, 91. The *Birba* temple has been abundantly described in the Arabic literature from the 12th century onwards; it was regarded as equivalent to one of the seven wonders of the world. For the Arabic historians who described the temple, see Kuhlmann, *SDAIK* 11, 25–31, 32–33. The most extensive description of this *Birba* is from Ibn Gobair, who visited Egypt in 1183, giving details of its measurements and its plan, and a vivid picture of its pillars, walls, ceiling, sculptures, and paintings. According to Ibn Gubair, the enormous temple was 86.5 or 106.5m. in width and 118 or 146m. in length, Kuhlmann, *SDAIK* 11, 26 no. 109. This means it was larger than the Edfu temple (79m. x 137m.), and smaller than the temple of Karnak. The temple would have contained 40 Hathoric columns measuring 4m. in diameter and 21m. in height, with a square shape. Ibn Gobair mentions that '*the temple consisted of reception halls, small niches, entrances and exits, ramps, staircases, corridors and entrance openings, so that in its whole groups of people get lost; only by loud screaming can one lead one other's way*', Sauneron, *BIFAO* 51 (1952), 123–35.; Kuhlmann, *SDAIK* 11, 33–35. Kuhlmann recorded the descriptions of modern travellers, Kuhlmann, *SDAIK* 11, 14–49. About this temple, see D. Arnold, *Temples of the Last Pharaohs* (New York, Oxford 1999), 164.; id., *Die Tempel Ägyptens, Götterwohnungen, Kultstätten, Baudenkmäler* (Zürich 1992), 174–76.; A. Basilus, 'Eine Bislang Unpublizierte Priester Statuette aus Dem Ptolemäischen Panopolis', in A. Egberts, B. Muhs, and J. Van Der Vliet (eds.), *Perspectives on Panopolis, an Egyptian Town from Alexander the Great to the Arab Conquest; Acts From an International Symposium, Held in Leiden on 16, 17, and 18 December 1998* (Leiden, 2002), 29.
[27] J. Kosciuk, 'The Architectural Record, General Description of the Individual Areas of the Town and their Monuments', in R. El-Sayed and Y. El-Masry (eds.), *Athribis I*, 133, fig. 2.3.24. From El-Salamuni, the limestone could be transported along canals to the downtown area of the city, Geens, 'Panopolis, a Nome Capital', 301.
[28] On the festival, see M. Fukaya, *The Festivals of Opet, the Valley and the New Year, Their Socio-Religious Functions*, BAR Publishing 28 (Oxford 2019).
[29] V. Altmann-Wendlig, 'Of Min and Moon, Cosmological Concepts in the Temple of Athribis (Upper Egypt)', in G. Rosati and M. Guidotti (eds.), *Proceedings of the XI International Congress of Egyptologists, Florence Egyptian Museum, Florence, 23–30 August 2015* (Oxford 2017), 7.
[30] C. Leitz, R. El-Sayed, D. Mendel, and Y. El-Masry, 'Die Inschriften des Torbaus Ptolemaios IX', in R. El-Sayed and Y. El-Masry (eds.), *Athribis I*, ins. 2, 5–8.
[31] Leitz et al., *Athribis I*, ins. 1, 3, 6, 8.

[32] Leitz et al., *Athribis I*, ins. 4, 5, 9.
[33] Altmann-Wendlig, 'Of Min and Moon' in G. Rosati and M. Guidotti (eds.), *Proceedings of the XI International Congress of Egyptologists*, 8.
[34] F. Petrie, *Athribis* (London 1908), pls. 17, 18, 25, 27, 31, 32. Another one of Min's consorts, named Thmesios, or 'the Midwife', was mentioned on mummy labels from Bompae as Θμεσιως and Ψενθμεσιως, E. Lüddeckens, H. Thissen, and W. Brunsch, *Demotisches Namenbuch*, *DNB* XIV, 1066–67.
[35] A. Gardiner, 'The Supposed Athribis of Upper Egypt', *JEA* 31 (1945), 109.
[36] M.-Th. Derchain-Urtel, 'Epigrafische Anmerkungen zu den Stelen aus Achmim', in A. Egberts et al. (eds.), *Perspectives on Panopolis*, 84.
[37] M. Derchain-Urtel, *Priester im Tempel. Die Rezeption der Theologie der Tempel von Edfu und Dendera in den Privatdokumenten aus ptolemaïscher Zeit*, GOF IV.19 (Wiesbaden 1989), 103–51.
[38] An inscription on the base of a statue of Ramesses II which was recently excavated in Akhmim mentions '(Ramesses) beloved of Horus, son of Isis; beloved of Min, who is in Akhmim; beloved of Horus, who is in Akhmim; beloved of Isis, mother of the god', Y. El-Masry, 'Further Evidence of a Temple of Ramesses II at Akhmim', *MDAIK* 59 (2003), 287.
The myths of Min and Horus were entangled; Min was assimilated with Horus since the Old Kingdom and worshipped as Min-Horus, *RÄRG*, 'Min', 465.; H. Junker, *Die Onourislegende, Die Stundenwachen in den Osirismysterien, Das Götterdekret über das Abaton III* (Wien 1917), 35–36.; H. Kees, *Der Götterglaube im alten Ägypten*, Mitteilungen der vorderasiatischaegyptischen Gesellschaft, E.V. 45 (Leipzig 1941), 199–203. Hence, Min was both the son and husband of Isis in Panopolis.
[39] A. Scharff, 'Ein Denkstein der Römischen Kaiserzeit aus Achmim', *ZÄS* 62 (1927), 88.; Kees, *Rec. Trav.* 36, 35. This combination of Min-Re also appears in the temple of Hapu and other Graeco-Roman temples, H. Gauthier, *Les fêtes du dieu Min*, *RAPH* 2(Cairo 1931) 181–82.; Kees, *ZÄS* 57, 132.
[40] M. Depauw, 'The Late Funerary Material from Akhmim', in A. Egberts et al. (eds.), *Perspectives on Panopolis*, 73.
[41] *LD* II, 167.
[42] *BM* 1215.; A. Budge, *A Guide to the Egyptian Galleries (Sculptures)* (London 1909), 287 no. 1036.

Panopolis in Upper Egypt[43]. The main register has over 430 entries, although there is no direct evidence for the size of Panopolis. However, the register does add more details to the picture of the city, listing several houses owned by priests in addition to several temples [44] in a sort of street-by-street view. According to the register, houses were located along small alleys or at angles to each other. One house-by-house inventory of a quarter of the city was found to contain more than 300 entries of houses (one of which belonged to Petetriphis, the son of Petearbeschinis)[45]. Some houses are recorded as being in ruins, while others have just been built. Each entry occupies one line and records the nature of the property and the property owner(s). Each individual plot (either a house, empty plot, workshop, or a combination of these) is recorded in a single entry, as a list. Borkowski charts 33 professions in Akhmim, as well as the number of people, the religious buildings, and the workspace for each[46]. Personal names found on the papyrus include Greek, Egyptian, and Latin elements, with the Egyptian elements strongly predominating. This may suggest that the population was largely indigenous. However, the use of mixed Egyptian and Greek in words and in names suggests a level of Hellenisation, or at least of multi-culturalism [47].

Since the Roman period, Panopolis has been distinguished by occupational differentiation, housing a variety of workshops of different types, as well as a famous linen textile industry[48]. Strabo[49] notes that Panopolis had the reputation of being an old centre of linen weavers, stonemasons, ship builders, and metal workers (particularly gold smiths), claiming 'and then (one comes) to Panopolis, an old settlement of linen workers and stone workers (Πάνω 'ν πουλίς λινουργῶν και; λυκούργῶν κατοικία παλαία)'[50]. Inhabitants of the city are identified as jewellers, carpenters, and others, and those practicing similar trades tended to live in the same neighbourhoods[51]. The Akhmim cemeteries have yielded an abundant trove of textiles such as linen, wool, and silk, dating especially to the Ptolemaic, Byzantine, and Islamic Periods. The P. Berl. Bork shows a considerable concentration of textile specialists living in the early fourth century: 22 men out of 61, or roughly 36% of all traders and craftsmen listed in the P. Berl. Bork are involved in textile manufacture and trade, with 13 different specialisations out of a total of 41 (roughly 32%) in Panopolis relating to its production, and about 13 out of 24 workshops (mainly linen weaving)[52]. Akhmim cemeteries, especially El-Hawawish A, housed a wealth of Roman and Coptic textiles[53]. Today, Akhmim is not only a great archaeological city, but also a major location for the manufacture of modern Egyptian textiles[54].

Herodotus claims that a vast Greek community had settled at Akhmim as early as the mid-fifth century BC, and remarks that the Greek culture flourished in Panopolis during that period. He mentions that Chemmis (Panopolis) was the only city in Egypt to have adopted Greek customs[55].

---

[43] This document most likely dates to 315–30 AD (part of the period after the persecution against the Christians), Z. Borkowski, *Une description topographique des immeubles à Panopolis* (=*SB* XVI 16000) (Warsaw 1975), 13. Thomas dates it to after 298 AD, J. Thomas, 'Chronological Notes on Documentary Papyri', *ZPE* 6 (1970), 177–80, while Youtie dates it to between 299–441 AD, H. Youtie, 'P.Gen. inv. 108= SB VIII 9902', *ZPE* 7 (1971), 170–71. Part of the roll is now in Geneva (published in 1962 by Martin (=SB VIII 9902)), and part is in Berlin. Both sets of rolls were published together by Borkowski as P. Berl. Bork, Borkowski, *Une description topographique*, 24–26. In the Oxyrhynchite nome, about 30 temples were recorded for Greek gods, and were built in either an Egyptian or Greek form, J. Whitehorne, 'The Pagan Cults of Roman Oxyrhynchus', *ANRW* II.18.5 (1995), 3053.
[44] P. Van Minnen, 'The Letter (and other Papers) of Ammon: Panopolis in the Fourth Century AD', in A. Egberts et al. (eds.), *Perspectives on Panopolis*, 179.
[45] W. Willis and K. Maresch, *The Archive of Ammon Scholasticus of Panopolis (P. Ammon), The Legacy of Harpocration, Texts from the Collections of Duke University and the Universität zu Köln*, PC 26/1 (Köln 1997), 5.
[46] Z. Borkowski, *Une description topographiquere*, 44–46.; McNally and Schrunk, *Excavations in Akhmim*, 9.
[47] V. Martin, 'Relevé topographique des immeubles d'une métropole', *Recherches de Papyrologie* II (1962), 45–46.
[48] Ten linen weaving workshops (λινουφειον) are recorded in Panopolis' P. Berl. Bork II 28, IX 20, IX 33, X 2, XII 9, XII 15, XVI 21, XVIII 10, A II 3, and A IV 14. Also see B. Mcging, 'Lease of a Linen-weaving Workshop in Panopolis', *ZPE* 82 (1990), 115–21.
[49] Strabo, XVII.1.41 C813.; Martin, *Relevé topographique*, 37–73.
[50] P. Berl. Bork XII, 17. Akhmim was famous as a quarry from the New Kingdom until at least the second century. Quarrying by stone workers took place both north of El-Salamuni and further away to the north and south, R. Klemm and D. Klemm, *Steine und Steinbrüche im alten Ägypten* (Berlin 1993), 168–83.
[51] Willis and Maresch, *The Archive of Ammon (P. Ammon)*, 5.
[52] C. Geens, *Panopolis, a Nome Capital in Egypt in the Roman and Byzantine Period (ca. AD 200–600)*, PhD thesis, (Leuven 2007), 290–91. Attempts at gathering the Akhmimic artefacts and materials dispersed throughout the world since Maspero's excavations were begun by H. Middleton-Jones in his thesis, titled *The Akhmim Project, the Analytical Catalogue of Material from the Late Period Cemeteries of Akhmim in Upper Egypt* (MPhil. thesis, Swansea University, (Swansea 1997). Later, in 2017, Marion Claude fulfilled her PhD thesis on 'La IXe province de Haute-Égypte (Akhmîm), organisation cultuelle et topographie religieuse de l'Ancien Empire à l'époque romaine', (unpublished PhD thesis, Paul-Valéry Montpellier 3, (Monpellier 2017).
[53] On the Akhmimic textiles, see R. Forrer, *Über Steinzeit–Hockergräber zu Achmim Naqada etc. in Oberägypten (Achmim–Studien I)* (Strasbourg 1901), 10–12, 14, 17f, 33, pl. 16–22, fig. 2–4.; id., *Mein Besuch in El-Achmim. Reisebriefe aus Aegypten* (Strasbourg 1895), 34–40.; R. Forrer, 'Antike Bucheinbände von Panopolis-Achmim', *Zeitschrift für Bücherfreunde* 8 (1904–05), 311–15.; E. Wipszycka, *L'Industrie Textile* (Wroclaw 1965), 44–46.; S. Schrenk, 'Spätrömisch-frühislamische Textilien aus Ägypten', in S. Emmel, M. Klause, and S. Richter (eds.), *Ägypten und Nubien in spätantiker und christlicher Zeit, Akten des 6. Internationalen Koptologenkongresses Münster, 20.–26. Juli 1996. 1. Materielle Kultur, Kunst und religiöses Leben, Sprachen und Kulturen des christlichen Orients* 4 (Wiesbaden 1998), 339–78.; M. Rutschowscaya, *Tissues Coptes* (Paris 1990) (textiles from Akhmim are printed on 17(VI), 34(VII), 52(XI), 69(IV), 83–87(IV), 90(IV), 106(V–VI), and 132(VI)).; R. Pillinger, 'Die Textilkunst der frühen Christen gezeigt am Beispiel der Funde aus Ägypten', in H. Harrauer and R. Pintaudi (eds.), *Gedenkschrift Ulrike Horak (P.Horak) 2 (Pap. Flor. XXXIV)* (Florence 2004), 429–35.
[54] D. Ammon, *Crafts of Egypt* (Cairo 1999), 28–31. In the 12th century conquest, Akhmim remained an important Coptic city and a centre of the textile industry. It exported its textiles via a well-travelled pilgrim and trade route to the Red Sea, Kuhlmann, *SDAIK* 11, 25 no. 101. Today, textiles from Akhmim can be seen in museums around the world. Between 2003 and 2010, the Canadian Aid in Egypt built 'Qaret El-Nassseg', which includes 174 textile houses in Akhmim. They gathered all of the local hand weaving practitioners to revive the textile craft. Unfortunately, the project failed, and the craft is nowadays a subject of extinction. According to the International Council of Museums (ICOM)'s Red List of Egyptian cultural treasures, issue 2011, the Coptic textiles are listed as endangered artifacts, M. Bruwier, 'Akhmim antique', in M. Jeanne Paule and M. Bruwier (eds.), *Akhmim, au fil des femmes, broderies et tissages de Haute–Égypte, 4000 ans d'art textile, MUMAQ* (Mariemont 2022), 15–16.
[55] Herodotus, II, 91.

Hellenistic-style games were organised there, the so-called Paneia for the local Greek god Perseus Ouranios, since the fifth century BC[56]. During the Graeco-Roman Period, Panopolis continued to be a thriving Hellenised metropolis with several major ethnicities and a densely packed population; in this city, Greeks and Romans lived alongside the indigenous Egyptian population. The city was one the most important strongholds of Greek culture in Upper Egypt, where the Egyptian and Hellenistic cultures intertwined in a productive way and where a Hellenised clientele thrived. Panopolis was a main spring of cultural diversity and is a paradigm for studying Graeco-Roman Egypt through the 'double style'. Hybridisation and multi-culturalism influenced the local religion, most notably in regards to local traditions, funerary beliefs, and burial customs[57].

In Roman Panopolis, the Hellenistic culture was fully established, with a Hellenised population and access to a Greek education and culture[58]. Panopolis was a hot-bed of Greek culture, with excellent libraries and educational opportunities[59]. The multi-cultural society of Panopolis was a centre for the merging of classical and Egyptian funerary art and iconography, showing multi-directional influences between the Egyptians and the Greeks. Hellenism was its so-called 'elite' culture, and the members of wealthy families were encouraged to participate in and learn the Greek language and ways. Social stratification was partially caused by one's ability to adapt to the Greek culture and language. The acquaintance with Greek culture became increasingly crucial as a means of obtaining status and prestige[60]. In Late Antiquity, the Christian community in Panopolis included an urban elite marked by a Greek cultural tradition. The community was known as a town of scholars and a centre of learning. Besides a newly developing political elite, Upper Egyptian Panopolis produced the most well-known poets of the Greek language in the fifth century. It was a major centre of Greek culture, with poets such as Triphiodorus, Cyrus, Pamprepius, and Nonnus, who wrote *Dionysiaca*. Nonnus is an extreme example of a Christian sharing in Greek culture. Besides famous poets being born in Panopolis, the alchemist Zosimus, a gnostic, became equally well-known[61].

---

[56] A. Lloyd, 'Perseus and Chemmis (Herodotus, II, 91)', *JHS* 89 (1969), 79–86.; id., Herodotus II, *Commentary:* 1–98.; *EPRO* 43 (Leiden 1976), 367–70.
[57] L. Castiglione, *Dualité du style dans l'art sépulcral égyptien à l'époque romaine*, *AAASH* 9 (Budapest 1961), 209–30.
[58] For the Greek culture in Panopolis, see A. Martin and O. Primavesi, *L'Empédocle de Strasbourg (P. Strasb. gr. inv. 1665–1666)* (Berlin, Strasbourg 1999), 43–51.; J. Hahn, *Gewalt und religiöser Konflikt, Studien zu den Auseinandersetzungen zwischen Christen, Heiden und Juden im Osten des römischen Reiches von Konstantinbis Theodosius II, Klio, Beiträge zur alten Geschichte, Beihefte N.F.* 8 (Berlin 2004), 243–46.; A. Cameron, 'The Empress and the Poet, Paganism and Politics at the Court of Theodosius II', *YCS* 27 (1984), 217–89.; G. Bowersock, *Hellenism in Late Antiquity* (Cambridge 1990), 55–69. Although Panopolis was a centre of Greek education and culture, only nine copies of Greek classical literature indisputably come from Akhmîm; the texts include P. Achm. 2–5 (LDAB 1269, 982, 2090, 10638), P. Ammon I.2 (LDAB 5626), II.26 (*LDAB* 1913), the Empedocles Papyrus published by Martin and Primavesi (*L'Empédocle de Strasbourg (P. Strasb. gr. inv. 1665–1666)* LDAB 824), and a mathematical exercise published by J. Baillet (*Le papyrus mathématique d'Akhmîm, MMFAC* IX.1 (Paris 1892),1–89 (LDAB 6240). The number of Coptic papyri discovered from eastern Akhmim is still few, and they date to the fourth and the fifth centuries AD. Most are written in Greek and/or Coptic, and are bilingual. These papyri likely come from El-Hawawish A, which was a distinctive cemetery for Coptic burials, U. Bouriant, *Les Papyrus d'Akhmîm, MMFAC* 1.2 (Paris 1885), 243–304.; id., *Rapport au Ministère de l'Instruction Publique sur une mission dans la Haute-Egypte (1884–1885), MMFAC* 1.3 (Paris 1887).; U. Wilcken, 'Die Achmîm-Papyri in der Bibliothèque Nationale de Paris' (Sitzungsber. Kgl. Preus. Akad.) (1887) 807–20.; P. Lacau, 'Textes coptes en dialectes akhmimique et sahidique', *BIFAO* 8 (1993), 43–109.; J. Gascou, 'Les codices documentaires égyptiens', in A. Blanchard (ed.), *Les débuts du codex (Bibliologia 9)* (Turnhout 1989), 71–101.; K. Treu, 'Christliche Papyri XIV', *AfP* 35 (1989), 107–16. On the other hand, the Panopolite nome was home to a famous Coptic papyrus, known as the Bodmer Papyrus, which was acquired by Martin Bodmer, a learned Swiss bibliophile and merchant of Geneva in the years 1955–56. There, the so called 'Chester Beatty Biblical Papyri' were discovered, being now located in Dublin. They are written in Coptic and Latin, and were used by the family of Alopex to record tax receipts dating between 339 and 346 AD. For more on these manuscripts, see J. Robinson, *The Pachomian Monastic Library at the Chester Beatty Library and the Bibliothèque Bodmer*, The Institute for Antiquity and Christianity, Occasional Paper 19 (Claremont 1990), 11–16.; id., 'The First Christian Monastic Library', in W. Godlewski (ed.),*Coptic Studies, Acts of the Third International Congress of Coptic Studies, Warsaw, 20–25 August, 1984* (Warsaw 1990), xxv–vi.; W. Brashear et al., *The Chester Beatty Codex Ac. 1390 Mathematical School Exercises in Greek and John 10:8–13:38 in Sub–Achmimic, Chester Beatty Monographs* 13 (Leuven, Paris 1990). Furthermore, the White Monastery library became the largest single find of Coptic (Sahidic) manuscripts known to-date. About 3,500 papers and fragments are now in the Bibliothèque Nationale thanks to Maspero, Bouriant, and Amélineau. See M. Foat, 'Shenuti: Discourse in the Presence of Heraklammon', *OLP* 24 (1993), 23–24. Large collections are now in the Cairo Museum, the IFAO, and the British Library, W. Crum, *Catalogue of the Coptic Monuments in the British Museum* (London 1905). The Austrian National Library, the Bibliotheca Nazionale in Naples, and the Vatican Library also contain some manuscripts, S. Emmel and C. Römer, 'The Library of the White Monastery in Upper Egypt', in H. Froschauer and C. Römer (eds.), *Spätantike Bibliotheken, Leben und Leser in den frühen Klöstern Ägyptens (Nilus. Studien zur Kultur Ägyptens und des Vorderen Oriens 14* (Wien 2008), 5–14.
[59] J. Dieleman, *Priests, Tongues, and Rites, the London- Leiden Magical Manuscripts and Translation in Egyptian Ritual (100–300CE)* (Leiden 2005), 291–93. Panopolis was a stronghold of revolts against the Ptolemies during the second century BC, and was once held captive after a prolonged siege which presumably occurred in 165 BC, Diod. Sic. XXXI fr. 17b.; A. Veisse, *Les 'révoltes égyptiennes', Recherches sur les troubles intérieurs en Égypte du règne de Ptolémée III à la conquête romaine, StudHell* 41(Leuven, Paris, Dudleya, 2004), 39–43. A second revolt led to the exclusion of Panopolis from the amnesty of 118 BC, P. Tebt. 5, ll.134–38= 147–54.; Veisse, *Les 'révoltes égyptiennes'*, 57, 63.
[60] The Romanisation of the local elite was a means of consolidating their positions of power, as attested by a man named Ammon, who was the scion of an Egyptian priestly family, but acquainted with Greek language and Greek culture, see R. Cribiore, *Writing, Teachers, and Students in Graeco-Roman Egypt, Am.Stud.* 36 (Atlanta 1996), 242. The urban elite Christian community in Panopolis was marked by a Greek cultural tradition, Hahn, *Gewalt und religiöser Konflikt*, 249.
[61] On the *Dionysiaca*, see G. Bowersock, 'Dionysius as an Epic Hero', in N. Hopkison (ed.), *Studies in the Dionysiaca of Nonnus* (Cambridge 1994), 156–66.; id., 'Selected Papers on Late Antiquity' (Bari 2000), 109–20.; A. Hollis, 'Some Allusions to Earlier Hellenistic Poetry in Nonnus', *CQ* 26 (1976), 142–50.; W. Liebeschuetz, 'The Use of Pagan Mythology in the Christian Empire with Particular Reference to the Dionysiaca of Nonnus', in P. Allen and E. Jeefreys (eds.), *The Sixth Century, End or Beginning?, Australian Association for Byzantine Studies, Byzantina Australiensia* 10 (Brisbane 1996), 75–91. On the alchemist Zosimus, see M. Mertens, 'Alchemy, Hermetism and Gnosticism at Panopolis c. 300 A.D: The Evidence of Zosimus', in A. Egberts et al. (eds.), *Perspectives on Panopolis*, 165–75.; B. Hallum, *Zosimus Arabus, the Reception of Zosimus of Panopolis in the Arabic/ Islamic World*, PhD dissertation for Combined Historical Studies, Warburg Institute (London 2010).; J. Lindsay, *The Origins of Alchemy in Graeco–Roman Egypt* (New York 1970).; M. Mertens, *Les alchimistes grecs, Tome IV, 1re partie, Zosime de Panopolis, Mémoires authentiques* (Collection des Universités de France) (Paris 1995).

In 298 AD, the Panopolite nome was subdivided into six administrative toparchies[62]. Two were located on the east bank. One was known as Τοπαρχια Μητροπόλεως, or the 'Toparchy of the Metropolis', corresponding to modern Akhmim. It comprised the fertile and productive river plain, and was bordered on the east and northeast by the high limestone ridges of the Eastern Desert, which taper towards the northern border near the Antaiopolite nome. The toparchy was also sometimes called Τοπαρχια Μητροπόλεως και Αραβια[63], or the 'Toparchy of the Metropolis and Arabia', the latter title being mentioned twice in papyri[64], and probably referring to the smaller fertile area of land bordering the Eastern Arabic Desert northwest of Akhmim. The second toparchy was called the 'Upper Toparchy'. It encompassed the southern part of the nome, and was situated on the Panopolite east bank, opposite the southernmost toparchy on the west bank. Four toparchies were situated on the west bank. The northernmost toparchy was the Τοπαρχια Συνορίας και Τοετώ[65], or the 'Toparchy of Synoria and Toeto'. It was situated on the northern border of the nome, on the west bank, corresponding to modern Tahta[66] (Toeto is undoubtedly the modern Tahta)[67]. The name 'Synoria', meaning 'borderland', may suggest that this location was the boundary between the Panopolite and Antaiopolite nomes[68]. Toeto and Synoria are occasionally mentioned in the papyri of Aphrodito and in texts from the Great Oasis[69]. Additionally, Τοπαρχια Πακέρκη-Ψιναβλα, or the 'Toparchy of Pakerke and Psinabla'[70], corresponds to modern Shandawil. Furthermore, ΜέσηΤοπαρχια, or the 'Mese Toparchy', was wrongly suggested by Skeat to have been situated on the east bank[71], while a recently published text from the Ammon Archive mentions that Bompae (modern Sohag) was one of the main sources of mummy labels from the west bank, situated within the Mese toparchy[72]. This would strongly imply that the Mese toparchy was located on the west bank, presumably opposite the metropolis of Panopolis. The sixth division was Τοπαρχια Φενεβύθεως (εος), or the 'Phenebythis Toparchy'. This was the southernmost toparchy on the Panopolite west bank[73], bordering the Thinite nome and including Athribis-with-Triphion[74]. The toparchies of Pakerke and Phenebythis were the smaller ones[75]. Later, in 307/308 AD, the six toparchies were replaced by an unknown number of *pagi*, only two of which were documented. The first *pagus* may have been near the nome capital, while the second one matches the middle toparchy, including Bompae and Nesos Apollinariados, as mentioned in the archive of Aurelius Heron (also known as Dionysodoro) (318-321 AD), who was the *praepositus* of the second *pagus* of the Panopolite nome[76]. Most likely, the Panopolite toparchies and *pagi* were subdivided into *merides*, as was the case in the Oxyrhynchite nome[77].

By the third century BC, Hellenism reached its zenith in the region, resulting in a newly-cultivated multi-cultural urban identity. In 201 AD, Septimius Severus finally granted the metropolis a city council (*boulē*) through which Panopolis became a Greek *polis*, gaining full urban status, and developing from a town to a fully Greek city with elite Greek citizens[78]. Due to the dramatic Romanisation and Hellenisation of the public architecture in the cities, by the second century AD, Panopolis possessed several civic buildings and had become larger and grander, with a theatre[79], at least three public baths (the windows of which

---

[62] *P. Panop. Beatty*, xxxv–ii.
[63] *P. Panop. Beatty*. 1.329.
[64] One is in the P. Ammon (I 3, v, 28), while the second is in the P. Bodm. (I 1 recto).
[65] J. Gascou and K. Worp, 'The Panopolitan Village Συνορία', *ZPE* 112 (1996), 163–64.
[66] On Tahta, see S. Timm, *Das Cchristlich-Koptische Ägypten in arabischer Zeit, Teil A-Z* (Wiesbaden 1992), 2467–69.
[67] In 298 AD, one Roman camp was known as 'the Camp of Toeto and Psinabla'. It was garrisoned by the Ala II Herculia Dromedariorum and served as a *mansio*, or 'resting place' on the main highway leading down the west bank, *P. Beatty. Panop*. 1.39, 87, 389, 406.
[68] Synoria relates to ὅρος, M. Lewuillon-Blume, 'P. Giessen inv. 263', *CdÉ* 52 (1978), 118–22. The noun συνορία derives from ὅρια, meaning 'boundary', C. Buck and W. Petersen, *Reverse Index of Greek Nouns and Adjectives* (Chicago 1945), 153. Husson connects it to ὅρος, meaning 'gebel', G. Husson, 'L'hospitalité dans les papyrus byzantins', in E. Kiessling and H. Rupprecht (eds.), *Akten des XIII, Internationalen Papyrologenkongresses, Marburg/ Lahn, 2.–6. August 1971, Münchener Beiträge zur Papyrusforschung und antiken Rechtsgeschichte* 66 (München 1974), 175 no. 39.
[69] *P. Grenf*. II 73.; *P. Kell. Gr*. I 30.
[70] Its ancient name was *Pa-kerkê* (variant *Pa-grg*), meaning 'the City of Foundation', S. Sauneron, *Villes et légendes, Bibliothèque d'études* 90 (Cairo 1983), 108 (=*BIFAO* 66 (1968), 18).; K. Worp, 'Localisation d'un camp de l'armée romaine à Psinabla', *Eirene* 52 (2016), 271–76.; H. Gauthier, 'Nouvelles notes géographiques sur le nome Panopolite' *BIFAO* 10 (1912), 120. Sauneron identifies *Psinabla* with modern Shandawil, Sauneron, *Villes et légendes*, 101–08.; K. Vandorpe, *Egyptische geografische elementen in Griekse transcriptie*, unpublished MA dissertation, KU Leuven (Leuven 1988), 146 no. 635, 156.
[71] Skeat, introduction to *P. Beatty. Panop*, xxxvi.
[72] *P. Ammon* II 50, ii.
[73] Chauveau connects Phenebythis with the Egyptian name *Pr-nb-wt*, M. Chauveau, 'Autour des étiquettes de momies de la Bibliothèque nationale de Vienne', *BIFAO* 92 (1992),108.; id., 'Rive droite, rive gauche, Le nome Panopolite au IIe et IIIe siècles de notre ère', in A. Egberts et al. (eds.), *Perspectives on Panopolis*, 47 no.8.; K. Zauzich, 'Verteidigung eines Mumienschildes', *ZÄS* 114 (1987), 97, n. 6. Smith declares that the Papyrus Harkness does not come from Akhmim, but from the Antinopolite nome, as previously assumed by Chauveau (who argued that *Pr-nb-wt* was identical with Phenebythis in the Panopolite nome), M. Smith, *Papyrus Harkness, MMA* 31.9.7 (Oxford 2005), 15–16. In the name Φεν-εβύθις, Φεν could means *P3 Hr n*, or 'side of Abydos', J. Quaegebeur, 'Mummy Labels, An Orientation', *P.L. Bat*. 19 (1978), 251. Furthermore, in the list of contributions in the P. Strasb. VI 587, Phenebythis is mentioned alongside villages in the Thinite nome, adding a further indication of its location as both south of the Panopolite nome, and beyond the Thinite nome.
[74] *P. Panop. Beatty*, xxxvii.; Chauveau, *BIFAO* 92, 108.; El-Sayed and El-Masry, *Athribis* I, 9.
[75] *P. Beatty. Panop*. 1.276–331.
[76] *SB* VI, 9544.
[77] J. Rowlandson, *Landowners and Tenants in Roman Egypt, The Social Relations of Agriculture in the Oxyrhynchite Nome* (Oxford 1996), 8.
[78] The earliest reference to the community of the Panopolites is a text dating to AD 288, *P. Oxy*. xxvii 2476.; *P. Beatty. Panop*. 1.60–62 (AD 298). The only attestations of *bouleutai* in Panopolis are from the following: P. Lips 45 r.6, 59.5 and 60.r.3 (371 AD), PSI xii 1233.2 (323/24 AD), and duplicate documents from the Ammon archive dated to 281 AD (P. Coll. Youtie II and 72), Willis and Maresch, *The Archive of Ammon (P. Ammon)*, 4–5.
[79] *P. Beatty. Panop*. 1.335–37.; G. Xanthaki-Karamanou, 'Hellenistic Drama and Alexandrian Culture', in C. Zerefos and M. Vardinoyannis (eds.), *Hellenistic Alexandria: Celebrating 24 Centuries: Papers Presented at the Conference Held on December 13–15 2017 at the Acropolis Museum, Athens, Archaeopress Archaeology (BAR Publishing)* (Oxford 2018), 139.

were glazed by the government)[80], a gymnasium with a bath[81], a *Komasterion* (a kind of festive hall)[82], a separate bath house, a *Paraetorium*, where the provincial governors would reside during their visits (and which also included a bath)[83], a *Logisterion*[84], and other public buildings[85]. It even had a philosophical school, albeit no doubt private rather than public[86]. Furthermore, the famous Panhellenic festivals were an important part of civic life from the third century onwards[87].

The language used in both the east and west banks of the nome may be employed as a general standard to measure the level of Hellenisation of the area. In this case, it reached its peak on the east bank, especially in the metropolis, in contrast to the west bank. Mummy labels[88] inscribed in Greek are common finds from Bompae and Nesos, located near the metropolis, while the proportion of discovered Demotic labels is generally remarkably low. In contrast, Demotic labels, many of which are still unpublished, are widely found in Psonis, which was located on the west bank, and further away from the metropolis[89]. The evidence for the belief in the Osirian afterlife in the third century AD is thus well attested from the mummy labels from the west bank, but less attested on the east bank[90]. Furthermore, the funerary culture also reflects the difference in Hellenisation between the city (on the east bank) and the west bank. On the west bank, the indigenous Egyptian religion remained generally more traditional, while the east bank it became more Hellenised.

The Egyptian cults were plugged into regional and national networks of culture and learning. From the fourth century onwards, the region of Panopolis became crowded with monasteries and nunneries, and Panopolis became home to some of the most well-known representatives of pagan literary culture. Members of leading families could look forward to a priesthood in the Pan/Min cult, and these priesthoods were often made hereditary, as exemplified by the archive of the aristocratic family of Aurelius Ammon (281-366 AD)[91]. However, around the first quarter of the fourth century AD, the traditional priesthood started to decline. In 325 AD, Ammon and his brother were still managing to preserve the priestly aristocracy and its hereditary rights to office and property, although with difficulty. This was combined with a devotion to the local cults[92], and the association of the two brothers with Hellenistic culture, as members of the intellectual, Hellenised, urban elite of the metropolis[93].

---

[80] A. Bowman, 'Public Buildings in Roman Egypt', *JRA* 5 (1992), 500–02.
[81] In the Hellenistic Period, the gymnasium and the bath were in two separate buildings, while in the Roman period, both institutions were typically placed inside one building, B. Mayer, 'Gymnase' et 'Thermes' dans l'Égypte romaine et byzantine', in B. Kramer, W. Luppe, H. Maehler, and G. Poethke (eds.), *Akten des 21. Internationalen Papyrologenkongresses, Berlin, 13.–19.8. 1995, AfP* 3.II (Stuttgart, Leipzig 1997) 691–95.; Van Minnen, 'The Letter (and Other Papers) of Ammon', in A. Egberts et al. (eds.), *Perspectives on Panopolis*, 179.
[82] *P. Got.* 7. *Komasterion* is a Greek word referring to a religious building or sanctuary attributed to the god Dionysius. It was used as a meeting place for the procession of the sun and star gods, and festivals were made inside the building by the *komasterei*, see H. Liddell and R. Scott, *Greek-English Lexicon* (Oxford 1925), 973.; W. Gemoll, *Griechisch Deutsches Schulund Handwörterbuch* (Wien 1997), 461.; W. Martini, *Sachwörterbuch der Klassischen Archäologie* (Stuttgart 2003), 171.; H. Cancik and H. Schneider, *Der Neue Pauly Enzyklopädie der Antike*, Band 6 (Stuttgart 1999), 706. Therefore, the *komasterion* of Panopolis may have been situated near the temple of Min/Pan.
[83] A temporary *palation* was installed in the *Triphion* to serve as a place of accommodation for the visit of Diocletian to Panopolis in AD 298, instead of erecting a new building, *P. Beatty. Panop.* 1.260.; Van Minnen, 'The Letter (and Other Papers) of Ammon', in A. Egberts et al. (eds.), *Perspectives on Panopolis*, 179.
[84] *P. Berl. Bork* I.27.; *P. Beatty. Panop.* 1.228, 346, 350 (AD 298).; *P. Panop.* 29, l. 8 (AD 332). On the *Logisterion*, see A. Luckaszewicz, *Les édifices publics dans les villes de l'Égypte romaine. Problèmes administratifs et financiers* (Warsaw 1986), 46 no. 21.
[85] There is no known date for the initial erection of these Hellenistic buildings in Panopolis, but in 253 AD, a conservation contract was made between three glass workers, the *proedros* Aurelius Theon (alias Demetrios), and the council of Panopolis, for the re-glazing of several sets of public baths in the *gymnasium*, the *praetorium*, near the *komasterion*, and in other city works, *P. Got.* 7, ll. 5–6.
[86] Van Minnen, 'The Letter (and Other Papers) of Ammon', in A. Egberts et al. (eds.), *Perspectives on Panopolis*, 179.
[87] Bagnall, *Egypt in Late Antiquity*, 55–57.; id., *Later Roman Egypt, Society, Religion, Economy, and Administration*, Variorum Collected Studies Series 758 (Burlington 2003), 101.; A. Bowman, 'Landholding in the Hermopolite Nome in the Fourth Century AD', *JRS* 75 (1986), 69–72.; id., 'Urbanization in Roman Egypt', in E. Fentress (ed.), *Romanization and the City: Creation, Transformations and Failures*, *JRA* suppl. 38 (2000), 183.; E. Schönbauer, 'Die rechtliche Stellung der Metropoleis im römischen Ägypten', *Epigraphica* 11 (1949), 123.; Van Minnen, 'The Letter (and Other Papers) of Ammon', in A. Egberts et al. (eds.), *Perspectives on Panopolis*, 179.; W. Van Regen, 'Les Jeux de Panopolis', *CdÉ* 46 (1971), 136–41.
[88] Mummy labels are tags or plaques made of wood or other materials. They have one or more holes through which a piece of string can be drawn to tie them to a mummy. They contain personal information about the deceased. The inscription relates to the mummy, its transport, and its burial. See Boyaval, 'Remarques sur la définition des étiquettes', *CRIPEL* 7 (1985), 91–92.; id., 'Conclusions provisoires sur les étiquettes de momies en langue grecque', *BIFAO* 86 (1986), 37–40.
[89] Almost 30% of the mummy labels from Bompae are in Greek (70 out of 256), whereas those of Psonis are almost exclusively bilingual or Demotic (58 out of 61). Chauveau's analysis of the mummy labels from the Louvre yield similar proportions; on 252 labels from Bompae, 68 are Greek, 178 bilingual, and 6 are Demotic; on 72 from Psonis, only 3 are Greek, 59 bilingual, and 10 Demotic, Chauveau, 'Rive droite, rive gauche', in A. Egberts et al. (eds.), *Perspectives on Panopolis*, 53. The earliest known label from the Akhmim region with a precise date was written in year 13 of the reign of Domitian, on 07 December, 93 AD, Vleeming, *Demotic and Greek-Demotic Mummy Labels*, 810. The latest known mummy label of a precise date that records the afterlife beliefs of its owner was written in year 15 of Gallienus, on 24 February, 268 AD, Vleeming, *Demotic and Greek-Demotic Mummy Labels*, 476 no. 846. However, Arlt suggests that the label with the latest date was written around 275 AD, C. Arlt, *Deine Seele möge leben für immer und ewig: Die Mumienschilder im British Museum* (Leuven 2011).; M. Stadler, 'Funerary Religion: The Final Phase of Egyptian Religion', in C. Riggs (ed.), *The Oxford Handbook of Roman Egypt*, 386.
[90] M. Smith, *Following Osiris, Perspectives on the Osirian Afterlife from Four Millennia* (Oxford 2017), 430.
[91] It was found in Akhmim in 1968, and was purchased via the antiquities market between 1968 and 1971. Currently, its rolls are divided, being held at Duke University, the University of Cologne, and the Vitelli Institute in Florence. It was written by Ammon in a rough, rapid 'draft-hand', W. Willis, 'Two Literary Papyri in an Archive from Panopolis', *ICS* 3 (1978),140–42.; id., 'The Letter of Ammon of Panopolis to his Mother', *Actes du XVe Congrès international de papyrologie, Bruxelles- Louvain 29 août- 3 septembre 1977. II, Pap.Brux.* 17 (Brussels 1979),98–115.
[92] F. Feder, 'Ammon und seine Brüder, Eine ägyptische Familie aus Panopolis (Achmim) im 4.Jh. zwischen ägyptisch-hellenistischer Kultur und Christentum', in M. Fitzenreiter (ed.), *Genealogie, Realität und Fiktion von Identität, Workshop am 04. Und 05. Juni 2004 in Berlin*, *IBAES* 5 (London 2005), 105–06.
[93] L. Tacom, *Fragile Hierarchies, the Urban Elites of Third-Century Roman Egypt*, Mnemosyne Supplements 271 (Leiden 2006), 117. The cultivated Hellenism continued as a striking feature of Late Antique paganism in Panopolis during the early fourth century AD, especially within the pagan priestly family of Ammon, Van Minnen, 'The Letter

The pantheon of Panopolis was rich. The Panopolite nome housed not only Egyptian deities, but also Greek cults and divinities. Greek cultural icons such as Dionysius and Heracles were still being used by Christian members of the elite to express their ideas about God and the world[94]. The study of onomastics provides useful indications of local cults and their topography[95]. Personal names derived from Greek theophoric names such as those of Apollo, Dionysius, Artemis, Hermes, Aries, Kronos, and Herakles are found in the Panopolite nome[96]. Some of these Greek gods were assimilated with Egyptian deities, and some Egyptian cults underwent Hellenisation. The P. Beatty Panop.[97] and P. Berl. Bork[98] provide two very interesting topographical surveys of buildings in the city of Panopolis during the last part of the third and the early fourth centuries AD. They highlight the pagan and Christian religious transformations occurring during this period. They demonstrate how Egyptian, Graeco-Egyptian, and Greek gods appeared side by side in Panopolis, a city with significant inter-cultural interactions.

Temples known from the Panopolite nome which follow the Greek style and cult are considerably fewer, no doubt due to a lack of sources[99]. Greek documentary texts such as P. Berl. Bork of the fourth century AD mention temples, priests, and priestesses at Akhmim. However, most of these served Greek cults rather than Egyptian ones[100]. The P. Berl. Bork also mentions several houses owned by priests[101]. In fact, in the third century AD, the city register lists nine Greek *Hiera,* or 'sanctuaries'[102] situated along the city streets. These include sanctuaries for:

- **Hermes:** God of knowledge, magic, and oracles. He had a special cult in Bompae, in the temple of 'Haryotes, Hermes, and Apollo'[103].
- **Chnoubis**[104]**:** The Hellenised form of the ram-headed god Khnum from Elephantine, who was assimilated with Ammon-Zeus.
- **Ammon/Amon:** He was probably identical to Min-Amun[105].
- **Araus:** His name was mentioned in sources from Bompae as Ἀραυς and ωψεντανάραυς[106]. His identity is still obscure, being perhaps a shortened form of Inaraus.

(and Other Papers) of Ammon', in A. Egberts et al. (eds.), *Perspectives on Panopolis*, 451, as well as in the Horapollon family, D. Frankfurter, *Religion in Roman Egypt, Assimilation and Resistance* (Princeton 1998), 223–24.; Hahn, *Gewalt und religiöser Konflikt*, 245–46. The Christian and pagan elite in Panopolis still marked and related to the Greek cultural traditions, Hahn, *Gewalt und religiöser Konflikt*, 249. In Roman Egypt, a priest who had a 'genuinely Hellenic culture' was regarded as a stoic ('a philosopher'), Fowden, *The Egyptian Hermes*, 54.

[94] Van Minnen, 'The Letter (and Other Papers) of Ammon', in: A. Egberts et al. (eds.), *Perspectives on Panopolis*, 181. Greek theophoric names known from the Panopolite nome were composed of or derived from the names of Greek cults and gods such as Apollo, Dionysius, Artemis, Hermes, Herakles, Apollonia/os (*P. Achm.* 9, ll. 39, 48, 53, 54, 120, 122, 130, 137, 138, 155, 156), Apollinarion (*P. Achm.* 9, l. 62), Apollinarios (*P. Achm.* 9, l. 52, 158), Artemis (*P. Achm.* 9, l. 142), Dionysios/arion (*P. Achm.* 9, ll. 68, 164, 165, 166), Herme(neu)s (*P. Achm.* 9, l. 44; *P. Bour.* 41a, l. 20), Hermion (*P. Achm.* 9, l. 169), Kronos (*P. Achm.* 9, l. 69, CEMG 1753, CEML 83, 94 and SB XX 14410), Herakleios (*P. Achm.* 9, ll. 180, 181?, 183, 184), and Herakleides (*P. Achm.* 9, l. 65).

[95] On the religious importance of onomastics, see R. Bagnall, 'Cults and Names of Ptolemais in Upper Egypt', in W. Clarysse, A. Schoors, and H. Willems (eds.), *Egyptian Religion, The Last Thousand Years, II, Studies Dedicated to the Memory of Jan Quaegebeur*, OLA 85 (Leuven 1998), 1093–101.; F. Colin, 'Onomastique et Société, Problèmes et methods à la lumière des documents de l'Égypte hellénistique et romaine', in M. Dondin-Payre and M. Th. Raepsatcharlier (eds.), *Noms. Identités culturelles et romanisation sous le haut-empire* (Brussels 2001), 3–15.; M. Abd El-Ghani, 'The Role of Ptolemais in Upper-Egypt Outside its Frontiers', in I. Andorlini (ed.), *Atti del XXII Congresso Internazionale di Papirologia, Florence, 23–29 agosto 1998, I* (Florence 2001).

[96] Including Apollonia/os (*P. Achm.* 9, ll. 39, 48, 53, 54, 120, 122, 130, 137, 138, 155, 156), Apollinarion (*P. Achm.* 9, l. 62), Apollinarios (*P. Achm.* 9, l. 52, 158), Artemis (*P. Achm.* 9, l. 142), Dionysios/arion (*P. Achm.* 9, ll. 68, 164, 165, 166), Herme(neu)s (*P. Achm.* 9, l. 44; *P. Bour.* 41a, l. 20), Hermion (*P.Achm.* 9, l. 169), Aries 'Arios Ἄρειος' (*P. Achm.* 9, l. 54; *P. Berl. Bork* I 17, X 32, XIV 27); Herakleios (*P. Achm.* 9, ll. 180, 181 ? 183, 184), and Herakleides (*P. Achm.* 9, l. 65). Local traditional names that were exclusively derived from the Panopolitan triad include Paniskos, Panodoros, Paniskion, Triphiodoros, Kolanthos, Hierakapollon, Perseus, Ouranios and Euodios, and the famous Petetriphis derived from Triphis, Z. Borkowski, 'Local Cults and Resistance to Christianity', *JJP* 20 (1990), 30. Though the god Petbe was worshipped in Panopolis, he was equated to Kronos, as suggested in E. Amelineau, *Oeuvres de Schenoudi*, I (Paris 1907–14), 383–84. Although names such as 'Panetbeus' are absent from Panopolite onomastics, 'Petbe' is mentioned in both Demotic literature and Coptic magical texts. In the Demotic legend of the Seth and Horus-bird, as well as in P. Insinger from Akhmim, Petbe is 'the avenging daemon', appearing standing at the end of a scene in which one animal devours the other. Some scholars see the assimilation of Petbe as Min, J. Van der Vliet,'Spätantikes Heidentum in Ägypten im Spiegel der koptischen Literatur', in D. Willers (ed.), *Begegnung von Heidentum und Christentum im spätantiken Ägypten, Riggisberger Berichte 1* (Riggisberg 1993), 114. Aufrère suggests that the name 'Petbe' is an imitation of Horus-imychénout, a local god in Panopolis who was depicted as a crocodile with a falcon head, S. Aufrère, 'Démons vus par les premiers chrétiens', in M. Rassart-Debergh (ed.), *Études coptes V, Sixième journée d'études, Limoges 18–20 juin 1993 et Sixième journée d'études, Neuchâtel 18–20 mai 1995*, CBC 10 (Leuven 1998), 81.; id., 'KRONOS, un crocodile justicier des marécages de la rive occidentale du Panopolite au temps de Chénouté?', in S. Aufrère et al. (eds.), *Encyclopédie religieuse de l'Univers végétal. Croyances phytoreligieuses de l'Égypteancienne (ERUV III), OrMonsp* 15 (Montpellier 2005), 77–93.

[97] K. Skeat, 'P. Panop. Beatty, Papyri from Panopolis in the Chester Beatty Library', *Proceedings of the IX International Congress of Papyrologie, Oslo, 19th–22nd August 1958* (Oslo 1961), 194–99. These two long rolls were acquired by Chester Beatty in 1956 together with a Greek grammar book, a biblical lexicon, and P. Bodm. II. The first roll records the correspondence of a *strategos* (probably Apollinarios) over the course of 13 days in September of 298 AD to his superior officials and to local officials and employees. The correspondence deals with the furbishing of the Triphion and the preparation of accommodations(?) for the upcoming visit of Diocletian and his troops to Panopolis. The second roll shows the incoming correspondence received by the *strategos* Apollinarios from the procurator of the Lower Thebaid in January and March of 300 AD, Skeat, *P. Beatty. Panop.*, 122–23.

[98] See Borkowski, *Une description topographique*, 24–26.

[99] In the Oxyrhynchite nome, about 30 temples were recorded for Greek gods. They were built using either Egyptian and/or Greek forms, Whitehorne, 'The Pagan Cults', 3053.

[100] M. Smith, 'Osiris and the Deceased in Ancient Egypt, Perspectives from Four Millennia', *Journal of Publications of the* École Pratique des Hautes Études (2014), 97.

[101] Van Minnen, 'The Letter (and Other Papers) of Ammon', in A. Egberts et al. (eds.), *Perspectives on Panopolis*, 179.

[102] They are mentioned respectively in P. Berl. Bork VIII 5, XV 27, XIV 27, IX 3, A II 5, A IV 12.; Borkowski, *Une description topographique*, 24–26.

[103] CEML 53.; J. Quaegebeur, 'Thot-Hermès, le dieu le plus grand', in *Hommages à François Daumas, II* (Montpellier 1986), 525–44. On Hermes Trismegistos, see Fowden, *The Egyptian Hermes*, 174.

[104] In the early fourth century, the people of Panopolis would still refer to the shrine of Chnoubis using the god's Egyptian name, Frankfurter, *Religion in Roman Period*, 107.

[105] Kuhlmann, SDAIK 11, 48 no. 230.

[106] SB XXVI 16764.; CEMG 171, 1679, 1681, 1713, 1723, 1738, 1740, 1751, 1868.; B. Boyaval, *Corpus des étiquettes de momies grecques, Publications de l'Université de Lille III, Série 'Etudes archéologiques'* (Lille 1976).

- **Agathos Daimon:** The Egyptian Shai,[107] known as 'the Good Fate', and 'the Beneficent Spirit of Alexandria'[108]. A *laura* in Panopolis was named after this god or after his sanctuary[109]. He was very popular in Panopolis and is still attested in the fourth and fifth centuries AD[110]. During the time of Saint Shenoute, Shai was apparently worshipped in local homes. Shenoute refers to 'Shai of the Village' or 'Shai of the Home', to whom lamps were burned and incense was offered[111]. A local shrine and cult for Agathos Daimon was still maintained by the community in the fifth century in the north of Panopolis[112]. Here, the locals maintained niches in their homes which housed an image of the god[113]. Furthermore, a special festival for Shai was still performed in Panopolis in the fifth century. During this festival, Shenoute once complained about homeowners who lit lamps in their houses to proclaim the festival of Shai[114].

- **Persephone:** It is unknown whether she was venerated in Panopolis as a Greek goddess or rather worshipped through her Egyptian equivalent character, being either Triphis or Isis[115]. Both were associated with fertility. Thus, the cult of Persphone-Triphis shows how the classical and Egyptian cultures had intermingled within the domain of fertility[116].

The syncretism of the Egyptian and Hellenistic practices and deities is significant in Panopolis during the Roman period. However, Smith has a *'naïve and uncritical use of literary, often highly rhetorical, sources as historical evidence;[and an] ignorance of traditional Egyptian religion and the forms which it took in and around Akhmim during the Graeco-Roman Period, resulting in an inability to distinguish it from the Greek religion which co-existed alongside it there'*[117]. He does not properly account for the religious syncretism of the area.

By the fourth century, the Greek divinities were still widely worshiped in Panopolis. Shenoute is known to have destroyed pagan idols in the domestic parts of the sanctuary of Atripe, as suggested by the fact that the idols confiscated from Gesios' house were the same as those that were rescued from a temple[118]. It is highly likely that the sanctuary once contained images of Kronos, Hecate, Zeus, and other Greek deities. This emphasises the home's traditional function as a site for religious practices, some of which were connected to local or regional temples and their festivals. In the Panopolite nome, the domestic cult, including the Eleusinian mysteries cult, was known, and its rites were likely performed in Panopolis, either in the houses or in the crypts of the temples of Min and Athripe. Frankfurter claims that religious practices 'shifted centrifugally from temple cult to village and domestic rites' in Roman period Egypt[119]. In one of his works, Shenoute criticizes the people who give thanks to daemons, saying *'It is (the time for) worshipping the tutelary spirit (ⲡⲩⲁⲓ) today'*. Smith proposes that *'the fact that he uses an Egyptian term to denote the tutelary spirits whose worship he castigates tells us nothing about their nature or that of the belief system to which they belong'*[120]. In the opinion of the author, a kind of mysteries cult was thus probably performed in the subterranean crypts of the temple of Athribis, and in the main temple of Min in Panopolis

---

[107] Amelineau, *Oeuvres de Schenoudi*, 379. Theophoric names in the Panopolite community sometimes derived from Shai (Ψαις, Ταψαις(Σεν) ψενταψαις, and Σερεμψαις), R. Bagnall, B. Frier, and I. Rutherford, *The Census Register P. Oxy.* 984.; *The Reverse of Pindar's Paeans (Pap. Brux. 29)* (Brussels 1997), 114–24.; Bagnall, 'Cults and Names', 1093–101. One even finds Min-Shai (Πετεμινσαις) on Demotic mummy labels in the IFAO collection, D. Devauchelle and J. Quaegebeur, 'Étiquettes de momies démotiques et bilingues de l'IFAO', *BIFAO* 81 (1981), 366 no. 31. The local names 'Agathos Daimon' and 'Hierakapollon' were common among the Hellenised elite population of the fourth century, N. Litinas, 'Hierakapollon, the Title of Panos Polis and the Names in-Apollon', *AncSoc* 37 (2007), 97–106.
[108] Borkowski, *Une description topographique*, 24–26.
[109] *CEMG* 1962. Agathos Daemon was also associated with Dionysus (the god of wine). When Dionysus was invoked or worshipped by the ancient Greeks for his command of the powers of discrimination, response, wisdom, healing, fertility, prophecy, and magic, he was considered Agathos Daemon, or 'the good daemon', R. Taylor-Perry, *The God who Comes: Dionysian Mysteries Revisited 6.* On Agathos Daimon, see D. Ogden, 'Alexander, Agathos Daimon, and Ptolemy, The Alexandrian Foundation Myth in Dialogue' in M. Sweeney (ed.), *Foundation Myths in Ancient Societies, Dialogues and Discourses* (Pennsylvania 2015), 129–50.
[110] *P. Berl. Bork* A II 5. In Egypt, Agathos Daemon was assimilated as one of the traditional divinities who controlled individual fates and fortunes. This association explains the regular invocations of Agathos Daemon in prayers for wellbeing, favour, and worldly success, R. Gordan, D. Joly, and W. Van Andringa, 'A Prayer For Blessings On Three Ritual Objects Discovered At Chartres-Autricum (France/Eure-Et Loir)', in F. Simón and R. Gordon (eds.), *Magical Practice in the Latin West: Papers from the International Conference Held at the University of Zaragoza, 30 Sept.- 1st Oct. 2005, EPRO* 168 (Leiden 2010), 515.
[111] J. Quaegebeur, *Le dieu égyptien Shaï dans la religion et l'onomastique*, OLA 2 (Leuven 1975), 39, 160–66.; Frankfurter, *Religion in Roman Egypt*, 63–64. Shenoute had a certain harshness towards the Panopolite pagan cults. Local religion shifted to the domestic sphere at the village level, and pagan cults and practices could still be maintained in private houses. Hence, Shai was still venerated at home, with the Panopolites continuing his worship in their household shrines, Van der Vliet, *Spätantikes Heidentum in Ägypten*, 114. Furthermore, in the Ammon Archive of the fourth century AD, the name of the local god Agathos Daimon (Egyptian Shai) was mentioned and indeed prominent in Panopolis, such as seen in *P. Ammon* II 37, l. 2; 41, l. 2; 46, l. 4. He sometimes occurred alongside Tyche and the *pronoia* of the gods (see *P. Ammon* II 37, l. [2]; 41, l. [2]).
[112] D. Frankfurter, 'Religious Practice and Piety', in C. Riggs (ed.), *The Oxford Handbook of Roman Egypt* (Oxford 2012), 332.
[113] D. Frankfurter 'Illuminating the Cult of Kothos, The Panegyric on Macarius and Local Religion in Fifth-Century Egypt', in J. Goehring and J. Timbie (eds.), *The World of Early Egyptian Christianity: Language, Literature, and Social Context.Washington, DC* (Washington 2007), 179–82.
[114] Frankfurter, 'Religious Practice and Piety', in C. Riggs (ed.), *The Oxford Handbook of Roman Egypt*, 323.

[115] Martin, 'Relevé topographique', 65.; Kuhlmann, *SDAIK* 11, 48 no. 230.
[116] A. Pelletier, 'Note sur les mots ΔΙΑΤΡΙΒΗ, ἹΕΡΟΝ, ΔΙΑΘΗΣΙΣ dans P. Gen. Inv. 108', *RechPap* 4 (1967), 186.
[117] Smith, 'Aspects of indigenous religious Traditions', in A. Egberts et al. (eds.), *Perspectives on Panopolis*, 245.
[118] S. Emmel, 'Shenoute of Atripe and the Christian Destruction of Temples in Egypt: Rhetoric and Reality', in J. Hahn, S. Emmel, and U. Gotter (eds.), *From Temple to Church, Destruction and Renewal of Local Cultic Topography in Late Antiquity, EPRO* 163 (Leiden 2008), 197, lines 22–23.; D. Frankfurter, 'Iconoclasm and Christianization in Late Antique Egypt: Christian Treatments of Space and Image', in J. Hahn et al. (eds.), *From Temple to Church*, 142–43.
[119] Frankfurter, 'Religious Practice and Piety', in C. Riggs (ed.), *The Oxford Handbook of Roman Egypt*, 319.
[120] On the domestic cults in Akhmim, see Smith, *Following Osiris*, 441–44.

as well. Then, when Shenoute started to complain, the villagers may have shifted their cult practices to take place inside of their homes instead, likely before the same ritual statues that were used for worship in the temples.

A Roman monument with an inscription reading 'the Monument [of] Ptolemagrios', which is also known as the *Agrios*[121], shows how the Egyptian and Greek cultures interacted in Panopolis, and reflects the fusion of the Egyptian and Hellenistic cultures and beliefs. It provides evidence of the milieu in which a well-to-do citizen of Panopolis lived. It is a square pillar monument that is 1.33m. high, tapering slightly towards the top, with Greek inscriptions running to the bottom of each of its four sides. This implies that the pillar originally stood on a base[122]. At the top of each side, in a bordered field, a bust of Ptolemagrios as a bearded military man with a crested helmet appears. The image is the same on all four sides. There is a symbol placed below him on each side. Each symbol is different, symbolizing the four gods invoked in the four inscribed poems which accompany the bust. The symbols include an eagle (the personification of Zeus), a seahorse of Poseidon, a shield with a gorgon in the centre and crossed spears resembling Ares, and another animal, which is probably a dog (Kerberos?), and which is addressed to Hades [123]. Below the panel, there are three or (on the wider sides) four canopic jars representing Egyptian gods and goddesses. In total, there are 14 jars on the sides. Each side also includes a complete Homeric poem corresponding to one of four gods; the poems are directed to Zeus and Ares on the wider sides, and Poseidon and probably Hades on the narrower[124].

Moreover, Egyptian gods of the Akhmim pantheon are also depicted on the monument's four sides. The first side shows a row of deities, including Osiris with an *atef* crown, Horus with a *pschent* crown, Isis with her distinctive emblem, and an unlabelled female head, which is probably Nephthys(?), although her emblem has disappeared. The second row shows the Ibis-headed god Thoth, crowned with a lunar disc, Amon, with a male human head and a helmet with double plumes, and Mut, who has a human female head, complete with a vulture and *pschent*. The third side depicts a damaged figure which is probably Shu or Maat judging from the appearance of a single feather. She is joined by Tefnout as a lioness, and Hathor or Sekhmet, who is depicted as a female with a lion's head and a sun disc with horns. The fourth and final side of the monument probably depicts Ra or Atum with the crown of Lower Egypt, and a female head that is crowned with a vase, most likely representing Nut (Figure 1.1)[125].

Ptolemagrios was an urban elite figure with a Roman military background, and combined Hellenism with his devotion to the traditional local cults[126]. He dedicated a temple garden and honoured the main divinities of the Egyptian pantheon by means of their *canopoi*. He also had a Greek background, as indicated by the metrical inscription on the monument and its depiction of Greek gods. Ares may have been his patron due to his military career. The three other gods depicted on the monument represent the universe. The inscription on the monument refers to the banquets in honour of Phoibos in the present tense. Hence, its use as an epitaph seems unlikely. Instead, the monument is probably an honourary piece, erected in honour of Ptolemagrios as a benefactor[127].

Akhmim has a rich collection of funerary materials and objects, especially from the Graeco-Roman Period. The religious beliefs and practices of the Graeco-Roman Panopolite nome are vibrant and distinctive. This is well attested through the vast amount of material discovered there, including temples, numerous funerary materials (such as stelae, coffins, and mummy labels), literary and documentary papyri, ostraca, graffiti, and inscriptions[128]. Although the extensive funerary sources are scattered throughout many museums and collections[129], ancient Panopolis is still poorly documented. There are gaps in the documentation of its artefacts, which is partly due to the illicit or flawed excavations of its cemeteries during the late 19th century. Thus, it often happens that the true provenance and date of many artefacts and papyri cannot

---

[121] This pillar entered the Cairo Museum in 1885 (inv. 26093) and was published by Milne in 1901. The first editor of these poems is J. Milne, 'Greek Inscriptions from Egypt', *JHS* 21 (1901), 287–90. Agrios was an important figure of Panopolis. Guéraud reconstructed the Ptolemagrios monument with the missing lower part of the pillar found in a private house in Akhmim, O. Guéraud, 'Notes gréco-romaines', *ASAE* 35 (1935), 1–3.; id., 'Le monument d'Agrios au Musée de Caire', *ASAE* 39 (1939), 279–303. On the inscription, see L. Criscolo, 'Nuove riflessioni sul monumento di Ptolemaios Agrios a Panopolis, in G. Paci and L. Gasperini (eds.), *Epigraphai. Miscellanea Epigrafica in onore di Lidio Gasperini I* (Tivoli, 2000), 275–90.; E. Bernand, *Inscriptions métriques de l'Egypte gréco-romaine, recherches sur la poésie épigrammatique des Grecs en Egypte*, Annales littéraires de l'Université de Besançon 98 (Paris 1961) (= I. Métriques).
[122] Guéraud, *ASAE* 39, 281.
[123] Guéraud, *ASAE* 35, 1–3.; E. Schönbauer, 'Die rechtliche Stellung der Metropoleis', 126.
[124] A. Wilhelm, *Die Gedichte des Ptolemagrios aus Panopolis, Anzeiger, Österreichische Akademie der Wissenscaft* (Wien 1948), 302–03. There is a problem with dating this monument. Milne relates it to the Augustan age, see Milne, *JHS* 21, 287–90. Bernand and Welles think it dates to the second or third century. Bernand bases this claim on the acclamations of the emperor, Bernand, *Inscriptions métriques*, no. 450. Welles presents his arguments in the following: B. Welles, 'The Garden of Ptolemagrios at Panopolis', *TAPA* 77 (1946), 192–206. Criscuolo also suggests this date, L. Criscuolo 'A Textuary Survey of Greek Inscriptions from Panopolis and The Panopolite', in A. Egberts et al. (eds.), *Perspectives on Panopolis*, 63.

[125] Guéraud, *ASAE* 39, 282–84.
[126] D. Frankfurter, "Things Unbefitting Christians': Violence and Christianization in Fifth-Century Panopolis', *Journal of Early Christian Studies* 8 (2000), 277.
[127] Wilhelm,'Die Gedichte des Ptolemagrios aus Panopolis', 306.
[128] M. Smith, 'Aspects of the Preservation and Transmission of Indigenous Religious Traditions in Akhmim and its Environs during the Graeco-Roman Period', in A. Egberts et al. (eds.), *Perspectives on Panopolis*, 241–43.
[129] Petrie wrote about the situation of the cemetery of El-Hawawish A in 1886: He states that '*at Ekhmim there had been great expectations, two or three years before, of results from a large and undisturbed cemetery of all periods; but a French Consul was put there (without any subjects to represent him), and he raided and stripped the place under Consular seal, which could not be interfered with*', F. Petrie, *Seventy Years in Archaeology* (New York 1932), 80.; McNally and Schrunk, *Excavations in Akhmim*, 2.

Figure 1.1. The *Ptolemagrios* monument, the so-called 'Agrios Pillar' of Panopolis, the Cairo Museum (inv. 26093), Bernand, I. *Métriques*, 114.

be positively identified, except by their documentation in museum archives, their dates of purchase, their style, and their textual content (for example, mentions of local gods, onomastics, titles, and genealogical links). Thus, Smith states that '*Akhmim remained, in a sense, the older Egypt's home of lost causes*'[130]. He also states, however, that 'it will become apparent that my own particular perspective on Akhmim or Panopolis is clouded to some extent by doubt and uncertainty'[131]. Van der Vliet notes that '*working on ancient Panopolis means working with fragments*'[132]. One of the main problems one faces in dealing with the different kinds of material and textual evidence is the issue of undated objects and manuscripts, as Smith highlights in his review of the religious traditions of Akhmim in the Graeco-Roman Period[133]. The data collected here will be incorporated into the study and analyses of the cemetery of El-Salamuni below.

The clergy of Panopolis was rich, with the higher priestly orders receiving a share of temple revenues. This is why they had to make bids to be appointed for their position by the state[134]. The Panopolite priests were qualified and professional in their knowledge of myths, rituals, wisdom, literature, medicine, astrology, and astronomy[135]. The high-status priestly category included the *archiereus* (high priest), who was a kind of annually appointed chairman, selected from among the higher clergy. His function was administrative rather than religious. Meanwhile, other priests performed the traditional rites. In Egyptian documents, several priests are attested as serving Min. The *stolistai*, for instance, were charged with dressing the divine statues, and were also involved in giving hymns and offerings, along with inspecting sacrificial animals for their

---

[130] M. Smith, 'Dating Anthropoid Mummy Cases from Akhmim, the Evidence of the Demotic Inscriptions', in M. Bierbrier (ed.), *Portraits and Mummies, Burial Customs in Roman Egypt* (London 1997), 70.
[131] Smith, 'Aspects of the Preservation and Transmission', in A. Egberts et al. (eds.), *Perspectives on Panopolis*, 234.
[132] J. Van der Vliet, 'Preface', in A. Egberts et al. (eds.), *Perspectives on Panopolis*, XI.
[133] M. Smith, 'Aspects of the Preservation and Transmission', in A. Egberts et al. (eds.), *Perspectives on Panopolis*, 238–41.

[134] U. Wilken, 'Kaiserliche Tempelverwaltung in Aegypten', *Hermes* 23 (1888), 592–606.
[135] In Late Antique Panopolis, astrology was unaccepted, and the astrologers and casters of horoscopes were regarded as magicians, poisoners, and idol worshippers. However, this was a rhetorical device rather than a historical reality. Shenoute denounces his opponents as 'interpreters of hours' who 'make calculations on the basis of the stars of heaven,' reacting against astrology being practiced in Roman Panopolis, Amelineau, *Oeuvres* 1, 379, 381.; D. Bell, *Besa: The Life of Shenoute*, CSS 73 (Kalamazoo 1983), 84–85.; M. Smith, 'Aspects of the Preservation and Transmission', in A. Egberts et al. (eds.), *Perspectives on Panopolis*, 244.

purity. The *pterophoroi* were sacred scribes in charge of the calendar. As for the scribe of the divine scrolls (*zx3 mD3.wt nTr.wt*)[136], he had a ritual function in the temple and the necropolis, and used specific magical spells which were recorded in divine scrolls[137]. The *hierogrammateis* read and wrote the religious books, and evaluated potential new priests based on their capabilities, such as their cultic purity and writing skills. The lower-status categories included the *pastophoroi* (bearers of sacred objects), who carried the barque of the gods through the major ritual festivals and processions, and the Θαλλοσόται (*Thallodoteoi*), who delivered branches to visitors of temples and shrines, and who were presumably also a kind of minor priest[138]. The scribe of the oracle (*zX3 bj3.t*)[139] was another distinguished priestly position attested at Akhmim (it was one of the titles of the two brothers Hor and Hor-resnet/ Hor-nesu), as well as the 'Reporting Prophet', or *Hm-nTr wHm*, who may have conducted the secret religious ceremonies at Akhmim[140]. Furthermore, the priestly titles *Hm nTr tpy/ 2-nw/3-nw/ 4-nw n Mn*, translating to mean the 'first, second, third, and fourth prophet of Min', as well as *Hm-nTr wHm n Mn*, or 'Heralding Prophet of Min', are also attested[141]. In funerary contexts, and especially on the east bank, Min is often accompanied by Horus and Isis. De Meulenaere suggests that the trinity Min-Horus-Isis is recorded by Μεναρης on three linen bandages of the mid-second century AD[142].

Panopolis has not yet been recognised for its great significance as a cultural heritage site, both as a Graeco-Roman city, and as a centre of Egyptian and Hellenistic religion and culture. Archaeological remains in the city of Akhmim are rare because the ancient city is covered by modern buildings. An in-depth study of its history and the respective significance of its archaeological cultural heritage and sites is still needed. Key areas and limitations of research in this region include:

1. The modern town of Akhmim (*Kom al-Tawr*)[143] lies on top of the ancient one. Aside from the evidence of former temples, recorded in texts as 'fields of ruins', the city itself remains virtually unexplored. This is because Akhmim has been continuously occupied. As a result, Akhmim's old temples, mansions, houses, palaces, workshops, granaries, markets, and other civic structures have been buried under the towering strata of the alluvial plain, and under the sprawling maze of the rapidly growing modern city. The remains of the temple of Min, located within modern Akhmim, are now buried under a public highway, extending under a modern Muslim cemetery. The highway and cemetery would need to be relocated in order to uncover the rest of the temple[144]. Thus, the written sources and the great mass of funerary mummy cases are still the only clues to form an approximate understanding of the ancient city; new sources may still be revealed by new excavations (Figures 1.2a-c).

2. Ancient Akhmim was a great city with a highly significant political-administrative, socio-economic, religious, and cultural centre. Furthermore, Akhmim is one of the main necropoleis to have provided materials and objects for study. Sauneron describes it as *'une region de toute façon passionante, qu'il faudra un jour mieux étudier. L'abondance des matériaux historiques, à toutes les périodes, est étonnante. Et c'est aussi un secteur où les aventures spirituelles les plus remarquables ont été tenées'*[145], which means '*a fascinating region anyway, which one day will have to be better studied. The abundance of historical materials, from all periods, is astonishing. Also, it is an area where*

---

[136] A. Gardiner, *Ancient Egyptian Onomastica. Text. 1.* (Oxford 1947), 55–59.
[137] P. Derchain *Le papyrus Salt 825 (B.M. 10051), rituel pour la conservation de la vie en Égypte, Mémoires de l'Académie Royale de Belgique VIII/1a. collection in–8, 2ᵉ série 58* (Brussels 1965), 73.
[138] A *thallodotes* from Psonis is mentioned in *CEML* 139 (=*CEMG* 2176).; *P. Oxy.* XLIII, 3094, II,. 40, 43.
[139] R. Parker, *A Saite Oracle Papyrus from Thebes in the Brooklyn Museum (Papyrus Brooklyn 47.218.3), BEStud* 4 (Providence 1962), 33–34.; J. Elias and T. Mekis, 'The yellow-on-black coffin of the oracle scribe Hor in the Swansea Museum', *CdÉ* 91, fasc. 182 (2016), 251–52.; M. Bruwier and T. Mekis, 'Diversity of the Akhmimic Funerary Art in the 4th–3rd centuries BC, a Case Study on a Priestly Family, and a Study on Canopic Chests of Akhmim in the Graeco-Roman Period: a Survey in the Antiquity Collections', in M. Mosher (ed.), *The Book of the Dead, Saite Through Ptolemaic Periods, Essays on Books of the Dead and Related Materials, SPBD Studies* (Prescott 2019), 6.
[140] J. Elias and T. Mekis, "Prophet-registers' of Min-Horus-Isis at Akhmim', *MDAIK* 76 77 (2020/2021), 83–112.
[141] Depauw, 'Late Funerary Material', in A. Egberts et al. (eds.), *Perspectives on Panopolis*, 73.
[142] H. De Meulenaere, 'Prophètes et danseurs panopolitains à la Basse Époque', *BIFAO* 88 (1988), 41–49. The bandages are published in G. Wagner, 'Bandelettes de momies et linges funéraires', in J. Vercoutter (ed.), *Livre du Centenaire de l'IFAO 1880–1980, MIFAO* 104 (Cairo 1980), 330–33 (now SB XVI 12435–37).

[143] Kuhlmann, *SDAIK* 11, 14. The Arabic name 'Karm al-Tawr', meaning 'Garden of the Bull', might refer to the white bull, the sacred animal of the sky god Min. On the bull of Min, see G. Wainwright, 'Some Celestial Associations of Min', *JEA* 21 (1935), 158–70.
[144] In 1987, excavations carried out by the Supreme Council of Antiquities (SCA) Inspectorate of Sohag unearthed a granite statue of Nakhtmin, the high priest of Min in the reign of Eje, along with a calcite statue of a Roman female, perhaps for Venus or Aphrodite, Y. El-Masry, 'Seven Seasons of Excavations in Akhmim', in C. J. Eyre (ed.), *Proceedings of the Seventh International Congress of Egyptologists, Cambridge, 3–9 September 1995, OLA* 82 (Leuven 1998), 761–62. In 1991, a queen statue and several fragments of a colossal, seated statue of Ramesses II were found roughly 45m. north of the Ramesside temple. The fragments included a base and were surrounded by mudbrick walls, El-Masry, *OLA* 82, 763–64.; id., *MDAIK* 59, 285–87. Illegal excavations in the Muslim cemetery situated about 100m. north of the area uncovered a huge head of another colossal statue of Ramesses II, El-Masry, *MDAIK* 59, 288. Later, in 2003, the Supreme Council of Antiquities (SCA), supervised by Z. Hawass, found the seated statue itself. The statue measures about 13m. in height and weighs 700 tons, making it the largest seated limestone statue ever found, Hawass, *KMT* 16.1 (2005), 20–21. Hawass suggests that upon the conversion of the temple of Min into a monastery, the Copts attempted to destroy the colossal statue of Ramesses II, and incorporated the base into a screen wall, Hawass, *KMT* 16.1 (2005), 22. In 1995, the archaeological area was opened to the public as an open-air museum located several metres below the modern ground level, where the Local Sohag Inspectorate Office is also situated (in the southern part of the area). Between 1978 and 1982, the University of Minnesota worked at five open sites in Akhmim, including two inside the town and three on its northern edges. There, they studied the urban development of Akhmim in the Later Roman and Early Islamic Periods. The excavations were concentrated on one of the sites located near the church of Abu Seifein. There, they found the remains of two houses, as well as stores with pins and pottery. These buildings were destroyed and reused during the Fatimid Period, McNally and Schrunk, *Excavations in Akhmim*, 45, 47, 48.
[145] Sauneron, *Villes et légendes*, 106–10.

Panopolis: An Overview

Figure 1.2a. The ruined temple of Min in Akhmim.

the most remarkable spiritual adventures have been held'. Current knowledge of the history of Panopolis as a Graeco-Roman town is based only on its various funerary artefacts, with unreliable information available about their descriptions, find circumstances, and dates. A colloquium on Panopolis, organised in 1998 in Leiden, was the most important study of the city. It was entitled 'Perspectives on Panopolis', and included discussions and the sharing of opinions and interdisciplinary approaches by Egyptologists, Classicists, Coptologists, Archaeologists, Papyrologists and Historians. In 2006, Peter van Minnen noted that *'Panopolis has received some attention in recent times, but this material still needs to be put together meaningfully'*[146]. In all honesty, studying Akhmim during the Graeco-Roman period means entering the labyrinth of doubt and imperfection.

3. For a long time, the Akhmim necropoleis were the victims of unscientific excavations, illicit looting, and treasure hunts, leaving behind important heritage sites which are now in a poor state of preservation. Ever since the 19th and early 20th centuries, many Nile steamers have stopped at Akhmim, which once had a thriving market designed especially for mummies and coffins from the Akhmim cemeteries. As Akhmim became an important centre for the antiquities trade, sales were not limited to objects that were actually discovered there[147].

Figure 1.2b. A Roman calcite statue of Venus(?) in the Open-Air Museum.

---

[146] As documented in PM V, 17–26.; K. Parlasca, *Mumienporträts und verwandte Dènkmäler* (Wiesbaden 1966), 41–43.; G. Grimm, *Die römischen Mumienmasken aus Ägypten* (Wiesbaden 1974), 26–27, 96–100, 146–48.

[147] People like Budge and Wilbour, for instance, purchased many objects in Akhmim. Budge made purchases on behalf of the British Museum, and the Wilbour amassed a private collection that was later transferred to the collections of the Brooklyn Museum, E. Budge, *By Nile and Tigris, A Narrative of Journeys in Egypt and Mesopotamia on Behalf of the British Museum Between the Years 1886 and 1913, I–II* (London 1920), 87.

The Afterlife in Akhmim

Figure 1.2c. A Roman Period structure which may be a magazine.

4. The lack of systematic excavation techniques represents the most serious problem for understanding the main town of Panopolis and its necropoleis. The El-Salamuni cliffs as well as the El-Diabaat hill are honeycombed with tombs dating from the Old Kingdom to the Coptic Period, but few of these tombs have been systematically recorded. Some are not recorded at all, and many remain hidden. Doubtless, future excavations in El-Salamuni will uncover more hidden tombs and funerary materials, and the hill will hopefully be recognised as an important site for the study of funerary iconography in the Graeco-Roman Period. Hence more information on Panopolis may still be revealed from its main necropolis. Investigating and publishing the El-Salamuni tombs will be a starting-point for discovering one of the great necropoleis of the Graeco-Roman Period, as well as for elucidating the history of the funerary art and burial customs of Panopolis.

2

The Necropoleis of Akhmim

The broader necropolis of Akhmim includes a large complex of burial places from various periods. The extensive cemeteries are situated on the edge of the Eastern Desert to the northeast of Akhmim, nearly touching the Nile at their southern part. Akhmim contains three main cemeteries, classified by Kuhlmann as cemeteries A, B, and C. The three necropoleis are situated within the Τοπαρχια Μητροπόλεως[1]. Rock-cut tombs seem to have been the most common architectural type in the three cemeteries, and most of the known funerary material was found there. None of the known tombs in the three necropoleis are well preserved (Figure 2.1).

Necropoleis B and C are cliff sites, while A is in the valley. All three burial sites contain pharaonic tombs. Necropoleis A and C also contain tombs of later periods, and especially the Graeco-Roman and Coptic eras. The three cemeteries were known to travellers ever since the 18th century, and were rediscovered in the late 19th and early 20th centuries. Although the Graeco-Roman cemeteries of El-Hawawish and El-Salamuni have been known since the 18th century, the cemeteries are still neglected and undocumented. Topographical maps for the recording and registering of the tombs are still needed.

2.1: El-Hawawish A (Naga al-Diabat[2], or 'the Ridge Cemetery')

This cemetery[3] is located about 4km. east of Akhmim, in the valley close to the village of El-Hawawish. The cemetery contains burials from the Predynastic Period up to Christian and Islamic times, although most of the tombs belong to the Graeco-Roman Period. Many of the tombs were consistently reused. Many natural clefts and faults in the cliffs were used for mass burials of the poor, in which simple mummies, without any coffin, were heaped upon the floor. Furthermore, a catacomb for sacred animals (including ibises, raptors, canids, cats, and snakes) has also been found here[4]. The archaeological hill is gently-sloped and is about 20-30m. in height and 3km. in length.

Its tombs are still unregistered and unexplored (Figure 2.2). It has three Coptic monasteries known as El-Deir El-Bahri ('the Northern Monastery'), El-Deir El-Wastani ('The Middle Monastery'), and El-Deir El-Qibli ('The Southern Monastery')[5]. It is located about 2km. south of El-Salamuni C (Figure 2.3).

Gaston Maspero (1846- 1916), the Director of the Egyptian Antiquities Service, learned that various burial objects had come into the possession of local people in the areas of Sohag and Akhmim. Maspero once stated that *'the first time that [he] thought about researching the cemetery, villagers were carrying to their homes sarcophagi of white stone, some in human form. The villagers, [when] questioned on their provenance, responded vaguely. They attached no value to these antiquities and gave no assistance to search for them'*[6]. Maspero's team searched the archaeological hill for over 3km. and bodies were discovered everywhere. From 1884 until the early 1890s, Maspero conducted many rapid and extensive field campaigns at the site, headed by Rais Khalil-Sakkar. Sometimes, this was with the absence of Maspero, and often it was with the engagement of local military personnel to undertake the actual work. Unfortunately, the excavation campaigns were haphazard and without any systematic documentation. Maspero once stated *'Jamais cimetière ne mérita mieux que celui d'Akhmîm le nom de nécropole. C'est vraiment une ville, dont les habitants se comptent par milliers...'*, which translates to say *'Never has a cemetery deserved the name of necropolis better than that of Akhmim. It really is a city whose inhabitants count in the thousands'*[7].

During Maspero's first visit, he recorded 20 tombs at the site within 14 days, observing a few pharaonic tombs, and numerous Graeco-Roman sepulchres. He found tombs crammed with bodies and artefacts in 'an almost apocalyptic order'[8]. He recorded 800 pieces of mummy cartonnage dating to the Graeco-Roman Period, and unearthed about 8,000 to 10,000 mummies with their burial items, *'la plupart sans valeur'*[9]. Maspero also mentions

---

[1] El-Sayed and El-Masry, *Athribis I*, 8.
[2] Y. El-Masry was the first scholar to name the location 'Naga al-Diabat', Y. El-Masry, 'Recent Explorations at the Ninth Nome of Upper Egypt', in Z. Hawass (ed.), *Egyptology at the Dawn of the Twenty-First Century, Proceedings of the Eighth International Congress of Egyptologists, Cairo, 2000, I. Archaeology* (Cairo, New York 2003), 335.
[3] The term 'ridge cemetery' was coined by J. Elias in 2005. See J. Elias, 'Akhmim', in R. Bagnal et al. (eds.), *Encyclopaedia of Ancient History* (Oxford 2013), 3. It is southwest of the cemetery, located on the ridge to the north side of the Coptic monastery of Deir El-Adhara/Deir El-Qibli, A. Klales, *Computed Tomography Analysis and Reconstruction of Ancient Egyptians Originating from the Akhmim Region of Egypt, A Biocultural Perspective*, Ph.D. Thesis, University of Manitoba (Winnipeg 2014), 30.
[4] S. Ikram, *Divine Creatures, Animal Mummies in Ancient Egypt* (Cairo 2005), XVIII.

[5] Kuhlmann, *SDAIK* 11, 52, 53–63, pl. 19–21.; U. Bouriant, 'Notes de Voyages', *Rec.Trav.* 11 (1889), 141, 145, no. 2.
[6] G. Maspero, *Études de mythologie et d'archéologie égyptiennes*, BE 1 (Paris 1893), 214–15.
[7] G. Maspero, *Sur les fouilles exécutés en Égypte de 1881 à 1885*, BIE 6–1885 (Cairo 1886b), 84 (=Etudes de mythologie), BE 1 (1893), 215.
[8] Depauw, 'The Late Funerary Material from Akhmim', in. A. Egberts et al. (eds.), *Perspectives on Panopolis*, 71.
[9] For more on Maspero's accounts, see Maspero, *'Sur Les fouilles exécutés*, BIE 6–1885, 84–90.; id. *'Trois années de fouilles'*, BIE 5–1885 (Paris 1886a), 69–91.; id. *'Rapport à l'institut Ègyptien sur les fouilles et travaux exécutés en Ègypt, pendant l'hiver de 1885–1886'*, BIE 7–1886 (Cairo, 1887), 210–23.; id., *'Etudes de mythologie'*, BE 1, 233–34. Baedeker mentions that thousands of mummies were found there by Maspero; Baedeker, *Egypte, Manuel du Voyageur*, 56.

The Afterlife in Akhmim

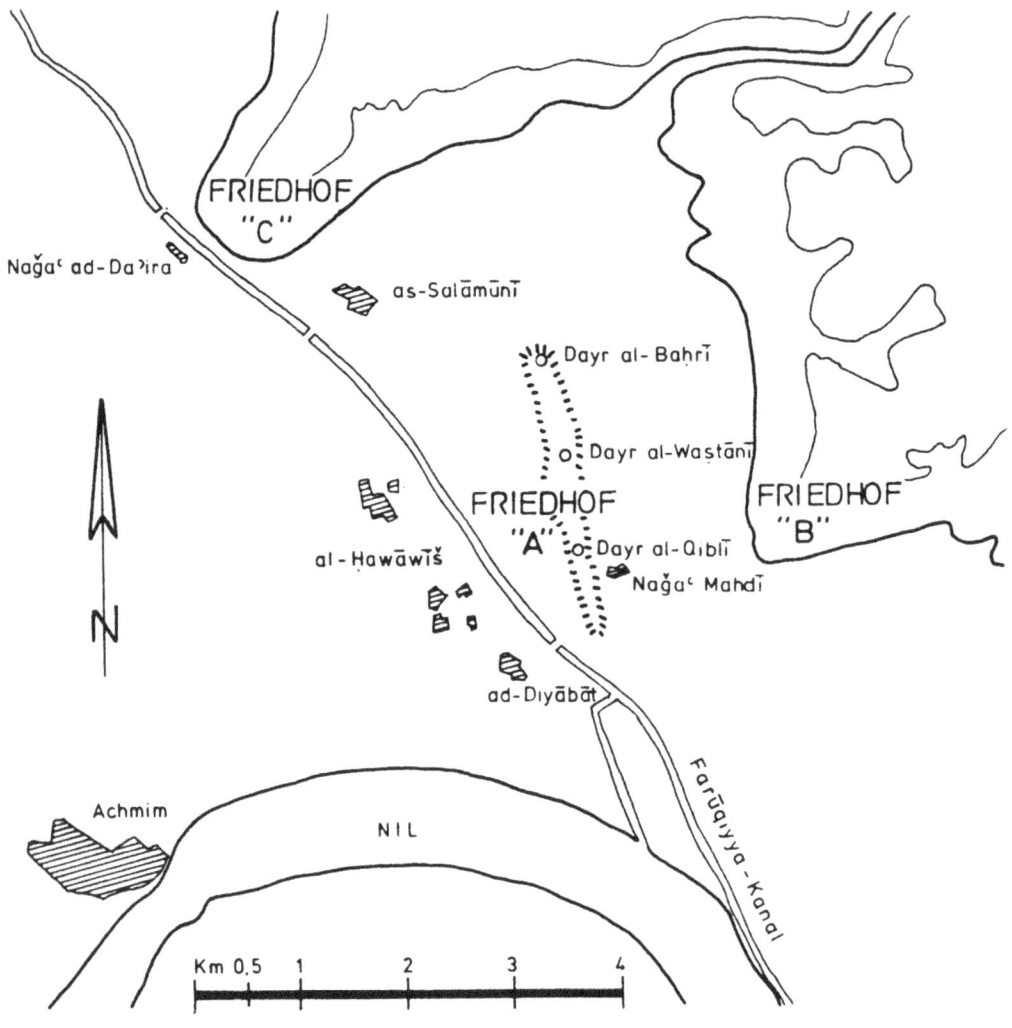

Figure 2.1. The Akhmim cemeteries, Kuhlmann, *SDAIK* 11, 53.

Figure 2.2. An overview of the cemetery of El-Hawawish A ('el-Tallah'), complete with the hewn openings of the tombs.

Figure 2.3. The location of El-Salamuni Mountain from El-Hawawish A cemetery.

that '*Les grottes surtout ont l'aspect de fosses communes. Les simples momies, emmaillotées mais sans cercueil, sont empilées sur le sol par lits réguliers, comme le bois des chantiers. Par dessus, on a entassé jusqu'au plafond les momies à cartonnage et à gaine de bois: tous les objets qui leur appartiennent sont jetés au hasard dans l'épaisseur des couches, tabourets, chevets, souliers, boîtes à parfum, vases à collyre et, pour ne rien perdre de l'espace, on a enfoncé de force les derniers cercueils entre le plafond et la masse accumulée, sans s'inquiéter de savoir si on les endommageait ou non*' ('*The tombs especially have the appearance of mass graves. The simple mummies, swaddled but without a coffin, are piled up on the ground in regular beds, like the wood of the building sites. On top, the mummies with cardboard and wooden sheaths have been piled up to the ceiling; all the objects that belong to them are thrown at random into the thickness of the layers, stools, bedside tables, shoes, perfume boxes, eyedrop vases and, in order not to lose any space, the last coffins have been forced between the ceiling and the accumulated mass, without worrying about whether they were damaged or not*')[10].

During Maspero's following campaigns, he revealed several animal burials, and the southern-most of two Coptic cemeteries, where famous Coptic textiles were found. Moreover, some licenses for digging in the necropolis were given to certain citizens of Akhmim. Thus, both the Antiquities Service and the local population worked on the site. In the years 1884-1888, the necropolis was thoroughly pillaged and destroyed. Wilbour attests to the fact that collecting the mummy textiles was a focus of Maspero,

stating: '*Maspero had an idea of stopping at Ekhmeem, not to find the famous tombs . . .but some graves where there are said to be fine mummy clothes* '[11].When Maspero left, the remaining burials were gradually exploited for the antiquities trade. Looting activities either by the local inhabitants or by foreign visitors also accompanied and followed the 'official' explorations[12].

The majority of pre-Christian burials in the cemetery of El-Hawawish date to the Ptolemaic Period, with many others date to the Roman period. In 1884, during the Universal Exhibition at the Trocadero, G. Maspero exhibited some of the Egyptian textiles discovered at the site[13]. During the winter of 1886/1887, the research was taken up by Urbain Bouriant (1849-1903), who complained about the almost complete destruction of the tombs of Akhmim[14].

On the recommendation of a compatriot, and in relation to the exhibition, Gaston Le Breton (1845-1922) was motivated to conduct his field campaign in the necropolis

---

[10] Maspero, *Études de mythologie*, 216.

[11] C. Fluck, 'Akhmim as a Source of Textiles', in G. Gabra and H. Takla (eds.), Christianity *and Monasticism in Upper Egypt I, Akhmim and Sohag* (Cairo 2008), 212.
[12] Kuhlmann, *SDAIK* 11, 51.; H. Kischkewitz, R. Gremer, and M. Lünig, *Berlinr Mummiengeschichten, Ergebnisse eines multidisziplinären Forschungsprojektes Gebundene Ausgabe- 13. Oktober* (Berlin 2009), 114.
[13] R. Cortopassi, 'Tissus de la cité égyptienne d'Akhmîm au musée de l'Homme', *La revue du Louvre et des musées de France* 3 (2001), 29–37.
[14] U. Bouriant, *Rapport au Ministère de l'Instruction Publique sur une mission dans la Haute-Egypte (1884–1885), MMFAC* 1.3 (Paris 1887).; id., *Rec.Trav.* 11, 140–41., 145–49.; G. Tallet, 'Fragments d'El-Deir (Oasis de Kharga) au tournant de notre ère- À propos de Carl Schmidt et de William Hornblower', in G. Tallet and C. Zivie-Coche (eds.), *Le myrte et la rose, Mélanges offerts à Françoise Dunand par ses élèves, Cahiers Égypte Nilotique et Méditerranéenne* 9. (Montpellier 2014), 392.

in 1889, searching for the missing textile pieces[15]. His campaign aroused an interest in the Graeco-Roman tombs and materials. On 07 February 1889, LeBreton sent a letter, which is now kept in the archives of the National Museum of the Middle Ages. In the letter, he laments the difficulty of finding intact tombs[16]. He notes how seriously the Akhmim necropoleis have been dismantled, as well as the great trafficking and dispersal of its antiquities. In his second letter (which was also written in February 1889)[17], he mentions the procedures being undertaken to transport six textile pieces, seven ceramic objects, and as many as three mummies to France for the exhibition. The two letters are addressed to Alfred Darcel.

The author has received a copy of the first letter which Le Breton had written in four pages[18]. On the fourth page, Le Breton mentions that he will ask for help from Le Comte d'Aunay ('the Count of Aunay'), who was the Plenipotentiary Minister in Egypt in 1885. His full name is Charles-Marie-Stephen Le Peletier (1840–1918), although people used to call him 'Le Comte d'Aunay'. The translation of the letter is as follows:

Akhmim 7 Février 1889
Mon cher Monsieur Alfred

Je ne puis résister au plaisir
de vous écrire et de vous donner
une bonne nouvelle concernant
le Musée de Cluny et celui des
Antiquités de la Seine Inférieure.
Arrivé en Égypte mon premier
soin a été de m'informer où
l'on trouvait ces fameux tissus
byzantins importés de l'orient
dont vous avez vu de si curieux
échantillons, la chose n'était
pas chose si aisée car on en a
découvert en plusieurs endroits
mais il me fallait trouver
la mine principale. J'ai fini
par réussir et me suis mis

en rapport avec un de nos
compatriotes qui habite Akhmim.
(à deux jours de Louqsor)

[second page]
les tombeaux en question
se trouvent à deux heures de
chez lui dans le sable près de
la montagne. Vous savez que
je suis un chercheur intrépide
aussi j'ai commencé par soudoyer
un arabe qui m'a conduit
dans le bon endroit où la nuit
les arabes vont fouilles les tombes
pour y trouver les fameux
tissus. C'est de là que le chanoine
Bock[19] a eu tous les siens. Je
connais l'individu qui les lui
a vendus en Europe.

J'ai commencé par embaucher
une trentaine d'arabes et me
suis mis à l'œuvre. Le premier
endroit ou j'ai commencé
mes fouilles est une petite
montagne de sable où l'on
a bien fouillé déjà trois à
quatre mille tombes sur une
superficie que j'évalue à une
cinquantaine ᵗʳᵉⁿᵗᵃⁱⁿᵉ d'hectares. Mes premières
recherches ont été vaines, les fouilles

[third page]
que je faisais ayant porté sur
des tombes déjà explorées dépouillées, mais
bientôt en explorant les endroits
environnants j'ai fini par découvrir
un terrain complètement vierge
et j'ai eu la joie de mettre au jour
seize momies entourées de ces fameuses
étoffes, j'en ai dépouillé la plus
grande partie de leurs tissus qui
les enveloppaient et j'ai fait emporter
par mes arabes trois momies très
bien conservées que l'on croirait
[?] d'hier dans leurs étoffes.
J'ai fait faire une caisse pour
les y mettres ainsi que les tissus
des autres momies. Parmi ces tissus
il y a une chemise brodée absolument
compète. C'est une pièce très intéressante.
Il s'agit maintenant d'expédier
tout cela en France, car je
destine ma trouvaille moitié
au Musée de Cluny moitié
au musée de Rouen. Vous verrez

---

[15] G. Gogny-Ghesquier, 'Le Breton: un collectionneur passionné', *Études Normandes* 1 (2005), 54–70.; F. Saragoza and P. Georges-Zimmermann, 'Doublement éternel, Quand les Égyptiens inhumaient leurs morts deux fois', *EniM* 7 (2014), 61–78.
[16] Saragoza and Georges-Zimmermann, 'Doublement éternel', 62.; M. Durand and F. Saragoza, *Égypte: la trame de l'Histoire, Textiles pharaoniques, coptes et islamiques, Sous la direction de Maximilien Durand et. (Catalogue d'exposition, Rouen, Musée des Antiquités, du 19 octobre 2002 au 20 janvier 2003)* (Paris 2002), 11–12.
[17] Unfortunately, Le Breton's letters do not refer to any details about the tomb's architecture, the burial methods, or the circumstances of the findings, Saragoza and Georges-Zimmermann, 'Doublement éternel', 63. For the letters, see M. Durand and F. Saragoza, 'Historique de la collection de textiles égyptiens du musée départemental des Antiquités', in *La trame de l'Histoire, Textiles pharaoniques, coptes et islamiques, cat. Exp.* (Roanne, Paris, 2002–2004),11–12.; S. Aufrère, *Collections égyptiennes, Collections des Musées départementaux de Seine–Maritime III* (Rouen 1987), 205.
[18] The author is grateful to Mrs Isabelle Bardiès-Fronty, the General Curator at the Musée de Cluny (Musée National du Moyen Âge) for sending a copy of this letter.

[19] I believe 'le chanoine Bock' is Franz Bock (1823–1899), who was a Catholic priest (a 'chanoine'/canon is a cleric). Franz Bock was also an art collector and extensively studied religious art and ecclesiastical treasures.

ainsi et mes compatriotes avec vous
de quelle manière et dans quelles

[fourth page]
conditions se trouvent les fameux
tissus.
    Maintenant la difficulté est de
faire passer la caisse en France en
évitant la douane égyptienne qui
saisirait probablement ma trouvaille,
je verrai pour cela en rentrant
au Caire le Comte d'Aubigny auquel
je demanderai ce service de faire
transporter cette caisse avec la
franchise diplomatique.
    Dans cette caisse il y a deux
momies d'enfants et une momie
d'adulte merveilleusement conservée.
    Vous voyez, mon cher Monsieur
Alfred, que j'utilise mon temps
dans la haute Égypte. Je suis
    émerveillé de ce que je fais et
je ne suis qu'au début de
mon voyage, j'aurais cependant
déjà un volume à vous écrire.
Veuillez vous charger de mille
choses aimables pour tous les
vôtres et croyez aux meilleurs
sentiments de votre
    tout dévoué et affectionné
Gaston Le Breton

Akhmim 7 February 1889
My Dear Mr Alfred

I cannot resist the pleasure
to write to you and give you
good news about
the Cluny Museum and the Antiquities of the Lower Seine.
When I arrived in Egypt, my first concern
was to inform myself where
one could find these famous
Byzantine fabrics imported from the East
of which you have seen such curious
samples, the thing was
not so easy, for they have been
discovered in several places
but I had to find
the main mine. I eventually
succeeded and got
in touch with one of our
compatriots who lives in Akhmim.
    (two days from Luxor)

[second page]
the tombs in question
are located two hours away from
his home in the sand near the
the mountain. You know that
I am an intrepid researcher
so I started by bribing
an Arab who led me
to the right place where at night
the Arabs go to dig the graves
to find the famous
cloths. It is from there that Canon
Bock got all of his. I
know the individual who sold them to him
sold them in Europe.
    I started by hiring
about thirty Arabs and set myself
to work. The first
place where I started
my excavations was a small
mountain of sand where
three to four thousand graves
have already been dig on an
area that I estimate to be around
fifty thirty hectares. My
initial
searches were unsuccessful, the excavations.

[third page]
that I was doing having targeted
graves already fully explored, but
soon, as I explored the surrounding
areas I ended up discovering
a completely virgin area
and I had the joy of uncovering
sixteen mummies surrounded by these famous
cloths, I have stripped most
of them of the cloths
that enveloped them and I had
my Arabs take away three very well-preserved mummies
that could be believed
[?] to be from yesterday in their clothes.
I had a crate made to
put them in with the fabrics
of the other mummies. Among these fabrics
there is an embroidered shirt that is absolutely
complete. It is a very interesting piece.
It is now a question of sending
all this to France, because I am designating half of my
findings
to the Cluny Museum and the other half
to the Rouen Museum. Accordingly you will see and my
compatriots with you
how and in what

[fourth page]
conditions the famous
fabrics are found.
    Now the difficulty is
to get the box to France
while avoiding the Egyptian customs who
would probably seize my find,
I will see for that back
in Cairo with the Count d'Aubigny, to whom
I will ask the service of having this box
transported with the

The Afterlife in Akhmim

diplomatic franchise.
    In this case there are two
children's mummies and one adult
mummy that are wonderfully preserved.
    You see, my dear Mister
Alfred, that I use my time
in Upper Egypt. I am
    amazed at what I am doing and
I am only at the beginning of
my journey, I would however
already have a volume to write to you.
Please receive a thousand
kind things for all of
your close ones and believe in the best
feelings of your
    very devoted and affectionate
Gaston Le Breton

Although Maspero's expeditions unearthed and highlighted an important cemetery in Egypt, it was also the main reason why the great heritage of this necropolis, which was particularly damaged by clandestine excavations, was dismantled. Unfortunately, in the years 1884-1888, the necropolis was thoroughly looted. By the 19th century, Akhmim had started to lose its great cultural heritage and property; thousands of its funerary objects were smuggled out of Egypt by diplomats, scholars, and travellers. Maspero removed many objects from the cemetery and transported them to France. During a short buying trip for the British Museum in Akhmim in January 1896, W. Budge declared '*I learned at first hand that the director of the Service of Antiquities had bought and disposed of antiquities, and exported them, which the British authorities in Cairo declared to be contrary to the law of the land*'[20]. Currently, many of the funerary stelae from the site are exhibited either in the local museums of Cairo and Alexandria, or in international museums, having been acquired through antique dealers or other public and/or private collections. In the latter case, the provenance is often lost, although most are believed to have been unearthed from the necropolis[21].

Due to the dissolution of certain private collections, some objects have been put back up for sale. Sometimes, this results in them being bequeathed to, donated to, or purchased by public museums. Both the French and British consulates had an illegal role in smuggling antiquities from Akhmim. Most of the objects that are recovered today had once ended up belonging to private collections from the last decade of the 19th century and the first half of the 20th century. Others have appeared on the art market when old private collections are sold[22]. On 08 January 1887, Budge stayed the night at Akhmim, writing '*I found that the French consular agent at Akhmim had about 200 vellum leaves inscribed with the Gospels and some of the early Coptic patriarchs and saints, and a box full of fragments of leaves. He was reserving them for Maspero and the Bibliotheque Nationale had agreed to buy them; but the agent needed money and as it seemed to me very desirable to buy them, I finally gave him £81 and brought them away with me*'[23].

Today, the Akhmimic mummies that largely originated from this cemetery can be found on every inhabited continent. The vast quantity of mummies and beautiful textiles attracted robbers and art dealers, who plundered the site. In the spring of 1894, a polymath named R. Forrer (1866-1947) was one of the most prominent scholars working with textiles to visit the site of Akhmim, shortly after the diggings of Maspero. He examined the destroyed Coptic necropolis in search of more Coptic textiles. When Forrer arrived at Akhmim, he already owned a considerable collection of more than 2,000 textiles, according to his own words, which he bought on the antiquities market in Cairo. They were supplied to him by agents who acquired the textiles from local finders[24]. The Byzantine tombs around the al-Qibli Monastery and the prehistoric cemetery near El-Westani Monastery were the focal points of Forrer's excavations. He discovered many mummies and textiles there[25], as well as various Christian ornaments such as hairpins of wood and bone, earrings, silver and bronze jewelry, belt buckles in the form of a Christian cross, ivory crosses, and some mummy labels. In reference to the looted cemeteries of Akhmim, Forrer wrote (in his fourth letter) to Gustav Müller, the director of the journal Antiquitäten–Zeitschrift, describing the nature of the site. He states '*Everywhere you look, you notice black holes in the mountains, where tombs have been opened, other holes become apparent, which turns out to be human bodies. Mummies that had been opened, their bindings and garments discarded*'[26].

The first comprehensive studies of the Akhmim finds were written by Forrer in 1891. During this time, he published one catalogue on textile finds, focusing mainly on woven tapestries featuring dyed wool, attributing the local silk production to Panopolis. In his travelogue, he reports that Akhmim is still suffering from illicit looting and antiquities trading. R. Forrer casts an uncompromising look at the

---

[20] Ismail, *Wallis Budge*, 113.
[21] L. Criscuolo, 'A Textual Survey of Greek Inscriptions from Panopolis and the Panopolite', in A. Egberts et al. (eds.), *Perspectives on Panopolis*, 57.
[22] M. Bruwier and T. Mekis, 'Diversity at Akhmim', in M. Mosher (ed.), *The Book of the Dead*, 62–64.
[23] M. Ismail, *Wallis Budge, Magic and Mummies in London and Cairo* (London 2021), 112–13.
[24] R. Forrer, *Die Gräber- und Textilfunde von Achmim-Panopolis* (Strasbourg 1891), 10.
[25] Most of the textiles from cemetery A are dated to the fifth, sixth, and seventh centuries; few are earlier. During Forrer's excavations, he noted that the elite were buried in colourful decorative clothing, while the lower classes were buried in plain linen cloth. The dressed bodies were then wrapped in a shroud, tied to a board, and placed in a grave, Forrer, *Mein Besuch in El-Achmim*, 44–45.; id., Über *Steinzeit-Hockergräber zu Achmim Naqada etc. In Oberägypten, Achmim-Studien I* (Strasbourg 1901), 10–12, 14, 17, 33, figs. 16–22, pls. 2–4. The two Forrer publications of the Akhmim textiles were later elaborated upon and their arguements refined by D. Renner-Volbach, *Diesogenannten Koptischen Textilien im Museum Andreasstift der Stadt* (Wiesbaden 2002).
[26] Forrer's text is written in German and is now in the atelier of Julian Laitzsch in the Staatliche Museen zu Berlin. It has been translated by Julian Laitzsch via a documentary film for the Akhmim project entitled 'Egypt's Forgotten City'.

world of Akhmim's antiquaries and necropolis raiders[27], explaining the devious ways of transporting antiquities abroad to Europe, as well as how they change hands until finally coming into the possession of Europeans. He recalls, for example, objects from Akhmim that were brought by a bedouin from Giza to Luxor. It is very likely that the Kharga Oasis was one of the stopping points for antiquities dealers. It was likely used as a location to hide artefacts acquired from different locations (including Akhmim) before transporting them abroad[28].

In 1891, Karl Baedeker (1801–1859) had confused the necropolis of El-Hawawish A with that of El-Hawawish B (El-Madina) in his guidebook[29]. This was perpetuated by Percy Newberry and in the well-known bibliography of Porter and Moss[30]. As a result, Cemetery A came to be forgotten. During Kuhlmann's survey of necropolis A in 1981/1982, he recorded the history of the necropolis and sketched its topography, documenting a great number of shallow graves in the hill. In relation to this, he states: '*Man sieht sich vor eine wahre Mondlandschaft flacher Krater gestellt, zwischen denen hie und da noch halb verschüttete Schächte die Gegenwart von Gräbern anzeigen*'[31]. He also recorded the prehistoric burials within the area of the Deir El-Wastani. Just south of here lie tombs from the Pharaonic to the Roman Periods. The part of the cemetery lying between Deir-El-Qibli and Deir El-Wastani belongs to the Ptolemaic Period[32]. Near the Ptolemaic cemetery, Maspero located a cluster of tombs dating exclusively to the Antonine Period[33]. The Coptic burials are scattered between the older tombs; one group is situated at the northern border, near the prehistoric burials, while the other lies in the south section, at Deir El-Qibli. The eastern section of the mountain is exclusively children's burials from the Old Kingdom to the Roman period, while in the Christian burial area, children are mingled with adults. On the other side, the western section has a *hypogeum* of mummified falcons, jackals, cats, baboons, and ibises[34].

Kuhlmann classifies three types of tombs in the necropolis[35]. Type A-1a are Ptolemaic tombs that are partly rock-cut and partly constructed of mud-brick (Figure 2.4),

Figure 2.4. Remains of some mudbrick constructions in the cemetery before the rock-cut Ptolemaic tombs.

with descending passages and stairs leading to separate burial chambers at a lower level[36]. The greatest quantity of stelae from Akhmim was found in these tombs. Type A-1b are shaft tombs of the Ptolemaic/Roman eras, where a shaft of roughly.15-20m. leads down to various terraces. Here, each shaft contains about eight to ten burial niches filled with roughly one dozen sarcophagi. Type A-2 refers to square-shaped animal tombs. Finally, type A-3 refers to Christian tombs with a shaft of roughly 1.3 to 1.5m.. They are about 2.8m. in length and usually have a west-east orientation. The deceased were buried with their clothes on a bare floor beneath two stones[37]. Besides burial chambers and shafts, every natural cleft and fault in the cliffs was used to bury dead bodies.

In 1985, the necropolis was excavated by the Egyptian Antiquities Organisation (EAO), supervised by Yahya El-Masry, the Head of the Inspectorate of Antiquities at Sohag. It was also excavated during three later seasons, from 1989 to 1999. These excavations revealed several tombs from the Ptolemaic Period in the area between Deir El-Qibli and Deir El-Wastani, and a tomb for ibis and falcon mummies[38].

---

[27] *Antiquitäten-Zeitschrift* 6 (1895), 131.; Forrer, *Mein Besuch in el-Achmim*. On the collection of R. Forrer at Akhmim and his *villa panopolitana*, see Martin and Primavesi, *L'Empédocle de Strasbourg (P. Strasb. Gr. Inv. 1665–1666)*, 39 no.7. Grimm refers to a great number of objects with unknown provenances which appeared on the antiquities market between 1891 and 1897, Grimm, *Die römischen Mumienmasken aus Ägypten*, 27–36.
[28] Tallet, 'Fragments d'El-Deir (Oasis de Kharga)', in G. Tallet and C. Zivie-Coche (eds.), *Le myrte et la rose*, 388.
[29] Baedeker, *Egypte, Manuel du voyageur*, 57.
[30] In 1912, Newberry took Maspero's description of the tombs 'opposite to El-Hawawish' to mean those of
cemetery B instead of A. In *PM* V, 18, the author adopts Newberry's interpretation (*The Inscribed Tombs of Akhmim'*, *AAA* 4 (Liverpool 1912), 99–120) and hardly mentions cemetery A, reinforcing the misunderstanding once again.
[31] Kuhlmann, *SDAIK* 11, 55.
[32] El-Masry, 'Recent Explorations at the Ninth Nome', in Z. Hawass (ed.), *Egyptology at the Dawn of the Twenty-First Century*, 335.
[33] Maspero, *Sur Les fouilles exécutés, BIE 6–1885* (1886b), 89 (=Etudes de mythologie, *BE* 1 (1893), 218).
[34] Kuhlmann, *SDAIK* 11, 55–60.
[35] Kuhlmann, *SDAIK* 11, 61–62.

[36] El-Masry, 'Recent Explorations at the Ninth Nome of Upper Egypt', in Z. Hawass (ed.), *Egyptology at the Dawn of the Twenty-First Century*, 335.
[37] E. Budge, *The Mummy, A Handbook of Egyptian Funerary Archaeology* (New York 1989), 217–18.
[38] El-Masry, 'Recent Explorations at the Ninth Nome', in Z. Hawass (ed.), *Egyptology at the Dawn of the Twenty-First Century*, 331–38.; Y. El-Masry, 'The Ptolemaic Cemetery of Akhmim', *OLA* 194 (Leiden 2010), 173–84.; G. Abd-El-Nasser, 'A New Discovery from the Ptolemaic Period in El-Hawawish', *GM* 92 (1986), 7-8. For more on the other excavations at the cemetery, see Baedeker, *Egypte, Manuel du voyageur*, 57. For the typology of the tombs, see Kuhlmann, *SDAIK* 11, 53–71.

The Afterlife in Akhmim

The cemetery was excavated in a haphazard manner and not to today's standards. Unfortunately, the cemetery is still a continuous target of illicit looting by robbers, both from the local community and from other regions in Egypt. Furthermore, the location of the three monasteries upon this archaeological hill is also a fiscal challenge. Recently, more campaigns were undertaken in the cemetery by the Akhmim Antiquities Office under the supervision of the Egyptian Ministry of Tourism and Antiquities (including excavations in December 2021 and January 2022, a school for excavations in August 2022, and an additional field campaign in November 2022). These excavations led to the unearthing of several painted Ptolemaic tombs, as well as shallow burials of a later date, and various funerary objects. The so-called 'El-Tellah'('the hill') is the area of the recent necropolis excavations, containing tombs of the Late Period and Early Ptolemaic Period (Figure 2.5). In April 2019, an Early Ptolemaic tomb belonging to Tutu/Totoes, a high priest of Min, as well as his son *Iw-hat* (*iw-h3t*), his mother (*Ir.n nbt Pr t3 Wsir*, or 'the Lady of the House Ta-Wsir') and his wife Ta-sherit-Iset (*T3 Srt. Ist*), a sistrum-player of Hathor[39], was discovered in the tell area between the western and northern monasteries, following looting activities that led the local authorities of the Akhmim Inspectorate to the area. Various mummified humans, animals, and birds were also found[40].

Figure 2.5. The entrance of the Ptolemaic rock-cut tomb of Tutu with a mud brick entrance.

Cemetery A revealed that a vast quantity of funerary materials originating from Akhmim especially date to the Ptolemaic Period, many of which were sold to private collections and museums around the world[41]. The more beautiful funerary material was often sold to visiting travellers. Only a few items ever made it into the inventory of the Egyptian Museum in Bulaq. Maspero's rapid and extensive excavations took place under his authority, but in his absence. Certain citizens of the local community received permission to dig in the necropolis alongside the Antiquities Service. This was followed by illegal looting on a large scale, leaving the necropolis totally looted. This resulted in the loss of the great heritage of one of the most important necropoleis of the Ptolemaic, Roman, and Coptic Periods in Egypt.

2.2: El-Hawawish B, or 'Bayt El-Madina'

El-Hawawish B is located 6km. east of Akhmim. Schiaparelli first visited the cemetery in 1885[42]. Near the end of 1888, after the excavations in cemetery A, Maspero discovered the cemetery of El-Madina. It is situated east of El-Hawawish A. Rais Khalil Sakkar conducted an excavation campaign here[43], on El-Hawawish Mountain, which is about 310m. in height. In 1919, Newberry visited the cemetery of El-Hawawish B, and dated one of the tombs to the Middle Kingdom. He counted only 29 tombs, dating to the end of the Old Kingdom and the Middle Kingdom. Later in 1927, Wreszinski visited the necropolis and noticed only the destroyed tombs[44]. Between 1979 and 1992, Naguib Kanawati of the Australian Centre for Egyptology excavated and recorded about 884 tombs dating back to the Old through Middle Kingdoms (ca.

---

[39] Tutu, the patron of the El-Diyabaat tomb, is a different priest from Tutu, the owner of the London BM EA 1215 stela. He was the son of Pa-di-Khonsu-iy and Aset-weret, who together with his father were prophets of Ptolemy III and Berenike II in the cult of the 'efficient gods'. The stela may be dated to around 190 BC, Taylor, *Journey Through the Afterlife, Ancient Egyptian Book of the Dead* (London 2010), 177 no. 85.; Bruwier and Mekis, 'Diversity at Akhmim', in M. Mosher (ed.), *The Book of the Dead*, 16, 69. There is also another Tutu who is the owner of *P. Twt*. He was the soltist of Min and the son of Hor, and probably lived in the second century AD, Bayer-Niemeier et al., *Ägyptische Bildwerke III, Skulptur, Malerei, Papyri und Särge* (Frankfurt 1993), 254–92. There is also another priestly figure named Ta-sherit, who was a sistrum player of Min, as well as the owner of a stela, Padova, 'Museo di Scienze Archeologiche e dell'Arte dell'Università di Padova, inv. No. 1357'.; F. Crevatin, 'Una Nuova stele da Akhmim', *Quaderni Digitali* 3 (2005),1–2.; id., 'Briciole epigrapfiche', *Rivista degli studi orientali* 85 (2012),155–59.

[40] Looting activities at the site led the Akhmim Inspectorate to uncover this tomb. It was opened and introduced to the media on 06 November, 2019. The painted scenes of the tomb were recently removed by the Egyptian Ministry of Tourism and Antiquities and transferred to be on exhibition in the new museum in Cairo. The tomb can be associated with Totoes, the soltist of Min, who was certainly engaged in the dressing and equipping of the divine statue in the Temple of Min, Gauthier, *Le personnel du dieu Min*, *RAPH* 3 (Cairo 1931), 39–51. He is also the owner of the famous *P. Twt*. He was the son of Horos, the soltist and the second prophet of Min. His mother was named 'Epoeris', and was a player of Min, E. Bayer-Niemeir et al., *Ägyptische Bildwerke III*, 254–92. Since Maspero's excavations, El-Hawawish A has become a spot of illicit looting activities, and Akhmim has remained an important centre for the antiquities trade. Budge and Wilbour, for instance, purchased many objects from Akhmim (most of which were probably found in El-Hawawish A), the former purchasing on behalf of the British Museum, and the latter amassing a private collection, much of which later entered the Brooklyn Museum, Budge, *By Nile and Tigris*, 87. The excavation school that was held at the site also led to the discovery of a beautiful painted tomb of the Ptolemaic Period belonging to one of the priests of Min. He was also probably related to Tutu's father. A conservation effort is now being undertaken in the tomb. In the opinion of the author, many of the priestly figures of Akhmim who were known from the Late Period and the Early Ptolemaic Period are likely buried in this section of the necropolis.

[41] Petrie, *Seventy Years in Archaeology*, 75.
[42] E. Schiaparelli, 'Chemmis (Akhmim) et la Sua Antica Necropolis', in *Études archéologiques, linguistiques et historiques dédiées à Mr. Le Dr. C. Leemans à l'occasion du cinquantième anniversaire de sa nomination aux fonctions de Directeur du Musée archéologique des Pays-Bas* (Leiden 1885), 85–88.
[43] Kuhlmann, *SDAIK* 11, 64.
[44] W. Wreszinski, *Von Kairo bis Wadi Halfa* (Leipzig1927), 63.

2350-1750 BC), recording one of the most extensive Old Kingdom provincial cemeteries. Several governors, viziers, and high priests from the fifth to sixth dynasties are buried in this cemetery[45]. Most of the tombs are undecorated, unfinished, or damaged[46].

El-Hawawish B is one of the most extensive Old Kingdom provincial cemeteries, paralleled only by the capital cemeteries of Giza and Saqqara. Kanawati also found indications of a rock-cut temple in the cemetery[47]. During their persecution, the Copts escaped and hid here; Christian crosses, Coptic graffiti, saints, and altars were found in the tombs (Figures 2.6a-b). Recently, on 26 February, 2021, a tourism development project was launched, where five tombs were opened for visitors. The tombs included those of Nehwet-Desher (G95), Shepsi-Pu-Min (H24), Ka-Hep/Tjeni-Iker (H26), Hesi-Min (M22), and Hem-Min (M43), all of which date to the 6th dynasty, with the exception of the tomb of Hesi-Min (M22), which dates to the fifth dynasty (Figure 2.7)[48].

2.3: El-Salamuni C

The mountain of El-Salamuni C lies 6km. northeast of Akhmim and about 2km. north of El-Hawawish B. The site is named for the nearby modern village, which lies south of it (Figure 2.8), while the village of Naga El-Sawâma-sharq lies north of El-Salamuni Mountain[49]. Naga El-Sheikh Ismail and El-Rabaab are the closest places north of El-Salamuni, and the modern Muslim cemetery of El-Sawamaa lies close to the archaeological site as well (Figure 2.9). The old road connecting Upper Egypt with Cairo runs in front of the mountain, with Naga El-Sawâma-sharq straddling the road. One must cross the El-Sheikh Ismail (or El-Raii) bridge to reach the north edge of the mountain. The cemetery contains rock tombs dating from the Old Kingdom to the Roman period[50]. Many of the Graeco-Roman tombs have been systematically recorded. The El-Isawieh (formerly El-Faraoukiya) canal

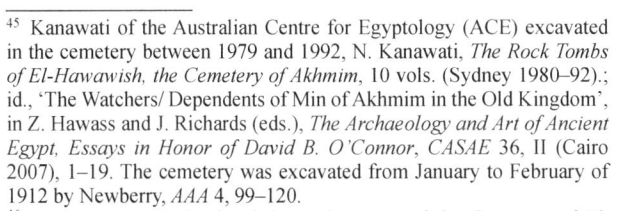

Figure 2.6a. The Coptic remains in the El-Hawawish B tombs.

Figure 2.6b. A Coptic inscription from El-Hawawish B.

lies at the foot of the mountain[51], and branches off from the Nile above Akhmim to turn northwest[52] alongside the cultivated land. On the northern section of the mountain,

---

[45] Kanawati of the Australian Centre for Egyptology (ACE) excavated in the cemetery between 1979 and 1992, N. Kanawati, *The Rock Tombs of El-Hawawish, the Cemetery of Akhmim*, 10 vols. (Sydney 1980–92).; id., 'The Watchers/ Dependents of Min of Akhmim in the Old Kingdom', in Z. Hawass and J. Richards (eds.), *The Archaeology and Art of Ancient Egypt, Essays in Honor of David B. O'Connor*, CASAE 36, II (Cairo 2007), 1–19. The cemetery was excavated from January to February of 1912 by Newberry, *AAA* 4, 99–120.
[46] E. Thompson, *A Study of the Architecture of the Cemetery of El-Hawawish at Akhmim in Upper Egypt in the Old Kingdom*, MA thesis, Macquarie University (Sydney 2001), 1.
[47] Kanawati, *The Rock Tombs of El-Hawawish I*, 6.; Kuhlmann, *SDAIK 11*, 12–13, 21.
[48] The project was funded by the International Bank under the auspices of the Sohag Governorate and the Sohag Inspectorate Office. It started in 2016 with a total fund of 17,0000000 LE.
[49] On its archaeological value, see T. Whittemore, 'The Sawamaa Cemeteries', *JEA* 1 (1994), 246–47.; J. Bourriau and A. Millard, 'The Excavation of Sawâma in 1914 by G.A. Wainwright and T. Whittemore', *JEA* 57 (1971), 28–57.
[50] F. von Bissing, 'Tombeaux d'Époque Romaine a Akhmim, Lettre ouverte au Dr Étienne Drioton', *ASAE* 50 (1950), 555.; id., 'Aus Römischen Gräbern zu Achmim (Panopolis) in Oberägypten', *JDAI* 61/62 (1946/1947), 1–16.

[51] The modern village of Isawiah Sharq is located 6km. upriver from Akhmim, bordering the Nile. It was named Θμόω, or 'Thmou', which probably means 'the large new land/island'. The fort of Thmou is mentioned in P.Beatty Panop., in the Notitia Dignitatum, and in the Antonine Itinerar, see Gauthier, 'Notes géographiques sur le nome Panopolite', *BIFAO* 4, 65–67.; id., *BIFAO* 10, 108–110.; K. Vandorpe, *Egyptische geografische elementen in Griekse transcriptie*, 2 vol., unpublished M.A. dissertation, KU Leuven (Leuven 1988), 99.
[52] On El-Salamuni cemetery, see Kuhlmann, *SDAIK* 11, 71–86, pls. 27–38.

The Afterlife in Akhmim

Figure 2.7. The tombs along the upper terraces of El-Hawawish B.

Figure 2.8. El-Salamuni village, to the south of El-Salamuni Mountain.

The Necropoleis of Akhmim

Figure 2.9. El- Sawâma- sharq village and the Muslim cemetery to the north of El-Salamuni Mountain.

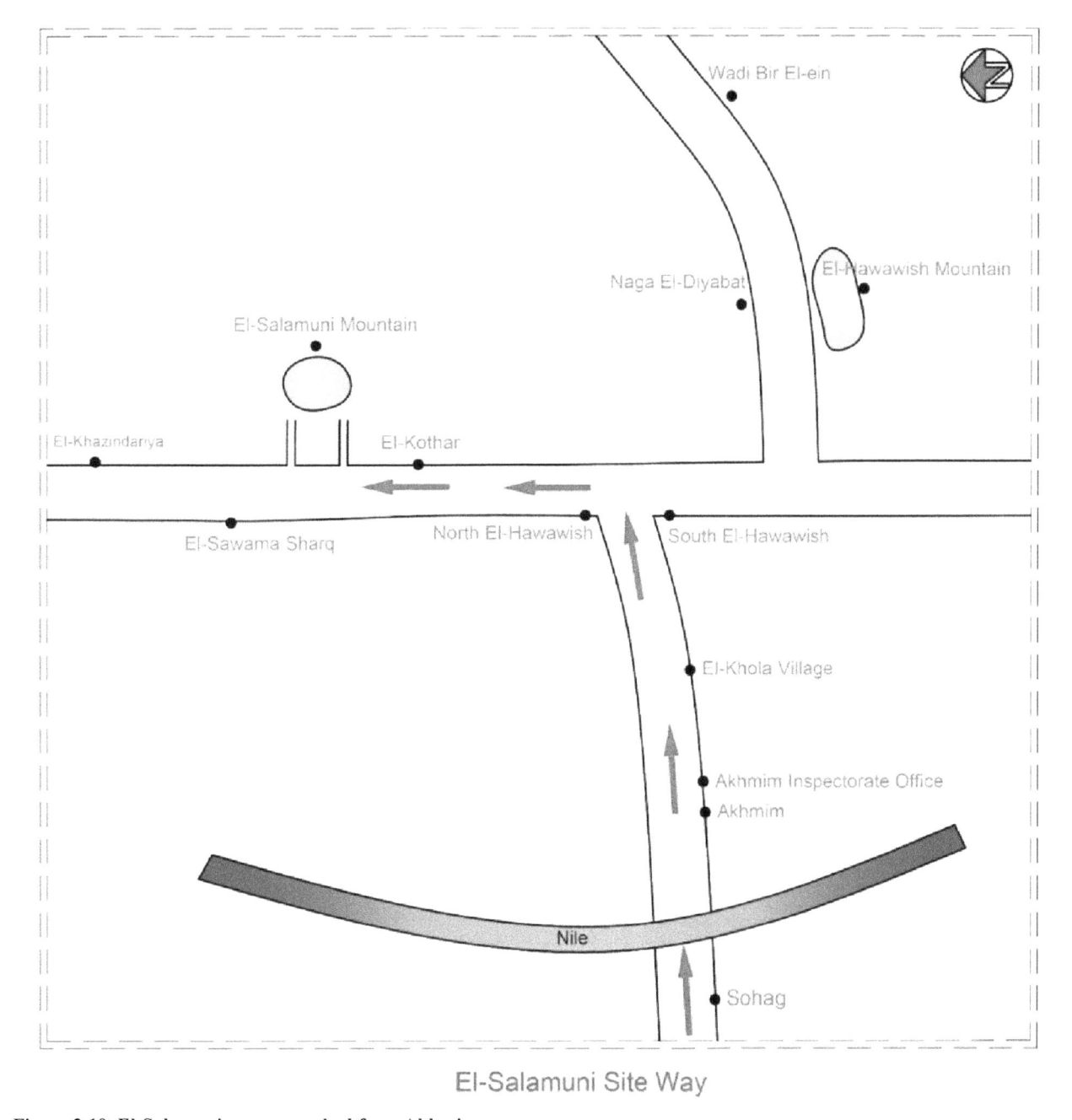

Figure 2.10. El-Salamuni, as approached from Akhmim

an impressive rock-cut temple of Min from the reign of Ay overlooks the cemetery. It was restored in the Ptolemaic Period, and was then used as a shelter by hermits and *anachoretes* during the Late Roman Period.

The El-Salamuni necropolis was home of significant quarrying activities from the time of the New Kingdom until at least the second century. The quarries were both directly north of El-Salamuni and further away, being located to the far north (Nazlet Haridi, 30km. north) and to the far south (Gebel Toukh, 13km. south). Three main quarries were used in the cemetery. The first one dates to the 18th dynasty and is located south of the rock-cut temple of Ay, being commonly known as Hawsh el-Gemaal. The second quarry is of the New Kingdom, but continued to be used in the Late Period. It was probably used until the Roman period, but with less frequency. This second quarry is located somewhat far from the cemetery itself, about 300m. south of the archaeological cemetery. The quarry from the Late Period contains large galleries, and is most recently known by the villagers as *el-Birba*. The third quarry is of the Ptolemaic Period. It is small, and located north of the rock-cut temple of Ay, in a register below that of the Old Kingdom tombs. The quarries of El-Salamuni produced fine, very white-coloured limestone of good quality. A paved white road connected the foot of the mountain with the quarries, facilitating the workers' activities and probably serving as a rubbish heap for stones and as a transport route[53].

To reach the eastern necropoleis of Akhmim, one must pass the village of El-Khiloah, which is 2km. east of the villages of Akhmim, El-Hawawish El-Qibliah (southern Hawawish), and El-Hawawish El-Bahariya (northern Hawawish). The public road separating the two villages lies 2km. farther east. The necropoleis of El-Hawawish B and El-Hawawish A are located opposite the village of El-Hawawish El-Qibliah. To reach El-Salamuni, one must go north and cross El-Hawaish El-Bahariya, the El-Kawthar district, El-Salamuni village, and then Naga El-Dairah, which is located opposite El-Salamuni Mountain. El-Dairah forms a part of the Naga El-Sawâma-sharq village (Figure 2.10).

---

[53] Kuhlmann, *MDAIK* 35, 185–86.; Kuhlmann, *SDAIK* 11, 40a.

3

A History of the Investigations and Surveys of El-Salamuni

An increased interest in travel to Egypt by Europeans began as early as the 13th century. However, many of these travellers were mainly restricted to the region north of and north of Cairo. An even larger interest in ancient Egypt by travellers and historians did not begin until later, during the Enlightenment (from the mid-17th century to the late 18th century). During this time, a fascination with ancient Egyptian culture prompted many Europeans to visit Egypt[1]. During the early 19th century, a wide-scale looting and exporting of material from Egypt began. There was, at that time, no Egyptian Antiquities Service, and therefore, mass quantities of materials and objects were plundered and shipped to museums and private collections all over the world.

The Akhmimic cemeteries at El-Hawawish and El Salamuni have been known since the 18th century. In 1884, they started to be unsystematically explored by Gaston Maspero (1846–1916) and the Antiquities Service. The cemetery of El-Hawawish A started to be widely looted by the arrival of Maspero. However, the plundering of El-Salamuni is recorded as beginning even earlier than this by N. L'Hôte (1838). The only systematic excavations to have taken place in these cemeteries were in the rock-cut tombs of El-Hawawish B, conducted by the Australian Centre for Egyptology of the Macquarie University, and headed by Naguib Kanawati (1979-1992).

3.1: Travellers and Visitors to the Site

From the 17th century onwards, European rulers, historians, literate visitors, and intellectuals began to recognise the political and archaeological value inherent in the appropriation of Egyptian artifacts. In the first half of the 18th century, Akhmim, and the cemetery of El-Salamuni in particular, was well-known as a regular stopping point, and attracted a multitude of European travellers, visitors, and Archaeologists. Between 1737 and 1738, Richard Pococke (1704-1765)[2] visited El-Salamuni, the Wadi El-Westani of Naga al-Diabat hill, and the Wadi Bir El-Aïn (the 'Valley of the Magic Spring', to the southeast of El-Salamuni). He gave a brief description of the different types of tombs in El-Salamuni, and noted that some are painted. In one of them, he states that found an ibis (probably a vulture) painted on the ceiling, plus a strange figure of a man lying on the back of a quadruped animal (which probably refers to the common image of a mummy on an animal-footed bier).

Pococke also noted a large block from the ruins of a temple dedicated to Pan and Triphis, which was built during the lifetime of the emperor Trajan. On one side of the block, there is a Greek dedicatory inscription to Pan, the most significant god at Akhmim. It was written by Tiberius Claudius Apollinaris in favour of Trajan and can be dated to year 12, on the 19th of *Pachons*, 109 AD (corresponding to either the 10th or 14th of May, 109 AD)[3]. In 1778, C. Sonnini mentioned the same limestone block. He deciphered the name Tiberius (Tiberio) on one side, and on the other side, he saw a zodiac engraved with the colour blue. It may have been part of a ceiling, perhaps of a tomb. Regarding the block, he said: '*I saw a huge mass of single stone, on one of these was a Greek inscription engraved in large characters, it is almost cleared and I could not distinguish it as the word Tiberio... ... ... we distinguish in the middle a sphere with twelve signs of the zodiac*'[4].

In 1799, M. Frenay, a member of Napoleon Bonaparte's expedition, noted disturbances at Akhmim, and the desecration of some mummies. In 1799, Saint-Génis, another member of the expedition[5], visited Akhmim. He visited the ruined temple of Min and recorded an architrave of a portico/gate (now lost). The architrave had a reference to the completion of a building for the temple of Min in 109 AD. The architrave measures 3ft. (about 90cm.) in diameter. On one side is a Greek dedication in six lines to Pan in favour of the emperor Trajan. To the left of the Greek inscription, there is a figure of Pan/Min with a Min-hut sign behind him. To the right of the inscription, there is a scene of a figure holding an *ankh* sign. Between this figure and the inscription, there is a narrow line of hieroglyphs. On the other side of the block, there is a depiction of a zodiac (Figure 3.1)[6]. Perhaps, a Greek-style

---

[1] See J. Vercoutter, *The Search for Ancient Egypt* (New York 1992), 30.
[2] R. Pococke, *A Description of the East and Other Countries*, I, *Observations on Egypt* (London 1743), 78–79.
[3] J. Abry, *Les Tablettes Astrologiques de Grand (Vosges) et L'Astrologie en Gaule Romaine, Actes de la Table-Ronde du 18 mars 1992 organisee au Centre d'Etudes Romaines et Gallo-Romaines de l'Université Lyon III* (Lyon 1993), 123, fig. 6. Many travellers from the 18th and 19th centuries observed and described this lost monumental block which lay in the ruins of Min's temple in Akhmim, see M. Claude, 'Du bloc au temple : nouvelles perspectives sur une architrave monumentale du temple de Min d'Akhmîm', *Dialogues d'histoire ancienne, 2022, Chronique des Travaux en Égypte Chronique* 2022, 48 (1), 345-364.
[4] C. Sonnini, 'Voyage dans la Haute et Basse Égypte, fait par ordre de l'ancien gouvernement III' (Paris 1800), 144.
[5] M. Saint-Génis, 'Notice sur les restes de l'ancienne Ville de Chemmis ou Panopolis, aujour'hui Akhmim,
et sur les environs', in C. Panckoucke (ed.), *Description de L'Egypte, ou Recueil des Observations et des
Recherches qui été faites en Égypte pendant l'Expédition de l'Armée Française*, 2nd ed. (Paris 1821), 45–47.
[6] The dedication is made by Tiberius Claudius Apollinaris, a former military tribune and temple *prostates* of Pan and Triphis, I. Pan no. 79. Ibn Battuta mentions that the *Birba* of Akhmim housed at least one zodiac, Kuhlmann, *SDAIK* 11, 29 (which probably refers to this zodiac). Scholars argue that the stone served as a large architrave of the roofed *pronaos* of the temple of Pan, O. Neugebauer and R. Parker, *Nag° Hammad A, B, Egyptian Astronomical Texts III, Decans, Planets, Constellations and Zodiacs*, *EAT* III (London 1969), 86.; Kuhlmann, *SDAIK* 11, 43–44.

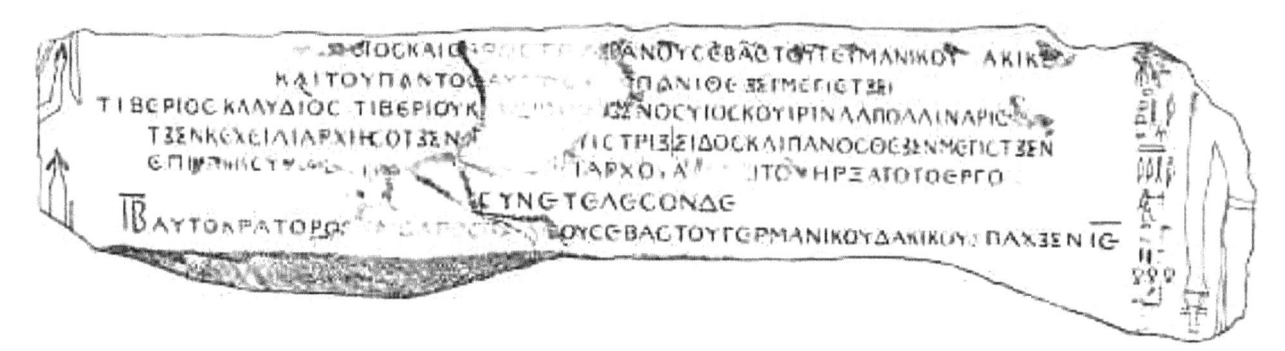

Figure 3.1. An architrave with a zodiac from the temple of Min, Kuhlmann, *SDAIK* 11, 44 after Wilkinson and Burton.

circular zodiac once covered the ceiling of the temple of Min, such as in the *pronaos* and the hypostyle hall[7].

Later, from 1838 to 1839, Nestor L'Hôte (1804-1842), a member of the Expedition française d'Egypte[8], visited the cemetery, where he noted a great number of tombs in an Egyptian-Greek style, as well as *'innombrables excavations taillées sans symétrie et avec la plus grande négligence'*. The first reference to the zodiacs of the El-Salamuni tombs was recorded by N. L'Hôte. He documented a circular zodiac which was divided into 12 sections, stating: *'quelques tombeaux m'ont offert des restes de peinture dans le gout égyptio-grec, c'est- à-dir des divinités égyptiennes combinees avec des ornaments du genre de ceux que j'ai déjà observés a Qau el Kebir. Dans un de ces tombeaux, j'ai reconnu les divinités de l'enfer égyptien, ... mais l'exécution de ces figures est bien grossière, on peut meme dire barbare. Ce que j'ai trouvé de plus remarquable dans ce tombeau, c'est un zodiaque circulaire a 12 compartiments, peint au plafond'* (*'Some tombs have offered me remains of paintings in the Graeco-Egyptian style, that is to say, Egyptian deities combined with ornaments of the kind I have already observed in Qau el Kebir. In one of these tombs, I recognised the divinities of the Egyptian underworld. But the execution of these figures is very crude, we can even say barbaric. The most remarkable thing I found in this tomb is a circular zodiac with 12 compartments, a painted ceiling'*). He also mentions: *'J'ai remarqué surtout, avec curiosité, dans les parties les moins dégradées de quelques plafonds, des portions de deux zodiaques à douze compartiments, où l'on aperçoit encore les figures du Sagittaire, du Taureau, du Scorpion, au milieu d'autres figures tout à fait méconnaissables ; au centre de l'un d'eux, j'ai discerné une tête humaine de forte proportion...'*, which translates to mean: *'I noticed especially, with curiosity, in the less degraded parts of some ceilings, portions of two twelve-compartment zodiacs, where the figures of Sagittarius, Taurus, and Scorpio can still be seen, in the midst of other completely unrecognisable figures; in the centre of one of them, I discerned a human head of great proportions...'*.

L'Hôte also sketched the temple of Ay[9].

From 1843 to 1845, Richard Lepsius (1810-1884) visited Akhmim and El-Salamuni. He recorded the impressive rock-cut temple of Min on the mountain. He described the temple's layout, translated some texts, and determined the different phases of its construction[10]. Maspero did not conduct excavations at El-Salamuni. The plundering of the cemetery by the local villagers revealed a few hundred tombs, but also caused great damage to them. It was reported that *'Notre chevauchée nous mena aux montagnes du Nord, mais sans résultat: les tombes sont peu nombreuses, et ne nous fourniront rien que Nestor L'Hôte et Lepsius n'eussent déjà signalé avant nous'* (*'Our ride led us to the mountains of the north, but without result: the tombs are few, and did not provide us anything that Nestor L'Hôte and Lepsius had not already reported before us'*)[11].

Ernesto Schiaparelli visited Akhmim and the cemetery of El-Hawawish A during the excavations of Maspero. He recognised three necropoleis in the city. One of these, El-Salamuni, is located at the entrance to a wadi in the Arabian Desert, opposite the plain of Akhmim. Schiaparelli wrongly dated the necropolis to be from the 18th and 19th dynasties, suggesting that the temple of Ay was a necropolis temple for the New Kingdom tombs[12].

In 1896, the Coptologist Carl Schmidt (1868–1938)[13] spent only a half of a day surveying the necropolis. He

---

[7] Neugebauer and Parker, *EAT* III, 204.
[8] N. L'Hôte, *Lettres écrites d'Égypte en 1838 et 1839, contenant des observations sur divers monuments Égyptiens nouvellement explores et dessinés* (Paris 1840), 86–87.
[9] J. Vandier d'Abbadie, *Nestor l'Hot (1804–1842), Choix de documents conservés à la Bibliothèque National et aux Archives du Musée du Louvre*, DMOA 11(Leiden 1963), fig. XVI.1. The reports and drawings of N. L'Hôte are now conservated in the Department of Manuscripts in la Bibliothèque nationale de France under the registration number NAF20396 142r, http://gallica.bnf.fr/ark:/12148/btv1b525045086/f284.image.r=nestor%201%C3%B4te.
[10] Lepsius, *LD* II, 163.; id., *Briefe aus Aegypten, Aethiopien und der Halbinsel des Sinai: geschrieben in den Jahren 1842–1845 während der auf Befehl Sr. Maj. des Königs Friedrich Wilhelm IV von Preußen ausgeführten wissenschaftlichen Expedition-Berlin* (Berlin 1852), 102f, 411 no. 22.
[11] Maspero, *Sur Les fouilles exécutés*, BIE 6–1885 (1886b), 87.; id., *Etudes de mythologie*, 215.
[12] Schiaparelli, 'Chemmis (Akhmīm) e la sua antica necropoli', 85.
[13] C. Schmidt, 'Ein Griechisches Mumienetikett aus Achmim', *ZÄS* 34 (1896), 80–81. For more about Schmidt's records, see Tallet, 'Fragments d'El-Deir (Oasis de Kharga)', in G. Tallet and C. Zivie-Coche (eds.), *Le myrte et la rose*, 390–92.

nevertheless unearthed an intact tomb, with undecorated walls and multiple mummies lying next to each other on a bare floor. One of them bore a mummy portrait, while two others had a mummy label. Given the damaged state of the mummies and the portraits due to moisture, Schmidt suggested that the numerous 'worthless portraits' which he saw in the antiquities shops at Akhmim might have come from this cemetery, together with 'forty better preserved portraits' in several museums[14]. The mountain was once used by the local Christian population for habitation, burials, and religious practices, and Charles Wilbour (1846–1916)[15] recorded that the El-Salamuni tombs were used as shelters for Coptic monks. He noted that many of the monk-caves in the hillside that had drawings on their ceilings had originally been tombs of the Ptolemaic-Roman Period. Fortunately, Maspero did not order for excavations to be carried out in El-Salamuni. He visited the site, but decided that it was too large of a project for him.

In 1897, Friedrich Wilhelm von Bissing (1873–1956) visited the necropolis alone for the first time. He later returned to the site in 1913 accompanied with Hermann Kees and his wife. He noted several Roman tombs at the desert's edge. During his first visit, the *fellahin* led him to discover the most famous tomb in the necropolis, and fifty years later, he published this Roman tomb, which is now numbered tomb C1 by the Akhmim Inspectorate. During his second visit in 1913, he found two other tombs on the southern section of the mountain[16]. The tomb had polychrome Egyptian-Hellenistic paintings showing red and green flowers, and small green twigs were scattered around the walls. At the corners were garlands with red berries[17]. Kees was also the first to examine the scenes and inscriptions of the temple of Min in detail. The so-called 'tomb of von Bissing of 1913' is located south of the rock-cut Temple of Ay.

In April 1903, Jean Clédat (1871–1943) visited what he called 'Qurnet es-Salamouni'. His interest in the necropolis is reflected in his very brief description of some of its tombs in an unpublished notebook entitled *Couvents Rouge et Blanc*. He recorded three tombs on the mountain and referred to them as tombs 1, 2, and 3 in his notebook,

which was later published by C. Meurice[18]. The tombs are now listed as tombs F2, F3 and F4; they were lost for a long time until having been re-excavated and registered by the Akhmim Antiquities Office.

In 1906, Otto Rubensohn (1867–1964)[19] came to El-Salamuni. He described a tomb in which the Egyptian deities appear together with representations of marble panels and garlands, confirming the mix of Egyptian and Hellenistic art in the tombs. According to von Bissing, the tomb which Rubensohn visited is most likely located to the south, at the foot of the desert slope opposite a sheikh's tomb built on a hill[20]. Regarding the tomb, Rubensohn mentions:

'*Das in den Felsen eingearbeitete Grab, eine einfache Anlage mit Vorraum und zwei durch ein schmales Stück stehen gebliebener Felswand getrennte Kammern, war ausgeraubt. Die Wände sind mit weiszem Stuck bedeckt, darauf ist mit bunten Farben gemalt. Das untere Drittel der Wand zeigt umlaufend in Vorraum und Kammern braunrot getônte quadratische Felder in geringen Abständen voneinander, mit verschiedenfarbigen Linien eingerahmt. Es ist also deutlich als Sockel mit Orthostatn gehalten. Oben abgeschlossen wird dieser Teil durch eine umlaufende breite Blumengirlande, die von parallelen Streifen oben und unten eingefaszt ist. Darüber, also auf der eigentlichen Dekorationsfläche, sind Bildfelder abgeteilt durch schlanke, mit Blumen umwundene Pfeiler, die auf dem Sockel sich erheben. Von Spitze zu Spitze der auch mit einem Blumenaufsatz gekrönten Pfeilerchen sind Blumengirlanden gehängt. In den so umgrenzten Bildfeldern begegnen sich die gewohnten Darstellungen aus ägyptischen Gräbern, Barke mit dem Toten, Anubis neben dem aufge- bahrten Leichnam, alles bunt auf weissem Grund. Die Decke des Grabes ist leicht gewülbt, und über ihre weiszgetünchte Fläche sind frei und regellos bunte Blumen und Vôgel verstreut. Das Ganze wirkt wie einer jener luftigen Baldachine, unter denen die Toten aufpebahrt wurden. Das Grab, das ganz ungeschützt in der Wüste liept, verdiente eine Publikation, ehe es zerstôürt wird*'.

This translates to mean:

'*The tomb is carved into the rock, a simple structure with an anteroom and two chambers separated by a narrow piece of rock wall that had remained standing, and had been robbed. The walls are covered with white*

---

[14] The seven portraits that were originally seen in Cairo in 1908 and that are now in the Metropolitan Museum have been attributed to one single family tomb in the cemetery of El-Salamuni by Parlasca, based on physiognomic similarities, K. Parlasca, *Mumienporträts und verwandte Denkmäler*, 41–42, pls. 27.1.2.4.; K. Parlasca and H. Seemann, *Augenblicke: Mumienporträts und ägyptische Grabkunst aus römischer Zeit* (Munich 1999), no. 231–33.; E. Doxiadis, *The Mysterious Fayum Portraits, Faces from Ancient Egypt* (London 1995) 153–55.; B. Borg, *Mumienporträts, Chronologie und kultureller Kontext* (Mainz 1996), 79, 166, 186. One portrait of a bearded, middle-aged man shows stylistic parallels with two portraits in the Art Institute in Chicago, inv. numbers. 224798 and 224799. Furthermore, inv. 09.181.5, a portrait of a young boy, may date to the second third of the third century AD.
[15] For further information about this visit, see J. Capart, *Travels in Egypt (December 1880 to May 1891, Letters of Charles Edwin Wilbour* (Brooklyn 1936), 98.
[16] Von Bissing, *ASAE* 50, 560–66, figs.7, 9, 10.
[17] Von Bissing, *ASAE* 50, 556.; id., *JDAI* 61–62, 7.; Kaplan, *BzÄ* 16, 169–70, pls. 89a, b.

[18] For Clédat's visit, see C. Meurice, *Jean Clédat en Égypte et en Nubie (1900–1914)*, *BdÉ* 158 (Cairo 2014), 69–70, 463 fig. 20. Although von Bissing's 1897 tomb was accidentally rediscovered by Kuhlmann in 1981 (Kuhlmann, *SDAIK* 11,73, 35c–d, 36), Kuhlmann did not find the three tombs of Jean Clédat.
[19] O. Rubensohn, 'Archäologische Funde im Jahre 1905', *AA* 21 (1906), cols.130–31.
[20] Von Bissing, *ASAE* 50, 555. Most likely, this tomb is one of the tombs C3-C5, which are located on the far southern part of the mountain, near El-Salamuni village. The Sheikh's mausoleum in the village still receives local villagers to this day, and has its own festival, which is known as 'Seidnah El-Hares' ('Our Lord, the protector').

stucco, painted with bright colours. The lower third of the wall shows square fields encircling the anteroom and chambers, tinted brown-red, at short distances from each other, framed with lines of different colours. So it is clearly seen as a base with orthostats. This part is closed at the top by a wide flower garland running around it, which is framed by parallel stripes at the top and bottom. Above it, that is, on the actual decorative surface, picture fields are divided off by slender pillars surrounded by flowers, which rise on the base. Flower garlands are hung from tip to tip of the pillars, which are also crowned with a flower cap. In the pictorial fields delimited in this way, the usual representations from Egyptian tombs meet, the barque with the dead, Anubis next to the laid-out corpse, all colourful on a white background. The ceiling of the tomb is slightly vaulted, and colourful flowers and birds are freely and randomly scattered over its whitewashed surface. The whole thing looks like one of those airy canopies under which the dead were laid out. The tomb lying quite unprotected in the desert deserves publication before it is destroyed'.

Three years later, in 1909, Michael Rostovtzeff (1870-1952)[21] visited the site, returning for a second time in 1914. He noticed that the necropolis was looted a long time ago and was continuing to be looted. During his first visit in 1909, he only spent a few hours in the necropolis. During his second visit, he was interested in searching for the painted tomb which Rubensohn had visited before, but unfortunately, he was unable to find the tomb. Instead, he recorded two Roman tombs which belong to the second to third centuries AD. Giving a precise date of these tombs is not possible, but through the hieroglyphic inscriptions visible on some of the tombs, Rostovtzeff proposed a date of no later than the third century AD. He additionally sketched a schematic plan of a tomb, as well as its classical wall paintings.

The tomb that Rostovtzeff sketched consists of two rooms with three burial niches, imitating the usual burial chambers of Alexandria in the Hellenistic Period. He only describes the anteroom, mentioning that it has the same composition as the burial one. His description stresses the classical aspects of the tomb and mentions that it is decorated with fields delineated by a pilaster, as well as panels with decorated *orthostats*, laurel leaves, and garlands. The pilasters and garlands feature scenes from the Egyptian funerary repertoire, which he did not care to record. In fact, he described the ancient Egyptian elements as not important and as the subject of trifles, stating: '*et les détails et autres brouilles n'ont pour nous aucune importance*' ('*and the details and other trifles are of no importance to us*'). The ceiling is covered with birds and flowers. Rostovtzeff compared the style of the classical floral motif in the tomb with the *arcosolium* of the tomb of 1905 (number 2086) in Chersonesos. Rubble covers the lower parts of the walls of the tomb. Information about the tomb and its similarities to the one that was explored by Rubensohn was provided to Rostovtzeff by his request[22]. He concluded that this classical style of painting in El-Salamuni is not the result of chance, but that it is a well-established decoration scheme with other ancient examples. He is only mentioned to have photographed the second tomb. Regarding the great importance of the El-Salamuni tombs, Rostovtzeff laments that '*nobody has tried to reproduce and to save the most important series of tombs near Akhmim*'[23]. The location of Rostovtzeff's tomb is still obscure. Unfortunately, in his publications, he did not describe the Egyptian scenes or provide photos of the tomb to help determining which tomb in the south section of the mountain he had visited.

In 1952, Charles Nims investigated El-Salamuni, focusing on the astronomical scenes. Six astronomical zodiacs in both the ante- and burial chambers of the tombs were later published by Otto Neugebauer and Richard Parker as Salamuni 3A and 3B, Salamuni 6, Salamuni 7, and Salamuni 8A and 8B[24].

In March 1957, the German Archaeological Institute in Cairo (DAIK) undertook an expedition to El-Salamuni that remained unpublished. Later, between 1977 and 1982, Klaus Kuhlmann of the DAIK conducted a brief survey of Akhmim, including its main temple and the necropoleis of El-Hawawish A, B, and El-Salamuni. Kuhlmann compiled an architectural typology of the tombs of El-Salamuni cemetery, and took some photos in the tombs. However, the photos are without descriptions or comments, or any plans of the tombs. He also described the rock-cut temple of Min[25].

In December 1989, while working at El-Hawawish B, Naguib Kanawati visited the tomb noted by von Bissing in 1897. Kanawati had been requested by the Egyptian Ministry of Culture to prepare a book on the touristic sites at Sohag, and therefore conducted a quick visit, spending only five minutes in the tomb, and making only three

---

[21] M. Rostovtzeff, *Anticnaja dekorativnaja zivopis na juge Rossi I* (St. Petersburg 1913–14), 494–95, figs. 92, 93.; id., 'Ancient Decorative Wall-Painting', *JHS* 39 (1919), 147, 158. M. Rostovtzeff is famous in the West for his work on ancient economy and his excavations with Yale at Doura Europos. He published a monumental (in both the literal and figural senses) monograph on the paintings in the tombs in Kertsch. The monograph is written in Russian, like all of his works. Therefore, to access his work, most scholars refer to the English article in *JHS* 39. Rostovtzeff's work is important because he parts from the idea of a cultural continuity that is mostly influenced by Hellenistic art forms. In connection to this, he became interested in visiting Akhmim. A French translation of the book of Rostovtzeff was published by A. Barbet, *La peinture décorative antique en Russie méridionale*, in *Mikhail I. Rostovtzeff Mémoires de L'Academie des Inscriptions et Belles-Lettres, Saint-Pétersbourg 1913/14*, I, Texte, description et étude des documents (Paris 2004), 622–25, figs. 92–93. The author would like to thank A. Barbet for sending him a copy of the book.

[22] The only difference is the existence of a *Blumengirlande*, or 'flower garland', in the tomb explored by Rubensohn.
[23] Rostovtzeff, *JHS* 39, 158.
[24] Neugebauer and Parker, *EAT* III, 98, 204–05.; Smith, 'Aspects of the Preservation and Transmission', in A. Egberts et al. (eds.), *Perspectives on Panopolis*, 243.
[25] Kuhlmann, *MDAIK* 35, 165–93.; id., *MDAIK* 38, 347–62.

photographs[26]. The tomb was known among the Akhmim Inspectorate as the 'Tomb of N. Kanawati', and the keys of the tomb were labelled 'N. Kanawati Tomb!'.

In 1999, for her MA degree, Irene Kaplan compiled and republished some funerary scenes from previously recorded tombs, using photographs of El-Salamuni that had been made by Kuhlmann during the German Archaeological Institute of Cairo (DAI Kairo) survey[27]. In particular, she named the two von Bissing tombs from 1897 and 1913 as 'El-Salamuni Tombs I and II'. She also briefly described other tombs that Kuhlmann, Neugebauer, and Parker had documented before, labeling them 'El-Salamuni tombs III, IV, V, VI, and VIII'[28]. Furthermore, she named Clédat's tomb 1[29] as 'tomb VII[30]', which is now tomb F2, and Clédat's tomb 2 as 'tomb VIII', which is now named 'tomb F4' in the nomenclature of the local Antiquities Office at Akhmim.

3.2: Recent Excavations

During two field excavations in 1) 1996/1997, and 2) 2018/2019, the Local Antiquities Office of Akhmim excavated and uncovered some ancient tombs that had been recorded before, as well as other new, decorated Graeco-Roman tombs. These new tombs also contained astronomical zodiacs on their ceilings. Some of the tombs' entrances are now hidden by the local Akhmim Inspectorate due to the looting activities at the site (Figure 3.2). The recently excavated tombs are situated on both the north and south sections of the mountain.

In 2014/2015, the Sohag Restoration Office conducted conservation processes in tombs C5, F2, and F3. Later, in 2018, the local Inspectorate Office of Akhmim conducted a field campaign on the south section of the mountain, in the area adjacent to the *ghaffirs'* hut. They uncovered and cleaned some lower façade tombs, most of which were unpainted, in levels A, B, D, and E. Here, many mummy-shrouds and bones were found. The excavated tombs were then labelled as A1-A7, B1-B4, D3-D6, and E2-E7. All of the tombs date to the Roman period. The lower western entrances of the tombs can be reached either via descending staircases or via a slightly low shaft. Some are one-chamber tombs with one niche, while most contain two rooms and two or three niches in the burial chamber. Pieces of wood were found in tombs D3 and D6, which suggest that the tomb once had a wooden door[31]. Tomb B1 is the most important painted example unearthed during this season. Unfortunately, the soot fully covers the paintings in the antechamber; only the classical figure of the deceased woman is still visible. Meanwhile, the funerary scenes are well-preserved on the eastern and southern walls of the burial chamber.

Figure 3.2. The attempts at hiding façade-entrances of certain tombs by the Akhmim Inspectorate.

3.3: Typology and Topography

The El-Salamuni cemetery was used from the Old Kingdom to the Late Roman Period (fifth century BC–third century AD)[32]. Unfortunately, because of the limited excavations and investigations of the area to-date, it is not easy to get a comprehensive picture of the chronology, topography, or architecture of this necropolis. The creation of a topographical and archaeological survey map, which would register and record all of the tombs in El-Salamuni, is still missing. The ideal map would show the tombs' locations, and number them according to the mountain's registers and periods of use. Moreover, the survey will also define the locations of still unexcavated tombs, the hewn entrances of which are visible, and which are widely spread all over the mountain's terraces.

During his quick survey of the mountain, Kuhlmann noted that the Old Kingdom, New Kingdom, and Late Period burials are mainly situated on the upper registers of the cliff (which are nowadays registers G and H). The Ptolemaic and Roman tombs are scattered throughout the lower registers (A-F). Kuhlmann divided the tombs chronologically into four typological architectural groups according to their historical phases:

C1: These are rock-cut tombs of the Old Kingdom lying north of the temple of Ay. Kuhlmann recorded about 29 tombs of this type. Some are scattered around the face of the rock, and others are just beneath the temple of Ay. All of the tombs are now looted and unpainted, containing either shallow trenches, pits for pottery vessels, niches and/or long mastabas. Most of the tombs are located north of the temple of Ay (Figures 3.3a-b). Some still have their traditional Old Kingdom façade entrances. Other tombs contain descending underground shafts, resembling

---

[26] Personal communication with N. Kanawati on 22 March 2020.
[27] Kaplan, *BzÄ* 16, 166–78, figs. 86a–100b.
[28] Kaplan, *BzÄ* 16, 171–77, pl. 90a–b, 91a–b, 93b, 94a–b, 95a–b, 98b, 99b, 100 a–b.
[29] Meurice, *BdÉ* 158, 69–70, fig. 20.
[30] Kaplan, *BzÄ* 16, 176, fig. 99a.
[31] The Inspectorate's report.

[32] Kuhlmann, *SDAIK* 11, 71–84.

The Afterlife in Akhmim

Figure 3.3a. The Old Kingdom tombs on both sides of the temple of Ay.

Figure 3.3b. Niches and damaged benches in one of the Old Kingdom tombs.

the Old Kingdom tombs of El-Hawawish (Figure 3.4), which also contain underground chambers. Most of these corridors are still covered with sand. In the past, robbers have tried to remove the sand to uncover the details of the tombs. An inscription can still be seen at the entrance of one of these tombs.

C2: These undecorated shaft tombs date to the Late and Ptolemaic Periods. The depths of the shafts are varied, and the shaft openings are covered with a large slab of stone. Kuhlmann mentions that this tomb type typically has a vertical shaft with an opening of about 0.50m.-1m.

Figure 3.4. An underground shaft of an Old Kingdom tomb, located north of the temple of Ay.

in width, and 5m. in depth, leading to a small antechamber with a burial niche and a large anthropoid trench. This is followed by another larger burial chamber with one or multiple niches (Figures 3.5a-b)[33]. The El-Salamuni C2 tomb style of the Late and Ptolemaic Periods is presumably similar to that of the Ptolemaic tombs in El-Hawawish A[34]. This shaft-type tomb is mainly found cut into the upper terraces of the mountain, especially on the mountain's north and middle sections. Currently, there is no evidence of the shaft-grave style at the southern section of the mountain. Many shaft tombs are yet to be unearthed, and their openings are still covered with sand. It is highly assumed that the majority of this type of tomb are still intact, and are still unvisited by robbers. Contrary to this type of shaft tomb, the A2 shaft tombs opposite Athribis, including the tomb of Psenosiris, date to the Early Roman Period[35].

C3: These are façade tombs of the Roman period from the first to the third century AD. They have a low façade, typically leading to two chambers on the same horizontal axis. Occasionally, some C3-type tombs contain up to five rooms, one of which is an antechamber that allows access to one or more burial chambers. These burial chambers contain burial niches in either an Egyptian or Greek style. For example, the presence of a *kline* in the wall of the so-called 'tomb 1913 of von Bissing' (Figure 3.6) probably suggests it is a family tomb. Most of the burial chambers contain burial niches and funerary pits in the ground that are similar to those found in Athribis[36]. Some of the older type C2 tombs were reused (Figure 3.7a-b)[37]. Some tombs of the C3 type additionally cut into the tombs of the C2 type, incorporating the latter's rooms. Most of the façade tombs have both of their niches in the burial chambers, as well as shallow trenches in their antechambers. They bear a close resemblance to the type 1 façade tombs in Athribis, where both mummies in burial niches and inhumations in shallow trenches alongside them are attested[38].

C4: These are one-chamber tombs dating to the Late Roman Period. Their layout typically consists of a single chamber, complete with a long bench or shelf that encircles the tomb and serves as a *klinium* for visitors. As the benches are too small to place any mummies on them, the mummies were heaped up along the narrow sides of the room, lying on the floor in front of the bench (as von Bissing had previously noted) (Figure 3.8)[39]. In one of these tombs, von Bissing recognised ten mummies on the

Figure 3.5a. A C2-type tomb of the Late and Ptolemaic Periods, Kuhlmann, *SDAIK* 11, 77, fig. 24.

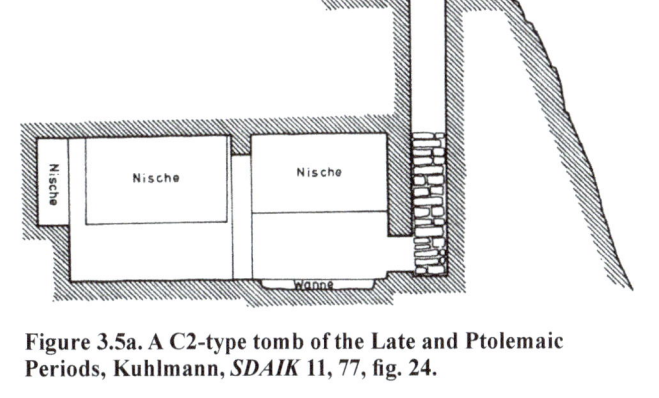

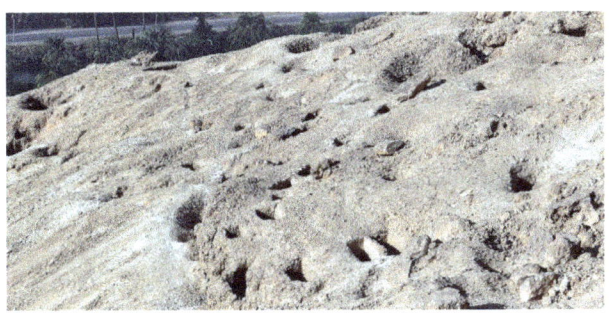

Figure 3.5b. Shaft tombs along the upper terraces of the southern section of El-Salamuni Mountain.

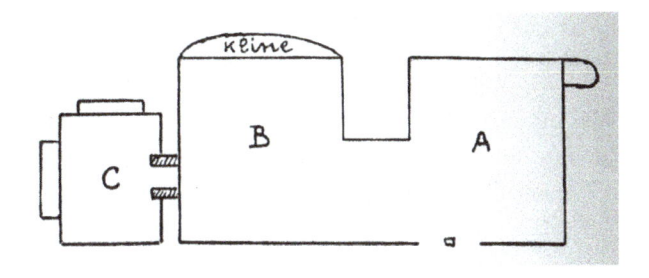

Figure 3.6. The layout of the so-called 'Tomb of von Bissing (1913)', von Bissing, *ASAE* 50, 560, fig.7

floor, lying on both sides of a narrow visitor's bench. He thus concluded that it is a tomb which, like so many others in Akhmim, was intended for the burial of a considerable number of people[40]. Tomb F4 is the best example of this Late Roman style.

3.4: The Rock-Cut Temple of El-Salamuni

El-Salamuni was of great importance during the New Kingdom and Late Period due to its quarries, which produced fine, very white limestone of good quality. In the New Kingdom, the quarries of El-Salamuni were only used for open-cast mining[41]. In the Late Period,

---

[33] Kuhlmann, *SDAIK* 11, 77–79, figs. 24–26.; id., *MDAIK* 38, 347, 352.
[34] Maspero, *Sur Les fouilles exécutés*, 89. The excavations of the Egyptian Antiquities Organisation (EAO) in the years 1986 and 1995 (under the direction of Y. El-Masry) resulted in the discovery of six tombs of this type between El-Deir El-Wistani and Dayr al-Qibli, G. Mohamed, 'A New Discovery from the Ptolemaic Period at El-Hawawish', *GM* 92 (1986) 7–10.
[35] R. El-Farag, U. Kaplony-Heckel, and K. Kuhlmann, 'Recent Archaeological Explorations at Athribis (ḥw.t Rpiit)', *MDAIK* 41 (1985), 5–6.
[36] Kuhlmann, *SDAIK* 11, 77, fig. 33c.
[37] Kuhlmann, *SDAIK* 11, 78.
[38] El Farag et al., *MDAIK* 41, 4.
[39] Kuhlmann, *SDAIK* 11, 81.

[40] Von Bissing, *ASAE* 50, 566, fig. 10.
[41] The builders of Akhmim caused the exploitation of quarries from the New Kingdom until at least the second century. The quarries were located both directly north of El-Salamuni and further away, to the north and south. The quarries of El-Salamuni produced fine, very white limestone of good quality in the New Kingdom and Late Periods, Klemm and Klemm, *Steine und Steinbrüche*, 172–75.; Kuhlmann, *SDAIK* 11, 185–86. No quarrying is attested in the region of Panopolis in the Late Roman Period.

The Afterlife in Akhmim

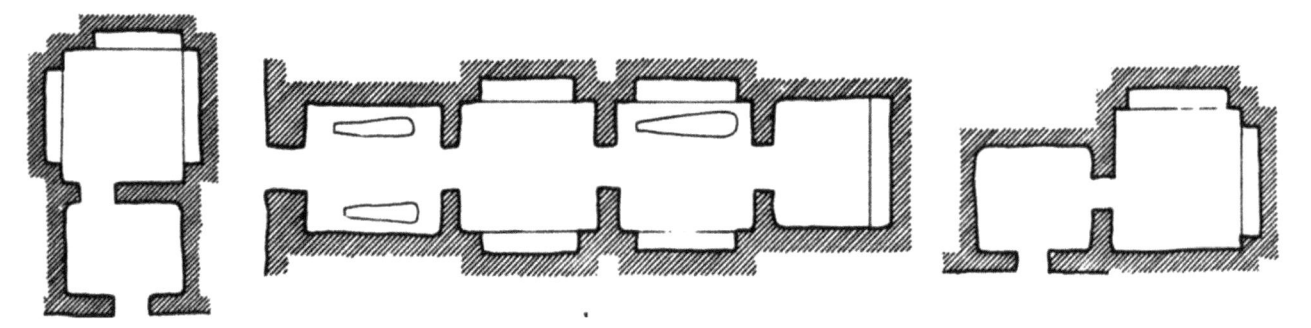

Figure 3.7a. A C3-type tomb of the Roman Period, Kuhlmann, *SDIAK* 11, 79, fig. 27.

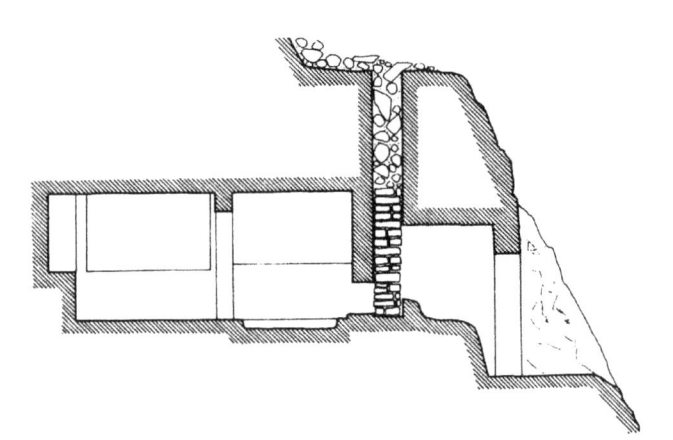

Figure 3.7b. Tombs of the C3-type, which are cut into some tombs of the C2-type, Kuhlmann, *SDAIK* 11, 78, fig. 26.

Figure 3.8. A C4-type tomb of the Late Roman Period, von Bissing, *ASAE* 50, 566, fig.10.

the mountain was connected through a road with the surrounding galleries of Nazlet Haridi (30km. northeast) and Gebel Toukh (13km. southeast). Kees declares that Thutmose III was the real founder of the temple, which was usurped by Ay, and was later restored by the Ptolemies[42]. However, Kuhlmann claims that King Ay constructed this impressive rock temple[43]. The temple now overlooks El-Salamuni Mountain at a height of about 240m. above the floodplain. It is situated in the middle of the mountain, in the area below the second quarry from the 18th dynasty (Figure 3.9)[44].

The construction of the temple was in two stages; it was first built by Nakht-Min, a high priest of Min during the lifetime of King Ay[45], and was then substantially refurbished and expanded upon by Hormaakheru, the *archiereus* (high priest) of Min during the reign of Ptolemy II Philadelphus[46]. Hormaakheru was also known as a '*sm3ty*[47], and as *Ḥm-nṯr w3ḏi.t Ḥr m33 ... ...-Nsw Ḥr*, which translates to mean 'the soltist' and the Priest of Wadjet, Hormaa [*chrew* ('son of'?)], Hor (the royal scribe)'[48]. Kuhlmann supports Schiaparelli's suggestion[49] that the sanctuary served as a cult space for the quarry workers who venerated Min, asking him for help and protection[50]. There is a Ptolemaic quarry located on a

---

[42] See Kees, 'Felstemple', *LÄ* II, 162–66.
[43] Kuhlmann proved his assumption by multiple lines of reasoning. First, Akhmim is the homeland of King Ay, and second, he also declares in his stela, which was found in front of the temple, that he is the founder of this temple, and that his architect Nacht-Min was responsible for erecting it. Thirdly, all of the scenes of King Thutmose III are inside the temple in chamber D, which was added during the Ptolemaic Period, Kuhlmann, *MDAIK* 35, 173–74,187.
[44] Kuhlmann, *SDAIK* 11, 82.; Kees, *Rec.Trav.* 36, 51.; von Bissing, *ASAE* 50, 555.; *PM.* V, 18.
[45] A granite statue of Nakht-Min was found in the famous temple of Ramesses II, with later additions discovered in *El-Birba*, which is in downtown Akhmim, El-Masry, 'Seven Seasons of Excavations', in C. Eyre (ed.), *OLA* 82, 759–66. For more about Nakhtmin, see M. Claude, 'Nakhtmin, High Priest of Min and Isis in Akhmim and Overseer of Works for Ay, His Career, his Tomb, and Ay's Memorial Temple', *MDAIK* 76/77 (2021/2022), 63–82.

[46] The *archiereus* was a high priest that was chosen yearly from among the higher clergy. His duties were more administrative rather than religious. Only the large temples were led by the *archiereus*, alongside various priests with various functions, Geens, *Panopolis, a Nome Capital in Egypt*, 320.
[47] The meaning of this ubiquitous title has long been uncertain, but it is now commonly believed that *sm3ty* means 'the soltist priest', Depauw, 'Late Funerary Material', in A. Egberts et al. (eds.), *Perspectives on Panopolis*, 73.
[48] Kuhlmann, *MDAIK* 35, 177.; Kees, 'Iin-ins-Mehit', *LÄ* II, 177.
[49] Schiaparelli, *Chemmis (Akhmim) et la Sua Antica Necropolis*, 85.
[50] Kuhlmann, *MDAIK* 35, 182–85, pl. 48. Kanawati found indications for a rock-cut temple in the El-Hawawish B cemetery, Kanawati, *The Rock Tombs of El-Hawawish, I* (1980), 6.; Kuhlmann, *SDAIK* 11, 12–13, 21.

Figure 3.9. The temple of Ay on the uppermost part of the northern section of El-Salamuni Mountain.

terrace north of and below the temple of Ay (Figure 3.10). Later, the temple was used as a necropolis sanctuary for the quarry workers of the Graeco-Roman Period[51]. During the Early Christian Period, the little caves were covered by stone and used by *anchorites*[52].

The temple is dedicated to Min-Pan[53], Repit/Triphis/Aperet-Isis[54], and the child-god Kolanthes/Harendotes, which all together represent the divine trinity of Akhmim[55]. Kess mentions that the goddess *Iin-ins* or *Iin-ins-MHjt* was also worshipped inside the temple as a local deity in Akhmim. She was called 'the Lady of Akhmim' and 'at the top of Akhmim'[56]. Upon visiting the area in 1843

---

[51] Kuhlmann, *MDAIK* 39, 347–48.; id., *SDAIK* 11, 20. Though Strabo mentions that Panopolis was a city of stonemasons, the list of buildings in the P. Berl. Bork XII 17 does not mention any quarry worker. This may be either related to the fact that quarry workers were usually of a low social class (being among the part of the Panopolis community who were not able to buy a house of their own), or because Panopolis was no longer a centre of quarry workers in the Late Roman Period, Geens, *Panopolis, a Nome Capital*, 301.

[52] Kuhlmann, *Orientalia* 51, 444. The martyrs Pachomius and his sister Daluscham received a church near the village of Naga El-Sawâma-sharq, north of El-Salamuni, R. Coquin and M. Martin, 'Dayr Anba Bakhum', *CE* III (1991), 730.; A. Papaconstantinou, *Le culte des saints en égypte des byzantins aux abbassides, L'apport des inscriptions et des papyrus grecs et coptes* (Paris 2001).

[53] Later, the temple was described by Kuhlmann, *MDAIK* 35, 165–93.; id., *MDAIK* 38, 347–54.; id., *SDAIK* 11, 82, pls. 27, 29. Recently, M. Gabolde studied the text of Nakhtmin in the temple, M. Gabolde, 'Le Grand Texte de Nakht Min dans la Chapelle d'Ay a Al-Salamouni', *Akhmîm, une tour d'horizon, Egypte, Afrique & Orient* 96 (2020), 3–14. Some of the titles of Pan are Ὀρεσσανύλοιο, meaning 'the one who lives in the mountains,' and Ὀρεοβάτης, which means 'running through the mountain,' A. Bernand, *Pan du deesert* (Leiden 1977), no. 1, no. 4.

[54] Repit's worship as *T3-Rpj.t* was focused particularly in Athribis/modern Waninnah, called the 'Mansion of Repit', F. Petrie, *Athribis*, 7–11. Repit was assimilated with Aperet-Ist (*ꜥpr-s.t*), who was mainly worshipped on the east bank of the nome, and who was known as the 'Mistress of Akhmim', U. Bouriant, 'Petits monuments et petits textes recueillis en Égypte', *Rec. Trav.* 8 (1886), 163–64, no. 38.; Gardiner, *JEA* 31, 109. Repit's name is widely inscribed on the funerary stelae excavated in the cemeteries of Panopolis, including CGC 22007, I, CGC 22053 (A. Awadalla, 'Une stèle cintrée de Ns-Mnw Caire CG 22053', *SAK* 25 (1998), 3–4), CGC 22095, I, 22139, 4, and the stela BM EA1139. Aperet-Isis in inscribed on CGC 22114, 2, CGC 22070, 2, and CG 22151. She carries the Nile-offering of the Panopolite nome in the Opet temple at Karnak, C. De Wit, *Les inscriptions du temple d'Opet à Karnak*, *BiAeg* 11 (Brussels 1958), 214 (right).; *LGG* II, 105.; A. Abdelhalim, 'A Lunette Stela of Pasenedjemibnash in the Cairo Museum, CG 22151', *BIFAO* 114.1 (2014), 3 no. 13.

[55] In the Ptolemaic Period, Kolanthese was substituted for Horus as the child in the triad, especially on the west bank of the Panopolite nome, Karig, 'Ahmim', *LÄ* I, 54. The 'Min-Hor-Isis' triad in Akhmim was known during the Late Dynastic and Ptolemaic Periods. The triad was treated as if it was a single entity named Menareti/Menares (Μεναρης), the 'supreme god' in Greek texts. A priestly function in service of the triad was known as *Hm ntr wHm*. For more about the Min-Horus-Isis triad, see J. Elias and T. Mekis, 'Prophet-registrars of Min-Hor-Isis at Akhmim', *MDAIK* 76/77 (2020/ 2021), 83–112.; Wagner, 'Bandelettes de momies', in J. Vercoutter (ed.), *Livre du centenaire, 1880–1980*, *MIFAO* 104, 332–33.; C. Bleeker, *Die Geburt eines Gottes: eine Studie über den ägyptischen Gott Min und sein Fest*, Studies in the History of Religions, supplement to Numen (Leiden, 1956), 18.; De Meuleanere, *BIFAO* 88, 47.; id., 'Un prêtre d'Akhmim à Abydos', *CdÉ* 44 (1969) 214–21. The names of the trinity Min-Triphis-Kolanthes are also found in the neighbouring nomes, including a Demotic inscription at Gebel Toukh, W. Spiegelberg, 'Miszellen, Der Gott Kolanthes', *ZÄS* 58 (1923), 155–56, as well as a Greek dedication from Ptolemais, *SB* III 6184, I. 9.

[56] Kees, Achmim, *LÄ* I, 54. Rössler-Köhler argues for the existence of *Iin-ins-MHjt* as a local goddess in the temple, and proposes that it is a wrong reading, Rössler-Köhler, *LÄ* II, 177.; Kuhlmann, *MDAIK* 35, 186.

The Afterlife in Akhmim

Figure 3.10. The Ptolemaic quarry to the north of the temple of Ay.

and 1845, Lepsius was the first to record the impressive rock-cut temple of Min, which he described as the 'grotto of Pan'[57]. Min was the god of the desert, mountains, and quarries[58]. Hence, he was worshipped by workers in the mines and quarries of the Eastern Desert around Ptolemais and Koptos[59]. Here, many natural features like caves and rock shelters (sometimes receiving architectural supports and additions), were used as cultic shelters and sanctuaries dedicated to Min[60]. Demotic inscriptions refer to the quarry of Gebel Toukh as the 'resting place of Min'[61]. According to the villagers of Abu El-Nasr and Nazlet El-Haridi, a Roman(?) road made of paved white stones once stretched from the Haridi quarries to Akhmim[62], most likely passing through El-Salamuni. At the foot of El-Haridi Mountain is a temple dating to the reign of Ptolemy III. It is partly rock-cut, and partly stone-built. The most important discovery within this was a large round-topped stela with a high-quality hieroglyphic inscription of the Canopus Decree[63]. The existence of this temple emphasis the Ptolemaic interest in promoting the cult of Min in the quarries of Akhmim.

The temple has a west-east axis, and consists of a forecourt, *pronaos* (F), sanctuary (G), and four side chambers to the left and right of the forecourt. Chambers A and C are on the left side of the temple, while chambers B and D are on the right side. Chamber D opens into a small chamber on the temple's northern side. Kuhlmann suggests that chamber D had a religious purpose as opposed to being a storeroom since many funerary hymns are inscribed on its walls. Hormaakheru substantially extended and refurbished the temple, attaching chambers C and A as storage rooms. The high priest also cut small openings as entrances leading to the court, and made another entrance from chamber C to the *pronaos* (F). This was to enable the priests to go to the *pronaos* through chamber C, rather than only having access from the court (Figure 3.11)[64]. The names of kings Thutmose III and Ramesses II are inscribed inside the temple and in the graffiti of the forecourt[65].

The temple is in very poor condition. It has a western façade facing opposite the El-Isawiah canal, which is 8.78cm. high. On the right side of the entrance, there is a niche that is 0.90cm. in height, 0.43cm. in width, and 0.46cm. in depth. Sanctuary G has a niche carved into its eastern wall, which is 1.40cm. high, 1.24cm. wide, and 1.10cm. deep. It also has a rising staircase, to the left of which is another smaller niche. This niche is on a higher level than the first one, with a 0.96cm. height, a 0.49cm. width, and a 0.46cm. depth[66].

Nowadays, steel doors lock both the outer entrance of the temple and the inner entrance which leads to chambers D and E. The inscriptions and paintings have been partially smashed and scraped. Furthermore, great parts of the walls and the ceilings of chamber C, *pronaos* F, and *naos* G are covered with soot. This vandalism was caused by the hermits who found shelter here during the Christian Period, and/or by the continuous and even recent looting of those who still have a firm belief that the temple contains treasures and gold inside one of its secret chambers[67]. A few scenes and inscriptions are still found in the tomb. On the left side of the door, for instance, King Ay and his wife Tiye are shown offering before an ithyphallic Min, along with Isis, Horus, and Aperet-Isis (Figure 3.12)[68].

On the right and the left sides of the façade of the tomb are representations of a winged solar disc. There are two hieroglyphic columns, with one on each side. The left-hand one includes a small text which is partially

---

[57] R. Lepsius, *Denkmäler aus Aegypten und Aethiopien, Text II: Mittelaegypten mit dem Faijum*, in E. Naville and K. Sethe (eds.) (Leipzig 1904), 16.; Kees, 'Achmim', *LÄ* I, 54.
[58] Gauthier, *Les fêtes du dieu Min.*; J. Yoyotte, 'Une épithète de Min comme explorateur des régions orientales', *RdE* 9 (1952), 125–37. On Min/Pan as a god of the desert and the mountains in the Graeco-Roman Period, see A. Bernand, *Pan du désert*, 269–78.; id., 'Pan du désert et ses adorateurs', in H. Maehler and V. Strocka (eds.), *Das ptolemäische Ägypten, Akten des internationalen Symposions 27–29. September 1976 in Berlin* (Mainz 1978), 161–64. *Proskynemata* were known for Min along the desert routes (in Wadi Hammamat), (*De Koptos à Kosseir* (Leiden 1972), 59–213), and asked for his protection. Perhaps Min's ithyphallic character warded off danger, J. Lesquier, *L'armée romaine d'Égypte d'Auguste à Dioclétien*, MIFAO 41 (Cairo 1918), 285.
[59] One of the main epithets of Min is the 'Guard or Watcher (of the desert)', and there are numerous examples of his titles in Panopolis, such as Γορσης and (Σεν) ορσενουφις, which are related to his attributes, J. Lindsay, *Men and Gods on the Roman Nile* (London 1968), 344.; J. Quaegebeur, 'A propos de Teilouteilou, nom magique et de Têroutêrou, nom de femme', *Enchoria* 4 (1974), 24–25 no. 27.
[60] W. van Regen, 'A new Paneion at Mons Porphyrites', *CdÉ* 70 (1995), 240–45.
[61] G. Legrain, 'Les carrières antiques de Ptolémaïs', *MMFAC* 8/3(1894), 372–73.
[62] C. Kirby and S. Ikram, 'Haridi's High Society', *EA* 4 (1994), 33.
[63] For more about this stela, see El-Masry, 'Recent Explorations in the Ninth Nome', in Z. Hawass (ed.), *Egyptology at the Dawn of the Twenty-First Century*, 331–38.

[64] Kuhlmann, *MDAIK* 35, 173.
[65] Their names may have been added by the Egyptian priest Hormaakheru as a kind of commemoration and means of glorification. Graffiti containing the figures and names of Thutmose III and Ramesses II were added later by local visitors, as their style is different from the decorations of the temple, suggesting a later date.
[66] Kuhlmann, *MDAIK* 38, 348.
[67] During the field campaigns in the mountain, the *ghaffirs* caught many robbers (unfortunately, young students) who roamed the site, trying to break the key of the steel door in an attempt to search for treasures, such as in chambers D and E. This is the opinion of the *fellahin* who live beyond the mountain.
[68] Kuhlmann, *MDAIK* 35, 176–77, no. 43, fig. 52.1. Lepsius recognised them as Pan (=Min), Hathor, Horus, and Triphis, Lepsius, II, 164.

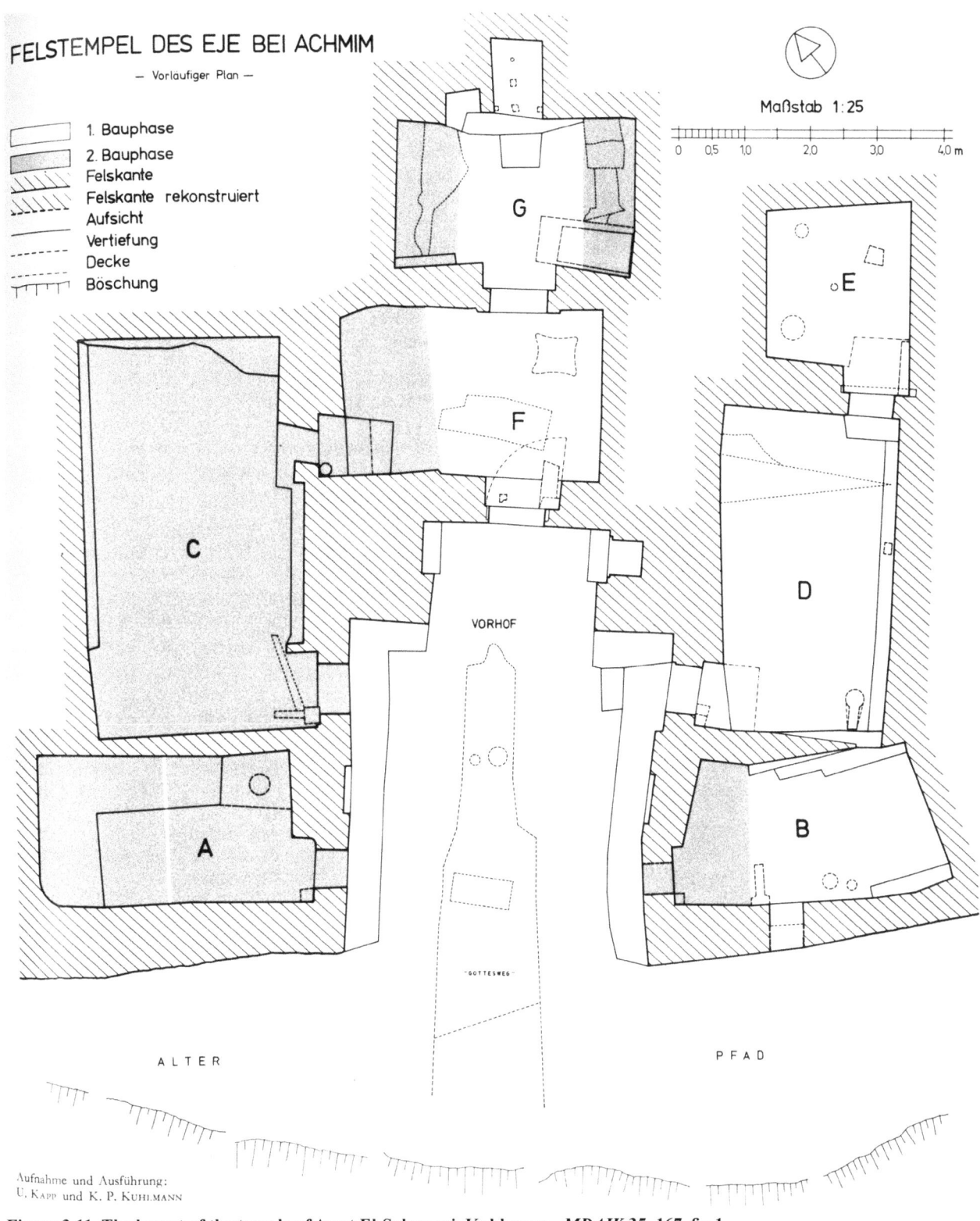

Figure 3.11. The layout of the temple of Ay at El-Salamuni, Kuhlmann., *MDAIK* 35, 167, fig.1.

demolished, while the right-hand one is larger and more preserved. Sethe translates the text[69], which refers to an unknown queen called Ptolemais[70]. She is the descendant of the Egyptian pharaoh Nectanebo I and a contemporary of Ptolemy II, his spouse, and his daughter. Kuhlmann suggests that Ptolemais is the daughter of Nectanebo I. The temple was a place of worship for the workmen exploiting the limestone quarries to the north of Akhmim. Nectanebo I engaged in rather extensive building-activities, so he made use of the Akhmimic quarries and put his daughter in charge of supervising the whole operation, elevating her on this occasion to a full regal rank as his representative.

---

[69] This text was first copied by Lepsius, *LD* II, 164. It was then was published by Sethe, *URK* II, 27.
[70] K. Kuhlmann, 'Ptolemaios- Queen of Nectanebo I, Notes on the Inscription of an Unknown Princess of the XXXth Dynasty', *MDAIK* 37, 276–79.

The Afterlife in Akhmim

Figure 3.12. Ay and Tiye in the act of adoring Min, Isis, Horus, and Aperet-Isis. Seen on the left side of the entrance.

The soot covering both sides of the doorway of *pronaos* F leads into sanctuary G as well (Figure 3.13a). The upper register on the left side of this room shows King Ptolemy II with his cartouche, wearing a blue crown and offering *sHyt* before an ithyphallic Min. Behind him is a goddess with a sun disc and two horns of a cow in between, probably representing Aperet-Isis. The lower register shows a king, presumably Ptolemy II, offering before a mummified figure of Osiris. The god wears a white crown(?) and is followed by Horus and a goddess (Isis?). The goddess wears a sun disc between two cow horns on her head[71].

On the right side of the doorway, the upper register shows another figure of Ptolemy II. His cartouche is still visible. He is wearing a *nemes* headdress and is shown making offerings before the figure of an ithyphallic Min and a goddess with a sun disc and two cow horns. Perhaps this is Repit-Triphis. The lower register shows a king with a blue crown who is perhaps Ptolemy II. He is situated before a damaged god (maybe Horus?), and another goddess with a sun disc between two cow horns[72].

Chambers A, B, and C are significantly damaged; the walls have been scraped and the paint is likely erased. Soot covers the ceiling of chamber C. Chambers A and B lie on either side of the forecourt of the temple. Their functions are unclear; perhaps they had a religious, administrative, or storage role. A large cut in the southern wall of chamber B is probably an irregular niche (Figure 3.13b). Meanwhile, chamber A contains two long benches and a deep niche that was cut into its outer south wall, overlooking the forecourt. The benches were probably use as a resting place for the quarry workers who climbed to the sanctuary to ask Min for protection and help.

Chamber D is the most important chamber in the temple, and is now closed by a door. Kuhlmann copied and translated some inscriptions inside the room[73]. On the south wall, to the right of the entrance, he noted a partially damaged hieroglyphic text of five lines. Because of the small break in the wall, which creates an entrance to chamber B, the inscription is probably a hymn to Min. Kuhlmann wrongly mentions that there is a procession of five ithyphallic figures of Min below the text. However, in reality, they are six in number (Figure 3.13c).

By the fifth century AD, Panopolis was a thriving centre of Christianity. The temple was used as a house by the Copts and was a victim of Shenoute's anti-pagan campaign in the nome. Shenoute plundered temples and took violent actions against pagan gods and heretics in Panopolis as far as Koptos[74]. Kuhlmann mentions that the temple was

---

[71] Kuhlmann, *MDAIK* 35, 180.
[72] Kuhlmann, *MDAIK* 35, 180.
[73] For more information, see Kuhlmann, *MDAIK* 35, 177–80, figs. 53, 54.
[74] F. Plevit was a hotbed of fanatical pagans, headed by charismatic anti-Christian priests and united through their homage to their ancestral deities, Frankfurter, *Religion in Roman Egypt*, 78, 82, 236. Shenoute destroyed this temple, and went to Plevit on a donkey to destroy the idols in the temple there. Some villagers buried charms in the road to obstruct Shenoute from entering the temple, but the donkey detected the charms and dug them up with his hoof. Shenoute ordered that these charms be collected and hung around the necks of the pagan villagers

A History of the Investigations and Surveys of El-Salamuni

Figure 3.13a. The soot that covers the doorway of the *pronaos* (F) into the sanctuary (G).

Figure 3.13b. Chamber B, to the left of the forecourt.

The Afterlife in Akhmim

Figure 3.13c. Hormaacheru shown making libations before six figures of Min on the southern wall of chamber D.

Figure 3.14. The *anachoretes* crypt in the sanctuary of the temple of Ay.

used by the Copts as a residence, and that there were pits in the floor and holes in the walls in which to put votive materials and wooden fittings. In fact, the temple has an underground crypt which is 1.15m. in height, 0.56cm. in width, and 0.82cm. in depth, being cut into the south-western side of a chamber, and being originally covered with a flat slab[75]. This crypt was probably used as a late tomb or by hermits (Figure 3.14). The Christian anchorites made the Gebel their hermitage; small caves covered by stones were used by the anchorites during the Early Christian Period, as well as the rock-cut temple of Min[76].

The anchorites[77] smashed many inscriptions and scenes, and others were entirely covered in clay[78]. The tomb below the temple was presumably occupied by the Copts. Furthermore, von Bissing documented red terracotta, Hellenistic pottery, a coin of the emperor Theodosius, amphorae, and fragments of Coptic vases in one of the tombs that he visited[79]. Two Coptic figures painted at a later date can also be found in tomb F2, the zodiac of which was also re-used with the inclusion of Coptic figures.

In modern times, the El-Salamuni temple is called 'Beit El-Binaiah ('the House of the Girl'), with the suggestion that a famous Sheikh is buried inside of it[80]. A popular myth is that the king of the jinn 'daemons' keeps his seven daughters alive inside the temple, along with gold and treasures, and that once a year, the temple will be opened when the king and his daughters smell onions. Once opened, people will run to plunder the gold, and those who come from far away on a lame donkey will obtain a great amount of the riches.

---

who concealed them. However, they escaped. Shenoute then entered the temple and overthrew the idols, F. Trombley, *Hellenic Religion and Christianization C. 370–529*, II, RGRW 115/1–2 (Leiden, New York, Köln 1993–94), 208. Panopolis was thus an epi-centre of religious conflict; Shenoute's anti-paganism and unlawful actions are proof of a pagan resistance in Panopolis. The pagan cults later shifted from public temples to households shrines. The religious conflict reached its climax through the struggle between Shenoute and Gessius, a rich landowner at Panopolis, as well as a heretic and Kronos worshipper. The fight between Shenoute and Gessius offers the most prominent picture of the conflict between Christianism and paganism in Late Antiquity Panopolis. For more about this conflict, see J. Leipoldt, *Schenute von Atripe und die Entstehung des national-ägyptischen Christentum, Texte und Untersuchungen zur Geschichte der altchristlichen Literatur* 25.1 (Leipzig 1903).; H. Thissen, 'Zur Begegnung von Christentum und «Heidentum»: Schenute und Gessios', *Enchoria* 19–20 (1992–93), 155–64.; Van Der Vliet, 'Spätantikes Heidentum in Ägypten', 102–06.; F. Trombley, *Hellenic Religion and Christianization C. 370–529*, RGRW 115/1–2, II (Leiden, New York, Köln 1993–94), 214.; Leipoldt, *Opera*, III, no. 28, 92, ll. 2–3. Together with seven monks, Shenoute had also stolen and destroyed pagan idols in Koptos. Hahn argues that paganism continued in Panopolis until about 450 AD, Hahn, *Gewalt und religiöser Konflikt*, 255. As Rémondon mentions, before this time, paganism was still very active, including during the lifetime of Shenoute. He states: '*Panopolis est un centre païen où les temples attirent encore les foules. Dans la region, il est des lieux où le christianisme n'a point pénétré: ... On comprend que Macaire et Schenoudi aient dû organiser contre les temples de véritables expéditions pour en venir à bout*', R. Rémondon 'L'Égypte et la suprême résistance au christianisme (Ve–VIIe siècles)', *BIFAO* 51 (1955), 70–71.

[75] Kuhlmann, *MDAIK* 38, 348.
[76] Kuhlmann, *Orientalia* 51, 444. The martyrs Pachomius and his sister Daluscham received a church near the village of Naga El-Sawâma-sharq, north of El-Salamuni, R. Coquin and M. Martin, 'Dayr Anba Bakhum', *CE* III (1991), 730.; A. Papaconstantinou *Le culte des saints en égypte des byzantins aux abbassides. L'apport des inscriptions et des papyrus grecs et coptes* (Paris 2001). According to the Upper Egyptian Coptic Synaxarium, the mountain of Athribis and particularly the towns of Edfa and Athribis on the west bank were frequented by Christian hermits, B. Ward, *The Sayings of the Desert Fathers, The Alphabetical Collection*

(Kalamazoo 1984). In a tomb of the reign of Tutankhamun, which was later reused at Awlad Azaz, many Coptic inscriptions and plaster pieces were found. Some larger tombs from the Pharaonic Period were used by Coptic monks, and one of these tombs was perhaps also used as a church, C. Kibry and W. Monkhouse, 'Filling the Gaps at Gebel El–Haridi', *JEA* 14 (1999), 11. Furthermore, to the east of Wadi bir El-Aïn, many holes in the rocks served as caves for monks, and a Coptic community lived there. The area was known as 'the Monastery of the Seven Mountains', Kuhlmann, *SDAIK* 11, 9. Coptic crosses, plaster pieces, and monograms of Christ were inscribed by the monks on the rocks of the Wadi bir El-Aïn, Bernand, I. *Pan* 1b, 11b, 12–14.
[77] *Anachoresis* is the step by which an ascetic, following the example of Saint Antony, leaves his village 'to withdraw' (Greek: *Anachorein*) to the desert and thus become an *anchorite*. The oldest attestation of this phenomenon relates to the social realm, as the monk would to the desert to separate himself from the world, meaning from people and things. This phenomenon is widely represented in the history of religions, and particularly in Judaism and early Christianity, even before the appearance of monasticism, A. Guillaumont , 'Anachoresis', in A. Attiya (ed.), *CoptEnc* 1 (New York 1991), 119.; H. Braunert, *Die Binnenwanderung Studien zur Sozial Geschichte* Ägzptens *in der Ptolemäer- und Kaiserzeit*, Bonner Historische Forschungen 26 (Bonn 1964).
[78] Kuhlmann, *SDAIK* 11, 17.; Kees, *Rec.Trav.* 36, 52.
[79] Von Bissing, *ASAE* 50, 565–67, fig. 11.
[80] Kuhlmann, *MDAIK* 35, 166.

Figure 3.15. El-Salamuni Mountain.

3.5: The Characteristics of El-Salamuni

El-Salamuni Mountain is about 300m. in height and 2500m. in length. The Akhmim Antiquities Office divided El-Salamuni Mountain into eight terraces, extending from the bottom of the mountain to the top. They are labelled as terraces A, B, C, D, E, F, G, and H. Numerous tombs are cut into the mountain, being next to or above one another. The outer-most cemetery was mainly used during the Late Pharaonic, Ptolemaic, and Roman Periods (fifth century BC–second/third centuries AD) (Figure 3.15). The necropolis of El-Salamuni is both significant for and unique in Graeco-Roman Egypt. Its special characteristics lie in the tombs' architectural layouts, burial customs, and funerary art.

3.5.1: Typology

It is precisely the fact that El-Salamuni Mountain has a wealth of materials and information that allows one to write a regional history of Akhmim. The mountain has been used as both a necropolis and as a quarry. The mountain's appearance has been strongly affected by the enormous piles of debris and huge cuttings and slopes caused by large-scale quarrying, earlier excavations, and human looting. There are about six large inner slopes of the mountain, aligned from the north to the south (Figures 3.16a-f). Most of the tombs are scattered within these slopes. In many parts of the mountain, its division into terraces is obvious, especially in the area beneath the temple of Ay, to the north of the mountain (Figure 3.17). Archaeologically, the mountain starts at the sixth southern-most slope, running about 70m. south of the *ghaffirs'* hut, and about 300m. north of El-Salamuni village. A few unpainted and partially painted tombs are found beyond this slope, and a great mass of mummy shrouds still covers it. On the other side, the northern-most burial is located where the mountain strongly bends to the north, continuing to embrace the Naga El-Sawâma-sharq village. A villager's house was erected on the foot of the southern border of the mountain. A wide flat area covered with sand is additionally located in front of the mountain, to its north. The area is south of the Muslim cemetery of El-Sawamaa, and is not considered to be part of the archaeological components of the mountain.

A security supervisor for the mountain (Mr Abdallah Mahmoud) claims that between 1960 and 1970, the area was heavily looted due to its hundreds of shallow pits of various dimensions, as well as its large amounts of scattered mummy shrouds and bones. The security guardian highly suggests that this area was concentrated with poor people, especially on the far northern part of the mountain, where shallow trenches are also attested (Figure 3.18)[81]. These are the only trenches to be found outside of the local tombs. Unfortunately, the electric lighting poles which provide electricity for the modern El-Sawamaa village are now standing on this flat area. However, many cuttings in the blocks of the mountain are still recognizable. The incisions highly suggest that the area once contained a funerary stela, which was erased by robbers. A rock-cut stela was found about 100m. south of the temple of Ay, showing a kneeling pharaoh, most probably of the Amarna Period. He wears a *khepresh* crown and is shown praying, with a hieroglyphic text above him (Figure 3.19). Another

---

[81] The area is still included within the archaeological site of El-Salamuni ('El-Tafteesh' in Arabic).

The Afterlife in Akhmim

Figure 3.16a. The first slope of El-Salamuni Mountain.

Figure 3.16b. The second slope of El-Salamuni Mountain.

Figure 3.16c. The third slope of El-Salamuni Mountain.

Figure 3.16d. The fourth slope of El-Salamuni Mountain.

Figure 3.16e. The fifth slope of El-Salamuni Mountain.

Figure 3.16f. The sixth slope of El-Salamuni Mountain.

incised stela can be found to the right of this, having been erased and cut off in various places by robbers. However, the cavetto, corniche, and colours have remained.

Tombs of the Ptolemaic-Roman Periods are located on terraces A-F, while terraces G and H contain tombs from the Old Kingdom, New Kingdom, and the Late Period. Most of the painted Graeco-Roman tombs are now documented in the mountain's zones C and F. The Akhmim Inspectorate labelled them as tombs B2, B6, B7, C1, C3, C4, C5, C6, F1, F2, F3, F4, and F5. Tombs C3, C4, C5, F1, F2, F3, F4, and F5 are located on the southern side of the mountain (Figures 3.20a-b), while tombs B2, B6, B7, C1, and C6 are located on the northern side (Figure 3.21). All of these tombs are now closed with steel doors to protect them, except for tombs B2, B6, and C6. The mud-brick security hut for the *ghaffirs* is located on the southern part of the mountain just above tombs C3, C4, and C5. All of these tombs are badly documented and remain currently unpublished.

The creation of a topographical map of the necropolis is still to be done. Unfortunately, many tombs on the mountain were registered in a random and unsystematic way, and

Figure 3.17. The terraces on the southern section of El-Salamuni Mountain.

many other tombs are not yet registered. The Akhmim Inspectorate registered the tombs in the southern and northern sections separately rather than as a unit, giving the same numbers to tombs in the northern and southern sections. For example, there are two tombs named 'tomb C1', located on both the southern and the northern part of the mountain. The one on the south section is painted, and is about 800m. north of the unpainted one. There are many other unregistered tombs in between them. Another example is that there are two tombs in the southern section registered with the same number F2; both are located on register F, but there is about 50m. between them. One has been closed with steel door, and the other has been left doorless. All of the shaft tombs are still unregistered.

Furthermore, hundreds of landslides have obscured the openings of some tombs, giving them the appearance of a honeycomb along the middle terraces of the southern section of the mountain (Figure 3.22). Many unregistered tombs of the Graeco- Roman Period also resemble beehives (Figure 3.23). Located on the upper terraces of the southern section of the mountain, these tombs have been mostly vandalized by robbers. They have crumbling walls that are damaged and empty of scenes. A fully systematic and correct registration system, as well as a topographical map, are still lacking for the mountain. Doubtless, future excavations at the site will uncover more hidden tombs and funerary materials. As of now, some of the registered tombs have been documented by travellers and ancient scholars, and some have been re-excavated and re-labelled by the Akhmim Inspectorate Office. Others

Figure 3.18. Shallow trenches on the lower terrace of the northern section of El-Salamuni Mountain.

Figure 3.19. A rock-cut stela of a kneeling pharaoh, located south of the temple of Ay.

The Afterlife in Akhmim

Figure 3.20a. The southern section of El-Salamuni Mountain, which is the location of El-Hawawish Mountain.

Figure 3.20b. An overview of the southern section of El-Salamuni Mountain.

have been discovered for the first time by the Akhmim Inspectorate. Only a few tombs on the mountain are not yet registered.

Most of the labelled tombs are oriented roughly west-east, with a low façade-entrance to the west. In its middle, El-Salamuni Mountain starts to be slightly bent to the east. Therefore, the tombs situated along the northern section of the mountain open with a southwest entrance. These tombs consist of only two rooms. The rooms are cut horizontally on the same axis, with one extending behind the other; only tomb C1 is off-axis. Tomb B7 is distinguished by the fact that it consists of three rooms; both the ante- and burial chambers run along the traditional west-east axis, while an unfinished side room is cut south of the anteroom, suggesting a later date (Figure 3.24). Only a few tombs are one-chambered, and are unfortunately still unregistered. The burial room of these tombs is typically larger than the anteroom, and

A History of the Investigations and Surveys of El-Salamuni

Figure 3.21a. The northern section of El-Salamuni Mountain.

Figure 3.21b. The distribution of the most important tombs on the northern section of El-Salamuni Mountain.

there are presumably two burial niches cut into their walls. Some exceptions are certain one-niche examples in tomb F4, and three-niche examples in tombs C1 and B7. These tombs are highly likely to date to the Roman Period due to their artistic and architectural layouts. Kuhlmann relates the façade tombs to those of the Roman period, dating from the first to the third century AD[82].

3.5.2: Heritage Significance

The painted tombs of El-Salamuni of the Graeco-Roman Period present the necropolis as being of high rank and importance. In the Egyptian *chora*, painted and well-structured Graeco-Roman tombs are very scarce. Except for the house-tombs of Tuna El-Gebel and the opposite rock-cut tombs of Athribis, the tombs of El-Salamuni are the only known painted tombs of a rather high quality to be discovered south of Tuna El-Gebel as far as Aswan. El-

---

[82] Kuhlmann, *SDAIK* 11, 79–80, fig.-27, pls. 27, 29a, 30, 32a, 33–38.

The Afterlife in Akhmim

Figure 3.22. The so-called 'honeycomb tombs', located on the middle register of the southern section.

Figure 3.23. Landslide Roman tombs on the lower terraces of the southern section of El-Salamuni Mountain.

Salamuni is one of the most artistically and architecturally interesting necropoleis of Graeco-Roman Egypt[83]. In the Egyptian *chora*, Akhmim is more suitable for study than Tuna El-Gebel; its necropoleis of El-Hawawish A and El-Salamuni contain a larger number of painted tombs, dating to the Late, Ptolemaic, and Roman Periods. However, it should be noted that in both regions, more tombs and materials are still hidden than which are already known.

---

[83] M. Cannata states that the tombs in Roman Egypt are almost non-existent, M. Cannata, 'Funerary Artists, the Textual Evidence', in C. Riggs (ed.), *The Oxford Handbook of Roman Egypt* (Oxford 2012), 597.

El-Salamuni is still relatively intact and largely archaeologically unexplored. Very little data concerning the tombs are scientifically and systematically published. The documentation and publication of the El-Salamuni tombs will enrich scholars' knowledge about funerary art and burial customs in Akhmim during the Ptolemaic and Roman Periods. The information gathered from and about the mountain provides new and improved information concerning the archaeologically inaccessible city. The specific regional characteristics of Panopolis are of particular importance. The new data will be the first contextual information from Akhmim's Graeco-Roman tombs. Because of gaps in the papyrological, epigraphic, and archaeological material, some periods and aspects of the history of Panopolis remain poorly documented. Studying the El-Salamuni tombs will certainly fill a larger part of that historical and archaeological vacuum. Unfortunately, some of the tombs which were visited in 2007 are now more damaged. Today, El-Salamuni is losing its architectural and archaeological cultural heritage faster than it can be documented. Therefore, the scientific and local communities should strive to preserve the great heritage and significance of the El-Salamuni tombs as much as possible. Though it is impossible to save everything, one of the options available is to document this heritage before it is lost.

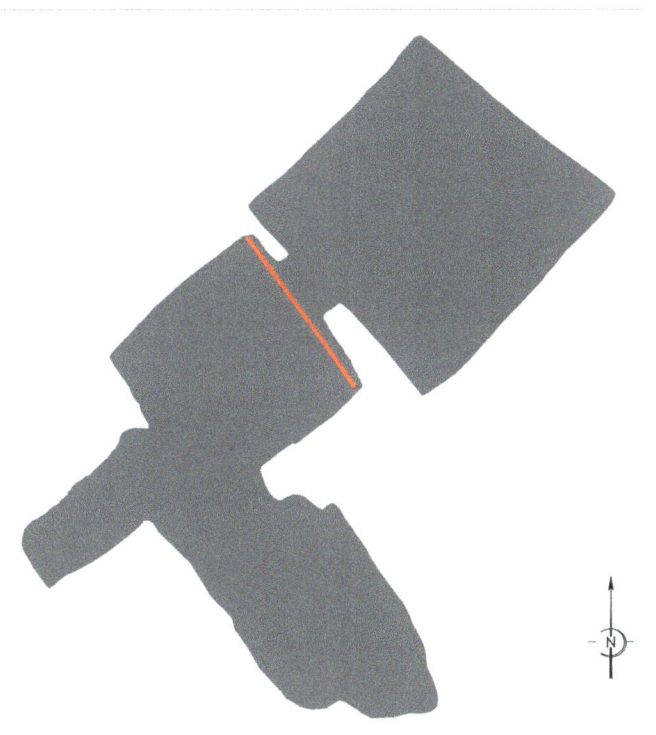

Figure 3.24. The layout of Tomb B7.

The lack of proper systematic excavations and the gaps in the documentation of the El-Salamuni tombs represents further unfortunate obstacles for drawing a definite conclusion about their precise dates. This also makes it difficult to figure out the names and characters of the tomb patrons and their filiations. The distribution of the deceased over the two main necropoleis of Graeco-Roman Period Panopolis remains vague and still requires a historical chronology. It is very likely that, ever since the reign of Ptolemy Philadelphus, El-Salamuni started to be more important than El-Hawawish A as the main burial centre of the city. This is possibly because the great additions which were undertaken by Hormaacheru in El-Salamuni cemetery's temple started to motivate the local people, and particularly the elite, to be buried beside Min, their main god. On the other hand, the El-Hawawish A necropolis was mainly used from the Early Ptolemaic to Early Roman Periods; its Roman tombs are plain in their architectural and artistic style, being largely shallow graves.

El-Salamuni cemetery flourished and replaced El-Hawawish A as the main burial centre from the Late Ptolemaic Period until the end of the third century AD. It reached its peak as the main burial centre for the urban elite during the Roman period[84], and particularly during the second and third centuries AD. Many mummy portraits and mummy labels were found that date to this period. It is noteworthy that a few red bricks of the Roman period were also found scattered around El-Salamuni. They probably belong to Late Roman graves. Unlike at Tuna El-Gebel, the use of mud and red bricks was rare here[85].

El Salamuni may have been contemporaneous with the cemetery of Athribis on the west bank, a site which includes burials dating exclusively to the Ptolemaic and Roman Periods. Athribis is characterised by the discovery of the most abundant and distinctive of Roman mummy labels found to-date; no other region in Egypt has yielded so many labels as the Panopolite nome, with mummy labels typically being discovered on the east bank[86]. In Late Antiquity, El-Hawawish A was again restored to its position of power, and it replaced El-Salamuni as the main cemetery of Coptic Panopolis, with new tombs being scattered in between the tombs of earlier dates. Systematic excavations and investigations in both El-Hawawish A and El-Salamuni are still required in order to understand the full relationship between the necropoleis, as well as to better understand and compare their chronology and social structures.

Egyptian ideology remained potent and powerful. The El-Salamuni tombs are notable in that they record the survival of traditional ancient Egyptian mortuary iconography

---

[84] Being a member of the elite in the Roman period was defined based on several criteria, including but not limited to one's background (family membership and marriage), economic status (wealth, income, and occupation), political status (power and authority), and culture (lifestyle, nomenclature, literacy, and education), P. Garnsey, *Social Status and Legal Privilege in the Roman Empire* (Oxford 1970), 234–59.

[85] In Tuna El-Gebel, by the Early Roman Period, mud-brick buildings had become increasingly numerous in the necropolis. The interiors and façades of the tombs in this area were plastered and painted, K. Lembke, 'City of the Dead, The Necropolis of Tuna El-Gebel During the Roman Period in Egypt in the First Millennium AD', in E. O'Connell (ed.), *Perspectives From New Fieldwork* (Leuven, Paris, Walpole 2014), 186.

[86] On the mummy labels from the Panopolite nome, see Depauw, 'The Late Funerary Material from Akhmim,' in A. Egberts et al. (eds.), *Perspectives on Panopolis*, 71–81.; Smith, *Following Osiris*, 427–29.

The Afterlife in Akhmim

and beliefs from as late as the fourth century AD[87]. The tombs are decorated with colourful Egyptian funerary iconography, showing a trend towards conservatism in mortuary practices and beliefs.

El-Salamuni Mountain was the cemetery of the local elite in the Hellenised metropolis of Panopolis and its adjacent villages. Judging from the quality of its architecture and art, it is likely that members of the high aristocracy such as priests, landowners, high ranking local officials, and veterans of the Roman army were buried there. It reflects the wealth of the Panopolite community, especially on the east bank. Strikingly, most stelae were found on the east bank of the Panopolite nome, while mummy labels for the poor were found on the west bank[88]. At a first glance, this also indicates a regional variation in the religious beliefs, burial practices, and cultural backgrounds of the people on the two banks[89]. Furthermore, the large classical portraits of the deceased[90], as well as the widespread appearance of zodiacs in El-Salamuni, also confirm the high social and cultural statuses of the deceased.

It makes sense that the high priest Hormaachreu, who enlarged the El-Salamuni rock-temple, could be buried in El-Salamuni under the full patronage of the god Min. However, as of now, his tomb has not been identified. The author highly suggests that El-Salamuni was the necropolis of high priests of the Ptolemaic-Roman Periods. This would answer the urgent question of the location of the tombs of the famous Panopolite figures whose names are inscribed on the Ptolemaic-Roman artefacts in international collections.

3.5.3: Funerary Art

The blending of Egyptian and Hellenistic features is extremely attested in the expression of afterlife beliefs in El-Salamuni. The unusual combination of Greek and Egyptian iconography in different styles is worthy of being noted. Despite the trend of sometimes following typical Egyptian iconography, the influence of Hellenistic art is also visible in the tombs. The funerary art at El-Salamuni combines Egyptian beliefs with Greek cultural habits and ideas; it can be 'almost exclusively' Egyptian, or combine features of the Egyptian, Greek, and Roman repertoires, proving the complex interaction between Egyptian traditions and Hellenistic ones, especially in the metropolis. The synthesis of the classical and Egyptian funerary elements reveals the predilections and desires of the tombs' patrons concerning beauty, political allegiances, and religious identities in their tombs. The combination of Egyptian and classical elements calls into question to what extent one can document the homogeneity and artistic similarities and differences in the tombs. Outside of Alexandria,

---

[87] In the gebels near Akhmim, anachoretic monasticism rose to popularity, based on the model of Saint Antony. On the east bank of El-Salamuni, the tombs were reused by *anachorets*. Some annexes in the rock-cut temple of Min in El-Salamuni contain little caves covered by stone, which were later used as a necropolis sanctuary, perhaps dating to the Christian Period, Kuhlmann, *SDAIK* 11, 347–48.; id., *Orientalia* 51, 444.

[88] The abundance of labels from the Panopolite nome, most of which bear a toponym, shed light on onomastics, local cults, and the lower strata of society. Some labels are bilingual in text, being written in both Greek and Demotic. Other texts are either entirely Greek, entirely Demotic, or Graeco-Demotic. There are also a few examples written in hieroglyphic, Hieratic, Old Coptic, Coptic, and these languages combined with Greek or Demotic. In some cases, a figure of a deity, a sacred animal, or a religious symbol (a life sign, palm branches, or the *chrismon* monogram) is included, Quaegebeur, 'Mummy Labels', *P.L. Bat.* 19, 239 no. 74, 240. The vast majority of labels from the Panopolite nome are dated to the second and third centuries AD, and especially to 175–275 AD, S. Vleeming, *Demotic and Greek-Demotic Mummy Labels and other Short Texts Gathered from Many Publications, Short Texts II 278–1200*, StudDem 8 A–B (Leuven 2008). Some Coptic mummy labels with crosses, formulae, and/or a Chi–Rho monogram are also attested, *CEMG* 104, 113, 1404.; *CEMG* 1512. For more about the mummy labels of Akhmim, see Bouriant, *Rec.Trav..* 11, 143–44. The most important collection of these objects is the collection of Robert Forrer, which has roughly 255 labels and is located in Strasbourg, Forrer, *Mein Besuch in El-Achmim*, 59–60. Further objects can be found in the Egyptian Museum of Berlin, F. Krebs, 'Griechische Mumienetikette aus Ägypten', *ZÄS* 32 (1894), 36–51 (1894).; G. Möller, *Mumienschilder, Demotische Texte aus den Königlichen Museen zu Berlin* 1 (Leipzig 1913).; S. Vleeming, *The Berichtungsliste of Demotic Documents in A. D. 2007* (Brauneberg 2008), 132–33., and in Leiden and Amsterdam, P. Pestman, 'Two Mummy-Labels in the Museum of Antiquities at Leiden', *OMRO* 44 (1963) 24–26.; id., 'Der demotische Text der Mumientäfelchen aus Amsterdam', *OMRO* 46 (1965), 44–51.; P. Sijpesteijn, 'Eine Sammlung von Mumientäfelchen im Allard Pierson Museum zu Amsterda', *OMRO* 46 (1965), 34–43.; id., 'Fourteen Ostraca from a Private Collection', *ZPE* 14 (1974), 229–39. The collection of the Louvre was mainly assembled by Bouriant and Revillout, and the Greek texts are published by F. Baratte and B. Boyaval, 'Catalogue des étiquettes de momies du Musée du Louvre (C.E.M.L.). Textes grecs, 1', *CRIPEL* 2 (1974) 155–26.; id., Catalogue des étiquettes de momies du Musée du Louvre (C.E.M.L.). Textes grecs, 2', *CRIPEL* 3 (1974), 155–264 no. 1–259, no. 151–261, no. 260–68.; id., 'Catalogue des étiquettes de momies du Musée du Louvre (C.E.M.L.), Textes grecs, 3', *CRIPEL* 4 (1976), 173–254 no. 689–99.; id. (1979), 237–90, no. 1000–209, index 291–339. The British Museum collection was acquired by E. Budge, *The Mummy, A Handbook of Egyptian Funerary Archaeology* (New York 1892), 224–25.; H. Hall, Greek Mummy-Labels in the British Museum', *PSBA* 27 (1905), 4. Some of these labels are now published in the collection of the Egyptian Museum of Cairo, W. Spiegelberg, *Die demotischen Denkmäler. I. Die demotischen Inschriften (CGC 30601–31166)* (Leipzig 1904), 13–20, 48–56, 83–91, 115–22, 159–65.; J. Milne, 'Greek Inscriptions', *Catalogue Général des Antiquités égyptiennes du Musée de Caire*, No. 9201– 400, 26001–123, 33001–37 (Cairo 1905), 5.; *SB* I, 742–843. For the collection in the IFAO, see G. Wagner, 'Étiquettes de momies grecques de l'IFAO', *BIFAO* 74 (1974), 45–46.; D. Devauchelle and J. Quaegebeur, 'Etiquettes de Momies démotiques et bilingues de l'IFAO', *BIFAO* 81 (1981), 359–77. For the mummy labels in the collection of the Austrian National Library in Vienna, see H. Klos, 'Griechische Mumientäfelchen der Papyrussammlung der Österreichische Nationalbibliothek', *CdÉ* 27 (1952), 282–88.; id., *Die griechischen Mumientäfelchen der Papyrussammlung der Österreichische Nationalbibliothek, Studia et Documenta Orientalia* 6 (Cairo 1956), 221–82.

[89] M. Chauveau, 'Rive droite, rive gauche', in A. Egberts et al. (eds.), *Perspective on Panopolis* 47. Bataille refutes the argument that the mummy labels are an indication of a lower-class burial, A. Bataille, *Les Memnonia*, RAPH 23 (Cairo 1952), 53. The large collection of funerary stelae in the Cairo Museum comes from Maspero's excavations at the cemetery of El-Hawawish A, having been published by A. Kamal, *CGC, Stèles ptolémaiques et romaines, Nos 22001–22208, 2 vols. Catalogue général des antiquités égyptiennes du Musée du Caire* (Cairo 1904–05). In his books (*Die spätägyptischen Totenstelen*, 2 vols., ÄF 25 (Glückstadt 1973), 117–15, 312–28.), Munro identifies a variety of typologies of the Akhmim stelae, P. Munro, *Die spätägyptischen Totenstelen*, 2 vols. *ÄF* 25, (Glückstadt 1973),132–54. Roughly150 Graeco-Roman hieroglyphic stelae and some Demotic funerary stelae from Akhmim are listed on https://www.trismegistos.org/geo/geotex_list.php?tm=1589&partner=all.

[90] Corcoran states that the patrons of the mummy portraits are seen as members of the 'elite', L. Corcoran, 'They Leave Behind Them Portraits of Their Wealth, Not Themselves': Aspects of Self-Presentation in the Dress of the Deceased in Mummy Portraits and Portrait Mummies from Roman Egypt', in A. Batten and K. Olson (eds.), *Dress in Mediterranean Antiquity, Greeks, Romans, Jews, Christians* (London 2021), 140.

it is arguable that the elite tombs are characterised by physical and cultural remains that distinguish the potential ethnicities of the tombs' owners. In El-Salamuni, the classical and Egyptian decoration styles merge to create a beautiful and symbolically significant place to rest for eternity. Surely, the hybridised iconographic repertoire from El-Salamuni presents a translatable visual language that was designed to communicate religious beliefs and cultural associations to a multi-cultural audience in Roman Egypt.

The paint layers on the walls of the Roman tombs are very weak, being made on a limestone base. The walls were covered with a layer of silt and sand before being finally coated with a rough plaster and painted. They were occasionally whitewashed and then decorated. The walls of the tombs are mostly divided into two friezes, and in a few cases, into three. The upper frieze typically illustrates ancient Egyptian afterlife iconography and other elements of the ancient Egyptian religious and symbolic system, while the lower one always features distinctive Roman *orthostats* (stone slabs set at the base of a wall) and/or *opus sectile/opus isodomum* decorations[91]. These serve to divide the walls into sections that are then painted above the plinth. Such Hellenistic decorations survive in Roman art, and indicate the exceptional permanence of the tradition of wall decoration in the city of Alexandria itself[92]. The painted *orthostats* contain geometrical rectangular polychrome plinths that are most often decorated with a smooth colour. These plinths are often meant to imitate the Egyptian precious stones of marble, granite, porphyry, and alabaster, thus revealing the Roman influence in these tombs[93]. The rectangles are separated by striped pilasters or frames, from which smaller fields of decoration can be additionally seen. The imitation of varying stones reflects the decoration of wealthy houses at Panopolis, and is related to Roman wall paintings in the northern Mediterranean.

The standard quality of the decorations in the tombs is attributed to the social status of the deceased; depending on how rich someone was, one could buy, prepare, and/or fully paint one's own tomb. Some tombs are only plastered without decorations, and others only feature lower geometrical panels (Figure 3.25). In some tombs, only the burial niches are decorated. It is also noteworthy that there are a few Graeco-Roman tombs that are completely lacking afterlife scenes and *orthostats*. Here, only floral motifs such as festoons (chains or garlands made of flowers), cover both the walls of the tomb, reflecting the use of flowers during the burial itself. Like the *kline*, it may illustrate the eternal *prothesis* of the dead. Furthermore, the commissioners of the tombs of the second and third centuries AD began to favour classical iconography, and especially Greek floral motifs[94] in order to better express their beliefs in a blissful afterlife. This was represented in the shape of lovely gardens.

The *orthostats* and geometrical panels are varied in their style, colours, and decorations (Figures 3.26a-b). In a few cases, only birds and animals (with no funerary scenes) decorate the walls and ceilings of the tombs, appearing alongside floral motifs, emphasizing that the deceased hopes to enjoy paradise in his or her afterlife (Figure 3.27). In contrast to this, in an unregistered tomb, birds adorn the *orthostats* (Figure 3.28)[95]. Green festoons adorn the *orthostats* in tombs E4 and M5 (Figure 3.29). In very rare cases, the interior of the *orthostats* show Macedonian *clipei*, with a circle imitating black marble in the centre. The use of *orthostats* is not only widely found in Graeco-Roman funerary structures, but is also part of the lower frieze of the chapel of the temple of Tutu in the Dakhleh Oasis. The close similarity of the architectural ornaments from Hermopolis to those of the chapel of the temple of Tutu encourages Lembke to claim that this type of decoration dates to the beginning of the second century[96].

The simple style of geometrical lines on *orthostats* is present in one New Kingdom or Late Period tomb at El-

---

[91] R. Ling, *Roman Painting* (Cambridge 1991), 12–22.
[92] G. Majcherek, "Crumbs from the table'- archaeological remains of Hellenistic Alexandria', in C. Zerefos and M. Vardinoyannis (eds.), *Hellenistic Alexandria: Celebrating 24 Centuries*, 77–78.
[93] Kuhlmann, *SDAIK* 11, 73, 81, fig. 28, pls. 37d, 38c. Besides at El-Salamuni, *orthostats* were widely used in Graeco-Roman Egypt, including in civic buildings, houses, and tombs. In Alexandria, some Roman tombs are attested, such as Sieglin's tomb of 1902. Here, the lower part of the pilasters is decorated with a pattern of intersecting lines. G. Botti notes that this decoration looks like the *opus reticulatum* of the first Pompeian style, C. Gaël, *Architecture des Tombes d'Egypte à L'Epoque Imperial*, 1, 71. The use of these blocks is also recorded in the civic buildings of the baths and villas of Kom El-Dikka, B. Tkacyow, 'An Imitation of Opus Alexandrinum in Wall Paintings? Two Wall Paintings from Kom El-Dikka (Alexandria)', *Rec.Trav.*.17 (1995), 324–25, 324–25. The blocks are also found in the necropolis of Mustafa Pasha and in the Ras El-Tin tombs 1 and 8, R. Pagenstecher, *Nekropolis, Untersuchungen über Gesalt und Entwicklung der alexandrerischen Grabenlagen und ihrer Malerien* (Leipzig 1919) 179–80.; A. Adriani, *Repertorio d'Arte dell 'Egitto Greco-Romano C I-II* (Palermo 1963), 126–29, figs. 365, 367, 382–86.; M. Venit, *Visualizing the Afterlife in the Tombs of Graeco-Roman Period* (Cambridge 2016) 57 no. 369, 183. Furthermore, they are used in Sakiya's tomb in El Wardian. At Marina el-Alamein, polychrome plinths are widely used in houses, G. Bakowska and R. Czerner, 'Marina el-Alamein as an Example of Painting Decoration of Main Spaces of Hellenistic-Roman Houses in Egypt', in *Arts* 11, (2022), 6–11. In the Egyptian *chora*, *orthostats* are also found in the northern chapel of the monument of Piyris in Ayn al-Labkha in the Kharga Oasis, A. Hussein, *Le Sanctuaire rupestre de Pyiris a Ayn al-Labakha, MIFAO* 116 (2000), 30–31, pl. 3–4. They are widely used in Roman house-tombs 4, 6, 21, and 22 of Tuna El-Gebel, C. Riggs, *The Beautiful Burial in Roman Egypt, Art, Identity and Funerary Religion* (Oxford 2005), 132, fig. 57.; K. Lembke, 'Neferu-aesthesis-pulchritude, zum Wandel des Schönheitsbegriffs im ptolmemäisch-römischen Ägypten am Beispiel der Petosiris-Nekropole von Tuna El-Gebel', in M. Flossmann-Schütze, F. Hoffmann, and A. Schütze (eds.), *Tuna El-Gebel, eine ferne Welt, Tagungsband zur Konferenz der Graduade School 'Distant Worlds' vom 16. bis 19.1.2014 in München* (München 2020),140–41, pl. 7, 8.
[94] Lembke, *City of the Dead*, in E. O'Connell (ed.), *Perspectives From New Fieldwork*, 87.
[95] This is similar to the birds which adorn the panels in the *triclinium* hall of the House of Leukaktios in Ptolemais, which may represent the painter's signature style (*pictor imaginarius*) of images of birds, J. Żelazowski, 'Painted Decoration from the House of Leukaktios in Ptolemais', in J. Żelazowski (ed.), *Ptolemais in Cyrenaica Studies in Memory of Tomasz Mikocki* (Warsaw 2012) 186–88, figs. 5, 8.
[96] Lembke, *City of the Dead*, in E. O'Connell (ed.), *Perspectives From New Fieldwork*, 87.

The Afterlife in Akhmim

Figure 3.25. An unregistered tomb that is only decorated with lower *orthostates*, found on the northern section of El-Salamuni Mountain.

Salamuni[97], located beneath the temple of Ay. Here, the geometrical panels cover the lower registers of the walls in both the ante- and burial chambers, though great parts of the panels in the antechamber are still covered with sand. The tomb is more delicately decorated in its antechamber than in its burial chamber (Figure 3.30). Certainly, the style was developed in Roman tombs, but this finding leads the author to strongly argue that the *orthostats* were known in Akhmim since the New Kingdom. The so-called *a pannelli* decorative scheme was popularly used in El-Salamuni's Roman tombs. The creation of the main frieze in an Egyptian style and the lower one in a classical manner is a hallmark of the tombs at Akhmim. However, it is also found in Athribis[98].

The tombs show varied deities that are not only from Panopolis but also from the adjacent nomes. Due to the close connection between Panopolis and Abydos, a strong overlap of cults between Panopolis and Abydos is attested. Since the Middle Kingdom, the cult of Min was known in Abydos (Mnw Hry-ib AbDw = Min who resides in Abydos)[99]. Osiris and Sokar-Osiris were, of course, prominent in the Panopolite nome, and Osiris still held the position of god of the dead and evaluator of their posthumous existence. Numerous texts from Panopolis date to the second and third centuries AD, but not thereafter. They attest to the fondness of the deceased for Osiris; the dead hope to enjoy the afterlife as members of his following. The latest text to list a precise date was inscribed on 24 February in 268 AD. It records the perspective of a dead female and is addressed to Osiris for the beneficiary's hopes of an afterlife. This suggests that the belief in the Osirian afterlife at Akhmim ceased after the third quarter of the third century AD. This does not mean that all polytheistic beliefs in the Akhmim region died out, however[100]. By Shenoute's time, almost all that survived of the old indigenous religion was subsumed into

---

[97] The *a*tomb is in a bad state of preservation, and is covered with sand and debris. Light soot covers its walls. The painting style presumably suggests a date of the Ptolemaic Period.

[98] The imitation of panelling in red and black granite as well as the use of porphyry for the lower parts of the walls is also attested in the necropoleis of Athribis, El-Sayed and El-Masry, *Athribis I*, 84, fig. 15.1.2.

[99] The title is inscribed on the stele of the Calvet A42 museum in Avignon and dedicated to Prince Montouhotep, J. Goyon and L. Postel, *Fastueuse Égypte, catalogue d'exposition du Musée Calvet à Avignon, 25 juin-14 novembre 2011* (Avignon 2011), 50.

[100] M. Smith, 'Osiris and the Deceased in Ancient Egypt: Perspectives from Four Millennia', *Conférences de l'année 2012–2013*, in *Annuaire de "École pratique des hautes études (EPHE), Section des sciences religieuses Résumé des conférences et travaux, Journal of Publications de l'École Pratique des Hautes Études* (2014), 97, openedition.org. A cartonnage coffin from Akhmim shows a dead child in the costume of a Pharaoh/Osiris, C. Spieser, 'Cercueils d'enfants dans l'Egypte ancienne et tardive', in F. Gusi, S. Muriel, and C. Olària (eds.), *Nasciturus, infans, puerulus vobis mater terra, la muerte en la infancia/ la mort dans l'enfance/ la mort a la infància/the death in the childhood* (Castellon 2008), 537–38, fig. 18.

Figure 3.26a. The Roman *orthostates* style, as seen in the antechamber of tomb C4 on the northern section of El-Salamuni Mountain.

Figure 3.27. Trees flanking a damaged figure of the deceased in tomb C8, which is on the southern section of El-Salamuni Mountain.

Figure 3.26b. Another example of the *orthostates* style, this time in an unregistered tomb from the northern section of El-Salamuni Mountain.

the broader framework of the then-dominant Hellenism. Particularly, evidence of the Osirian belief had already ceased to exist in the Akhmim region by the time that Shenoute's career began.

The cult of Osiris-Sokar, or Ptah-Sokar-Osiris, the so-called 'Great God and Lord of Abydos', was introduced into the Akhmimic pantheon, and a related funerary festival was celebrated in both Abydos and Akhmim[101]. The great number of funerary stelae written either in hieroglyphic or Demotic that were found in the cemeteries of the east

---

[101] According to the stelae from Abydos and Akhmim, Derchain-Urtel concludes that a close religious connection between the two areas had existed since the Late Period, continuing through the Ptolemaic Period, Derchain-Urtel, 'Die Beziehungen zwischen Achmim und Abydos', in *Priester im Tempel, Die Rezeption der Theologie der Tempel von Edfu und Dendera in den Privatdokumenten aus Ptolemäische Zeit*, GOF IV.19 (Wiesbaden 1989), 240 (see: JE 22209 (Akhmim), 22173 (Abydos), and 22151(Akhmim)).

Figure 3.28. A bird that adorns some *orthostates* of an unregistered tomb located north of tomb F5, on the register below it. The tomb is on the southern section of El-Salamuni Mountain.

The Afterlife in Akhmim

Figure 3.29. Festoons and flowers that decorate the ceiling of tomb C8 on the southern section of El-Salamuni Mountain.

Figure 3.30. Some geometrical decorations from a New Kingdom tomb(?), just to the south of the temple of Ay.

bank emphasise the common belief in Osiris as a god of the afterlife in Panopolis[102]. Later, during the time of Roman Panopolis, huge numbers of mummy labels were written in the nome (after the second century AD); they refer to the Osirian afterlife[103]. A common Demotic religious formula written frequently on mummy labels from the Athribis/Triphion cemetery is often addressed to either Osiris-Sokar or Sokaris, including his name or his figure in ink[104]. The formula states: 'May his soul live before Osiris-Sokaris, the Great God, Lord of Abydos', or

---

[102] Smith, *Following Osiris*, 426–27.; 'Transformation, Retracing Ptah-Sokar-Osiris Figures from Akhmim in Museums and Private Collections', in T. Gillen (ed.), *(Re)productive Traditions in Ancient Egypt: Proceedings of the Conference Held at the University of Liège, 6th-8th February 2013* (Liège 2017), 445–74.; id., 'Two Ptah-Sokar-Osiris Figures from Akhmim in the Egyptian Collection of the Museum of Fine Arts', *BMH* 119 (Budapest 2014), 13–41. On the Akhmimic types of Ptah-Sokar-Osiris, see Bruwier and Mekis, 'Diversity of the Akhmimic Funerary Art', in M. Mosher (ed.), *The Book of the Dead*, 20–25.

[103] Smith, *Following Osiris*, 427.
[104] Vleeming, *Demotic and Greek*, A: Texts, 127–525, B, 799–801.

similarly, 'His Ba will serve Osiris-Sokaris, Great Lord, Lord of Abydos'[105]. The same formula in hieroglyphs was recorded by von Bissing in the burial chamber of the tomb. It reads: *'May his soul live forever for Osiris... (lost)'*[106]. Osiris and Osiris-Sokar are simply variant names for the same divinity in Panopolis, at least until the beginning of the fourth century AD[107]. The *fekty* ('shorn-priest'), who was presumably related to the mysteries of Osiris, was responsible for the preparation of the Sokaris figure in the House of Life[108]. The great cultic importance of Osiris-Sokar in Panopolis encourages M. Smith to assume that the so-called 'tomb of 1897' at El-Salamuni attests to a belief in the Osirian afterlife[109], and leads him to attribute the papyrus in the Bodleian Library in Oxford to Akhmim's provenance because of the references to Osiris-Sokar in its texts[110].

The funerary texts of the rock-cut temple of Ay describe Osiris-Sokar as the god of *Ipu*[111]. On the stela of Pasenedjemibash from Akhmim, Sokar-Osiris is also titled 'the Lord of Akhmim'[112]. The famous Panopolite wisdom text P. Insinger, which is most likely from a tomb, as Smith suggests[113], ends with a prayer requesting that the *ba* of a certain Paheb flourishes forever in the following of Osiris-Sokar. This request is very similar to those found on mummy labels and funerary stelae[114]. The funerary texts in the temple of Auletes at Wannina also mention a special cult of Sokar-Osiris at Akhmim, stating *Skr -Wsir ntr c³ hr –ib ipw*, or 'Sokar-Osiris, the Great God, Chief of Panopolis'[115]. Another mummy label mentions that Osiris–Sokar is both the Lord of Abydos and of Athribis[116].

Many other deities who are typical for mortuary contexts (such as Horus, Thoth, Anubis, Khepri, Isis, Hathor, Sekhmet, Neith, Maat, Geb, and Onouris) are also depicted in the tombs. Deities that are typical for the region of Akhmim are widely depicted in the tombs, especially the triad of Panopolis (Min-Re, Isis/Repit, and Horus). Likewise, Horudja/Haryotes, the locally deified human-god who combined divinity and humanity, and whose cult flourished in Bompae[117], being venerated together with Hermes and Apollo[118], also has a special appearance and function in the tombs. Here, some deities appear in unique iconographic contexts, such as Bes and Ptah. The desert god Tithoes is also frequently depicted in the tombs; he is illustrated twice, accompanying the deceased in a barque in tomb F2, and guarding the mummy of the deceased as it is transported in a burial cart in tomb B7[119].

From the Ptolemaic Period onwards, Akhmim, and especially El-Salamuni and El-Khazindariyah, has maintained a close connection with the Great Oasis (Dakhla and the El-Kharga Oasis), as attested in the sources[120]. Hence, funerary cults

---

[105] Quaegebeur, 'Mummy Labels' in *P.L. Bat* 19, 251–55.; Vleeming, *Demotic and Greek*, StudDem 8B, 795. Most of the mummy labels from the Panopolite nome were written by two distinct scribal schools of the villages of Bompae and Psonis, Vleeming, *Demotic and Greek*, StudDem 8B, 796–97.
[106] Von Bissing, *ASAE* 50, 559. As for the formula which was widely mentioned in the funerary and wisdom texts of Akhmim, the prayer is mentioned in the P. Insinger, and is very similar to those found on mummy labels and funerary stelae, *P. Insinger*, xxxv.; K. Worp, 'The Greek Text of the P. Dem. Insinger: A Note to the Date', *OMRO* 63 (1982), 39–41.; Lexa, *Papyrus Insinger*. The Instructions of Ankhsheshonqy, which was found rolled up together with the mortuary texts of P. BM 10507, were both certainly recovered from a tomb. Thus, Smith supposes that the other literary manuscripts from the area were probably also found in tombs, and wonders where these tombs may have been located, Smith, 'Aspects of the Preservation and Transmission of Indigenous Religious Traditions', in A. Egberts et al. (eds), *Perspectives on Panopolis*, 237. The well-attested existence of this religious formula in the El-Salamuni tombs may lead one to assume that El-Salamuni indeed contains the tombs for which Smith searched.
[107] Van Minnen, 'The Letter (and Other Papers) of Ammon' in A. Egberts et al. (eds.), *Perspectives on Panopolis*, 179–80, no. 16.
[108] Derchain, *Le papyrus Salt 825 (B.M. 10051)*, 69–70, 73–74.; F. von Känel, 'Les prêtres-ouâb de Sekhmet et les conjurateurs de Serket', *Bibliothèque de l'Ecole des hautes études, Sciences religieuses* 87 (Paris 1984), 84.
[109] Smith, *Following Osiris*, 427.
[110] M. Smith, 'Bodl. Ms. Egypt. A.3 (P) and the Interface between Temple Cult and the Cult of The Dead,' in *Ägyptische Rituale der griechisch-römischen Zeit, Heraugegben von Joachim Friedrich Quack* (Tübingen 2014), 145-55. The festival of Sokar was prominent in the Theban area. About 20 private tombs record the existence of the Sokar barque, dating from the time of Horemheb to the end of the 20ᵗʰ dynasty, M. Saleh, *Das Totenbuch in den thebanischen Beamtengrabern des Neuen Reiches. Texte und Vignetten, AV* 46 (Mainz 1984) 39. Later, during the Roman period, the Sokar barque was further represented in a series of painted plaster and linen mummy masks from Deir El-Bahari, Grimm, *Die romischen Mumienmasken*, 93–96, pls. E, 112.; S. Walker and M. Bierbrier, *Ancient Faces, Mummy Portraits from Roman Egypt, A Catalogue of Roman Portraits in the British Museum IV* (London 1997) 156–59 no. 175–78.; M. Stadler, 'The Funerary Texts of Papyrus Turin N. 766, A Demotic Book of Breathing (Part II)1, D. The Theban Context of Papyrus Turin N. 766', *Enchoria* 26 (2000), 111.
[111] Kees, *Rec.Trav.* 36, 5.; S. Sauneron and J. Vercouter, 'Perses, Dieu de Khemmis', *RdÉ* 14 (1962), 53 no. 2.
[112] Abdelhalim, *BIFAO* 114.1, 7.
[113] M. Smith, 'Budge at Akhmim, January 1869', in C. Eyre, A. Leahy, and L. Leahy (eds.), *The Unbroken Reed: Studies in the Culture and Heritage of Ancient Egypt in Honour of A. F. Shore* (London 1994), 300.

[114] *P. Insinger*, xxxv, 13–15.; Lexa, *Papyrus Insinger*, 113.; Smith, 'Aspects of the Preservation and Transmission', in A. Egberts et al. (eds.), *Perspectives on Panopolis*, 237.
[115] Petrie, *Athribis*, pl. 21.
[116] Louvre Inv. Prov. 50.; Chauveau, 'Rive droite, rive gauche', in A. Egberts et al. (eds.), *Perspectives on Panopolis*, 47.
[117] Bompae is probably identified as modern Sohag, Chauveau, 'Rive droite, rive gauche', in A. Egberts et.al. (eds.), *Perspectives on Panopolis*, 48.; id., *BIFAO* 92, 107.; Smith, 'Aspects of the Preservation and Transmission', in A. Egberts et al. (eds), *Perspectives on Panopolis*, 242. The object Louvre E 9471 refers to Haroudja Haryotes, and combines the Greek gods Hermes and Apollo, who were assimilated with the Egyptian gods Thoth and Horus, Chauveau, 'Rive droit, rive gauche', 53. The so-called 'Haryotes names' were familiar names of the community there; derivites of the name Haryotes comprise 103 out of 714 names, or about 15%, *CEML* 7, 9, 10, 13, 15, 17, 18, 22, 23, 30, 36, 41, 44, 46, 51, 58, 61, 64, 66, 71, 77, 78, 79, 81, 82, 84, 93, 94, 95, 100, 101, 601, 1101; CEMG 156, 160, 164, 349, 955, 1142, 1281, 1671, 1677, 1680, 1689, 1693, 1701, 1703, 1707, 1709, 1710, 1715, 1716, 1719, 1720, 1722, 1724, 1726, 1730, 1734, 1735, 1736, 1740, 1743, 1745, 1746, 1747, 1750, 1752?, 1753, 1760, 1764, 1767, 1768, 1769, 1770, 1775, 1781, 1782, 1787, 1788.; *P. L. Bat.* XIX 41. Object *CEMG* 1752 is a mummy label of Haryotes, the son of Haryotes and grandson of Haremephis. It has a picture of a Horus falcon on its back. The Haryotes names also appear in relation to local people in Panopolis, *P. Achm.* 9, ll. 124, 135, 148, 149, 200.; *CPR* XVIIB 15, l.11, as well as on the island of Apollinaria, *CEMG* 1968, 1975, 1981, 1982, 1986, 1990, 2003, 2004, 2007, 2010.
[118] The mummy label *CEML* 53 mentions a 'priest of Haryotes, Hermes and Apollo', while another mentions a 'Priest of Horoudja of Bompae', Chauveau, *BIFAO* 92 no. 44.
[119] The publication of the tomb is forthcoming.
[120] Worp's paper, entitled 'From Dakhleh to Panopolis and Vice Versa, First Explorations', which he read at the Leiden colloquium on Panopolis, was unfortunately not submitted for publication, Geens, *Panopolis, a Nome Capital in Egypt*, 289 no. 1268. Caravan roads connected Panopolis, Toeto, and Psinabla in the Panopolite nome with the military station of Hibis and El-Deir (20km. north of Hibis), R. Bagnall and D. Rathbone, *Egypt from Alexander to the Copts, An Archaeological and*

were transferred[121]. A major desert road connected the two places. Even nowadays, caravan routes depart from Akhmim to Hibis (El-Kharga, the capital of the Great Oasis). This connection delivered not only products[122], but also the local cult of Tithoes from the Great Oasis to El-Salamuni[123].

The astronomical decorations are the most prominent and interesting characteristics of the El-Salamuni tombs, as they represent the largest number of astronomical zodiacs known from a necropolis in Graeco-Roman Egypt, and are also the best preserved. Astrology and astronomy were important interests of the priests from the Panopolite nome. In addition to the six zodiacs in Greek style that Neugebauer and Parker recorded, the newly discovered tombs contribute to the hitherto unpublished ones. All six of the zodiacs are dated to the second century AD. In the middle of these tombs' circular zodiacs, Isis-Sothis appears twice, and Harpocrates is shown squatting at the centre of the zodiac three times[124]. Meanwhile, another zodiac can be recognised from a fragment of a painting which now only has Virgo and Libra preserved. Nowadays, the paintings are all somewhat damaged and the tombs have been resealed for some time. The zodiacs cover both the ante- and burial chambers' ceilings.

The 'Zodiac tombs' represent a group of tombs whose vertical syntax admits both Greek and Egyptian elements, confirming that local traditions proliferated within the Hellenistic context of Panopolis. The Egyptian sky goddess Nut is shown giving birth to the new sun in some tombs, while the classical image of Isis-Sothis, mounted side-saddle on a dog, is depicted in other zodiac tombs. The scene evokes the celestial realm, recalling Isis as the 'Mistress of the Heavens, of the Earth, and of the Underworld'. The high number of zodiacs suggests that immortality in El-Salamuni was not imagined to be only accessed through a chthonic deity (Osiris). It was also possible through a cosmic approach, with the zodiac representing a celestial afterlife. Several texts confirm the match between Sokar and the rising sun[125]. Therefore, Sokar, who was characterised by a dual nature of being both chthonic and celestial, was widely depicted in the El-Salamuni tombs.

The great number of zodiacs depicted in El-Salamuni is mainly related to the reputation of the Panopolite nome as a centre for the study and interpretation of astral phenomena. The local priests may have been priests of Thoth, being called 'those who know the forms of the ancestors, and scribes, wise men, who enter the library, [as] servants of Thoth, the staff of the House of Life'[126]. The House of Life in the temple of Min at Akhmim played a distinct role in the survival and transformation of local Ancient Egyptian funerary rituals, burial practices, and language. There, scribes and artists were trained to gain highly specialised skills that required more knowledge, emphasizing the continued use and development of the local language and the art forms traditional to both local temples and tombs. The House of Life continued to function during the Graeco-Roman Period[127]. In El-Salamuni, it was the funerary and artistic decisions of the priests and the school of artists who supervised the construction of the necropolis to create tombs with astronomical decorations.

On the west bank of the Panopolite nome, a significant village whose name is Ψωνις, or 'Psonis' (*psooyn* in Coptic, and *Pr-swn* (with variants *Pa-swn* and *P3-swn*) in Demotic), and which is also known as modern 'Bassouna', lying 20km. northwest of Sohag[128], was well attested in documents dating from the first to the eighth century AD. Its name was especially common on mummy labels[129]. The name of the village may have been popularly reinterpreted as meaning 'House of Knowledge' or simply 'knowledge'[130], which is appropriate, given its role as a centre for the composition, or at least the

---

Historical Guide (London 2004), 249–50, 255, 257.; G. Wagner, *Les Oasis d'Egypte, Bibliothèque "Etude* 100 (Cairo 1987), 140–46, 155–96.; R. Morkot, 'The Darb El-Arbain, the Kharga Oasis and its Forts', in D. Bailey (ed.), *Archaeological Research in Roman Egypt, The Proceedings of the Seventeenth Classical Colloquium of the Department of Greek and Roman Antiquities, British Museum, JRA Supplementary Series* 19 (Ann Arbor 1996), 82–89.; M. Reddè, 'Sites militaires romains de l'oasis de Kharga', *BIFAO* 99 (1999), 377–96.

[121] In the temple of Deir El-Haggar, the emperor Domitian presents offerings to Min and Repit, M. Claude, 'Le prêtres d'Akhmim de L'Ancien Empire a L'épogue romaine', *Akhmim, une tour d'horizon, Egypte, Afrique & Orient* 96 (2020), 27, fig.1. As early as 300 AD, some Christian *nekrotaphoi* of Toeto in the Panopolite nome had contacts with the well-organised Christian community in Kysis, in the Great Oasis, *P. Grenf.* II 73 = W. Chr. 127.

[122] *P. Thomas* 23.

[123] On the cult of Tithoes in El-Salamuni, see W. Omran, 'Tithoes in El-Salamuni Necropolis', *GM* 261 (2020), 157–64. On the combination of Tithoes and Bes, see O. Kaper, 'Bès et Toutou, comparer les dieux égyptiens', *Bès, une puissante figure divine (seconde partie), Égypte, Afrique & Orient* 100 (2020), 27–34.

[124] In the texts of the Roman period, Horus was called the 'Totality of Time' or, one who 'thinks of the years beforehand', and is sometimes shown carrying a harp, which is an attribute of Saturn, R. Witt, *Isis in the Graeco-Roman World* (London 1971), 210–11.

[125] C. Graindorge-Héreil, *Le dieu Sokar à Thèbes au Nouvel Empire, GOF* 4; 28 (Wiesbaden 1994), 9, 14–15, 185–86.

[126] M.Th. Derchain-Urtel, *Thoth à Akhmîm*, in *Homages a Francois Dumas* I (Montpellier 1986), 174.; K. Nordh, *Aspects of Ancient Egyptian Curses and Blessings, Conceptual Background and Transmission, Uppsala Studies in Mediterranean and Near Eastern Civilization* 26 (Uppsala 1996), 194–95.; Smith, 'Aspects of the Preservation and Transmission', in A. Egberts et al. (eds.), *Perspectives on Panopolis*, 242–43. Two mummy labels from Psonis mention a priest of Min who is called an 'astronomer', *P. Louvre E* 9895, 10400.; M. Chauveau, 'Les étiquettes de momies de la 'Ny Carlsberg Glyptotek' [Ét. Carlsberg 1–17]', *BIFAO* 91 (1991), 136. A special priestly function was the role of *ihb* or *xbj*: a dancer-priest in the service of Thoth at Akhmim. Derchain-Urtel suggests that Thoth had an important role in the pacification of the angry sun's eye. He did so by dancing in front of the distant Hathor-Tefnut, in order to restore her peaceful spirit and drive her back to her lord, Re (in the Akhmimic context of Min-Re), Derchain-Urtel, *Thoth à Akhmîm*, 175–76. For the House of Life, see A. Gardiner, 'The House of Life', *JEA* 24, 157–79.

[127] Nordh, *Aspects of Ancient Egyptian Curses*, 194–95.

[128] E. Amelineau, *La géographie de l'Égypte à l'époque copte* (Paris 1893), 505.; C. Alrt, *Deine Seele Möge Leben für immer und Ewig, Die Demotischen Mumienschilder im British Museum*, *StudDem* 10 (Leuven 2011), 107.

[129] Sauneron, *Villes et Legendes d'Egypte*, 104.; id., 'Notes Geographiques sur le Nome Panopolite', *BIFAO* 4 (1905), 72–73.; H. Thissen, *Der Verkommene Harfenspieler, Eine altägyptische Invektive (P. Wien KM 3877), DemStud* 11 (Sommerhausen 1992), 60.

[130] W. Spiegelberg, *Ägyptische und Griechische Eigennamen aus Mumienetiketten der römischen Kaiserzeit auf Grund von grossenteils unveröffentlichen Material* (Leipzig 1901), 71.

copying, of Demotic wisdom literature[131]. The extensive corpus of mummy labels originating from the nome gives information about the villages of the nome and provides a unique opportunity to gain insight into the local cults. Here, the god Min was titled 'the Great Astronomer' (*imj-wnw.t a3 n pr-swn*) of Psonis[132]. Unfortunately, many faded and smashed zodiacs cover the ceilings of Graeco-Roman tombs that are still open to the public, without doors (Figure 3.31).

The zodiacs from the Akhmim region all exclusively come from the ceilings of private tombs, either in El-Salamuni or in Athribis, with the exception of a single zodiac that was recorded upon an architrave of the temple of Min-Pan at the *Birba* of Akhmim. The architrave features a Greek dedication to Pan in the favour of Trajan (109 AD), written by a temple prostate of Pan and Triphis. On one side of the stone, there was once a zodiac, though it no longer exists. It is known to scholars through the incomplete drawings of Wilkinson and Burton[133]. Furthermore, four zodiacs are found in the Roman tombs of Athribis, a pair being depicted in the tomb of Mery-Hor, and another pair being depicted in the tomb of Psenosiris[134]. The El-Salamuni zodiacs offer a crucial clue as to the wealthy status of the deceased, and are also indicative of a once-royal privilege of having private tombs.

At the El-Salamuni necropolis, one can observe a rare glimpse of an old Egyptian town in the process of Hellenisation. The typical Hellenised deceased wears a traditional civic costume, which can include a tunic, a mantle, a *clavus* or *clavi*, and sandals, and is surrounded by traditional Egyptian funerary imagery, displaying the creative license and agenda of both the deceased and the artist[135]. The deceased is posed with one hand raised and an outward-facing palm. It is additionally a special, extensively depicted, characteristic in the El-Salamuni necropolis for the deceased to hold objects in his or her hands, such as a garland, a myrtle branch or other greenery, a *rotulus*, or the *situla* of Isis. The deceased is typically dressed in a classical garment, which, for men, consists of a striped under-tunic, a tunic with a narrow striped *clavi*, and a white cloak. The cloak is draped around the lower body and dropped over one's shoulder[136]. This naturalistic classical depiction of the tombs' patrons confirms a kind of greatness, power, and wealth. It is the same costume of the dead as that which appears on the mummy portraits of the eastern necropoleis. These portraits belong to a wealthy elite who were both acquainted with the Hellenistic culture and loyal to local funerary traditions.

The popular figure of the deceased, as framed within the proliferation of the traditional sphere of Egyptian mortuary practices, is misleading, as it downplays the interest in Greek identity[137]. The combination of both Hellenistic and Egyptian visual elements is a result of a fusion between two rival cultures in Panopolis. The combination contributed to the increased use of naturalistic portraits for the Roman elite in domestic and funerary spheres. Portraiture in this mode offered a new means of self-presentation with an elite

---

[131] The Demotic wisdom literature was a special product of Panopolis, Smith, 'Aspects of Indigenous Traditions', in A. Egberts et al. (eds), *Perspectives on Panopolis*, 238. For more information about this wisdom literature at Panopolis, see *P. Insinger*, 35, 13–15.; F. Lexa, *Papyrus Insinger, Les enseignements d'un scribe égyptien du premier siècle après J.-C., I-II* (Paris 1926), 113. Also see the P. BM EA 10508, which is known as 'the Instructions of Ankhscheschonqy', S. Glanville, *The Instruction of 'Onchsheshonqy (British Museum Papyrus10508), Catalogue of Demotic Papyri in the British Museum* 2 (London 1955).; H. Thissen, *Die Lehre des Anchscheschonqi (P. BM 10508), Papyrologische Texte und Abhandlungen* 32 (Bonn 1984). A new fragment of the papyrus was recently published by J. Quack in 'Neue Fragmente der einleitung Erzählung der Lehre des Chascheschonqi', *Enchoria* 36 (2018/2019) 129–43. For the P. Spiegelberg, see W. Spielgerberg, *Der Sagenkreis des Königs Petubastis* (Leipzig 1910).; I. Grumach, *Untersuchungen zur Lebenslehre des Amenope, Münchener ägyptologische Studien* 23 (München, Berlin 1972). On the Panopolis mortuary papyri, see M. Smith, *The Mortuary Texts of Papyrus BM 10507* (London 1987).; id., *The Liturgy of Opening the Mouth for Breathing* (Oxford 1993). Akhmim housed other Demotic literature such as the Instructions of Ani, the Instructions of Cheti, and the Instructions of P. Brooklyn, see H. Thissen, 'Achmim und die Demotische Literatur', in A. Egberts et al.(eds), *Perspectives on Panopolis*, 249–60.

[132] ²⁴⁴An inscription can be found on two mummy labels in the Louvre, namely E9895 and E10400, Chauveau, 'Rive droite, rive gauche', in A. Egberts et al. (eds), *Perspectives on Panopolis*, 48. People with various titles that can be designated as astronomers are attested from the Old Kingdom (fifth dynasty) until the Roman period, J. Fissolo, 'Les astronomes egyptiens', *EAO* 21 (2001), 15–24.; V. Altmann-Wendling, *Mondsymbolik-Mondwissen, Lunare Konzepte in den ägyptischen Tempeln griechisch-römischer Zeit*, *SSR* 22 (Wiesbaden 2018). A. Winkler assumes that the English translation of the priestly titulary *imj-wnw.t* or *wnw. ty* as 'astronomer' is quite inaccurate; the title literally translates to mean 'who is in the hour'. He argues that the priestly duties of this person are well-known, including the length of each day, season, and year of the work, and the exact hour for performing each ritual, A. Winkler, 'Stellar Scientists: The Egyptian Temple Astrologers', *JNES* 8 (2021), 108.

[133] Saint-Genis, 'Notice sur les restes', 46.; Neugebauer and Parker, *EAT* III, 86–89, pl. 45A. According to Ibn Battuta, the *Birba* temple contains at least one zodiac, Kuhlmann, *SDAIK* 11, 37–38, 41–42.; Arnold, *Temples of the Last Pharaohs*, 263. To the north of the Trajanic block, Wilkinson notes a (naos?) fragment of red granite, with two winged globes, J. Wilkinson, *Manners and Costumes of the Ancient Egyptians* II (London 1843), 105.

[134] For astronomical zodiacs in the Panopolite nome, see Petrie, *Athribis*, 13. Petosiris' tomb was considered to have been lost since 1952.

However, during the excavations carried out by the Sohag Inspectorate (1981–1985), it was rediscovered. For more about this tomb, see Venit, *Visualizing the Afterlife*,148–54, figs. 4.43, 4.45, 4.47, 4.48.; El Farag et al., *MDAIK* 41, 1–8, figs.10–12. Petrie also discovered many Demotic ostraca, some of which he characterised as 'interesting astronomical ones, with entries of stars', Petrie, *Athribis*, 11–13, pls. xi, xli, xxxvi, xxxviii. During the fourth century AD, there was a well-documented knowledge of and interest in the study and interpretation of astral sciences among Akhmim's local community and especially among priests. This is why Shenoute denounced some of his local opponents as casters of horoscopes and as astrologers. During this time, the belief in and knowledge of astrology in Akhmim was likely met with a punishment equal to that of sorcerers, potion-mixers, and idol worshippers, J. Leipoldt, *Sinuthii Archimandritae Vita et Opera Omnia 3*, *CSCO* 42 (Paris 1908), 88.

[135] W. Omran, 'The Deceased in El-Salamuni Necropolis: Following Osiris in Classical Gesture', MDAIK 79 (forthcoming, 2023).

[136] C. Riggs, 'Facing the Dead, Recent Research on the Funerary Art of Ptolemaic and Roman Egypt', *AJA* 106 (2002), 86–87, 96.

[137] The deceased are shown in the same everyday Graeco-Roman costumes as those found on Roman mummy cases and portraits from Panopolis in the second century AD. However, the deceased were also eager to associate with an Egyptian deity (mainly Osiris or Anubis) and/or to act as a participant in scenes of the Egyptian afterlife, such as those chosen from the Book of the Dead or the Book of the *Amduat*, Riggs, *AJA* 106, 86–87, 96.; Schweitzer, *BIFAO* 98, 342–43.

The Afterlife in Akhmim

Figure 3.31. A partially faded zodiac on the ceiling of an unregistered tomb on the northern section of El-Salamuni Mountain.

and highly inter-cultural form[138]. Thus, the designers and artists of El-Salamuni balanced Egyptian and Hellenistic elements in the tombs.

Bi-scriptural texts in hieroglyphs and Demotic are widely recorded in the tombs. Unlike at Tuna El-Gebel and the Triphion necropolis[139], no Greek texts are attested from this area as of now; the *lingua franca* in Middle Egypt during the second and third centuries AD predominated[140]. This confirms the survival of Egyptian indigenous scripts among the local community of Akhmim until the Late Roman Period. In fact, Roman Panopolis continued to be an important centre for the production of Demotic funerary, wisdom, and literary texts[141]. The bi-scriptural contracts, ostraca, and mummy labels originating from the Panopolite nome suggest that many individuals were at least bilingual[142]. For instance, scenes from El-Salamuni are characterised with more images and less text, suggesting that the visual language of these scenes was more powerful and prominent than the textual language.

In Roman Egypt, figurative images had a strong visual impact, being capable of expressing meaning without any additional medium, as opposed to texts, which are mainly dependent on the audience knowing the language or script in which it is written[143].

Indigenous scripts remained the most popular choice in the Roman tombs of El-Salamuni, while Greek was also sometimes used[144]. Although no Greek or Latin scripts appear in the tombs of El-Salamuni, the local Egyptians learnt Greek and Latin for various reasons, such as in order to fulfil administrative roles. Additionally, some learned Demotic, which was used for religious purposes[145]. Lines of Demotic text found in tombs F2[146] and C5 present the name of their patrons, while short hieroglyphic inscriptions are

---

[138] Riggs, *The Beautiful Burial*, 246.
[139] Greek inscriptions on the lintels of the tombs' doors identify their owners by name as Ερμιον τον Αρχιβιον ταφος and Αριππον, El-Farag et al., *MDAIK* 41, pl. 9a.
[140] Lembke, 'City of the Dead', in E. O'Connell (ed.), *Perspectives from New Fieldwork*, 87.
[141] Smith, *The Mortuary Texts of Papyrus BM 10507*.; id., 'Aspects of the Preservation and Transmission of Indigenous Religious', in A. Egberts et al. (eds.), *Perspectives on Panopolis*, 237–38.; H. Thissen, 'Achmim und die demotische Literatur', in A. Egberts et al. (eds.), *Perspectives on Panopolis*, 249–60.
[142] The mummy labels offer a glimpse into the spread of Hellenism between the east and west banks of the Panopolite nome in the second and third centuries AD.

[143] W. Abell, *Representation and Form, A Study of Aesthetic Values in Representational Art* (Connecticut 1971), 122. Reynolds suggests that the scenes are vital interpretations of the texts, and that they have the same efficacy as the texts. However, their visual effect on observers is more immediate and powerful, J. Reynolds, *Discourses on Art* (New Haven, London 1997), 241.
[144] Greek script is found in the Tomb of Isidora, tombs 18 and 21 at Tuna el-Gebel, tombs 6, 7, and 8 at El-Salamuni cemetery C, the Tomb of the Two Brothers at Wannina, and the tombs of Kitynos, Petubastis, and Petosiris in the Dakhla Oasis, Abdelwahed, *Egyptian Cultural Identity*, 129.
[145] In Graeco-Roman Egypt, bilingual writing was frequently used for a variety of documents, such as official decrees and official texts, M. Depauw, 'Bilingual Greek-Demotic Documentary Papyri and Hellenisation in Ptolemaic Egypt', in P. Van Nuffelen (ed.), *Faces of Hellenism, Studies in the History of Eastern Mediterranean (4th Century B.C.- 5th Century A.D.)* (Leuven 2009), 114.
[146] Kaplan named the tomb 'tomb VII'. Here, one line of hieroglyphs and one line of Demotic was written, having been translated by S. Vleeming, *Demotic Graffiti and Other Short Texts Gathered from Many Publications, Short Texts III 1201–2350, StudDem* 7 (Leuven 2015), 272.

visible in tombs F2, F4, F5, and C1, being addressed to the god Osiris. Unfortunately, there are no texts in tombs C3, C4, or F3; some parts of the walls of these tombs are now destroyed, but may have once contained texts. Tomb B7 is the only one that contains a long hieroglyphic text, covering the upper-most walls of the burial chamber. In other cases, the complete or partial lack of texts leads one to assume a probable date rather than a strictly accurate one. Long hieroglyphic inscriptions are also found in the Roman tomb of Psenosiris and the 'Zodiac tomb'[147]. The hieroglyphic texts found in El-Salamuni reveal the inaccuracy of Petrie's assumption when he claimed that only the tomb of Psenosiris and the 'Zodiac tomb' possess a hieroglyphic text[148].

So-called pseudo-hieroglyphic columns[149] are another characteristic of El-Salamuni. These columns of short, cursive hieroglyphs are solidly painted in either vertical or horizontal boxes, mimicking cartouches. They are placed before the heads of the gods, and are intended to contain their names, like normal cartouches. Due to the pseudo-hieroglyphic writing method, environmental issues, and the local community's history of either scrapping off texts or writing over them with white chalk, most of the names are now rubbed out or otherwise demolished, and are hardly readable.

Black, fleshless, corpse-like shadow figures in silhouette are widely represented in the Roman tombs of El-Salamuni. They are either positive or negative in nature, representing the shadow of either the (good or bad) deceased, or the bad, impious enemies of Egypt who will perish in the judgement ceremony[150].

El-Salamuni presents a strong example of the use of a hybrid style in tombs, combining typically Egyptian and Hellenistic artistic styles. The author agrees with Whitehouse, who states: '*of the Greco☐Roman tombs so far discovered in Egypt, that of Petosiris offers probably the most vivid evidence for that mixture of cultural and religious traditions which… have become a focus of interest in the study of post☐pharaonic Egypt*'[151].

3.5.4: Burial Customs

The types of burial customs are numerous in El-Salamuni. Mummification remained the standard treatment practiced in the area, with carefully mummified bodies being covered in cartonnage and/or encased in coffins, and then deposited into long, shallow niches in the burial chambers[152]. Hence, the mummified dead in Roman El-Salamuni still 'become Osiris', as is widely depicted in portraits of the dead[153]. The existence of burial niches attests to the fact that mummification was a common burial custom[154].

The niches of the Graeco-Roman tombs vary in their length and height. They are mostly flat, with a plastered floor that is coloured and made to hold the mummy (Figure 3.32). In a few cases, the niche is hollowed out and then coated to contain the mummy (Figure 3.33a). Occasionally, the flat and hollowed-out burial niches are found adjacent to each other in the same tomb (Figure 3.33b). Tomb B8 in El-Salamuni[155] has a new style of burial niche, which takes the Egyptian form of a hollow, deep sarcophagus. The mummy is entombed inside rather than above the niche. Meanwhile, a small Egyptian niche in the rear wall of tomb B8 was supposed to contain a small statue, stela, or lamp. Sometimes, there are two burial niches cut into the same wall, being either adjacent to each other or stacked with the smallest one on the bottom (Figure 3.34). These niches are found not only in the inner burial chambers, but also in the antechambers of the tombs.

In a few Graeco-Roman tombs on El-Salamuni Mountain, a specific architectural style is used; an underground shaft is cut under the niche of the burial chamber (Figure 3.35). However, one unregistered tomb lacks the existence of a burial niche, featuring only a shallow trench in the floor of the antechamber. The niches of these tombs are mostly painted with Egyptian repertories on their ceilings and walls, showing afterlife scenes, a winged vulture or falcon, hieroglyphic inscriptions, and/or traditional recumbent jackals alternating with *khekrew* decorations. Rarely, alternating black and white squares may cover the rear wall of the niche[156], while sandal decorations may be painted on the lateral wall, referring to the location

---

[147] It most likely dates to the Early Roman Period, El-Faraag et al., *MDAIK* 41, 5–6.
[148] Petrie, *Athribis*, 13.
[149] The pseudo-hieroglyphs also appeared outside of El-Salamuni, such as in Alexandria, in the Habachi and Persephone tombs, M. Venit, *The Monumental Tombs of Ancient Alexandria, The Theatre of the Dead* (Cambridge 2002), 121, fig. 99.; A. Guimier-Sorbets and M. Seif El-Din, 'Les Deux tombes de Perséphone dans la necropole de Kom al-Shuqafa', *BCH* 121/I (1997), 355–410. They are also found in tomb 3 at Oxyrhynchus, J. Padró, 'Recent Archaeological Work', in A. Bowman et al. (eds.), *Oxyrhynchus, A City and Its Texts*, EES (London 2007), 130–33, figs. 10. 4–5, pl. xv.
[150] On the use of the silhouette in the El-Salamuni tombs, see W. Omran, 'Virtuous or Wicked: New Occurrences and Perspectives on the Black Silhouette in Graeco-Roman Egypt', *JARCE* 56 (2020), 143–67.
[151] H. Whitehouse, 'Roman in Life, Egyptian in Death, The Painted Tomb of Petosiris in the Dakhla Oasis', in O. Kaper (ed.), *Life on the Fringe, Living in the Southern Egyptian Desert During the Roman and Early Byzantine Periods, Proceedings of a Colloquium Held on the Occasion of the 25th Anniversary of the Netherlands Institute for Archaeology and Arabic Studies in Cairo 9–12 December 1996* (Leiden 1998), 253.

[152] In El-Hawawish A, Kuhlmann recognised a type of tomb layout called type A-1b. It refers to steep shaft tombs of the Ptolemaic/Roman Periods, of ca. 15–20m., having been constructed in several levels, and, in some cases, containing about eight to 10 burial niches starting from the shaft. This explains the unusual measurements of the shaft. Moreover, each niche contains a common burial of a dozen sarcophagi, Kuhlmann, *SDAIK* 11, 62. During the fourth century AD, the Copts still practiced mummification for their dead, with the dead now being buried in luxurious examples of garments worn during life.
[153] C. Römer, 'Das Werden zu Osiris im römischen Ägypten', *ARG* 2 (2000), 141–61.
[154] On the funerary art and burial customs in El-Salamuni see, W. Omran, A. Oksana, and A. Abu-Gebel, 'Resurrection in Panopolis; the Graeco-Roman Period at the El-Salamuni Necropolis', *EA* 59 (2021), 16–19.; id., "Berg der Toten'-Die Felsgräber von El-Salamuni', *SOKAR* 41 (forthcoming, 2023).
[155] Unfortunately, the tomb is still open and without a door, and its floor is filled up with heavy debris. Though there are no decorations in its burial chamber, the painted *orthostats* cover the lower *dado* of its antechamber, which suggests a Roman date of the tomb.
[156] It is quite similar to the chequer pattern of Greek decoration attested in Ras el Tin 8, in the *kline* niche. The same chequer pattern also fully

The Afterlife in Akhmim

Figure 3.32. The plastered floor of the burial niche in tomb C6, located on the southern section of El-Salamuni Mountain.

of the mummy in the burial niche (Figure 3.36). In a few cases, the niche may contain a shelf for the deposition of the dead, and imitate the Greek *kline* décor of a funerary bed, complete with legs, a mattress (Figures 3.37), and a glass on a nearby table for the deceased's recreation (Figure 3.38). However, niches were mostly adorned with classical festoons. They were also sometimes decorated with white and black geometrical patterns that were painted on the rear walls of the tomb[157]. The *loculi* burial

---

covers the walls of the tomb of Anfushy II, Venit, *Monumental Tombs*, 72, fig. 55.; Venit, *Visualizing the Afterlife*, 57–58, figs. 2.6, 2.7.

[157] In Tuna El-Gebel, huge floor burials called *loculi* were found, where mummies were laid in a supine position alongside one another until the room was filled. The sorts of burials at Tuna El-Gebel include solid funerary beds, wooden funerary beds, white-washed mudbrick tomb obelisks, burials on benches, and individual burials with either the absence or presence of mummification. The body was placed in a shallow grave dug directly into the sand, or in *kline* niches, which were often placed under a shell or a baldachin. For more on the burial customs of Tuna El-Gebel, see F. Awad, 'The Development of Burial Types at Tuna El-Gebel During the Graeco-Roman Era', in M. Flossmann-Schütze et al. (eds.), *Tuna El-Gebel- eine ferne Welt*, 100–09. A burial niche with a shell is found in GB 45 (M1), while the use of a baldachin is recorded in GB 8 (M2). There is an *Arcosolium* in tomb GB 25, K. Lembke, 'The Petosiris-necropolis of Tuna El-Gebel', in K. Lembke et al. (eds.), *Tradition and Transformation, Egypt Under Roman Rule, Proceedings of the International Conference, Hildesheim, Roemer- and Pelizaeus- Museum, 3–6 July 2008* (Leiden 2010), 243–44, fig. 12, pl. xxiv. As demonstrated on the Terenouthis funerary stelae, placing the dead on a *kline* allowed them to simultaneously take part in an eternal symposion banquet and an eternal prosthesis. For more on the laying out of the dead for mourning, see K. Lembke, 'Terenuthis and Elsewhere, the Archaeology of Eating, Drinking and Dying in Ptolemaic and Roman Egypt', in D. Robinson and A. Wilson (eds.), *Alexandria and the North-Western Delta, Joint Conference Proceedings of Alexandria, City and Harbour (Oxford 2004) and the Trade and Topography of Egypt's North-West Delta, 8th Century BC to 8th Century AD (Berlin 2006)* (Oxford 2010), 259–67.

Figure 3.33a. A hollowed niche in tomb B2, which is located on the southern section of El-Salamuni Mountain.

Figure 3.33b. A flat and hollowed-out burial niche from tomb B2, on the northern section of El-Salamuni Mountain above Tomb C1.

A History of the Investigations and Surveys of El-Salamuni

Figure 3.34. Two adjacent burial niches placed in the same wall, as seen in an unregistered tomb from the southern section of El-Salamuni Mountain, above register F.

style was also attested in one unregistered tomb on the mountain. This tomb is located on the northern section of the mountain, close to tomb B7. Two *loculi* are cut into the burial chamber of this tomb, with walls that are smoothed and plastered. Further excavations of the mountain could reveal and confirm more examples of the use of this style.

It is unclear whether the House of Embalment was located somewhere on the mountain, or if it was situated somewhere else. Perhaps it was located in the city of Panopolis itself, or in an adjacent village at the foot of the mountain (the ancient Salamuni villages were not yet mentioned in texts), or even in the necropolis. Considering the lengthy procedure of mummification[158], it seems quite improbable that embalment took place in the town of the living. However, although lacking sufficient archaeological and textual documentation, the author suggests that the embalming house may have been situated in a village located at the foot of the mountain (such as ancient El-Salamuni). This is because funeral processions of the mummy of the deceased are widely depicted in the El-Salamuni tombs[159]. One example is the depiction of a mummy being transported in a wheeled funerary cart. The mummy is shown ready to 'climb' the mountain to be placed in the tomb on the mountains' terraces. This highly suggests that the House of Embalment was located outside of the necropolis itself.

The popular inhumation burial style was mainly used in antechambers, where shallow mummiform trenches were

---

[158] Herodotus mentions that the mummification process could last for 70 days, *Herod.* II, 88.
[159] W. Omran, 'Transporting the Deceased by the Wheeled Cart in the Greco-Roman Tombs', *International Journal of Association of Arab Universities for Tourism and Hospitality*, Suez Canal University 17, no. 2 (2019), 40–42.

Figure 3.35. An underground shaft located below the burial niche of an unregistered tomb on the southern section of El-Salamuni Mountain.

The Afterlife in Akhmim

Figure 3.36. The sandal decorations found in the burial niche of an unregistered tomb on the southern section of El-Salamuni Mountain.

Figure 3.37. The leg of a funerary bed (Greek: *kline*), found in tomb C6 on the southern section of El-Salamuni Mountain.

typically dug into the bare floor[160]. However, inhumation burials are occasionally found in the burial chamber. In the antechamber, the mummified bodies, having been wrapped in mats, are placed directly in the ground, in shallow pits that are wide and long enough to inhumate the mummy. These pits are coated and plastered on their floor and lateral sides, and closed with a slab of stone (Figure 3.39).

---

[160] Von Bissing states that the use of these shallow sarcophagi is like the style which is found in the Fort Saleh tomb. He dates this style to between the 26th dynasty and the Ptolemaic Period. However, he warns that the existence of this style is not enough to date the necropoleis in a precise manner, von Bissing, *ASAE* 50, 566.

Figure 3.38. A glass on a table located to the right of a niche in the burial chamber of tomb F2. The tomb can be found on the southern section of El-Salamuni Mountain.

60

Rarely, very narrow, shallow pits also appear in the tombs. The existence of these burial pits likely suggests that the tombs were first used as family or public tombs, and that the inhumation pits were added later[161]. In a few cases, the shallow trenches were found in the burial chamber alongside the burial niches. The shallow pits are also recorded in the opposite Triphion cemetery [162], as well as in Tuna El-Gebel, where they are one of the various forms of burials.

The cremation burial style is not yet attested in El-Salamuni. While a small niche has been found beside the burial niche in tomb B8 and also in another unregistered tomb (both of which were closed by slabs), modern scholars have no clear idea of their purpose. It seems possible that they contained urns, or perhaps were meant for the installation of ushabtis. Nevertheless, examples of cremation in Egypt are quite rare, even in Alexandria[163]. The use of cremation cannot be proven at El-Salamuni. Further excavations can perhaps determine the use of or absence of this style[164]. Unfortunately, the remaining bodies have been damaged by repeated plundering in search for valuable items.

The Panopolite nome was distinguished by the worship of sacred animals[165] during the Graeco-Roman Period, as is evidenced by the discovery of a number of cemeteries of mummified jackals, cats, baboons, ibises, falcons, and other creatures, including insects[166]. El-Salamuni was not only a cemetery for mummified humans, but also for sacred animals and birds. In 2018, because of illicit looting,

Figure 3.39. A shallow pit in the antechamber of tomb F1, which is located on the southern section of El-Salamuni Mountain.

and during the daily investigations of the *ghaffirs* on the mountain, who were working 120m. north of the so-called 'von Bissing tomb', the remains of mummified falcons, ibises[167], and a mouse were discovered. This highly suggests that El-Salamuni, like El-Hawawish A, was also a necropolis for mummified animals and birds. Future excavations in this area could uncover other mummified species. The *hypogeum* of sacred mummified animals and birds suggests its use during the Late, Ptolemaic, and Early Roman Periods[168].

The location of the rock-cut temple of Ay on the northern section of the mountain leads to the speculation that this section was probably used for burials ever since the Ptolemaic Period, being older than the southern section, which includes Roman tombs (Figures 3.40a-b). It also

---

[161] A dozen mummies lying on the floor was noted by Schmidt in one of the El-Salamuni tombs of the Roman Period, Schmidt, 'Ein Griechisches Mumienetikett aus Achmim', 80–81. As for the registered tombs, shallow mummiform pits are found in the antechambers of tombs F1, F5, and B7.
[162] Kuhlmann, *SDAIK* 11, 77, fig. 33c.; El-Farag et al., *MDAIK* 41, 4. Two anthropoid-shaped coffin basins cut into the floor of a Roman tomb were recently excavated, having been discovered to the left of the famous tomb of Sennedjem at Awlad Azzaz, B. Ockinga, *A Tomb from the Reign of Tutankhamun at Akhmim*, ACER 10 (Warminster 1997), pl. 24, sect. T-T.
[163] G. Cartron, *L'architecture et les pratiques funéraires Dans l'Égypte romaine, I* (Oxford 2012), 42–43. In Alexandria, cremations are present in simpler and less expensive forms than inhumations and mummification, Venit, *Monumental Tombs of Ancient Alexandria*, 11. Cremation had basically disappeared as a practice by the Roman period, I. Morris, *Death-Ritual and Social Structure in Classical Antiquity* (Cambridge 1992), 53. However, cremation and inhumation were more common than mummification in the Roman period at Alexandria, M. Venit, 'The Stagni Painted Tomb, Cultural Interchange and Gender Difference in Roman Alexandria', *AJA* 103.4 (1999), 666.
[164] In the Gabbari cemetery, the mummies had been placed over earlier cremations and inhumations, J. Empereur and M. Nenna, *Necropolis 1, Tombes B1 B2, B3, B8*, EtudAlex 5 (Cairo 2001), 523.
[165] In Late Antiquity, Shenoute faught against the worship of (idols of) falcons, serpents, crocodiles, and other creatures. He states: '*Woe upon those who will worship wood, stone, or anything made by man's craftwork with wood and stone, or (moulded by putting) clay inside them, and the rest of the kind, and (making from these materials) birds and crocodiles and beasts and livestock and diverse beings!... Consider your foolishness, O pagans who serve and worship (things) that have no power to move whatsoever (and) especially (no power) to do something prodigious!... Where are the crocodiles and all the things in the water, those things that you serve? Where is the sun and the moon and the stars- that God placed to illumine the earth? You are deceived, you who worship them as gods!*', Frankfurter, *Religion in Roman Egypt*, 78.
[166] For a list of animal cemeteries discovered in the Akhmim region, see D. Kessler, *Die heiligen Tiere und der König* 1 (Wiesbaden 1989), 21–22.

[167] There existed a small village or hamlet known as *Ιβιον*, or 'Ibion', M. Drew-Bear, 'Le nome Hermopolite, Toponymes et sites', *Am.Stud. Pap.* 21 (Atlanta 1979), 122–23. In Demotic, it was known as '*hj*, referring to a burial for sacred birds, and mainly ibises, K. Vandorpe, 'Les villages des ibis dans la toponymie tardive', *Enchoria* 18 (1991), 115–22 (esp. 119–20). The Ammon Archive shows that Ibion was in the Panopolite nome, near El-Salamuni. It was in the Metropolis toparchy on the east bank, *P. Ammon* II, 50, ll, 10–11, 20.
[168] For the necropolis which was unearthed in Asyut, see J. Kahl, A. Sbriglio, P. Del Vesco, and M. Trapani, *Asyut, the Excavations of the Italian Archaeological Mission (1906–1913)* (Modena 2019), 35–36.

Figure 3.40a. The first slope of El-Salamuni Mountain, which is the location of many mummified animal and a bird *hypogeum*, as well as looting activities. The slope is located on the northern section of El-Salamuni Mountain.

seems probable that the residents of individual villages were buried together in specific areas of the cemetery. It is remarkable that villages in the northwest of the Panopolite nome, such as Toeto, Synoria, Psinabla, Pakerke, and Sentanelol, are not mentioned on the mummy labels from the opposite Triphion cemetery[169]. This highly suggests that the deceased of these villages were not buried here, or that they were buried in parts of the necropolis that were not excavated or do not survive.

The El-Salamuni necropolis is associated with significant local folklore and stories which were passed down through generations. Some of the stories are recorded below:

1. During the first part of the 19th century, the tombs were left open. Therefore, torrential rainfall swept the mummies down to the foot of the mountain. According to the stories, local people then used the mummies as flood fenders in the El-Faraoukiya canal, in order to prevent their lands from sinking.
2. **Hawsh El-Gemaal:** Translated as 'the Yard of Camels', this large building is on the upper terrace of the southern section of the mountain. It is very wide and roofed, with a large entrance and a visible staircase. It lies just above the fourth slope of the mountain, south of the temple of Ay. It was once recorded by Kuhlmann as being a quarry

Figure 3.40b. Some species of mummified birds and animals from the northern section of El-Salamuni Mountain.

---

[169] Pakerke is only attested once, in *CEMG* 2018.

of the New Kingdom. It measures about 75m. in length and 40m. in width[170]. The *ghaffirs* told the author that their grandfathers remember this building got its name from the merchants and travellers in the Eastern Desert who used to rest here with their camels. The building contains about seven damaged structures which are probably sanctuaries or tombs. Damaged mastabas and benches(?) are still visible along with small niches. Later, the location most likely served as a sacred sanctuary during the Graeco-Roman Period. This is especially true for when it was abandoned, and the quarry workers switched their focus to a Ptolemaic quarry that is located north of the temple of Ay. The cutting of niches, which are now removed by robbers, was also recorded at its entrance. Shallow mummy trenches are documented on its floor, which further highly suggest that it has a religious and burial purpose. Bats are now living inside the structure (Figures 3.41a-b).

3. **Wadi El-Batikh:** Known as the 'Valley of the Watermelon', it was named by local people. This is because the top of the mountain contains scattered blocks resembling watermelons. The villagers used to smash them, suspecting a diamond inside (Figures 3.42). The villagers were so eager to climb to Wadi El-Batikh to destroy the blocks in search of the diamonds thought to be hidden inside them, that some of the villagers commemorated their journey, writing their names in the nearby sand.

4. **El Birba:** This is a huge, wide building located on the upper limit of the mountain, just about 300m. south of the *ghaffirs'* hut, opposite the El-Salamuni village. The building contains three galleries, the first of which is the main and largest one. To its west and east sides, there are two small galleries lying in ruins; their entrances are still covered with heavy sand, and no one can enter. Both the east and west minor galleries contain a paved way (a *dromos*?) with low walls that are still visible today. Kuhlmann assumes that this building was used as a southern quarry ever since the New Kingdom, and possibly even up until the 30th dynasty. Its location, which is away from the necropolis itself, leads Kuhlmann to suggest that it was substituted for the north quarry. This may have been partially due to the desire to avoid making significant noise in the necropolis. A noisy quarry can hardly be reconciled with the reverence and calm that one would likely consider appropriate for a cemetery dedicated to the god of the dead[171]. Nearby, there is a paved, ascending white slope that could have been used by the quarry workers to connect the foot of the mountain with the quarries. This path was later used by the villagers, who used it to climb to the *Birba* (Figures 3.43a-b). The quarry's walls and ceilings are cracked and smashed, and blocks of its ceiling have fallen. Probably, the worship of Min was also performed inside the quarry. Demotic graffito of the Ptolemaic Period as well as a labyrinth graffito are found in the west hall of the quarry[172]. Furthermore, an incomprehensible graffito in red ink has been written on a column. It shows a man with frizzy hair, holding something (probably a stick?) with his upraised hands upon his head. Meanwhile, another human figure stands behind him, and holds something in his hands, which is probably a rope. A figure of an animal (a griffin or a jackal) is in front of him. The two human figures are probably standing in a barque. This graffito is not recorded by Kuhlmann. Therefore, one cannot determine if it was added recently (Figure 3.43c). Additionally, another buried building is located about 100m. north of the *Birba*. It is identified by Kuhlmann as the west section of the quarry gallery[173]. To recognise its layout and details, excavators had to remove the sand that covered it. The building is roofed, with a partially damaged *dromos* leading to its entrance (Figures 3.44a-b).

5. **The Barrel:** Located on the roof of the mountain, just 100m. south of the temple of Ay, the villagers think it was used as a sign to help military helicopters land safely on the mountain.

6. **Taket El-Diik:** Known as 'the Cock's Window', Taket El-Diik is a niche 'window' carved into the southern-most section of the mountain. It was given its name by villagers who saw that at daybreak every day, a crowing cock used to rest in it. According to legends, one day, while a female farmer was walking at the foot of the mountain towards her farm, the cock opened the window on which he rested. The female saw mounts of gold appear behind the window, and she fainted for a while. When she woke up, the window was closed again (Figure 3.45).

7. **'El-Dohrija':** This area of the mountain describes the far northern section, where the mountain starts to deviate northward. It is opposite the modern Muslim cemetery of Naga El-Sawâma-sharq. In the recent past, the villagers, and especially sterile females, used to climb to the slope located north of the temple of Ay and tumble down it, asking for pregnancy. Furthermore, in the adjacent village of Nagaa El-Rabaab, which is on the north of the mountain, a great local festival took place annually in July in relation to the Sheikh of El-Salamuni Mountain.

8. **El-Hadidah:** Meaning 'the Iron', this area is located on the northern-most part of the mountain. In the recent past, the officials of the Endowment Authority used to climb the mountain in this area to check the appearance of the crescent moon to declare the beginning of the Ramadan fast's month.

3.6: A Risk Assessment of El-Salamuni

In the time of the French campaigns and the British occupation of Egypt, there were wide-scale archaeological explorations of Egypt. During this time, European Archaeologists received a share of their finds via an official arrangement with the local authorities known as

---

[170] Kuhlmann, *MDAIK* 35, 185–86, fig. 56 a, b.
[171] Kuhlmann, *SDAIK* 11, 81–82, figs. 39, 40–43.
[172] The author was unable to locate the two graffiti in question.
[173] Kuhlmann, *SDAIK* 11, 41b.

The Afterlife in Akhmim

Figure 3.41a. 'Hawsh El-Gemaal', a quarry of the New Kingdom, located south of the temple of Ay in the southern section of El-Salamuni Mountain.

partage. Licensed dealers also sold antiquities to visitors, since the artifacts were considered personal possessions and were undocumented. The smuggling and the illegal trade of antiquities even extended to markets in the United States and other countries worldwide. Ever since the fast and wide-scale excavations conducted by Maspero, illegal excavations have continued to be conducted on a wider scale in the Akhmim necropoleis. Akhmim thus became an important centre for the antiquities trade, which was not limited to objects found directly there. El-Salamuni and El-Hawawish A were permissible areas for European antiquities collectors who dug with and/or negotiated with local peasants and traders. Most of the Akhmimic objects exhibited in museums lack reliable information as a result. They often lack a date, location, and information on the circumstances of their discovery.

Figure 3.41b. Some rock-cut shrines from 'Hawsh El-Gemaal'.

Figure 3.42. The so-called 'Wadi el-Batikh' on the flat roof of the mountain.

A History of the Investigations and Surveys of El-Salamuni

Figure 3.43a. 'El Birba', the main gallery-quarry located opposite El-Salamuni village.

Figure 3.43b. The damaged *dromos* of 'El Birba'.

Figure 3.43c. A graffito in 'El Birba'.

The looting and sale of objects in the area became worse after the Egyptian Revolution of 2011, when increased political instability made many archaeological sites vulnerable. El-Salamuni Mountain was an important target for the violent robbers, who came either from its adjacent villages or from other cities in Egypt. Indeed, many of the opportunistic looters were (and are) not targeting antiquities in order to sell them, but rather in hopes of finding the gold which they are convinced was buried by the ancient Egyptians. Therefore, there are many random holes at the site, and especially on the northern section of the mountain. This has destroyed the local stratigraphy as well as de-contextualized various objects. As a result, it is now quite difficult to determine the topography, chronology, burials, and burial customs in Akhmim. Though El-Salamuni is arguably one of the most important necropoleis in Egypt, it is largely neglected and unknown. El-Salamuni is certainly suffering from many threats and risks, including severe deterioration and architectural vulnerabilities. It is negatively impacted by the chaotic excavations and tomb robberies.

During one of the author's campaigns to the area, looters spotted his position on the mountain, broke down the steel door protecting the tomb, and tried to enter the tomb at night. In the morning, after the workers removed the simple debris which was placed their daily to hide the tomb's entrance, the author found the door lying on the ground. Fortunately, the robbers did not cause any damage in the tomb. They most likely thought that the author had

The Afterlife in Akhmim

Figure 3.44a. Overview of the western gallery of the 'El Birba' quarry, covered with sand.

Figure 3.44b. A damaged *dromos* in front of the eastern gallery of the 'El Birba' quarry.

3.6.1: Heritage Risks

The site of El-Salamuni is still widely unknown, and its tombs are continuously subjected to damage and other threats. A full photogrammetric documentation of the tombs is the primary tool needed for recording, preserving, and sharing the great significance of the site.

Security is missing at the site. Since the 19th century, the necropolis has been continuously plundered. The area remains a continuous target for chaotic excavations and illicit looting. The encroachment by tomb robbers has caused great damage to the site's walls and inscriptions. Much of the illicit digging has been carried out on the mountain's terraces, while damage inside the open tombs is also attested. The dig spots, tools, and motors of the robbers and excavators are widely found on the mountain. No objects are known to have been discovered in the uncovered and registered tombs, since the necropolis was fully exhausted by the chaotic excavations and tomb looters. Furthermore, a large mass of mummy shrouds and human bones are scattered both inside the tombs and over the mountain, especially near the tombs' entrances (Figures 3.46a-b). The only security hut of the local *ghaffirs* is situated on the south section of the mountain, near the village of El-Salamuni. Therefore, tombs C3, C4, and C5 are fully protected, as they are situated beneath the *ghaffirs'* cave. So far, tombs F1-F5, which lie about 70m. above the hut, are still visible by the *ghaffirs* from their post; some of the steel doors of these tombs are visible to the *ghaffirs*. Hence, looters always attack the mountain from its north section, which is considered a weak point because of the non-existence of a security post. Therefore, the tombs and temples that are located there, especially tombs B7 and C1, and the temple of Ay, suffer from vandalism, despite their entrances being heaped with heavy debris to try to deter this. Many archaeological sites were looted in Egypt following the January 2011 Revolution. At El-Salamuni, the looters dug into the mountain. Many looting pits are recorded on the mountain, and the looters have also directly threatened the local *ghaffirs*. It appears that a mafia element is involved with the looting here, which is harder to stop.

Figure 3.45. 'Taket el-Diik', which is located on the southern-most part of El-Salamuni Mountain.

found the gold first, and had hidden it somewhere inside the tomb. Only two guards currently protect the vast mountain. Their shelter is a simple mudbrick cave that is situated on the southern section of the mountain. It was built during Kuhlmann's investigation at the site. The tombs are in urgent need of cultural conservation projects, including stabilisation, documentation, and the reviving of their features. In this section, the most important threats and issues facing El-Salamuni are outlined.

Figure 3.46a. Mummy shrouds inside an unregistered tomb on El-Salamuni Mountain.

Figure 3.46b. Mummy shrouds on the terraces of the northern section of El-Salamuni Mountain.

Furthermore, the tombs are generally not well preserved. This is largely due to their history of chaotic excavations, tomb robbers, and poor attempts at preservation, especially over the past two decades. In fact, the recently closed tombs were accessible for people in ancient times. Since ancient times, many people have drawn or carved their names and memories on the walls of the accessible tombs, and the mountain has served as a focal point for many travellers and visitors. An inscription in English dates to the year 1891 and is written by a person named 'Gordon' (Figure 3.47). It could be related to Sir William Gordon-Cumming, a fourth Baronet (20 July, 1848– 20 May, 1930), and a member of both the cavalry and of a good family, who had distinguished himself in Egyptian campaigns. As a member of the army, he saw service in South Africa, Egypt, and the Sudan. He participated in the Battle of Tel El-Kebir in Egypt. The author of the inscription could also be 'Eka', or Constance Frederica Gordon-Cumming (1837–1924). She was a traveller, author, and painter who visited Egypt[174]. Other inscriptions in the tombs date to 1923 and 1937. The mountain also served and still serves as a safe residence for criminals who are seeking to escape from their crimes. Furthermore, the local community has been historically eager to hike the mountain and spend time at the top of it, with the oldest known memory of this dating to 1923. The hazardous actions of the local community towards the tombs have caused damage, including the disappearance of the scenes' colours over the years.

The limited awareness of and interest in heritage by the local community near the mountain of El-Salamuni is a big risk. The local community does not generally appreciate the history and the archaeological value of the site. Therefore, they tend to have a negative or indifferent attitude towards the site. The empowerment of local communities, both by involving them in their own history and by highlighting their role as main stakeholders and beneficiaries of their own heritage, is a central tactic for ridding the community of damaging behaviours and bad feelings towards the site.

The history and documentation of the mountain's investigations and excavations is poor (it has been 39 years since Kuhlmann's quick survey). The site is in dire need of documentation, restoration, and excavations to uncover its

---
[174] F. Gordon-Cumming, *Via Cornwall to Egypt* (London 1890), 301.

The Afterlife in Akhmim

Figure 3.47. The name 'In Gordon', as found in an unregistered tomb above register F on the southern section of El-Salamuni Mountain.

great heritage and value, and to convert it into one of the most fertile and rich archaeological sites in not only Upper Egypt, but the whole land.

3.6.2: Urban Risks

Like most rural archaeological sites in Egypt, El-Salamuni is under enormous strain from Egypt's population growth crisis. The sprawl of the local village of El-Salamuni along the foot of the mountain, with its houses and agricultural lands, is a big threat to the mountain and its archaeological sites. Animals belonging to the villagers are scattered about, and often try to climb the mountain. Some of the local people who operate their agricultural lands close to the heritage sites have taken advantage of the security chaos in order to expand their land, to the point that they are now encroaching a few meters into the heritage sites' lands (Figure 3.48). They have also paved a new road on the mountain to reach their cultivated lands, which are irrigated by extending pipes to the El-Faraoukiya canal. Moreover, the archaeological remains and objects which are scattered all over the mountain can easily be trampled under the feet of the villagers and visitors. Erecting a wall to encircle the mountain's borders is essential.

3.6.3: Environmental Risks

There are numerous environmental risks facing El-Salamuni. As El-Salamuni Mountain is a part of the Eastern

Figure 3.48. The expansion of the agricultural lands into the archaeological belt of El-Salamuni Mountain.

Desert of Egypt, the effects of wind erosion are the most damaging and the most important factors regarding the weathering and deterioration of the tombs. The erosion caused by wind increases progressively from November to January, and reaches a peak from March to May, causing dust storms that are famously known as 'El-Khamasin'. At night, these storms may reach a speed of 140 km./hr.. What multiplies the effect of this wind is the absence of any barriers to decrease its impact; the tombs are in an open area, and many tombs are still without doors. Furthermore, the tombs have all been constructed upon the upper terraces of the mountain, which increases the effects of the wind and accelerates the erosion of their walls. Erosion and exposure problems have caused significant cracking and the deterioration of the raw blocks and walls of the tombs. The carvings, inscriptions, and paintings are also demolished, their colours suffering from fading and even full removal.

The second issue is bird droppings and nesting, which distorts the walls of the tombs. The fungi which live in the excrement of the birds (rather than the excrement itself) are the causative agents that erode the stones. The fungi enter through the pores of the stones, producing acids, which in turn begin to interact with the stones, increasing the porosity of the stone's structure[175]. This expansion allows rainwater to penetrate through the stone's pores, causing the cracking of the stone. Furthermore, bats, insects, wild wolves, and wild foxes are also found in the tombs. They pose a big risk, as they dig their dens under the archaeological buildings.

One of the natural risks affecting the El-Salamuni tombs is the biodeterioration process. Several types of micro-flora and micro-bacteria can be found on the walls of the historical buildings, which are an appropriate habitat for their growth, especially in the presence of humidity, temperature, and sunlight. It is noteworthy that the high temperatures at El-Salamuni accelerate the chemical reactions of the algae, thereby also accelerating its growth. The so-called 'silverfish' which cover the walls are additionally harmful to the colours and the scenes of the tombs.

3.6.4: Black Bitumen

As mentioned prior, the El-Salamuni tombs were reused as an early Christian hermitage. Panopolis reveals an important picture of the impact of the persecution of Christianity; a great majority of Christians no doubt tried to escape their execution rather than face a heroic death. Schmidt notes the presence of cave shelters in El-Salamuni, and many ancient caves in the mountains near Akhmim (Bir El-Aïn) were used as hiding places[176]. The Coptic people lived there for long periods, cooking and making fires which harmfully covered the coloured scenes with black soot. The chaotic excavations and tomb robberies of the 19th and 20th centuries may also be the partial cause of the black soot and/or bitumen which now covers the walls and ceilings of many tombs in El-Salamuni (Figure 3.49).

---

[175] On the effects of bird droppings, see A. Harith, S. Khattab, and M. Al-Mukhtar, 'The Effect of Biodeterioration by Bird Droppings on the Degradation of Stone Built', *Engineering Geology for Society and Territory* 8 (2015), 515–20.; P. Tiano, 'Biodegradation of Cultural Heritage, Decay Mechanisms and Control Methods', *Proceedings of the ARIADNE Workshop* 9 (Florence 2002), 7–12. The birds have a detrimental effect on the buildings. They can affect the archaeological remains by damaging the weaker parts of the architecture via their repeated standing and perching, and via pecking at the buildings with their beaks, P. Baedecker and M. Reddy, 'The Erosion of Carbonate Stone by Acid Rain', *Journal of Chemical Education* 70, No. 2 (1993), 104–08.
[176] Saint-Genis, 'Notice sur les restes', 29–30.

4

Tomb C1: The So-called 'Tomb of von Bissing' (1897)

The history of Panopolis as a Ptolemaic-Roman *polis* is mainly based on the analysis of its vast number of mummy cases and other funerary materials from the Graeco-Roman Period[1]. The corpus comprises mummy coffins, stelae, statues, offering tables, funerary papyri, inscriptions, graffiti, ostraca, mummy labels, textiles, various animal and bird species, as well as inscribed linen bandages. The most up-to-date information about Panopolis centres on its mummies. Until now, little funerary data has been produced from El-Salamuni and Naga al-Diabat, which represent the two main necropoleis of Akhmim during the Ptolemaic-Roman Period.

The northern section of the mountain is located between the first and the fourth slopes, in the area south of the temple of Ay. It is the part of the mountain that curves north to face the modern Muslim cemetery of Naga El-Sawâma-sharq village. The northern section has an older history of use than the southern one; it contains tombs of various periods, including the Old and New Kingdoms, the Late Period, and the Ptolemaic and Roman Periods. A great number of shaft tombs (probably of the Late and Ptolemaic Periods) are also recorded. Because of illicit looting, in 2016, the shrouds of multiple mummified animals and birds were discovered by robbers in a low-lying indentation (a *hypogeum*?) in this northern section. The rock-cut tomb of Ay is located on the upper-most part of the northern section of the mountain. The tombs of the Old Kingdom are located north of the temple of Ay. About 29 tombs are recorded by Kuhlmann. As for the tombs of the Ptolemaic and Roman times, these are located on the lower terrace, below the temple. The New Kingdom tombs, only one of which is painted, lie on the lower terraces of the mountain, south of the temple of Ay. The so-called 'tomb of von Bissing of 1897' is in the same area.

Unfortunately, tombs of El-Salamuni Mountain are not recorded as a single unite. The tombs on the northern section of the mountain are registered with numbers such as B1, B2, C1, C3, C4, etc., which are the same numbers used for the tombs on the southern section of the mountain. Furthermore, new codes were given to tombs M1, M2, M5, which are located on the middle register of the mountain, south of tomb C1. More tombs are still unregistered. Looting has been widely undertaken in this section because it is far away from the *ghaffirs'* cave; robbers almost always attempt to plunder the tombs via the northern-most part of the mountain. As of now, there are no tombs found on the lower terraces of this section. Mummy shrouds, bones, and ostraca are scattered all over the terraces. Only tombs C1 and B7 (which is now damaged)[2] are guarded with doors. The Ptolemaic(?) quarry is on the most northern part of this section (Figures 4.1a-b).

4.1 Location and History of Investigations

Tomb C1 is located on the mountain's register C, on the northern side of the cemetery, below the rock-cut temple of Ay, which is nearby, to the south (Figure 4.1c). It is about 523m. south of the northern entrance of the mountain (Figure 4.2a-b), and 977m. north of the southern entrance of the mountain, being about 41m. high when measuring from the surface of the mountain. Von Bissing has published a simple topographical description of El-Salamuni Mountain, mentioning that the El-Salamuni tombs have been dug into a promontory. These tombs appear to belong exclusively to between the Roman and

---

[1] For a preliminary survey of the Akhmimic material, see Depauw, 'The Late Funerary Material from Akhmim,' in A. Egberts et al. (eds.) *Perspectives on Panopolis*, 71–81. The inscribed materials from Panopolis can now be traced via the Trismegistos database (https://www.trismegistos.org/index.html). Akhmim is well-known among scholars for having a specific tradition of producing Book of the Dead manuscripts. These papyri often contain unique spells and spell sequences that are not known from the traditions of Memphis and Thebes. Furthermore, a distinctive feature of the Akhmim papyri is the retrograde disposition of the vertical hieroglyphic columns from left to right. The papyri are mainly written for members of Min's clergy, and were most likely found in the El-Hawawish A cemetery. They include P.BM EA 10479 and P. MacGregor, M. Mosher, *The Papyrus of Hor (BM EA 10479), with Papyrus McGregor, Late Period Tradition at Akhmim, Catalogue of the Books of the Dead in the British Museum II* (London 2001). Mosher's results caught the attention of H. De Meulenaere, H. De Meulenaere, *Compte-rendu sur Mosher, M. Jr.- The Papyrus of Hor*, Bibliotheca Orientalis 59 (No. 5–6) (London 2002), 491–93.; A. Niwiński, *Review: Mosher Jr., Malcolm 2001, The Papyrus of Hor (BM EA 10479), with Papyrus McGregor, Late Period Tradition at Akhmim, Catalogue of the Books of the Dead in the British Museum 2, London: British Museum Press*, JEA 90 (reviews suppl.), 49–50. Other examples from El-Hawawish A include P. Nesmin (J. Clère, *Le Papyrus de Nesmin, Un Livre des Morts hiéroglyphique de l'époque ptolémaïque*, BiGen 10 (Cairo 1987)), P. Twt (Bayer-Niemeier et al., *Ägyptische Bildwerke III*), P. Berlin 10477, P. Hildesheim 5248 (B. Lüscher, *Die Totenbuch Handschrift pBerlin 10477 aus Achmim (mit Photographien des verwandten pHildesheim 5248)*, HAT 6 (Wiesbaden 2000)), P.Louvre E. 11078, P. Berlin 3064 A–B (U. Kaplony-Heckel, *Ägyptische Handschriften III, Verzeichnis der orientalischen Handschriften in Deutschland* 19.1 (Stuttgart 1986)), and finally, the Omar Pacha Pap. 408 (Collection of Omar Pacha Sultan 1929, plate lxvi.). Examples of the Liturgy of Opening of the Mouth for Breathing, of which P. Louvre E 10607 is the best preserved, were also found. Versions of spells 25 and 32 of the Pyramid Texts (spells for 'Presenting Offerings to Spirits', and other compositions) are now in the Bodleian Library in Oxford, Smith, *The Mortuary Texts of Papyrus BM 10507*, 650–62.; id., 'New Middle Egyptian Texts in the Demotic Script', *Sesto Congresso Internazionale di Egittologia: Atti* II (Turin 1993), 491–95. Stadler proposes that the latest Book of the Dead papyri come from Akhmim; they have been dated to the first century BC on stylistic grounds, as well as due to the degree of the text's corruption, Stadler, 'Funerary Religion', in C. Riggs (ed.), *The Oxford Handbook of Roman Egypt*, 388.

[2] Unfortunately, in 2018, looters broke the steel door of this painted tomb and damaged its niches and great parts of its walls. However, in 2014, the author was luckily able to photograph and document the tomb.

The Afterlife in Akhmim

Figure 4.1a. The topography of the northern section of the mountain.

Figure 4.1b. The location of the Ptolemaic quarry on the most northern part of El-Salamuni Mountain.

Coptic Periods and the Middle Ages. Von Bissing also recorded the existence of a modern cemetery on the northern side of the mountain. However, he falsely claims that the Old Kingdom tombs are located on the southwest part of the mountain.

Von Bissing dates all of the tombs to between the sixth and 12th dynasties. All of these tombs consist of one room without any inscriptions. They generally have tunnels on an inclined slope (the so-called 'shaft' of the tomb) leading to a vault. A vertical shaft is only recorded as appearing in one tomb. Furthermore, some of the tombs differ in that they have two shafts. The oldest tombs seem to be

Figure 4.1c. The location of tomb C1.

Tomb C1: The So-called 'Tomb of von Bissing' (1897)

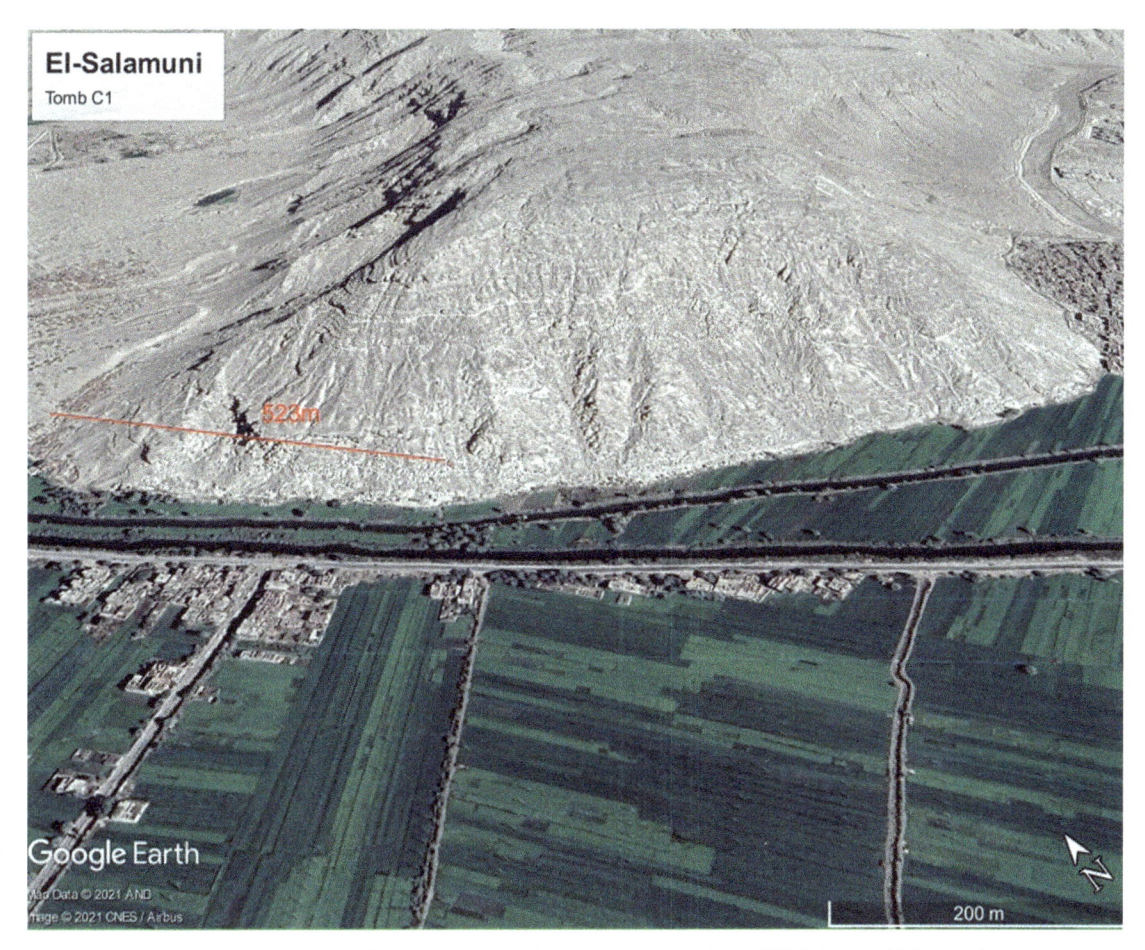

Figure 4.2a. The location of tomb C1 at the start of the northern section of El-Salamuni Mountain.

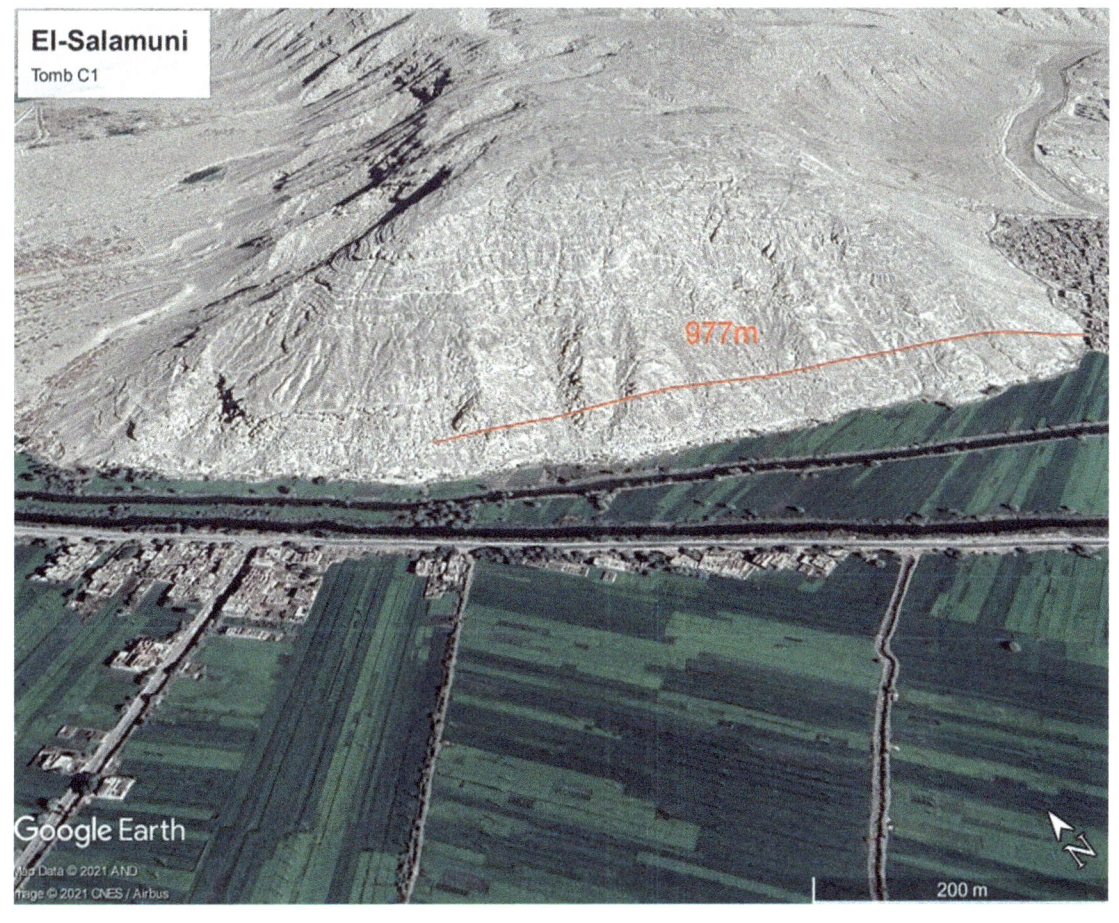

Figure 4.2b. The location of tomb C1 from the start of the southern section of El-Salamuni Mountain.

near the part of the mountain closest to Siflaq, but they face Akhmim. Von Bissing believed that, together with H. Kees, he had found the New Kingdom temple of Ay, with New Kingdom tombs scattered along the mountain below.

While the Late Period burials of the necropolis are located right at the foot of the desert slope, a group of multi-coloured, painted Graeco-Roman tombs, like the tombs which are described by Rubensohn, is located along the southeast corner of the mountain. They are near a sheikh's tomb, which was built on a hill located 10m. above a row of cultivated fields (the area beyond the *ghaffirs'* cave). The Graeco-Roman tombs are at most the height of a man, and the door frames are therefore very low. The doors of the tombs have been destroyed by looters, and one must now enter the tombs through the damaged holes in their ceilings or elsewhere[3]. Von Bissing describes how he and Dragendorff once slid down a shaft to the bottom of tomb C1, thus sinking into a pile of mummies. He states: '*C'est ainsi que quand, le D'Dragendorff et moi-même, nous nous laissâmes glisser d'en- haut dans la tombe, nous nous enfonçâmes jusqu'aux hanches dans des momies*'. When they entered the tomb in 1897, they entered through a crack. The exterior of the tomb was covered in sand, and the door was blocked with sand and debris. Dragendorff only sketched part of the tomb's layout, and the sketch is very inaccurate. The tomb was full of heavy debris and piles of mummies, so it was very difficult to give precise dimensions.

The tomb consists of two chambers connected by a door, the axis of which does not correspond to that of the entrance. The three niches of the second chamber are not symmetrical, and the author and the team found similar irregularities in almost all the tombs inspected at Akhmim[4]. The walls of the tomb are all in a poor state of preservation, including their smoothed surfaces, their whitewash, and their painted layers. The floor is covered with debris and mummies, making it impossible for the author and his team to measure the exact height of the walls. The ceiling of tomb C1 is relatively flat, and the stone is covered everywhere with a coating. The contours, which are very wide, are black. Other colours used in the tomb are dark brown, a lighter brown, red, and green[5].

With the help of the *fellahin*, the tomb was first documented by von Bissing in 1897, during his first visit to Egypt. He recorded the location of the tomb, which he found at the desert's edge at the foot of the north section of the mountain. When it was excavated by von Bissing, the tomb was covered with sand, and the door was also blocked with sand and debris. Furthermore, it was full of the remains of mummies[6]. Von Bissing recorded the discovery of many human bones in the burial chamber[7]. About 50 years after von Bissing's visit to the tomb, he finally published a book about his research[8]. However, he only described the scenes of the antechamber in detail, and he provided very limited data about the burial chamber, which was full of debris, with heavy soot covering its walls. He hardly noted many of the details inside the tomb. He only included a drawing of the judgement court scene in his article [9].

A short time after having discovered the tomb, von Bissing sent a letter to Maspero. The letter was sent from near Akhmim, on 05 February 1897, when von Bissing was traveling with Hans Dragendorff (1870–1941), a German Archaeologist specializing in Roman pottery. The letter shows that von Bissing was not alone when he visited El-Salamuni, and that when he discovered tomb C1, he was accompanied by Hans Dragendorff. The letter is provided below, in both French (original) and in English (translated). The French text of the letter says:

'*Au Sud d'Achmim*[10]
1897. Febr. 5.

Très cher Monsieur le professeur,

C'est à Achmim que Vôtre [sic] aimable lettre m'est parvenue, dans un des plus delicieux site [sic] de l'Egypte. Je n'ai pas besoin de Vous decrire le cirque pittoresque des montagnes qui entourent la necropole ou [sic]Vous avez executé de si heureuses fouilles. Nous avons visité, mon ami et moi, les tombeaux très [p. 352, r.] *réduits qui se trouve [sic] à l'entourage du monastère copte et nous y avons ramassé des morceaux de sarcophages et de toile de momie pour le musée de Bonn et mes propres collections. Plus loin dans la montagne vers le nord, j'ai decouvert(?) à l'aide des fellahin un magnifique tombeau romain admirablement conservé, à peu près du IIIème siècle. Il n'y a plus de hiéroglyphes, du moins ceux qui y sont, sont ornementales [sic]. J'essayerai de faire comprendre aux autorités du Musée que ce tombeau, peut-être unique dans sa conservation, contenant par exemple le 'Totengesicht' transformé en vraie ψυχοστασία avec* [p. 352, v.] *des εἴδωλα en noir, mériterait d'être conservé et d'être dessiné, ou photographié par un membre de la mission peut-être.*

Sinon j'en publierai dans mon petit rapport pour la Zeitschrift les calques pris à la hâte et tacherai

---

[3] Von Bissing, *ASAE* 50, 555.
[4] Von Bissing, *ASAE* 50, 555–56, fig. 1.
[5] Von Bissing, *ASAE* 50, 556.
[6] Von Bissing, *ASAE* 50, 556.; Kuhlmann, *SDAIK* 11, 166.
[7] Von Bissing, *JDAI* 61/62, 2.

[8] He published two articles: one in French (*ASAE* 50 (1950), 547–84.), and one in German (*JDAI* 61/62, (1946/1947), 1–16.). His article in French was more notable for its accuracy, *ASAE* 50, 576.
[9] Von Bissing's publication in French (von Bissing, *ASAE* 50, 554–73.), is considered the most complete and precise record. On von Bissing's two tombs, see Venit, *Visualizing the Afterlife*, 183–84, 185–92.; Riggs, *The Beautiful Burial*, 164.
[10] Two letters were sent by von Bissing to Maspero in commemoration of his two visits to El-Salamuni (in 1897 and in 1913). The letters are now registered in the La bibliothèque de L'Institut de France, under the reference number ms. 4005. The letter from 1897 is located between paragraphs number f352–55. Many thanks to Lebee Thomas (École du Louvre and the Musée du Louvre-département des antiquités grecques, étrusques et romaines), for sending the author copies of the two letters.

[sic] de faire mieux plus tard. Il y a aussi le portrait du défunt. Je n'ai pas mal ramassé de poterie à Tell el Amarna, à Siout (ou [sic] on est en train de voler toute la vieille necropole au dessous du Hapzef ') à Achmim etc., de sorte que nous sommes à même de ranger d'une façon certaine les vases de l'ancien empire, de la XVIII-XX (Tombeau de Snnoudjem), des basses époques. Nous avons des vases datés [p. 352, v.] pour le moyen empire aussi pour la XIème dyn. Ici une question grave s'élève: d'après nos résultats pour le développement des vases, d'après les résultats des fouilles de Mr. Petrie (au- torité dont malheureusement il faut se méfier un peu, si je puis juger d'après Tell el Amarna et Koptos surtout) et d'après une indication que Vous avez bien voulu me donner il y a quelques ans, les prétendus vases préhistoriques dateraient de la VII-XI dyn. Il me semble qu'il n'y a dans le livre de Mr. de Morgan pas une preuve effective du contraire, il m'est absolument impossible d'ad- mettre avec lui ces constructions [p. 354, r.] très doctes peut-êtres, mais très invrai-semblables sur les origines de l'Egypte.

Et la poterie des peuples barbares a tant de ressemblances aux poteries des origines grecques qu'il m'est impos- sible de l'en séparer tout-à-fait. Ce n'est pas la [sic] de la poterie égyptienne, bien sur, mais c'est une poterie qui a grandement influencé la poterie non de l'ancien empire mais précisément du moyen empire et des temps postérieurs. La poterie a vernis rouge ne se trouve que dans des formes [et?] des tombes (etc) qui sont contemporaines des dynasties thébaines; c'est dans la [p. 354, v.] haute Égypte que se trouvent seulement ces vases 'préhistoriques'. Si Mr. Amelineau, au lieu d'écrire des gros volumes su la préparation de la tombe (je Vous remercie sincèrement de la critique que Vous avez bien voulu m'envoyer) nous donnait un compte rendu précis de ses fouilles, on saurait peut-être à quoi s'entenir. Je vais chercher à voir plus claire dans tout ça à Abydos même, inš Allah! mais Vous nous obligeriez beaucoup en me communiquant une petite note, si Vous avez trouvé de ces vases dans un sarcophage où [sic] une tombe intacte où [sic] dans des circonstances excluantes tout [sic] les doutes sur l'âge de la [p. 355, r.] poterie. Je viendrai cherchér [sic] tout [sic] les détails, si Vous permettez, moi-même à Paris enautomne.

Je Vous remercie de tout mon cœur de toutes Vos bontées [sic] envers moi. Je Vous parlerai, si celà [sic] ne Vous ennuie pas, à Paris du triste état dans lequel se trouvent ici les choses. Mr. de Morgan est très libéral lui-même : grâce à lui Mr. Borchardt a été appelé pour faire l'inventaire des statues. Mr. de Morgan m'a donné un permis pour estamper etc dans les musées et ruines et Brugsch m'a promis d'ecrire au ghaffir de Thèbes pour me permettre à faire de petits nettoyages. Je ne puis pas me plaindre de personnes [sic] pour mon propre conte [sic], mais il y a bien des choses lamentables ailleurs [p. 355, v.]. Mr. Vôtre [sic] frère a été très bon envers moi; malheureusement comme tout le monde a terriblement à faire le jour et que la distance entre

Cairo et le musée est tellement considérable, je suis privé du plaisir de le voir plus souvent.

Mais voilà que je Vous aie retenu bien longtemps, monsieur; je Vous en demande pardon et Vous prie de me rappeler à la mémoire de Madame et de Vos enfants en me croyant Vôtre [sic] tout dévoué et très sincèrement respectueux.

Fritz v. Bissing

Ne craigniez rien pour ma santé, une dahabieh avec des vents contraires ne permets guère de nuire à elle, ou fait plustôt [sic] trop!'.

Meanwhile, the English translation of the letter, as created by the author, is the following:

South of Akhmim
February 5, 1897

Very Dear Mr Professor,

Your kind letter reached me in Achmim, in one of the most delightful places in Egypt. I need not describe to you the picturesque cirque of the mountains which surround the necropolis where you have carried out such happy excavations. My friend and I visited the very small tombs around the Coptic monastery and have collected pieces of sarcophagi and mummy cloth for the Bonn Museum and my own collections. Further up the mountain to the north, I discovered(?) with the help of the fellahin, a magnificent and beautifully preserved Roman tomb from the third century or so. There are no remaining hieroglyphs, besides those that are ornamental. I shall try to make the museum authorities understand that this tomb, perhaps unique in its preservation, as it contains, for instance, the 'Totengesicht,' transformed into a real ψυχοστασία with εἴδωλα in black, deserves to be preserved and drawn, or photographed by a member of the mission perhaps.

If not, I will publish the hastily taken tracings in my little report for the Zeitschrift and try to do better later. There is also a portrait of the deceased. I have collected a lot of pottery at Tell el Amarna, at Siout (where the whole old necropolis below the Hapzef[11] 'is being robbed) at Achmim etc., so that we are able to classify the vases of the Old Kingdom, of the XVIII-XX [dynasties] (Tomb of Sennedjem), of the Late Period, in a certain way. We have vases dated to the Middle Kingdom as well as to the eleventh dynasty. Here a serious question arises: according to our results for the development of the vases, and according to

---

[11] Hapzef is an old transcription for Hapydjefay/Djefaihapi, and "the Hapzef" points to his tomb in Asyut. On this tomb, see M. El-Khadragy, 'The shrine of the rock-cut chapel of Djefaihapi I at Asyut', GM 212 (2007), 41–62; G. Reisner, 'The Tomb of Hepzefa, Nomarch of Siût', JEA 5/2 (1918), 79–98; and M. Shaw, 'Ceiling Patterns from the Tomb of Hepzefa', AJA 74/1 (1970), 25–30.

the results of Mr Petrie's excavations (an authority which unfortunately one must distrust a little, if I may judge from Tell el Amarna and Koptos especially) and according to an indication that You kindly gave me a few years ago, the so-called prehistoric vases would date to the VII-XI dynasty. It seems to me that there is no effective proof of the contrary in Mr de Morgan's book, and it is absolutely impossible for me to agree with him on these conclusions, which may be very doctrinaire, but are highly implausible on the origins of Egypt.

And the pottery of the barbarian peoples has so many similarities to the pottery of the Greek origins that it is impossible for me to separate it completely. It is not Egyptian pottery, of course, but it is pottery that has greatly influenced the pottery not of the Old Kingdom but precisely of the Middle Kingdom and later times. Red-glazed pottery is only found in forms [and?] tombs (etc.) that are contemporary with the Theban dynasties; it is in Upper Egypt that these 'prehistoric' vessels are found. If Mr Amelineau, instead of writing large volumes on the preparation of the tomb (I thank You sincerely for the criticism You kindly sent me) would give us a precise account of his excavations, we would perhaps know what to expect. I will try to see this more clearly at Abydos itself, inš Allah! But You would oblige us a lot by communicating to me a small note, if You found these vases in a sarcophagus or in an intact tomb, or in circumstances excluding all doubts about the age of the pottery. I will come to Paris myself in the autumn to find out all the details, if You allow me.

I thank You with all my heart for all Your kindnesses towards me. I will speak to You, if You do not mind, in Paris about the sad state in which things are here. Mr de Morgan is very liberal himself: thanks to him Mr Borchardt was called in to make an inventory of the statues. Mr de Morgan has given me a permit to stamp etc. in the museums and ruins and Brugsch[12] has promised to write to the ghaffir of Thebes to allow me to do some small cleaning. I cannot complain about people on my own account, but there are many lamentable things elsewhere. Mr Your Brother has been very kind to me; unfortunately, as everyone has so much to do during the day and since the distance between Cairo and the museum is so great, I am deprived of the pleasure of seeing him more often.

But now I have kept You a long time, sir; I beg Your pardon and ask You to keep in mind the memory of your Madame and your children, believing myself to be yours most sincerely and devotedly.

Fritz v. Bissing

Do not fear for my health, a dahabieh with counterwinds hardly allows harm to be done to it, or rather does too little!

At the end of his article in French (ASAE 50), von Bissing implicitly alludes to his superior, presumably Maspero, thanking him. Von Bissing also boldly expresses the hope that with Maspero's broad knowledge, Maspero will be able to complete and perhaps also correct von Bissing's research. Von Bissing stresses that he would be grateful for any contributions and any criticism, and that he is grateful to Maspero for the care he has kindly taken in printing this article, helping with its illustrations, and correcting its French grammar. Finally, von Bissing offers his most sincere gratitude and his entire devotion to Maspero. The French text says the following: '*En vous soumettant, cher maître, ces humbles notes, qui ont au moins le mérite de sauver des témoins détruits depuis plusieurs dé- cades, j'ose espérer qu'avec vos larges connaissances vous pourrez compléter et peut-être aussi corriger mes propres recherches; soyez certain que je serai reconnaissant de toute contribution et toute critique comme Je vous suis reconnaissant du soin que vous avez bien voulu apporter à l'impression de cette lettre, à ses illustrations, et aussi à la correction de mon français, et veuillez agréer l'assurance de ma plus sincère gratitude et de mon entier dévouement*'[13].

During his second visit to the site, von Bissing was so worried about the bad state of tomb C1's preservation that he asked the Archaeological Institute of Moscow for help with cleaning, documenting and closing it. He sent another letter to Maspero mentioning that '*Avant de rentrer au Caire je voudrais rendre visite encore une fois à Léfebure et peut-être le prier de venir avec moi à Akoris. J'ai signalé l'autre jour à l'institut archéologique de Moscou les tombeaux gréco-romains d'Achmim qui ont grandement besoin d'être nettoyés et fermés et copiés: les Russes pourraient s'y mettre, ne pensez-Vous pas ?*'[14]. This translates to mean '*Before returning to Cairo I would like to once again visit Léfebure and perhaps pray to him to come with me to Akoris. I reported the Graeco-Roman tombs of Akhmim to the Archaeological Institute of Moscow the other day, which seriously need to be cleaned and closed and recorded: the Russians could start, don't you think?*'. Apparently, von Bissing was so enthusiastic to excavate and preserve the tombs that he searched for funding and support. When he was appointed as an honourary member of the Russian Imperial Archaeological Institute in 1913, he seized the opportunity to propose a mission to methodologically excavate the Graeco-Roman necropolis of Akhmim. He proposed to do so with the assistance of M. Rostovtzeff, a Russian Archaeologist who was an expert in the antiquities of southern Russia, from which he could potentially draw analogies. The idea was for Rostovtzeff to direct the excavation with von Bissing's student Ballod (who died after having taken refuge in Stockholm, where he taught at the university). Von Bissing hoped that his collaboration with a Russian Archaeologist would make it

---

[12] Émile Brugsch was Maspero's assistant, and assumed responsibility for the excavation of the great mummy cachette at Deir el-Bahri.

[13] Von Bissing, *ASAE* 50, 576. In his footnote, he refers to the excavations conducted by T. Whitemore and M. Wainwright in the adjacent necropolis of Naga El-Sawâma-sharq, which contains Roman tombs, and is located north of El-Salamuni.

[14] The paragraphs of the letter are documented as numbers f627–28, with the paragraph referring to El-Salamuni numbered as f628, v.

possible to determine a more accurate date for the tombs of Akhmim. The idea was to compare them with the *hypogea* of Kertsch and Olbia[15].

When von Bissing returned to El-Salamuni in 1913 in search of the tomb he visited in 1897, he entered several other tombs that were obviously from the same period as the one he sought. However, he could not find the one he visited in 1897, and he believed it had been destroyed [16]. Luckily, Kuhlmann of the German Archaeological Institute in Cairo (DAIK) conducted a brief survey of Akhmim from 1979 to 1982, and accidentally rediscovered the 'missing' tomb in 1981. He photographed the tomb, which was heaped with debris[17], but he did not clean it up. Later, by the time of N. Kanawati's visit in 1989, the tomb had been completely cleaned, with no remaining debris in either of the rooms. The entrance was closed with a metal door, which was visible, without any debris covering it[18]. This means that most likely, the Akhmim Inspectorate cleaned the tomb sometime in the period between the end of Kuhlmann's survey (1982) and Kanawati's visit (1989). Unfortunately, after Kanawati's visit, the tomb was again covered with a deep accumulation of debris, prompting looters to break through it. Hence, some of the painted scenes were harmfully attacked and destroyed at that time. Later, in 1996, the Akhmim Inspectorate Office registered the so-called 'von Bissing tomb' as tomb C1. To preserve the tomb from grave robbers, the Inspectorate covered its main entrance with more debris. This was especially importance since it is located on the northern side of the mountain, and is about 830m. away from the *ghaffirs'* security hut.

In January 2015, the author visited the tomb, which was in a bad state of preservation. Its entrance was fully covered by heavy crushed stones and sand. Its burial chamber was in a worse condition than the anteroom; its walls and ceiling were covered with heavily ingrained bitumen. Hence, some of its funerary scenes were hardly visible. On many parts of the walls, the burial niches and the ceiling were almost black, and the scenes were destroyed, which suggests a deliberate burning. On the other side of the tomb, the layers of soot were less present on the walls and the ceiling of the antechamber. The reason for the soot could be related to the Coptic monks, or to the local villagers. The tomb was once used for mass burials; the mummies were swaddled and stacked in the tomb in a way reminiscent of the adjacent necropolis of El-Hawawish A. The *ghaffirs* told the author that their grandfathers used to climb the mountain and play with mummies, either by burning them inside the tombs, or by throwing them in the El-Faraoukiya canal (which is located on the foot of the mountain to reduce the risk of the Nile overflowing during the annual inundation). Furthermore, the tomb was a continuous target of grave robbers, who caused great damage to the burial niches, destroying its scenes, and trying (though sometimes unsuccessfully) to cut and pluck them out from the wall.

The author was hardly able to enter the tomb, as the antechamber was full of stones which varied in size and covered great parts of the lower friezes on the walls. Moreover, a big, heavy block was in the centre of the room. The black burial chamber was not accessible at all because of the heavy debris (Figures 4.3a-c). Using a

Figure 4.3a. The heavy debris in the antechamber of tomb C1, as photographed in 2015.

Figure 4.3b. The heavy debris in the antechamber of tomb C1, as photographed in 2015.

Figure 4.3c. The heavy debris in the burial chamber of tomb C1, as photographed in 2015.

---
[15] Von Bissing, *ASAE* 50, 554.
[16] Von Bissing, *ASAE* 50, 560.
[17] Kuhlmann, *SDAIK* 11, 73, pls. 35c, d, 36a, b, c.
[18] N. Kanawati, *Sohag in Upper Egypt, A Glorious History*, Prism Archaeological Series 4 (Giza 1990), pls.40–42.

The Afterlife in Akhmim

mobile phone's lighting to discover the walls and scenes, the author was hardly able to enter more than roughly 1m. inside the antechamber to take some photos.

Later, in January 2020, the author visited the tomb again, and was able to remove great parts of the debris from the antechamber, also cleaning the floor of the room except for the big block in the middle. The illicit activities of the robbers are evidenced by their attempts to try to cut some of the friezes away from the walls by digging holes around them to loosen them (Figures 4.4). On 05 April 2020, the author received the approval of the Ministry of Tourism and Antiquities to begin cleaning the layers of soot and dirt, as well as to undertake a full restoration process in the tomb (Figures 4.5a-b). Later, during two field campaigns (October-November 2020, and May-June 2021), the conservation work in the tomb took place. Once again, the antechamber was completely cleaned of debris (Figure 4.6). The workers, with their equipment, succeeded in crumbling a great part of the heavy block in the centre of the antechamber. They then lifted the rest of the block out of the tomb. The burial chamber was also cleared of its heavy rubble (Figure 4.7). The workers cleaned the soot covering the walls and ceilings of the tomb, consolidated the weak parts, and reconstructed certain damaged walls and burial niches. While examining the debris, the remains of mummy shrouds, small human bones, small painted pieces of the damaged walls, and parts of pottery vessels were found. Moreover, after removing the debris, a part of the original floor of the tomb became visible along the north-east corner of the burial chamber, as well as in the doorway leading into the burial chamber (Figure 4.8).

4.2: Layout of the Tomb

Tomb C1 is a façade tomb (Figure 4.9). Because of the slight bend of the mountain, the tomb is oriented on a roughly south-north axis. It has a low south-east entrance, and the remains of descending staircases have been found. The tomb consists of two chambers, with one behind the other despite being off-axis to one another. The ground floor of the antechamber is lower than the entrance of the tomb, measuring an elevation of 30cm. (Figure 4.10). The burial chamber is larger than the antechamber, with three asymmetric niches cut into its northern, southern, and eastern walls. They are varied in their dimensions, and highly suggest a family tomb (Figure 4.11a-c). Tomb B1 is unpainted, and is about 2m. in elevation, while the painted tomb B2 lies 4.75cm. northwest of tomb C1 (Figure 4.12a-b). Creating a layout of the tomb was possible by fixing two main spots on the mountain as points of reference (ES1 and ES2), and by using a Universal Transverse Mercator (UTM) along with a Global Positioning System (GPS) and a Total Station. The results of the measurements of the two stations ES1 and ES2 are displayed in Table 4.1:

Figure 4.4 The looters' attempts to cut out some of the scenes in the antechamber of tomb C1.

Table 4.1: Stations Created to Document El-Salamuni (First Step)*

Station	North	East	Elevation	Description
ES1	2944522.021	376208.393	86.82	A newly-created station on El-Salamuni Mountain, called ES1. It lies to the south of C1. It is comprised of metal pegs in cement bases.
ES2	2944524.819	376192.565	87.422	A new station created on El-Salamuni Mountain, called ES2. It lies to the north of tomb C1, and is in front of tomb B2. It is comprised of metal pegs in cement bases.

* The architectural layout of the tomb was recorded by M. Gamal, an inspector from the Akhmim Office.

Table 4.2: More Stations Created to Document El-Salamuni (Second Step)

Station	North	East	Elevation	Description
ES3	2944526. 23	376200.185	83.93	Longitudinal hall
ES4	2944525.450	376200.671	84.324	Longitudinal hall
ES5	2944530.119	376197.844	83.603	Burial chamber
ES6	2944530.332	376196.763	83.092	Burial chamber

Figure 4.5a. The state of the tomb C1 burial chamber and the southern burial niche, as photographed in 2019.

Figure 4.5b. The state of the tomb C1 east burial niche in 2019.

Through the use of the Total Station, four other points of reference were additionally taken. They are shown in Table 4.2:

The rock-cut C1 tomb was carved of local limestone, and its walls were covered with white stucco, being coated with white plaster made from lime and sand. This acted as a background for the intended decoration; the tomb is patterned with scenes[19]. The painted scenes are mostly arranged into two registers with a black line in between. The only section to have scenes in three registers occurs on part of the west wall to the left side of a niche. Traditional afterlife funerary scenes as well as the influences of classical art are shown on the tomb's walls. The tomb is distinguishable by the non-existence of its lower *orthostats*, the presence of which was a special and known artistic characteristic of the El-Salamuni tombs.

Venit claims that the tomb is 'one of the most 'Egyptianising' of the Akhmim tombs', and 'the most enigmatic', being 'the most completely recorded painted tomb at Akhmim'[20]. The author disagrees with Venit's claims; the tomb is not the most 'Egyptianising' in El-Salamuni, and it is not completely recorded, as its burial chamber is still quite covered under soot and rubble. Regarding the current state of the tomb's records, Venit mentions that she is 'unaware of any published photographs of the burial chamber, except for the west wall captured in a photo by Kanawati, and another photo, which is nearly unreadable, being published by Kaplan'[21]. A description of each room of tomb C1 is provided below.

---

[19] Kaplan, *BzÄ* 16, 166.

[20] Venit, 'Referencing Isis in Tombs of Graeco-Roman Egypt, Tradition and Innovation', in L. Bricault and M. J. Versylus (eds.), *Isis on the Nile, Egyptian Gods in Hellenistic and Roman Egypt, Proceedings of the IV*th *International Conference of Isis Studies, Liège, November 27–29 2008*, EPRO 171 (Leiden 2010), 99.; Venit, *Visualizing the Afterlife*, 186.

[21] Venit, 'Referencing Isis', in L. Bricault and M. Versylus (eds.), *Isis on the Nile*, no. 60.

The Afterlife in Akhmim

Figure 4.6. The antechamber of tomb C1 after cleaning.

Figure 4.7. The burial chamber of tomb C1 after cleaning.

Tomb C1: The So-called 'Tomb of von Bissing' (1897)

Figure 4.8. Part of the original floor of tomb C1, showing the southeast corner of the burial chamber.

Figure 4.9. The tomb C1 entrance, showing the damaged descending staircases.

Figure 4.10. The level of the antechamber floor, which is lower than the entrance of the tomb.

4.2.1: The Antechamber

Venit mentions that '*The tomb stands as one of the most considered, one of the most 'Egyptianising', as well as [one of] the most confounding of the Akhmim tombs*'[22]. The scenes in the antechamber are better preserved than those of the burial chamber, and the best reports are those by von Bissing. An astronomical zodiac covers the ceiling of the antechamber. The height of the ceiling is about 1.85cm.. The antechamber serves as a meeting point between the worlds of the dead and the living.

4.2.2: The Southern A3 Wall: Left Jamb of the Entrance, The Upper Register

In the layout of the tomb as created by von Bissing, he wrongly defined the location of the scene as belonging to wall B, to the left of the doorway of the burial chamber. Unknown to him, von Bissing had accidently reversed the locations of the scenes on walls B and D; the scene is actually depicted on wall D, not B (Figure 4.13).

The upper frieze on the wall located to the left of the main entrance shows the god Anubis. He stands facing the entrance of the tomb, and holds a large green disc before Min[23]. This is the only known representation of Min in

---

[22] Venit, *Visualizing the Afterlife*, 186.
[23] Von Bissing, *ASAE* 50, 557, 563.; Kaplan, *BzÄ* 16, 169.

The Afterlife in Akhmim

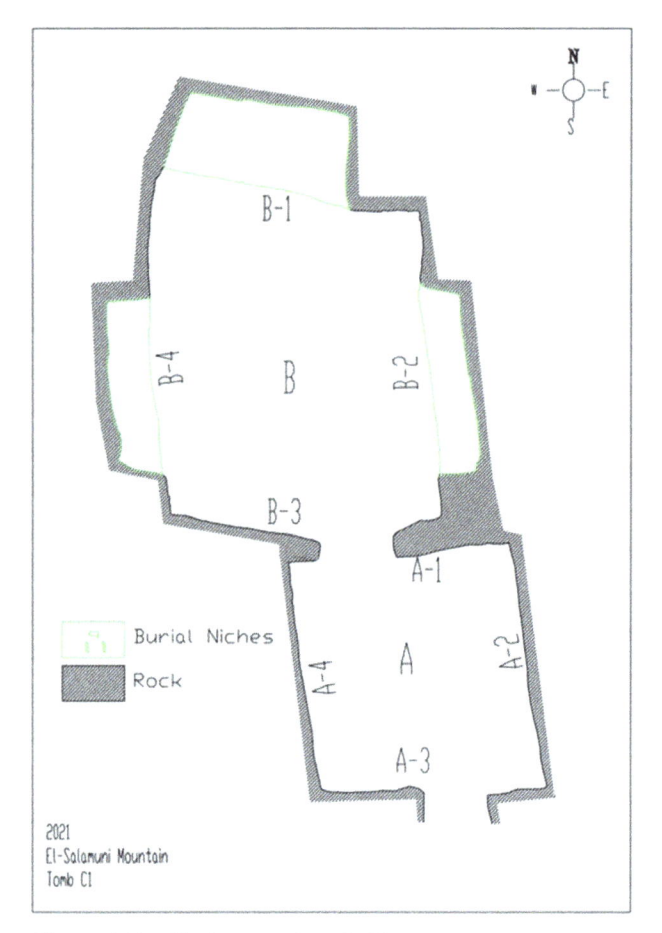

Figure 4.11a. The layout of tomb C1.

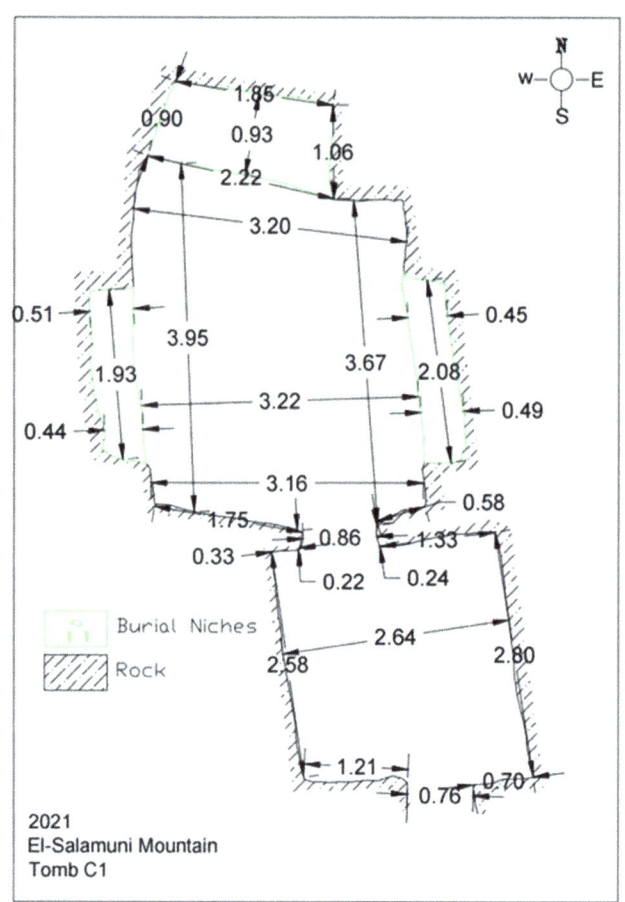

Figure 4.11b. The dimensions of tomb C1.

the Graeco-Roman tombs of Egypt in general, and of El-Salamuni in particular. Min[24] stands close to the doorway, and is depicted with a frontal view. He stands upon a *naos* that is outlined in black, and is characterised by the two-feathered crown upon his head. Unfortunately, Min's face is partially damaged, and the rest of the wall behind him is cracked[25]. Von Bissing suggests that in this tomb, Min is mainly connected to his local ritual festival, called the *pr.t Mnw*, or 'Going Out of Min'[26]. The festival took place in Panopolis, where a statue of the god was taken out of the temple and carried on a barque by a group of *pastophori* along a *dromos* to the metropolis. The festival took place via a *komasia* procession, with attendants stopping in certain places in the city and the countryside

---

[24] Von Bissing suggests that Min is represented in the scene as the local god of Panopolis, von Bissing, *ASAE* 50, 557 no. 3.
[25] Kaplan, *BzÄ* 16, 167–77, pl. 86 (a4).; Von Bissing, *JDAI* 61/62, 4, pl. 2(a–f). Min's traditional form was that of an ithyphallic, bearded, mummiform male, standing with both legs together, and wearing two feathers on his head. He typically holds a whip in his raised right hand, while his left hand is either hidden or grasping the base of his erect penis, S. Schoske and D. Wildung, *Gott und Götter im alten Ägypten* (Mainz, 1992), 28.; F. Dunand, *Religion populaire en Égypte romaine, Les terres cuites isiques du Musée du Caire*, EPRO 76 (Leiden 1979), no. 367, pl. cxxvii.
[26] Von Bissing, *ASAE* 50, 563.; id., *JDAI* 61/62, 8. The festival of *pr.t Mnw* was the most important of the festivals dedicated to Min, and was celebrated throughout Egypt each year from at least the third century BC onwards. It took place in Akhmim during the *shemu* month, H. Gauthier, *Les fêtes du dieu Min*, RAPH 2 (Cairo 1931), 15.

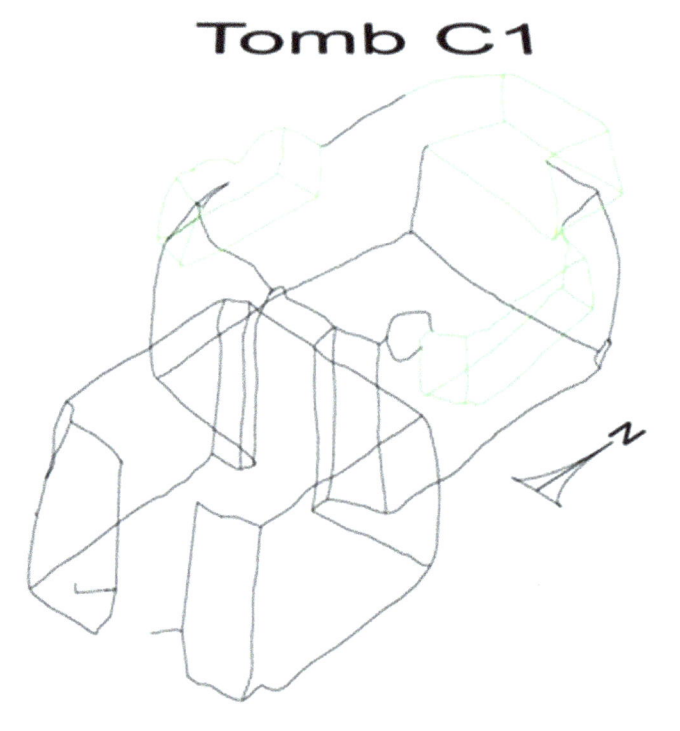

Figure 4.11c. A 3D model of tomb C1.

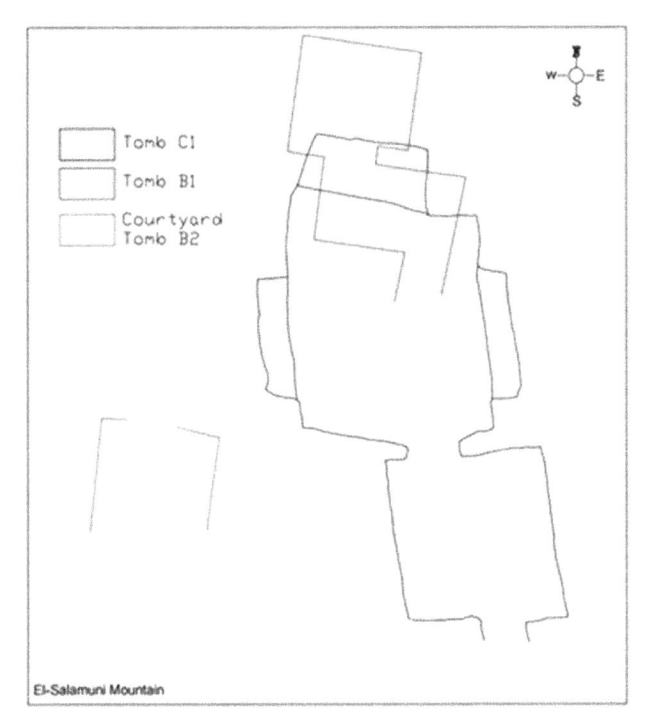

Figure 4.12a. The locations of tombs B1 and B2.

Figure 4.12b. Tomb B2, which is located north of tomb C1.

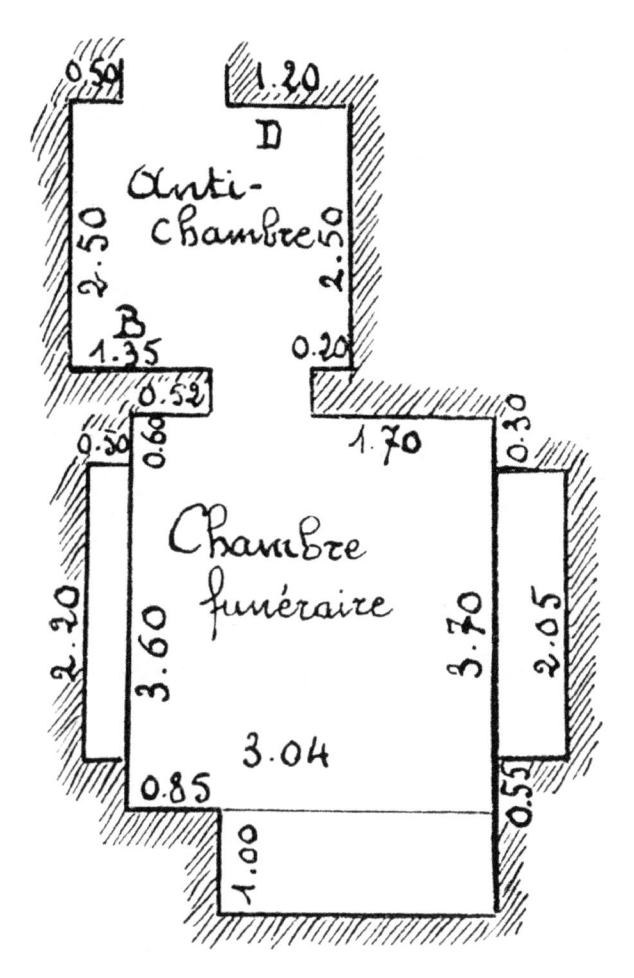

Figure 4.13. Von Bissing's layout of tomb C1.

for public ritual celebrations[27]. Scholars have connected the appearance of Perseus to the Going Out of Min festival[28]. Two Roman graffiti in the so-called *Asklepeion* in the Triphion cemetery attest to the fact that the festival was still celebrated at this time[29]. It is apparent that this festival was still celebrated in the fourth century AD. In Shenoute's reference to 'images of priests with shaven heads holding an altar in their hands'[30], he is most likely referring to an altar containing a statue of the god Min.

In the scene, the jackal-headed Anubis holds a large lunar disc (a green tambourine) before Min (Figure 4.14), justifying the close connection between Anubis as the *B3w* of *PsDntyw*[31] and the lunar disc. The relationship between Anubis and his disc is unclear, but in several temples' scenes, Anubis tends to a disc that represents Osiris[32] and quite possibly also the invisible moon[33]. The scene is connected to circumcision rituals, the divine king, birthing houses, and cyclical rebirth[34]. The representation of Anubis with a tambourine in tomb C1 remains unusual, as it is not depicted in other Graeco-Roman tombs [35], despite its prophylactic role in funerals.

---

[27] Von Bissing, *JDAI* 61/62, 8.; id., *ASAE* 50, 563. For more on this festival, see C. Bleeker, *Die Geburt eines Gottes, eine Studie über den ägyptischen Gott Min und sein Fest, Studies in the History of Religions: suppl. to Numen* 3 (Leiden, 1956), 59–66. For more about the festival, see Gauthier, *Les fêtes du dieu Min*, 25–35.

[28] L. Castiglione, 'Hérodote II 91', in *Mélanges offerts à K. Michalowski* (Warsaw 1966), 45–46.

[29] Geens, *Panopolis, a Nome Capital in Egypt*, 322–23.; Lindsay, *Men and Gods*, 353–54.

[30] Emmel, 'Shenoute of Atripe', in J. Hahn et al. (eds.), *From Temple to Church*, 170.

[31] *CT* II, 155, 308a–308b.

[32] R. Ritner, 'Anubis and the Lunar Disc', *JEA* 71 (1985), 149–55.

[33] G. Priskin, *Coffin Texts Spell 155 on the Moon*, *BEJ* 1 (2013), 50.

[34] For information on the scene in Deir El-Bahari, see E. Naville, *The Temple of Deir El-Bahari* II (London, 1896), 18, pl. 4.; Von Bissing, *ASAE* 50, 563. For Edfu, see E. Chassinat, *Le Mammisi d'Edfou*, *MIFAO* 16 (Cairo 1910), 21, pl. 13.

[35] On the Ramesside tomb A26 at Thebes, Anubis is shown playing the tambourine, L. Mannische, *Ancient Egyptian Musical Instruments*, *MÄS* 34 (Berlin, 1975), 3.; *PM* I, 455. The amulets of the drummer Bes are familiar. He also beats a drum for Hathor in the temple of Hathor, C.

The Afterlife in Akhmim

Figure 4.14. The upper frieze on the south A3 wall of the tomb C1 antechamber.

The sound of the tambourine was likely to have inspired fear, 'attacking' enemies and keeping them at a distance from the mummy[36]. The instrument also had a symbolic role in confirming the rebirth of and provision of farmable land for the deceased[37].

The lunar disc, which represents the moon, is the light-giving celestial body of the night. Thus, lunar rites had a funerary and regenerative nature. Consequently, lunar symbols had erotic connotations. The moon was mainly attributed to Osiris [38]; the lunar aspect of Osiris is hinted at by his title 'the Lunar God'. He was also associated with vegetation and sexual pleasure (*nb nDmnDm*), being the 'Lord of Love'[39].

In connection to this, the appearance of Anubis as a funerary deity in a birthing relief may at first seem surprising, but his nature as the god of mummification and thus as a guarantor of rebirth embodies the Egyptian concept of the transition from death to life. Hence, the deceased in his tomb may have wished for the 'repeating of births like the moon'[40,] and the power to be 'rejuvenated like the moon'[41].

The musical aspect of Anubis is a special feature in the iconography of El-Salamuni. In the so-called tomb of von Bissing from 1913, three women are shown dancing while Anubis beats a green tambourine to accompany them[42]. One can associate the moon with the rebirth of the deceased, as the moon is 'rebirthed' every night. Hence, when Anubis bends over the moon with his torso, and when his arms roll the disc, it is directly related to mummification scenes[43].

Graves-Brown, *Daemons & Spirits in Ancient Egypt, Lives and Beliefs of the Ancient Egyptians* (Cardiff 2018) 40.
[36] On the protective role of the sound of tambourine, see S. Cauville, *Le temple de Dendara, Les chapelles osiriennes, I, IFAO, BiEtud* 117 (Cairo 1997).; Dendara X/2, pl. 37, 54.; R. Herbin, *Le livre de parcourir l'éternité, OLA* 58 (Leuven 1994), VI, 5.; R. Faulkner, *The Papyrus Bremner-Rhind, BiAeg* III (Brussels 1933), 1,l.1.; P. Barguet, *Le papyrus N. 3176 (S), du musée du Louvre, BiEtud* 37 (Cairo 1962), 9–10.
[37] An example is depicted in the temple of Dendera, where Anubis tends to a tambourine before the naked body of the deceased in what to seems to be a sarcophagus, S. Cauville, *Osiris aux sources du Nil* (Leuven, 2021), 45.
[38] J. Griffiths, 'Osiris and the Moon in Iconography', *JEA* 62 (1976) 153–59.; id., *The Origin of Osiris and His Cult* (Leiden 1980), 239–40.
[39] On the astral myth of Osiris see, G. Priskin, 'The Astral Myth of Osiris: The Decans of Taurus and Libra', *eNiM* 9 (2016), 79–111.

[40] *Urk* IV, 2161, 6.
[41] H. Grapow-Erman, *Die Bildlichen Ausdrücke des Aegyptischen* (Leipzig 1924), 34–35.
[42] Von Bissing, *ASAE* 50, 562.
[43] A. Piankoff, *Mythological Papyri* (New York 1957), pl. 22. The connection between Anubis and the lunar disc still appears during the Byzantine Period, D. Millard, 'St. Christopher and the Lunar Disc of Anubis,' *JEA* 73 (1987), 237–38.; M. Edgar, *Graeco-Egyptian Coffins, Masks and Portraits* (Cairo 1905), 33–36, pl. 19.; K. Michalowski, *The Art of Ancient Egypt* (London 1969), 428.

Min was also a moon god[44], and ancient texts mention his lunar invisibility[45]. Min was believed to replace the moon at certain times, and it is Min who lights the first day of the new lunar cycle[46]. Here, in El-Salamuni, the temple of Min-Re was known as the 'House of the Moon', or *Hw.t- iaH*, and Min was regarded as the king of the gods (*'nswt- (nTr-w-) m – Hw.t-iaH*)[47]. taking up residency there as the so-called *Hry-ib-Hw.t-iaH*[48]. He was also known as the 'Lord of the House of the Moon', or *xnty- Hw.t-iaH*[49]. Min was additionally assigned as the moon god of Athribis (*nb ipw wpi Abd xaj.ti m iaH*). He is called the 'Lord of Akhmim, who opens the month, having appeared as Iah (the moon)'[50]. Furthermore, in the Wadi Bir El-Aïn, one can find rough drawings of an ithyphallic Min, complete with a lifted arm, two plumes on his head, and a large circular encasement[51].

Since the time of Ptolemaic Panopolis, Min has shown evidence of an assimilation with Osiris. On an anthropoid coffin from Akhmim belonging to a man called Inaros, his name is listed with the title *Wsir-Min*, or 'Osiris-Min'[52]. Here is perhaps an example of the locution '*Osiris- Min n NN*', reflecting the syncretism of Osiris and Min in Akhmim, especially if Inaros was a priest in the cults of both deities. A Demotic mummy label from Ptolemaic-Roman Panopolis also mentions the name of the deceased in connection to Osiris-Min[53]. Another example is found on an anthropoid coffin of Inaros from Akhmim; the name of the owner is preceded by *Wsir-Mn* ('Osiris-Min')[54], a word that was most often associated with a priest in the cults of both deities. It is an example of the locution 'Osiris-Min of NN', which strongly suggests syncretism between Osiris and Min in Panopolis[55]. The inclusion of Min in the tomb might have been based not only on the god's fertility, but also on his association with Panopolis and his role as a burial god. The depiction of Anubis with a tambourine, standing on a shrine before the ithyphallic form of Min, is also closely connected to the Sokar festival; it is depicted on both the southern Maat chapel of the temple of Deir El-Medina[56] and on the coffin of Soter[57], followed by the Sokar barque. Regarding the lunar aspect of Osiris and the feathered crown of Min, the author believes that the god for whom Anubis beats the lunar disc is the god Osiris-Min. He is typically dressed in a white garment which mimics the garment of the deceased, confirming his glorification as well as confirming the tomb owner's dual cultic affiliations with both Osiris and Min.

Tomb C1 is unique; it documents the only known figure of Anubis playing the tambourine in Graeco-Roman tombs. It also records the first known depiction of Min as a burial god in the Graeco-Roman tombs of Egypt. It is, in fact, logical to depict the chief god of Panopolis in the tombs. El-Salamuni tomb B7 shows yet another traditional figure of an ithyphallic, bearded, mummiform Min, standing with both legs together, with two feathers on his head. He holds a whip in his raised right hand, while the left arm is either hidden or with his hand grasping the base of his erect penis[58]. He is depicted behind the barque of Osiris,

---

[44] Stephanus Byzantinus, who wrote *De Urbibus et populis*, describes a statue of Pan in Akhmim, even referring to Min as an *eidolon* of the moon. According to the inscriptions, Min was regarded as the moon god of Athribis, Altmann-Wendlig, 'Of Min and Moon', in G. Rosati and M. Guidotti (eds.), *Proceedings of the XI International Congress of Egyptologists*, 9.

[45] S. Cauville, 'Le Pronaos d'Edfo: une voute étoilée', *RdÉ* 62 (2011), 42–43. On the lunar attributes of Min, see J.Olette- Pelletier, « Le dieu Min "protecteur de la lune" : aspects et rôles lunaires du dieu de la fertilité », *ÉAO - Supplément au numéro* 72 (n° 2), (2014), 9-16.

[46] *Esna* IV, I, no. 399C. If two new moons occurred in the same civil calendar month, the second one was referred to as a 'black moon', in reference to Min as a god of regeneration, Cauville, *RdÉ* 62, 41.

[47] *LGG* III, 337b.; *LGG* III, 338c. It is mentioned on a stela of Hadrian (Scharff, *ZÄS* 62, 88.), and on several reliefs from the temple of Triphis (*RÄRG*, 'Min', 466).

[48] *LGG* V, 336c.

[49] *LGG* V, 828b.

[50] Altmann-Wendling, 'Of Min and Moon', in G. Rosati and M. Guidotti (eds.), *Proceedings of the XI International Congress of Egyptologists*, 9, 10. Within the lunar cycle, there is a close connection between Min and the moon, and the phrase 'give appearance to (the god) Min every new moon', or *sh'j(.t) Mnw n psdn.tyw nb*, is known. For the festival of Min, which was one of the main festivals in the temple of Kom Ombo, see A. Grimm, *Die altägyptischen Festkalender in den Tempeln der griechisch-römischen Epoche*, ÄAT 15 (1994), 124f.; G. Burkard, *Spätzeitliche Osiris-Liturgien im Corpus der Asasif-Papyri: Übersetzung, Kommentar, formale und inhaltliche Analyse*, ÄAT 31 (Wiesbaden 1995), 108f.

[51] Bouriant, *Rec.Trav.* 11,148.; Bernand, *Pan du désert*, pl. 14. During the day of the new moon, when the moon was still invisible and was believed to attacked by enemies, the recitation of funerary rituals was needed to protect it. For more about the 'Book of the New Moon Festival', see the most recent publication by S. Vuilleumier, *Un rituel osirien en faveur de particuliers à l'époque ptolémaïque. Papyrus Princeton Pharaonic Roll 10*, SSR 15 (Wiesbaden 2016), 176–221. Another new moon ritual that involves the ritual destruction of enemies is examined in C. Leitz, *Geographisch-osirianische Prozessionen aus Philae, Dendara und Athribis, Soubassementstudien II*, SSR 8 (Wiesbaden 2012), 127–29. Also see V. Altmann-Wendling, 'Shapeshifter-Knowledge of the Moon in Graeco-Roman Egypt', in J. Althoff, D. Berrens, and T. Pommerening (eds.), *Construction and Transfer of Knowledge about Man and Nature in Antiquity and the Middle Ages* (Bielefeld 2019), 215.

[52] The coffin is now in San Francisco. A brief description of it was included by Ruth Brech in her study on the coffins of Panopolis, where she examined 85 examples from different collections, R. Brech, *Spätägyptische Särge aus Achmim, Eine typologische und chronologische Studie* (Gladbeck 2008), 302–05, 309. In Athribis, Min was identified as Horus, and was regarded as the son of Osiris, who collected his body parts, Altmann, 'Of Min and Moon', in G. Rosati and M. Guidotti (eds.), *Proceedings of the XI International Congress of Egyptologists*, 12. In Roman Panopolis, Min was also associated with Amun, Kuhlmann, *SDAIK* 11, 48 no. 230.

[53] Vleeming, *Demotic and Greek*, StudDem 8, 569 no. 967. On a mummy label of the Early Roman Period from Dendera, the name of the deceased is also preceded by that of Osiris-Min, Vleeming, *Demotic and Greek*, StudDem 8, 40 no. 329.

[54] R. Brech, *Spätägyptische Särge aus Achmim*, 302–05, 309.

[55] In the temple of Hibis, Baqué Manzano has assessed the role of the god Min as a counterpart of Osiris and Horus. This is an eclectic religious component which attests to the link between the theologies of Coptos and Abydos, L. Baqué Manzano, 'Min-Osiris, Min-Horus: a propósito de un relieve del templo de Hibis en el oasis de El Jarga', in J. Autuori and A. Álvarez (eds.), *...ir a buscar leña: Estudios dedicados al Prof. Jesús López*, Avla Aegyptiaca : Stvdia 2 (Barcelona 2001), 35–49. The syncretistic form of Osiris-Min-Harsiesis is also cited in C. Leitz, *LGG* II, 546. On a mummy label from Dendera from the Early Roman Period, the name of the deceased is preceded by the word *Wsir-Mn*, Vleeming, *Demotic and Greek-Demotic Mummy Labels*, 40 no. 329.

[56] P. Bourguet and L. Gabolde, *Le temple de Deir al-Médîna*, MIFAO 121 (Cairo 2002), 58.

[57] BM EA 6705. For more on the coffin, see C. Riggs, 'Archaism and Artistic Sources in Roman Egypt: The Coffins of the Soter Family and the Temple of Deir El-Medina', *BIFAO* 106 (2006), 320–22, fig. 1.

[58] For more on the traditional figure of Min, see Schoske and Wildung, *Gott und Götter*, 28.; Dunand, *Religion populaire en Égypte romaine*, no. 367, pl. cxxvii. Min was depicted in an unusual form in the tomb of Thyty (26th dynasty) in Baharyia. Here, Min has a lion's head surmounted by a cobra, which is unusual, C. De Wit, 'Le Rôle et le sens du lion dans l'égypte ancienne' (Luxor 1980), 235. He also appears in an unusual fashion in the temple of Hibis, where he is depicted in an Osirian form or with a falcon head, N. Davies, *The Temple of Hibis in El-Khargeh Oasis* III (New York 1953), pl. 20, no. 3, pl. 4, no. 3.

The Afterlife in Akhmim

on the rear wall of the burial niche. His characteristic attribute of a great white bull, a sacred animal connected with the *sHnt*, is depicted behind him (Figure 4.15).

4.2.3: The Southern A3 Wall: Left Jamb of the Entrance, The Lower Register

Terrible threats could occur on the passage through the underworld, which the deceased had to overcome. Slaughtering by daemons was the fate of unrighteous sinners who failed the final judgement before Osiris. The lower register on the left wall of the entrance depicts three protective daemons, or genii, who act as gatekeepers. They are most frequently represented in human form, but are also sometimes shown as semi-anthropomorphic figures with a human body and the head of an animal. They have knives in their hands and stride towards the entrance of the tomb, a gate with a protective snake inside of it being positioned before each gatekeeper. The static function of the gatekeepers does not allow them to leave the place they guard. Their protective function is related to the vigil of Osiris, which takes place during the hours of the night, when the mummified body of the god needs protection before his rebirth[59]. The iconography of the daemons may be confusing because of the similarity of their appearances to that of the main gods, such as the jackal-headed Anubis and the crocodile-headed Sobek. Their images are luckily labelled with their names, which helps to distinguish them from the main gods.

In tomb C1, the first daemon has a lion head with a red sun disc, and the second has a jackal head. The third has a falcon head and wears a *pschent* crown. A gate is placed before each of the daemons. The daemons brandish knives to destroy the enemies of Re, confirming their protective role in the tomb[60]. Both knives and snakes are thus shown as apt tools for protecting the portals of the night[61]. During the journey to the afterlife, the deceased are attacked by snakes, crocodiles, and insects. There are also many underworld gods who guard the gateways through which the deceased must successfully pass. If they do not give the right answers to their questions at the gates, the daemons can attack them with the knives and snakes in their hands. Unfortunately, the left side of the west wall of tomb C1 is heavily damaged, and it is hardly possible to distinguish the painted scenes on it, despite the evidence of daemons (Figure 4.16). The wall is fully documented, both before and after the author's conservation efforts (Figures 4.17a-d).

Figure 4.15. A figure of Min from tomb B7.

Figure 4.16. The lower frieze on the south wall of the antechamber of tomb C1.

4.2.4: The Southern A3 Wall: Right Jamb of the Entrance

The southern A3 wall is so narrow that it features no scenes on its upper and lower registers, despite the presence of plaster. This is just one of many parts of the tomb walls that are plastered but left unpainted by the artist.

4.2.5: The Western A4 Wall: Overview

Common funerary beliefs in El-Salamuni included the view that the journey to the afterlife led to the Hall of Judgement, where the deceased's heart was weighed and judged. By receiving a good burial and funerary rites, the dead would be ready to successfully pass through the Court of Judgement of Osiris and enjoy eternal rejuvenation, including the free movement of one's *ba*

---

[59] R. Lucarelli, 'Death, Gods, Daemons of the Book of the Dead', in F. Scalf (ed.), *Book of the Dead, Becoming God in Ancient Egypt, Oriental Institut Museum* 39(Chicago 2017), 134.

[60] The depiction of daemons holding knives with feet becomes more common from the New Kingdom onwards. Bes and the hippopotamus are the earliest deities to hold footed knives. In the Graeco-Roman Period, Tutu is shown holding knives with his hind-paws, C. Graves-Brown, *Daemons & Spirits*, 33, no. 59.

[61] C. Graves-Brown, *The Ideology of Flint in Dynastic Egypt*, Unpublished PhD thesis, UCL Institute of Archaeology (London 2011), http://discovery.Ucl.ac.UK/1306709/.

and the obtainment of divine offerings. The Court of Judgement is a standard scene in the El-Salamuni tombs.

The A4 wall was previously photographed by the German Archaeological Institute in Cairo (DAIK) (Figure 4.18). It is divided into two registers bordered and divided with a black line. Light soot covers the wall, with heavier soot layers on the uppermost and lowermost portions of the wall.

4.2.6: The Upper Register of the Western A4 Wall

The uppermost part of the wall shows the judges of the deceased, who are local to the nome. The image includes 21 squatting judges who are painted in red, yellow, and green. The judges face the burial chamber, sitting on a black line, and each holding a feather of Maat. The judges' numbers, which are 7, 9, 10, 16, and 17, are destroyed (Figure 4.19). In connection to this, the artist depicted the other 21 crouching judges on the parallel east wall. The artist thus provides a complete representation of the traditional 42 local judges, all of whom hear cases, representing the 42 nomes of Egypt during this period. The deceased would recite his negative confession to these judges in order to become forgiven[62]. The representation of local judges in the Court of Judgement is widely depicted in El-Salamuni.

When the deceased spirit journeys to the afterlife in ancient Egyptian mythology, the most important stage is the trial in the lawcourt of Osiris. The Court of Judgement for the deceased is thus the main scene on the A4 wall, showing a remarkable version of the Book of the Dead's spell 125. Before the presiding god Horus[63], the deceased announces his 'declaration of innocence'[64]. The court scene starts on the southern corner of the wall, closest to the main entrance of the tomb. It shows Maat with the traditional feather upon her head, dressed in a red fitted garment, and guiding the deceased male to the court [65]. The deceased male is garbed in a fringed, white, calf-length garment. Unfortunately, the face of the deceased is now partially destroyed. Maat salutes the falcon-headed Horus with her raised left hand and holds the deceased male by his left wrist, while the dead man salutes Horus with his right hand. As a parallel, the introduction of the deceased to the court by Maat is also depicted on the tomb of Psenosiris in Athribis (Figure 4.20). At the far northern end of the A4 wall, Horus sits on a throne, wear a white crown, and supervises the court, facing the entrance of the tomb[66].

The middle and main part of the upper register on the A4 wall preserves a depiction of the Egyptian Weighing of the Heart ceremony. In this scene, Anubis and Horus[67] are both shown beneath a scale, taking charge of the weighing. They support the main beam of the scale with their upraised hands, turning their heads to face one another and placing their other arms in support of the pans of the scale[68]. Meanwhile, Thoth in his baboon form is perched on the scale's cross-beam, which is now damaged[69]. To the left of the scale is the devourer Ammit (*mwtw*) who was believed to eat the hearts of the unjustified dead. She sits on a low Egyptian shrine with a cornice, and is a constant presence during the final judgement, licking her lips and sharp teeth, and awaiting her meal of the unjustified's heart with relish[70].

The scene in tomb C1 also features four black silhouettes shown as part of the trial, some of which play a positive role, and others a negative role. One silhouette stands stolidly beneath the beam of the scale, facing the viewer with a frontal form. The tiny second silhouette is drawn in the right-hand pan of the scale, being weighed against a seated figure of Maat (personifying truth and cosmic order) in the left pan. The third silhouette, which is shown frontally, stands before the forelegs of the drooling devourer, its feet being placed irregularly, and its arms dangling to indicate a restless shift of weight from foot to foot. Finally, the last silhouette, which is damned, bounces inside a large fiery cauldron. It is drawn with an outline and is coloured red inside. The silhouette's legs emerge from the sides of the cauldron, which is shown to be a white *skyphos*-shaped vase that is coloured red inside in

---

[62] Lucarelli, 'Death, Gods, Daemons of the Book of the Dead', in F. Scalf (ed.), *Book of the Dead*, 133.
[63] In the absence of text, it could be Osiris-Sokar, the god that is widely addressed by the dead on Akhmimic mummy labels of the Roman period.
[64] The function of the Book of the Dead spell 125 in priestly initiations extended into the Graeco-Roman world. A Roman novel by Apuleius from the second century AD describes the initiation of the protagonist Lucius into the mysterious cult of Isis in Corinth. Here, the Egyptian rituals were performed by Lucius, including purification, abstaining from certain foods, and asserting one's innocence to the deities. Purification oaths sworn by the Roman priests reflect the direct influence of and similarity to the Book of the Dead spell 125, Y. Barbash, 'The Ritual Context of the Book of the Dead', in F. Scalf (ed.), *Book of the Dead; Becoming a God in Ancient Egypt* (Chicago 2017), 82.
[65] In the tomb of Petosiris in the Dakhla Oasis, Maat is shown leading the deceased to the Court of Judgement. Here, she is shown at a high level, and the court is on a lower level, Kaplan, *BzÄ* 16, pl. 106b. For more about this tomb, see Whitehouse, 'Roman in Life', in O. Kaper (ed.), *Life on the Fringe*, 253–70.

[66] Von Bissing, *ASAE* 50, 557.; id., *JDAI* 61/62, 2.; Kuhlmann, *SDAIK* 11, pl. 35c.; Kaplan, *BzÄ* 16, pl.86b.; Venit, *Visualizing the Afterlife*, 189, fig. 5.31.
[67] For Anubis as a weigher of hearts, see H. Willems, 'Anubis as a Judge', in W. Clarysse, A. Schoors, and H. Willems (eds.), *Egyptian Religion, the Last Thousand Years, Studies Dedicated to the Memory of Jan Quaegebeur* (Leuven 1998), 728–43.
[68] Prior to the 21st dynasty, Thoth or Horus took charge of the weighing, but during the 21st dynasty, Anubis shared this task, H. Willems, 'Anubis as a Judge', in W. Clarysse et al. (eds.), *Egyptian Religion*, 719–43.
[69] In the Book of the Dead spell 17, the baboons in the court are said to remove evil and blot out sins, T. Allen, *The Book of the Dead or Going Forth by Day, Ideas of the Ancient Egyptians Concerning the Hereafter as Expressed in their Own Terms* (Chicago 1974), 102.
[70] This hybrid monster is always shown crouching near the balance. The monster has a crocodile's head, a lion's body, and the hindquarters of a hippopotamus. On the different forms and names of the 'Devourer of the Dead' in Chapter 125 of the Book of the Dead, see C. Seeber, *Untersuchungen zur Darstellung des Totengerichts im Alten Ägypten*, *MÄS* 35 (Munich 1976), 163–84. This creature was believed to eat the hearts which were heavier when balanced against the feather of Maat, emphasizing their damnation. The monster is sometimes shown to be crouching by the side of a lake of boiling water or fire (the so-called 'Lake of Fire'), W. Budge, *The Egyptian Religion of Resurrection Osiris* I (New York 1961), 320–21. Ammit's alternative position at the foot of the throne of Osiris, being turned away from the balance, is characteristic of the 21st dynasty, L. Berman, *Catalogue of Egyptian Art, the Cleveland Museum of Art* (Cleveland 1999), 318–19.

The Afterlife in Akhmim

Figure 4.17a. Photogrammetry of the south A3 wall of the tomb C1 antechamber, before its restoration in 2019.

Figure 4.17b. Photogrammetry of the south A3 wall of the tomb C1 antechamber after its restoration in 2021.

imitation of blood or fire[71] and the wrath of the god. A judgement scene with black skeletal figures and a huge image of Ammit is also depicted in the so-called 'von Bissing tomb' (Figure 4.21)[72]. The devourer, licking her lips, is also attested in the judgement court depiction in the Ptolemaic tomb of Psenosiris at Athribis.

The frieze to the left of the scale scene shows a partially damaged figure of a deity striding before Horus. His head is damaged, and only the lower part of his body and a small part of his crown are still visible. He is most certainly the ibis-headed god Thoth, who is particularly identified as the indicator (or plummet) of balance[73]. According to von Bissing and Kaplan's photos, Thoth wears an *atef* crown and acts in his traditional role as the reporter of the judgement results to Horus[74]. Thoth is sometimes shown holding a palette and a notched date-palm branch, and sometimes a papyrus roll, where he records the verdict of the judgement of the deceased. He is depicted on a larger

---

[71] On the judgement scenes, and on the depiction of silhouettes in general, see von Bissing, *ASAE* 50, 557, 562, 568–76. Von Bissing (*ASAE* 50, 573) interpreted the red interior of the vessel as the Lake of Fire. Seeber (*MÄS* 35, 186), called it a 'cauldron of fire', as did E. Brunner-Traut, *Gelebte Mythen, Beiträge zum altägyptischen Mythos* (Darmstadt 1981), 76.
[72] Von Bissing, *ASAE* 50, 562.; Kuhlmann, *SDAIK* 11, 37c.; Kaplan, *BzÄ* 16, pl. 89b.
[73] C. Manassa, 'The Judgement Hall of Osiris in the Book of Gates', *RdÉ* 57 (2006), 127.
[74] Kaplan, *BzÄ* 16, 166, fig. 86b.

Tomb C1: The So-called 'Tomb of von Bissing' (1897)

El Salamouni, Tomb C1, Anti Chamber, South Wall, A3.

Figure 4.17c. A facsimile of the south A3 wall of tomb C1.

Figure 4.18. The west A4 wall, as photographed by the German Archaeological Institute (DAI), Kaplan, *BzÄ* 16, fig. 87b.

89

The Afterlife in Akhmim

Figure 4.19. The upper frieze of the west A4 wall of the tomb C1 antechamber, showing the judgement court (before the restoration in 2019).

Figure 4.20. The introduction of the deceased to the judgement court by Maat, as shown in the tomb of Psenosiris at Athribis.

scale than the figures of Horus and Anubis, who oversee the scale. Here, at tomb C1, the figures on the balance are far smaller than Thoth, Ammit, and Osiris, just like in the scene of the judgement court in the tomb of Petubastis.

In tomb C1, Horus wears the white crown[75]. His body is encased in a typical rhombic wrapping of the Roman Period, as shown by the drawing of intersecting diagonal lines with black and red panels. His hands are crossed over his chest. He sits on a throne which is patterned with geometrical designs and chequers coloured in black and white. The winged goddess Isis-Maat stands behind him and protects him with her outstretching arms. She raises her right hand with an offering of the *ankh* sign, while holding the ostrich feather of truth in her lowered left hand, which is close to her body.

---

[75] Von Bissing, *ASAE* 50, 557.; id., *JDAI* 61/62, 2.

Figure 4.21. The judgment court in the so-called 'von Bissing tomb (1913)'.

The cult of Thoth was well-attested in the Panopolite nome, and the House of Life in the temple of Min at Akhmim continued to function during the Graeco-Roman Period[76]. The large quantity of sacred baboon and ibis mummies found in El-Hawawish A attests to the great cult of Thoth in Panopolis[77]. Many of the priests and scribes of the House of Life who served roles related to Thoth preserved and transmitted knowledge about their religious traditions[78]. Thoth, who is sometimes referred to as 'Thoth Who Listens', had his own sanctuary in Akhmim[79]. Känel suggests that the title 'Prophet of Thoth who dwells in the House of Life (*Ḥm nTr ḎHwtj HrJ-jb pr cnx*)' links Thoth to the personnel of the House of Life who were engaged in medicine, the interpretation of dreams and oracles, teaching, and other duties[80]. A stela was found at Akhmim that refers to Thoth with the name *dhwti-sdm*, meaning 'Thoth hears'. It also mentions Thotsytmis as *dhwti-sdm-wtr-ᶜ3 hr-ib Ipw*, or 'Thotsytmis, the Great God, resident at Akhmim'. Furthermore, a village named Ibion[81] may have had an ibis sanctuary[82].

Venit mentions that in the Court of Judgement scene in tomb C1, Horus replaces the traditional figure of Osiris as the presiding judge, emphasizing the celestial connotations of the tomb[83]. Unfortunately, human intervention has caused a significant amount of damage in the tomb, and the wall has crumbled near the image of Horus. Therefore, great parts of Thoth's arms and legs, as well as great parts of the scene, are now demolished. Von Bissing recorded the damaged part of the wall, which depicts small mummiform figures of the four sons of Horus emerging from a huge blue lotus bloom as a symbol of primeval birth[84]. The lotus bloom was also later photographed by Kuhlmann[85].

The use of silhouettes is widespread in the judgement court scenes of El-Salamuni's Graeco-Roman tombs. The concept of punishment after death, as suggested in the judgement scene, continued to be shown in tombs of the Roman period[86]. Punishments awaiting the guilty were described in particularly imaginative ways; their souls were either swallowed by Ammit, or were placed in fire. The devourer's punishment did not differentiate between the poor and the rich, as suggested by the Roman-era Demotic story of Setne II (*P. BM EA 10822*)[87].

The silhouettes sometimes hold negative meanings, and were initially regarded as negative figures[88], representing the godless enemy against whom protection is sought by the deceased. Therefore, the deceased had to get rid of these wicked silhouettes and justify his or her innocence

---

[76] Nordh, *Aspect of Ancient Egyptian Curses and Blessings*, 194–95.
[77] Kuhlmann, *SDAIK* 11, 57 no. 285–86.
[78] Derchain-Urtel, 'Thot à Akhmîm', 173–80.; K. Jansen-Winkeln, 'Die Hildesheimer Stele der Chereunach', *MDAIK* 53 (1997), 91–94.
[79] Derchain-Urtel, 'Thot à Akhmim', 177–17.; Kuhlmann, *SDAIK* 11, 57, no. 285, 286.
[80] Von Känel, *Les prêtres-ouâb de Sekhmet et les conjurateurs de Serket*, 27.; Nordh, *Aspect of Ancient Egyptian Curses*, 106f, 194.; Smith, 'Aspects of the Preservation and Transmission', in A. Egberts et al. (eds.), *Perspectives on Panopolis*, 242.
[81] It is located in the metropolis of the east bank. It may have been a fairly small cultic place, such as a hamlet rather than a village, *P. Ammon* II 50, ll. 10–11, 18, 20.
[82] A sanctuary of Asclepius, where healing of the sick was practiced, was also found in Athribis, El Farag et al., *MDAIK* 41, 1–4, pls. 7–8.
[83] Venit, 'Referencing Isis', in L. Bricault and M. Versylus (eds.), *Isis on the Nile*, 102.
[84] According to the Heliopolitan creation myth, the lotus flower gave rise to the first solar god. In the Coffin Texts, four other primeval male creator gods exist, who may be loosely representative of or related to the four sons of Horus, S. Bickel, *La Cosmogonie egyptienne avant le Nouvel Empire*, OBO 134 (Freiburg 1994), 123–67. From the 18th dynasty until the Roman period, each canopic jar had a head in the shape of a particular figure or son of Horus, Graves-Brown, *Daemons & Spirits*, 112.
[85] Kuhlmann, *SDAIK* 11, fig. 35c.
[86] Venit, *Visualizing the Afterlife*, 110. According to ancient Egyptian beliefs, the deceased would ask the tribunal gods to save his *šwt* from Ammit, who was labelled as the 'Soul-Eater' or the 'Swallower of the Damned'. In CT 335 and 336, the deceased pleads with Atum to save him and his *šwt* from the swallower. The earliest representation of Ammit-Amemet dates to the end of the 18th dynasty, Seeber, *MÄS* 35, 163–84.; C. Leitz, *Lexikon der ägyptischen Götter und Götterbezeichnungen* II (Leuven 2002), 114.; M. Gabolde, 'Une interprétation alternative de la 'pesée du cœur' du Livre des Morts', *Égypte, Afrique & Orient* 43 (2006), 11–22. The Ammit creature guarded the *nsrt* ('Lake of Fire'), E. Abbas, *The Lake of Knives and the Lake of Fire, Studies in the Topography of Passage in Ancient Egyptian Religious Literature* (Oxford 2010).; D. Brewer, 'Shadow', in D. Redford (ed.), *The Oxford Encyclopedia of Ancient Egypt*, III, 277; E. Hornung, *Altägyptische Hollenvorstellung* (Berlin 1968), 29–30.
[87] The Demotic papyrus describes the visit of Setna Khaemwaset and his son Siosiris to the underworld. There, Setna sees two men that are being judged. One is rich, and the other is poor. The judge finds that the rich man's misdeeds outweigh his good deeds, while the poor man's good deeds outweigh his misdeeds. The judges place the poor man, clad in the garments of the wealthy man, 'among the noble spirits, as a man of god who serves Sokar-Osiris and stands near the spot where Osiris is…[while] it was ordered to imprison [the wealthy man] in the netherworld…', with the pivot of a door being eternally fixed in his eye, Lichtheim, *Ancient Egyptian Literature, A Book of Readings, Volume III, The Late Period* (Berkeley, Los Angeles, London 1980), 140–41. For more about the story of Setna, see F. Hoffmann and J. Quack, *Anthologie der demotischen Literatur* (Berlin 2007), 118–37, 340–43.; F. Dunand and C. Zivie-Coche, *Dieux et hommes en Égypte: 3000 av. J.-C. 395 apr. J.-C., Anthropologie religieuse* (Paris, 1991), 313.; M. Smith, *Traversing the Afterlife, Texts for the Afterlife from Ptolemaic and Roman Egypt* (Oxford 2009), 27–29.; Smith, *Following Osiris*, 365, 369, 371. Scholars suggest that the author of the Demotic Setna text may have derived the story from the Greek mythological story of Oknos and Tantalos, who were given the same torments, F. Hoffmann, 'Seilflechter in der Unterwelt', *ZPE* 100 (1994), 339–46.; G. Vittmann, 'Tradition und Neuerung in der demotischen Literatur', *ZÄS* 125 (1998), 68–69.
[88] W. Wreszinki, *Der Grosse medizinische Papyrus des Berlinr Museums* (Leipzig 1909), 17, 19, 70, 73.; M. Lichtheim, 'The Songs of the Harpers', *JNES* 4 (1945), 195, fig. 7.

The Afterlife in Akhmim

in the court to secure a blessed afterlife and enjoy immortality. Those who were deemed too sinful would meet their end either through boiling in the Lake of Fire[89], burning in the fire-cauldron of the Place of Annihilation[90], or being relished as a fatty meal for the devourer, as shown on a fragmentary shroud illustrated by Brunner-Traut[91]. Spells were placed in the tombs of those who had suffered violent deaths in order to counteract the vengeful spirits[92]. Von Bissing suggests that the red interior of the vessel placed before the devourer manifests the Lake of Fire[93]. Likewise, Venit suggests that the silhouettes before Ammit in von Bissing's tomb serve as images of sinners in the fire-cauldron, as depicted in various books of the afterlife[94].

The images of Ammit devouring silhouettes in tomb C1 are interesting because they are unique. Though the devouring of silhouettes is depicted on the Berlin coffin 11652, tomb C1 documents the only known scene of the silhouettes being punished in Graeco-Roman tombs, either by being devoured or by being set on fire. Ammit shows aggressive daemonic behaviour towards the damned silhouettes, which include those of arch-enemies and those with evil pasts who have not been absolved of their sins in the divine tribunal. Those who have been judged to be innocent are automatically out of her reach[95]. Here, the scene also includes a depiction of the 42 judges of the netherworld, called *cm am Sw. wt* or the 'Swallowers of Shadows[96]' (or 'Swallowers of Corpses')[97].

The use of the silhouette is a distinctive feature of the Graeco-Roman tombs of El-Salamuni, where it is characterised by several features. The most important feature is that the silhouettes are only shown in connection to the judgement of the deceased[98]. In fact, the helpful and benevolent actions of some of the black silhouettes in these scenes suggest that these are not the souls of the damned, but rather helpers aiding the deceased in his or her preparation for the afterlife[99]. El-Salamuni is thus the only necropolis with evidence of the ambivalent nature of a silhouette figure within a judgement scene. Here, the silhouette plays a double role, functioning both benevolently and malevolently, as a manifestation of the blessed deceased, and as a tortured victim and/or stubborn enemy who hinders the deceased's transfiguration. This double role of the silhouette gives El-Salamuni a special funerary character, and helps to create a more nuanced understanding of the role these black figures play in the funerary beliefs of Roman Egypt. In this judgement scene, the silhouette functions as a counterweight for the scale[100]. In the El-Salamuni tombs, devouring the silhouettes of

---

[89] S. Quirke, 'Judgement of Dead,' in D. Redford (ed.), *Oxford Encyclopedia of Ancient Egypt* II (Oxford 2001), 211, 214.; J. Zandee, *Death as an Enemy According to Ancient Egyptian Conceptions, Studies in the History of Religions* V (Leiden 1960), 176–77.

[90] Venit, 'Referencing Isis', in L. Bricault and M. Versylus (eds.), *Isis on the Nile*, 114. The shadows are consigned to a cauldron in the Book of the Caverns, alongside other (sometimes decapitated) figures of enemies, shadows, and *bas*. This could be a whole figure, or just body parts, including hearts and heads, A. Piankoff, 'Le Livre des Quererts,' *BIFAO* 42 (1944), 56–57, pl. LI.; E. Hornung, *The Ancient Egyptian Books of the Afterlife* (Ithaca 1999), 88, 89, fig. 45.

[91] Brunner-Traut, *Gelebte Mythen*, 76, 79.

[92] R. Ritner, *The Mechanics of Ancient Egyptian Magical Practice* (Chicago 1997), 180–81.

[93] Von Bissing, *ASAE* 50, 573. Seeber calls it the 'cauldron of fire', citing parallels between the devourer and the Lake of Fire, Seeber, *MÄS* 35, 186.

[94] Venit, 'Referencing Isis', in L. Bricault and M. Versylus (eds.), *Isis on the Nile*, 114. Boiling the shadows (the enemies of Osiris) in either the fiery cauldron or in the Lake of Fire was previously depicted in pharaonic funerary art. The boiling of the shadows is depicted in the 11th hour of the *Amduat* in the tomb of Thutmose III, S. Schott, 'Das blutrünstige Keltergerät', *ZÄS* 74 (1938), pl. vIb.; P. Bucher, *Les textes des tombes de Thoutmosis III et d'Aménophis II*, MIFAO 60 (Cairo 1932), pl. 10. For shadows in the Lake of Fire, see Louvre 3297 (the Papyrus of Bakenmut) in A. Piankoff and N. Rambova, *Mythological Papyri* (New York 1957), 127, pl. 12. The damned shadows are captured before being pressed and roasted according to the court's decree, von Bissing, *ASAE* 50, 573.

[95] R. Lucarelli, 'Demons in the Book of the Dead', in I. Munro, and S. Stöher (eds.), *Totenbuch- Forschungen, Gesammelte Beiträge des 2. Internationalen Totenbuch- Symposiumus 2005*, SAT 11 (Wiesbaden 2006), 207–08.

[96] This is mentioned in the P. Nu, G. Lapp, *the Papyrus of Nu (BM EA 10477), Catalogue of the Books of the Dead in the British Museum* I (London 1997), pl. 66.4.

[97] This is mentioned in P. Neferoubenef, S. Partie, *Le Papyrus de Neferoubenef (Louvre III 93)*, BdÉ 43 (Cairo 1968), pl. 17.684.

[98] Omran, *JARCE* 56, 162, fig.15.

[99] On four Roman mummy shrouds from Saqqara (which are now in the Berlin Ägyptisches Museum (11651)), the Moscow Pushkin Museum of Fine Arts (4229/ I 1a 5749 and 4301/I 1a 5747), and the Paris Louvre (N 3076)), the silhouettes are depicted in the act of rowing a boat, on which they all stand. Other figures are shown drawing water, erecting canopic jars, dressing the deceased, mourning the dead, and possibly performing the Opening of the Mouth rituals by extending an adze-like object to the mouth of the deceased, Riggs, *The Beautiful Burial*, 168–74, fig. 82, pls. 7–9, 277–78.; I. Régen, 'Une iconographie singulière du mort sur des « linceuls » d'époque romaine provenant de Saqqâra', in A. Gasse, F. Servajean, and C. Thiers (eds.), *Et in Ægypto et ad Ægyptum, Recueil d'études dédiées à Jean-Claude Grenier*, CENiM 5 (Montpellier 2012), 612–13, 621–22, 34 figs. 1–4. Parlasca paid great attention to these four shrouds, K. Parlasca, *Mumienporträts und verwandte Denkmäler* (Wiesbaden, 1966), pls. 12.1, 35.1, 61.2.; K. Parlasca et al., *Repertorio d'arte dell'Egitto Greco-romano* (Rome 1977).; K. Parlasca and H. Seemann, *Augenblicke: Mumien-porträts und ägyptische Grabkunst*.; K. Parlasca, 'Osiris und Osirisglaube in der Kaiserzeit', in D. Françoise and P. Lévêque (eds.), *Les syncrétismes dans les religions grecque et romaine: Colloque de Strasbourg, 9–11 juin 1971* (Paris 1973), 95–102.

[100] Silhouettes are also depicted on the coffin of Didyme of the second century AD, found at Zaweit el-Meitin, D. Kurth, *Der Sarge der Teüris, Eine Studie zum Totenglauben im römerzeitlichen Ägypten*, Aeg.Trev. 6 (Mainz 1990), pl. 5. They are also depicted on the Roman-era coffin Louvre AF 13027 from Antinoupolis, dating to the second or third century AD. Here; the silhouette lies on one of the scale's pans while being weighed against a heavy spherical object, E. Brunner-Traut, *Gelebte Mythen*, 70.; Seeber, *MÄS* 35, 77, fig. 23.; Régen, 'Ombres, Une iconographie singulière du mort sur des « linceuls » d'époque romaine provenant de Saqqâra', in A. Gasse, F. Servajean, and C. Thiers (eds.), *Et in Ægypto et ad Ægyptum, Recueil d'études dédiées à Jean-Claude Grenier*, CENiM 5 (Montpellier 2012), 614, fig. 10.; M. Aubert and R. Cortopassi, *Portraits funéraires de 'Égypte romaine, Tome I, masques en stuc. Paris, Réunion des musées nationaux* (Paris 2004), 219–20. Silhouettes are shown in the judgement scene from house-tomb 20 at Tuna El-Gebel. Here, there is a unique depiction of a near skeletal figure in the *orans* gesture, emerging from a vessel that is set on the scale's right pan. Unfortunately, the other pan is now lost. Anubis and Horus, crowned with a solar disc, stand below the crossbar attending each pan. Meanwhile, Thoth (partially damaged) stands in the middle of the beam, S. Gabra, *Fouilles d'Hermoupolis Ouest (Touna El-Gebel) (Avec la collaboration d'Ét. Drioton, P. Perdrizet, and W. Waddell)* (Cairo 1941), 102–03.; Kaplan, *BzÄ* 16, 161–62, pl. 78c, fig.; Venit, *Visualizing the Afterlife*, 112–13. Žabkar suggests a sort of sexual power inherent in these silhouettes, where the black colour of the shadow can be associated with the black earth that makes seeds grow. Likewise, the darkness of the night gives life to a new sun, and the dark colour of Osiris assumes his second birth, L. Žabkar, *A Study of the BA Concept in Ancient Egyptian Texts*, SAOC 34 (Chicago 1968), 104.

the damned was a necessary prelude for rebirth. This is quite similar to the ancient funerary sacrifice of the bull as a representation of Seth[101]. The Lake of Fire or fire-cauldron was also depicted as a means of transforming and revitalizing the sun god and blessed dead[102].

4.2.7: The Lower Register of the Western A4 Wall

Unfortunately, the lower register is partially damaged and suffers from being covered in soot. At the far north end of the wall, closest to the doorway of the burial chamber, a deceased female is depicted. She is garbed in a traditional white garment, complete with a curly wig of hair. She raises her arms, venerating a partially damaged, mummified figure of Osiris, who is wearing the remains of an *atef* crown. A high-footed altar is topped with three loaves of bread and is placed before the deceased. A goddess, probably Isis, stands behind Osiris, embracing him. She is dressed in a green fitted garment with a red disc on her head. During the author's visit in 2015, the figure of Osiris and the altar were still clearly visible (Figures 4.22a-b). Unfortunately, due to the illicit looting of the tomb, the Osiris figure and the altar before him are now partially effaced and faded.

Behind the deceased, a procession of nine knife-wielding daemons stands, each with their back to the figure (Figures 4.23a-b). Six of them are depicted on this wall, while the other three are found on the adjacent A3 wall to the south. The six gatekeepers have the heads of a lion, a bull, a serpent, a crocodile, an ibis, and an equine. The lion and the bull-headed daemons are covered with soot. That the daemonic guardians are associated with the central mortuary themes of protection (such as spell 145) and justification (such as spell 125) can be suggested by their role in spell 145 of the Book of the Dead. Here, they are described as being close in function to the judges of spell 125[103]. In connection to this, the daemons are represented below the Court of Judgment in the tomb scene. Because of the heavy debris covering the lower frieze, von Bissing and Venit mention only four daemons on the wall[104]. These daemons stand menacingly in front of their respective afterlife gates, with guardian snakes from the Book of Gates depicted inside. The daemons wield their attributed knives in their hands[105], and are shown to be hurrying towards the entrance to drive away the evil of the tomb-owner. Wall A4 is fully documented through photogrammetry[106], the creation of a facsimile[107], and the making of a deterioration map (Figures 4.24a-c).

Figure 4.22a. An image of the deceased adoring the mummified figure of Osiris (before the scene's restoration in 2015).

Figure 4.22b. The same scene as that of fig. 22a, this time recorded in 2019. The figure of Osiris is partially damaged, and the altar is destroyed.

The protection of one's tomb by gatekeepers is a widely depicted scene in the Roman funerary iconography of Alexandria and the *chora*. The scenes often show the *ꜥḥ-kheker* pedestal, which is also depicted in ancient Egyptian books of the afterlife such as the Book of the Dead, the Book of the Gates, and the Amduat. The pedestal symbolises that the netherworld gate must be traversed by the deceased on his way to the Field of Reeds. The benevolent daemons deal with the secret knowledge of the netherworld and, more specifically, the names of its doors and its inhabitants. They are always in a protective and static position before their gate, in order to prevent the deceased from passing through it[108]. Hence, the deceased

---

[101] Graves-Brown, *Daemons & Spirits*, 73, 85.
[102] Abbas, *The Lake of Knives and the Lake of Fire*, 397.
[103] As depicted on the exterior of the coffin of Padiamun, A Dautant et al., 'Creativity and Tradition in the Coffin of Padiamun (Liverpool 53.72): A Case–Study of 25th Dynasty Mortuary Practice', in K. Kóthay (ed.), *Proceedings of the International Conference Burial and Mortuary Practices in Late Period and Graeco-Roman Egypt, July 17th–19th, Museum of Fine Arts Budapest* (Budapest 2017), 190.
[104] Von Bissing, *ASAE* 50, 557.; Venit, 'Referencing Isis', in L. Bricault and M. Versylus (eds.), *Isis on the Nile*, 103.
[105] Von Bissing, *ASAE* 50, 557.
[106] It was conducted by W. Asaad of the Sohag Inspectorate.
[107] The facsimile drawings of the tomb were undertaken by A. Abdel-Halim of the Akhmim Inspectorate.

[108] It is depicted in vignette 145 of the Book of the Dead, J. Osing, *Denkmäler der Oase Dachla, aus dem Nachlass von A. Fakhry* AV 28 (Mainz 1982), 77. It is also found in the Book of the Dead spells 148 and 149, S. Quirke, *Going Out in Daylight, Prt m hrw, the Ancient Egyptian Book of the Dead, Translation, Sources, Meaning*, GHP Egyptology 20 (London 2013), 330–31.; E. Hornung, *The Ancient Egyptian Books of the Afterlife* (Ithaca 1999) 57–58.

The Afterlife in Akhmim

Figure 4.23a. A procession of daemons along the lower frieze of the west A4 wall in the antechamber of tomb C1 (before the restoration in 2015).

Figure 4.23b. The procession of daemons along the lower frieze of the west A4 wall in the antechamber of tomb C1 (after the restoration in 2021).

Figure 4.24a. Photogrammetry of the whole west A4 wall (including the upper and lower friezes) of tomb C1.

Tomb C1: The So-called 'Tomb of von Bissing' (1897)

El Salamouni, Tomb C1, Anti Chamber, West Wall, A4.

Figure 4.24b. A facsimile of the whole west A4 wall (including the upper and lower friezes) of tomb C1.

El Salamouni, Tomb C1, Anti Chamber, West Wall, A 4, reconstruction.

Figure 4.24c. A facsimile/reconstruction of the whole west A4 wall (including the upper and lower friezes) of tomb C1.

95

The Afterlife in Akhmim

must get near these doorkeepers, and face and greet them, knowing the names of each portal and its guardian. Such a password is needed in order to obtain passage into the gates of the netherworld of Osiris, and in order to be one of his subjects in the realm of the dead [109]. Consequently, the daemons can be understood to have a positive and beneficent role, their names providing a general glimpse into their function. For each portal, the deceased must also declare that he has been purified in the waters wherein a god is purified, and that he wears a certain type of clothing and holds a particular kind of sceptre, among other things.

One of the features of the El-Salamuni tombs is the widespread depiction of daemons standing before gates (or sometimes standing without gates), brandishing knives (Figure 4.25a). Outside of El-Salamuni, these scenes are also depicted in places such as the tomb of Psenosiris at Athribis (Figure 4.25b). Venit suggests that the 'daemonic protection' offered in the Egyptian tombs of the *chora* was a new phenomenon that only appeared in the early first millennium AD, and that this phenomenon 'does not arise from an Egyptian context', but rather from Greek practices regarding the sanctity of the tomb, recalling the guarding of early Greek tombs by monsters such as sphinxes and sirens. Examples of this can be found in the Moustapha Pasha Tomb I, in the Agathodaemon at Kom El-Schoqafa, and in the tombs at Tigrain [110]. Here, the author disagrees with Venit's idea, believing that the daemonological protection of the tomb is an ancient and traditional iconographic theme.

An altar featuring loaves of bread is additionally common in the funerary art of the El-Salamuni tombs. From the Pharaonic Period onwards, loaves of bread are widely depicted on the offering tables and altars of Akhmim, which are either of a 'canal', or 'Nut' type. In the recently excavated Ptolemaic tomb of Tutu in El-Hawawish A, the loaves are depicted in a more elegant style than at El-Salamuni. The objects which surmount the altars in the El-Salamuni tombs are quite different to the egg-altars in the tomb of Tigrain, where the egg was a main symbol of rebirth and resurrection [111].

4.2.8: The Northern A1 Wall: Left Jamb of the Doorway

The northern A1 wall of tomb C1 contains a doorway into the burial chamber. Only the left door jamb is still preserved. The wall shows a deceased male, who is depicted in a Hellenistic posture. He flanks the doorway into the burial chamber, spanning the size of two registers. This disproportionate size helps confirm his identity as the patron of the tomb. The tomb owner inhabits a spot directly opposite the entrance, and welcomes visitors to the tomb as the first image seen by them [112]. He stands in a frontal, three-quarter view, with his weight shifted onto one foot, evoking the fifth century BC style of sculpting Greek figures [113]. He is dressed in a white everyday garment in a Roman style [114], with a *pallium* (mantle) and a tunic featuring two vertical purple *clavi* stripes [115]. A *himation* is wrapped around his torso; it is placed around his right hip and thrown over his left arm. Two woven *gamma* shapes are depicted on the garment's *cilia* along his left leg [116]. The deceased male has curly hair and a short beard, and wears black leather sandals on his feet with a *lingula* fastening. The knee of his left leg is slightly flexed and the representation of the foot suggests that it is ready for movement. The objects in both of his hands have various religious meanings. Von Bissing mentions that he holds a small brown egg-shaped object in his left hand, which Dr Dragendorff thinks may be a roll of papyrus. Meanwhile, he holds a metal vase with two handles in his right hand [117]. Venit claims that he holds a *rotulus* and a laurel branch, which is a sign of victory, in his uplifted left hand, while holding a *situla* in his lowered right one [118]. However, Kuhlmann believes that he instead holds an olive twig and a papyrus roll in his left hand, and an egg-shaped vessel above another vessel in the other hand [119]. Riggs suggests that the objects are a book roll and a spring of myrtle in his left hand, and a floral garland in the right, and that he

---

[109] Vignette 149 is entitled 'Spell for knowing the mounds of the House of Osiris in the field of Rushes', R. Lucarelli, *The Book of the Dead of Gateschen, Ancient Egyptian Funerary Religion in the 10th Century BC* (Leiden 2006), 173.; R. Lucarelli, 'Daemons in the Book of the Dead', in B. Backes, I. Munro, and S. Stöher (eds.), *Totenbuch-Forschungen*, SAT 11, 209–12.; id., 'Demonology During the Late Pharaonic and Greco-Roman Periods in Egypt', *Journal of Ancient Near Eastern Religions* 11, no. 2 (2011), 115. For more on the guardian daemons in spells 144–47, see id., 'The guardian-demons of the Book of the Dead', *British Museum Studies in Ancient Egypt and Sudan*, BMSAES 15 (2010), 85–102.
[110] Venit, *Visualizing the Afterlife*, 200. The earliest version of Vignette 149 starts with an adoration of Osiris. Later versions of this vignette are placed next to vignette 148, which ends with the adoration of Osiris in his form of Ptah-Sokar-Osiris, R. Lucarelli, 'The Inhabitants of the Fourteenth Hill of Spell 149 of the Book of the Dead', in L. Morenz and A. El Hawary (eds.), *Weitergabe, Festschrift für Ägyptologin Ursula Rössler Köhler zum 65. Geburtstag*, GOF IV, Reihe, Ägypten 53 (Wiesbaden 2015), 275–91.
[111] Eggs are also a Greek symbol of rebirth and regeneration, as depicted in the tombs, D. Kurtz and J. Boardman, *Greek Burial Customs* (Ithaca 1971), 77. The object Syracuse 22789 may also depict a woman holding an egg, A. Fairbanks, *Athenian Lekyothi with Outline Drawing in Glaze Vanish on a White Ground* (New York 1907), 167.
[112] Von Bissing, *ASAE* 50, 558.; id., *JDAI* 61/62, 5.
[113] Venit, *Visualizing the Afterlife*, 187–88.
[114] Von Bissing, *ASAE* 50, 558.; Kuhlmann, *SDAIK* 11, 73, pls. 35c–d, 36a–b.
[115] Venit, *Visualizing the Afterlife*, 188. Venit suggests that, despite the purple stripes, the garment should not be considered to be a *toga praetexta*, Venit, *Visualizing the Afterlife*, 235 no. 1204. Many textiles from Egypt and Akhmim were, however, dyed with other substances of a purple colour. Purple was a symbol of economic capability, social status, and official rank. Jorgensen proposes that the *calvi* are not indicative of one's *equitus* or of one's senatorial class. Furthermore, in Egypt, the purple *calvi* attached to a tunic did not equate with the wearer having Roman citizenship, L. Jorgensen, 'Calvi and Non-calvi, Definition of Various Bands on Roman Textile', in C. Alfaro Giner et al. (eds.), *Textiles y tintes en la ciudad antigua, actas del III Symposium international sobre textiles y tintes del Mediterraneo en el mundo antiguo, Naples, 13 al 15 de noviembre, 2008*, CNRS-EFR, (Valencia 2011), 75–76. Riggs assumes that the Akhmim coffins, where the deceased are dressed in red or purple tunics with *calvi*-like stripes, represent a style of fashion rather than an indication of one's high social status, Riggs, *The Beautiful Burial*, 123.
[116] Riggs, *The Beautiful Burial*, 164. This style of clothing was commonly found on the coffins of males from Roman Panopolis, Riggs, *The Beautiful Burial*, 88–94.
[117] Von Bissing, *ASAE* 50, 558.
[118] Venit, 'Referencing Isis', in L. Bricault and M. Versylus (eds.), *Isis on the Nile*, 104.
[119] Kuhlmann, *SDAIK* 11, 73 no. 373, pls. 36 a, b.

Figure 4.25a. The daemons with their knives, as seen in an unregistered tomb from the northern section of El-Salamuni Mountain.

Figure 4.25b. The daemons standing before their gates, as seen in the tomb of Psenosiris at Athribis.

The Afterlife in Akhmim

is in an offering stance[120]. Outside of the tombs, the same classical figure is also depicted in the tomb of Petosiris at El-Mazawaka, as well as in the Roman temple of Akoris[121].

On the northern A1 wall, to the left of the classical figure of the deceased, the wall is divided into two registers. The upper register shows another taller and slenderer figure of the deceased in profile. He is clean-shaven with short black hair, and wears a long, white, fringed garment. He venerates a fetish of Abydos which is topped with a red sun disc and the feather-crown of Amun. The fetish is flanked with two recumbent rams topped with solar discs[122]. Two Egyptian deities face each other as they erect the effigy. The face of the right one is partially destroyed, but it can be determined that the figure is falcon-headed, resembling Horus. Unfortunately, the upper part of the left deity is effaced, but it may have once shown the ibis-headed god Thoth[123].

The lower register of the north A1 wall shows two offering bearers that face each other. One wears a typical Egyptian costume while the other is partially damaged and garbed in classical clothing. The Egyptian bearer is bald and wears a loincloth with a fringed edge, holding a *hes* libation vase in his lowered left hand and a palm branch in his upraised right hand[124]. The classical figure is missing his face and hair, with only his feet and his white classical garment capable of being distinguished by the viewer[125]. He is meant to be shown presenting offerings. He is bare-footed, and the position of his feet affirms his classical connection, with his weight resting on his left leg and his right leg trailing behind him. Two offering tables heaped with *hes* vases and bread loaves are depicted in between the two bearers[126], ensuring provisions for the deceased[127]. On the southern corner of the wall, behind the Egyptian figure, a *naos*, chapel [128], or entrance to the tomb is depicted, being cut off by an image of what may be a leafy tree (Figures 4.26a-c)[129]. Von Bissing mentions that the scene contains two identical vertical inscriptions upon the libation offerings[130]; which comprise of two *qebeh* vases and two loaves of bread, and the word 'to make/to do' in hieroglyphics[131]. However, in his plan of the tomb, he wrongly defined the location of this scene as wall D, to the left of the tomb's entrance. The partially damaged classical figure, who stands to the right of the offering table, is described by von Bissing as receiving libations[132]. Venit notes that there is also another smaller figure of the deceased shown in a different stance[133]. Because of the damage done to the wall, it is difficult to determine the action that the smaller person is making. However, in reference to the similar libation scene in the tomb of Petosiris, it is likely that the smaller classical figure is meant to be serving the larger classical figure of the deceased.

Distinguishing what kind of tree is depicted in von Bissing's tomb is easy, since the early third century land register P. Bodm. I 1 recto refers to palm trees, olive trees, and vineyard lands that were cultivated in Panopolis[134].

---

[120] Riggs, *The Beautiful Burial*, 164. For more on this figure, see Kaplan, *BzÄ* 16, 167, pls. 86a2, 87a.; Kuhlmann, *SDAIK* 11, pl. 36b.; Von Bissing, *JDAI* 61/62, fig. 2d-e.

[121] Bergmann attests to the fact that these figures are a part of the category of 'Hellenistic-Egyptian' images of Roman Egypt, M. Bergmann, 'Stile und Ikonographien im kaiserzeitlichen Ägypten', in K. Lembke et al. (ed.), *Tradition and Transformation* (Leiden 2010), 1–36 (esp. 16–20), 7b, 10d. Large classical military figures are also depicted in the private house of Kysis, where their iconography reveals their high rank and heroics, G. Bassem et al., 'Wall-Paintings in a Roman House at Ancient Kysis, Kharga Oasis', *BIFAO* 113 (2013), 157–82.

[122] The figure of the fetish in Kaplan's publication shows a recumbent ram at the top right of the fetish, which is now destroyed, Kaplan, *BzÄ* 16, 87a. The traditional *djed* pillar is widely depicted on the chests of Akhmim (*NAM* (Athens), 75), and are typically shown as being either flanked by Isis and Nephthys appearing as women (Alexandria, *GRM*, inv. n. 1623; Strasbourg, IES, inv. n. 1600), or by the animal-headed Anubis and Horus (Paris, Louvre, E 13321 (4589)), Bruwier and Mekis, 'Diversity of the Akhmimic Funerary Art', in M. Mosher (ed.), *The Book of the Dead*, 53, figs. 19, 20, nos. 223–27.

[123] Von Bissing assumes that Thoth is another deity who supports the fetish, von Bissing, *ASAE* 50, 558. Kaplan describes the object as the 'Abydenian fetish', and states that the deities who are shown erecting it are Horus and Thoth, Kaplan, *BzÄ* 16, 167. The Abydos fetish can be used as a replacement for the *djed* pillar, as it has the same attributes. It is widely represented on the rear parts of canopic chests from Akhmim. Here, it is depicted either alone (London BM EA 8532), or accompanied by Anubis and the two sisters of Osiris (London BM EA 8537). Sometimes, it is shown accompanied by Horus, Thoth, Isis, and Maat (Turin, ME cat. no. 2433), M. Bruwier and T. Mekis, 'Diversity at Akhmim', in M. Mosher (ed.), *The Book of the Dead*, 55–56, nos. 241–43.

[124] Von Bissing describes it as an olive twig, von Bissing, *ASAE* 50, 558.

[125] It was in this same damaged state when von Bissing entered the tomb.

[126] Von Bissing, *ASAE* 50, 558, fig. 4.; Kaplan, *SDAIK* 11, 167, pl. 86a.2, 87a. The presentation of offering tables for the deceased recalls the ancient Egyptian funerary practices meant for nobles and high officials. It confirms the high status of the deceased as someone who receives honours in death via the tomb.

[127] The Book of the Dead Papyrus W867 illustrates several rites necessary for the deceased, such as the presentation of the offering table by a priest, who stands behind a lector priest, Graves-Brown, *Daemons & Spirits*, 73.

[128] Von Bissing, *ASAE* 50, 558.

[129] Venit, *Visualizing the Afterlife*, 188–89. In ancient Egypt, exotic flora and fauna were highly desired by royalty and the elite as a source of prestigious luxuries for the tomb owner, D. Abu Stet, 'New Insights into the Significance of Exotic Plants & Animals in Ancient Egypt', in A. Maravelia and N. Guilhou (eds.), *Environment and Religion in Ancient and Coptic Egypt, Sensing the Cosmos Through the Eyes of the Divine*, Archaeopress (BAR Publishing) 30 (Oxford 2020), 25. A classically-clad deceased female is also painted in the Ptolemaic tomb of Petosiris in Tuna El-Gebel, where she is shown standing beside a leafy tree and receiving offerings. She is probably Renpetnofrit, the wife of Petosiris, M. Lefebvre, *Le Tombeau de Petosiris, première partie*, Publications du Service des Antiquités de l'Égypte (Cairo 1924), 107.

[130] This libation table is similar to the traditional 'canal-type' altars that are widely known from Akhmim during the third century BC, Bruwier and Mekis, 'Diversity of the Akhmimic Funerary Art', in M. Mosher (ed.), *The Book of the Dead*, 14–16, no. 71.

[131] Von Bissing, *ASAE* 50, 558, fig. 4.

[132] Von Bissing, *ASAE* 50, 558.

[133] Venit, *Visualizing the Afterlife*, 188.

[134] The Panopolite nome was known for its cultivated lands. A village named Σενπανενωλ, or 'Shenaloletas', which was the birth place of Shenoute, is nowadays the modern village of Shandawil. It is located about 15km. north of Akhmim, and was famous as the land of vines and trees, being called *T3-s.t-n3-3rly.w*, K. Zauzich, 'Drei demotisch-koptische Ortsnamen aus der Gegend von Achmim', *Enchoria* 11 (1982), 118. Amelineau identifies the land as Shandawil (Chandaouil), Amelineau, *La géographie de l'Égypte*, 426–427. Sauneron however, identifies Shandawil as Psinabla, S. Sauneron, *Villes et legends*, 101–07 (=*BIFAO* 66 (1968), 11–17); Gauthier, *BIFAO* 10, 93. The author is convinced that this debate suggests the existence of two villages named Shandawil, or rather, of one named Shandawil and another known as the Jazirat of Shandawil, lying ca. 1.5km. east of Shandawil. Both of them are on the west bank of the Nile, and only the Sohag-Assiut highway separates them. This area is still famous for its gardens and farms. Hence, Amelineau must have meant the Jazirat of Shandawil, while Sauneron meant that Psinabla is the village of Shandawil itself. For the lands in the Panopolite nome, see T. Derda, *P. Bodmer I Recto, A Land List from the Upper Panopolite Nome in Upper Egypt (after AD 213/4)*, *JJP*

Min is closely associated with the date palm, which represents wealth and fertility[135]. The persea tree, or *persicum*, was also familiar in Panopolis, as a symbol of the god Perseus/Min. The Greek and Latin sources state that Perseus introduced the persea plant into Egypt, and that it was a sacred tree in his festivals[136], being widely found in the sacred areas near Panopolite temples and tombs[137]. This is because the deceased wanted to surround themselves with beautiful, idealized landscape scenes in the hopes that their afterlives would be as carefree and blessed as the land[138].

Many different types of clothing have been recovered from Late Roman cemeteries in Egypt. They include tunics, mantels, cloaks, shawls, scarves, and sashes[139]. The artistic representations of clothing reflect the opulent fashion of elite ancient Egyptians, especially during the Roman period. Though it is difficult to say if Panopolis transformed from a temple city into a classical metropolis in the Roman period, one can say that Panopolis became more Hellenised and Romanised. Plain, classical models of the deceased are extensively depicted in the tombs of El-Salamuni. Venit suggests that this classical model, as seen in both tomb C1 and in the tomb of Petosiris at El-Mazawaka, marks a point of intersection between the classical world and that of Egypt. It recalls the idealistic ancient Egyptian portraits of the honoured elite dead found in Old Kingdom tombs. In these scenes, figures of the dead span multiple registers and are often the largest figures in the tomb, showing the inheritance of the so-called 'Egyptianising' artistic style in Roman Egypt[140]. In contrast to typical classical funerary art, in this model, the Greek gods are depicted on a greater scale than humans[141]. Riggs claims that these classical models of the dead, which appear on shrouds and in tombs, evoke a Greek identity as their reference point rather than a Roman one, especially since they follow the Greek fashion of dress[142]. On the contrary, Whitehouse argues for Hellenistic influences in the figure of Petosiris, as evidenced by his style of dress and pose, which is derived from Hellenistic and Roman sculptures[143]. Castiglione mentions that the classical style of the deceased shows both real and spiritual aspects, and is a vivid indicator of the so-called 'double style', where the patron represents himself in his tomb with a two-sided character. The deceased is garbed in a realistic Hellenistic style, but is placed among examples of an Egyptian spiritual iconography[144].

Reconstructing the funerary rituals performed at tomb C1 is quite difficult due to its long period of reuse, its continuous history of looting, and the lack of proper excavations and documentation. Von Bissing suggests that the antechamber was meant for the cult of the deceased, and that a ritual veneration of the deceased took place inside the tomb[145]. In both von Bissing's and Petosiris' tombs, the owners enjoyed a kind of cult where they received and offered ritual acts[146]. Garbing the deceased in a *pallium* suggests that the deceased held a higher status, especially since the *pallium* was the traditional dress of philosophers, scholars, and those who appear cultured[147]. In Roman Egypt, the cult of the dead was prominent; before burial, mummies were kept on display in local houses for a period of time in order to participate in their family life and ritual customs[148]. After the burial, regular family visits and funerary banquets took place at the tombs on specific days that were set aside for practicing the cult

---

suppl. 14 (Warsaw 2010). Trees were a traditional feature of Egyptian art in the Ptolemaic and Roman Periods, and had a cultic function; the choice of trees was based upon religious and symbolic considerations, C. Thiers, 'Les jardins de temple aux époques tardives', in S. Aufrère (ed.), *Encyclopédie religieuse de l'Univers végétal, Croyances phytoreligieuses de l'Égypte ancienne I*, OrMonsp 10 (Montpellier 1999), 107.

[135] M. Lurker, *The Gods and Symbols of Ancient Egypt, An Illustrated Dictionary* (London 1980), 94.; I. Wallert, *Die Palmen in alten Ägypten. Eine Untersuchung ihrer praktischen, symbolischen und religiösen Bedeutung*, MÄS 1 (Berlin, 1962), 109–10.

[136] Arboriculture was widespread in Panopolis, and orchards are mentioned in several land leases in the following: P. Panop. 14, P. Ammon II 50–56, and P. Cair. Masp. II 67170, D. Hagedron, 'Papyri aus Panopolis in der Kölner Sammlung', in D. Samuel (ed.), *Proceedings of the Twelfth International Congress of Papyrology*, Am. Stud. Pap. 7 (Toronto 1970), 209. On the persea tree and its symbolic meaning in Graeco-Roman Egypt, see S. Caneva, 'The Persea Tree from Alexander to Late Antiquity, a Contribution to the Cultural and Social History of Greco-Roman Egypt', AncSoc 46 (2016), 46, 58.; M. Malaise, 'Le persea, l'olivier, le lierre et la palme dans la religion égyptienne tardive', in T. Duquesne (ed.), *Hermes Aegyptiacus, Egyptological Studies for B.H. Stricker on his 85th Birthday*, DE, special number 2 (Oxford 1996), 131–44.; S. Amigues, 'Sur le perséa d'Égypte', in *Hommages à Francois Daumas*, I (Montpellier 1986), 25–31. Ptolemagrios planted persea trees along the *dromos* to the main entrance of the Pan temple, while palm trees were planted inside its precinct, to the right of the temple building, Thiers, 'Les jardins de temple aux époques tardives', in S. Aufrère (ed.), *Encyclopédie religieuse*, 111. The modern Arabic name 'Karm al-Taur', meaning the 'Garden of the Bull', was most often attributed to the beautiful gardens of the temple of Pan/Perseus at Akhmim, Wainwright, JEA 21, 158–70.; A. Lloyd, 'Herodotus on Egyptian Buildings, a Test Case,' in A. Powell (ed.), *The Greek World* (London, New York 1995), 291. Furthermore, persea trees were widely planted in Panopolis for religious purposes. Persea wood was also used for ship building, along with acacia wood, L. Casson, 'Documentary Evidence for Greco-Roman Shipbuilding (P. Flor. I 69), BASP 27 (1990), 15–19.

[137] Theophr. H.P. IV, 2.5.

[138] The lettuce plant of Min was wrongly identified as a persea by A. Gayet, *Le Temple du Louxor*, IFAO 15 (Cairo 1894), 42, 50, 73, 84.

[139] P. Hooft, *Pharaonic and Early Medieval Egyptian Textiles* (Leiden 1994), 149–50.; S. Lewis, *Early Coptic Textiles* (Stanford 1969), 8.

[140] Venit, *Visualizing the Afterlife*, 189–99. In ancient Egypt, large statues of the elite dead were placed in their tombs as a means of enabling them to achieve a position in the underworld and the next world, J. Baines, 'Society, Morality, and Religious Practice', in B. Shafer et al. (eds.), *Religion in Ancient Egypt, Gods, Myths, and Personal Practice* (Ithaca, London 1991), 183.

[141] Venit refers to a popular Roman relief from the Lateran Museum, which shows one of the humans on a larger scale than the other figures in the scene, Venit, 'Referencing Isis', in L. Bricault and M. Versylus (eds.), *Isis on the Nile*, 199. An exception to this can be found on a Roman portrait which is possibly from Ostia, and is now in the Lateran Museum, B. Bandinelli, *Rome, the Centre of Power, 500 BC to 200 AD* (New York 1970), 263, fig. 294.; id., *Visualizing the Afterlife*, 199, 238, no. 1300.

[142] Riggs, *The Beautiful Burial*, 165.

[143] Whitehouse, 'Roman in Life', in O. Kaper (ed.) *Life in the Fringe*, 259.

[144] Castiglione, *Dualité du style dans l'art*, 209–30.

[145] Von Bissing, ASAE 50, 559.

[146] Riggs, *The Beautiful Burial*, 164.

[147] A. Groom, *Roman Clothing and Fashion* (Gloucestershire 2010).

[148] The so-called mummy label of Takhenmet, the daughter of Petarsomtheus, records a period of a year and four months between the time of her death and burial, D. Montserrate, 'Death and Funerals in the Roman Fayum', in M. Bierbrier (ed.), *Portraits and Masks, Burial Customs in Roman Egypt* (London 1997), 38.

The Afterlife in Akhmim

Figure 4.26a. The north A1 wall, located in the antechamber of tomb C1, Kaplan, *BzÄ* 16, fig. 87a.

of the dead[149]. This custom was presumably performed in El-Salamuni; von Bissing reports the finding of a long bench encircling a Late Roman tomb. This bench served as a *klinium*, or a place of rest, for the tomb visitors. Moreover, as mentioned above, numerous burial gifts such as vases and amphorae were also found, providing the deceased with a comfortable lifestyle in the afterlife[150]. Benches were found in the forecourt of many El-Salamuni tombs such as tomb B2. These benches are in the form of banqueting couches and are all are cut from living rock. Unlike the typical Egyptian tradition of performing rituals in the entrance to the tomb, the practice of performing rituals inside the tomb at El-Salamuni was uncommon. This is because the smell must have been intolerable, as is attested by a Greek inscription: '*Wanderer, do not pass me in silence, me, the son of Epimachos! Stay, the odour of cedar oil shall not make you sad. Remain and listen a bit to the good smelling deceased*'[151]. Furthermore, the

---
[149] The banquets could take place in the tomb itself, as the *triclinium* dining room of Kom El-Schouqafa suggests, or may have taken place near the tomb in the necropolis, as in Tuna El-Gebel, D. Montserrat, 'The Kline of Anubis', *JEA* 78 (1992), 301–07.; id., 'The Representation of Young Males in 'Fayum Portraits', *JEA* 79 (1993), 215–25.; id., 'Death and Funerals', in M. Bierbrier (ed.), *Portraits and Masks*, 33–44.; J. Willeitne, 'Tomb and Burial Customs after Alexander the Great', in R. Schulz and M. Seidel (eds.), *Egypt, the World of the Pharaohs* (2004), 313–21.
[150] Von Bissing, *ASAE* 50, 565–66, fig. 10.; Kuhlmann, *SDAIK* 11, 81.
[151] This quote is cited by Lembke as being found in Tuna El-Gebel, K. Lembke, 'A 'Beautiful Burial' at Tuna El-Gebel, Burial Customs

Figure 4.26b. Photogrammetry of the north A1 wall of tomb C1 (after the restoration in 2021).

El Salamouni, Tomb C1, Anti Chamber, North Wall, A1.

Figure 4.26c. A facsimile of the north A1 wall of tomb C1.

mounds of pottery sherds found on the mountain, and especially in the area between tomb C1 and the temple of Ay, include remnants of many drinking cups and small flasks (*unguentaria*) (Figure 4.27)[152]. Dragendorff, a Roman pottery specialist, collected several fragments of matte red pottery from the rubble that were made to imitate the shape and appearance of *terra sigillata*[153]. This suggests that family visits and funerary banquets most probably took place outside the tombs itself[154].

The offering frieze shown on wall A1 is multi-cultural and multi-faceted, depicting both Egyptian and classical offering bearers as they present their offerings for the classical-style deceased. The offering bearers are associated with both the supply of water and food for the deceased, confirming the intended presence of a ritual funerary cult in the tomb. Generally, in Ptolemaic cemeteries, a mortuary priest would have performed the religious services and presented the purificatory offerings for the deceased[155]. The offering bearers that are depicted in tomb C1 are therefore probably acting in the traditional function of the *choachyte*, or '*Χοαχύτης*-priest', a role which involved being in charge of the tombs in the Theban necropolis during the Graeco-Roman Period[156]. These priests served various functions, including acting as *w3ḥ-mw.w* priests. The term *w3ḥ-mw.w* translates to mean 'the One Who Offers Water', but the title is also sometimes the 'Pourer of the Water'. Later, this type of priest was called a *choachyte* in Greek[157].

---

and Commemorative Culture from the Ptolemies to the Romans', in M. Nenna, S. Huber, and W. Van Andriga (eds.), *Constituer la tombe, honorer les défunts en Méditerranée antique, Etudes Alexandrines* 46 (Alexandria 2018), 160–61.; id., 'City of the Dead', in E. O'Connell (ed.), *Perspectives from New Fieldwork*, 90.

[152] M. Naguib, a pottery specialist and the Director of the Abydos Inspectorate Office, claims that some of the discovered pottery vessels date back to the late fourth century AD. This suggests that the funerary rituals in El-Salamuni continued at this date.

[153] Von Bissing, *ASAE* 50, 566, fig. 11.

[154] Fireplaces are not yet recorded for the necropolis of Tuna El-Gebel, K. Lembke, 'A Beautiful Burial', 160, fig.18.

[155] See P. Turin 2130 (99 BC), P. Berlin P. 3106 (98 BC), P. Berlin P. 3139 (98 BC), and P. Turin 2132 (98 BC).

[156] The *choachyte* is also attested in Edfu (M. Cannata, *Three Hundred Years of Death 10, the Egyptian funerary Industry in the Ptolemaic Period, Culture and History of the Ancient Near East* (Leiden, Boston 2020), 110, 51–52.), in Hawara (Cannata, 65–66, 68–69, 84.), in Memphis (Canaata, 54–55, 57–61.), and in Middle Egyptian necropoleis (Canaata 91, 101–03.). Cannata discusses the Theban *choachytes* as well (Cannata, 159–66.).

[157] The *W3H-mw* acts on behalf of the deceased's relatives to make the funeral arrangements. Their duties typically include delivering the body to an embalmer, purchasing the necessary materials for mummification, obtaining a burial place, and transporting the mummy to the tomb. After the funeral, the *W3H-mw* is in charge of the cult of the deceased, including the act of regularly visiting the tomb to provide offerings such as water, food, and prayers. For the burial tasks of the *W3H-mw* in the Ptolemaic Period, see M. Cannata, *The Regalia of Egyptian Burial Practices in the Ptolemaic Period (332–30 BC)* (Oxford 2009).

Figure 4.27. Dumps of pottery sherds beneath the temple of Ay.

In Akhmim, the *imi r3 x3s.wt* ('Overseer of the Necropolis'), is known from the Saite Period onwards. The main duties of this overseer involved collecting burial taxes and supervising various affairs concerning the necropolis[158]. Another priestly title, *imy-iset* (meaning 'chamberlain/officer'), frequently occurs together with the title *hezek*[159], who assisted in watching over funerary worshippers in the tombs of the necropolis[160]. The *hezek* had a more administrative function than religious; '*he presided more particularly over the reserves of cult objects, the clothing stores, [and] the treasury where the garments were kept, and supervised the preparation of ointments*'[161]. The presentation of food and water to the deceased by two offering bearers on wall A1 helps to identify the offering bearers as *choachyte* priests in the act of performing cultic funerary activities[162]. Their donated cultic water[163] symbolises the Nile's inundation and guarantees longevity and cosmic integration[164]. Von Lieven mentions that '*in fact, the choachytal acts are by no means the only sources proving that Greeks or at least persons with Greek names could receive an Egyptian cult as deified persons*'[165]. As for the offering of water, it continued to be an essential rite conducted by the funerary cult for the deceased during the Roman period[166]. After all, the El-Salamuni necropolis

---

[158] Iah-mes, the eldest among four brothers (the others being Hor, Herresenet, and Heremeheb), inherited this important title of 'Overseer of the Necropolis' from his father, Djed-Hor, M. Malinine 'Taxes funéraires égyptiennes à l'époque Gréco-Romaine', in M. Mariette, *BdÉ* 32, *IFAO* (Cairo 1961), 138–45, Pls. i–vi.; Von Känel, *Les prêtres-ouâb de Sekhmet*, 90. Iah-mes was a real scientist; he was both the Overseer of the Physicians (*jmj-rA wab-xm.t*) and the Prophet of Thoth Who Dwells in the House of Life (*Hm-nTr +Hwtj Hrj-jb pr-ꜥnx*), a position which also involved medicine, the interpretations of dreams and oracles, teaching, and other responsibilities, C. Nordh, *Aspects of Ancient Egyptian Curses and Blessings, Conceptual Background and Transmission, Uppsala Studies in Ancient Mediterranean and Near Eastern Civilizations* 26. (Uppsala 1996), 106f, 194.; Smith 'Aspects of the Preservation and Transmission', in A. Egberts et al. (eds.), *Perspectives on the Nile*, 242. Together with his three brothers, Iah-mes officiated Min's oracular ceremonies. Meanwhile, his son, Iret-Hor-ru, gained the position of First Prophet. Recently, a statue of him from Cuma (ancient Cumae), Italy was discovered and unearthed, together with a statue of Isis and a statue of a sphinx dating to somewhere between the first century BC and second century AD, C. Cozzolini, 'Recent Discoveries in Campania', in R. Pirelli (ed.), *Egyptological Studies for Claudio Barrocas, Serie Egittologica 1. Istituto Universitario Orientale* (Napoli 1999), 21–36.; M. Bruwier and T. Mekis, 'Diversity of the Akhmimic Funerary Art', in M. Mosher (ed.), *The Book of the Dead* 7, no. 36.

[159] Parker 'A Saite Oracle Papyrus from Thebes', 30, 33. The title *hezek* is mainly associated with the Osiris cult, Gauthier, *Le personnel du dieu Min*, 68–69.; H. Meulenaere, 'Le clergé abydénien d'Osiris à la Basse Époque', *OLP* 6/7 (1975/1976), 33–151.

[160] Gauthier, *Les Fêtes du dieu Min*, 67.

[161] J. Goyon, *Rituels funéraires de l'ancienne égypte, Litteratures anciennes du Proche-Orient* 4 (Paris 2000), 97.; S. Aufrère, 'Études de lexicologie et d'histoire naturelle, IV-VI', *BIFAO* 84 (1984), 2–3.

[162] On the roles of the priest, see O. El-Aguizy, 'The Priesthood of the Temple of 'Medinet-Habu' in the Ptolemaic Period Through the Demotic Texts' (in Arabic), in N. Grimal et al. (eds.), *Hommages a Fayza Haikal*, *BdÉ* 138, *IFAO* (Cairo 2003), 4–15. In the Ptolemaic Period, the *choachytes* performed the ancient Egyptian priestly function of the *w3H ix.t*, or 'the One who Makes Offerings'. These tasks included not only funeral preparations, but also the presentation of food offerings after the funeral, as well as the upkeep of the mortuary cult of the deceased in his tomb. In ancient Thebes, up until the Roman Period, the *choachytes* carried out the performance of the cult on Amenope's behalf, preparing weekly feasts either as part of the funerary cult or as part of the cult of divine ancestors, F. Cenival, *Les associations religieuses en Égyp'e d'après les documents démotiques*, *BdÉ* 46 (Cairo 1972), 103. On the *choachytes* in the Theban necropolis in the Ptolemaic Period, see P. Pestman, *The Archive of the Theban Choachytes (Second Century BC)* (Leuven 1993).; S. Vleeming, 'The Office of a Choachyte in the Theban Area', in S. Vleeming (ed.), *Hundred-Gated Thebes, Acts of a Colloquium on Thebes and the Theban Area in the Graeco-Roman Period, P.L. Bat.* 27 (Leiden 1995), 246–48.

[163] M. Bommas, 'Situlae and the Offering of Water in the Divine Funerary Cult, A New Approach to the Ritual of Djeme,' in A. Amenta et al. (eds.), *L'acqua 'ell'antico Egitto, vita, rigenerazione, incantesimo, medicamento; Proceedings of the First International Conference for Young Egyptologists, Italy, Chianciano Terme, October 15–18, 2003* (Roma 2005), 258–62.

[164] M. Bommas, 'Schrein unter, Gebel es-Silsilah im Neuen Reich', in G. Heike, E. Hofmann, and M. Bommas (eds.), *Grab und Totenkult im alten Ägypten, Festschrift Jan Assmann* (München 2003), 88–103.

[165] A. von Lieven, 'Of Choachytes and Saints, Demotic Documentary Texts as Sources for Religious Practices,' in R. Jasnow and G. Widmer (eds.), *Illuminating Osiris, Egyptological Studies in Honor of Mark Smith* (Atlanta 2017), 242.

[166] The formula 'May Amenope pour out water on his day of coming to the valley' is repeated on funerary monuments dating up until the Roman period in Thebes, F. Herbin, *Le Livre de Parcour'r l'éternité*, *OLA* 58 (Leuven 1994), 140–45. A Roman shroud from Thebes is now in the North Carolina Museum of Art, classified as Inv. L. 57.14. 95. It shows the deceased facing Osiris, and the inscription reads: 'may you receive

was under the full auspices of the god Min, and water tends to be a constant element when Min is worshipped, especially in desert areas. This is certainly related to Min's role as a fertility god[167]. Sacred water continued to be an important mortuary element of the local community of Panopolis during the Coptic Period as well[168].

Furthermore, when an Egyptian priest is depicted holding a palm branch in his right hand, it may identify him as a θακλλαδότης priest, or a 'a Deliverer of Branches'[169] to visitors in temples and shrines. This was a known position in the Panopolite clergy[170]. When the palm frond is held by the deceased, or is shown lying upon a coffin, it is meant to symbolise the overcoming of death, and the promise of eternity in connection to rebirth[171].

The holding of the *rotulus* and the *situla* in the hands of the deceased also has its funerary meanings. The typical Hellenistic image of the elite deceased involves a formal fashion and the holding of a scroll. The scroll is a symbol for the wealthy and elite, as it refers to Roman sculptures where scrolls are depicted in a basket placed near intellectual or public figures[172]. The Egyptian iconography of the *rotulus*, as held in the hands of the deceased, is associated with multiple words, such as *mD3.t* ('books'), *sfdw* ('rolls'), *sS* ('knowledge'), and others[173]. The magical knowledge recorded in these rolls includes the *rn*, or 'name', of the owner. Such names were used as magical and powerfully protective symbols, helping the deceased along his or her journey to the afterlife[174].

The ancient Egyptian custom of depicting the deceased with a papyrus roll in his or her hands continues in the funerary art of Roman Egypt, developing a new and syncretic classical model. Besides the tombs of Petosiris and von Bissing, the holding of the *rotulus* by the deceased is also frequently shown on Roman coffins and shrouds[175]. Quaegebeur concludes that these folded and stamped papyri, which were written in Demotic and placed in the hands of the deceased, were 'letters of recommendation' written by Thoth to usher the deceased into the beyond[176]. Whitehouse claims that the papyrus roll which Petosiris holds in his hands thus acts as a 'letter of recommendation' which he can present to Anubis as a passport or as proof that he should be accepted into the realm of Osiris and

---

the offering of water by Amenope', K. Parlasca, 'Bemerkungen zum ägyptischen Gräberwesen der griechisch-römischen Zeit', in *Ägypten, Dauer und Wandel, Symposium anlässlich des 75jährigen Bestehens des DAI Kairo am 10. und 11. Oktober 1982, SDAIK* 18 (Mainz 1985), 99, no. 6, pl.4a. On Late Roman mummy masks from Thebes, the dead appear to be holding a chalice of wine in their hands, Grimm, *Die römischen Mumienmasken*, pl. 112.; C. Riggs, 'Roman Period Mummy Masks from Deir El-Bahari', *JEA* 86 (2000), 121–44.; id., *The Beautiful Burial*, 233–43, figs. 117, 119–21.

[167] Bernand, *Pan du désert*, 270–71. Graffiti at Wadi Bir El-Aïn shows that the large, inscribed rock and the *bir* were consecrated to Sheikh Shakhoun, who is said to have had the gift of being able to fertilize women who come to him, begging him for help, and drinking his water, O. Meinardus, 'Bir al-'Ain, eine volkstümliche Kultstätte bei Akhmim', *OstkStud* 34 (1985), 185. Sheikh Shakhoun was said to be the modern representative of the fertility god Min, disguised in an Islamic cloth. A local festival was celebrated yearly in Bir El-Aïn in his honour. Here, the people of Akhmim, including both Christians and Muslims, gathered and performed rituals, celebrating for three or four days. They believed that a drink or a bath from the holy water would help them achieve their desires to have children and would bring other kinds of fortune as well, Kanawati, *Sohag in Upper Egypt*, 39. In Thebes, Min was assimilated with the primeval god Amon, presumably because of the fertility aspect of both gods. Like Amon, Min was also a sky god, combining weather and fertility, Wainwright, *JEA* 21, 152–70.

[168] Ever since Jesus is said to have blessed the Bir El-Aïn spring, the bedouins of the Wadi Bir El-Aïn have had the practice of mixing water from the well at Mecca with the water of this spring, Meinardus, 'Bir El-Aïn', 185.

[169] The title of *Pr-swn* is mentioned in a *thallodotes* from Psonis (*CEML* 139= *CEMG* 2176: P. Oxy. XLIII 3094, ll. 40, 43). This was a resting place for the royal troops in 298 AD, in preparation for the impending visit of Diocletian to the Panopolite nome, *P. Beatty. Panop*. 1.262. Palm branches are also depicted next to the text of some mummy labels from Akhmim, Quaegebeur, 'Mummy Labels', *P.L. Bat.* 19, 240.

[170] The palm branch was used in funerary iconography, and mainly symbolised longevity, conveying the idea of the deceased's triumph over death, and confirming one's positive posthumous state. The palm branch was laid on the mummy's chest, P. Dils, 'Stucco Heads of Crocodiles: A New Aspect of Crocodile Mummification', *Aegyptus* 70 (1990), 82.; H. Willems and W. Clarysse, *Les Empereurs du Nil, à la mémoire de Jan Quaegebeur* (Leuven 2000), 282–83, cats. 217–18. The branch was also associated with the jubilant figure of the deceased in the judgement court, representing the positive result of the Weighing of the Heart, Seeber, *MÄS* 35, 101–08, figs. 35–40.; D. Kurth, *Materialien zum Toten glauben im römerzeitlichen Ägypten* (Hützel 2010), 80, fig. 5. In the ancient Roman world, the palm branch was also considered a sign for victory, K. Dunbabin, *Mosaics of the Greek and Roman World* (Cambridge 1999), 70, fig. 71. It was stamped onto imperial coinage, R. Pool, *Catalogue of Coins of Alexandria and Its Nomes* (London 1892), I no. 4, 27 no. 218, 29 no. 233, 31 no.251, 45 no. 365, 46 no. 381, 53 nos. 438, 442 and 443, 61 no. 508, 63, no. 526.; Venit, *Visualizing the Afterlife*, 235 no. 1208. The palm was most closely associated with the Isiac cycle and Anubis. In a Greek papyrus of the Roman Period, which is now in Leiden, Anubis states '*I am the tree which is called Palm (bais), I'm the efflux of the blood of the palm branches from the tomb of the great one (i.e., Osiris)*', K. Preisendanz, *Papyri Graecae Magicae* II (Leipzig, Berlin 1931), 73. The palm branch was one of the main offerings for the god during the festival of *Khoiak*, P. Koemoth, *Osiris et les Arbres, Contribution à l'étude des Arbres sacrés 'e l'Égypte ancienne*, Liège, AegLeod 3 (Liège 1994), 272.

[171] Kaplan, *BzÄ* 116, 119, pls. 26 b, c.

[172] See, for instance, the statue of Sophocles in the Musco Gregorian, Venit, 'Referencing Isis', in L. Bricault and M. Versylus (eds.), *Isis on the Nile*, 198–99, nos. 1292–93.

[173] *BD* 42, 157.

[174] Many faience models of papyrus rolls were found in the royal burials, A. Wiese and A. Brodbeck, *Tutankhamun, Das goldene Jenseits, Grabschätze aus dem Tal der Könige* (München 2004), 156–57, cat. 14. During the Late Period and the Ptolemaic Period, papyrus rolls were attached to the body of the deceased for protective functions, and rolls of papyri featuring the Book of the Dead were also wrapped into the mummies of the Ptolemaic Period, Bayer-Niemeier et al., *Ägyptische Bildwerke III*, 254, abb. 62A.; O. Illés, *An Unusual Book of the Dead Manuscript from TT 32, Acta Antiqua* (2006), 119–27.; J. Budka, 'Neues zu den Nutzungsphasen des Monumentalgrabes von Anch-Hor, Obersthofmeister der Gottesgemahlin Nitokris (TT 414)', *Ägypten und Levante* 18 (2008), 70–71.; C. Martin and R. Kim, 'Put My Funerary Papyrus in My Mummy, Please', *JEA* 92 (2006), 270–74.

[175] Some examples include a mummy shroud in the Pushkin Museum (inventory number I.1a. 5749), the coffin Berlin *ÄM* 17126 from Abusir El-Meleq, as well as the Roman P. London BM EA 9995. One is found in the Fitzwilliam Museum as number E. 103.1911 (Parlasca, *Mumienporträts und verwandte Denkmäler*), and two others are in the Louvre as E 12379 (Aubert and Cortopassi, *Portraits funéraires de l'Égypte romaine*, 161, cat. D19), and Louvre AF 21587. For further information about the papyrus rolls in vignettes of the Book of the Dead, see M. Tarasenko, 'Images of papyrus rolls in vignettes of the Book of the Dead', in K. Kóthay (ed.), *Burial and Mortuary Practices in Late Period and Graeco-Roman Egypt: Proceedings of the International Conference Held at the Museum of Fine Arts, Budapest, 17–19 July 2014* (Budapest 2017), 73–80, pls. 8–12.

[176] J. Quaegebeur, 'P. Brux Dem. E. 8258, une lettre de recommandation pour l'au-delà', in S. Israelit-Groll (ed.), *Studies in Egyptology Presented to Miriam Lichtheim* II (Jerusalem 1990), 776–95.

The Afterlife in Akhmim

the afterlife[177]. Depauw argues against this interpretation due to the lack of epistolary elements; he has some reservations about using the term 'letter' to describe the texts. Nonetheless, Depauw confirms the relationship between these short Demotic texts and the Hieratic Books for Breathing in his publication from 2003; he shows how two papyri that were written for the same deceased individual were likely intended for placement beneath the head and feet of the body[178]. Smith proposes that the classification of these texts as letters for breathing depends not so much on their actual contents, but rather on their intended functions. These texts were used by the deceased, who presented them upon their arrival at the gates of the underworld in order to obtain the privileges that were bestowed upon the blessed[179]. The labels found on the versos of the *cnḫ p3* papyri indicate that their ultimate destination was the netherworld, to be presented before Osiris[180].

The Isiac attributes in tomb C1 suggest that the mortal figures depicted on its walls are initiates into the cult of Isis. Here, the *situla* is not only an artistic feature, but also carries a funerary association, providing clues into the meanings of the tomb's Isiac elements[181]. In the Roman world, the *situla* was firmly associated with Isis as one of her cultic attributes in her *Iseum*[182]. The bronze *situla* was related to elite banquets and symbolic drinking rituals in Rome[183]. Hence, in El-Salamuni, the holding of a *situla* by the deceased identifies the deceased as an adherent of Isis[184], and suggests that the deceased person may be a *wn-pr*, or *pastophoros*, which translates to mean 'shrine bearer' or 'shrine-opener' in English[185]. This was an important position in Roman Egypt[186]. The portrayal of the classical-style deceased in El-Salamuni as a worshipper of Isis and as an adherent of her cult helps the deceased to conquer death, overcoming the agony of dying and justifying the desired posthumous state[187]. The cult of Isis

---

[177] Whitehouse, 'Roman in Life' in O. Kaper (ed.), *Life in the Fringe*, 26.; S. Vleeming, 'A Priestly Letter of Recommendation (P. CtYBR inv. 4628)', in R. Jasnow and G. Widmer (eds.), *Illuminating Osiris, Egyptological Studies in Honor of Mark Smith* (Atlanta 2017), 375–78. On the veneration of Petosiris, see W. Omran, 'Petosiris in his Tomb at Dachla, Venerating the Deceased in Roman Egypt', *Journal of the Association of Arab Universities for Tourism and Hospitality* 19, no. 3 (2020), 97–112.

[178] M. Depauw, 'A 'Second' Amuletic Passport for the Afterlife: P. Sydney Nicholson Museum 346 b', *SAK* 31 (2003), 93–99.

[179] M. Smith, 'A Demotic Formula of Intercession for the Deceased', *Enchoria* 19–20 (1992–93), 131–54.

[180] Smith mentions that '*they are addressed to the inhabitants of the underworld by an unnamed sender, and their purpose is to request that the person for whom they were written be admitted to the company of those in the West and granted the favours which they enjoy. One of the most important of these is the freedom to travel freely between this world and the next and receive libations in conjunction with Osiris. Thus, the texts seek to benefit the deceased and enhance their status in both worlds*' (Smith, *Traversing Eternity*, 558). For more on the passports of eternity, see F. Scalf, *Passports to Eternity: Formulaic Demotic Funerary Texts and the Final Phase of Egyptian Funerary Literature in Roman Egypt*, PhD Thesis, The University of Chicago (Illinois 2014).

[181] Supplying water was one of the main funerary functions of Isis, R. Wild, *Water in the Cultic Worship of Isis and Serapis*, EPRO 87 (Leiden 1981). During the Roman period, the *situla* was always depicted in the right hand of the deceased, and had several forms and functions, M. Lichtheim, 'Situla n. 11395 and Some Remarks on Egyptian Situlae', *JNES* 6 (1947), 169–79, pls. iv-vii.; W. Walters, *Attic Grave Reliefs that Represent Women in the Dress of Isis*, Hesperia Supplement XXII (Princeton 1988), 20–25.; R. Merkelbach, 'Der Eid der Isismysten,' *ZPE* 1 (1967), 55–73.; id., *Isis Regina-Zeus Serapis. Die Griechisch-Ägyptische Religion nach den Quellen Dargestellt* (Stuttgart, Leipzig 2001), fig. 216. Normally, the garments of priests and other members of the Isiac cult were long, and the priests were shown beardless, without a headdress. An example of this is the classical male figure in the von Bissing tomb. This man acted as a priest of Isis, Venit, 'Referencing Isis', in L. Bricault and M. Versylus (eds.), *Isis on the Nile*, 106–07. Other examples of Isis priests outside of Egypt can be found in paintings from Herculaneum, E. Arslan, *Iside, Ilmitoilmistero la Magia, Palazzo Reale* 22 (Milano 1977), 447, no. V.77. The *situla* is known in the funerary art of ancient Egypt from the 18th dynasty onwards, and is one of the most distinguishable ceremonial vessels to have been used in temples and the mortuary cult in private tombs, A. Ragheb, 'Situla Pelizaeus-Museum inv. no. 4592, Roemer- und Pelizaeus-Museum, Hildesheim', *GM* 219 (2008), 73–78. The *situla* was also a common object for the *pastophori* of Isis in her shrines and temples in Rome. The *situla* is characterised by a high, looped handle, flaring mouth, and round or piriform shape with a knob at the bottom, M. Venit, 'Ancient Egyptomania, the Uses of Egypt in Graeco-Roman Alexandria', in E. Ehrenberg (ed.), *Leaving No Stones Unturned, Essays on the Ancient Near East and Egypt in Honor of Donald P. Hansen* (Winona Lake 2002), 274 no. 39.

[182] Walters, *Attic Grave Reliefs*, 20.

[183] E. Pergo, 'Between Religion and Consumption, Culinary and Drinking Equipment in Venetic Ritual Practice', in A. Smith and M. Bergeron (eds.), *Pallas, Revue d' Etudes Antiques, the Gods of Small Things* (Toulouse 2011), 243.

[184] Roman membership in a mystery cult, a practice which was inherited from classical and Hellenistic Greece and the East, came with promises of a richer, happier, and more god-like afterlife, J. Toynbee, *Death and Burial in the Roman World* (Baltimore 1971), 38.

[185] M. Cannata, 'God's Seal-Bearer, Lector-Priests and Choachytes, Who's Who at Memphis and Hawara', in G. Widmer and D. Devauchelle (eds.), *Actes du IXe Congrès International des Études Démotiques: Paris, 31 août – 3 septembre 2005, IFAO, BdÉ* 147 (Cairo 2009), 58–59. The *pastophores* of the Hellenistic and Roman world were priests who spread the belief in the Egyptian gods, H. Schönbron, *Die Pastophoren im Kult der ägyptischen Götter, Beiträge zur klassischen Philologie* 80 (Meisenheim 1976).

[186] On the *pastophoros*, see F. Hoffmann and J. Quack, '*Pastophoros*,' in A. Dodson, J. Johnston, and W. Monkhouse (eds.), *A Good Scribe and an Exceedingly Wise Man, Studies in Honour of W. J. Tait*, GHP 21 (London 2014) 127–55.; H. De Meulenaere, 'Pastophores et Gardiens des Portes', *CdÉ* 31 (1956), 299–302.; F. Dunand, 'Une Plainte de Pastophoros', in *CdÉ* 44 (1969), 301–12. In house-tomb 21 of Tuna El-Gebel, a female *sem* priestess is depicted. She is crowned with two feathers and wears a leopard skin of the priesthood, reciting from a papyrus scroll (*rotulus*). An offering table with three Egyptian vessels stands before her, Gabra, *Rapport sur les Fouill's d'Hermoupolis* 45. Venit identifies her as a lector priest reading from a scroll, resembling the deceased herself, Venit, *Visualizing the Afterlife*, 125–26. The lector priest is titled (*sS mD3t-ntr*), as can be seen inscribed on a statue in the Egyptian Museum, H. Bakry, 'A Statue of Pedeamun-Nebnesuttaui', *ASAE* 60 (1968), 17–25. The author proposes that she may be a priestess that is shown reading out the appropriate spells and presenting the appropriate offerings for the deceased in his tomb. Furthermore, according to Hellenistic iconography, the two feathers on her head also identify her as a *pterophoros*. The priestess combined these functions and served both as a lector priest and as a *pterophoros* priest in Kom El-Schukafa, Venit, *Monumental Tombs of Ancient Alexandria*, 138. Kaplan further identifies her based on the lustration vessel on her plate, Kaplan, *BZÄ* 16, 36. Reciting funerary hymns and making offerings to the deceased were important funerary customs often depicted in Roman tombs in Alexandria, in the Egyptian *chora* (Tuna El-Gebel, El-Salamuni, Thebes), and in the Oases (Petosiris), carried out by the priest. A lector priest, reciting from a relevant scroll, is depicted in the 26th dynasty tomb of Djedamenefanch in El-Baharia, H. Schäfer, *Kunstgeschichte in Bildern, I, Das Alterum* (Leipzig 1913), fig. 22. A lector priest is also depicted on a Roman period mummy shroud in the Ägyptische Museum in Berlin (Kaplan, *BZÄ* 16, 35–36, fig. 5b), as well as on a coffin from Siwa that is now at the Graeco-Roman Museum of Alexandria (Kaplan, *BZÄ* 16, 35–36, fig. 6a).

[187] Apuleius recounts how his hero, Lucius, as a newly initiated devotee of Isis, dresses himself in an ornamented, high quality tunic indicating wealth, and carries a flaming torch in his hand. On his head is a garland of palms, J. Griffiths, *Apuleius of Madauros: the Isis-book, Metamorphoses, book XI*, EPRO 39 (Leiden 1975), 100–01, 313–15.

was prominent in the Panopolite nome, where a village was even named Θμονησις (*T3-m3j-(n) Is.t*), or 'the New Land/Island of Isis'[188]. The village was located near the metropolis.

The combination of Greek and Egyptian mythological and religious themes in El-Salamuni shows a high degree of inter-cultural awareness by the deceased himself and/or by his commissioned artist. It also speaks to the ability of the deceased or artist to condense a diverse and complex funerary repertoire and tradition into individual tombs. During the Roman period, Hellenism was viewed as an elite culture. Thus, the ability to dress oneself in a classical style was indicative of an elite status. The urban elites in Panopolis wanted to emphasise their new urban status in numerous ways, and to reflect the great influence of the Greek civic culture of the *polis* in their religious and artistic visions[189]. The acquaintance with Greek culture became increasingly important as a means of obtaining status and prestige. The tombs and art of the wealthy reveal their self-conscious adherence to an elite group identity in the Panopolite nome; either these people are Greeks, Romans, Egyptians, or some combination of these options. The El-Salamuni tombs thus offer a clear example of the conception of duality (and even plurality) in the funerary art of the *chora* of Roman Egypt[190]. Though the deceased were interested in representing their Greek culture, they were also eager to express their affinity with and pride for local cults and the Egyptian afterlife. Furthermore, the representation of the deceased at El-Salamuni suggests that the local school of artists was both well-versed in the Egyptian representational system and in the Greek imagery that was circulating in cosmopolitan environments during that period.

The classical portraits that characterise the wealthy deceased are just one of the many accoutrements deemed necessary for a felicitous and beneficent afterlife. These representations are common on Roman shrouds[191]. They both reflect the attitude of the living for their dead and help the dead obtain a high status in the afterlife. One example is the depiction of warrior-heroes and their costumes on stelae from Alexandria[192]. Here, the image of the deceased mirrors the classical figure of the deceased at El-Salamuni; they are shown receiving reverence in their tombs and enjoying a priestly service. They carry proof of their justification to show Osiris, and they present themselves as adherents of Isis. Representations of trees and gardens, which can supply water to the tombs, are additionally indicative of a blessed afterlife, both in Greek and in Egyptian funerary iconography[193]. In studying the El-Salamuni tombs, it is important to remember that the wearing of a classical style in combination with an otherwise entirely Egyptian decorative program is not indicative of an absolute ethnicity of the deceased, but at least of a knowledge of the cultural 'other'.

4.2.9: The Inner Right Side of the Doorway Leading Into the Burial Chamber

The right side of the doorway leading into the tomb C1 burial chamber is narrow and does not contain any scenes. The inner part of the doorway is covered with a light layer of soot, and is also undecorated.

4.2.10: The Eastern A2 Wall: Overview

Wall A2 is divided into two registers, featuring a black line in between. Both registers show afterlife scenes. The lower frieze and some other parts of the wall are covered with debris. Some parts of the wall are cracked because of illicit activities.

4.2.11: The Upper Register of the Eastern A2 Wall

On the upper part of the scene on the eastern portion of the A2 wall, closest to the main entrance, 21 squatting judges are depicted[194]. Since they help to judge the deceased for the afterlife, they all hold an ostrich feather of truth. All of the judges are depicted with human heads except for the seventh one, which has a serpent head. This seventh figure resembles Nehebkau. Normally, the deceased must recite their negative actions in the presence of 42 judges to assert the extent of their good behaviour on earth. The daemons, numbered 5, 6, 17, and 19, are partially demolished, with number 18 being entirely damaged (Figure 4.28)[195].

---

[188] *P. Panop.* 2, l. 4 (308 AD).
[189] A. Bowman and D. Rathbone, 'Cities and Administration in Roman Egypt', *JRS* 8 (1992), 109.; L. Tacoma, *Fragile Hierarchies, the Urban Elites of Third-Century Roman Egypt, Mnemosyne Supplements* 271 (Leiden 2006), 3–4.
[190] Castiglione, *Dualité du style dans l'art*, 209–30.; id., *Kunst und Gesellschaft im Römischen Ägypten, AAASH* 15 (Budapest 1967), 107–52.
[191] On one shroud, a female named 'Tashy' is shown attending her judgement court. She is dressed in a classical style. It is clear that she has had a successful judgement. The shroud was bought by Henry Wellcom at an auction on 13 January, 1931, and has been published by Griffiths, 'Eight Funerary Paintings with Judgement Scenes in Swansea Wellcome Museum', *JEA* 68 (1982), 228–52. According to Tashy's hairstyle, Riggs dates the shroud to 140–160 AD. For more on this shroud, see C. Riggs, *Art and Identity in the Egyptian Funerary Tradition, c. 100 BC to AD 300*, unpublished DPhil thesis (Oxford 2001), 262.; C. Riggs and M. Stadler, 'A Roman Shroud and its Demotic Inscriptions in the Museum of Fine Arts', *JARCE* 40 (2003), 69–87, fig.1.; Riggs, *The Beautiful Burial*, 98–103, fig. 39; id., *AJA* 106, 88.

[192] Guimier-Sorbets. 'L'architecture et décor funéraire, de la Grec en Égypt', in C. Müller and F. Prost (eds.), *Identités et cultures de la monde méditerranéen antique, Mélanges Fr. Croissant* (Paris 2002), 159–80.
[193] According to Homer, the land of the blessed is a pleasant, bright, shaded, fresh, airy, and fertile place. This is presented in New Kingdom tombs, Wallert, *MÄS* 1, pls. v, xi.; W, El-Saddik, 'Garten darstellungen in Gräbern', in C. Tietze (ed.), *Ägyptischen Gärten* (Weimer 2011), 90–100. It can be seen in tomb 5 in El-Anfushi, A. Tricocohe, *L'eau dans les espaces et les pratiques funérair's d'Alexandrie aux époques grecque et romaine, IVe siècle av. J.-C.-IIIe siècle ap. J.-C., BAR Publishing International Series* 1919 (Oxford 2009). Various types of trees, including a palm tree, and various types of reeds are also depicted in this tomb's funerary chamber 5.2 and in the *loculus* of its chamber 5.5, A. Guimier-Sorbets, 'Le Jardin pour l'au-delà de bienheureux, Archéologie des jardins, analyse des espaces et méthod's d'approche', *Arceologie et histoire romaine* 26 (2014), 151–60.
[194] Von Bissing mentions 22 judges, von Bissing, *ASAE* 50, 558.
[195] Von Bissing, *ASAE* 50, 557–58.

The Afterlife in Akhmim

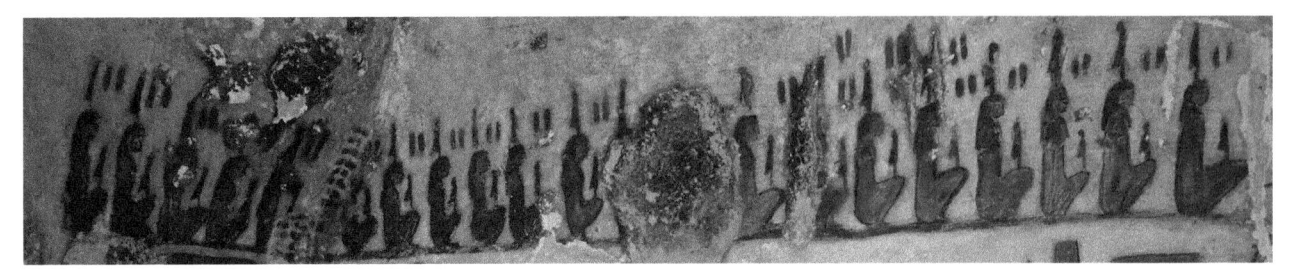

Figure 4.28. The 21 local judges in the afterlife court, as seen on the north A1 wall of tomb C1.

On the northern part of the eastern A2 wall, an enthroned Osiris is flanked by two female deities with prominent bare breasts. They are probably his adjuncts Isis and Nephthys, or Isis and Hathor, as von Bissing suggests[196]. The faint lines of the throne hieroglyph of Isis is still visible on the head of the goddess as she stands before Osiris. Osiris crosses his arms over his chest, holding his attributed royal insignia of the crock and the flail. His body is shrouded in a net with geometrical patterns in red, with black ends. His face is green, which is the colour of fertility and resurrection[197]. He wears a broad collar and an *atef* crown in yellow, which is adorned with two *uraei* painted black. His chequer-pattern throne is partially damaged and is decorated with a diamond grid pattern that imitates a small lattice of beads.

Isis and Nephthys are both depicted with one arm raised in adoration of Osiris, and they touch his arms with their lowered hands. Both are represented with a bare-breasted sheath dress. One goddess is dressed in green and the other is in red. The two act as intercessors between the god and the deceased, intending to petition Osiris on the deceased's behalf; the deceased approaches the throne in an adjacent scene. Here, the *psychopomp* Anubis, the divine messenger, acts in his role of guiding souls to the afterlife[198], as he leads and introduces the deceased to Osiris. Unfortunately, because of damage to the wall, a great portion of the figure of Anubis is now destroyed. The previous photo taken by Kanawati and the German Archaeological Institute (DAI) shows a better preserved figure of Anubis than what is now currently visible in the tomb (Figure 4.29)[199]. The deceased male that is also depicted in the scene is dressed in a traditional white and fringed Roman garment; his upper body is now entirely destroyed. In the scene, the deceased male grips the left wrist of Anubis with both hands, reflecting his worry, fear, and hope before Osiris.

At the southern end of the eastern A2 wall, Anubis acts in another role, making a ritual cleansing and lustration for the deceased. Anubis stands behind the deceased and conducts the ritual for washing the corpse with *hes* vessels[200]. Meanwhile, the deceased turns his back to Anubis and raises his hands in veneration before the four sons of Horus[201]. Although a great part of the body of the deceased is now destroyed, it is still clear that he is dressed in a traditional white fringed garment and a black wig. This traditional classical form was also adopted for deceased females, and purification rituals are also attested in the house-tomb 21 of Tuna El-Gebel[202]. Because of the great damage done to wall A2, only two of the four sons of Horus are still visible; only the legs of the first son remain, and the second is entirely damaged. The third son is Hapi, complete with his typical baboon head and green face. The fourth son is the best preserved, although his

---

[196] Von Bissing mentions that the scene is partially destroyed, von Bissing, *ASAE* 50, 557.
[197] The use of a net shroud on mummies is first attested in the 25th dynasty. It is frequently worn by Osiris in iconography, and therefore is widely worn by the deceased to enhance their association with Osiris. It also confers the protection of Nut through the blue colour of its nets, H. Taylor, *Death and the Afterlife in Ancient Egypt* (London 2001), 206–07.
[198] In Greek mythology, the typically Egyptian god Anubis, acting as a *psychopomp*, conducts the souls of the deceased to the shores of the river *Styx* and leads the deceased to the afterlife, acting as a sort of key to the next world. He is identified with Hermes as Anubis-Hermes or 'Hermanubis'. For Anubis as a *psychopomp*, see J. Grenier, *Anubis Alexandrin et Romain*, EPRO 57 (Leiden 1977).; D. Doxey, 'Anubis,' in D. Redford (ed.), *The Oxford Encyclopedia of Ancient Egypt* I (Oxford 2001), 98.; Riggs, *The Beautiful Burial*, 126–28, figs. 53–54, 165–73. Hathor was also responsible for leading deceased women to the court of Osiris, A. Abdalla, *Graeco-Roman Funerary Stelae from Upper Egypt* (Liverpool 1992), 112, cat. nos. 5, 62, 89, 117 (pl. 45), 166, 81.
[199] Venit, *Visualizing the Afterlife*, 189, fig. 5.31.
[200] In ancient Egypt, lustration was an essential step in passing from death to rebirth and in preparing the body for the spiritual journey towards the afterlife. A sort of baptism was used to initiate the deceased into the Isis cult, V. von Gonzenbach, *Unterschunungen zu den knabenweihen im Isiskult der römischen Kaiserzeit, Antiquitas I; Abhandlungen zur alter Geschichte* (Bonn 1957).; Venit, 'Referencing Isis', in L. Bricault and M. Versylus (eds.), *Isis on the Nile*, 94. The earliest depiction of purification appears on a 12th dynasty temple at Medinet Maadi. Here, the king is purified by Horus and Thoth, A. Gardiner, 'Addendum to 'The Baptism of Pharaoh', *JEA* 36 (1950), 3–12. Gardiner suggests that Horus and Thoth represent two of the four gods making up the four cardinal points, while Corcoran (*Portrait Mummies from Roman Egypt (I–IV Centuries AD), with a Catalog of Portrait Mummies in Egyptian Museums*, SAOC 56 (Chicago 1995), 59 (citing G. Jécquier, *Considérations sur les religions* égyptiennes (Neuchâtel 1946), 80–83, 133–36)) notes that the choice of the two gods may have been influenced by their substitution for '*Sia and Hu[,] who journeyed with Re in the solar boat and who were responsible for the resurrection of the sun from the primeval waters*'. The rite was later depicted on non-royal coffins and in private tombs dating to the Ramesside Period, as well as on cartonnage coffins of the Third Intermediate Period, L. Corcoran, 'Mysticism and the Mummy Portraits', in M. Bierbrier (ed.), *Portraits and Masks*, 47 (including the revision of her chronology as given in *Portrait Mummies from Roman Egypt*, 59).
[201] Von Bissing, *ASAE* 50, 557.
[202] Venit, *Visualizing the Afterlife*, 122. Riggs notes that this classical depiction of the deceased woman in the process of purification (in house-tomb 21) ensures that she is still connected to the world of the living, Riggs, *The Beautiful Burial*, 135–36. Venit also emphasises that the deceased woman is ready to undertake the voyage to the afterlife, Venit, *Visualizing the Afterlife*, 122. Smith and Riggs claim that the representation of the deceased in a non-Egyptian style of dress signals that the deceased is at the beginning of the posthumous transfiguration process, while the mummiform iconography shows the deceased at its end, as a transfigured spirit, Smith, *Following Osiris*, 364–65.

Tomb C1: The So-called 'Tomb of von Bissing' (1897)

Figure 4.29. The east A2 wall of tomb C1, as photographed by the German Archaeological Institute (DAI), Kaplan, *BzÄ* 16, fig. 87b.

head is too destroyed to distinguish his identity. The four sons hold their relative attributes in their hands, which is similar to the image of the sons of Horus shown in housetomb 20 at Tuna El-Gebel[203]. The sons are portrayed as mummiform; the wrapped body often symbolises ancestors, including primeval gods[204]. A shrouded body was thus a common practice for the deceased in Roman Egypt[205]. Unfortunately, during the first visit of the author to the tomb in 2015, the tomb C1 wall was more preserved than it is now (Figures 4.30a-b).

Pseudo-columns are depicted either horizontally or vertically along the wall, and are painted in a red colour with a black border. These columns are supposed to contain the names of deities or short inscriptions in black cursive hieroglyphs. The existence of a pseudo-text to accompany a funerary image was important, as it complemented the other the elements of the funerary iconography. However, due to the poor quality of the initial writing, environmental issues, and the threat of looters in the tombs, most of the names are now demolished, and are hardly recognizable; even the use of infrared photography and fluorescence does not uncover the full text of the now-invisible scripts. Although the use of pseudo-hieroglyphs may suggest a lack of familiarity with indigenous scripts in a certain region, the accompanying images could help illustrate the meanings of these symbols by relying on their visual and symbolic potency[206]. The pseudo-hieroglyphic columns are a distinctive feature in the El-Salamuni tombs[207].

4.2.12: The Lower Register of the Eastern A2 Wall

During Kuhlmann's visit, the lower frieze of wall A2 was mostly hidden by heavy debris[208]. During the first visit of the author to tomb C1, the frieze was more visible than in Kuhlmann's time, though great parts of it were still hidden with rubbish and debris.

The far northern corner of the wall is mostly destroyed. It shows the deceased female standing in veneration of a

---

[203] Kaplan, *BzÄ* 16, 161, fig. 77a.
[204] C. Riggs, *Unwrapping Ancient Egypt* (London, New York 2014), 146. The net pattern, representing the bodies of the four sons of Horus in faience, may allude to the feathers of the sun god, or perhaps to a costume worn by the goddesses. Alternatively, the net pattern may represent the stars of the night sky or imitate the net which catches evildoers and through which the justified are able to float. The net bodies of the four sons of Horus connect to both the solar and lunar aspects of rebirth, Graves-Brown, *Daemons & Spirits*, 113.
[205] C. Arnst, 'Vernetzung Zur Symbolik des Mumiennetzes', in M. Fitzenreiter (ed.), *Die ägyptische Mumie, ein Phänomen der Kulturgeschichte, Beiträge zum Workshop am 25. und 26. April 1998, Humboldt-Universität zu Berlin, Seminar für Sudanarchäologie und Ägyptologie* I (Berlin 1998), 79–94.
[206] Y. Abdelwahed, *Egyptian Cultural Identity in the Architecture of Roman Egypt (30 BC–AD 325), Archaeopress Roman Archaeology (BAR Publishing)* 6 (Oxford 2015), 107–09.
[207] The pseudo-columns are also well-preserved in the so-called 'von Bissing tomb of 1913', and in El-Salamuni tombs III and IV, Kaplan, *BzÄ* 16, 166–74, pls. 86–93.
[208] Kuhlmann, *SDAIK* 11, pl. 35d.; Kaplan, *BzÄ* 16, pl. 87b.

The Afterlife in Akhmim

Figure 4.30a. Osiris flanked by two female deities. The scene is located on the lower frieze of the east A2 wall of tomb C1, and was best preserved in 2015.

Figure 4.30b. The damage done to the previous scene (figure 4.30a) in 2019.

mummiform, falcon-headed figure of Horus. Isis stands behind him, embracing him and holding his effigy[209]. An altar is placed in front of Horus[210]. This scene parallels the scene on the lower register of the opposite west wall, which shows Isis supporting the mummy of Osiris. Here, the deceased, having successfully passed through the gates of the underworld, is shown to have conquered death[211]. Isis is dressed in a red garment with a sun disc surmounting her head, while meanwhile a tall altar is placed in between the deceased and Horus [212]. Nowadays, only the legs of Isis and Horus are visible, as grave robbers have destroyed the scene.

The next scene shows the deceased with upraised hands, adoring a procession of four daemon gatekeepers, complete with knives in their left hands. The first daemon (with a falcon head) wears the *pschent* crown, while the head of the second one is partially damaged, and is comprised of the head of a horse and a sun disc. The third one has a ram head with a sun disc, while the last daemon has a jackal head. The pseudo-columns lie either horizontally or vertically before the figures (Figures 4.31a-b). Von Bissing does not refer to them as daemons. Instead, he identifies them as Anubis (Chnoubis), a bird-headed god with a red disc on his head (either Horus or Thoth(?)), and a divinity

of which only the double crown remains. Between each pair of deities, there is a *naos* with crossed swords[213].

On the west end of the wall is a unique erotic scene (Figures 4.32a-b). Kaplan refers to this erotic scene in her publication, but she does not define its location in the tomb. She mentions that the scene shows the deities Bes and Beset practicing sex[214]. Tomb C1 thus documents the only known sexual scene to occur in the Graeco-Roman tombs of Egypt[215]. During von Bissing's visit, the scene

---

[209] In the tomb of Siamun, Imentet is shown embracing a mummiform falcon-headed figure who is undoubtedly Osiris-Sokar, Venit, *Visualizing the Afterlife*, 139. Fakhry identifies the figure as Duamutef, A. Fakhry, *The Egyptian Deserts, Siwa Oasis, Its History and Antiquities* (Cairo 1944), 148.
[210] Von Bissing assumes that it is an incense burner, von Bissing, *ASAE* 50, 558, fig. 2.
[211] Venit, 'Referencing Isis', in L. Bricault and M. Versylus (eds.), *Isis on the Nile*, 118.
[212] Von Bissing, *JDAI* 61/62, 5, fig. 9.

[213] Von Bissing, *ASAE* 50, 558.
[214] Kaplan, *BzÄ* 16, 87, 168, pl.88b. It seems that the role of Bes also extended into the sexual realm. Beset was very popular in the Graeco-Roman Period, and often appears (unnamed) on amulets, depicted either as a full-sized naked female with a lion's ears and tail, or as a female dwarf with a human face and flowing hair. She is usually depicted nude and sometimes is pregnant or plump. Sometimes, she is shown carrying Bes on her shoulder, and/or standing on an antelope, a frog, or a papyrus stalk, J. Bulté, *Talismans Egyptiens d'Heureuse Maternité* (Paris 1991). The female dwarf figure found on the famous travertine model boat in the tomb of Tutankhamun has recently been suggested to be Beset, J. Quaegebeur and N. Cherpion, *La Naine et le Bouquetin, Ou L'Énigme de la Barque en Albâtre de Toutankhamon* (Leuven 1999).
[215] Depictions of sex are known in funerary art from as early as the Old Kingdom, see L. Manniche, *Sexual Life in Ancient Egypt* (New York 1987), 9, 19, 61, 119, figs.1, 9, 53. A sexual plaque was given as a votive offering at the Osiris Temple in Kom El Sultan. It is now in the collection of the Institute of Fine Arts at New York University, M. Marlar, 'Sex as a Votive Offering at the Osiris Temple,' in Z. Hawaas and J. Richards (eds.), *The Archaeology and Art of Ancient Egypt, Essays in Honor of David O'Connor, Annales du Service des Antiquites de L'Egypte, Cahier* 36, II (Cairo 2007), 111–20. Sexual depictions continued to be used through the Graeco-Roman Period. Though there is no prior evidence of a truly erotic scene on a tomb wall, a great number of erotic magical texts from the Graeco-Roman Period have been found in Egypt, K. Preisendemz, *Papyri Graecae Magicae, Die Griechischen Zauber Papyri, Vols. 1–II* (Leipzig 1928–31). A gemstone showing a couple making love in the 'Milenion and Atlanta position', where a woman's legs is placed on a man's shoulders, has been discovered in Damnhur, and dates to the third century BC, Kaplan, *BzÄ* 16, 215. Furthermore, Eros

Tomb C1: The So-called 'Tomb of von Bissing' (1897)

Figure 4.31a. The lower frieze scene on the east A2 wall of tomb C1 (before the restoration in 2019).

Figure 4.31b. The lower frieze scene on the east A2 wall of tomb C1 (after the restoration in 2021).

was completely covered with rubble, so von Bissing did not document or mention it, stating that it was '*en grande partie ensevelie sous les decombres*'[216]. Venit assumes that the figures in the so-called erotic scene, like the silhouettes and Ammit, the drooling devourer, act as damned figures in the various Egyptian books of the afterlife[217]. E. Bresciani describes the scene as erotic[218]. Venit deplores the existence of this erotic scene, saying that it is wholly inappropriate for a tomb decoration, and that it represents something completely different[219]. Klotz deeply studied the scene and suggests many theories regarding the religious meanings of this amorous sexual depiction. Perhaps it is meant to evoke Greek mythology and the seduction of Paulina as recounted by Flavius Josephus.

The most acceptable interpretation is that the deceased, dressed in the guise of Anubis (as a sexual god), is having sex with a woman figure, who is painted with a dull brown colour. Her long hair, which flows over her shoulders,

---

and Psyche are depicted in a sexual position on a second century AD wall painting from Oxyrhynchus, which is now in Florence. The so-called *Hierodouleia*, or 'prostitution rooms', can be found east of the pyramid of Teti, within the enclosure of the *Anubeion*. The rooms are decorated with three polychrome figures of the fertility god Bes, flanked by female worshippers. The rooms date to the mid-second century BC and are known as the 'Bes-chambers', where Bes was honoured as the giver of sexual energy. A cache of 'erotic' figurines was also found in these rooms, consisting of phallic statutes of Bes and other anthropomorphic figures, H. Bonnet, *RÄRG*, 105.; F. Velazquez, *El dios Bes: aspectos iconográficos en el ámbito fenicio-púnico con especial referencia a la Península Ibérica e Ibiza, Tomo I* (Madrid 2001), 88. On the so-called *Symplegmata* style of interlocked couples making love, see Kaplan, *BzÄ* 16, 125, pl. 8.; G. Martin, "Erotic' Figurines: The Cairo Museum Material', *GM* 96 (1987), 71–84.The Greeks found Bes to be reminiscent of phallic deities in their own religion, such as Driapus and Silenus. At Saqqara, a number of Roman terracottas have been discovered which depict two priests and two figures of Bes carrying an enormous phallus in procession, D. Montserrat, *Sex and Society in Graeco-Roman Egypt* (London 1996), 173.

[216] Von Bissing, *ASAE* 50, 557–58.

[217] Venit, 'Referencing Isis', in L. Bricault and M. Versylus (eds.), *Isis on the Nile*, 118.

[218] E. Bresciani, 'Un insolita figura di'concubina in terracotta: la suonatrice di tamburo', in P. Buzi, D. Picchi, and M. Zecchi (eds.), *Aegyptiaca et Captica, Studi in onro di Sergio Pernigotti*, BAR Publishing 2264 (Oxford 2011), 28, 32, fig. 7.

[219] Venit, 'Referencing Isis', in L. Bricault and M. Versylus (eds.), *Isis on the Nile*, 116.

The Afterlife in Akhmim

Figure 4.32a. The erotic scene from tomb C1, as photographed in 2015.

signifies sex[220], inspiring the virility of Anubis. She rests her left arm on a pillow and wraps her legs around the Anubis figure. They sit upon a type of classical couch called a *kline*. Two *hes* vessels and lettuce plants (a common Egyptian symbol of sexuality) are frequently depicted beneath the *kline*[221]. The scene attests to the fact that the deceased hopes to enjoy his full sexual power in the netherworld. Klotz claims that this erotic scene is proof of the transfiguration of the deceased[222]. Here, the deceased is capable of having sexual intercourse with the living in his *ba* and *Swt* forms [223].

The scene found on wall A2 is currently the only record of an erotic image in Graeco-Roman tombs, with the exception of the scene from house-tomb 20 at Tuna El-Gebel. Although it is now destroyed, the Tuna El-Gebel example once depicted a strange, humorous, and folkloric scene of

---

[220] M. Valdesogo, *Hair and Death in Ancient Egypt in Ancient Egypt, Mourning rites in the Pharaonic Period* (Zandvoort 2019), 93.
[221] Klotz refers to amphorae, flowers, and other objects that are typically stored under the coach, D. Klotz, 'The Lecherous Pseudo-Anubis of Josephus and the 'Tomb of 1897' at Akhmim', in A. Gasse, F. Servajean, and C. Thiers (eds.), *Et in Ægypto et ad Ægyptum, Recueil d'études dédiées à Jean-Claude Grenier, CENiM* 5, II (Montpellier 2012), 387. The author suggests that these are three heads of lettuce, rather than flowers, and that they are being offered in order to increase the sexual desire and fecundity of the deceased male.
[222] D. Klotz, 'The Lecherous Pseudo-Anubis', 385–92, fig.1. Kaplan identifies the two figures as Bes and Beset, Kaplan, *BzÄ* 16, 87, pls. 88b.
[223] As mentioned in CT 71, A. de Buck, *The Ancient Egyptian Coffin Texts I, Texts of Spells 1–75* (Chicago 1935), 297, T2C d–e.; Žabkar, *A Study of the Ba Concept*, 98.

Figure 4.32b. The erotic scene from tomb C1, as recorded by the German Archaeological Institute (DAI), Kaplan, *BzÄ* 16, 87, 168, fig. 88b.

Tomb C1: The So-called 'Tomb of von Bissing' (1897)

a man with a batrachian's head and an oversized phallus in the act of mating with a naked squatting woman. This scene was likely painted by an amateur painter who did not pay attention to the proportions of the figures; the man is painted in a smaller size than the woman[224]. Another similarly disproportional and sexual representation in the same tomb depicts a man mating with a lady who bends forward[225]. The sexual scenes are exclusive to this house-tomb, and are depicted in a folkloric style. The iconography is possibly unique because it may have been made in reference to the evil brought by the burial of a female mummy in the house; she was supposedly dead and lacking a uterus because of an incubus. The uterus is represented by a toad's head, drawing on the similarity of the shapes of a uterus and a batrachian[226]. This kind of scene is typically dominated by the feeling of immorality and promiscuity that reflects the stereotypical ancient Roman spirit[227].

In fact, the virility of the dead was itself a sign of revival and resurrection. Certainly, there is a link between vegetation and eroticism. Therefore, the sexual depictions and penile erections of the deceased were still main factors in the deceased's transfiguration. The funerary iconography of the wall A2 scene is largely Egyptian. It represents a positive sexual meeting of the male deceased in the guise of Anubis with a divine or daemonic female, a story which was documented in the literature of Pharaonic Egypt[228]. Thus, the deceased showed his sexual abilities and confirmed his resurrection.

Wall A2 is fully documented through photogrammetry, drawings, and the creation of a deterioration map (Figures 4.33a-d).

4.2.13: The Zodiac Ceiling

A zodiac is a composite diagram of the Egyptian, Mesopotamian, and Greek traditions that depicts the sky, and which can include a representation of planets, decans, and other constellations[229]. The inclusion of constellations in the zodiac shows a Greek influence that was possibly unknown to the Egyptians before the Persian or the Ptolemaic Periods, coming either directly from Greece or indirectly from Greece via Mesopotamia[230]. The zodiac has been popular in Egypt ever since Ptolemaic times, and was widely attested in Roman Egypt, not only through written evidence like charts and horoscopes, but also through imagery found on the ceilings of tombs and temples[231].

The reason for the use of a zodiac in the mortuary sphere is that the deceased of the Graeco-Roman Period were interested in being granted eternal renewal. This could be achieved via the heavenly zodiacs that were placed overhead in the tombs. The zodiac represents the world, the heavens at the moment of creation, and the new year. Occasionally, it is personalised, either through the depiction of the Sothic new year or the first rise of the sun (Harpocrates). From the ancient Egyptian iconographical point of view, the zodiac represents the material creation from which the soul must escape, either via the Egyptian model of travelling through the hours of the night in a solar barque and overcoming the various gates, or via the Greek model of the planetary gates of Saturn, Venus, Jupiter, Mercury, Mars, the moon, and the sun[232]. Zodiacs became popular in the Roman period[233], confirming the age-old traditional funerary beliefs of Egypt, complete with its the focus on the solar cycle, which continued to flourish as a means of securing the deceased glorification, transfiguration, and the opportunity to be a follower of Re and Osiris in the *Duat*.

The ceiling of tomb C1 is enlivened with a Greek-style zodiac as a circular feature. In the middle of the zodiac is a largely damaged figure of Isis-Sothis, who is depicted riding on a dog[234]. Her long hair is crowned with a solar

---

[224] Gabra, *Rapport Sur Les Fouill's D'Hermopolis*, 102.; E. Pfuhl, *Masterpieces of Greek Drawing and Paintings* (New York 1979), figs. 129, 130, 133.
[225] S. Gabra, *Peintures à Fresques et Scènes Peintes À Hermoupolis-Ouest (Touna El Gebel)* (Cairo 1954), pl. 12.
[226] Gabra, *Rapport Sur Les Fouill's D'Hermopolis*, 103.
[227] I. Saad, 'Tuna El-Gebel, Analytical Study of Architecture and Painting' (in Arabic), Published MsC degree, Alexandria University (Alexandria 1986), 210.
[228] H. Navrátilová and R. Landgráfová, *Sex and the Golden Goddess II, World of the Love Songs* (Prague 2015), xvi–ii.
[229] For more about the zodiac, see T. Barton, *Ancient Astrology* (London, New York 1994), 10–31, 178.; F. Cumont, *L'Egypte des Astrologues* (Brussels 1973).
[230] Altmann-Wendling, 'Shapeshifter- Knowledge of the Moon', in J. Althoff et al.(eds.), *Construction and Transfer of Knowledge*, 238–40.

[231] Out of the 24 which were recorded by Neugebauer and Parker, nine zodiacs depict a Greek style of signs, Riggs, *The Beautiful Burial*, 57 no. 32.
[232] Whitehouse, 'Roman in Life, Egyptian in Death', in O. Kaper (ed.), *Life in the Fringe*, 266.
[233] Although temples are generally dominated by Egyptian traditions, the Greek-style zodiac appears as a unique scene executed in the Dendera Temple, reflecting a Greek influence, E. Graefe, 'Über die Verabeitung von Pyramidentexten in den späten Tempeln', in U. Verhoeven and E. Graefe (eds.), *Religion und Philiosophe im alten Ägypten, Festgabe für Philippe Derchain*, OLA 39 (Leuven 1991), 130.
[234] In the Late Period, Isis became a universal goddess by virtue of her assimilation with deities such as Sothis and Sirius, with whom she merged. She was worshipped under the name of Isis-Sothis, B. Watterson, *The Gods of Egypt* (London 1984), 97. 'Sothis' was the Egyptian name for Sirius, the dog star, and was thought to be the goddess responsible for the inundation, Watterson, *The Gods of Egypt*, 186. Stars appear in various ways in the funerary symbolism of the Egyptian cults during the Graeco-Roman Period. It is Nut who gives birth to the sun and the stars, and swallows them at sun set. This has led to her being called 'the Sow', which is an allusion to the sow as a devourer of her its offspring. In the Hellenistic Era, the connection between Isis and Nut is conveyed in art by depictions of Isis riding on a sow. In the astral world, Isis is identified as the bright Star 'Sirius' or 'Sothis' (Sepedet) in the constellation Orion, D. Bredford, *The Ancient Gods Speak, a Guide to the Egyptian Religion* (Oxford 2002), 171. Sothis is equated with Osiris, and their sexual union was said to produce Horus Sopd. Lepsius mentions that the representation of Isis-Sothis is known from the Pharaonic Period, having appeared on the ceiling of the Ramesseum under the name and the form of Isis, LD III, 171.; J. Hani, *La Religion Egyptienne dans La Pensee de Plutarque* (Paris 1976), 200–04. The representation of emperors with animals, and especially on dogs or with dogs, dates to the reign of the emperor Caligula, and is especially depicted on coins dated to 71 AD of the year of the emperor Vespesian. However, some suggest that the image which was found in the Iseum of Rome shows Isis-Sothis, dating to the lifetime of Caligula, von Bissing, *ASAE* 50, 567.; W. Weber, *Die Ägyptische-Griechischen Terrakoten* (Berlin 1914), 36–37, 51, pl. 3. Here, the representation of Isis-Sothis provides a sign of protection to the deceased, M. Vermasern, *Etudes Preliminaires aux Religions Orientales da's L'Empire Romain* (Leiden 1925).; S. Hollios, *Five Egyptian Goddesses, Their Possible Beginnings, Actions, and Relationships in the Third Millennium BCE, Bloomsbury Egyptology* (London 2020), 83.

The Afterlife in Akhmim

Figure 4.33a. Photogrammetry of the east A2 wall of tomb C1 (before the restoration in 2019).

Figure 4.33b. Photogrammetry of the east A2 wall of tomb C1 (after the restoration in 2021).

Tomb C1: The So-called 'Tomb of von Bissing' (1897)

Figure 4.33c. A facsimile of the east A2 wall of tomb C1.

Figure 4.33d. A reconstruction/facsimile of the damaged parts of the east A2 wall of tomb C1.

disc. In her right hand, she holds the stem of a lotus, while her left hand rests on her knee[235]. Unfortunately, because of damage done to the middle of the wall, the figure of Isis-Sothis no longer remains. In the Hellenistic Era, the connection of Isis and Nut was conveyed in art by depictions of Isis riding on a sow, announcing the Nile's inundation and prosperity[236]. In the astral world, Isis was identified as the bright star Sirius (*Sothis/Sepedet*) in the constellation Orion[237]. This was the most southern constellation in the decan list. When Orion is clear on the horizon, Sirius appears, so it makes sense that they were usually represented together in the scenes[238]. In tomb C1, the circular zodiac is distinguished by the lack of female deities carrying it, despite Isis-Sothis being on a dog in the centre, as photographed by Kuhlmann.

Unfortunately, recent looting of the tomb has resulted in the damage of a great part of the centre of the zodiac, including the image of Isis-Sothis on a dog. The head and the body of Isis-Sothis are destroyed; only her raised right hand is still visible, and a great portion of the dog is also demolished.

Reconstruction efforts to save the zodiac revealed that, as usual, the dog's head once turned back to gaze at Isis[239]. The signs of the zodiac are arranged clockwise, in the order of: Taurus, Gemini, Cancer, Leo, Virgo, Libra, Scorpio, a partially damaged figure of Sagittarius, Capricorn, Aquarius, a partially damaged figure of Pisces, and finally, a partially erased Aries (Figures 4.34a-e). Neugebauer has documented two further zodiacs in El-Salamuni 3A and 8A which also show Isis-Sothis, this time as a lady with long heavy hair, wearing a folded Roman garment, and riding a typical dog[240]. The depiction of the dog-star Sothis (alpha *Canis majoris* or alpha *CMa*)[241] in the central circle of the zodiac is also repeated on 1) the ceiling of the burial chamber of the so-called tomb of von Bissing of 1913 (which was later registered as Salamuni 3A by Neugebauer and Parker)[242], and 2) Salamuni 8A. Both of these tombs date to the Roman period[243].

R. Lupus writes that in the time of Tiberius, Isis-Sothis can be described as 'the Great Isis, the Mother of the Gods, Sothis, Regent of the Stars, Mistress of the Heavens, of the Earth, and of the Underworld'[244]. The mother Sothis is thus associated with the ascending of the deceased to the sky, confirming one's rebirth in the beginning of the year. She also gives birth to the sun (Horus, son of Sothis) at the time of her rising[245]. Implicitly, the depiction of Isis-Sothis in the middle of the zodiac suggests that the patron of the tomb was an adherent of the cult of Isis[246].

Von Bissing proposes a Roman date for tomb C1, not only due to the funerary art in the tomb, but also due to the representation of Isis-Sothis riding on her dog. The dog as an attribute of Isis-Sothis is a Greek influence; the Greek days of summer are marked by the morning rise of Sothis[247]. The earliest example of Isis seated side-saddle on a dog has a Roman origin and iconography. Von Bissing wrongly states that the first appearance of Isis-Sothis with a dog is on coins of Antonius Pius (86–161 AD)[248] but an earlier appearance of the goddess riding on a dog can be found on

---

[235] Kaplan, *BzÄ* 16, 168, pl.88a.; Von Bissing, *ASAE* 50, 556.; id., *JDAI* 61/ 62, 6.

[236] Isis was a universal and celestial goddess. She had different representations throughout ancient Egypt, and played many important roles in the religion and astronomy of the civilization as well. She is sometimes depicted in astronomical scenes as Sothis Sirius, and as Sopdet. She was called 'Sopdet' by the Egyptians and 'Sothis' by the Greeks, G. Deyoung, 'Astronomy in Ancient Egypt', in H. Selin and S. Xiaochun (eds.), *Astronomy Across Cultures, The History of Non-Western Science*, (New York 2000). The helical rising of Sothis coincided with the Nile inundation and the summer solstice, thus making it a herald of the inundation and the beginning of the Egyptian year, E. Krupp, *In Search of Ancient Astronomies*, (New York 1977).; P. Casanova, 'Qulques legends astronomiques arabes considérées dans leurs rapports avec la mythologie Egyptienne', *BIFAO* 2 (1902), 1–39.; G. Tallet, 'Isis, the Crocodiles and the Mysteries of the Nile Flood: Interpreting a Scene from Roman Egypt Exhibited in the Egyptian Museum in Cairo (SE 30001)', in C. Scibona and A. Mastrocinque (eds.), *Demeter, Aphrodite, Isis, and Cybele: Studies in the Greek and Roman Religion in Honour of Giulia Sfameni Gasparro.* (Stuttgart 2012), 137–60. In the Graeco-Roman Period, Isis was also called *spdt-3st* (meaning 'Sothis-Isis'). During this time, she was sometimes depicted as a large dog, or as a lady riding side-saddle on a dog, which was a symbolic animal, H. Kockelmann, *Praising the Goddess, A Comparative Annotated Re-Edition of Six Demotic Hymns and Praises Addressed to Isis* (New York 2008). Astronomical scenes are rich with depictions of the goddess Isis-Sothis-Sopdet-Sirius from the New Kingdom until the Gaeco-Roman Period. During this period, she was depicted in various ways. She is sometimes shown as a lady with a typical throne headpiece, holding a *w3s* sceptre, such as is visible in the fifth strip of the rectangular zodiac of the Dendera Temple. Here, on the eastern half of the ceiling of the third eastern Osirian chapel, she is additionally shown as a lady. She wears a *st* throne sign on her head and holds an *ankh* sign in her hand. In the temple of Deir el-Haggar in the Dakhla Oasis, she is depicted wearing a sun disk above her head with a star inside of it. She is also widely depicted in zodiacs as a recumbent cow in a barque, with a star between her two horns. Examples of these scenes are that of Ib-Pmeny, the rectangular zodiac in the hypostyle hall of the Dendera Temple, the circular zodiac of Dendera, the eastern half of the ceiling of the third eastern Osirian chapel of Dendera, the southern strip of Esna A, and the astronomical frieze of the hypostyle hall of the Edfu temple, H. Amer, *Astronomical Representations of Egyptian Goddesses in Tombs and Temples from the New Kingdom to the End of the Graeco-Roman Period, (An Archaeological Religious Study)*, Alexandria University (Alexandria 2021), 140–49.

[237] Bredford, *The Ancient Gods Speak*, 171.

[238] The Greeks regarded her as the faithful dog of Orion. Sothis was considered his dog, and Orion himself was a hunter, H. Guerber, *Greece and Rome: Myths and Legends* (London 1996). The ancient Egyptians regarded Sirius as a companion of Orion, G. Wainwright, 'Orion and the Great Star', *JEA* 22 (1936), 45–46.

[239] As shown in El-Salamuni 3A and 8A.

[240] Neugebauer and Parker, *EAT* III, 52, 55. Venit suggests that the precise form of the dog is difficult to make out, Venit, *Visualizing the Afterlife*, 237 no. 1268.

[241] A. von Bomhard, *The Egyptian Calendar, A Work for Eternity* (London 1999).

[242] Neugebauer and Parker, *EAT* III, 99, 100, cat. no. 73. The author was able to locate the tomb of von Bissing of 1913. It is still unregistered and doorless, lying south of the temple of Ay, in a terrace below it. Unfortunately, the zodiac no longer exists.

[243] Neugebauer and Parker, *EAT* III,101, no.77, pl. 55b. It was labelled by Kaplan as tomb III (El-Salamuni 8), Kaplan, BzÄ 16, 171, fig. 91a.; Venit, *Visualizing the Afterlife*, 184, fig. 5.26. Tomb III (El-Salamuni 8) is now named tomb F5. It is located on the southern part of the mountain. Its publication is forthcoming by the author.

[244] Clerc, 'Isis-Sothis dans le monde romaine', in *Hommages à M. J. Vermasern, recue'l d'études offert par les auteurs de la série Études préliminaires aux religions orientales da's l'empire romain à Maarten J. Vermaseren'à l'occasion de son soixantième anniversaire le 7 Avril 1978* (Leiden 1978), 281.

[245] For the attributes of Sothis, see P. Wallin, *Celestial Cycles, Astronomical Concepts of Regeneration in the Ancient Egyptian Coffin Texts, USE* I (Uppsala 2002), 28–49.

[246] Venit, *Visualizing the Afterlife*, 193–94.

[247] Clerc, 'Isis-Sothis dans le monde romaine', 254.

[248] Von Bissing, *ASAE* 50, 567.; id., *JDAI* 61/62, 6.

coins of Vespasian created in 71 AD[249]. The earliest known Alexandrian depiction of the goddess with the dog is from coinage struck in years 13–16 of the reign of Trajan[250]. The image continued to be used for the festivals of Isis in Rome during the time of the Christian emperor Valentinian II (400 AD)[251]. The image of Isis-Sothis riding on a dog is also depicted in temples to the goddess in the Campus Martius in Rome, which was rebuilt by Caligula (37–41 AD). Clèrc claims that the appearance of Isis-Sothis riding side-saddle on her dog first appears on coinage by the beginning 139 AD[252] as an announcement of a new Sothic era and the beginning of a new year[253]. Hence, giving an overly precise date of the tomb, in relation to the coinage, is still illogical[254]. However, it can be said that the circular layout of the zodiacs within a square field representing a starry firmament is an innovation of the Roman period.

The zodiacs from the Akhmim region all come from the ceilings of private tombs, except for one that was probably located on the ceiling of the temple of Min. All are in a Greek style, or in a combination of Greek and Egyptian styles. Some scholars suggest that the depiction of Isis-Sothis or Harpokrates in the middle of the zodiac was a means of announcing the beginning of the new year[255]. Likewise, Venit argues that the inclusion of Isis in the zodiacs of El-Salamuni refers to a specific calendrical event. During the Graeco-Roman Period in Egypt, the zodiac was not attributed to the Alexandrian calendar. Instead, it was a Hellenistic way to represent the sky. In El-Salamuni, the Greek-style of zodiac decorations are not always the main preference of the deceased; the Egyptian style, which uses Nut, is also depicted. Thus, the representations of Isis-Sothis in the Akhmimic tombs are meant to highlight the celestial and eschatological elements of the goddess, who makes the sky like Nut[256]. The deceased in El-Salamuni were eager to pass the celestial realm into the afterlife. However, there was a preference for the use of zodiacs in a Greek style, possibly since it provides a more precise description of the heavens than the Egyptian star map, thus helping them reach their goal[257].

4.2.14: The Burial Chamber

During the first visit of the author to tomb C1, the burial chamber was in a poor state of preservation. Some of the most important reasons for this include the following:

1. Heavy debris covered the walls of the tomb until the middle, hiding great portions of the scenes on the lower friezes. In many cases, the debris extended until the lower parts of the upper frieze. The debris is harmful for the scenes and its colours and has already caused damage to some of the walls. During the visits of von Bissing and the Kuhlmann survey, the tomb was still covered with debris. In his publications, von Bissing does not refer to the heavy block in the middle of the antechamber that was still *in situ* during the time of Kuhlmann and Kanawati's publication. It is therefore possible that the block had slid down into the anteroom through the low entrance of the tombs, either by the villagers or through natural environmental movements that are common in the mountains. At the request of the Egyptian Ministry of Culture, and in relation to his editing of a tourism monograph about Sohag, Kanawati visited the tomb in December 1980. Because Kanawati planned on photographing the tomb, the Sohag Inspectorate fully cleaned it, with the exception of the heavy block. Later, in 2011, the lack of security due to the 25th Egyptian Revolution resulted in tomb robbers badly damaging the tomb's burial niches. They attempted to scrape and cut off some of the scenes, which once again caused heavy rubble to fall inside the tomb.

2. Heavy soot covered the walls and the ceiling of the burial chamber, which hid the scenes either entirely or partially. Most of the scenes were faded and/or nearly fully erased. The percentage of layers of soot varied on the walls and the ceiling. The burial niches and the ceiling had the most soot. Presumably, there was once a fire burning directly under the scenes, which badly damaged the upper friezes and the ceiling. The soot on the lower frieze was probably lighter because of the heavy layer of debris protecting it. Thus, the fire was concentrated to the upper parts of the tomb. No one can determine exactly why and when the soot was created. While von Bissing describes a few scenes in the C1 burial chamber in his publication, as well as a hieroglyphic column on the back wall of the central niche, the text was completely covered with soot. When the author visited the tomb, it had to be cleaned. It is confusing that von Bissing does not refer to any soot in the tomb in his publications. However, his overly brief

---

[249] Neugebauer and Parker, *EAT* III, 99.; Clerc, 'Isis-Sothis dans le monde romaine', 255.; Venit, *Visualizing the Afterlife*, 193.
[250] Clerc, 'Isis-Sothis dans le monde romaine', 281.
[251] Neugebauer and Parker, *EAT* III, 99.
[252] Clerc suggests that the first apparence of Isis-Sothis in Egypt is on Alexandrian coinage struck in years 13 and 16 of the reign of Trajan, G. Clerc, 'Isis-Sothis dans le monde Romaine', in M. de Boer and T. Eldridge (eds.), *Hommages à M.J. Vermaseren, recue'l d'études offert par les auteurs de la série Études préliminaires aux religions orientales da's l'empire romain à Maarten J. Vermaseren 'à l'occasion de son soixantième anniversaire le 7 Avril 1978 1*, 247–281. Leiden, I (Leiden 1978), 255, 260, 264. Dunand refers to some terracottas from Egypt showing Isis-Sothis on dogs, Dunand, *Religion Populaire en Égypte romaine*, 177, pl. xxiii. The appearance of Isis-Sothis on a dog continues until about 400 AD, Neugebauer and Parker, *EAT* III, 99.; A. Alföld, *A Festival of Isis in Rome Under the Christian Emperors of the IVth Century* (Budapest 1937), 22, pl. xvi.
[253] The placement of Isis-Sothis or Harpocrates in the centre of the circular zodiac serves as a sign of the new year, R. Bagnall and D. Rathbone, *Egypt from Alexander to the Copts, An Archaeological and Historical Guide* (London 2004), 204.
[254] Neugebauer and Parker, *EAT* III, 99.
[255] K. Vandorpe, 'Contributions' in R. Bagnall and D. Rathbone (eds.), *Egypt from Alexander to the Copts, An Archaeological and Historical Guide* (London 2004), 204.; C. Leitz, 'Die Sternbilder auf dem rechteckigen und runden Tierkreis von Dendara', *SAK* 34 (2006), 287–89.; J. Quack, 'Egypt as an Astronomical-Astrological Centre between Mesopotamia, Greece, and India', in D. Brown (ed.), *The Interactions of Ancient Astral Science* (Bremen 2018), 92.; S. Nagel, *Isis im Römischen Reich, Teil I, Die Göttin im griechisch-römischen Ägypten, Philippika 109* (Wiesbaden 2019), 264.; Winkler, *JNES* 8, 92.

[256] Venit, *Visualizing the Afterlife*, 193.
[257] Venit, 'Referencing Isis', in L. Bricault and M. Versylus (eds.), *Isis on the Nile*, 100, no. 61.

The Afterlife in Akhmim

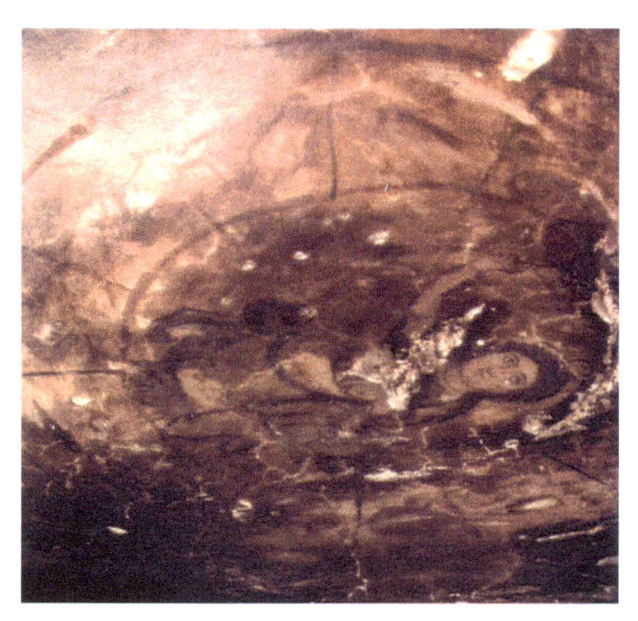

Figure 4.34a. The circular zodiac in tomb C1, as recorded by the German Archaeological Institute (DAI), Kaplan, *BzÄ* 16, 168, pl.88 a.

Figure 4.34b. Photogrammetry of the tomb C1 zodiac (before the restoration in 2019).

Figure 4.34c. Photogrammetry of the tomb C1 zodiac (after the restoration in 2021).

Tomb C1: The So-called 'Tomb of von Bissing' (1897)

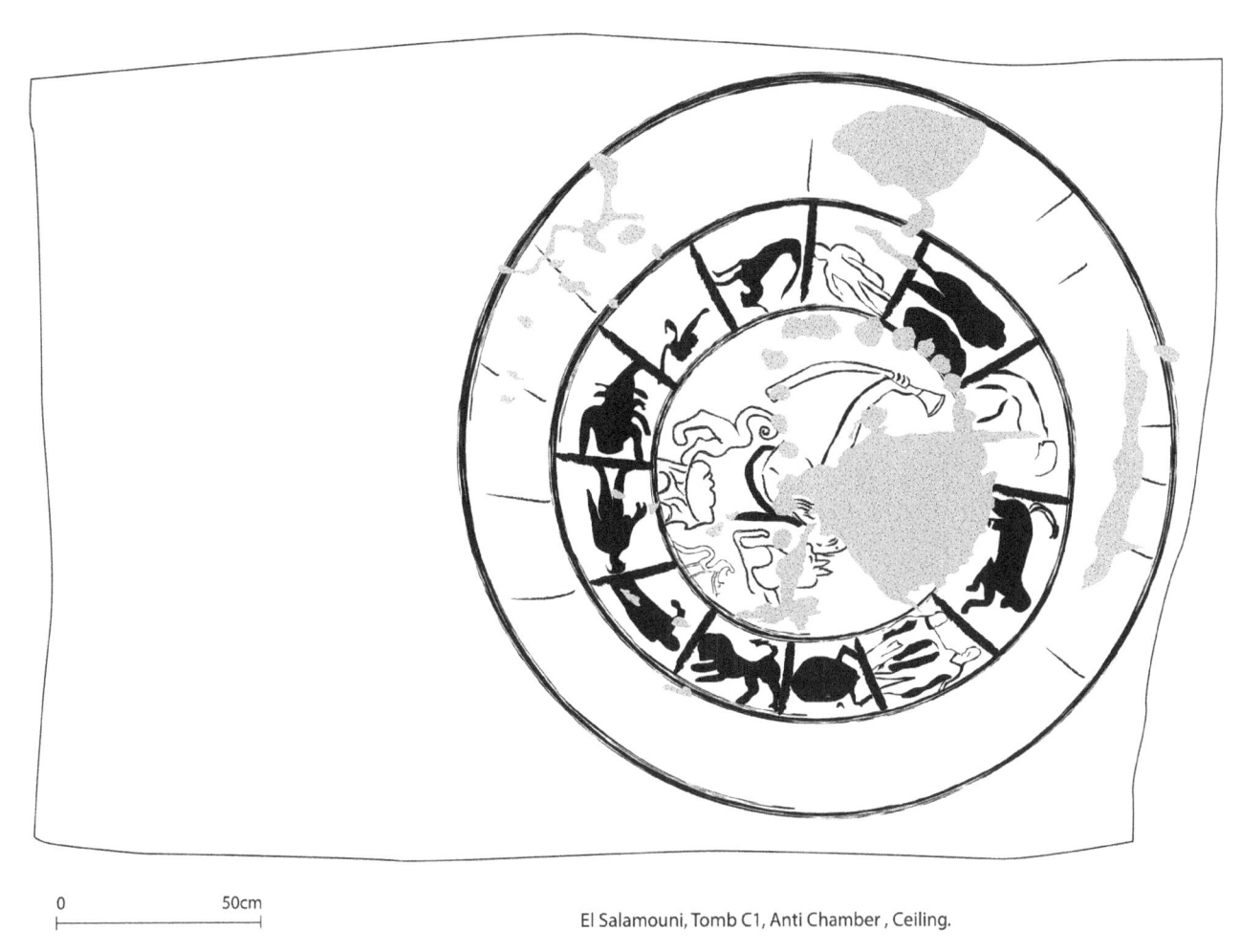

0 50cm

El Salamouni, Tomb C1, Anti Chamber, Ceiling.

Figure 4.34d. A facsimile of the tomb C1 zodiac.

Figure 4.34e. A reconstruction/facsimile of the damaged parts of the tomb C1 zodiac.

The Afterlife in Akhmim

description of only a few selected scenes in the burial chamber is apparently due to the fact that heavy rubble still covered the lower registers and great parts of the niches, making further recording impossible. Attempting to determine the source of the soot in the tomb resulted in various interpretations and speculations. It is possible that during the Coptic persecution, the hermits who escaped and lived in the temple above may have caused a layer of light soot to cover certain areas in the tomb, especially in the burial chamber. Later, after the visit of von Bissing, there was very likely a large-scale fire that consumed the pile of mummies originally documented as filling the tomb during his visit. This fire caused great damage to the painted scenes of both the walls and the ceilings. After the fire, the locals may have covered the entrance of the tomb with sand and rubble. Thus, after 16 years, von Bissing failed to find the tomb again during his second visit.

3. Since the tomb was open and accessible to the local community for a long period of time, people entered and spent time inside of it, damaging it. They wrote their names on the walls of the tomb, and probably burnt fires inside of it. Furthermore, illicit looting is still a big problem in the mountain region in general, and particularly inside the tomb. Although the steel door of the tomb is completely hidden by debris, looters still occasionally break into the tomb. This has caused the cracking and destruction of some of the walls of the chamber, and especially its niches and scenes.

4. There are multiple environmental threats which can potentially harm the tomb, including the scenes and its colours. One problem is the chemical reactions of the algae in the tomb, which leads to biodeterioration. Another issue is the existence of silverfish, which feed on the chemical elements of the colours (Figure 4.35).

Due to the above-mentioned threats, it was very difficult to get access to the burial chamber of tomb C1. Furthermore, due to the presence of heavy debris, von Bissing only noticed the lower portion of the right wall. Here, the deceased is depicted in a long white robe. He stands in front of various gods, including Shu, who is coming up from the ground. There is a *khekrew* frieze, as well as a line of hieroglyphic writing. The writing mentions a wish by the deceased for an eternal life with Osiris[258]. The text says: 'May his soul live forever for Osiris… (lost)'[259].

In tomb C1, the burial chamber is larger than the antechamber. It is in a *triclinium* shape, with three trabeated burial niches of varying size cut into its north, east, and west walls, creating a cruciform plan. Von Bissing proposes that each lateral niche was intended to contain one sarcophagus, while the central one was meant to house two[260]. The ceiling of the chamber is not flat; the artist smoothed and plastered the ceiling without levelling it. The greatest thickness of the ceiling is about 1.90cm.,

Figure 4.35. The presence of silverfish in the burial chamber of tomb C1.

while its smallest thickness is about 1.75cm. in its centre. The burial chamber contains a decorative program of Egyptian iconography.

4.2.15: The Southern B3 Wall

The southern B3 wall of tomb C1 includes a doorway to the burial chamber. When first examined by the author, it was found that the left side of the wall was full of debris and was therefore more damaged than the right side (Figure 4.36).

4.2.16: The Eastern Upper Frieze to the Right of the Doorway

The upper frieze to the right of the doorway, on the east side of the tomb, is dark. It has been fully covered with heavy soot (Figure 4.37). After removing the soot, it could be determined that the wall is divided into two friezes. The upper frieze expresses the idea of the heavenly cow-goddess Mehet-Weret, who gives birth to the sun god by transforming him from his underworld form of Osiris into his celestial form of a young sun god[261]. The celestial cow faces the doorway of the burial chamber. She crouches upon a coffin containing the mummified body of the deceased, which rests on a bier. The scene resembles that of the Book of the Dead spells 148 and 162, where the heavenly cow guides the deceased safely through the sky. In the tomb, the cow is painted in yellow, while the middle part of her body is red with black borders. She wears a *djed* pillar emblem on a cord around her neck. The mummy is painted red and rests on a yellow bier[262] with six symbolic objects are placed beneath it (Figure 4.38). They are probably a rushed version of those which were photographed by Kuhlmann in one of the El-Salamuni tombs[263]. The objects may be votive offerings[264], which

---

[258] Kaplan, *BzÄ* 16, 168.
[259] Von Bissing, *ASAE* 50, 559.; Kaplan, *BzÄ* 16, 168.
[260] Von Bissing, *ASAE* 50, 559.
[261] Kurth, *Materialien zum Totenglauben*, 85.
[262] A similar scene in the tomb of Petosiris depicts Mehet-Weret carrying the mummy of the deceased, Osing, *AV* 28, 83.
[263] Kuhlmann, *SDAIK* 11, pl. 35b. Kaplan named it 'tomb VI', Kaplan, *BzÄ* 16, 175, fig. 98b. Venit suggests that the unclear objects under the bed are the expected canopic jars, Venit, *Visualizing the Afterlife*, 185.
[264] Schweitzer, *BIFAO* 98, 341.

Tomb C1: The So-called 'Tomb of von Bissing' (1897)

Figure 4.36. The south B3 wall of tomb C1, which is covered with debris and soot.

are deposited by the living to help the deceased in his or her transfiguration[265]. The transport of the deceased by Mehet-Weret is a featured scene in the El-Salamuni tombs. Below this scene, the second frieze shows a recumbent figure of Anubis on a shrine, facing the burial niche. He is painted yellow and black, and wears the same *djed* pillar emblem on a cord around his neck as the heavenly cow. Eight symbolic objects are shown below the shrine.

4.2.17: The Eastern Lower Frieze to the Right of the Doorway

On the lower frieze to the right of the doorway, the deceased is shown in his traditional fringed garment. He has a beardless face and raises his hands in a gesture of veneration before the four sons of Horus, who are all depicted on an adjacent east wall. Only the figure of the deceased and the traditional high altar are depicted in the lower frieze (Figure 4.39).

4.2.18: The Western Left Side the Entrance

The western left side of the entrance of tomb C1 was fully covered with soot. This was especially true for the upper register. The destruction caused by looters and the significant cracks in the wall are especially visible on the lower register (Figure 4.40).

Figure 4.37. The upper frieze of the south B3 wall of tomb C1, to the right of the doorway. It is covered with soot.

---
[265] In the Roman cemetery of Dush, a tall cylindrical jar filled with the fruit of the dom palm is found next to a large granite sarcophagus, M. Smith, *Traversing Eternity, Texts for the Afterlife from Ptolemaic and Roman Egypt* (Oxford 2009), 45.

The Afterlife in Akhmim

Figure 4.38. The B3 wall of tomb C1 after removing the soot.

Figure 4.39. The deceased male in a gesture of veneration in tomb C1.

4.2.19: The Upper Frieze to the Left of the Entrance

After having undergone a restoration process, the upper frieze is now capable of being deciphered. The scene shows the deceased in his traditional garb, with his arms raised in veneration of a jackal-headed daemon. The frieze to the left of this depicts another similar custom of the deceased; two goddesses, presumably Isis and Nephthys, flank an anthropomorphic shrouded figure of a *djed* pillar. Here, Osiris is depicted with his arms crossed over his chest, holding two sceptres. His torso emerges from the upper part of the *djed* pillar, and is crowned with two feathers[266]. The *djed* pillar is said to represent the upright spinal column of

---

[266] The Osirian *djed* fetish, being flanked by Isis and Nephtyhs, is widely depicted on the chests of Akhmim, Freiburg MNM AE953.; Leiden RMO F.1953/11.1.; Paris Louvre E 13321 (4589).; Strasbourg IDE, inv.no. 1600.; Bruwier and Mekis, 'Diversity of the Akhmimic Funerary Art', in M. Mosher (ed.), *The Book of the Dead*, 53–54, fig. 20, no. 229. Venit notices that the *djed* pillar fetish is quite similar to the one in the house-tomb 21 of Tuna el-Gebel, though it is vastly different in its style and imagery, Venit, *Visualizing the Afterlife*, 186.

Osiris, and symbolises stability and resurrection[267]. The goddess on the right side of the pillar touches the right hand of Osiris with her right hand and the *djed* pillar with her left. The goddess on the left has the same gesture, although her hands are farther away from the pillar. There is a bit space between her and the pillar, which could be a mistake from the artist. Horizontal and vertical pseudo-columns are placed above the heads of the figures. Here, the deceased possess the qualities of Osiris, who is called the 'Osiris of NN'. The deceased are therefore meant to enjoy bodily rejuvenation. A persistent and powerful link with Osiris is prominent in this scene through the adoration and erecting of the pillar (Figure 4.41).

4.2.20: The Lower Frieze to the Left of the Entrance

The lower frieze to the left of the tomb C1 entrance suffers from being badly damaged. Therefore, its scene is now demolished. Soot also covers the wall. Fortunately, during Kanawati's visit, he photographed the wall; it is the only scene from the burial chamber to be included in his publication (Figure 4.42). The scene shows Isis and Nephthys venerating an anthropomorphised fetish of Osiris, which is composed of a *djed* pillar capped by a male figure and the feathered crown of Atum. To the right of the fetish, there is the head of a human figure bearing the same facial features as the deceased. It protrudes from a lotus blossom and is flanked by four canopic jars, arranged in groups of two. In one row, the jar of Qebehsenuef is above, and that of Hapi is below. Next to it, Duamutef's jar is above, and Imsety's jar is below. Unfortunately, because of the damage of the wall, only the remains of the Duamutef, Imsety, and Hapi jars are still visible. The scene alludes the rebirth of the deceased in the guise of Khepri.

The adjacent frieze to the left of the *djed* fetish shows the deceased with his hands raised to adore the four sons of Horus, complete with their net-pattern bodies. Each of them holds a long strip of mummy bandages, and a composite sceptre made of the *ꜥnḫ*, *ḏd*, and *wꜣs* sceptres/signs. Only the human-headed Imsety is shown on this wall (as opposed to Duamutef, Hapi, and Qebehsenuef, who are depicted on the adjacent south wall). The traditional high altar with three loaves of bread is visible[268]. The wall

is fully documented via the use of photogrammetry, the creation of drawings, and the creation of a deterioration map (Figures 4.43a-c).

4.2.21: The Western B4 Wall: Overview

The western B4 wall contains the western burial niche, which has been largely destroyed by looters. Debris almost completely covers the niche, as well as great parts of the lower register of the adjacent wall. Furthermore, heavy soot covers the niche and the B4 ceiling. Thus, the figures behind the soot are almost impossible to see; the soot is lighter on the adjacent wall left of the niche, making the figures here more easily visible (Figures 4.44a-b).

4.2.22: The Lower Frieze on the Western B4 Wall

Due to the damage caused to the niche, a great part of the lower register of the B4 wall is destroyed. Furthermore, soot covers the lower part of the wall below the niche. However, some of the scene can still be read. The lower frieze of the wall documents a procession scene before an enthroned figure of Horus, who is protected by Isis standing behind him (Figure 4.45). At the southern corner of the wall, three of the four sons of Horus are depicted: Duamutef, Hapi, and Qebehsenuef. Their bodies are enveloped in shrouds, and they hold composite sceptres made of the *ꜥnḫ*, *ḏd*, and *wꜣs* signs. The sons look towards the doorway of the burial chamber.

Behind the depiction of the four sons of Horus, there is a hieroglyphic column addressed to Osiris. It is still covered with bitumen, which hides its lower part. Only its upper part is currently visible. Removing the heavy soot via the use of chemical materials could also accidently remove parts of the hieroglyphic signs. Therefore, one must be very careful when cleaning the wall. To the left of the column is a human deity who acts as a *psychopomp*, leading the deceased to Horus. He turns his back and faces the deceased, grasping the deceased's left wrist by his right hand. He leads him forward, while saluting Horus with his upraised left hand. Unfortunately, a great part of the deceased's figure is still covered with bitumen, but it is nonetheless clear that he is garbed in a traditional white garment. A hieroglyphic column located behind the deceased is heavily covered with soot. Unfortunately, the wall is thickly burnt. Only the upper part of the text has been cleaned. It reads *ꜥnḫ.f Ḥr r nḤḤ Ḏt* ('May he live, Horus, forever'), which is a traditional formula used in the tombs. The author suggests that here, the male *psychopomp* is probably Haryotes (?), the local deity of adjacent Bompae. This god combines divinity and humanity within a single person, and is seen to widely accompany the deceased via his use on Roman mummy labels. Haryotes was a traditional figure guiding the deceased in El-Salamuni (Figure 4.46).

The next frieze on the lower register shows a procession of seven male deities who stride towards Horus. He is depicted with a falcon head, and is seated on the far northern side of the wall. He wears a white crown, and his

---

[267] The *djed* pillar refers to the resurrection of Osiris. It is therefore often represented inside the bottom of the coffin case, É. Liptay, 'The Wooden Inner Coffin of Takhenemet in the Czartoryski Museum', *Studies in Ancient Art and Civilization* 13 (Krakow 2009), 108.; P. Koemoth, 'Le rite de redresser Osiris', in J. Quaegebeur (ed.), *Ritual and Sacrifice in the Near East, Proceedings of the International Conference Organised by the Katholieke Universiteit Leuven from the 17th to the 20th of April 1991*, OLA 55 (Leuven 1993), 157–74. The Book of the Dead spell 155 associates the *djed* with the backbone and vertebrae of Osiris, and the deceased have to know this spell to safely traverse the gates of the west, M.Abouelata and M.Hossain, 'Continuity of Themes Depicted on Co–n Lids from the Third Intermediate Period to Graeco-Roman Egypt', in A. Amenta and H. Guichard (eds.), *Proceedings of the 1st Vatican Coffin Conference, 19–22 June 2013, A cura di Alessia Amenta e Hélène Guichard* (Vatican 2017), 27.

[268] Bread has always been a basic commodity. The length of the loaves varies in size, including broad loaves with a rim, bread baked in a *bd3* mould, and longer, straight loaves formed without a rim and baked in a *ꜥpr.t* mould, L. Roeten, *Loaves, Beds, Plants and Osiris, Considerations About the Emergence of the Cult of Osiris* (Oxford 2018), 144–45.

The Afterlife in Akhmim

Figure 4.40. The west side of the south B3 wall of tomb C1 (before the restoration in 2019).

Figure 4.41. Photogrammetry of the upper frieze on the west side of the south B3 wall in tomb C1 (after the restoration in 2021).

body is shrouded in black and red. His arms are crossed over his chest in the traditional Osirian posture. A female deity, presumably Isis, is also shown. She has bare breasts and wears a fitted red garment, as well as bracelets, a collar, and a crown with two cow horns framing a red sun disc. She touches the elbow of Horus with her lowered left hand and holds up her right one in a protective stance.

At the head of the entire procession is another image of Horus as a falcon-headed god who wears the *pschent* crown. He raises his hands and offers an image of a falcon in his left hand[269]. Behind him, there is a partially damaged deity. While his upper part is damaged, it can be determined that he is crowned with a large solar disc placed on a yellow *nemes* headdress. He could possibly be the god Ra-Horakhty with a falcon-head. He is shown presenting an object to Horus. Furthermore, in this scene, a ram-headed deity is shown. He wears an *atef* crown, and is probably Amun, who was widely worshipped in the *chora*, especially in Thebes and the Oases[270]. The figure presents a libation vase in his left hand, and holds up his right hand in praise or reverence. Behind Amun walks a serpent-headed deity, who wears a large solar disc. He is in the same gesture as Amun, holding a libation vase with his left hand, and showing reverence to Horus with his upraised right hand. He is followed by the ibis-headed Thoth, who is depicted wearing an *atef* crown. He holds a tall palm branch with his lowered left hand, while saluting Horus with his upraised right hand. Finally, two partially damaged deities can be seen at the rear of the procession. Only their lower parts and the bottom part of the second one's crown can still be seen. They are probably both making the same gesture as Thoth, holding a long palm frond in their left hand, and venerating Horus with their upraised right hand. Heavy soot covers the damaged figure of the second deity.

It is interesting to note that on the north wall of both the antechamber and the burial chamber, Horus is the presiding and dominant god in the depictions. However, all of the funerary practices are addressed to Osiris. The two gods appear simultaneously on the northern and southern wall of the antechamber. Here, while Horus supervises the Court of Judgement on the upper register of the antechamber wall, the deceased pays homage to the mummiform figure of Osiris below. On the opposite wall, Osiris dominates the upper scene, while the deceased venerates Horus below. There is a procession of seven male deities striding before Horus along one wall, while seven female deities make offerings before Osiris in the burial chamber. This latter scene is a traditional recurring scene in the El-Salamuni tombs, and is always depicted in the burial chamber.

Figure 4.42. The west side of the south B3 wall of tomb C1, Kanawati, *Sohag in Upper Egypt*, pl. 41.

Evidence of the solar-Osirian cycle is prominent in El-Salamuni; Re (Horus) and Osiris are scrupulously drawn in the tombs. The requests of the deceased are addressed to each god individually, in hopes of the deceased achieving celestial resurrection[271]. The hope was that the spirit of the deceased would become associated with the solar-Osirian cult and would therefore be entitled to mortuary offerings of it own. The zodiac thus represents a celestial afterlife, referencing the events of the Judgement Court before Horus, and confirming the solar connections of the tomb owner. The solar circuit was viewed as consisting of two parts: the sky and the underworld. While Re had dominion over both parts, Osiris only reigned over the second. Thus, in the tomb, Re is ultimately in charge of regulating and supervising the afterlife of the deceased, along with Osiris. Because of the damage done to the El-Salamuni tombs, the Court of Judgement scene is not always capable of being discerned. Among the few remaining (known) scenes, the previously mentioned scene is the only one in which Horus supervises the Judgement Court instead of Osiris. In other examples from outside El-Salamuni, Re-Horakhty sometimes appears as the Lord of the Court[272].

---

[269] The offering of a falcon by Thoth to Osiris is attested twice in Kom El-Schukafa, A. Guimier-Sorbets and M. Seif El-Din, 'Life after Death, an Original Form of Bilingual Iconography in the Necropolis of Kawm al-Shuqafa', in A. Hirst and M. Silk (eds), *Alexandria, Real and Imagined* (Alexandria 2004), 138, figs. 7.1, 2.; A. Guimier-Sorbets, A. Pelle, and M. Seif El-Din, *Resurrection in Alexandria: the Painted Greco-Roman Tombs of Kom al–Shuqafa, ARCE Press* (Cairo 2017), 78, figs. 112, 116.
[270] Venit suggests that the ram-headed god in SiAmun's tomb is Amun, given the patronage of Siwa, Venit, *Visulaizing the Afterlife*, 139.

[271] On the solar-Osirian unity, see Smith, *Following Osiris*, 271–355.
[272] Kurth, *Der Sarg der Teüris*, fig. 9.2.

The Afterlife in Akhmim

Figure 4.43a. Photogrammetry of the west side of the south B3 wall of tomb C1.

El Salamouni, Tomb C1, Burial Chamber, South Wall, B 3.

Figure 4.43b. A facsimile drawing of the south B3 wall of tomb C1.

124

Tomb C1: The So-called 'Tomb of von Bissing' (1897)

El Salamouni, Tomb C1, Burial Chamber, South Wall, B 3, reconstruction.

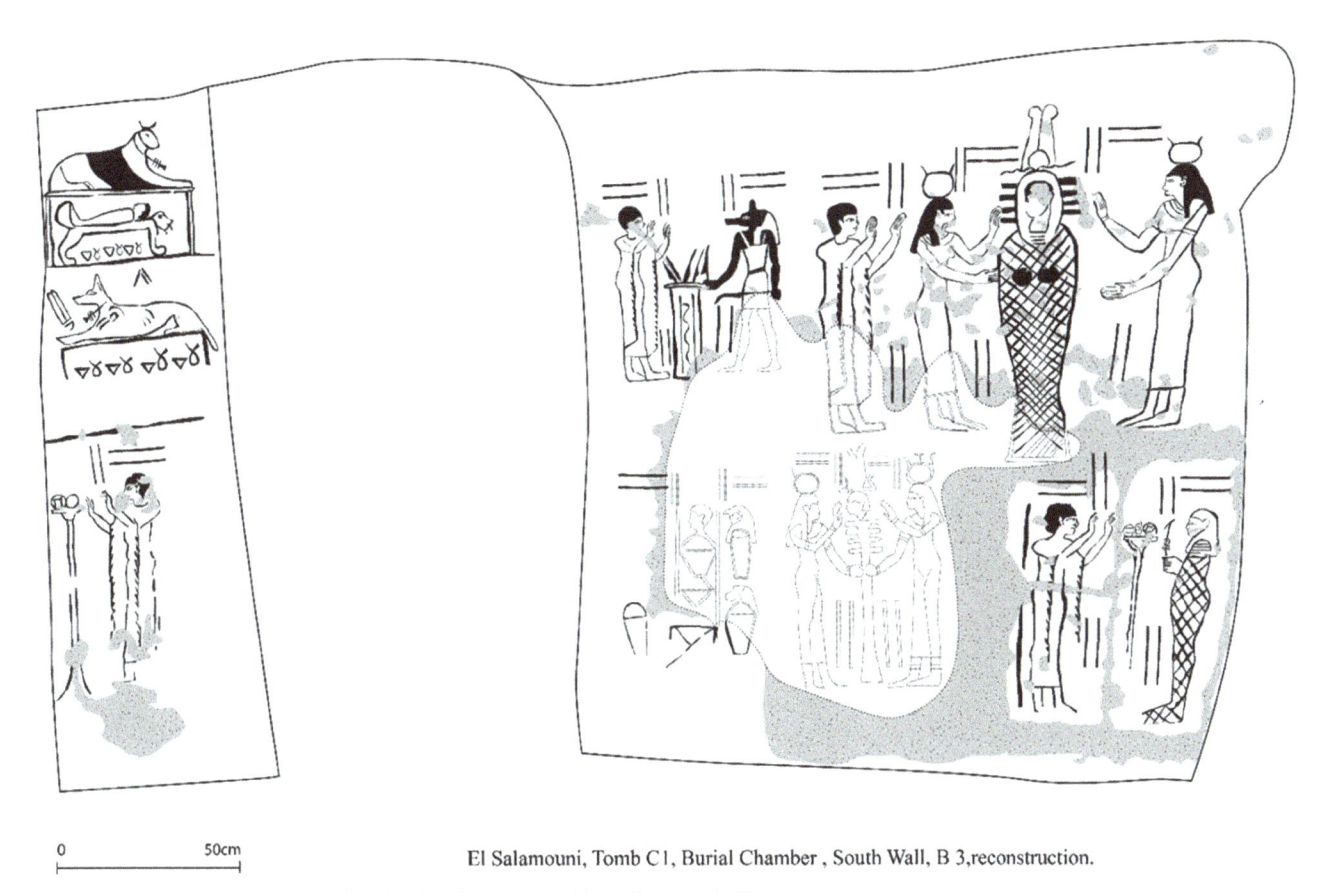

Figure 4.43c. A reconstruction/facsimile of the south B3 wall of tomb C1.

4.2.23: The Wall B4 Niche

Wall B4 contains a burial niche to the west, which has been largely damaged by looters, and which is still covered with a heavy layer of soot. The looters created a deep hole in the rear wall of the niche, searching for treasures which they wrongly believed were stored behind it (Figure 4.47).

Even after conservation efforts targeting the remaining part of the niche's rear wall, the niche's colours are faded. The niche is decorated in an Egyptian style, with *khekrew* decorations and recumbent jackals. This style is common in the tombs of El-Salamuni and Athribis[273].

The rear wall of the niche has three *khekrew* decorations representing eternity; there is one green symbol in the middle, flanked by two red ones. The niche wall has faced significant damage, and only the rear part of the crouching Anubis jackal, together with the upper parts of the other three *khekrew* signs, are still visible. Another crouching jackal is located on the far southern part of the niche. Ointment jars can be found under the funerary bed. The ointment jars may have been combined with canopic jars or bags of eye paint (*afr wDw*). Eye paint became a common offering to deities during the Graeco-Roman Period[274]. Anubis serves as a guard of the deceased, and is occasionally associated with the tombs' entrances. He is

Figure 4.44a. The heavy debris covering the west B4 wall of tomb C1.

Figure 4.44b. The west B4 wall of tomb C1 after removing the debris.

---
[273] Petrie, *Athribis*, pl. 40.
[274] S. Cauville, *Offerings to the Gods in Egyptian Temples* (Leuven 2012), 126.

125

The Afterlife in Akhmim

Figure 4.45. The male deities' procession before Osiris-Sokar, as depicted on the lower frieze of the west B4 wall of tomb C1.

Figure 4.46. Haryotes(?) shown guiding a deceased male in tomb F3, which is located on the southern section of El-Salamuni Mountain.

Figure 4.47. The damaged west burial niche in the B4 wall of tomb C1.

thus an attendant for the deceased along their passage to the Court of Judgement, and a keeper of the key for the door of the afterlife[275]. The damaged part of the niche is about 1.09cm. thick and most probably contained a traditional crouching Anubis, complete with *khekrew* signs. Because the niche was exposed to direct fire, its green colour suffered corrosion and oxidation. Thus, improving its legibility and preserving its colour was important during the conservation work.

The left lateral wall of the niche shows a human-headed bird (*ba*) of the deceased receiving water from a tree goddess. The adjacent frieze has an image of a rearing, anthropomorphised, snake-headed deity named *NHb-K3w*, or Nehebkau. He is said to be half human and half serpent, as a man with a serpent's head and tail. Unfortunately, his head is only partially preserved due to damage caused to the wall.

The right lateral wall of the niche shows three *khekrew* signs and a jackal crouching on his shrine, complete with traditional signs below (Figures 4.48a-c). The *khekrew* frieze was widely used as a royal symbol. Its use was first limited to temples and royal tombs[276], but later, it began to be used in the imagery of tombs of private people, and became commonly included in the tombs of the *chora*[277].

---

[275] Kurth, *Der Sarg der Teüris*, 11. Anubis is often shown guarding the doors of the Akhmimic canopic chests. Their doors are often covered with the beginning of a formula meant to be recited by Osiris (Bremen ÜM, B14732, and Edinburgh NMS, inv. no. 1907.689+A). However, these formulas could also be recited by Anubis, as is the case with two examples from Akhmim (Berkeley PAHMA, inv. no. 6–11749, and Tübingen UT, ÄS 977). M. Bruwier, and T. Mekes note that the presence of Anubis as a guard for the body of the deceased may be a special feature of Akhmim, as it is not yet observed for the caskets found in other necropoleis, 'Diversity at Akhmim', in M. Mosher (ed.), *The Book of the Dead*, 50, nos. 212, 213.

[276] The *khekrew* frieze was a common ornamentational element used in the royal tombs of King Thutmose III and Amenhotep II in the Valley of the Kings, E. Hornung, *Exploring the Beyond* (trans. D. Roscoe), in E. Hornung and B. Bryan (eds.), *The Quest for Immortality, Treasures of Ancient Egypt* (Washington 2002), 38, fig. 22.

[277] Kurth, *Der Sarg der Teüris*, 59. *Khekrew* signs also ornament the burial niche of the zodiac tomb (the tomb of the Two Brothers) at Athribis, Petrie, *Athribis*, pl. xl. This is also the case in the tomb of Siamun at Siwa, A. Fakhry, *The Egyptian Deserts, Siwa Oasis, its History and Antiquities* (Cairo 1944), pl. xxixa.; Venit, *Visualizing the Afterlife*, 139–40, fig. 4.33. The *khekrew* frieze ornaments one of the gates of the underworld in the tomb of Petubastis at Dakhla (Osing, *AV* 28, 77), as well as the tomb of Petosiris, N. Cherpion, J. Corteggiani, and J. Gout, *Le Tombeau de petosiris a Touna El-Gebel, Relevé Photographique, BiGen* 27, IFAO (Cairo 2007), 53, 152.

Tomb C1: The So-called 'Tomb of von Bissing' (1897)

Figure 4.48a. The back of the west burial niche on wall B4 of tomb C1 (after the restoration in 2021).

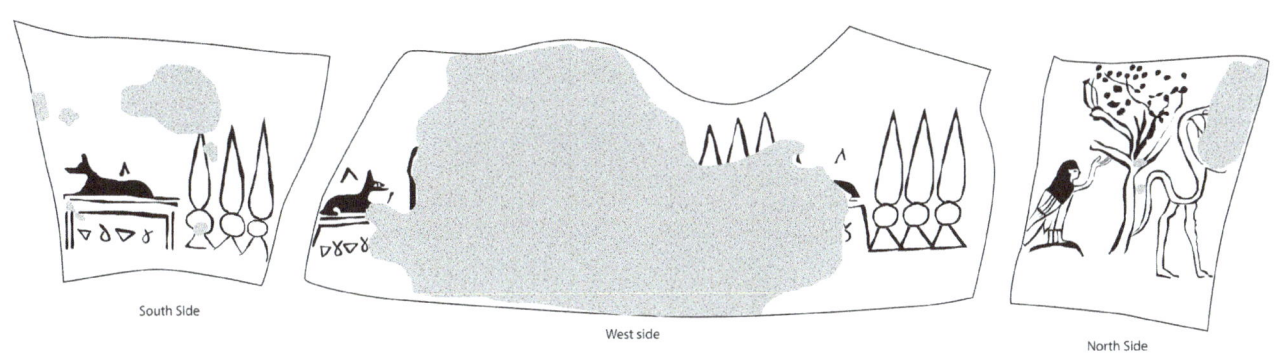

Figure 4.48b. A facsimile of the west burial niche in tomb C1.

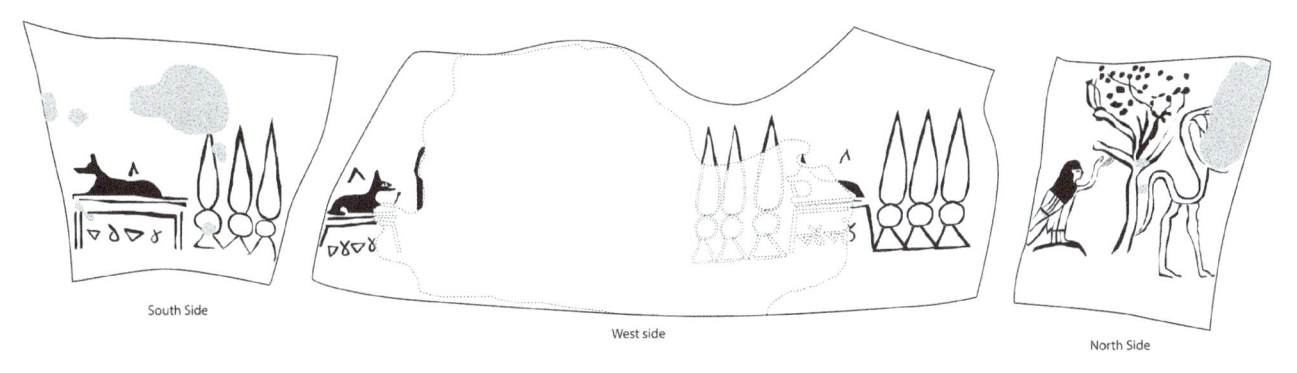

Figure 4.48c. A reconstruction drawing of the west burial niche in tomb C1.

Venit notes the link between the high position of the patrons of the Graeco-Roman tombs and the use of royal signs and symbols[278].

The snake is one of the apotropaic gods listed amongst the guardians of the doors of the netherworld, and is one of the most widespread symbols of magic during the Graeco-Roman Period[279]. Nehebkau was one of the 42 judges in the Court of Judgement. He absolved the souls of sin, and provided the justified deceased with food and drink.

Therefore, the deceased could have hopes of becoming Nehebkau himself[280]. The god was ultimately considered a powerful, benevolent, and protective deity[281], and could be recognised by the deceased as a fierce protector of the dead, and as a guardian of the entrance to the *Duat*[282].

---

[278] As depicted in house-tomb 21 at Tuna El-Gebel, Venit, *Visualizing the Afterlife*, 197.
[279] Lucarelli, 'The So-Called Vignette of Spell 182', 86.

[280] *CT* V, 371; *i Ink NHb-K A w*, or *Hpr m nHb-Kaw*.
[281] Nekhebkau is first attested in the Pyramid Texts as a protective deity who looks after the pharaoh and the Egyptians in the afterlife. He is said to be the son of Geb and Renenutet. In CT 762, it is stated: '*O Osiris N, you are Nekhebkau, son of Geb, born of your mother Renenutet*' (*H3 Wsir n pn, twt NHb-K3. w s3 Gb, ms (w).n Rnnwt.t*).
[282] T. Wilkinson, *The Complete Gods and Goddesses of Ancient Egypt* (New York 2003), 223. The snake-daemon with human legs (two or four) or with both legs and arms are widely depicted in the Books of the Afterlife. Sa-ta with two human legs is depicted in BD 87, while

127

The Afterlife in Akhmim

Nehebkau is occasionally represented as a personal guard of Osiris. In later mythology, he is described as a companion of the sun god Re and as an attendant of the deceased. The serpent evokes spell 87 of the Book of the Dead, where the deceased hopes to be transformed into a snake. Here, Nehebkau is meant to help make the deceased happy, filling their hearts with joy and justice. In the Book of the Dead, Nehebkau states: '*I am a long-lived snake; I pass the night and am reborn every day. I am a snake which is in the limits of the earth; I pass the night and [am] reborn, renewed and rejuvenated every day*'[283]. Nehebkau is thus one of the characteristics of the sun god, and eventually became the servant and partner of him. In the mythology, the snake assists Re in moving the solar boat through the sky throughout the day, from the east to the west. Therefore, Nehebkau protects the deceased during their journey in the barque of Re to the underworld[284]. However, this serpent-headed figure can also represent the serpent Khepry, who is depicted in the lower register of the tenth hour of the *Imyduat*[285]. Khepry is the snake that protects Re during his transit through the netherworld, its voice circulating through the 'mysterious place' where Re enters the sky[286]. In the Hellenic magical papyri, this

Figure 4.49a. The wall left of the niche in tomb C1 (before the restoration in 2019).

gnostic pantheistic image is attributed to Agathos Daimon, holding the rising sun[287].

4.2.24: The B4 Wall to the Left of the Niche

Multiple scenes appear on the upper and the lower friezes of the B4 wall to the left of the niche; a black line was used to separate them (Figures 4.49a-b). The upper scene shows three identical figures of the deceased in his traditional white garment. Each figure holds up his hands in reverence before a daemon, who holds two knives and stands before a gate with a protective snake inside. The first daemon has a falcon head and wears a *pschent*, while the second daemon has a cow's head. The third daemon has the head of a lion. The adjacent scene to the left shows the god Shu with a sun disc upon his head. He raises the *pt* sign for the sky with his hands, alluding to vignette 15 of the Book of the Dead, titled *Hymns to the Creator Sun-God* (Figure 4.50)[288]. The figure of Shu has previously been documented by von Bissing as appearing with a *khekrew* frieze[289]. Shu is well known as the protector of the sun god, as illustrated by his role in the myth of the sun god's eye[290]. On the B4 wall, Shu is flanked by seven feathered *ba* birds with different heads. Three are on each side, while the last bird is directly below Shu. The top four birds have human heads, symbolizing the *ba* of the deceased, while the three lower birds have baboon heads[291].

Nehebkau is widely shown in the 10th mound of BD 149 as the 'Bull of Nut', as well as in BD 162 as Atum, and BD 163 portrays a snake with two human legs and a solar disk on a pair of horns. For the god Nehebkau see, A. Abdelhalim, 'Snakes with Human Arms and Legs in Ancient Egyptian Books of the Afterlife', *ASAE* 88(2015), 291-300; M. Massiera, *Les divinités ophidiennes Nâou, Néhebkaou et le fonctionnement des kaou d'après les premiers corpus funéraires de l'Égypte ancienne*, Thèse de Doctorat Montpellier 3, (Montpellier 2013); W. Ramadan, 'Was There a Chapel of Nehebkaw in Heliopolis?', *GM* 110 (1989) 55-63; A. Moussa, 'A Seated Statue of nHb-kA.w from Heliopolis', in *Hommage J. Leclant*, BdE 106/1 (1994), 479-483; N. Omar, 'The God Nehebkau in Heliopolis', *Abgadiyat* 7 (2012), 32–38.; A. Shorter, 'The God Nehebkau', *JEA* 21(1935), 41–48. Nehebkau is depicted on the coffin of Teüris as one of the deities alongside the four sons of Horus, and the deceased is shown in a procession before Osiris, Kurth, *Der Sarg der Teüris*, figs. B, 3.2.

[283] R. Faulkner, *The Ancient Egyptian Book of the Dead* (New York 1972), 84, 86.; Allen, *SAOC* 37, 184. The snake deity is widely depicted on wooden stelae and coffins. The coffin Berlin 17940 names the snake as Atum, in association with Osiris or Ra-Horakhty. The double crown that it wears represents the god Osiris-Atum in the Book of the Dead vignette 125, Seeber, *MÄS* 35, 131, fig. 576, 134, fig. 586. On the connection between the snake and Atum, see M. Lichtheim, *Ancient Egyptian Literature, A Book of Readings, The Late Period* III (Berkeley, Los Angeles, London 1980), 214. Atum also appears as a snake on the Cairo Stela (Egyptian Museum SR 9447). Regarding the appearance of the snake deity on stelae and coffins, see H. El-Leithy, 'Iconography and Function of Stelae and Coffins in Dynasties 25–26', in J. Taylor and M. Vandenbusch (eds.), *Ancient Egyptian Coffins, Crafts, Traditions, and Functionality*, British Museum Publications on Egypt and Sudan 4 (Leuven 2018), 66–69.

[284] In the Book of the Dead vignette 115a, it is stated: *DA.k n Hrii m ꜥnx WAs NHb-Kaw m anDt rSi wDA.k ib.k*, which translates to mean '*you sail over the sky in life and health, Nehebkeau being in the mandjet barque, your barque rejoices your heart*', A. Shorter, 'Two Statuettes of the goddess Sekhmet-Upastet', *JEA* 18 (1932), 45.

[285] E. Hornung, *Das Buch von den Pforten des Jenseits: nach den Versionen des Neuen Reiches*, Teil 2, Übersetzung und Kommentar, *Aegyptiaca Helvetica* 8 (Geneva 1984), 240–41.

[286] J. Darnell and C. Darnell, *The Ancient Egyptian Netherworld Books* (Atlanta 2018), 315.; M. Minas-Nerpel, *Der Gott Chepri, untersuchungen zu Schriftzeugnissen und ikonographischen Quellen vom Alten Reich bis in griechisch-römische Zeit*, OLA 154 (Leuven 2006), 194–97. This snake is mentioned in the Demotic story of Setne, P. Piccione, 'The Gaming Episode in the Tale of Setne, Khamwas as a Religious Metaphor', in D. Silverman (ed.), *For His Ka: Essays Offered in Memory of Klaus Baer*, SAOC 55 (Chicago 1994), 201–03.

[287] The Bes *Pantheos* has been depicted in the P. Brooklyn 47.218.156 of the Ptolemaic Period, M. Tarasenko, 'Gliedervergottung Texts and Theogonic Ideas in Ancient Egypt', in A. Maravellia and N. Guilhou (eds.), *Environment and Religion* (Summertown 2020), 438–39.; J. Assmann, 'Primat und Transzenden, Structure und Genese der ägyptischen Vorstellung eines 'höchsten Wesens'', in W. Westendorf (ed.), *Aspekte der spätägyptischen Religion*, GOF 9 (Wiesbaden 1979), 7.

[288] By the Late and Ptolemaic Periods, sun hymns were often inscribed on wooden stelae that were placed with the coffin in the burial chamber, Quirke, *Going Out in Daylight*, 33.

[289] Von Bissing, *ASAE* 50, 559. He did not recognise the gatekeepers.

[290] M. Smith, 'Demotischer Mythos vom Sonnen-auge', *LÄ* V (1984), 1082–87.; W. Spiegelberg, *Der ägyptische Mythus vom Sonnenauge (der Papyrus der Tierfabeln-„Kufi")*. *Nach dem Leidener demotischen Papyrus I* 384 (Strasbourg 1917).

[291] Occasionally, a god in baboon form is labelled 'Isdes', which is a form of Thoth that occurs in the Roman period, C. Leitz, *LGG*, 558–61.; P. Boylan, *Thoth, The Hermes of Egypt* (London 1922), 201.; C. Bleeker, *Hathor and Thoth, Two Key Figures of the Ancient Egyptian Religion* (Leiden 1973), 107. Thoth and Isdes were both associated with judgement

Figure 4.49b. The wall left of the niche in tomb C1 (after the restoration in 2021).

This scene is similar to the one depicted on the south side of the east wall of room 1 at the tomb of Petosiris in El-Mazawaka. The only difference is that at El-Mazawaka, Shu is surrounded by eight *ba* birds with human or jackal heads, rather than seven. Osing identifies the scene as indicating the sun's journey during the day; the sun's journey at night is appropriately depicted on the west wall[292].

Onouris (*InHrt*)-Shu[293], who was the god of Thinis and especially Naga ed-Der, was transported to and worshipped in Akhmim[294] as the son of Re. Onouris is one of the 14 gods depicted on the famous Roman pillar of Ptolemagrios, where he is shown wearing a single feather[295]. He is related to the god Shu in the solar barque of Re, and in Akhmim, he is characterised by his traditional crown with four feathers. Onouris is depicted at El-Salamuni because he was regarded as a hunter and warrior god who was associated with the desert and its tricks[296]. Furthermore, many popular theophoric names are found in the papyri and mummy labels from Panopolis, including Shu as *Ns-Šw* and *Wdȝ-Šw*[297].

The lower frieze on the wall left of the niche shows a unique depiction of vignette 17 of the Book of the Dead.

Figure 4.50. A depiction of Shu raising the *pt* sign of the sky in tomb C1.

It illustrates the journey of the sun god in his boat through the 12 hours of the night in the subterranean netherworld in order to unite with the dead body of Osiris. A papyrus barque carries the mummy of the deceased upon a bier. Five traditional objects are depicted beneath the bier. A crouching figure of the ram god Atum, representing the nocturnal version of Re, as well as a manifestation of the *ba* (*bȝ ꜥnx*), surmounts the mummy. The face of the mummy is painted green, representing the flesh tone of the god Osiris[298]. The Egyptians believed that the colour

---

and the moon. Egyptian kings, the sun, and Re were also depicted as baboons, J. Darnell, *The Enigmatic Netherworld Books of the Solar Osirian Unity, Cryptographic Compositions in the Tombs of Tutankhamun, Ramesses VI and Ramesses IX*, OBO 198 (Göttingen 2004), 403–04.

[292] Osing, *AV* 28, 85, figs. 25a, 33b.
[293] *LÄ* IV, 573–74.
[294] Depauw, 'The Late Funerary Material from Akhmim,' in A. Egberts et al. (eds.), *Perspectives on Panopolis*, 73.; J. Karig, 'Achmim,' *LÄ* I, 54–55.; Sauneron and Vercouter, *RdÉ* 14, 53–57 no. 2. Onouris was merged with the air god Shu by the New Kingdom, Junker, 'Die Onouris Legend', *DAWW* 59 (Vienna 1917), 56–57. Ares correspondes to the Egyptian god Onouris in the Panopolite nome, J. Bremmer, 'Aëtius, Arius Didymus and the Transmission of Doxography', *Mnemosyne* 51(1998), 157–58, no. 14.
[295] G. Clerc and J. Leclant, *Lexicon Iconographicum Mythologiae Classicae LIMC* VI (Zürich, 1981–99).
[296] Junker, *Die Onouris Legend*, 130.; M. Valloggia, 'This sur la route des Oasis', *BIFAO* suppl. 81 (1981), 187. One of the desert routes connecting the oases of Dakhla and Kharga ends at Girga and attests to the prominence of Onouris at Thinis, E. Brokvarski, *Naga ed-Der in the First Intermediate Period* (Boston 2018), 63.
[297] M. Depauw, 'The Late Funerary Material from Akhmim', in A. Egberts et al. (eds.), *Perspectives on Panopolis*, 74.

[298] This is known since the sixth dynasty, and during the New Kingdom, it was typical for both males and females, R. van Walsem, *The Coffin of Djedmonthiufankh in the National Museum of Antiquities of Leiden, I: Technical and Iconographic/Iconological Aspects*, EU 10 (Leiden 1997), 109.; id., 'The Coffin of Djedmonthuiufankh in the National Museum of Antiquities at Leiden', *DE* 43 (1997), 55–56.

possessed an apotropaic power, being the colour of rebirth[299]. The deceased would need to identify himself with the creator god Atum, and appeal to Atum to secure a place in his solar barque. On the wall left of the niche, the barque is rowed by six sailors in the guise of kings, resembling the kingly followers of Re (the spirits of the *ba* and Nekhen) in his solar barque[300]. They are shown flanking the mummy of the deceased in two groups; each group has three members which face the mummy as well as each other. At the prow of the barque, the first group of sailors wear the red crown, and are led by a falcon-headed deity. The deity, who is probably Horus, turns his head towards the mummy and holds the rudder rope. He stands at the front of a queue of sailor deities who are responsible for both the protection of the deceased voyagers on the barque and their safe departure from the vessel. At the stern of the boat, the other three sailors wear the white crown. The sailors will help the deceased to transverse the endless waters of the Primeval Chaos of Nun. The vignette thus signifies the cyclical resurrection and victory of the deceased, and the impotence of the enemies of the gods[301].

Two mourning goddesses flank the bier. They may be *drt* women, who are personifications of the mourning and protective aspects of Isis and Nephthys. Hence, they assist the mummy and weep in a symbolic way. They are shown kneeling respectively upon the ground before the deceased. Both are with bare breasts. The goddess at the head of the bier wears a red fitted garment, while the other at the rear wears a green one. They both raise one hand to touch the mummy, and they both touch the bier with their other hands, which are lowered. Among the regeneration rites for the deceased, this mourning ritual, as executed here by the two female mourners, recalls the Opening of the Mouth rite, and evokes the protection laments of Isis and Nephthys. The women also represent the funerary attendants (so-called 'vigilants') who are responsible for the constant protection of the mummy and for keeping the nightly vigil (in German, *Stundenwachen*) maintained over Osiris' prepared mummy[302]. They guard the deceased during their travel through the divisions between the 12 hours of the day and night, securing safety for the deceased in their periodic attempts at transfiguration[303]. The depiction of funerary 'vigilants' alongside six crouching deities is widely attested on numerous coffins from Panopolis[304]. R. Lucarelli proposes that this sort of depiction, where a mummy on a funerary bed is being protected by the kneeling or squatting figures of Isis and Nephthys and the four sons of Horus, is a special representation of the nightly vigil of the mummy of Osiris[305].

In chapter 17 of the Book of the Dead, the solar-Osirian connection is confirmed. Osiris and Re embrace when they meet in Djedu[306]. The ram symbolises the solar-Osirian union, and is associated with the *ba*, being an indication of the location of the *Duat* [307]. The ram is also linked to the reborn Osiris. The deceased identifies himself with the creator-god Atum in order to cross to the Island of the Just, using the same road that Atum took when he proceeded to

---

[299] H. Kockelmann, *Untersuchungen zu den späten Totenbuch, Handschriften auf Mumienbinden. I: Die Mumienbinden und Leinenamulette des memphitischen Priesters Hor, Band II: Handbuch zu den Mumienbinden und Leinenamuletten, SAT 12 (Wiesbaden 2008),* 55–58.; Smith, *The Mortuary Texts of Papyrus BM 10507,* 95.; Corcoran, *Portrait Mummies,* 28–29.
[300] Pyr. 478–79, 1253.
[301] For more about the Book of the Dead vignette 17, see S. Ibrahim, *The Vignette of Spell Seventeen of the Book of the Dead and its Development to the End of the Greek and Roman Periods,* unpublished PhD thesis, Cairo University (Cairo 2015).
[302] A different approach to studying Akhmim was launched by the Akhmim Mummy Studies Consortium (AMSC) in 2005, headed by Jonathan Elias and Carter Lupton. Their goal is to examine the mummies originating from Panopolis via the use of CT scans, in order to increase the current knowledge about 'the processes and rituals of Egyptian mummification' (http://www.amscresearch.com/consortium.html). Also see J. Elias, 'Overview of Lininger A06697, an Akhmimic Mummy and Coffin at the University of Nebraska, Lincoln', *AMSC Research* 16–3 (Pennsylvania 2016), 13.; J. Elias and C. Lupton, 'Gods at all Hours: Saite Period Coffins of the 'Eleven-Eleven' Type', in R. Sousa (ed.), *Body, Cosmos and Eternity, New Research Trends in the Iconography and Symbolism of Ancient Egyptian Coffins* (Oxford 2014), 131–32. The holy vigil (*Stundenwachen*) was recited on the night before the day of the burial of the deceased. It was recited at the embalming place, during the 12 nocturnal hours. The ritual text was then deposited into the tomb, ensuring the efficacy of the embalming rites, S. Töpfer, 'Theory and Practice/ Text and Mummies, The Instructions of the 'Embalming Ritual' in the Light of Archaeological Evidence', in K. Kóthay (ed.), *Burial and Mortuary Practices,* 22. One of the epithets of the gods Ptah and Osiris was *nfr Hr,* meaning 'the Beautiful of Face'. The word *nfr* is associated with rebirth and the green colour of the Nile valley after inundation. Ptah-Tatenen is shown in green, and is also associated with vegetation. For more on the word *nfr,* see A. Donohue, 'Pr-nfr', *JEA* 64 (1978), 143–48. In vignettes 1073, 1079, and CT 1081, these gods are called *m3s.w,* meaning 'the Kneeling Ones', and *m3st.w,* meaning 'the Squatting Ones', in reference to their posture, R. Lucarelli, 'The So–Called Vignette of Spell 182 of the Book of the Dead', in R. Lucarelli, M. Müller-Roth, and A. Wüthrich (eds.), *Herausgehen am Tage, Gesammelte Schriften zum altägyptische Totenbuch, SAT* 17 (Wiesbaden 2012), 87 no. 45.
[303] For the so-called *Stundenwachen,* see Pries, *Die Stundenwachen im Osiriskult, eine Studie zur Tradition und späten Rezeption von Ritualen im Alten Ägypten,* 2 vols., *SSR* 2 (Wiesbaden 2011). The mummification scene in house-tomb 21 at Tuna El-Gebel shows two solar deities raising their hands in reverence. One has a jackal head, and the other has a baboon head, being depicted behind Isis and Nephthys, and representing Thoth and Anubis, Gabra, *Rapport sur les Fouilles d'Hermoupolis,* 49.; Venit, *Visualizing the Afterlife,* 127–29, fig. 4.22. The mourning goddesses are still present on Late Roman coffins until the fourth century AD, F. Dunand and R. Lichtenberg, *Les mommies et la mort en Egypte* (Paris 1998), 106.
[304] Elias and Lupton, 'Gods at All Hours', in R. Sousa (ed.), *Body, Cosmos, and Eternity,* 131–32. In addition to the 85 examples of coffins studied by Brech ('Spätägyptische Särge aus Achmim'), T. Mekis studied seven other examples, T. Mekis, 'Données nouvelles sur les hypocéphales', *Kút* 7/2 (2008), 38–40.
[305] Lucarelli, 'The So-Called Vignette of Spell 182', 90.
[306] P. London BM 10470 of the 19th dynasty shows a falcon-headed *ba* bird with a solar disc, and a human-headed *ba* bird with a white crown. They are shown perching on two adjacent pylons between two *djed* pillars, H. Milde, *The Vignettes in the Book of the Dead of Neferrenpet, EU* 7 (Leiden 1991), 33, 38.; T. DuQuesen, *At the Court of Osiris, Book of the Dead Spell 194, Oxfordshire Communications in Egyptology* 4 (London 1994), 33, 62.
[307] T. Bács, 'Amun-Re-Harakhti in the Late Ramesside Royal Tombs', in U. Luft (ed.), *The Intellectual Heritage of Egypt, Studies Presented to László Kákosy on the Occasion of His 60th Birthday* (Budapest 1992), 43–53.; W. Budge, *A Catalogue of the Egyptian Collection in the Fitzwilliam Museum* (Cambridge 1893), 49. In the Coffin Texts, the ram can be used as an alternative to the *ba* bird, thus strongly associating the *ba* of the deceased with the united *bas* of Osiris and Re, T. DuQuesne, 'The Osiris-Re Conjunction', with particular Reference to the Book of the Dead', in B. Backes, I. Munro, and S. Stöhr (eds.), *Totenbuch-Forshungen, gesammelte Beiträge des 2. Internationalen Totenbuch-Symposiums, Bonn, 25. bis 29. September 2005, Studien zum Altägyptischen Totenbuch* 11 (Wiesbaden 2006), 26.

the Field of Reeds. The deceased, in his association with the sun god, aims to pass through the gate of the *Duat*. This is the same door through which Atum passes when he proceeds to the eastern horizon of the sky, reinforcing the concept of the daily rebirth of the sun god. In the Book of the Dead spell, Atum and Re are syncretistic; Atum is the 'distant god' who created the universe, while Re is the 'closed god', resembling the two incarnations of the sun[308]. The six kings indicate what is called the 'battle-place of the gods'. Here, the creator and sun god is referred to as 'creating his names', with a following of 'the unopposed'. In vignette 17, the deceased expresses the wish to identify with the solar creator, saying *ink Ra-nb*, or 'I am Re every day'[309].

Chapter 17 of the Book of the Dead is also illustrated on the south wall of the antechamber of tomb F2 in El-Salamuni. However, it differs in the fact that the ram is crowned with a sun disc, and a falcon stretches out its wings upon the ram's head, which could symbolise the *ba* of the deceased (Figure 4.51). The vignette is also illustrated in the recently discovered Ptolemaic tomb of Tutu in El-Hawawish A, or 'Naga al-Diabat' (Figure 4.52). Here, only four sailors surround the ram. Two are shown wearing the white crown, and the other two are depicted with the red crown. Part 17 of the Book of the Dead is closely linked to the god Min, whose burial iconography is associated with the transition from death (linked to Osiris) to resurrection (linked to the sun god)[310]. Therefore, chapter 17 of the Book of the Dead is a major scene in most of the funerary papyri from Akhmim, such as the Papyrus of Nesmin (where the only difference in the image is that the two groups of sailors are not facing each other)[311]. The scene also appears on the Papyrus of Hor (BM EA10479)[312], on papyrus 10477 of Berlin[313], and on papyrus Hildesheim 5248. The widespread depiction of the Book of the Dead chapter 17 in the tombs of El-Salamuni can be explained through the words of Tarasenko[314], who writes that the phenomenon '*represents a relatively short but quite complete account of cosmological myth[s, which]... offers the deceased fusion with the sacred world by means of [a] magic[al] reproduction of the events connected with the act of creation. This may explain the wide popularity and long lasting utilization of [the] BD chapter 17 [for] a full two millennia*'.

4.2.25: The Northern B1 Wall: Overview

Wall B1, which is to the north, includes a burial niche which is now largely destroyed due to robbers. It has been covered with a layer of heavy debris (Figures 4.54a-c).

4.2.26: The Lower Register of Wall B1

Due to looting, a great portion of wall B1 is damaged. Moreover, soot covers parts of the wall. Kuhlmann includes a photograph of an embalming scene located below the wall's niche in his monograph (Figure 4.55a)[315], and another coloured photograph of the niche is also included by Kaplan in his work (Figure 4.55b)[316]. The lower part of the wall beneath the niche shows a procession of various male deities flanking an embalming scene on both sides. The concept of mummification is closely linked to the justification of the deceased[317]. On the B1 wall, the scene references the canonical image of the death of Osiris; the mummy lies on a bier, and wears a *nemes* headdress and a green face to associate it with Osiris[318]. Unfortunately, soot covers a great portion of the mummy and the body of Anubis. Thus, it is difficult to determine whether or not the mummy is wrapped in contemporary Roman period reticulated bandaging.

Unfortunately, the embalming scene and the four deities to the right of the embalming tent are now demolished, while the procession of deities to the left is still preserved. In the scene, four male deities are led by a deity with a damaged head. Of his head, only his yellow *nemes* headdress remains, as seen in the photo of Kuhlmann. He is nonetheless visible as a human-headed deity, who is dressed in green, with a solar disc upon his headdress. He raises up his hands, while his face is partially covered with bitumen. Behind him strides the god Atum, the primordial god of the Heliopolitan creation myth, shown as a human deity. He is crowned with his identifying double *pschent* crown, and holds a libation vase in his left hand. He salutes with his right hand. Unfortunately, even after restoration, the face of the god is still covered with bitumen, hiding his facial features. In addition, his figure was often directly exposed to fire, causing further damage. The falcon-headed Horus is depicted as next in line. He wears a *pschent* crown, and holds a red vase in his right hand, raising his left hand in the same salutation gesture as Atum. Finally, the ibis-headed god Thoth appears, complete with a crescent upon

---

[308] M. Tarasenko, 'Mythological Allusions Connected with Cosmogony in BD 17', in B. Backes et al. (eds.), *Totenbuch-Forshungen*, 342–43.; S. Quirke, *The Cult of Ra, Sun-Worship in Ancient Egypt* (London 2001), 25.
[309] Tarasenko, 'Mythological Allusions', 353.
[310] M. Hassoun, *The God Min and His Role in the Egyptian Beliefs Until the End of the New Kingdom*, Unpublished PhD thesis, Cairo University (Cairo 1999), 92, 211, 297–303.
[311] J. Clère, *Le Papyrus de Nesmin, un Livre des Morts Hiéroglyphique de l'Epoque Ptolémaïque*, *BiGen* 10 (Cairo 1987), pl. iv.
[312] The papyrus is one of the six Books of the Dead of Akhmim, and is now in the British Museum, Mosher, *The Papyrus of Hor (BM EA 10479)* pl. 3.
[313] Lüscher, *Das Totenbuch p.Berlin P. 10477 aus Achmim*, fig. 6.
[314] M. Tarasenko, 'Mythological Allusions', in B. Backes et al. (eds.), *Totenbuch-Forschungen*, 354. In the version of vignette 17 in P. Iufankh, Iufankh stands before the boat with his kingly sailor deities. He pays homage to a small image of Min held up by a man who also holds a branch, Quirke, *Going Out*, 64.

[315] Kuhlmann, *SDAIK* 11, fig. 36c.
[316] Kaplan, *BzÄ* 16, fig. 88c.
[317] Smith, *Traversing Eternity*, 6.
[318] Riggs concludes that the mummy and the mummy portraits from Akhmim (nos. 6–37), date to between 50 BC and the early first century AD. In these examples, the dead obtain characteristics and attributes of Egyptian funerary gods based on their gender; males obain traits of Osiris, and females become similar to Hathor, Riggs, *The Beautiful Burial*, 61–94.

The Afterlife in Akhmim

Figure 4.51. Vignette 17 of the Book of the Dead, as depicted on the south wall of the antechamber of tomb F2.

his head. He holds a palm branch in his lowered right hand and raises his left hand in a salutation gesture. At the rear of the line, the deceased female, dressed in her traditional fringed garment, raises her hands in an attitude of homage; her figure was only uncovered after the restoration.

Mummification and its associated rites were linked to the deceased's justification, and continued to be practiced in the Ptolemaic Period and onwards[319]. In the middle of the B1 wall, there is a depiction of an embalming tent, where the mummy of the deceased, calling upon Osiris, rests on a lion-headed bier. The mummy represents the god Osiris as he lays in the embalming workshop during the *Stundenwachen* (nightly vigil). Anubis attends to the mummy, performing verification rites, and acting in his traditional role as an embalmer of the deceased. He places his left hand on the head of the mummy, while his right one, which is entirely covered with soot, is supposed to hold an unguent vase. The representation of the deceased on a lion-headed couch, being attended to by Anubis, is the most frequently depicted scene in the afterlife iconography of Graeco-Roman Egypt. Just as Anubis had mummified the dismembered body of Osiris, the deceased was keen to be mummified by Anubis, and thus to be associated with Osiris. In the example from wall B1, the fact that Anubis reaches towards the mummy, touching its face with his left hand, refers to the fact that Anubis was personally responsible for the parts of the embalming ritual that concerned the head of the deceased. Anubis is most often depicted holding a small incense cup above the mummy to purify the surrounding area and to ward off evil forces[320].

The two grieving sisters Isis and Nephthys stand on both sides of the bier depicted on wall B1. They are shown lamenting the Osirian deceased[321]. Isis and Nephthys support the edges of the embalming tent [322]. However, the deceased, whose legs are hobbled, does not find a way to respond to their lamentations. Silence may have been imposed at this precise moment in the rituals in the hopes of 'waking up' the spirit[323]. It is said that during the enactment of the *Stundenwachen*, Isis and Nephthys would lament the death of Osiris through loud cries and lengthy liturgies. Their mourning serves the dual purpose of 1) protecting the embalmer's workshop from being compromised by Seth and 2) aiding in the resurrection of Osiris by crying out to him and begging him to return to them[324]. Through their appeals and cries, the Osirian deceased is exhorted to return to the world of the living. To the right, the scene shows a procession of four deities. They are hardly recognizable because of the debris around the wall and the soot which cover their figures. The photo which had been taken of them by Kuhlmann is from far away, and was probably taken from the antechamber. The procession of these four deities is led by the falcon-headed god Re-Horakhty, who wears a large red solar disc and holds a libation vase in his left hand, saluting with his right hand. Re-Horakhty is followed by the ibis-headed god Thoth, who wears a crescent moon on his head. He holds a libation vase in his left hand and salutes with the right one. Soot covers the heads of the other two deities, making them hardly recognizable. However, it seems that they are in the same gesture (Figure 4.56).

---

[319] Smith, *Traversing Eternity*, 6. In the Graeco-Roman Period, people were often interested in documenting the mummification process in texts and iconography in order to keep their corpses from being lost, Abouelata and Hossain, in Amenta and Guichard (eds.), *Proceedings of the 1st Vatican Coffin Conference*, 25–26.

[320] During the crucial act of mummification, an attack from Seth was to be feared, as the corpse of Osiris had not yet recovered all of its abilities. To ward off any danger, the embalming tent was placed under the protection of numerous deities, S. Emerit, 'À propos de l'origine des interdits musicaux dans l'Égypte ancienne', *BIFAO* 102 (2002), 209.

[321] On the gestures of lamentation, see Y. Volokhine 'Tristesse rituelle et lamentations funéraires en Égypte ancienne.' *Revue de l'histoire des religions* 2 (2008), 176–82.

[322] Kaplan, *BzÄ* 16, 29–30. The embalming tent, or 'Golden House' (*Hwt-nbw*) was originally surrounded by a procession of four deities. The mourning images of Isis and Nephthys are first known from the Ramesside Period, but later became common. See, for instance, the object known as 'Vatican 25016', A. Gasse, *Les Sarcophages de la troisieme periode intermediatere du Museo Gregoriano Egizio* (Vatican 1996), pl. xxiv/2.; Turin 2237/1.; A. Niwinski, *Sarcofagi della XXI dinastia (CGT 10101–10122), Catalogo del Museo Egizio di Torino* (Turin 2009), pl. IV.1.; A. Kucharek, 'Mourning and Lamentation on Coffins', in J. Taylor and M. Vandenbeusch (eds.), *Ancient Egyptian Coffins*, 88.

[323] J. Goyon, *Le papyrus d'Imouthès, Fils de Psintaês, MMA 35.9.21* (New York 1999), 32, col. 5, 14–15, 47, col. 17, 15.

[324] J. Assmann, *Altägyptische Totenliturgien. Band 1: Totenliturgien in den Sargtexten des Mittleren Reiches. Supplemente zu den Schriften der Heidelberger Akademie der Wissenschaften, Philosophisch-Historische Klasse* 14 (Heidelberg 2002), 105.

Figure 4.52. Vignette 17 of the Book of the Dead, as seen in the tomb of Tutu at El-Hawawish cemetery A.

4.2.27: The Upper Frieze to the Left of the B1 Niche

The part of the B1 wall to the left of the niche was once covered with heavy soot, making it nearly impossible to recognise the depiction of the winged goddess that was hidden underneath. After undergoing restoration, it became possible to determine that the scene shows a deceased male in a traditional white Roman garment. He raises his hands to venerate an enthroned figure of Osiris, while the winged goddess Isis-Maat[325] stands behind him. Unfortunately, the colours were applied in a very smooth manner. Therefore, the cleaning of the soot resulted in the fading of some colours. In the scene, Osiris is garbed in red and wears an *atef* crown in yellow. He is seated upon a throne and has his hands crossed over his chest. His legs rest on a low base. Isis-Maat wears a fitted garment in red, and a solar disc sits upon her head. She offers the *ꜥnx* to Osiris with her upraised hand and holds the ostrich feather of truth in her lowered left hand (Figures 4.57a-c).

4.2.28: The Eastern Burial Niche in Wall B1.

The rear wall of the eastern burial niche was once covered with soot, and the details behind were entirely hidden. After undergoing restoration, the wall now shows three identical figures of a deceased male. He venerates three of the four sons of Horus in the form of birds. The first son is the baboon-headed Hapi, the second is the jackal-headed Duamutef, and the third is Qebehsenuef (with a falcon head). A solar disc fronted with a *uraeus* is depicted behind each god (Figure 4.58). Two hieroglyphic columns are inscribed behind two of the three figures of the deceased (Figures 4.59a-b). The hieroglyphic inscriptions contain traditional religious formulas that were frequently inscribed on the Roman mummy labels of Akhmim. These formulas involve a request from the *ba* of the deceased to serve Osiris or, more often, Osiris-Sokar. The deceased asks to live 'in the presence of Osiris', which was a popular phrase[326]. The formula is widely found in the tombs of El-Salamuni.

The two hieroglyphic columns inscribed behind the figures of the deceased male are identical. They read: *ꜥnx Hr r HH Dd n Wsir nTA aA r. . .*, which translates to mean 'Life for Horus for eternity, words spoken by Osiris, the Great God in . . .'. An alternative translation is the following: *ꜥnx.f Hr r nHH Dt wAH Wsir n RA-aA* ('May he live, Horus, for ever and ever! May Osiris of Ro-aa(?) live forever and ever'). According to Gauthier, 'Ro-aa' (*âa* or *our*) is most likely an unknown village, or a place north of the village of Chenoboskion, to the east of Akhmim. The name translates to mean 'big door'[327].

Von Bissing recognised the hieroglyphic text of the two columns, and copied and translated it. According to him, it represents a wish by the deceased for an eternal life with Osiris, stating: 'May his soul live forever for Osiris... (lost)'[328]. Von Bissing hesitated to offer a clear translation for the last five signs of the hieroglyphic inscription, which he praised for its complexity. The signs that he could not recognise may be a priestly title of Min[329], possibly reading as *Cnh f Hr R NHH hnc Wsir ntr c3 nb*.

After removing a thick layer of soot, the details of the scene on the left wall of the B1 niche appeared. The depiction shows a kneeling figure of a tree goddess with a lioness head, who is presumably Hathor. She uses *hes* vessels to supply water to the deceased in the form of a *ba*

---

[325] Kaplan, *BzÄ* 16, 168, pl. 88c.

[326] Vleeming, *Demotic and Greek, StudDem* 8B. Concordances, Appendices, Indexes, and Plates, 795. Most of the mummy labels from the Panopolite nome were written by two distinct scribal schools of the villages of Bompae and Psonis, Vleeming, *StudDem* 8B, 796–97.

[327] Gauthier, *Dictionnaire des noms Géographiques* III, 114.; id., *BIFAO* 4, 60.

[328] Von Bissing, *ASAE* 50, 559, fig. 4.; Kaplan, *BzÄ* 16, 168.

[329] He cites the word *wb* (II, 242, according to the Edfu inscriptions), and translates the following: 'the priest of Min presented himself before Osiris'. He also refers to the text in P. Insinger (éd. Bozser, p. XLIV/LXXVII, 35), von Bissing, *ASAE* 50, 559–60.

The Afterlife in Akhmim

Figure 4.53a. Photogrammetry of the west B4 wall of tomb C1.

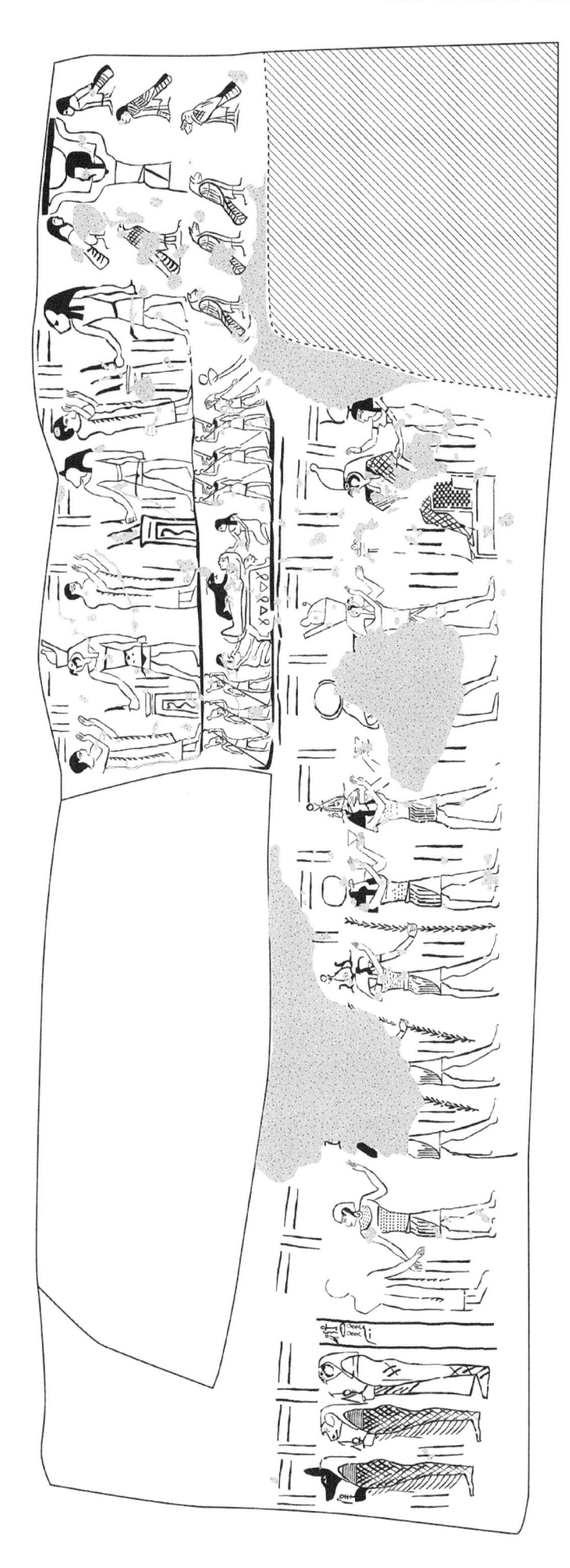

Tomb C1: The So-called 'Tomb of von Bissing' (1897)

El Salamouni, Tomb C1, Burial Chamber, West Wall.

Figure 4.53b. A facsimile of the west B4 wall of tomb C1.

The Afterlife in Akhmim

Figure 4.54a. The north B1 wall of tomb C1 (before the restoration in 2019).

Figure 4.54b. The damaged burial niche on the north B1 wall of tomb C1.

Figure 4.54c. The north B1 wall of tomb C1 (after the restoration in 2021).

Figure 4.55a. The wall below the burial niche in tomb C1, as photographed by the German Archaeological Institute (DAI), Kuhlmann, *SDAIK* 11, fig. 36 c.

Figure 4.55b. A coloured photo of the damaged north B1 niche in tomb C1, Kaplan, *BzÄ* 16, fig. 88c.

The Afterlife in Akhmim

El Salamouni, Tomb C1, Burial Chamber, North Wall, Reconstruction, B 1.

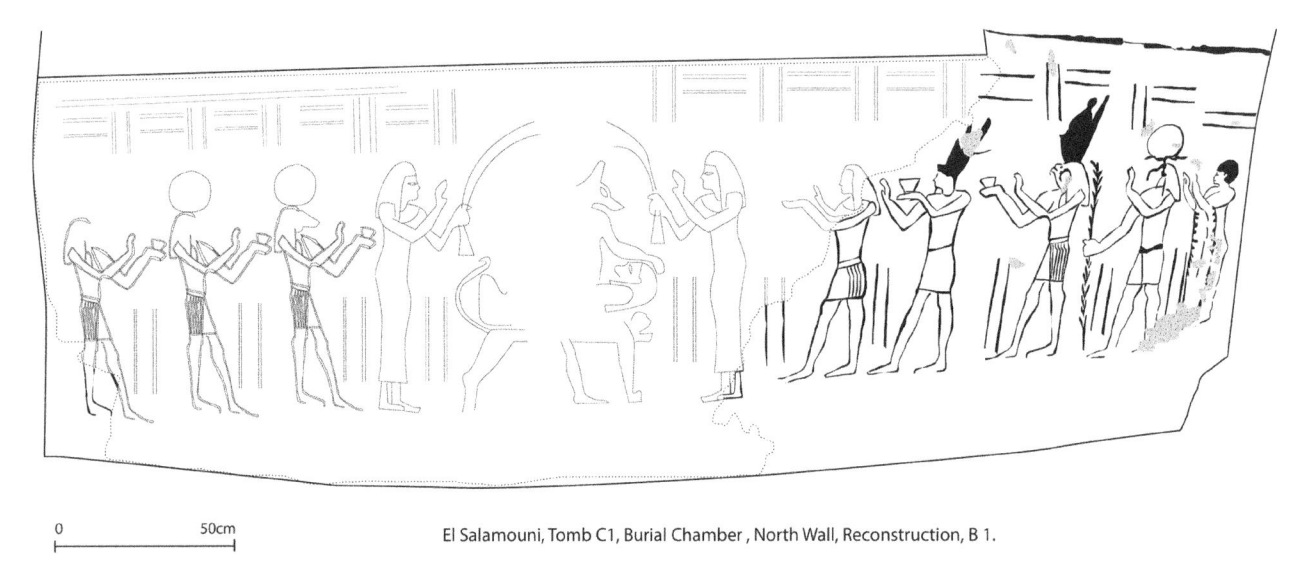

Figure 4.56. A reconstruction/facsimile of the whole procession scene of the B1 niche, found in tomb C1.

bird with a human head[330]. The bird stretches his hands to receive the streams of water, while a solar disc surmounts his head. The *ba* bird may be the figure of Imsety, the last of the four sons of Horus (the other three being illustrated on the rear wall of the niche). A sycamore tree with sycamore figs (*ficus sycomorus*) is behind the goddess. Free movement was an important aspect of the *ba*; every night the *ba* was believed to leave the tomb and descend to the *Duat* through the *Akhet*[331], and then return to the body. The fear that it might lose its way is well-depicted in the Book of the Dead, such as in vignettes 92 and 188. This is because the *ba* was believed to be closely linked with the physical body, and it needed the body for both food and drink[332]. Behind the tree goddess, a rearing, serpent-headed *sa-ta* daemon is depicted. A long feather extends from his back. The daemon looks behind himself, towards the tree goddess, and his stride is towards the entrance of the tomb[333]. On the register below this scene, on the north side of the wall, three *khekrew* signs and crouching jackals are depicted. The rest of the wall is empty of decorations (Figures 4.60a-c).

The heavy layer of soot covering the scene of the tree goddess highly suggests that the figures were directly exposed to fire. The details of the tree and its colours are still not clear, and increasing the use of chemical materials to remove the soot on the tree will very likely cause the erasure of its details. Nonetheless, some remains of the tree's branches and fig-like fruit can be distinguished. The tree goddess is as a nursing figure that supplies the deceased with drink in the netherworld. If this is indeed Hathor, then she is shown offering the *ba* of the deceased the water of life with two *qebeh* vases. Water is one of the necessities noted in the afterlife texts. It was common that either Nut, Hathor, Isis[334], or the goddess of the west[335] would assume the role of the tree goddess, providing water to the deceased and/or his *ba* in the tomb. As for the tree itself, it was most often a palm, sycamore, or dom palm, all three of which were sacred trees in Ancient Egypt. Hathor is the goddess with the oldest relationship to trees, being described as a sycamore-(*nht*) goddess and being named an *im3* goddess[336]. As for the *ba* of the deceased, it was mostly depicted as a bird with a human head, which signifies the intimate union of the bird with the deceased.

4.2.29: The Eastern B2 Wall

The east wall of the tomb, labelled B2, includes a burial niche which has been largely damaged by looters. Their intrusion has caused the destruction of the scenes of both the B2 niche and the B2 wall itself. To further complicate things, the wall is covered with heavy debris (Figures 4.61a-b).

---

[330] The *ba* bird of the deceased is known from the Saite Period, and was still in use during the second century AD, Graves-Brown, *Daemons & Spirits*, 95.
[331] For more about the *ba* going in and out of the *Duat*, see Žabkar, *A Study of the Ba Concept* (Chicago 1968), 99.
[332] Žabkar, *A Study of the Ba Concept*, 145–46.; H. Stewart, *Mummy Cases and Inscribed Funerary Cones in the Petrie Collection* (Warminster, 1976), pls. 4–6.
[333] There are several serpent deities with male human heads known from Graeco-Roman Egypt, many of which were probably associated with the god Shai, C. Barrett, *Egyptianizing Figurines from Delos, A Study of the Hellenistic Religion* (Leiden, Boston 2011), 232–34.

[334] In the tomb of Thutmose III, Isis is depicted sucking milk from a sycamore tree for the young king, B. Lesko, *The Great Goddess of Egypt* (1999), 170–71.; M. Buhl, 'The Goddess of The Egyptian Tree Cult', *JNES* 6 (1947), 93–95. The tree goddess had local variants, such as Naunet, Nephtys, Amenet, Neith, Maat, and Thoeris, see N. Baum, *Arbres et Arbustes de l'Egypte Ancienne* (Leuven 1988), 61, 69.; Wallert, *Die Palmen*, *MÄS* 1, 101–03.; H. Refai, 'Hathor als Gleichzeitig West- und Baumgöttin', in *Timelines Studies in Honour of Manfred Bietak*, *OLA* 149, I (Leuven 2006), 287–90.; id., 'Die Göttin des Westens in den Thebanischen Gräbern der Neun Reiches: Darstellung, Bedeutung und Funktion, *ADAIK* 12 (1996).
[335] N. Billing, 'You are Not Alone: The Conceptual Background of Nut as the Eternal Abode in Text & Iconography', in A. Maravelia and N. Guilhou (eds.), *Environment and Religion*, 79.
[336] R. M. ᶜAbdelwahed, 'Reflections on the Tree Im3/ I3m in Ancient Egypt', in A. Maravelia and N. Guilhou (eds.), *Environment and Religion*, 3.

Tomb C1: The So-called 'Tomb of von Bissing' (1897)

Figure 4.57a. The soot covering the upper frieze to the left of the B1 niche in tomb C1 (before restoration).

Figure 4.57b. The deceased adoring Osiris while Isis stands behind him. The scene is found on the upper frieze to the left of the B1 niche in tomb C1 (after the restoration in 2021).

Figure 4.57c. A facsimile of the B1 wall in tomb C1.

4.2.30: The Upper Frieze to the Right of the Wall B2 Niche

Heavy black soot covers the B2 wall, making it difficult to determine if anything is underneath. However, a cleaning of the soot uncovered a scene. The image shows the deceased raising his hands in an attitude of homage before an enthroned figure of the jackal-headed Anubis[337]. The god crosses his hands over his chest in the same traditional gesture of Osiris and wears a *pschent*

---

[337] Anubis sitting on a throne is also depicted in a niche in the Stagni tomb, showing the combination of both Greek and Egyptian ideas and forms, K. Savvopoulos, *Alexandrea in Aegypto, The Role of the Egyptian Tradition in the Hellenistic and Roman Periods, Ideology, Culture, Identity, and Public Life*, PhD thesis, University of Leiden (Leiden 2011), 241.

The Afterlife in Akhmim

Figure 4.58. The back wall of the north B1 niche of tomb C1.

Figure 4.59a. A hieroglyphic column on the north B1 niche of tomb C1.

Figure 4.59b. A second hieroglyphic column on the north B1 niche in tomb C1.

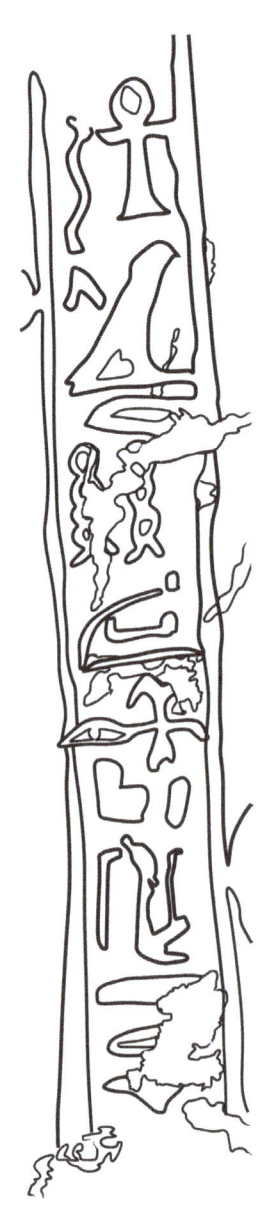

Figure 4.59c

140

Tomb C1: The So-called 'Tomb of von Bissing' (1897)

Figure 4.60a. The left side of the wall of the B1 niche in tomb C1.

Figure 4.60b. A facsimile of the wall to the left of the B1 niche in tomb C1.

North Side

East side.

El Salamouni, Tomb C1, Burial Chamber, North Wall Nich, B 1.

Figure 4.60c. A facsimile of the back and lateral east walls of the burial niche on wall B1 of tomb C1.

crown. Isis-Maat stands behind him, holding her traditional feather in her lowered left hand. She raises her right hand to Anubis in an attitude of protection. However, she does not hold the ^cnx sign (Figures 4.62a-b)[338]. The paying of homage by the deceased to Osiris and Anubis on two separate adjacent walls of tomb C1 confirms that Anubis had a high rank in El-Salamuni, and that he collaborated with Osiris. The deceased would have to be subordinate to them in order to be granted a good burial and the permission to travel on the beautiful roads to the afterlife.

4.2.31: The Upper Frieze to the Left of the Wall B2 Niche

There is also evidence of a frieze being located to the north of the B2 niche. The removal of soot along this wall has revealed a crouching figure of the jackal-headed Anubis on his shrine. Below the shrine, there are traditional geometrical signs (Figures 4.63a-b).

---
[338] Since the fifth dynasty, the dead are known to have expressed the wish to be *imakh* in the presence of Anubis, Smith, *Following Osiris*, 70.

4.2.32: The Wall B2 Niche

Looters have damaged a great part of the niche; the rear wall of the niche is largely destroyed, and heavily covered with soot (Figure 4.64). After the conservation efforts, the rear wall could be determined to be covered in traditional *khekrew* signs and crouching jackals. On the far north side of the wall, there are also two *khekrew* signs, one being painted green, and the other being red. To the left of this are two crouching jackals that are shown facing each other, with an altar heaped with bread loaves in between. The back part of the second jackal is damaged. The wall is also damaged, with only the remains of three *khekrew* signs remaining nearby. On the far southern part of the niche, there are two other *khekrew* signs (Figure 4.65). The damaged part of the niche's rear wall measures about 1.09cm. in thickness. By measuring the distance between each *khekrew* and crouching jackal sign, it can be determined that the damaged part of the wall originally contained two *khekrew* signs, two crouching jackals, and another altar in between (Figures 4.66a-c). The decoration of the burial niche with a frieze of recumbent

The Afterlife in Akhmim

Figure 4.61a. The east B2 wall of tomb C1 (before the restoration in 2019).

Figure 4.61b. The east B2 wall of tomb C1 (after removing the debris).

Tomb C1: The So-called 'Tomb of von Bissing' (1897)

Figure 4.62a. The soot covering the upper frieze to the right of the B2 niche in tomb C1 (before the restoration in 2019).

Figure 4.63a. The soot covering the upper frieze of the wall to the right of the B2 niche in tomb C1 (before restoration).

Figure 4.63b. A recumbent Anubis on the upper frieze of the wall left of the B2 niche in tomb C1 (after the restoration in 2021).

Figure 4.62b. The deceased adoring a seated Anubis, with Isis behind the god (after the restoration in 2021).

jackals and *khekrew* signs is widely popular in the El-Salamuni tombs.

The right lateral wall of the niche shows the deceased as he advances from his transitory state to be reborn by the sky goddess Nut. The *ba* bird of the deceased is shown receiving water from Nut, as the goddess of the tree[339]. Unfortunately, the head of the goddess is damaged. A hand (of the goddess) protrudes from the tree and holds a *hes* vessel, which pours streams of water. Meanwhile, the *ba* raises his hands to receive the water from the dom palm tree. As stated earlier, water was one of the necessities noted in the afterlife texts[340]. The tree goddess thus supplies food and water to the human-headed *ba* bird of the deceased, while a red sun disc fronted with a protective uraeus hovers above it. An offering table beneath the scene has three loaves of bread on it, as well as three vessels (two *hes* vessels and another wide one) below it (Figure 4.67).

The left lateral wall of the niche depicts a partially damaged figure of the deceased. His head is destroyed, and he raises his hands to venerate a crouching figure of Anubis on his shrine, with the traditional symbolic objects placed beneath it (Figure 4.68).

---

[339] The significance of Nut pouring out a libation for the *ba* bird is discussed by H. Kockelmann, 'Die Götting Nut und der Ba-Vogel', *BIFAO* 118 (1918), 225–31.

[340] This is mentioned in the fifth hour of the *Amduat*, in which the blessed dead are permitted access to water.

The Afterlife in Akhmim

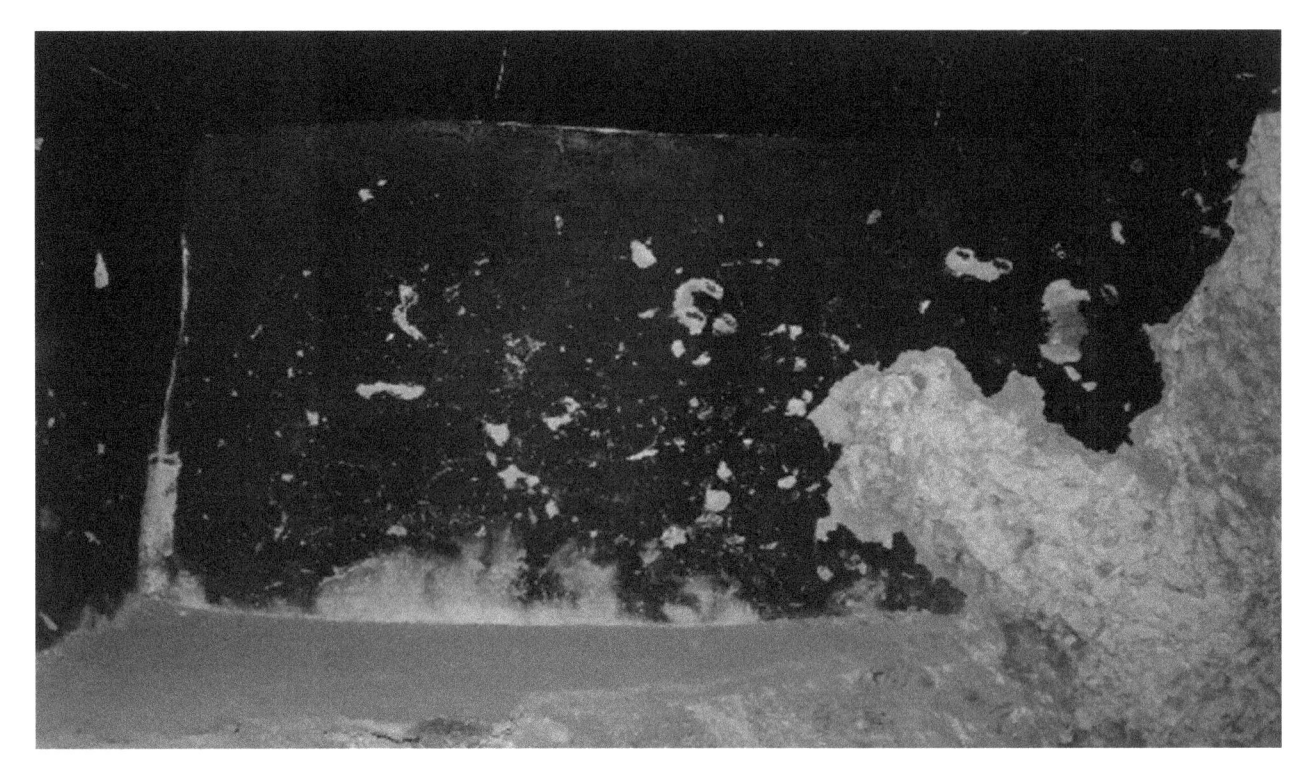

Figure 4.64. The back wall of the B1 niche in tomb C1 (before restoration).

4.2.33: The Lower Register of Wall B2

On the far southern part of the B2 wall, the four sons of Horus, complete with chequer pattern bodies, are shown holding a composite sign consisting of the *djed* pillar, the *w3s* sceptre, and the *shen* sign. They are labelled as Imsety, Duamutef, Hapi, and Qebehsenuef (whose falcon head is partially damaged). The four sons of Horus are venerated by the deceased, who is depicted on the right side of the western B3 wall. The veneration of the four sons of Horus by the deceased is widely depicted in the El-Salamuni tombs. Behind the four sons of Horus is a procession of deities standing before Osiris. Unfortunately, the looters destroyed the rest of this part of the wall.

On the far northern part of the wall, an incomplete figure of the deceased is shown adoring the enthroned Osiris, who is garbed in red and who wears an *atef* crown. This is the only figure of Osiris in tomb C1 to appear without a shrouded body. The scene is covered with soot, and the wall behind Osiris has crumbled. However, one can still decipher the remaining image of a female deity standing behind him. Presumably, this is Isis, as is found on the opposite procession wall. However, only her legs and her green dress are still visible. In the scene, a traditional high altar is placed before Osiris, although its top part is not preserved. Due to the damage caused to the niche, a great part of the wall below the niche is no longer preserved. However, it can be determined that a procession of female(?) deities is depicted. They stride towards Osiris. Some of them are entirely destroyed, while others have only their lower parts still visible. They hold palm branches in their hands. Traditional processions consisting of male and female deities are always depicted separately in the burial chambers of the El-Salamuni tombs. Each procession is always of seven figures standing before either Osiris (for the female processions) or Horus (for the male processions). The order of the figures is not always the same; the deceased can be depicted either at the front or at the back of the row. By comparing the scene to scenes of female processions in other tombs, the damaged row of female deities can be suggested to include (in order): Nut, the cow-headed goddess Hathor, Wadjet, three lioness headed-goddesses (probably Sekhmet, Tefnut, and Repit), and finally, Neith. All of the figures hold the *w3s* sceptre in one hand and are shown presenting various offerings to Osiris. The B2 wall is fully documented (Figures 4.69a-b).

4.2.34 The Ceiling of the Burial Chamber

The ceiling of the burial chamber of tomb C1 is fully covered with the heavy soot. It is considered the darkest area in the tomb, and is fully exposed to any fires that are lit here. It is larger than the zodiacal ceiling in the antechamber. The team enthusiastically cleaned the ceiling in hopes of uncovering a large astronomical horoscope or zodiac. The team conducted many preliminary tests using small amounts of various chemical materials on the four corners of the ceiling. The hope was to uncover the initial outlines of the zodiac. All of the tests led to frustrating results; the areas were unpainted. Every day, the team still maintained a great hope that they would find something behind the soot. It seemed unusual that the artist would leave this large and special area without any astronomical, geometrical, or floral decorations. To-date, this ceiling

Tomb C1: The So-called 'Tomb of von Bissing' (1897)

Figure 4.65. Recumbent jackals and *khekrew* signs, shown adorning the back wall of tomb C1 (after restoration).

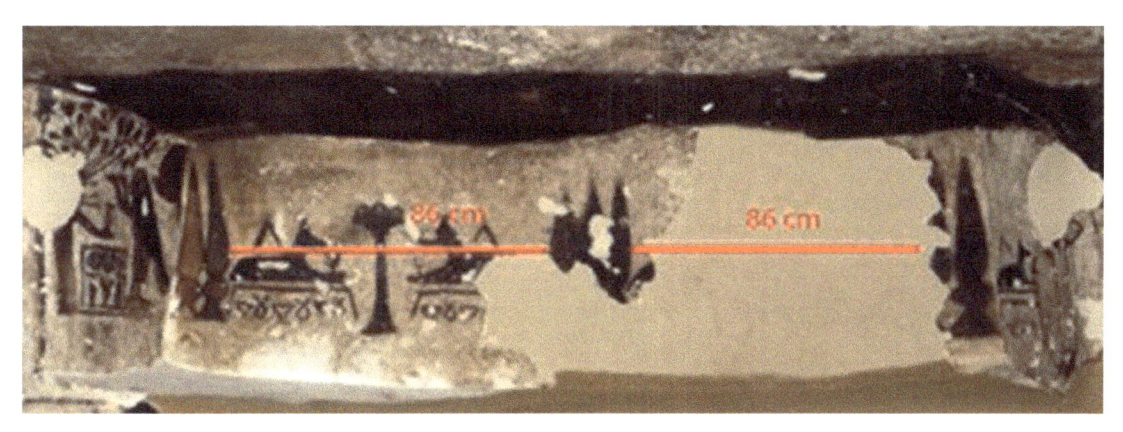

Figure 4.66a. The dimensions of the damaged part of the B2 niche back wall, found in tomb C1.

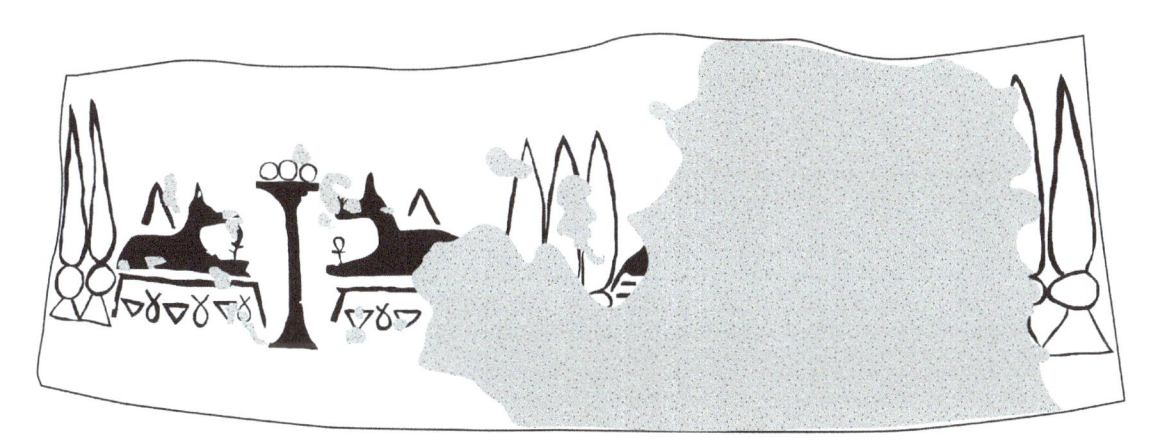

Figure 4.66b. A facsimile of the back wall of the B1 niche, found in a tomb C1.

Figure 4.66c. A reconstruction drawing of the damaged parts on the back wall of the B1 niche, as seen in tomb C1.

The Afterlife in Akhmim

Figure 4.67. A depiction of a tree goddess pouring water for the *ba* of the deceased. The image is on the right lateral wall of the B2 niche.

Figure 4.68. The deceased adoring a recumbent jackal, as seen on the left lateral wall of the B2 niche.

is the only one in the necropolis which has been left unpainted. The reason for this decision is unknown. The other confusing aspect of the tomb is that the ceilings of the three burial niches are unpainted. In El-Salamuni, it is normal for a winged vulture or falcons to be painted on the ceilings of the niches.

4.3: The Patron of the Tomb and its Date

Unfortunately, the hieroglyphic inscriptions in the burial chamber of tomb C1 do not indicate the name or character of the deceased. In the past, the heavy layer of debris proved to be an obstacle for von Bissing, Kuhlmann, and Kanawati, blocking their access to the burial chamber and their ability to discover its details. Surely, the removal of more of this debris will provide more valuable information. More recently, looting activities in the burial chamber caused damage to the burial niches, and probably resulted in the destruction of some of the hieroglyphic and/or Demotic inscriptions that are expected to have mentioned the name of the deceased. It seems that recording the name of the deceased was not a requirement in the El-Salamuni tombs. Besides C1, some other tombs in the area are completely missing both hieroglyphic and Demotic texts. Others contain only a short line of hieroglyphic text which is addressed to Osiris but which lacks the name of the deceased. If the name of the deceased is inscribed in the tomb, it is usually written in Demotic, rather than in hieroglyphs.

Von Bissing dates tomb C1 to the second century AD due to the appearance of Isis-Sothis in its zodiac. However, in his letter to Maspero, he describes the tomb at first glance as a 'Roman tomb from the third century or so'. Venit suggests a later date of the middle of the second century AD, based on the appearance of Isis-Sothis and the classical figure of the deceased[341]. Meanwhile, Riggs proposes a date of the late first to mid-second century AD because of the classical style of the bearded deceased, noting his curly wig and the fact that he holds a book-roll and a sprig of myrtle[342]. The short hairstyle and clean-shaven face of the deceased is a feature in the funerary portraits of both the von Bissing and Petosiris tombs. Osing[343] and Whitehouse[344] point out that these artistic features should prevent the tomb from being assigned a date later than the first quarter of the second century AD, and particularly, the reign of Hadrian, during which the Roman fashion was short beards. Venit refutes this suggestion, pointing out that the tomb of Si-Amun is later than the time of Hadrian. Furthermore, the harvesters and vintners in the tomb of Petosiris at Tuna El-Gebel, which is clearly post-Alexander in date, are bearded[345].

The tomb is distinguishable by its lack of flowery *orthostat* panels; it is currently the only known tomb in the necropolis to lack this characteristic Roman feature. The existence of three burial niches (couches) placed against the back and

---

[341] Venit, 'Referencing Isis', in L. Bricault and M. Versylus (eds.), *Isis on the Nile*, 101.; id., *Visualizing the Afterlife*, 193.
[342] Riggs, *The Beautiful Burial*, 164, fig. 77.
[343] Osing, *AV* 28, 71.
[344] Whitehouse, 'Roman in Life', in O. Kaper (ed.) *Life in the Fringe*, 262.
[345] Venit, *Visualizing the Afterlife*, 232, no. 1077.

Tomb C1: The So-called 'Tomb of von Bissing' (1897)

Figure 4.69a. Photogrammetry of the whole B2 wall in tomb C1.

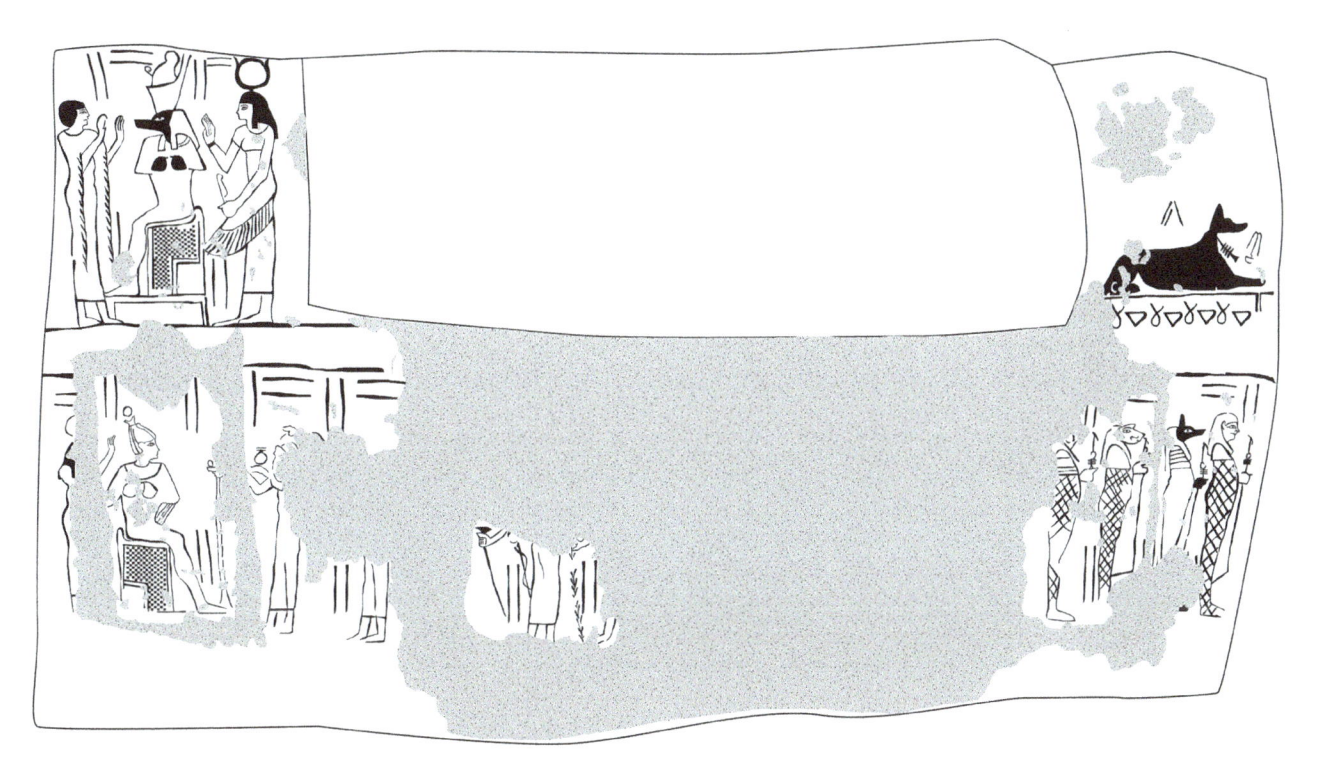

Figure 4.69b. A facsimile of the whole B2 wall of tomb C1.

side walls of the tomb suggests that it is a family tomb. However, Venit suggests that the niches were mainly used for banquets and celebrations[346]. The *triclinium* style of burial chamber is widely found in Alexandria, such as in the tombs of Kom El-Schukaf, Tigrain, Ramleh, and the grand catacomb of Wardian, all of which are dated between the first and the second centuries AD. The *triclinium* tomb shape also appears on coins dating between the reigns of Trajan and one of the sons of the emperor Licinius (after 324 AD)[347]. This style of burial chamber thus primarily dates to the Roman period. Von Bissing suggests that this shape dates to a time between the reigns of Vespasian and Hadrian[348].

---

[346] M. Venit, 'The Tomb from Tigrain Pasha Street and the Iconography of Death in Roman Alexandria', *AJA* 101, no. 4 (1997), 708.; id., 'Alexandria', in C. Riggs (ed.), *The Oxford Handbook*, 117.

[347] Crtron, *L'architecture et les Pratiques funéraires*, 82.

[348] F. von Bissing, *La Catacombe nouvellement decouverte de Kom el Chougafa* (Munich 1901), 3.; id., 'Zu den grieschish-ägyptischen Darstellungen', in *Expedition von Sieglin, Die Nekropole von Kom-esch-Shukafa* (Leipzig 1908), 147.

The Afterlife in Akhmim

Though some scholars have claimed that the first appearance of Isis-Sothis is on coins from the reign of Antonius (138–161 AD), Winkler argues that such images already existed by the end of the Ptolemaic Period/Early Roman Period, although in a funerary context. He discusses the P. Kramer 17[349], a papyrus with a depiction of a zodiac in which there is something resembling a dog, but no image of a goddess. It should be noted that the image is difficult to decipher. The text dates to ca 55 BC, based on both a consideration of the planetary positions it records, and on its palaeography (which indicates the first century BC). Winkler had previously recorded some images of the dog and the goddess. These date to at least the mid-first century AD, and probably already to the reign of Augustus[350]. Hence, it is still fair to provide a more precise date of the tomb, specifically that of the Antonine Period of the second century AD. Basing dates on the appearance of Isis-Sothis on a dog is arguably reliable. Furthermore, the long and elegant looped tail of the Capricorn does not appear until the first century AD, and is a widely typical second century feature[351].

It is apparent that the burial process in the necropolis was systematically organised and not done randomly. Burials were first placed on the northern section of the mountain. This section contains tombs of the Old and New Kingdoms, shaft burials of the Late and Ptolemaic Periods, animal and bird *hypogeums*, and Early Roman façade tombs. Meanwhile, the southern part of the mountain contains the final datable tombs of the late second and third centuries AD. Tomb C1 is located beneath both the temple of Ay and the Ptolemaic façade tombs which lie on the upper terraces or to the north. In the author's opinion, the register which contains tomb C1 probably dates to the period of the late first century or early second century.

In tomb C1, the deceased male is the largest figure and is costumed in a typically classical style. This makes the issue of ethnicity in Graeco-Roman Egypt, and indeed in this tomb specifically, very problematic. The fusion of the Egyptian and Hellenistic cultures in the Panopolite community suggests that ethnicity was socially and culturally determined, and was not necessarily connected to politics or religion[352]. Answering how many bodies were buried inside this tomb is very difficult; the existence of the three niches logically suggests three deceased people.

However, von Bissing supposes the tomb contained four people, with one in each lateral niche and two in the largest central one. In another publication, he declares that a male and female are buried there, suggesting only two bodies. One cannot ignore the fact that the local community had a damaging practice of burning the mummies inside the tombs. The soot in the tomb could be a result of this practice, especially since the mummies into which von Bissing and Dragendorff dived have not been found. Re-use of burial spaces was a common practice in Roman Egypt, and mass tombs were found in El-Salamuni.

The combination of Greek and Egyptian mythological and religious themes in the tomb represents a high degree of inter-cultural awareness, which was perhaps mostly limited to Roman citizens and those with an education. In the Roman tombs, the largest classical image of the deceased is typically a generic model that has a social and eschatological role. Von Bissing assumes that a male and female were buried in tomb C1, and that they were intended to receive a kind of divinity[353]. Surely, the deceased individual in tomb C1 was of a high, elite status in the Panopolite community, and his classical figure might suggest elements of a Roman identity. However, in Roman Egypt, the social importance of a person was defined more by cultural affiliations than by ethnicity[354]. The similarities between the classical style in tomb C1 and the tomb of Petosiris (which dates to the late first century AD[355]) could suggest that tomb C1 is of a similar date.

4.4: The Most Recent Conservation Work

Tomb C1 was carved into a limestone base. The craftsmen evened its surface with a layer of *hiba* (mountain powder). In some cases, aggregates of limestone were used to thicken the surface. The craftsmen mixed the *hiba* with straw and then placed layers of lime or gypsum mortar on top of it until the surface was ready for painting. An application of lime wash was immediately used prior to adding colours.

The conservation work in tomb C1 started in November 2019 and finished in December 2021. Four conservation field campaigns were conducted in the tomb by four Egyptian conservators, all of whom are affiliated with the Sohag Conservation Office. The conservators were Mohamed Abo El Makarem, a supervisor and conservator at the Sohag National Museum, and his assistants, named Ramadan Ahmed, Hossam Faisal, and Mahmoud Ahmed (from the Akhmim Conservation Office). All of these people have sufficient experience in the conservation of tombs, and they have both supervised and participated in many conservation projects related to the American Research Centre in Egypt (ARCE) The author appreciates

---

[349] It is a papyrus palimpsest that measures 21.1 x 8.7cm., having been extracted from a piece of mummy cartonnage found at Abusir el-Melek in Middle Egypt during the excavations of O. Rubensohn (1903–1908). The palimpsest is now kept in Berlin (Ägyptisches Museum, Papyrussammlung). Its Greek text consists of agricultural records. On paleographical grounds, the text can be dated to the late second or the early first century BC.
[350] The author would like to thank A. Winkler for sending him the article, A. Winkler and M. Zellmann-Rohrer, 'Zodiacs and Monuments: An Early Pictorial 'Horoscope' from Egypt', *JHA* 54 (forthcoming, 2023).
[351] M. Huxley, *The Signs of the Zodiac in the Art of the Near and Middle East Up to and Including the Early Islamic Period*, School of Oriental and African Studies (London 1985), 155, 166, 447, 555.
[352] On the topic of ethnicity in Graeco-Roman Egypt, see K. Gourdiaan, *Ethnical Strategies in Graeco-Roman Egypt*, in P. Bilde (ed.), *Ethnicity in Hellenistic Egypt* (Arahus 1992), 76–95.

[353] Von Bissing, *ASAE* 50, 559.
[354] K. Goudriaan, *Ethnicity in Ptolemaic Egypt* (Amsterdam 1988), 8–13, 75–77.
[355] Osing, *AV* 28, 71.; Whitehouse, 'Roman in Life', in O. Kaper (ed.), *Life on the Fringe*, 253.

their help, and is honoured by the great quality of their work[356].

4.5: Previous Documentation and Conservation Efforts

Though von Bissing is the first to have visited and fully documented the antechamber of tomb C1, the heavy debris and the black soot prevented him from discovering its burial chamber. Some parts of the tomb walls are glossy, which probably signifies that they have undergone a cleaning and/or consolidation process. Unfortunately, there is no information and no reports to prove this assumption. Therefore, the work conducted by the author and his team is the first known conservation treatment undertaken in this tomb. It is crucial that future generations know what was done to the tomb, as well as why it was done, when it was done, and by whom. Producing adequate records of the investigation of the tomb, as well as its treatment, is an ethical obligation that benefits the tomb and the ability of the researchers to find results.

4.6: An Assessment of the Condition of the Tomb

A small hill of debris was heaped in front of the tomb, as well as many scorpions and serpents. Small, heavily-painted pieces of damaged niches, as well as mummy shrouds, bones, and damaged pottery pieces were found. When the conservators entered the tomb for the first time to prepare a consolidated assessment, they noted its great heritage and significance. Both its layout and the scenes found in its antechamber distinguishes it from other tombs on the mountain. Moreover, the conservators realised the severe nature of the damage to the built-in and movable elements of the tomb. The official assessment report created by the conservators includes a brief description of each instance of damage to the tomb, including its type, its location (with reference to the base map, site map, and floor or sketch plan, where relevant), and its possible causes. Each entry includes a photograph to document the damage. The poor state of the tomb's preservation inspired the conservators to safeguard, stabilise, and recover it from the dirt. The on-site damage and risk assessment involved the visual inspection and documentation of the tomb's damaged areas. Likewise, immediate threats to the preservation of the tomb were noted, along with their respective mitigation measures.

Sohag's main area of illicit activities is concentrated in Akhmim. In the wake of the Egyptian Revolution of 2011 and the power vacuum that existed thereafter, many archaeological sites have become increasingly vulnerable to illegal digging[357]. In 2015, robbers destroyed great parts of the tomb. Other threats to the tomb involve its walls, which have differing levels of (sometimes superficial) decay. The walls have issues such as the presence of surface deposits and cracks, the loss of thickness of the preparatory and pictorial layers, the detachment of some of its pieces, the covering of some of its elements by debris and/or soot, and other signs of damage caused by robbers. In addition, the walls are home to multiple wasp nests, silverfish, and spiders. The presence of heavy soot poses the largest risk to the walls and ceiling of the burial chamber. Mitigating the consequences of the physical damage to the tomb was one of the most recent conservation goals. When Kuhlmann and later Kanawati visited the tomb, no looting or damaging activities were being undertaken there, at least, according to the security *ghaffirs*. However, the looters did successfully enter the tomb during the 25 of January Revolution. They caused significant damage, especially to the three burial niches. A consolidated damage and risk assessment report was thus created, and was used to create a plan for implementing necessary on-site stabilisation and conservation actions.

4.7: Some General Observations on the Construction and Decay of the Tomb

Tomb C1 is carved into El-Salamuni Mountain. Its walls are made of limestone, and are covered with a layer of silt and sand, before being finally coated in a layer of plaster and painted with scenes. Soot covers its walls and ceilings, and is most severe in the burial chamber. The overall condition of the tomb is bad; it suffers from various manifestations of damage, as explored in the following sections.

4.7.1: The Superficial Decay of the Walls and Ceilings

The superficial decay of the tomb and its walls has multiple facets. The first is the intentional mechanical damage caused to the tomb. Due to the continuous illicit looting activities on the mountain, many of the tomb scenes have suffered from the attempts of robbers to cut them away from the wall. Some scenes have also been scratched as an act of vandalism. This was despite the fact that the tomb's main entrance was hidden and covered with heavy debris and blocks. Chisel marks, grooves, and other damages were observed around some frieze scenes, suggesting that the looters had attempted to remove them. One of the most severe instances of damage in the tomb was done to the three burial niches, which caused the demolition of their painted scenes. Moreover, many important architectural elements of the tomb's layout are now lost. The thick, oily soot that covers the walls could be the result of the robbers, the ignorance of the local community (especially since the tomb was doorless for a period of time), and/or the ancient Copts, who used the tomb as a dwelling.

The superficial decay of the tomb has also been the result of the intense layer of soil that covers the ceiling of the antechamber, the ceiling of the burial room, and most of the burial room walls (Figures 4.70a-b). The soot causes the scenes to appear blurry. Furthermore, there is evidence

---

[356] M. Abo El Makarem is currently the main supervisor of the Chicago expedition at Medinet Habu. All of the people have participated in various projects, such as the conservation of tombs TT110 and TT 286 in Luxor, and the Tübingen conservation mission at the temple of Athribis.

[357] M. Hanna, 'Documenting Looting Activities in Post-2011 Egypt', in *Countering Illicit Traffic in Cultural Goods. The Global Challenge of Protecting the World's Heritage* (Paris 2015), 47.

The Afterlife in Akhmim

Figure 4.70a. The superficial decay and dirt covering the upper frieze of the west A4 wall of the antechamber.

Figure 4.70b. The soil covering the lower wall of the north B1 niche of the burial chamber.

of fire being used in the tomb, and the penetration of the fire into the layers of plaster has resulted in the loss of colours in many places. Unfortunately, many of the scenes are unable to be fully restored by the conservation process, especially when the original tomb artist had used a very light layer of colour. Furthermore, because of the great quantity of debris, dust covers the walls and ceilings of the tomb, which also causes damage.

Furthermore, the presence of surface deposits is widely apparent in tomb C1. These deposits include things such as wasp nests, spider webs, and mud deposits (Figure 4.71). They are often very well attached to the surfaces of the tomb's walls and ceilings. Wasp nests can cause severe damage, as wasp saliva is mixed with mud. The attachment of their nests therefore poses a severe risk to the walls and ceilings of the tomb, obstructing the scenery and distorting its form. The collection of mud also causes damage to the plaster and paint layers. Therefore, the colours and scenery of the tomb have been severely affected.

Besides leaving surface deposits, insects have damaged the tomb in other ways as well. The damage caused by insects has been significantly and clearly monitored. This includes monitoring the presence of silverfish. These insects often feed on the organic components of the tomb's ceilings and walls, and especially on the preparatory and final painted layers of the tomb scenes. Because El-Salamuni sometimes receives torrential rain, the tomb also suffers from acid rain mixed with dust. This has distorted the surface of the paint layers and made them susceptible to microbiological growth. Furthermore, insects and reptiles (including scorpions and serpents) often hide inside the tomb, within its gaps and large cracks. This is very detrimental to the surface of the scenery, and results in a poor visual effect. As the insects feed, they burrow into the layers of paint and plaster, forming holes and gaps that lead to further damage.

Finally, it should be noted that an unknown material or mortar has been previously applied to the tomb in order to treat its many problems. The old material still remains on the ceiling of the antechamber (Figure 4.72), and may have been used to blur out some of the original scene. This suggests that the material may have been applied by a Coptic person who lodged in the tomb during the Coptic persecution.

4.7.2: The Decay of the Paint Layer on the Walls and Ceilings

There is significant evidence for the decay of the paint layer on the walls and ceilings of tomb C1 (Figure 4.73). Evidence includes the following:

1. The total loss of paint in some areas.
2. The presence of spotting on some parts of the walls.
3. The fact that the layers of colour sometimes turn into 'scales'.
4. The flaking of the colours of some scenes. Flaking refers to the loss of adhesive material between two

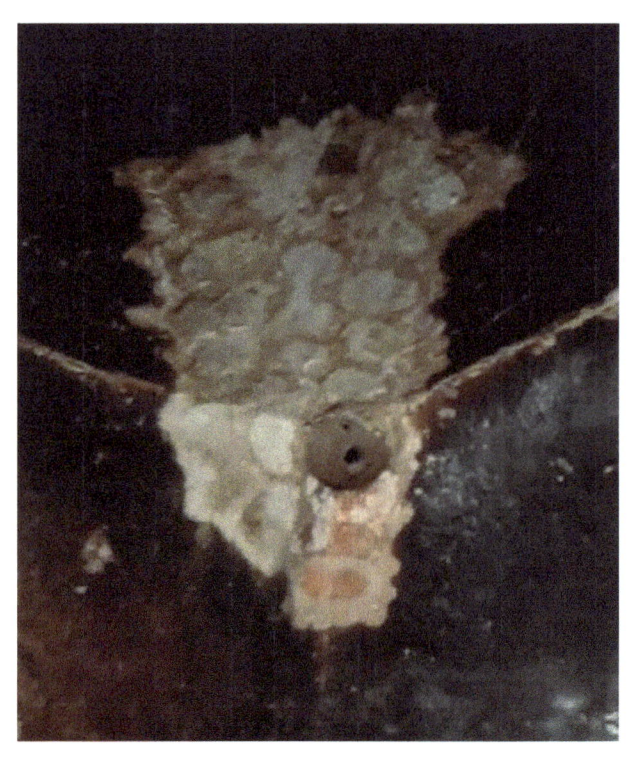

Figure 4.71. The presence of surface deposits such as wasp and spider nests on the ceiling of the burial chamber.

Figure 4.72. The use of ancient mortar on the ceiling of the antechamber, probably during the Coptic hermitage in the tomb.

   layers. It mainly occurs on the layers of colour, as is evidenced by cracks between the paint and plaster layers.
5. The fact that some of the colours have turned into powder.

Furthermore, one of the biggest weaknesses of the layers of colour used in tomb C1 is the fact that they were painted lightly, and with weak lines. This is evident in regards to the painted scenes in the antechamber, for instance. Unfortunately, the artist only used one or a few dabs of colour on his paintbrush. Furthermore, after some preliminarily tests, it was determined that the substance used to bind the raw colour was likely Arabic gum, which is very weak.

4.7.3: The Decay of the Pictorial and Preparatory Layers of Paint

The decay of some of the pictorial and preparatory layers of paint in tomb C1 can be observed in multiple areas. On multiple parts of the tomb walls and ceiling, there are superficial, medium, and deep cracks in the layers of material used in the preparation of the painted scenes. This includes separations between the paint layers and pictorial layers, and between the preparatory layers and support layers. In connection to this, there are missing parts of the prepared surface. Parts of the superficial layers of paint have also been lost, along with the disintegration of some of the paint into granules. On the plastered and painted

Figure 4.73. An image of the decay of the wall's paint layer, showing the patron of the tomb. The image is of the left doorjamb on the north A1 wall of the antechamber.

walls, there are remnants of wasp and spider nests, as well as bee hives. Furthermore, the painted scenes have sometimes separated from their plaster background, and are left with spaces behind them. Finally, one may notice the change of colour on the plastered and prepared areas of the walls and ceilings; there are many black spots due to burning, as well as discolouration because of dust and soot.

4.7.4: The Decay of the Support Layer of the Walls and Ceilings

The support layer of the tomb's walls and ceilings has been largely negatively affected by decay. In many areas in the tomb, one can see the loss of the support that is normally widely present. Cracks are visible in many parts of the support layer, ranging from shallow to deep. Some parts of the support layer are detached, fragmented, discoloured, or a combination of these. Furthermore, numerous bumps can be found in many of the support layers, especially on the wider parts of the walls and ceilings of the tomb.

4.8: The Methodology of the Treatment of Tomb C1

The risk assessment and monitoring carried out by the conservation team included the careful consideration of all known damages to the tomb. Samples and tests were made to remove the tomb's soot, with the hopes of uncovering the scenes and the inscriptions behind it. Six different samples of a poultice used to treat the damages were made, according to the degree of damage caused by the soot; the ratio of ingredients varied according to the soot type and strength. The effectiveness of the poultice samples with treating the soot covering each part of the walls and the ceilings was tested. The samples were added in gradual concentrations until the best and most effective samples could be determined. The samples were applied onto multiple sections of the ceilings of the ante- and burial chambers, as well as on the southern and northern walls of the burial chamber.

The ceiling of the burial chamber is not polished evenly; rocky outcrops still appear. To test whether or not the dark ceiling of the burial chamber has been painted, samples of different parts of the ceiling were made with equal squares measuring 10x10cm.. The conservators highly suspected that a zodiac covers the wide ceiling of the burial chamber. Unfortunately, all of the tested parts of the ceiling proved to be empty of colour, and nothing was found. This may be because the tomb was not completed, although the reason for this is unknown. In fact, other parts of the tomb are also free of painted scenes, such as the right side of the tomb's entrance and the wall in the burial chamber to the right of the northern niche.

The empty ceiling could be related to the cost of the tomb; the artist was probably not paid for this work. It could also reflect the attitude of the artist, who could have simply decided that the zodiac of the antechamber would be enough. However, there are other tombs that include two zodiacs, both in their ante- and burial chambers. Despite the negative sample results, the researchers are still optimistic and hopeful to find something interesting on the ceiling. Reviving tomb C1 through appropriate conservation treatments was one of the main challenges and goals of the research team.

4.9: The Processing of the Tomb To-Date

The initial processing of tomb C1 included the careful study and documentation of the tomb's vulnerabilities and decayed parts, as well as attempts at treating the damage, which were noted in a detailed report. The tomb has suffered from several phases of decay for multiple reasons. Soot is currently considered the most harmful threat to the tomb. The soot may have been caused by the use of fire by the Coptic hermits who once found shelter in the tomb. It may have also been caused by the local community of El-Salamuni at a later date. The use of fire and cooking would have caused a significant amount of soot and damage. After inventorying all of the various types of damage in the tomb, a deterioration map was designed. It includes suggestions for which type of conservation method is best for each threat, and outlines the materials which should be used. For two weeks, many preliminary tests were conducted to select the best proportions of chemical materials needed to clean both the heavy and light soot on the tomb walls and ceilings. The workers also established the causes of the deterioration of the wall paintings via a comprehensive program of visual examination, condition monitoring, and scientific investigation.

4.9.1: The Documentation of the Tomb

Before the start of the conservation process, the tomb was documented in its existing state; all of the scenes on the walls and ceilings of the tomb were photographed (Figure 4.74). The conservation team recorded all of the threats

Figure 4.74. The documentation of the damage by the conservators.

to the preservation of the tomb, as well as evidence of deterioration throughout the tomb. They recorded the damage done to each separate layer of the walls and ceilings, rather than only the top layer. The walls have been photographed and divided into plates with their own unique identifications. The plates can be traced and used to record and map the existing condition of a section of the ceiling or wall, including its various layers. In the documentation, symbols, rather than colour, are used in conjunction with a glossary to identify each layer of the damaged walls and ceilings. The documentation includes a report of the planned, and ultimately performed, conservation techniques. A digital map of the deterioration was also designed. Here, one can use signs to label each type of damage on each layer of plaster and paint via a certain key on Adobe Photoshop. This map of the tomb's deterioration was used as a guide to continue the systematic preservation work.

4.9.2: The Pre-Consolidation of the Damaged Areas

Upon assessing tomb C1, it became clear that immediate stabilisation actions were needed, as a sort of first aid. The pre-consolidation of the unstable edges of plaster, which needed immediate intervention, was thus the second step for the conservation team. The work included cleaning the selected areas with air pumps and soft brushes before placing binding strips on them. All of the vulnerable and decayed areas of the ceilings and walls which were prone to fall down during either mechanical or chemical cleaning were strengthened (Figures 4.75). Scales and microcracks were strengthened and fixed using KG 3%, syringes, and brushes. All of the decayed edges, small, fragile pieces that were still attached to the wall, and small, weak gaps that have turned into powder, were strengthened by using acrylic material. The specific formula was AC33, with a concentration of 1:5 and 1:2, applied by brushes, spray, and syringes.

4.9.3: The Mechanical Cleaning of the Tomb

The mechanical cleaning of the painted areas of tomb C1 was the next step of the conservation process. Dust and surface deposits such as wasp, insect, and spider nests were removed using soft brushes, and a rubber blower was used for removing superficial dust from the upper paint layers. The team also relied on the use of scalpels and spatulas for the removal of the wasp nests. Hand-held blowers and fibre tools were used to remove the accumulated soot on the stone surfaces. A *wishab* (an eraser) and a soot sponge were used to reduce the effects of the dust and soot as much as possible before the application of the chemicals.

4.9.4: The Chemical Cleaning Process

After manually cleaning the walls and ceilings of tomb C1, the chemical process could begin. Poultices and solutions consisting of the following materials were used: distilled water, ammonium carbonate, EDTA, carboxymethyl cellulose, Arbosil, and Japanese chio paper (Figures 4.76a-c). These materials were previously used by the team during their conservation work in tomb TT110 in El-Qurna (the Tomb of Djehuty), which was funded by the American Research Centre in Egypt (ARCE). The condition of this tomb was very similar to tomb C1 before the conservation process, especially in regards to the soot; its type and concentration was similar in both tombs. Many samples were taken and tests conducted before starting the main conservation work. This was in order to choose the best and most suitable poultices for each area of the walls and ceilings.

The poultice used to remove the soot on the ceiling of the burial chamber consisted of 125ml. of distilled water, plus 1g. of Edta, 1g. of Ammonium carbonate, 1g. of CMC, and Arposel. The poultice was left on the area for about 10–20 minutes, according to the quantity of soot. Meanwhile, the poultice used on the walls of the burial chamber consisted of 100ml. of distilled water, plus 1.5g. of Edta, 1.5g. of Ammonium carbonate, 1g. of CMC, and Arposel. The poultice was left on for about 10 minutes.

Regular *wishab* sponges were used in order to reduce the quantity of the soot and dust as much as possible, helping conservators to detect the lines of the figures beneath. To treat areas that were severely affected by the soot, a solution of EDTA and Ammonium carbonate at a concentration of 1.5% was used, being applied by wooden sticks and cotton. It was then neutralized with distilled water. When the borders and lines of the images started to appear beneath the soot, a poultice was placed on the areas surrounding the drawings. The poultice was held in place with Japanese paper and covered using food-grade plastic. After 10 minutes, it was removed. Finally, the area was cleaned with soap and cotton, and neutralized with distilled water.

After revealing the drawings and cleaning the drawings' backgrounds, the work became concentrated on the scenes themselves. To uncover the details, either a solution or a quick application (and removal) of a small amount of poultice was used. Finally distilled water was applied to each line and each colour separately. As for the ceiling of the burial chamber, it was cleaned after making sure that it

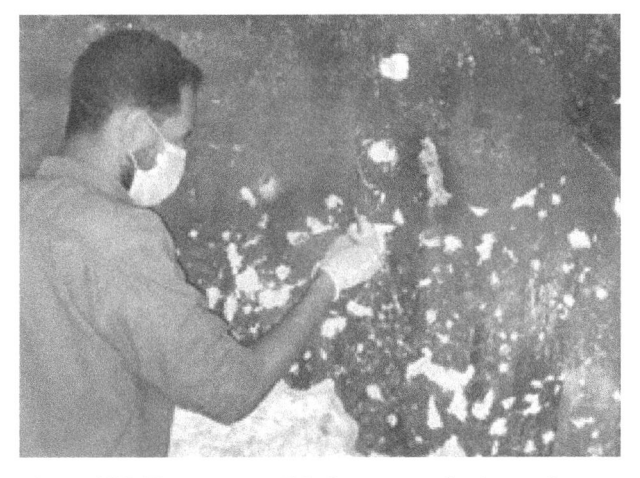

Figure 4.75. The pre-consolidation process in the tomb, as carried out by the conservators.

The Afterlife in Akhmim

Figure 4.76a. The mechanical cleaning carried out in tomb C1 with the help of a *weishab* sponge.

Figure 4.76b. The chemical cleaning of the soot by use of a suitable poultice on the walls of the tomb.

Figure 4.76c. Another example of using a poultice for the chemical cleaning process, this time on the ceiling of the burial chamber.

was completely free of any inscriptions. This was done by making several tests in separate places on the ceilings, and then following the previously described cleaning steps and concentration of poultice, followed by the solution with distilled water.

4.9.5.: The Consolidation Process

After removing the soot from the damaged scenes of tomb C1, a consolidation process to connect the separated parts of the stone was started (Figure 4.77). The team used Klucel G with a percentage of 3%, applied by means of a brush. The consolidation efforts were undertaken for all decayed edges of the plaster, by use of Paraloid B72 with a concentration of 1.5%. The weak areas of the scenes were covered with the acrylic material Acrill C33 (Ac33), with a concentration of 1:5.. The consolidation of the pictorial layer was also conducted by carefully cleaning the surface with an air pump. It was especially important to be careful because the plaster was very weak. The team also applied a lime and water solution as a spray.

4.9.6: The Treatment of the Fragments

After cleaning and consolidating the small, fragile, plaster pieces with the help of injections by small syringes, the pieces were 'fixed' by re-gluing them into their original locations on the wall (Figure 4.78). The more damaged

Figure 4.77. The consolidation of the vulnerable edges of the plaster.

Figure 4.78. Fixing and re-gluing the small, fallen pieces of wall.

pieces were fixed to the wall after verifying them. The re-attachment of the fragments to the walls was done using Ac33 at a concentration of 40%, and then fixing the edges with a lime mortar.

Using grout to secure the detached material between the mud layer and support was one of the main priorities of the team. The goal was to connect the separated areas together via the use of grout. The grout used was PLM stucco mortar and distilled water. The grouting process started along the lower level of the tomb, and continued to the higher level. The injection process was completed as follows:

1. Potential holes for the tubes were identified so that the grouting material could be injected to cover the largest possible area.
2. The team made sure that any visible holes and cracks were filled. This process could potentially cause leakage.
3. The holes were then examined, with attention to their sizes and depths. An order was established for which holes the team would work with first.
4. Before the application of the grout, each area to be filled with grout received a syringe full of alcohol in order to clean the dust and prepare the hole for the injection.
5. During the process of applying the liquid mortar, the team carefully monitored the adjacent gaps to avoid any damage or spillage that may occur.
6. The team applied 1 syringe full of material to one area each day, and recorded the amount that was applied in a table.
7. After completion of the grouting process, the plastic tubes were removed from the holes, and any remaining spaces were closed with a suitable mortar.

4.9.7: The Cracks in the Walls and Their Treatment by Injections

The cracks and detached sections of the tomb C1 walls were injected with a mixture of BLM dissolved with distilled water at a ratio appropriate to the type of damage on the wall. Acrylic was used with a concentration of 1:2 for microcracks. These materials were injected into the walls using hoses of different sizes, as well as various syringes. The syringes ranged from an insulin syringe to veterinary syringes (Figure 4.79). They were selected based on their ability to deliver the liquid material as far as possible into the detached areas and cracks. However, before being filled, the damaged areas were first flushed with a syringe containing alcohol and water in a ratio of 1:1. This was used to test the flow of the material and to assess the amount of leakage that can be expected to appear outside of the crack. The Table 4.3 presents some examples of the injections of different substances into the cracks and detached sections of the tomb walls:

Figure 4.79. The injection of material into a crack in the tomb C1 wall.

Table 4.3: Examples of the Use of Materials for the Grout Injection Process

No.	Location	Wall	Material	Date	Quantity
1	South Wall	B3	BLM	27-5-2021	5cm.
2	South Wall	B3	BLM	27-5-2021	3.5cm.
3	South Wall	B3	BLM	27-5-2021	45cm.
4	South Wall	B3	BLM	27-5-2021	107cm.
5	East Wall	A2	Ac33	30-5-2021	15cm.
6	North Wall	B3	BLM	30-5-2021	283cm.
7	North Wall	B3	BLM	30-5-2021	256cm.
8	North Wall	B3	BLM	30-5-2021	30cm.
9	South Wall	B1	BLM	30-5-2021	121cm.
10	South Wall	B1	BLM	31-5-2021	50cm.
11	South Wall	B1	BLM	31-5-2021	23cm.
12	South Wall	B1	BLM	31-5-2021	18cm.
Total	-	-	-	-	956.5cm.

4.9.8: The Masonry Work Undertaken for the Niches

The niches of tomb C1 were almost completely destroyed due to ancient vandalism, with the exception of parts of their lateral walls. These remaining parts help as a guide to determine the actual dimensions of the original niches, and to calculate the original dimensions of the burial chamber.

The masonry work to repair the niches involved many steps. First, the damaged niches were photographed. Then, the measurements of the lost parts of the niches were determined. This was done by drawing the niches manually and calculating the measurements of the parts that were destroyed. The detached spaces on the damaged niche wall were then levelled, and the walls were cleaned thoroughly. Then, the damaged parts were rebuilt using limestone blocks of irregular shapes and sizes, which were taken from the mountain outside the tomb. The stones were connected using a mortar consisting of sand and slaked lime in a ratio of 3:2. This was completed with consideration of the interior layout of the building, which was relatively determined by the layout of the original face of the mountain. A space of sufficient size was determined and set aside for the conservation work. Then, the layers of the walls were lined with a modern mortar. This was covered with a mortar consisting of sand and lime in a ratio of 3:1. Polyurethane foam was used to fill the gaps below the exposed face of the wall. The foam provides a stopping point within the deep gaps, allowing a secure and tight fill. Finally, a layer of mortar consisting of fine yellow sand, matt lime, and oxidized colours was applied (Figures 4.80a-c).

4.9.9: Filling the Gaps in the Tomb Walls

The final conservation efforts conducted in tomb C1 were carried out with the purpose of treating the gaps in the walls, which were either large, medium, or small in size. Many steps were conducted to fill the gaping areas of the walls. A mechanical cleaning of the gaps was carried out using brushes. Any moving parts on the walls were fixed, and their edges consolidated. Then, the gaps were flushed with distilled water. The mortars were applied using fine spatulas, and the surface was roughened to increase its porosity. A mortar consisting of sand and lime was added to the wall and fixed strongly in place using small trowels and spatulas. The process also included isolating the edges of any scenes with a Paraloid B72 solute in acetone and xylene before applying the mortar. This was done in order to avoid the creation of any yellowish spots. As for the pieces of limestone that had fractured off the niche, they were mixed into the mortar, and then fixed back in place. Then, they were covered with a layer of mortar and made level. This layer was purposely scratched to enable the final mortar layer to stick to it well after the 'lining layer' had dried (Figures 4.81a-b).

After the mortar lining was fully dry, and to be sure that there was no cracking, the final mortar was added only

Figure 4.80a. The damaged north B1 burial niche, as shown in the burial chamber, before the conservation work.

Figure 4.80b. Masonry work in the north B1 burial niche.

Figure 4.80c. The north B1 burial niche after the masonry work.

after conducting several tests. These tests helped the conservators prioritize and select the best mortar in terms of colour, strength, and shape. After many trials, sample number 1 was selected, which consisted of the following: 3g. of fine sand, 1g. of hydrated lime, 2g. of brown oxide, 5g. of yellow oxide, and distilled water. The removal of the soot and the status of the tomb walls both before and after the conservation processes is documented above (in the description of the funerary scenes).

Figure 4.81a. The addition of a mortar lining to the upper register of the eastern A2 wall of the tomb C1 antechamber.

Figure 4.81b. The scratching of the mortar lining on the upper register of the eastern A2 wall of the tomb C1 antechamber.

5

Tomb C3

The northern section of El-Salamuni Mountain is more crowded with tombs than the southern part. This section of the mountain includes façade tombs, shaft tombs, and hundreds of landslide tombs with entrances that are lower than the mountain's terraces. These tombs with lower entrances are mainly located on the lower terraces A and B. The mountain's northern section extends north of El-Salamuni village, and includes the area between the sixth slope and the third slope, south of the rock-cut temple of Ay. This part of the mountain is systematically divided into eight terraces ranging from A-H.

The tombs which are scattered on the fourth slope of the southern part of the mountain in the area around and below the *ghaffirs'* hut include façade and landslide tombs of the Late Roman Period (the second and third centuries AD). Presumably, the last burials on the mountain took place within this section. The northern part of the mountain, which includes the area between the third and the fourth slopes, contains many shaft tombs on its upper terraces (G and H), scattered along the ascending slope to the temple of Ay. The central part of the mountain contains the least amount of recorded tombs to-date. The looting in this section is less than in the northern part of the mountain, which is likely because of the existence of the security *ghaffirs'* cave. The recent excavation campaigns by the Akhmim Inspectorate Office (2012/2013, 2018/2019) were concentrated within the area beyond and below the *ghaffirs'* hut. The lower tombs in registers A and B were unearthed through these field campaigns. Tomb B1 is considered the most painted tomb to have been recently excavated in the area.

5.1: The Location and Layout

Tomb C3 is located on terrace C, on the southern section of El-Salamuni Mountain, just below the *ghaffirs'* cave/hut. It is adjacent to tombs C4 and C5, which are separated from each other by about 2m.. Tomb C3 is now closed with a steel door (Figures 5.1b-c). It consists of two rooms and a low west façade and entrance. Two niches are cut into the south and west walls of the burial chamber (Figure 5.2). The tomb is distinguished by the fact that it is one of the very few Graeco-Roman tombs in the necropolis to be devoid of a zodiac on its ceiling.

5.1.1: The Antechamber

The walls of the antechamber are divided into two registers, separated by a black line. Though the El-Salamuni tombs generally feature the distinctive Hellenistic *orthostat* decoration, the Greek chequerboard *orthostat* style is totally missing in the lower register of the tomb C3 antechamber[1]. Scenes of the Egyptian funerary afterlife only cover the upper friezes of the south, north, and west walls, while the lower friezes are unpainted. Only the east wall is decorated with funerary scenes on both its upper and lower registers.

5.1.2: The Northern A4 Wall

The northern A4 wall shows the beginning of a scene of the Hall of Judgement, which spans over both the north and east walls of the anteroom. The scene starts with the *psychopomp* Anubis, the divine messenger, leading the deceased to the court[2]. Anubis holds the left wrist of the deceased in his right hand, while the right hand of the deceased is raised in an adoration gesture. The deceased is dressed in a white and calf-length fringed garment, which is the same clothing as the deceased was wearing in tomb C1. The head of the deceased is destroyed, with only short, curly hair being visible. A partially damaged silhouette, with only its thin black legs preserved, is shown between Anubis and a damaged female goddess. The goddess is certainly either Hathor[3] or Maat[4]. Anubis turns his head towards the silhouette and holds it with his left hand, while Hathor(?) holds the same silhouette with her right hand, and another silhouette with her left hand. Anubis is painted in black and wears a red kilt with a yellow wig. Anubis' belly is also painted red. The damaged Hathor wears a red fitted garment, while her feet are painted yellow. The image of Anubis and Hathor leading the silhouette to the divine tribunal of Osiris confirms the positive beneficent function of these black figures as manifestations of the posthumous deceased, rather than as images of tortured

---

[1] Venit suggests that the absence of *orthostats* on the lower part of the wall in room 2 in El-Anfushi tomb II indicates a much less careful execution of the decoration of this room, Venit, *Monumental Tombs of Alexandria*, 83. It seems that the painter conducted his work in a hurry, possibly to finish the tomb for the burial.
[2] In the court, Anubis is assimilated with the Greek god Aiakos, the son of Zeus and Aigina, who was worshipped by the Greeks as the protector of the deceased in the afterlife, S. Morenz, 'Anubis mit dem Schlüssel', in S. Morenz (ed.), *Religion und Geschichte des alten Ägypten* (Vienna 1975), 516–17.
[3] Hathor is sometimes substituted for Anubis as the guide for the deceased woman to Osiris, Riggs, *The Beautiful Burial*, 128, fig. 54. Deceased women are more closely associated with Hathor than Osiris in texts and funerary art from Ptolemaic-Roman Egypt, Riggs, *The Beautiful Burial*, 71–78.; V. Rondot, *L'Empereur et le petit prince: les deux c'losses d'Argo, iconographie, symbolique et datation*, in V. Rondot, F. Alpi, and F. Villeneuve (eds.), *La pioche et la plume, autour du Soudan, du Liban et de la Jordanie, Hommages archéologiques à Patrice Lenoble* (Paris 2011), 428–31.; V. Rondot, *Derniers visages des dieux d'Égypte, iconographies, panthéons et cultes dans le Fayoum hellénisé des IIe-IIIe siècles de notre ère*, Passé présent (Paris 2013), 265, 355–56.; Smith, *Following Osiris*, 385–89.
[4] The middle register of the east wall of the tomb of Petubastis also shows the deceased (Petubastis) being led before Osiris by Anubis and Maat, fig. 22c.

The Afterlife in Akhmim

Figure 5.1a. The topography of the southern section of El-Salamuni Mountain.

Figure 5.1b. The location of tomb C3, below the security hut.

Figure 5.1c. The façade-entrance of tomb C3.

victims and stubborn enemies who hinder the deceased's transfiguration. The scene records the only known representation of a silhouette led to the Court of Judgement by a *psychopomp* deity in an ancient Egyptian tomb.

To the right of the image, the adjacent frieze shows a damaged, hybrid, and feathered daemon who strides towards the main entrance. Unfortunately, the upper part of this image is completely damaged; only the black legs and long, feathered wing extending from the back of the figure have survived. The feather is painted white and yellow, with black stripes. The daemon can hold weapons in his hands to protect the tomb from any evil (Figures 5.3a-b).

The cult of Anubis was quite popular in Panopolis, especially on the east bank. Mummified jackals were discovered in the El-Hawawish A cemetery[5], which may suggest that Anubis was the patron there. A sanctuary of Anubis in Akhmim is mentioned in the famous Demotic P. Berl. Bork of the fourth century AD. While the text reports the inventory of the buildings in the city, it also mentions that 'we have gone to the house of Melas', which was a generally well-known building in the city. The officials also mention 'we have reached the temple of An(. . .)'[6]. The rest of the text is missing, but it most probably refers to the temple of Anubis, the god who is connected to the funerary banquet meals. Furthermore, a sanctuary dedicated to Anubis is known from the opposite city of Athribis. It was a type of *Asklepeion*, and it was suggested that this building could be an *Anubieion*[7].

---

[5] Kuhlmann, *SDAIK* 11, 57 no. 283.

[6] *P. Berl. Bork A* II, 18–19.; *P. Berl. Bork VI*, 2–4.

[7] For the Greek inscription reading 'ANOUBIDI KRATHS' above the south entrance, see R. El-Farag et al., *MDAIK* 41, pl. 8d. The *Asklepeion* consists of a forecourt, two rock-cut chambers, and a niche for a cult statue, which lies behind a columned façade, the purpose of which is still unclear. S. Lippert recorded about 70 inscriptions on its walls. Out of these, 65 are written in Demotic, while five are in Greek. In addition, eight painted sketches and one recessed rectangular panel with a painting

Tomb C3

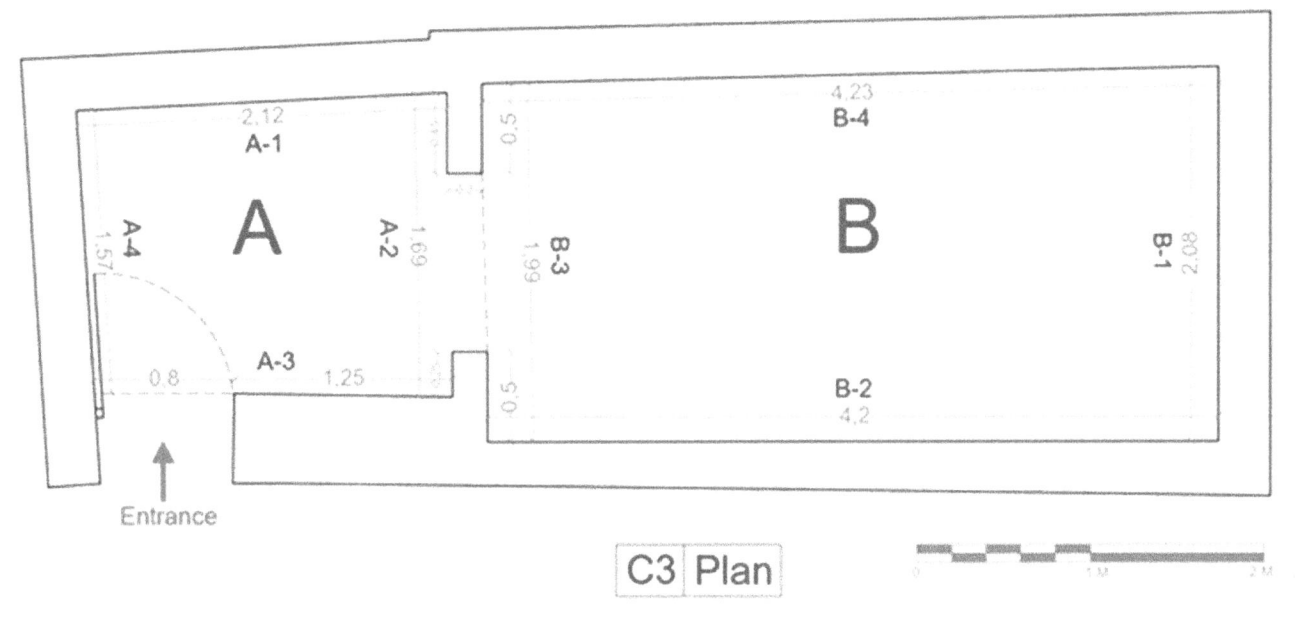

Figure 5.2. The layout of tomb C3.

5.1.3: The Eastern A1 Wall: An Overview

Scenes of the afterlife are depicted on both the upper and the lower registers of the A1 wall.

5.1.4: The Upper Register of the Eastern A1 Wall

The upper register of the A1 wall shows a scene of the Court of Judgement, where the deceased's heart is weighed and judged by the enthroned Osiris-Sokar, sitting on the far north side of the wall. Horus and a damaged figure, presumably Anubis, stand beneath the balance, and its beam is supported by their upraised hands. The crossbar of the beam is surmounted by a green ape. The two deities turn their heads and face each other, resting their free hands on a pan of the scale. A partially damaged silhouette (with only his legs being still visible) stands frontally beneath the centre of the scale. Meanwhile, another silhouette is shown being weighed on the right pan of the scale. The other pan is damaged. In this scene, Horus is represented with a black falcon head, a red chest, green arms, a red belly, and a yellow lower torso. The head of Anubis is damaged. He wears a red kilt and a yellow wig, and his body is multi-coloured, featuring a black chest, black arms and legs, and a yellow belly.

To the left of the scale, another silhouette awaits its destiny before the devourer Ammit, who is painted red, with a partially damaged head. Another partially damaged silhouette is submerged inside a fiery cauldron, painted white with a yellow frame[8]. This representation of a damned silhouette in a fiery cauldron is similar to the one shown in the von Bissing tomb. The El-Salamuni tombs preserve the only known examples of such silhouette punishment scenes in tombs, either by the devourer or by the cauldron of fire at their judgement.

To the right of the scale stands a large, partially damaged, ibis-headed depiction of Thoth, holding a papyrus scroll

---

underneath one line of Demotic have also been found. Inscriptions are found on the tomb's façade, on the doorframe leading into the first room, on all four walls of the first room, and on the back wall of the second room. Lippert mentions that only the Greek inscription in the entrance area makes a reference to the god Asklepios. However, while none of the other over 60 Demotic inscriptions found here mention Imhotep/Asklepios, they do mention other deities such as Min-Re, Repit, Horus Senedjem-ib, Haroeris (the Lord of Letopolis), Kolanthes, and Osiris-Sokar (the Lord of Abydos). The *Speos* was mainly used as a resting place for falcon mummies. The Greek inscription on its lintel dates to either much earlier or much later than the beginning of the first century AD, when the cult of the sacred falcons of Athribis was in full swing (especially the cult of *p3 bi k* and *ȝr-wr nb sxm*). One of the inscriptions also mentions a group of people bearing titles that seem connected to a falcon cult, S. Lippert, 'Ostraca, Graffiti, and Dipinti from Athribis in Upper Egypt', in M. Depauw and Y. Broux (eds.), *Acts of the 10th International Conference for Demotic Studies, Leuven, 26–30 August 2008*, OLA 231 (Leiden 2014), 145–53. On the *Asklepion* of Athribis, see W. Omran, 'The Egyptian and the Hellenistic Characteristics of the Asklepion', *Journal of Faculty of Tourism and Hotels, Fayoum University*, 8, no. 2 (2014), 76–78. The worship of sacred falcons was popular on the west bank of the Panopolite nome. Two mummy labels from Edfa mention a priestly office of the *sbty* of Haroeris, who was perhaps concerned with the mummification of the sacred falcons, M. Chauveau 'Les cultes d'Edfa à l'époque romaine', *RdÉ* 37 (1986), 37, no. I.3. At Awlad Azaz, many falcon burials are attested, B. Ockinga, 'The Tomb of Sennedjem at Awlad Azzaz (Sohag)', *BACE* 2 (1991), 81–89.

[8] Omran, *JARCE* 56, 143–67.; Régen, 'Ombres, Une iconographie singulière', 603–47.; K. Dunbabin, 'Sic erimus cuncit: The Skeleton in Graeco-Roman Art', *JDAI* 101 (1986), 185–255. The damned silhouette is relished as a fatty meal by the devourer, as shown on a fragmentary shroud illustrated by E. Brunner-Traut, *Gelebte Mythen*, 76.; E. Brunner-Traut, H. Brunner, and J. Zick-Nissen, *Osiris, Kreuz und Halbmond, Die Drei Religionen Ägyptens* (Mainz 1984), 137.

The Afterlife in Akhmim

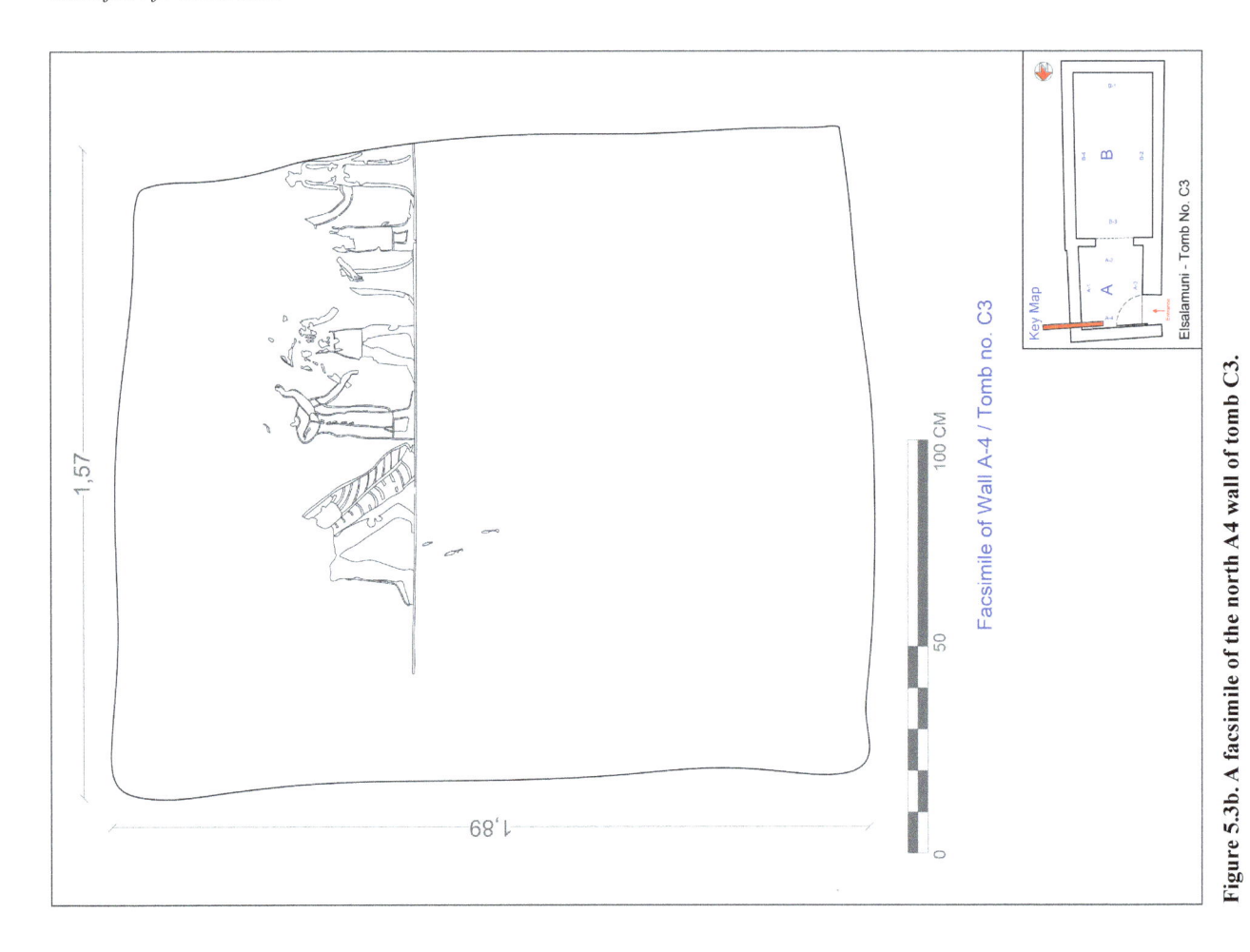

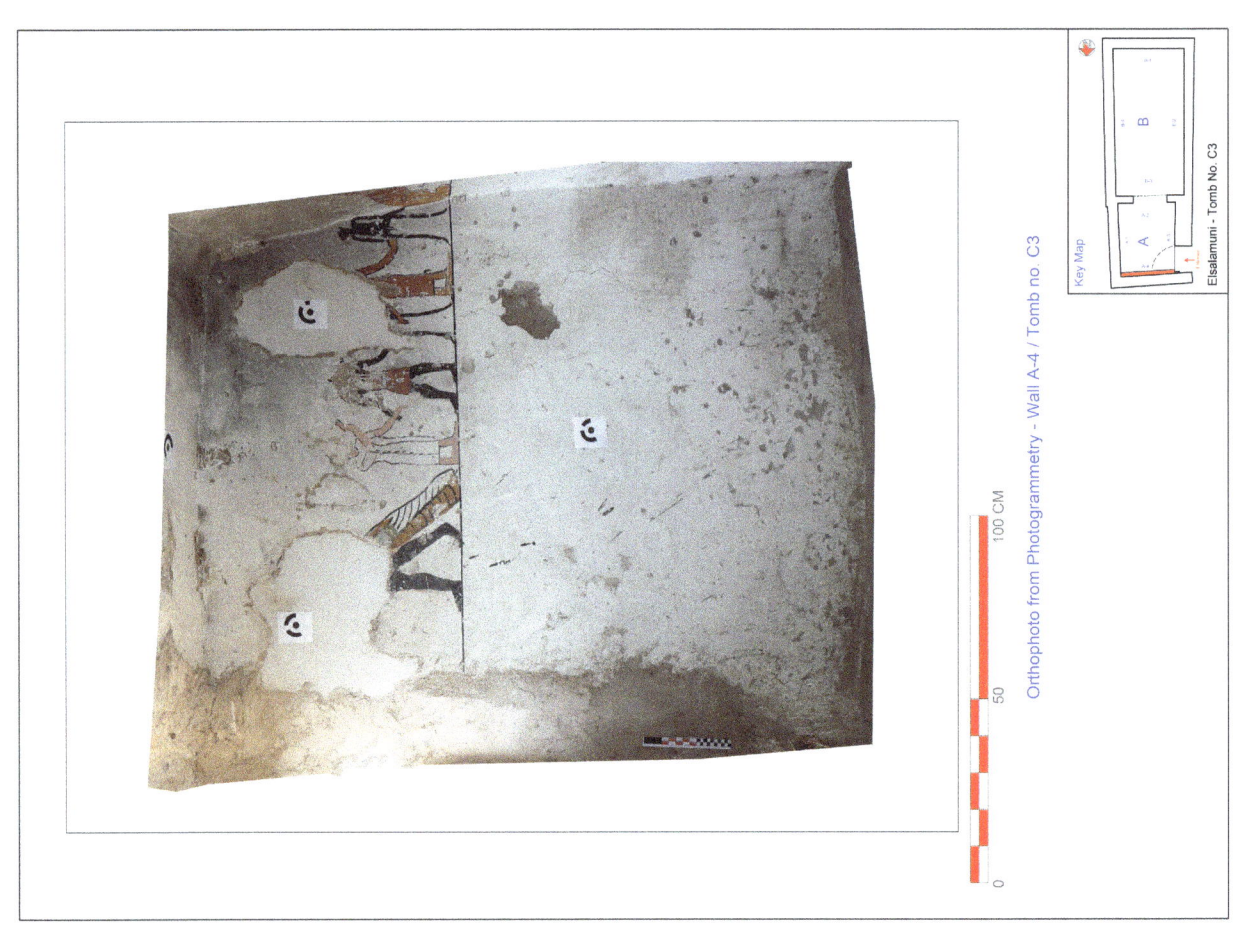

Figure 5.3b. A facsimile of the north A4 wall of tomb C3.

Figure 5.3a. Photogrammetry of the north A4 wall of the antechamber in tomb C3.

in his right hand. He is shown reporting the results of the court, and striding towards Osiris. He is painted green, and wears a yellow *nemes* headdress and a kilt with a black belt. Osiris faces the scale, holding his traditional royal insignia. The *nḥ3* flail can still be seen in his left hand, while he is supposedly holding the typical *hq3* crook in his damaged right hand. A great part of Osiris' body is damaged, even though the remains of his *atef* crown are still visible. His body is shrouded in red patterns with black dots inside, while the chequered throne is ornamented with red and yellow panels with black dots. A winged female deity, presumably Isis-Maat, stands behind Osiris and holds the ʿnx- sign with her upraised right hand. A black Maat feather rests in her lowered left hand. Isis-Maat is dressed in a red garment and a black headdress, with feathers painted black and yellow (Figure 5.4). Unfortunately, a lot of damage has occurred on the wall between Osiris and Thoth, so that only the base of a large vase remains. One could suggest that the four sons of Horus would have been shown here, protruding from a lotus bloom like in tomb C1.

The judgement scene shown on the upper register is quite like the one in tomb C1, with only small differences. Here, Osiris wears an *atef* crown and acts as the supervisor of the court, while in tomb C1, it is Horus who wears the white crown and presides over the court. Here, in tomb C3, Ammit crouches near a fiery cauldron shown to the right of the scale, while she appears to the left of the scale in tomb C1. The scene in tomb C3 shows the largest number of silhouettes; six figures are shown acting in various ambivalent roles in the court scene, while only four are depicted in tomb C1. Furthermore, in tomb C3, Anubis and Hathor attend to the deceased male, as well as to his incarnation as a silhouette in this court scene. Meanwhile, in tomb C1, Maat is responsible for introducing the deceased male to the court.

5.1.5: The Lower Register of the Eastern A1 Wall

The far southern side of the lower register shows the remains of a partially damaged, shrouded deity, sitting on a throne. The upper part of the figure is destroyed, but because its hands are crossed on its chest in an Osirian form, it is most likely Osiris. The frieze right next to this entity shows a figure in profile, costumed in a classical white dress and standing on a black base. The head is too destroyed to distinguish the gender of the figure, but it was probably a male. He holds a tall palm branch in his upraised left hand, while another taller branch is depicted behind him. He carries a big damaged libation vase painted yellow, which is probably a cultic *situla*, in his lowered right hand. He makes libations over an offering table containing two *hes* vessels and a lotus flower.

The vignette to the right of this scene is of a a bald man playing a flute[9]. He wears a long white garment, which is tied around his chest. His upper torso is naked. His face and his left arm are partially destroyed, and only his right eye remains. A female figure who is seated on the ground listens to the flautist. She is dressed in a white Roman garment which covers her chest, while her back is naked. Unfortunately, her face is partially damaged. However, it is still clear that she wears a black curly wig and that she faces the flautist, bending over slightly and raising her left hand to her face in the traditional Greek mourning posture[10], expressing her grief over the deceased. Next to the female mourner, Osiris sits on his traditional striped throne. He wears a white crown and a black curved beard; his face being painted green. His body is covered by a shroud decorated with black spots inside red squares. His throne is patterned with yellow panels with black dots, and a broad green panel adorns the throne's corner.

Behind Osiris, strips cover the body of a jackal-headed deity. He is probably Duamutef, one of the four sons of Horus. Like Osiris, his face is painted yellow, and he wears a black headdress. He stands in front of a partially damaged high altar. Although the offerings on it are damaged, it probably once held traditional bread loaves (Figure 5.5). Although the wall behind Duamutef is unpainted, the space could have contained the other three missing figures of the sons of Horus. The artist either did not pay enough attention to his work, or was in a hurry to move onto another part of the wall. Wall A1 is fully documented through the use of photogrammetry, the making of a facsimile, and the creation of a map of the deterioration of its scenes (Figures 5.6a-c).

The female mourner from the scene is quite similar to the male mourner depicted on the left wall of the central niche of a tomb at Kom El-Shukafa, who has been identified by Rowe as the weeping son of the deceased[11]. Therefore, the female mourner in tomb C3 is probably one of the relatives of the deceased. Perhaps she represents the grief experienced by the deceased's mother or wet-nurse[12]. In this scene, both the male figure who makes libations with a *situla* and the flautist presumably act as priests, just like the two priests in tomb C1. This confirms the presence of a funerary cult of the deceased in his tomb.

Tomb C3 provides the first (or rather, the only) known musical scene in a Graeco-Roman tomb of Egypt. The flautist (*wDny*) performs music with an *aulos* instrument in the presence of Osiris and a mourning squatting female. While the flautist is supposed to cover all the finger holes of his intrument, his left hand leaves the bottom hole

---

[9] A long flute is the oldest known representation of a wind instrument. It is depicted on a mudstone palette of the Predynastic Period, J. Quibell and F. Green, *Hierakonpolis II, Egyptian Research Account Memoir* 5 (London 1902), pl. XXVIII.
[10] Venit, *Monumental Tombs of Ancient Alexandria*, 138.; G. Holst-Warhaft, *Dangerous Voices: Women's Laments and Greek Literature* (Routledge 1992), 103. Various mourning postures were depicted in Pharaonic art, see Valdesogo, *Hair and Death*.
[11] A. Rowe, 'Excavations of the Graeco- Roman Museum of Kom El-Shukafa During the Season 1941–42', *BSRAA* 35 (1942), 22, 23.; Venit, *Visualizing the Afterlife*, 74, fig. 2.23.
[12] S. Walker and D. Montserrat, 'A Journey to the Next World: The Shroud of a Youth from Roman Egypt', in *Apollo* 148, no. 437 (July 1998), 18.

The Afterlife in Akhmim

Figure 5.4. The Court of Judgement, as shown on the upper register of the east A1 wall in tomb C3.

Figure 5.5. The whole scene of the lower register of the east A1 wall in tomb C3.

open. It is interesting to note that the flautist performs before Osiris, who is the Lord of Silence, and the god who prohibited music in his temples, especially during the Graeco-Roman period. This is attested in his *abatons* in Biggeh, Philae, Kom Ombo, Esna, and Abydos, as well as in the Tale of the Judgement[13]. This prohibition may come from liturgical taboos which were determined according to local theology and which were specific to each province. However, S. Emerit assumes that silence was only imposed at certain times in the Osirian rituals, and that music was not completely prohibited. It seems that, along with singing, playing music had a role in the rites of rebirth for the deceased and Osiris. Musical taboos are intrinsically linked to the lamentation rites of which

they punctuate certain stages, and their origin is clearly rooted in old Egyptian beliefs that the world is in a cycle which endlessly opposes nothingness, triumphing in creation. The cycle brings the triumph of life over death, and noise over silence. From this eternal struggle, Osiris emerges forever triumphant, incarnating all of the justified deceased of whom he is the model[14]. El-Salamuni tomb C3 records the first known musical ritual to happen before Osiris in ancient Egypt, confirming the transfiguration of the Osirian deceased through mourning rites.

The musical scene in tomb C3 is reminiscent of traditional New Kingdom banquet scenes with musicians and serving

---

[13] R. Parkinson, *Tale of the Eloquent Peasant* (Oxford 1991), 57–58.

[14] S. Emerit, 'À propos de l'origine des interdits musicaux dans l'Égypte ancienne', *BIFAO* 102 (2002), 189–210.

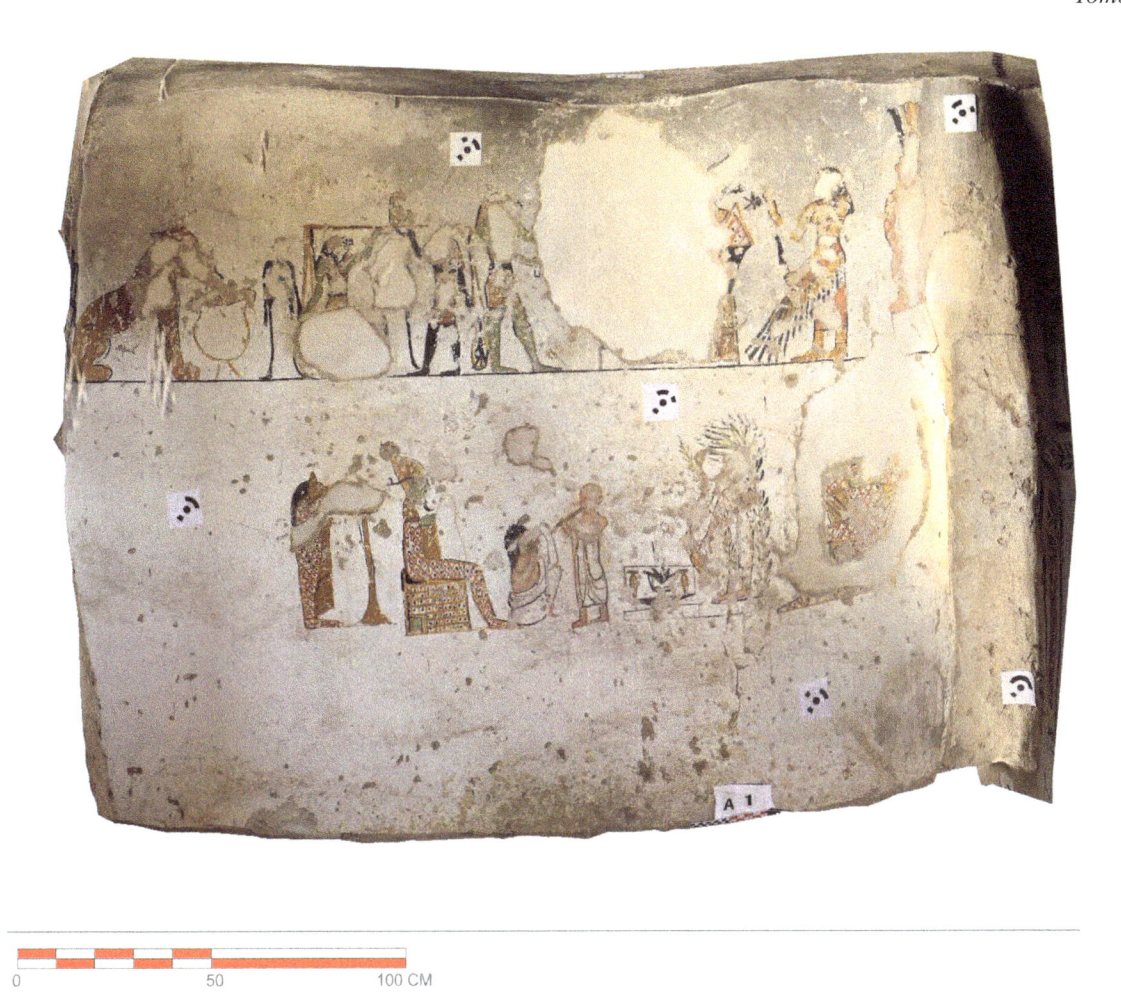

Figure 5.6a. Photogrammetry of the whole east A1 wall of tomb C3.

Figure 5.6b. A facsimile of the east A1 wall of tomb C3.

The Afterlife in Akhmim

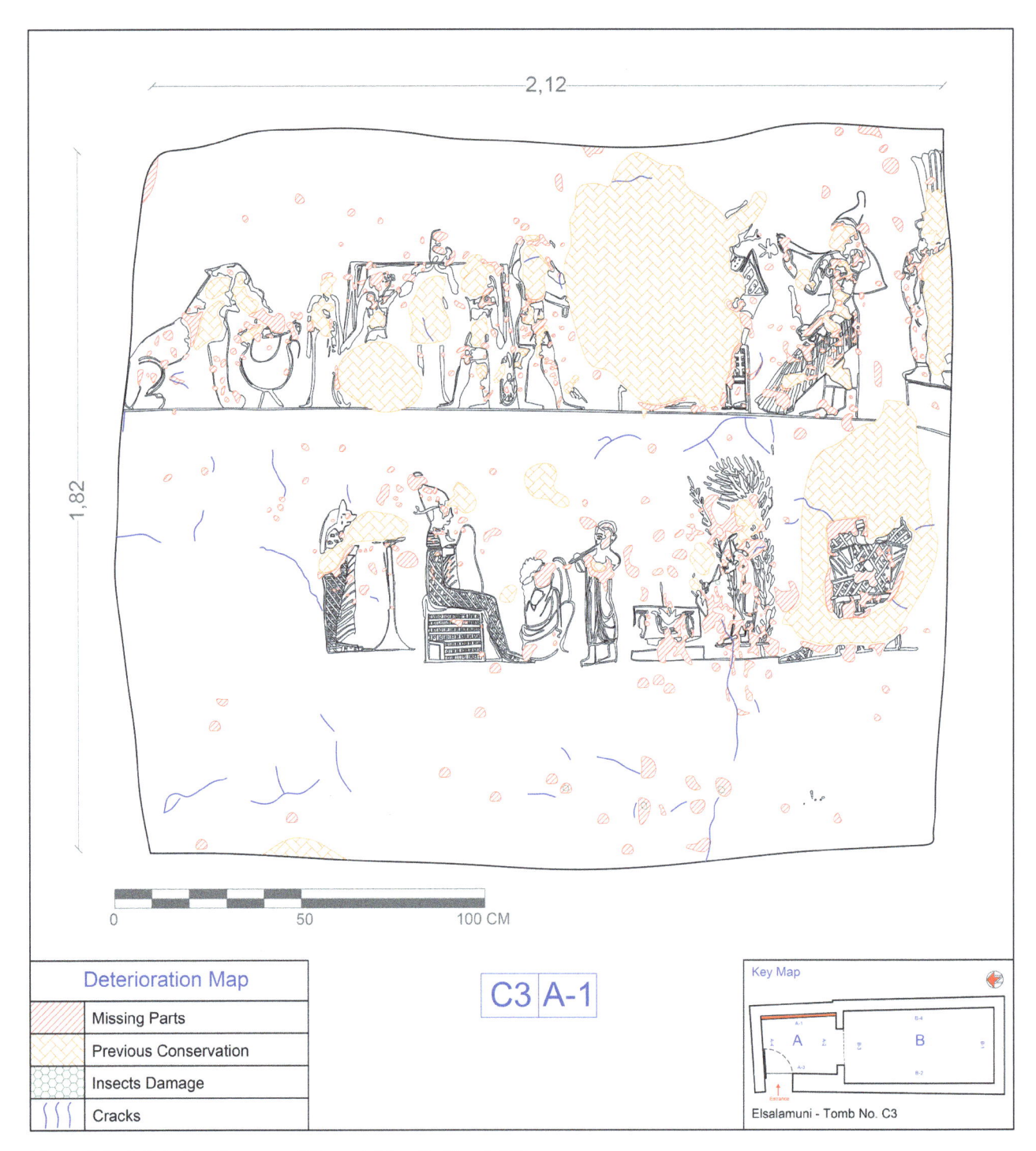

Figure 5.6c. A deterioration map of the east A1 wall of tomb C3.

girls[15]. The iconography of the funerary banquet scenes is mainly concerned with the rebirth of and the supply of provisions for the deceased. Here, the banquet can be understood as a divine meal. The music played during the banquet could be regarded as either an offering in itself or as a means of transmitting the offering[16]. The performance of musical instruments was a way to repel evil forces. Music was seen as apotropaic, being used to scare away birds and venomous animals and insects, and was also a tool for those facing the gods at funerals and at births[17]. In fact, musicians

---

[15] Musical instruments were depicted in New Kingdom tombs, and many were also found buried in the tombs of the Theban necropolis, S. Emerit, 'Trois Nouvelles harpes decouvertes a Thebes oust: Quel apport pour l'egyptologie?', in G. Rosati and M. Guidotti (eds.), *Proceedings of the XI International Congress of Egyptologists, Florence Egyptian Museum, Florence, 23–30 August 2015* (Oxford 2017), 192–98.

[16] C. Graves-Brown, 'Hathor, Nefer, and Daughterhood in the New Kingdom Private Tombs', in H. Navratilova and R. Landgráfová (eds.), *Sex and the Golden Goddess* II, 20.

[17] Music, perfume, alcohol, and sexual power were essential aspects of the Beautiful Festival of the Valley, E. Teeter, *Religion and Ritual in Ancient Egypt* (Cambridge 2011), 70–72.

often held multiple functions in ancient Egyptian society. It was usually a position in the priestly hierarchy[18], so that the male flautist could act as a priest while playing the flute. The lamentation rite enabled the mourners to sing a funeral dirge in honour of the dead and in order to appease the soul of the departed[19]. In this way, the flautist could rejoice the existence of the *ba* of the deceased and contribute to his or her rebirth while also animating religious festivities.

Furthermore, music was (and still is, in many cultures) associated with sex. Herodotus tells of how the erotic associations of music have been manifested on ritual occasions. The Hathor temple of Philae confirms this close association, as it contains a scene in which a woman plays the double oboe and lyre, accompanied by a monkey holding a lute and Bes, a sexual deity, playing the angular harp[20]. The funerary context of the music also highly suggests its sexually symbolic purpose, as music invokes the transformation and rebirth of the deceased. It is frequently represented in *mammisi*, such as images of naked women playing the tambourine before Bes[21]. In Greek prose and poetry, musicians, including harp players, were commonly viewed as dipsomaniacal, voracious, sexually perverse, and arrogant, and were often the objects of mockery and ridicule[22]. The flute and the oboe were often not the favourite choice of instrument for temple musicians. However, the oboe is frequently depicted in scenes of ritual ceremonies. Especially when a priest is shown presenting offerings to a deceased person, a musician of Hathor may follow him[23]. The musicians of the funerary estate were thus very likely to have assisted in the transmission of offerings to the deceased tomb owner and his family[24]. The ancient Egyptians believed that the music would drive away evil spirits and offer protection to the deceased in his tomb[25].

The god Min is often depicted with music being played during his feasts, as shown in the mortuary temple of Ramesses III at Thebes. Here, the scene shows a flautist playing military music alongside players of drums and trumpets[26]. In Panopolis, Min had a clergy with several priests at his service[27]. The clergy included musicians, singers, and dancers[28]. A priestly title that was often given to females in Akhmim is the term *iHy.t Mn*, which means 'Musician of Min'. Occasionally, it is specified that someone is *nfr.t* (a 'good' musician). However, this may be due to the date of the monument rather than the intrinsic qualities of the musician. A few other titles are also attested, such as *Sma*, meaning 'instrumentalist', *Hs.t*, meaning 'singer', and *iHb*, meaning 'dancer', all of whom were in the service of Min[29]. Singers and dancers held great importance in ancient Egypt, and performed at some of the cultic rituals and events of Min, although the exact nature of their singing and dancing remains unknown. The *jhb* or *xbj*, for example, was a special type of Akhmimic dancer in the service of Thoth[30]. In Roman Panopolis, music was a main feature in multiple events, such as the Panhellenic festival[31] and other athletic contests (including in festivals). The Panhellenic festivals included athletic contests and dramatic and musical performances provided by the Dionysiac artists[32]. The existence of the funerary musical scene thus confirms the presence of a ritual cult for the deceased in the El-Salamuni tombs.

5.1.6: The Southern A2 Wall

The southern A2 wall of tomb C3 contains the doorway of the burial chamber. The lower register of this wall is not painted. On both the right and left jambs of the doorway, there are two figures of the dwarf god Bes, depicted in his typical frontal pose and standing on a plinth. The Bes figures are painted red and wear a traditional high-plumed crown, which is painted yellow, red, green, and black. The deities themselves are painted red. Unfortunately, their faces are partially damaged, but they are supposed to have bulging eyes, a flat nose, protruding ears, and a visible tongue, which sticks out of a dishevelled beard to threaten or to tease evil spirits (Figure 5.7)[33]. The image of Bes

---

[18] S. Emerit, *Music and Musicians, UCLA Encyclopedia of Egyptology*, 2013, 9.

[19] In Greek burial customs, music played a key role; Music was present in several stages of the funeral, and especially during the exhibition of the body. During prothesis, mourning females would stand around the bier and sing a ritualised lament. The mourning singer would usually cradle the head of the deceased person between her two palms, S. Vermeule, 'Aspects of Death in Early Greek Art and Poetry', *Sather Classical Lectures* 46 (London 1979), 14–15. The *aulos* was clearly favored by the professional female mourners for accompanying a *threnody* (a song, hymn or poem of mourning that was composed and/or performed as a memorial to a dead person), R. Rehm, *Marriage to Death, the Conflation of Wedding and Funeral Rituals in Greek Tragedy* (Princeton 1994), 28.; M. Keller, 'Expressing, Communicating, Sharing and Representing Grief and Sorrow with Organised Sound (Musings in Eight Short Sentences)', *Humanities Research: One Common Thread the Musical World of Lament* 19 (2013), no. 3, 3–14.

[20] Hathor was regarded as the mistress of dancing and music, S. Schott, *Das schöne Fest vom Wüstentale, Festbräuche einer Totenstadt* (Wiesbaden 1952), 77–78.

[21] L. Manniche, *Music and Musicians in Ancient Egypt* (London 1991(, 116–19. Music is also associated with Hathor, C. Graves-Brown, 'A Gazelle, a Lute Player, and Bes, Three-Ring Bezels from Amarna', in A. Dodson et al., *A Good Scribe and an Exceeding Wise Man*, 113–26. Six terracotta figurines of Bes carrying a phallus, of priests, and of a figurine playing the tambourine, are preserved at the Petrie Museum as UC 33596–33601 from Memphis.

[22] Thissen, *Der Verkommene Harfenspieler*, 82.

[23] Manniche, *Music and Musicians*, 62.

[24] Manniche, *Music and Musicians*, 24.

[25] P. Spencer, 'Dance in Ancient Egypt', *NEA* 66, no. 3 (2003), 112.

[26] Manniche, *Music and Musicians*, 72.

[27] Gauthier, *Le personnel du dieu Min*.

[28] A special type of Akhmimic dancer in the service of Thoth was known within the Akhmimic context of Min-Re. These dancers may have performed at some of the cultic events taking place from the fourth century BC to at least the second century BC, Derchain-Urtel, 'Thot à Akhmim', 175–76. There are no further records of this priestly function from Roman Panopolis.

[29] Depauw, 'Late Funerary Material', in A. Egberts et al. (eds.), *Perspectives on Panopolis*, 74.

[30] There are numerous attestations of this priestly title, the owner of which was involved in funerary cultic acts. The title is attested from as early as the fourth century BC to at least the second century BC, Meulenaere, *BIFAO* 88, 47–49.

[31] J. Strasser, 'Les Olympia d'Alexandrie et le pancratiaste M. Aur. Asklèpiadès', *BCH* 128–29 (2004–05), 424, n. 20.

[32] *P.Oxy.* XXVII 2476, ll. 18, 25, 29, 31, 35, 44.; Frisch, *Pap.Agon.* (1986), 64.

[33] By the Graeco-Roman Period, Bes was associated with the headless Osiris (*Akephalos theos*). Bes-Akhephalos was associated with oracles, being called 'the Headless One', Smith, *Following Osiris*, 478. There is also a connection between Bes and the Greek satyrs, as Bes is sometimes

The Afterlife in Akhmim

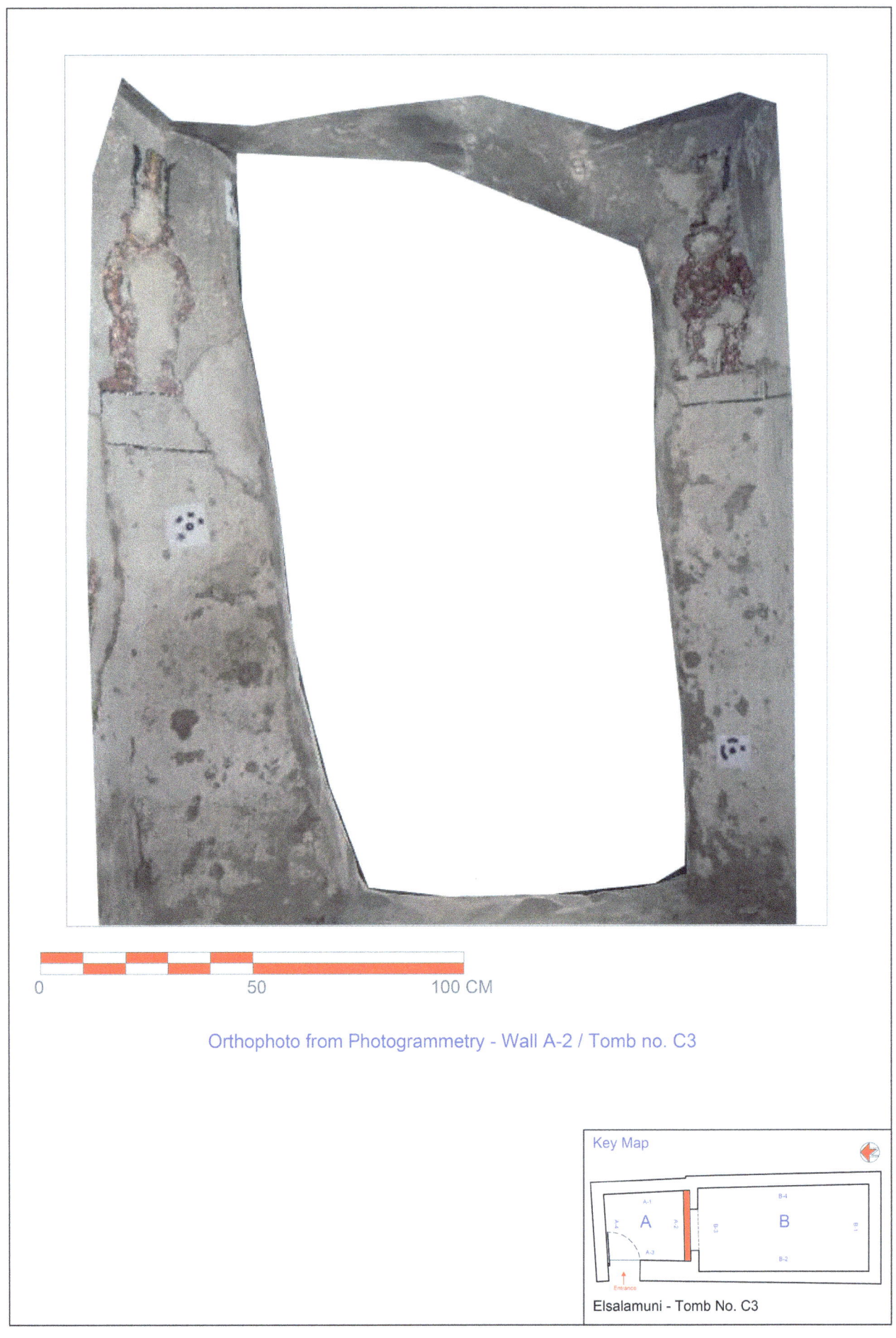

Figure 5.7. Photogrammetry of the south A2 wall of tomb C3.

does not reflect the ancient Egyptian ideal of beauty; he has short and thick arms and legs, a prominent stomach, fat buttocks, and a tufted tail[34].

Bes does not only repel wickedness, but also offers happiness and rejoicing. Bes' representation adjacent to the music scene on the west wall emphasises his musical attributes, which are widely depicted in temples, *mammisi*, and tombs. In these scenes, it is shown that Bes is a drummer, a flautist, a harpist, and even a bell-player[35]. The musical attributes of Bes are also attested on the wreaths of coffins and shrouds[36], reinforcing their festive character[37].

Both the ugliness and the grimacing face of Bes are meant to be scary. Bes was believed to have a wide field of protection that could defend against all the dangers of wicked powers. For this reason, he is often shown carrying knives and frightening spirits with his music[38]. Bes' depiction flanking the doorway of the C3 burial chamber ensures that his protective attributes are felt by the deceased. Bes is the most popular of the apotropaic[39], pantheistic gods[40]. He is the perfect example of a benevolent daemon, and has an important role in ancient Egyptian cults in regards to music, fertility, and protection against evil forces. Bes' representations in the Roman tombs of Egypt only depict him within this traditional role, as a protective daemon-god brandishing knives. In this way, Bes repels evil to protect newborns, killing the enemies of the sun. He is shown as ready to strike next to the entrance of the tomb of Petubastis [41]. Although Bes is not depicted with knives in tomb C3, his figure does flank the jambs of the doorway to the burial chamber, as opposed to just being depicted in the judgement scene. Thus, the doorjambs are surrounded and protected by two daemons; a partially damaged daemon is shown at the beginning of the scene on the eastern side, while Bes appears at the end of the whole scene on the western one. His representation next to the flautist suggests his musical attributes in the tomb.

One of the funerary characteristics of the El-Salamuni tombs is the participation of Bes in the court of the deceased. The depictions of Bes adjacent to the judgement court and in the musical scene are important, as they document a new, unique character of the god in El-Salamuni. In the Hall of Judgement, with reference to his fertility, magic, and protective powers, Bes protects the deceased and drives evil away. In the El-Salamuni tombs, Bes is regarded as more than just a protective god. He has a funerary, festal character. This is an important element for the deceased's reconfiguration, justification, and jubilance, as depicted in El-Salamuni tomb F2 (Figure 5.8), and in the tomb of von Bissing from 1913. Here, Bes is depicted at the entrance to the burial chamber, beside the upraised posthumous figure of the deceased[42].

By the Roman period, because of his oracular worship, Bes was the most important divinity in Abydos, his popularity being abundantly documented on later Greek graffiti from the temple of Seti I. His cult continued until the time of the emperor Constantinus II[43]. The belief was spread from Abydos to Panopolis, especially in the Roman period, and the cult of Bes was transported to Panopolis. Bes had a special cult centre in Panopolis, and evidence of his worship survives in Greek and Coptic magical texts[44]. Moreover, many theophoric names deriving from the apotropaic deity Bes, such as βηοις, Τβη(οι)ς, and Σεν (βηοις), are attested[45]. Bes is one of the divinities that is mentioned even in the Greek and Coptic Christian magical texts[46]. Therefore, Bes is widely depicted in the El-Salamuni tombs.

5.1.7: The Western A3 Wall

The lower register of the western A3 wall of tomb C3 is separated from the upper ones by only a black line; it is not painted. A female figure of the deceased, clad in a classical

---

shown holding wine cups and dancing with grapes. Bes is linked to water, wine, kohl, and perfumes as well, Graves, *Daemons & Spirits*, 50.; A. Nifosi, *Becoming a Woman and Mother in Graeco-Roman Egypt, Women's Bodies, Society and Demostic Space* (Routledge 2019), 111.

[34] J. Romano, *The Bes Image in Pharaonic Egypt*, Ph. D. Thesis (New York 1989), 89.

[35] For more about the flute, see Leiden F 1964/1.4.; P. Giovetti and D. Picchi, *Egypt, Millenary Splendour, The Leiden Collection in Bologna* (Milan 2016), pl. 347. For the harp, see Louvre accession number AF 12864, Graves, *Daemons & Spirits*, 40, no. 35.

[36] This was depicted on the coffin of a deceased female from Akhmim, which is now in Amesterdam. The coffin is adorned with the lion-faced dwarf Bes beside several *wedjat* eyes, H. Willems and W. Clarysse, *Keizers aan de Nijl* (Leuven 1999), 230–31, no. 141.; id., *Les Empereurs du Nil*, 230–31, no. 141.; Parlasca and Seemann, *Augenblicke: Mumienporträts*, 335, no. 229.; W. Van Haarlem, *Corpus Antiquitatum Aegyptiacarum, Allard Pierson Museum, Amesterdam, IV, Sarcophagi and Related Objects* (Hildesheim 1998), 78–80.; Grimm, *Römischen Mumienmasken*, 99, pl. 118, 3.

[37] The musical role of Beset is also symbolised by a double-sided disc of uncertain use, complete with a *wedjat* eye on one side and a Bes head on the other, E. Bresciani, *Kom Madi 1977 e 1978, Le pitture murali del centafo di Alessandro Magno* (Pisa 1980), 23, pl. 9c–d. For the musical role of Bes, see S. Khaksar, 'Bès et les musiciens aux jambes arquées du médio-élamite', *Bès, une puissante figure divine (seconde partie)*, Égypte, Afrique & Orient 100 (2020), 35–46.

[38] G. Pinch, *Magic in Ancient Egypt (*London 1994), 44.

[39] H. Altenmüller describes these apotropaic gods, stating '*in ihrem Wesen stehen sie den Dämonen nahe, sind jedoch von diesen zumeist durch ihre schärfer konturierte XXX* [? Something must be missing here, as the German sentence is incomplete) *unterschieden*'.; H. Altenmüller, 'Götter, apotropäische', *LÄ* II, 635.

[40] On the pantheistic gods, see J. Quack, 'The So–Called Pantheos on Polimorphic Deities in Late Egyptian Religion', *Egyptus et Pannonia* 3 (2006), 175–86.

[41] Osing, *AV* 28, 73, figs. 20b, c.; Venit, *Visualizing the Afterlife*, 158–59, fig. 5.1.

[42] Von Bissing, *ASAE* 50, 562.

[43] A. Piankoff, 'The Osireion of Set I at Abydos During the Graeco-Roman Period and the Christian Occupation', *BSAC* 15 (1958–60), 127–28.

[44] S. Pernigotti, 'La Magia copta: I testi', *ANRW* II.18.5 (1995), 3685–730.

[45] *SB* XVI 12438–439, XX 14413, XXIV 16086.; *CEML* 109, 115.; *CEMG* 163, 1133, 1610, 1675, 1702, 1704, 1763, 1780, 1800, 1806, 1902, 1923, 1924, 1927, 1979, 1991, 1992, 1998, 2044, 2059, 2072, 2134, 2163, 2171, 2176, 2177.; *P. Coll.Youtie* II, 144.; Chauveau, *BIFAO* 91, 136, no. 2, p. 145, no. 15.; *P. Achm.* 7, ll. 23, 26, 51, 103, 105, 116; 9, ll. 49, 57, 72, 88, 130, 178, 192.; *CPR* XVIIB 1, l. 69; 11, l. 10;12, l. 9; 19, l. 10; 15, l. 11; 37, l. 5.; *P. Bodm.* I 1 recto ng, l. 9, nd, l. 8, xa, ll. 7, 8, xe, l. 4, xz, l. 2, xq, l. 17, o, ll. 4, 10, oa, l. 11, oq, ll. 2, 17, 21, 22.; *P. Oxy.* LXIII, 4360; *P. Lond.* III, 1261b.

[46] Pernigotti, *ANRW* II.18.5 (1995).

The Afterlife in Akhmim

Figure 5.8. Bes in the Court of Judgement scene, as depicted in the burial chamber of tomb F2.

traditional white garment, is depicted on the upper register. Unfortunately, her head is damaged, but she raises her arms in an attitude of adoration, and is probably intended to be shown venerating the damaged figure of a deity. The rest of the wall is destroyed. With its back to the deceased female, a rearing, anthropomorphised Nehebkau snake is shown, facing the main entrance of the tomb for protection (Figures 5.9a-b). The Nehebkau snake is widely depicted in the El-Salamuni tombs and represents a direct model for the eternity of the deceased; just like the snake repeatedly sheds its skin, the deceased achieves daily renewal[47].

5.1.8: The Ceiling

The ceiling of tomb C3 is undecorated, and has layers of demolished material (Figure 5.10). The undecorated ceiling and the unpainted lower friezes of the antechamber walls attest to the unfinished state of tomb C3. Even though its surfaces were smoothed and plastered in preparation for the paintings, it can be assumed that the deceased died suddenly and was buried quickly, so that the tomb was not ready, and the artist had to draw the funerary scenes in a hurry.

5.1.9: The Burial Chamber

The burial chamber of tomb C3 is larger than the antechamber. Two niches are cut into its south and west walls. The scenes have classical motifs such as green garlands, which are pinned to the wall, hanging with red tassels. The scenes are on two registers. A black line tops the upper part of the upper register as a border. A green festoon made of twisted petals and a black bold line separate the two registers. Funerary afterlife scenes decorate the upper register, while traditional, geometrical, multi-coloured *orthostats* decorate on the lower one.

This style of the classical ornamentation, which includes garlandes and festoons, resembles the artisitc style of the so-called 'tomb of von Bissing' from 1913[48].

5.1.10: The Inner Part of the Wall B3 Doorjamb

The B3 wall contains a doorway into the burial chamber. Slightly above and on both sides of the interior of the entrance doorjambs, two mirror images of a deceased female are depicted, using a three-quarter view. The depiction on the interior of the left jamb is better preserved. Here, the woman raises her arms in a welcoming gesture to the visitors of the burial chamber. She is dressed in a classical garment that is bound around the waist by use of a knot. It drapes over her abdomen, hips, and legs. The upper part of her body is naked, showing bare breasts. She has tightly curled black hair that falls loosely over her shoulders (Figures 5.11a-b). On the interior of the right doorjamb, the other female figure is partially damaged. However, it is clear that she is costumed in the same way. Unfortunately, only her upraised right hand and parts of her curly hair are still visible.

The two women depicted on the north B3 wall are quite similar to those who are depicted in house-tomb 21 at Tuna El-Gebel. They are located above the entrance of the anteroom, and are shown with raised arms. Grimm and Kaplan identify the women in house-tomb 21 as additional representations of the deceased, who is the patron of the tomb[49]. This is especially based on the fact that their facial features resemble those of other depictions of the deceased female. Riggs argues that they might be mourners because of their bare-breasted attire, dishevelled hair, and arm gestures. In this case, which would be quite unusual, the deceased woman would act as a mourner for the dead girl[50]. Because of the damage done to the wall in between the two women and directly above the door, Venit finds it difficult to propose an identity for the figure they venerate[51]. However, the mirror images of the female help to resolve this debate, as they match other representations of the deceased woman (for whom the tomb is dedicated) in the tomb. In tomb C3, the deceased is depicted paying homage to various deities in the burial chamber. Since there is only one burial chamber cut in the room, it is highly likely that this is the patron of the tomb. The images of women are therefore those of mourners. These images would have welcomed the visitors to the burial chamber, employing traditional ancient Egyptian etiquette.

The knotted garment worn by the two female figures is commonly found on female coffins from Akhmim, and is a familiar feature of the everyday dress of the Panopolite community. The garment carries a divine association,

---

[47] Quirke, *Going Out in Daylight*, 203.
[48] Von Bissing, *ASAE* 50, pl. 2.
[49] G. Grimm, 'Tuna El-Gebel 1913–1973, eine Grabung des deutschen Architekten W. Honroth und neuere Untersuchungen in Hermopolis-West (Tanis Superior) ', *MDAIK* 31 (1975), 231.; Kaplan, *BzÄ* 16, 163, pl. 80b.
[50] Riggs, *The Beautiful Burial*, 138–39.
[51] Venit, *Visualizing the Afterlife*, 121.

Figure 5.9a. Photogrammetry of the west A3 wall of tomb C3.

being linked to the iconography of Isis and her devotees in the Hellenistic world[52]. Riggs proposes that this style was widely worn by women in Panopolis, but the use of this sort of clothing cannot be firmly dated as appearing prior to the Roman period[53]. Moreover, the function of the knotted garment associates the deceased female with Hathor[54]. During the Graeco-Roman Period, Hathor was perhaps mostly recognised as Osiris' female counterpart[55].

The hairstyle of the female figures constitutes an element of power and vigour[56]. The corkscrew curls of the deceased female have a religious function as a symbol of divinity and the blessed abode. The curls resemble the distinctive hairstyle used in representations of Isis in the Roman period, known as 'Isis-locks'. This hairstyle is especially common in Greek art. Since the Ptolemaic Period, these hair curls have been a fashion choice of queens, elite women, and goddesses, and they became a custom for the dead in Roman Egypt, especially in Panopolis[57]. Here, female hair was worn long and loose, in a dark and curly style that represents fecundity and sensuality, and thus

---

[52] This was especially true for Roman cultic statues, J. Eingartner, *Isis und ihre Dienerinnen in der Kunst der römischen Kaiserzeit* (Leiden 1991).; E. Walters, *Attic Grave Reliefs That represent Women in the Dress of Isis* (Princeton 1988).
[53] Riggs, *The Beautiful Burial*, 75. Bianchi thinks that the knotted costume has no relation to ancient Egyptian beliefs and Isis, R. Bianchi, 'Not the Isis Knot', *BES* 2 (1980), 19.
[54] On the appearance of the knotted garment on coffins of females from Akhmim, see Riggs, *The Beautiful Burial*, 71–78.
[55] Smith, *Traversing Eternity,* 7. The titles of Ḥ.t-Ḥr n NN and Ḥ.t Ḥr NN, which date to as early as the 23rd dynasty, were applied to the sarcophagi and statues of elite women, M. Smith, 'New References to the Deceased as Wsir n NN from the Third Intermediate Period and the Earliest Reference to a Deceased Woman as Ḥ.t- Ḥr NN', *RdÉ* 63 (2012), 193–96.

[56] S. Mayassis, *Le Livre des Morts de L'Egypte Ancienne est un Livre d'initiation* (Athens 1955), 354. In ancient Egypt, '*women's hair had [an] erotic significance, helping to mark women as icons of sexuality and fertility*', G. Robins, 'Hair and the Construction of Identity in Ancient Egypt, c. 1480–1350 BC', *JARCE* 36 (1999), 63.
[57] Riggs, *The Beautiful Burial*, 193. Corkscrew curls is a hairstyle that was made popular by the Flavian dynasty (69–96 AD). It continued to be used as a fashionable imperial Roman hairstyle, Riggs, *The Beautiful Burial*, 123.

The Afterlife in Akhmim

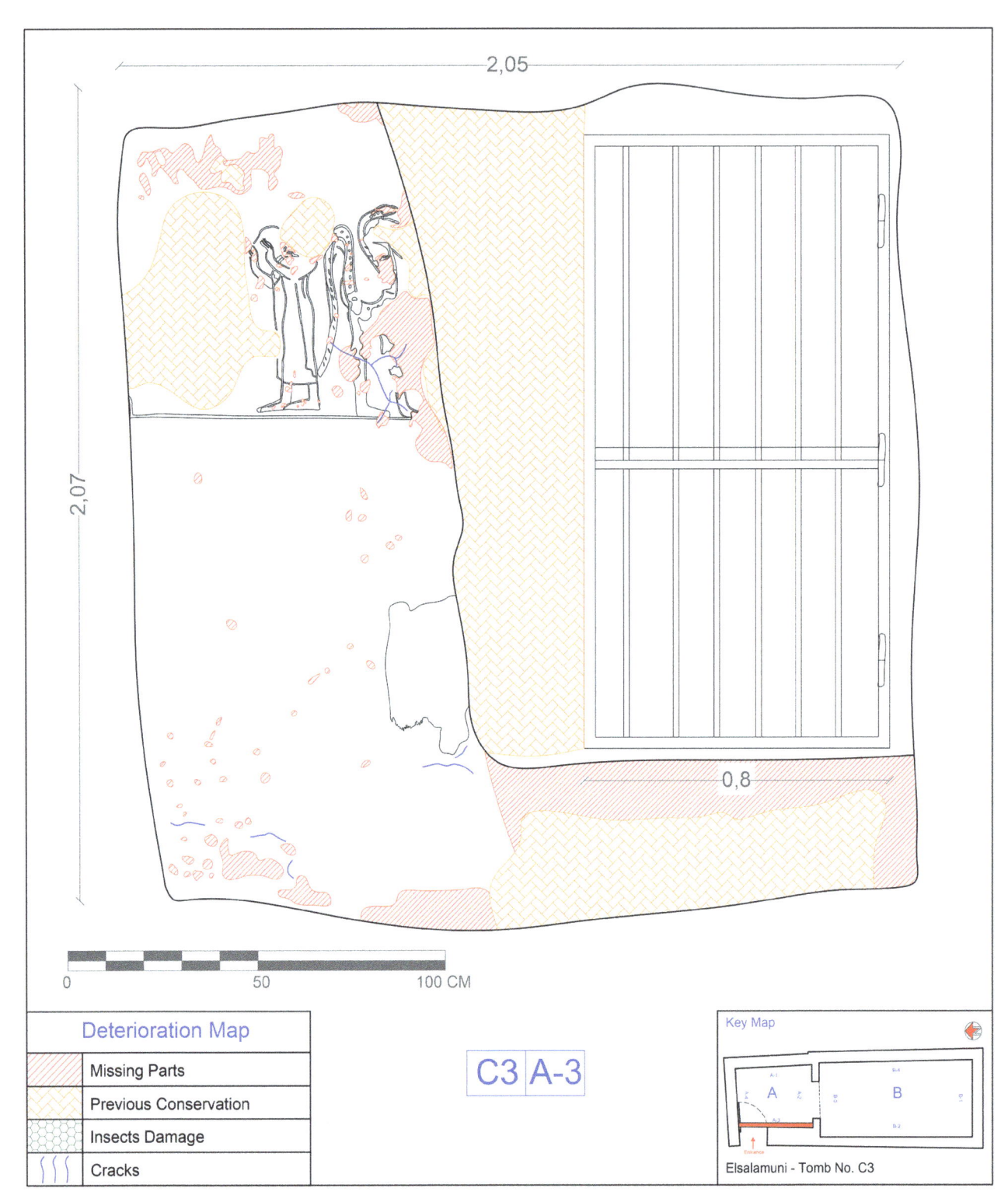

Figure 5.9b. A deterioration map of the west A3 wall of tomb C3.

the goddess Hathor[58]. Overall, the representation of a deceased female with an abundance of unrestrained hair can help determine the gender of the tomb owner, and directly links the tomb owner's image to the eroticism and fertility associated with the goddess Hathor.

5.1.11: The Lower Frieze on the Northern Part of Wall B3

The lower frieze on the northern B3 wall has a traditional rectangular *orthostat* decoration, with three twisted parts in varying sizes and an outer black border line. The outer twisted part is painted black, the inner one is red, and the middle one is yellow (Figure 5.12).

---

[58] Riggs, *The Beautiful Burial*, 125.

Tomb C3

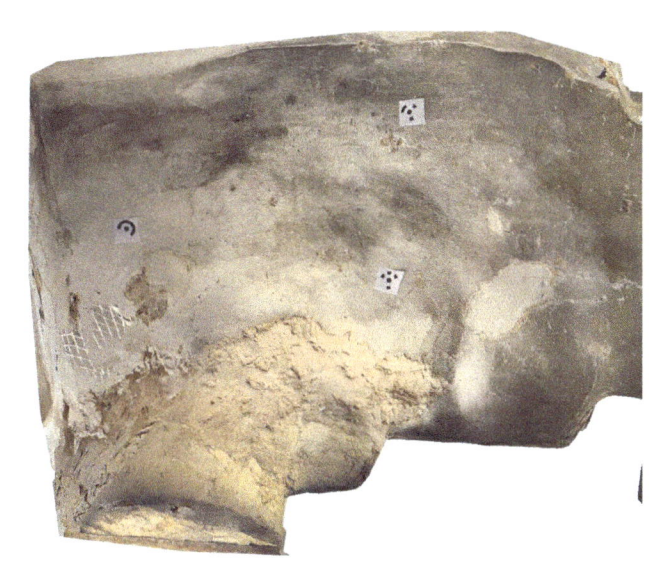

Figure 5.10. The ceiling of the antechamber of tomb C3.

Figure 5.11a. A female (a mourner) shown welcoming a visitor on the interior right side of the doorway into the burial chamber of tomb C3.

Figure 5.11b. Another figure of a damaged female (a mourner). The scene comes from the interior left side of the doorway into the tomb C3 burial chamber.

5.1.12: The Eastern Side of Wall B3: The Upper Frieze

On the left side of the doorway, there is a scene of a personified goddess in a tree. She is painted green, and extends her yellow human hands[59]. She holds a yellow the tree. She was said to receive the deceased in the sky in preparation for his rebirth. She also gives him water in his afterlife. The earliest representation of the tree goddess is from the fifth dynasty, namely the tombs of Ptahhotep and Akhethotep, N. Billing, *Nut, The Goddess of Life in Text and Iconography*, *Uppsala Studies in Egyptology* 5 (Uppsala 2003), 224. As the goddess of the tree, Nut is also widely shown on stelae, coffins, sarcophagi, ushabti boxes, and mythological papyri, Buhl, *JNES* 6, 93–95. As a tree goddess, Nut is also depicted in the famous Roman tomb of Si-Amon in Siwa, where the deceased is shown pouring water onto a sycomore fig tree. However, the Siwans refer to this tree as an olive tree rather than a sycomore fig, as it is abundant in Siwa, A. Fakhry, *The Oasis of Egypt, Siwa Oasis*, I (Cairo 1973), 194, fig.71.; F. Dunand and R. Lichtenberg, *Oasis Egyptiennes, Les Iles de Bienheureux* (Arles 2008), 110. Hathor also serves as a goddess of the tree, being *nb.t nh.t*, or 'the Lady of the Sycomore Fig Tree, Refai, 'Hathor als Gleichzeitig West,' in E. Czernyet al. (eds.), *Timelines Studies*, 287–90.

---

[59] The goddess of the tree can be identified as Hathor. The sycamore fig tree was one of the famous attributes of Hathor; the deceased would hope to be placed under the tree, A. Zingarelli, 'Some Considerations About the Water Offered (Poured) by the Tree-Goddess at TT49,' in *L'Acqua Nell'Antico Egitto, Vita, Rigenerazione, Incantesimo, Medicamento, Proceedings of the First International Conference for Young Egyptologists, Italy, October 15–18, 2003* (Rome 2005). Nut is the mostly frequently depicted goddess of

173

The Afterlife in Akhmim

providing water for the deceased is an important scene in El-Salamuni, promising a blessed celestial afterlife through Nut[61]. This scene further suggests the appropriation of once-royal imagery into a private context.

5.1.13: The Western Side of Wall B3: The Upper Frieze

The right side of the doorway into tomb C3 shows a damaged figure of the deceased in a traditional fringed garment. He is depicted paying homage to a damaged recumbent figure of an Apis bull, who is the incarnation of the living Osiris. Unfortunately, the head of the Apis bull is now destroyed, but it is clear that it was mounted on a *naos*-like pedestal adorned with vertical red stripes. The remains of a black *djed* pillar hang from Apis' neck[62]. The bull was also a fecundity symbol, and might have been the sacred animal of the ithyphallic Min, being celebrated in honour of him. The B3 wall is fully documented (Figures 5.13a-b).

Apis had a special cult in Akhmim. An inscription in the Opet temple of Karnak mentions that Akhmim was named *niw.t n(.t) kA psj*, or the 'City of the Raging Bulls'[63]. The ithyphallic Min, who is a fertility god, was frequently called a bull himself[64]. The sacred area of Akhmim was called the 'Garden of the Bull' ('Karm Al-Tawr' in Arabic). This may refer to the white bull, which was the sacred animal of the sky god Min[65]. The transportation of the deceased by Apis is widely represented in the Book of the Dead papyri from Akhmim, where the dead are placed either on the back or between the horns of the bull.

Figure 5.12. The lower *orthostates* on the north B3 wall of tomb C3.

qebeh vase in her upraised right hand, pouring libations upon a damaged offering table. On the table, a damaged *hes* vessel and a plant (probably lettuce, the main food of Min) are still visible[60]. The image of a goddess of a tree

---

[60] The lettuce plant was considered an aphrodisiac, as its milky sap was associated with the sperm of Min. Min's procreative power is further emphasised by the fact that his erect phallus was given the name 'His Beauty' and 'His Power', L. Keimer, 'Die Pflanze des Gottes Min', *ZÄS* 59 (1924), 140–43.; Gauthier, *Les fêtes du dieu Min*, 138–41. On Min and his link to aphrodisiac plants such as lettuce, see R. Germer, 'Die Bedeutung des Lattichs als Pflanze des Min', *SAK* 8 (1980), 85–87.; M. Defossez, 'Les laitues de Min', *SAK* 12 (1985), 1–4.; A. Bellucio, 'Le pianta del dio Min e la suo funzione sulitualmitico-rituale', *DE* 31 (1995), 15–34.; P. Norris, 'Lettuce as an Offering to Mnw (MIN)', in A. Maravelia and N. Guilhou (eds.), *Environment and Religion*, 317–29.

[61] Wilkinson, *The Complete Gods and Goddesses*, 161.
[62] Apis, the chief deity of Saqqara, was the incarnation of Ptah and Osir-Hapi, G. Kater-Sibbes and M. Vermasseren, *Apis, I, The Monuments of the Hellenistic-Roman Period from Egypt* (Leiden 1975). Since the beginning of the 18th dynasty, the Apis bull was a common deity in Alexandria, and was a familiar figure in the the tombs there. It is depicted on the walls of the tombs of Gabbari, Kom El-Shukafa, and Tigrain, D. Kessler, *Die Heiligen Tiere und der König, Teil 1, Beiträge zu Organisation, Kult und Theolgie der Spätzeitlichen Tierfriedhöfe*, ÄAT 16 (Wiesbaden 1989), 82–85.; Kaplan, *BzÄ* 16, 51a, b,110a.
[63] *Opet* I, 286, 19, the left scene, col. B. III.5.; V. Altmann-Wendling, *Mond Symbolik, Mond Wissen*, 847.
[64] *LGGG*, VII, 246. The syncretisim of Osiris-Apis and Serapis is widely attested in the textual evidence of the Panopolite nome from the Roman period. Most of the bilingual Demotic and Greek mummy labels found in Athribis, which date back to the second and third centuries AD, include a Greek formula referring to 'the Lord Sarapis' (variant: 'the Great Lord Sarapis'). The *ba* of the deceased was thought to serve Osiris-Sokar, the Great God and Lord of Abydos, M. Chauveau, *Les Etiquettes de momies démotiques et bilingues du Musée du Louvre provenant de la nécropole de Triphion*, unpublished PhD thesis, University of Paris III (Paris 1987), 188, 197. At Abydos, on certain stelae which feature a depiction of Osiris, the Greek texts may refer to the god as Serapis, J. Stambaugh *Sarapis Under the Early Ptolemies*, EPRO 25 (Leiden 1972), 37–38. A limestone offering table from Kom Abu Billu, which is now in Cairo (CG 23182), contains both hieroglyphic and Greek texts. While the hieroglyphic text is addressed to Osiris, the Greek one is addressed to Serapis, A. Kamal, *CGC: Tables d'orandes* (Cairo 1909), 133, pl. 46.; W. Spiegelberg, *CGC: Die demotischen Inschriften* (Leipzig 1904), 71, pl. 24.
[65] For the bull of Min, see Wainwright, *JEA* 21, 158–70. For the ibexes depicted on the rock and mentioned in the inscriptions of hunters at Wadi Bir El-Aïn, see Bernand, *Pan du désert*, 28–30. The sacred area dedicated to Min is discussed in Bernand, *Pan du désert*, 15. Hunting apparently took place here at the beginning of the new moon, *I. Pan* 11, ll. 2–3. This suggests that the ibex was a sacred animal exclusive to Pan/Min in Panopolis. Interestingly, the ibex is not depicted at all in the necropoleis of Akhmim, Kuhlmann, *SDAIK* 11, 7.

Tomb C3

Figure 5.13b. A facsimile of the north B3 wall of the tomb C3 burial chamber.

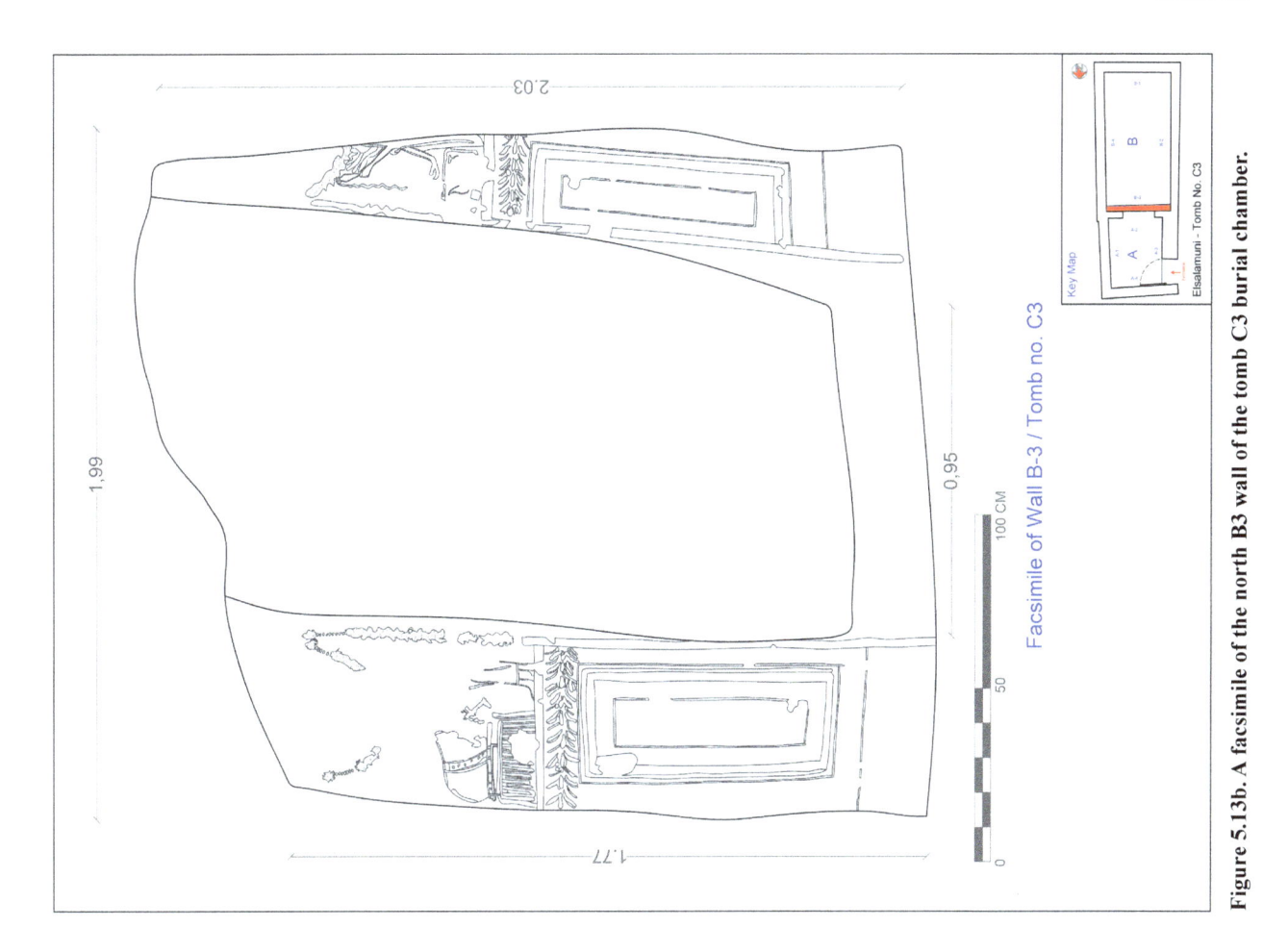

Figure 5.13a. Photogrammetry of the north B3 wall of the tomb C3 burial chamber.

The Afterlife in Akhmim

In later periods, Apis is related to Osiris, and he is said to accompany Horus in his search for the scattered body parts of Osiris. Apis carries these parts on his back, earning him the titles 'Companion of the Kings' and 'the Helper God'. Ancient Egyptians sometimes hoped to be embalmed in Memphis, as this is where Apis had delivered the mummy of Osiris[66]. Some hoped to have the sacred bull carry their mummy in a 'hurried run' in hopes of guaranteeing themselves a secure journey to their tomb[67].

5.1.14: The Eastern B4 Wall

The eastern B4 wall of tomb C3 is divided into two registers. The lower one has traditional *orthostats,* while funerary afterlife scenes cover the upper register. The scenes on the upper register are arranged as eight separate vignettes, each of which is bordered by two festoons. An additional festoon is placed above the uppermost of these friezes (Figures 5.14a-e).

The first vignette on the upper register shows a deceased male who is clad in a classical white fringed garment and a black curly wig. His face is partially damaged. He raises his hands in a venerating gesture before eight deities, who are depicted in two groups. A festoon tops the figure of the deceased, while another one separates him from the eight deities. The first group of deities is comprised of three figures with human bodies and falcon heads. Their bodies are of chequered yellow with black borders. They all wear black wigs, and have a high altar containing loaves of bread in front of them. This three-deity frieze is bordered by two festoons, but there is no festoon above them. The first deity is painted yellow, with a red frayed outfit and a black wig, while the second and the third deities are painted red with black dots inside. They hold linen (depicted here as a small strip of frayed fabric) painted yellow.

The second group includes five shrouded deities with human bodies. The first deity is shown with a falcon head, while the others have serpent heads. A festoon hovers above the figures, and two festoons border the group. The falcon-headed deity is painted yellow, and the first two serpent gods have red bodies. The other two serpent gods are painted yellow. The first three deities hold a frayed yellow strip of linen, while the other two have a red one. The artist did not divide the two groups of deities into equally numbered sections. It could have been an artistic mistake to include a fourth (falcon-headed) deity in the first group. The eight deities can be regarded as protective mummiform genii with falcons and serpent heads. They are the *akhou* spirits, the invisible powers and followers of Osiris who are responsible for protecting the bodily integrity of the deceased and for taking part in the *Stundenwache*[68]. The fact that they are depicted in the burial chamber possibly connects them to the hours of the nightly vigil, during which the Osirian deceased is mourned, protected, revived, and justified.

The second vignette of the upper register shows the deceased male in the same costume as in the first vignette. His arms are raised in a sign of exultation and reverence towards the ibis-headed Thoth, who sits on a cushion without a back. He wears an *atef* crown and his body is shrouded in a cloth that is chequered with red panels and black spots (inside the panels). Due to the poor condition of the wall, Thoth's seat is partially damaged, but a falcon head still adorns its front.

The third vignette shows two jackal-headed figures of Anubis facing each other. They venerate a partially damaged fetish which standing between them. The jackal figure to the right of the fetish has a black face, black arms, black legs, a red chest, and wears a yellow wig and kilt. The other figure has a yellow face, yellow arms, yellow legs, a black wig, a red chest, and a green kilt. Two festoons surround the vignette, while other hangs above the scene.

The fourth vignette shows two females erecting a black *djed* pillar. Both females are dressed in red and have curly hair, resembling Isis and Nephthys. The erection of the *djed* pillar is associated with Osiris, as the pillar is his spine. It is sometimes used to represent the deceased man or woman as Osiris, or in an Osirian form.

The fifth vignette depicts the ibis-headed Thoth and the falcon-headed Horus facing each other. They erect an Abydos fetish that terminates in the two feathers of Amun, with a yellow sun disc in between. A ram flanks the crown of Amun, along with a figure with a damaged head, which is probably a bull or a lion. Only its upwards-coiled tail is still visible. The scene is bordered by two festoons, while another one hovers above. Horus has a white face with a black wig, black arms, black legs, a red chest, and a yellow kilt. Meanwhile, Thoth has green arms, a green chest, and green legs. His wig and belly are yellow.

Horus was widely worshipped in the Panopolite nome, and as a result, several forms of Horus are attested here, including 'Horus who Rejoices the Heart' (Horus *senedjemib*)[69]. This form of Horus was known as the son of Osiris and Isis, and was also called 'Horus the Great', or

---

[66] A. Kucharek, *Altägyptische Totenliturgien, Die Klagelieder von Isis und Nephtys in Texten der Griechisch- Römischen Zeit* IV (Heidelberg 2010), 655.
[67] E. Otto, *Beiträge zur Geschichte in Ägypten*, UGÄA 13 (Leipzig 1938), 13–14.; H. Bonnet, 'Apis', in *LdÄR/RÄRG* (Hamburg 2000), 49.; A. Wiedemann, 'Der Apis als Totenträger', *OLZ* 20 (Leipzig 1917), 298–303.

[68] They are the lords of truth, and they punish sinners, evil–doers, and bad people by bringing terror to them. Normally, they are seven in number and receive several names. While they later become more numerous, here, they are eight in number. According to P. Jumilhac, they act under the control of Anubis, J. Vandier, *Le Papyrus Jumilhac* (Paris 1961), 203 no. 629. For more on the number and representation of the mummiform genii on Akhmimic chests, see M. Bruwier and T. Mekis, 'Diversity at Akhmim', in M. Mosher (ed.), *The Book of the Dead*, 56–60.
[69] For Ptolemaic stelae bearing this name, see Kamal, *Stèles ptolémaïques et romaines (CGC 27–28)*, no. 22017, 18, 22141, 123. For Hadrian's stela that was probably erected in the temple of Min, see Scharff, *ZÄS* 62, 89.; Petrie, *Athribis*, pl. 28.

Figure 5.14a. Photogrammetry of the east B4 wall in the tomb C3 burial chamber.

Figure 5.14b. A facsimile of the east B4 wall in the tomb C3 burial chamber.

'Haroeris, Lord of Letopolis'[70]. He was venerated in this form at Edfa. He was associated with the cult of Horus Iounmoutef (Harmouthes) in the Roman period, being called *Hr-iwn-mw.t.f*, or 'Horus, the Pillar of His Mother'[71].

---

[70] Haroeris, the '*Lord of Letopolis, [the] Great God, [being a] guest in Ipu, [who is] great in power, [and is] the strong one*', is mentioned in Scharff, *ZÄS* 62, 90. A Demotic inscription from the quarries at Gabal Tukh addresses Triphis, Kolanthes, and Haroeris, the Lord of Letopolis, El-Sayed and El-Masry, *Athribis I.*, 12.

[71] Sauneron, *Villes e légendes*, 71–77.; Chauveau, *RdÉ* 37, 36–37. Tell Edfa is situated 3km. south of the Red Monastery. Excavations were led by the Sohag Inspectorate in 1992. They uncovered three layers of the tell, the upper one consisting of a group of Coptic mudbrick tombs. The middle layer contained some Graeco-Roman granaries of mudbrick, in which various objects were found, such as big red jars, a group of lamps, Demotic and Coptic ostraca, and fragments from statues and terracotta figurines. A gate was also uncovered. For the publication of these finds, see E. Fathi, *Tell Edfa,* Unpublished MA thesis, Higher Institute of Civilizations of the Ancient Near East, Zagazig University (Zagazig 2000). The cult of Haroeris and Harmuthes is noted to have existed at Edfa, and Chauveau identifies a group of mummy labels from Edfa/Itb based on the presence of these gods, Chauveau, *RdÉ* 37, 31–43. There was once a Roman temple for Horus in *T3-ḥw.t-Ty* (Toeto, modern Tahta), near the northwest border of the ninth nome. This area gave its name to the toparchies of Toeto and Synoriaits. Blocks from here have been found to carry the name of Maximinus Daia (305–313 AD), as well as the last known cartouche of a Roman emperor, M. Minas-Nerpel, 'Egyptian Temples', in C. Riggs (ed.), *The Oxford Handbook of Roman Egypt* (Oxford 2012), 362. The name of a Roman called 'Commodus' is also recorded in this temple, *PM* V, 5.

The Afterlife in Akhmim

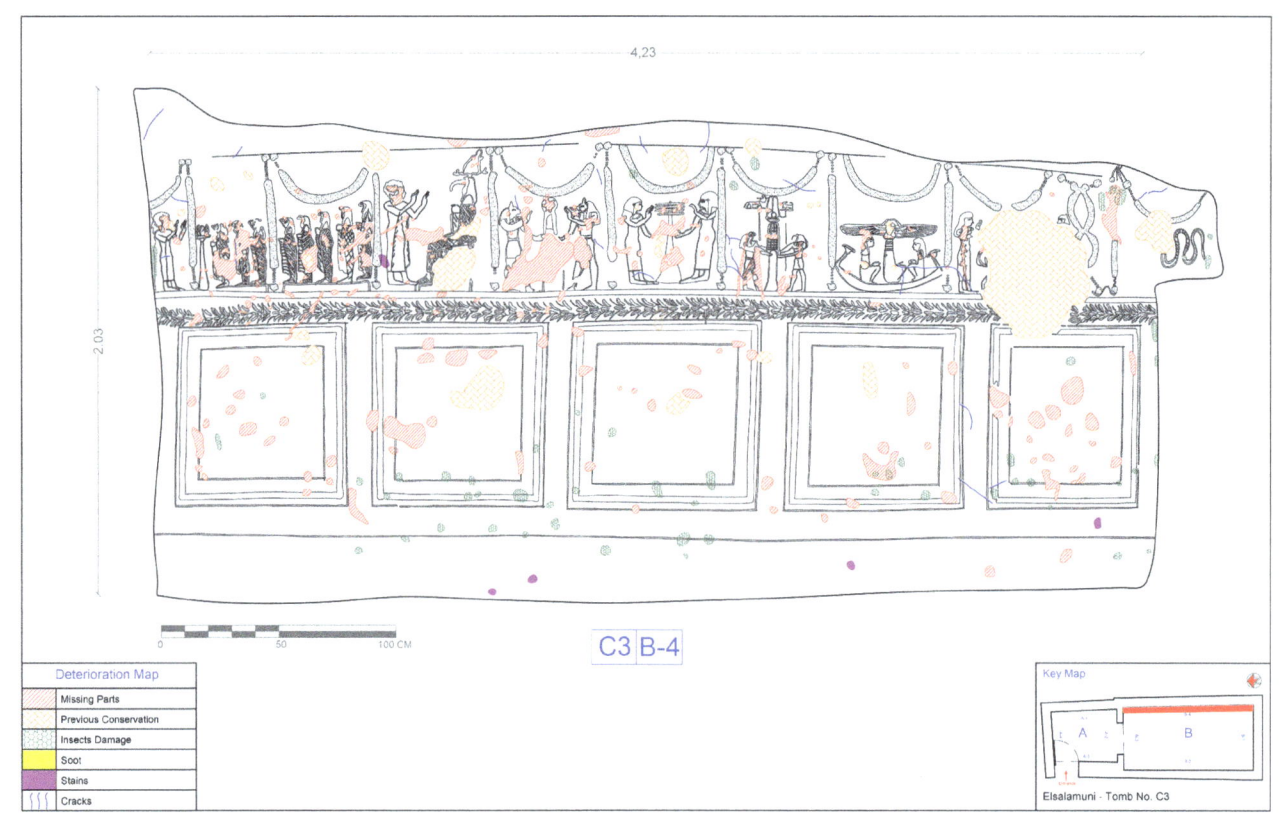

Figure 5.14c. A deterioration map of the east B4 wall in the tomb C3 burial chamber.

Figure 5.14d. An image of the deceased shown adoring some *genni* mummiform figures. The scene comes from the first and second vignette of the east B4 wall in the tomb C3 burial chamber.

Figure 5.14e. Photogrammetry of the east walls A1 (in the antechamber), and B4 (in the burial chamber) of tomb C3.

Moreover, the cult of *Ḥr-wḏ3* ('Horus is Healthy'), which was also known as the cult of Harudja/Haryotes, was popular in Bompae[72].

The sixth vignette shows two females squating on a papyrus barque; they are certainly Isis and Nephtyhs. They face each other and flank a third squatting human figure. The neck of the latter is in the form of a *djed* pillar, and is topped with an outstretched *khepri* (scarab beetle), signifying the newly created sun. The scene is surrounded by two festoons, while another one is depicted above the scene (Figure 5.15). Here, the squatting deceased man, in the guise of Osiris, is ferried on a solar barque made of papyrus. The scarab head confirms the justification and rebirth of the deceased male[73]. The scene therefore recounts the myth of the resurrection of Osiris (represented by the mummy), who became a *ḫpr* (the scarab symbol, meaning 'to exist'), united with Re (represented by the solar barque). At the same time, it alludes to the creation myth of the Heliopolitan cosmogeny[74]. From the New Kingdom onwards, and with an increasing frequency in the Third Intermediate Period, vignette 15 of the Book of the Dead commonly depicts Osiris as a *djed* pillar, with arms stretched to welcome the scarab as he ascends from the morning horizon[75]. In the sixth vignette, the two women who flank and protect the deceased almost definitely resemble Isis and Nephthys. A similar scene is depicted in an unregistered tomb located to the south, below the temple of Ay. It shows Isis and Nephthys with their attributed emblems on their heads. Here, they squat in their boat, protecting the squatting deceased, whose head is in the form of a solar disc with outstretched wings (Figure 5.16). The scene represents the deceased's final stage of transformation after

Figure 5.15. A depiction of the reborn tomb owner in a solar barque, flanked by two ladies (Isis and Nephthys).

having successfully completed the necessary funerary rites for a successful afterlife. Like Osiris, he has been justified, mummified, protected, and reborn as a transfigured spirit who is now destined for the afterlife.

Depictions of the afterlife from Ptolemaic-Roman Egypt mainly emphasise the syncretism of Re and Osiris, and the deceased's hope to join the solar-Osirian cycle. This close relationship between Re and Osiris secures the deceased person protection from every evil, and permits him to enter and leave the West without being turned away at the gates of the underworld[76]. Furthermore, when

---

[72] *CEML* 53.; Chauveau, *BIFAO* 92, 107.
[73] Minas-Nerpel, *Der Gott Chepri*, 152, 435–62. In the New Kingdom Tomb of Nefersecheru (TT926), a *djed* pillar representing Osiris and a goddess work together to elevate or embrace a sun disc, attesting to the union of Re and Osiris, G. Lapp, *Die Vignette zu Spruch 15 auf Totenpapyri des Neuen Reiches* (Basel 2015), 26, fig. 37.
[74] A. Niwiński, 'The Solar-Osirian Unity as Principle of the Theology of the 'State of Amun', in *Thebes in the 21st Dynasty*, *JEOL* 30 (1989)101–02, 104.
[75] For more on the *djed* pillar holding a sun disc, see Quirke, *Going Out in Daylight*, 37.; Lapp, *Die Vignetten zu Spruch* 15, 74.

[76] W. Budge, *Book of the Dead, The Chapters of Coming Forth by the Day, the Egyptian Text According to the Theban Recension in Hieroglyphic, ed. from Numerous Papyri* (London 1909), 99, lines 2–5.

Figure 5.16. A scene of the reborn tomb owner in a solar barque, flanked by two ladies (Isis and Nephthys). The scene comes from an unregistered tomb on the northern section of El-Salamuni Mountain, above tomb C1.

the deceased attempts to secure his rebirth in the *Duat*, he follows the solar deity's nocturnal passage, sailing through the sky each day to reach the eastern horizon at dawn, before starting the cycle again[77]. In Roman Egypt, the deceased was fully integrated within the solar-Osirian cycle, and the sun, which was sometimes called the *ba* of Osiris, was said to unite with Osiris on a daily basis, to be reborn in an endless cycle[78]. The depiction of the Osirian deceased as emerging from a lotus blossom as Khepri or Harpocrates is common in the Roman tomb of Petubastis at Dakhla[79] and in Roman tomb number 7 at Tuna El-Gebel[80]. The importance of the Solar-Osirian

unity is mentioned in funerary books for the afterlife; the Book of Caverns shows the revitalized Osiris with a sun disc on his head[81], and the final hour of the *Amduat* often shows Osiris as ithyphallic and mummiform[82]. In tomb C3, the figure of the deceased, with his elements of both Osiris and Khepri, confirms that the funerary beliefs in the El-Salamuni necropolis involved reverence for the Solar-Osirian cycle. The deceased hoped to be embraced by both the unified and revivified Re and Osiris.

The seventh vignette is damaged, but two females can still be seen. Unfortunately, whatever once appeared between the two females no longer exists. To whom (or to what) the females are addressing their reverent posture has been lost due to damage. The left female is entirely damaged, except for the uppermost part of her head and the remains of her black hair. The female deity to the right is dressed in a red fitted garment. She raises her arms in posture of adoration, and has long, black, curly hair. The author believes that the scene shows the mummification of the deceased on a bier. In fact, the rear leg of the bier, with its curved lion tail painted in yellow, is still visible, as well as the hand of a figure painted in red. Presumably, Anubis stood in the centre of this scene, behind the bier. He

---

[77] Smith, *Following Osiris*, 304.
[78] DuQuesne, 'The Osiris-Re Conjunction', in B. Backes et al. (eds.), *Totenbuch-Forschungen*, 25–30.
[79] Osing, *AV* 28, 79, pl. 31e.; Venit, *Visualizing the Afterlife*, 161–62, fig. 5.6.
[80] In Roman tomb 7 at Tuna El-Gebel, the deceased is shown squatting in an Osirian form. He wears an *atef* crown and rises from a lotus bloom between two females (Isis and Nephthys), D. Kessler and B. Patrick, *Ägyptens letzte Pyramide: das Grab des Seuta(s) in Tuna El-Gebel* (München 2008), 30.; M. Flossmann and A. Schütze, 'Ein Römerzeitliches Pyramidengrab und seine Ausstattung in Tuna El-Gebel, Ein Vorbericht zu den Grabungskampagne 2007 und 2008', in K. Lembke et al. (eds.), *Tradition and Transformation*, 79–110. Also see the coffin of Kephaesa from Akhmim. This coffin documents the rebirth of the deceased as a new *khepri* child; it is now in the NY Carlsberg-Copenhagen collection. It has been dated by S. Ikram to the 22nd dynasty, S. Ikram and A. Dodson, *The Mummy in Ancient Egypt, Equipping the Dead for Eternity* (London 1998), 236, fig. 312. Jorgensen dates it to between 900 and 700 BC, M. Jorgensen, *Catalogue Egypt III, Coffins, Mummy Adornments and Mummies from the Third Intermediate, Late, Ptolemaic, and the Roman Periods (1080 BC-AD 400)* (Copenhagen 2001), 184. Meanwhile Koefoed-Petersen connects the coffin to the Ptolemaic Period, O. Koefoed-Petersen, *Catalogue des Sarcophages et Cercueils Egyptiens* (Copenhagen 1951), 38.; Kessler and Patrick, *Ägyptens letzte Pyramide*, 30.
[81] C. Manassa, *The Late Egyptian Underworld, Sarcophagi and Related Texts from the Nectanebid Period, I: Sarcophagi and Texts, II: Plates, Egypt and Old Testament* 72 (Wiesbaden 2007), 114–17.
[82] É. Liptay, 'II/1, the Iconography of a 21st Dynasty Funerary Papyrus (Inv. No. 51.2547)', *BMH* 104 (2006), 38.

likely embalmed the mummy as he did with Osiris, thus enhancing the assimilation of the deceased with Osiris. The two ladies are identified with Isis and Nephthys. They stand in a venerating posture to the right and left of the bier. The scene is flanked on both sides by a festoon, with a third festoon above it. While this motif is rather typical, the existence of a fourth braided festoon is exceptional, probably referencing the embalming tent.

Mummification is a standard scene that affirms the corporal integrity of the deceased and involves an important mythic phase of his or her resurrection. Therefore, the scene of a mummy lying on a lion bed is frequent in Ptolemaic and Roman tombs. In El-Salamuni, the mummification scene is often depicted on the wall adjacent to the burial niche, as is the case with the lower wall of the burial niches in tombs C1, F2, and Kaplan's so-called tomb VI [83]. The scene is also known to occur outside of El-Salamuni[84].

Finally, the eighth vignette shows a coiled snake with a damaged head. Protection is the main function of the snakes in the tombs. Snakes are also identified with the cult of Isis, especially when they are crowned with either a sun disc and horns, imitating Isis-Thermousis, or with a *pschent* crown and beard, like Serapis, Agathos Daimon (the consort of Isis-Thermousis), or Isis in her role of Agatha-Tyche[85].

5.1.15: The Southern B1 Wall

The southern B1 wall is divided into two friezes. A burial niche covers the whole upper section of the wall. Painted green garlands made of twisted petals are pinned to the wall, with red tassels hanging from them. A serpent is shown on the left side of the wall. The winged vulture goddess Nekhbet hovers over the ceiling of the niche, spreading her wings to protect the mummy of the deceased. She has three layers of wings, the outer and inner sections of which are black, and the middle of which is red. She holds *shen* rings in her talons. The burial niche is about180cm. long, 43cm. wide, and 130cm. high (Figures 5.17a-b). The deceased would be placed under the burial niche's ceiling, which is painted to look like the garden of the afterlife, complete with flowers and garlands, and protected by the multi-coloured vulture. The burial niche

shows the blending of both Egyptian and Roman art styles; the Egyptian vulture occurs alongside the classical garlands, which are frequently used to adorn the *kline* in the tombs of Alexandria. On the right lateral wall is a coiled serpent meant for the protection of the mummy. Meanwhile, the left wall is only adorned with a festoon. Traditional *orthostat* panels cover the lower register. Beyond El-Salamuni, ceilings of burial niches ornamented with flowers are also attested in the Tigrain tomb (on the right-hand side of the niche), on the vault of a tomb in Ramleh, and in the funerary chapel of Tuna El-Gebel[86].

5.1.16: The Western B2 Wall

The western portion of the B2 wall contains a burial niche cut into its southern-most portion. Meanwhile, the northern part of the wall is divided into five vignettes, each of which are bordered and topped with festoons painted in green and black (Figures 5.18a-d). The far northern side of the wall, which is the closest to the doorway, is unfortunately in. a poor state of preservation because of damage.

The first of its five vignettes shows a partially damaged figure of a deceased male in a venerating pose. Two festoons surround the scene, while another one hovers above. The deceased wears a traditional white garment, and only the lower part of the deceased and his upraised hands are still visible. He stands before a high altar with loaves of bread. He adores the four sons of Horus, who are depicted in the next vignette. Behind him strides a deity. Unfortunately, the deity's face is completely damaged. The male deity is painted black, and wears a white kilt. Of his head, only the uppermost part of his crown remains. The author believes that this is the god Amun/Atum, as the remains of a *ṯ3w* sign painted in black are still distinguishable. The *ṯ3w* sign is mainly attributed to Atum, who is symbolically supposed to provide the deceased with air to breathe[87]. Here, the deceased asks the creator god Atum to provide him with the sweet air that the god enjoys, which comes from the god's nostrils. Atum had a special cult at Akhmim[88].

---

[83] Kaplan, *BzÄ* 16, 176, fig. 98b.
[84] In Alexandria, the embalming process was associated with the burial niche, and especially the central niche, as seen in the principal tomb of Kom El-Schukafa, F.von Bissing, *La catacombe nouvellement découverte de Kom el Chougafa (Les bas-reliefs de Kom el Chougafa) (drawings by E. Gillieron), Société archéologique d'Alexandrie* (Munich 1901), pl. VI. For the Tigrain tomb, see A. Adriani, 'Ipogeo dipinto della Via Tigrain Pascia', *BSRAA* 41 (1956), pl. II.2. It is also depicted in the Habachi A tomb at Gabari, Habachi, 1937, 275, fig.4a. For more on the *loculus* burial in tomb 1 of the Hall of Caracalla, see T. Schreiber, *Expedition Ernst Sieglin, Ausgrabungen in Alexandria, Die Nekropole von Kom-esc-schukafa* (Leipzig 1908), 129, fig.75. In the *chora*, the scene is found in the burial room of house-tomb 21, Venit, *Visualing the Afterlife*, 127–28, fig.4.22. It is also depicted on the rear wall of a niche in the burial chamber of the tomb of Petosiris, Venit, *Visualizing the Afterlife*, 172, fig. 5.15.
[85] Venit, *Visualizing the Afterlife*, 79.

[86] Guimier-Sorbets, Pelle, and Seif El-Din, *Resurrection in Alexandria*, 133.
[87] The Coffin Text spell 223, known as the 'Spell for Breathing Air in the Realm of the Dead', is a request from the deceased to Atum for air. It reads: 'O Atum, give the sweet air which is in your nostrils to N', CT III, 208c–d.
[88] Besides the triad of Akhmim, other finds including a chapel dedicated to Atum as an oracle god, and a striking figure of a falcon-headed snake (*ẖns i3wt*), were discovered during looting activities at Akhmim. They were found in one of the houses in Akhmim, lying south of the Ramesside temple. It is possible that the so-called 'necropolis of primeval gods' and the chapel functioned as a doorway, leading to a specific district of Akhmim in which the necropolis of the primeval gods and the local tomb of Osiris were located, G. Abdel Nasser, S. Baumann, and C. Leitz, 'Une Nouvelle Chapelle Pour Atoum a Akhmim', *Akhmîm, un tour d'horizon, Egypte, Afrique & Orient* 96 (2020), 15–26.; id., 'A Newly Discovered Edifice of Atum in Akhmim, Part of the Necropolis of the Primeval Gods?', *ENiM* 8 (2015), 187–221.; id., 'A New Doorway for Atum in Akhmim', *EA* 47 (2015), 3–6. The chapel of Atum uncovered new elements concerning the local cults and more specifically the yet unknown cult of the agathodaimon Atum-ḥns-j3.wt. The different writings of the anthroponym P3/T3-dj-ḥns-j3.wt show that it was first built on the

The Afterlife in Akhmim

Figure 5.17a. A winged vulture surmounting the ceiling of a burial niche on the south B1 wall of tomb C3.

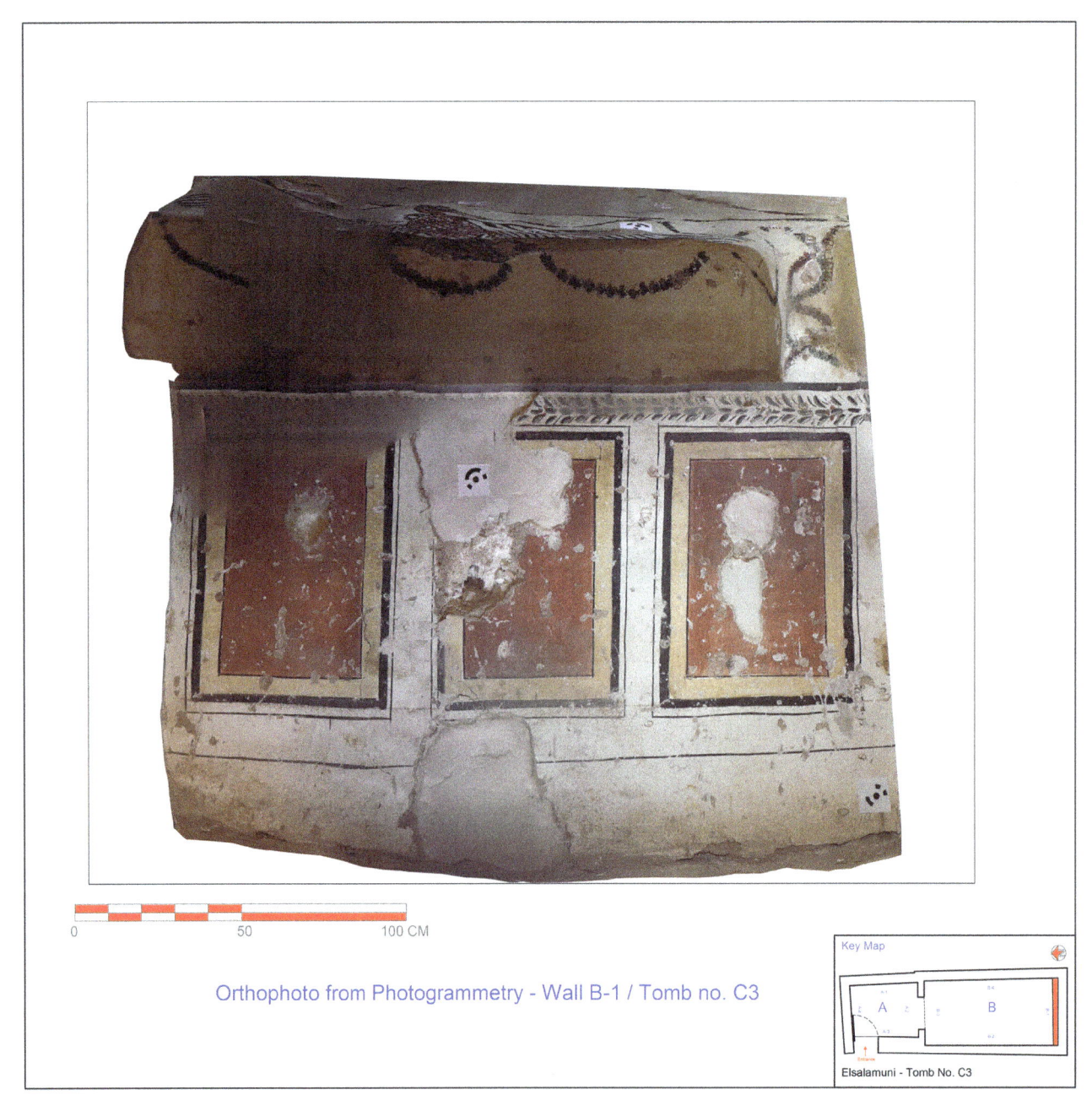

Figure 5.17b. Photogrammetry of the south B1 wall of tomb C3.

Figure 5.18a. Photogrammetry of the west B2 wall of tomb C3.

Figure 5.18b. A facsimile of the west B2 wall of tomb C3.

In order to ensure that the deceased would be appropriately provided with air to breathe, the Books of Breathing and Traversing Eternity became very popular by the second half of the Ptolemaic Period. They gradually replaced the famous Book of the Dead and its compositions[89]. The *ṯ3w* (or 'sailing') sign of breath is documented in vignettes 38 and 59 of the Book of the Dead, which are meant 'for breathing air and having power over water'[90]. The signs are also mentioned on various offering tables from tombs in Akhmim for this purpose of providing air[91]. Outside of El-Salamuni, the offering of Atum's *ṯ3w* ('breath') to the deceased is also depicted in house-tomb 21 at Tuna El-Gebel [92]. Here, the deceased, who are Petubastis[93] and Si-Amun [94], are represented holding the sign in their hands, confirming their transfiguration and portraying themselves as virtuous. The use of the breath sign by the wealthy Petubastis and Si-Amun suggests that a kind of a funerary cult was enjoyed in their tombs. In his scenes, Si-Amun receives praise and offerings from his eldest son and wife (named Rait). Meanwhile, it is a priestly figure who presents these things to Petubastis. The fact that Atum is

---

name of the sacred snake before it was reinterpreted phonetically into the seemingly better known, though meaningless, P3/T3-di-Ḫnsw-jj, see M. Claude, 'À propos de la relecture d'un anthroponyme à la lumière des inscriptions d'une chapelle d'Atoum récemment découverte à Akhmîm', *RdÉ* 68 (2018), 217-221.

[89] I. Munro, 'The Significance of the Book of the Dead Vignettes', in F. Scalf (ed.), *Book of the Dead, Becoming God in Ancient Egypt* (Chicago 2017), 54.

[90] Quirke, *Going Out into Daylight*, 111–12.

[91] Y. Barbash, 'The Ritual Context of the Book of the Dead', in F. Scalf (ed.), *The Book of the Dead, Becoming God in Ancient Egypt*, 77.

[92] Gabra describes this sign as a net, Gabra, *Rapport sur les Fouilles d'Hermoupolis*, 41.

[93] Venit, *Visualizing the Afterlife*, 163–64, fig. 5.7.

[94] Venit, *Visualizing the Afterlife*, 142, fig. 4.34.

The Afterlife in Akhmim

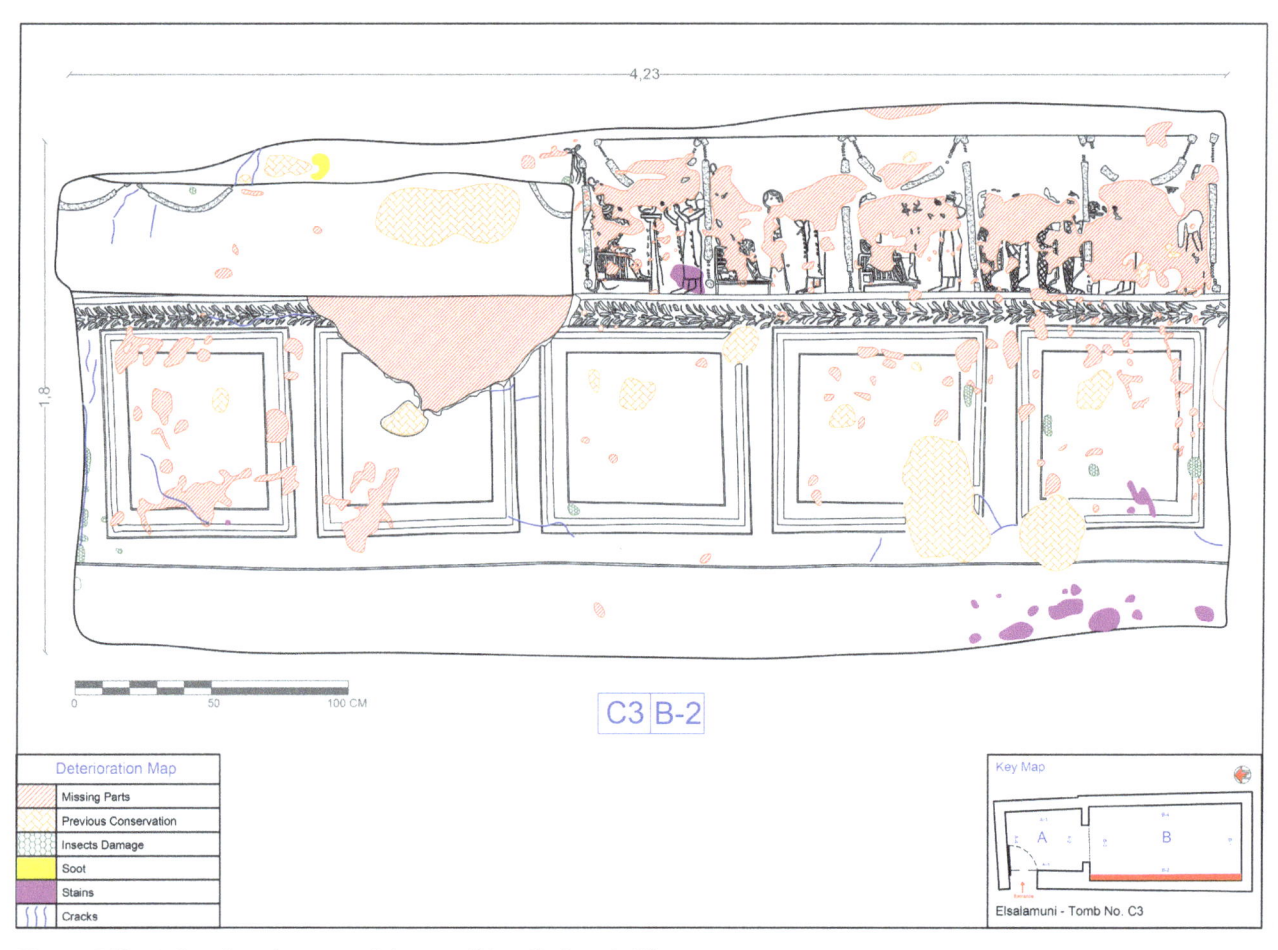

Figure 5.18c. A deterioration map of the west B2 wall of tomb C3.

Figure 5.18d. Photogrammetry of the west walls A3 (the antechamber), and B2 (the burial chamber) of tomb C3.

shown offering the sailing sign in tomb C3 might confirm that the patron of the tomb is related to one of the elites of the Panopolite community, and that he enjoyed a funerary cult[95].

The second frieze shows the four sons of Horus. Unfortunately, their heads are damaged; only the second figure still shows the black jackal head of Duatemutef. Their bodies are chequered in red, with only Duatemutef being shown in yellow. The frieze is bordered by festoons, although it lacks the common festoon placed above the scene.

The third vignette depicts the deceased male in an act of venerating a damaged god. The god sits on a cushioned throne. Only his black forehead remains; it could be Anubis without a crown. The god's body is wrapped in a

---
[95] W. Omran, 'The Deceased is Breathing', *GM* 263, no. 2 (2021), 173–80.

net shroud with red markings and black spots, while the throne is patterned with yellow squares containing black spots. A partially damaged but traditional high altar stands between the deceased and the god. Two festoons surround the scene, while a third one is placed above it (Figure 5.19).

The fourth frieze portrays the deceased in the same gesture of veneration as has already been described. He worships a seated god on the same style of cushion-throne as seen in the third vignette. A great part of the deity's body is damaged, and only the uppermost part of the crown, which is probably the white crown, is still visible. The god in question might be Horus, even though the evidence is rather fragmentary. The god and the throne are chequered in red, with black dots. An altar stands between the deceased and Osiris. Two festoons adorn both sides of the scene (Figure 5.20).

The fifth vignette shows the same venerating gesture of the deceased, this time before a partially damaged god, who is seated on a throne. The remains of the god's yellow *atef* crown and green face are highly reminiscent of Osiris. The damaged body of the god is shrouded in red squares containing black spots. His throne is patterned in yellow, with black dots. Here, the same altar as shown being placed between the deceased and Osiris in other vignettes is shown (Figure 5.21).

A burial niche is located at the south end of the wall. It measures 187cm. in length, 43cm. in width, and 130cm. in height. The niche's ceiling is also painted. A winged vulture, which decorates the ceiling of the niche, holds a *shen* sign between its claws. Festoons adorn the side and rear walls of the niche. The existence of two niches on the south and west walls of the burial chamber suggests that a couple was buried inside this tomb. Perhaps it was a man and his wife, as both a deceased male and female are depicted in the scenes of the tomb (Figures 5.22).

5.1.17: The Lower Registers in the Burial Chamber

Geometrical square *orthostats* cover the lower registers of the south, east, and west walls of the burial chamber, while rectangular panels cover the north wall. Each panel consists of four intertwined squares. The first square in this pattern is bordered with thin black lines, while the second one has broader and bolder lines on a yellow and black ground. The third square has thin black lines drawn on a broad red background (Figure 5.23). A thin black line lies beneath the *orthostats*, separating them from the *dado* of the chamber.

5.1.18: The Ceiling

The ceiling is decorated in a typical Hellenistic style, and is divided into two sections. Both sections have geometrical and floral patterns. Close to the doorway, there are twisted festoons in a geometrical, square form. Meanwhile, the interior section of the ceiling has twisted green and red festoons, which cover the southern half of the ceiling (Figures 5.24a-c). The geometrical squares that adorn the ceiling of tomb C3 are quite similar to the interwoven squares that are pinned with red tassels to the four corners of the ceiling of the so-called 'tomb of von Bissing' of

Figure 5.19. The offering of *ṯ3w* breath (first vignette), along with the veneration of the four sons of Horus (second vignette), and the adoring of a damaged seated Anubis (third vignette).

The Afterlife in Akhmim

Figure 5.20. An image of a deceased male venerating a seated damaged deity (either Osiris or Osiris-Sokar). The scene is from the west B2 wall of tomb C3.

Figure 5.21. A deceased male shown venerating a seated damaged Osiris. The scene is from the west B2 wall of tomb C3.

Figure 5.22. A winged vulture surmounting the ceiling of a burial niche on the west B2 wall of tomb C3.

Figure 5.23. The lower *orthostates* of the tomb C3 the burial chamber.

1913 (Figure 5.25)[96]. The style of the decoration is quite similar to the 'trellis and tapestery' design which ornamets the vaulted ceiling of room 2 in El-Anfushi (tomb II). It is decorated with multi-figured scenes in its squares[97].

5.1.19: The Floor

The current floor of tomb C3 is unpaved. The original floor could have been paved and damaged later-on, especially as the tomb has been accessible to the public and doorless for a long period of time (Figure 5.26).

5.2: The Patron and Date of the Tomb

Unfortunately, no text from tomb C3 has survived to offer hints as to the name and character of the deceased. However, the author assumes that the tomb dates to the first half of the second century AD. This observation has been made due to the use of *opus-sectile*, where monochromatic panels of the so-called *a pannelli* type are used. The style gained popularity for use in paints during the second century AD[98]. It is a distant relative of the fourth Pompeian style, and indicates major innovations in the painted decorations of the Mediterranean world from the reign of Hadrian onwards[99].

The ribbed dome ceiling of the tomb is quite similar in its pattern to the interwoven squares found along the four corners of the ceiling of the so-called 'von Bissing tomb' of 1913. The style imitates the 'trellis and tapestry' design which ornaments the vaulted ceiling of room 2 in El-Anfushi tomb II. The Greek-inspired painted decorations are widely utilized in El-Salamuni on flat ceilings, rather than on vaulted ones[100]. Venit assumes that this linear motif may represent a ribbed vault, like that of Tigrain's tomb[101], which dates back to the period of Hadrian and the second century AD.

Tomb C3 is situated on the far southern end of the mountain, where the last burials took place. Von Bissing and Rostovtzeff date the tombs in this area to the third century. The tomb lies adjacent to the painted Roman tombs C4 and C5. These tombs appear to be a coherent group, as they share common features in their decoration and in the distribution of scenes on their walls. This suggests that they date to a certain chronological horizon within one century, forming a coherent group by sharing the same typology. It could be that the tomb owners belong to the same family, or that they at least share the same social status. Pottery amphoras dating to the third and the fourth centuries AD were found in tomb C4[102]. A Demotic text in tomb C5 mentions the name of Senechnebis of Tatriphis, the patron of the tomb. Opposite this, the name of Senechnebis, daughter of Tapes (or daughter of Bes), is written in both Greek and Demotic. This Greek/Demotic mummy label (Berlin Staatliche Museen ÄM 10547-TM 50869[103]), which dates to the third century (225–275 AD), was found in a cemetery of the ninth nome. This same name is also mentioned in Greek in TM Ref 466066 from the ninth nome)[104]. Therefore, the tomb probably dates to either the late second century or the beginning of the third century AD.

---

[96] Von Bising, *ASAE* 50, 561, fig.9.; id., *JDAI* 61/62, 9, fig.12. Von Bissing notes that the same composition of branches and scattered flowers is also attested in Antaeopolis (Qaw al-Kebir), von Bissing, *ASAE* 50, 553, 563.
[97] Venit, *Monumental Tombs of Alexandria*, 85.
[98] H. Mielsch, *Römische Wandmalerei* (Darmstadt 2001), 93–106.
[99] H. Joyce, *The Decoration of Walls, Ceilings, and Floors in Italy in the Second and Third Centuries A.D*, Archaeologica 17 (Rome 1981), 33–40.
[100] The adjacent tomb C6 contains the same decorative style.
[101] Venit, *Visualizing the Afterlife*, 78-79, fig. 2.29.; id., *Monumental Tombs*, 148-49, fig. 129.
[102] Ashraf Sinwsi, a potter, dates them to the late third century AD. The publication of the tomb is forthcoming by the author.
[103] *SB* 1, 1220.; F. Krebs, 'Griechische Mumienetikette aus Ägypten', *ZÄS* 32 (1894), 48 no. 47.; Boyaval, *Corpus des étiquettes de momies grecques*, 124.; *Short Texts* II, 815.; P. Pestman, *Recueil des textes démotiques et bilingues* I, (Leiden 1977), 127, note 4 (=BL VII 178).
[104]

The Afterlife in Akhmim

Figure 5.24a. Photogrammetry of the ceiling of the tomb C3 burial chamber.

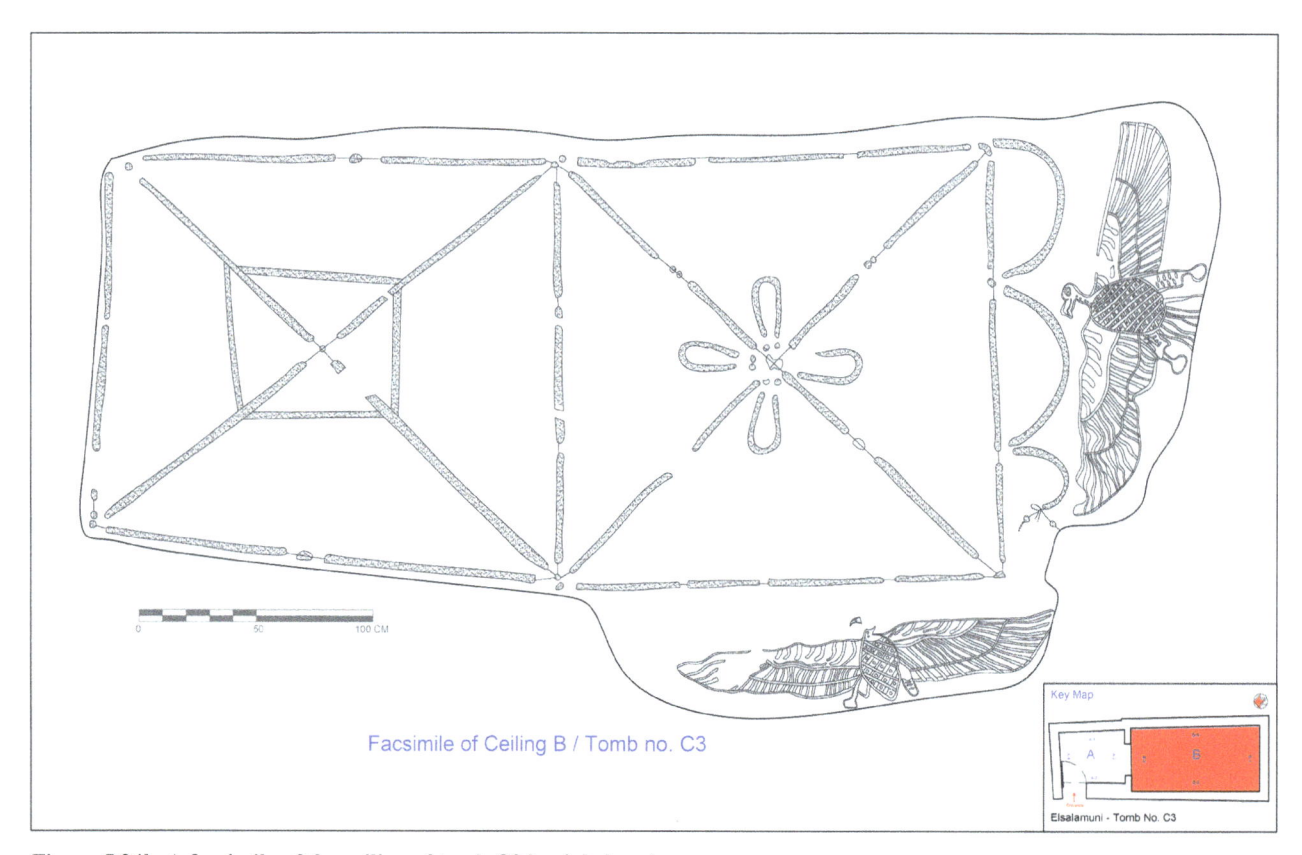

Figure 5.24b. A facsimile of the ceiling of tomb C3 burial chamber.

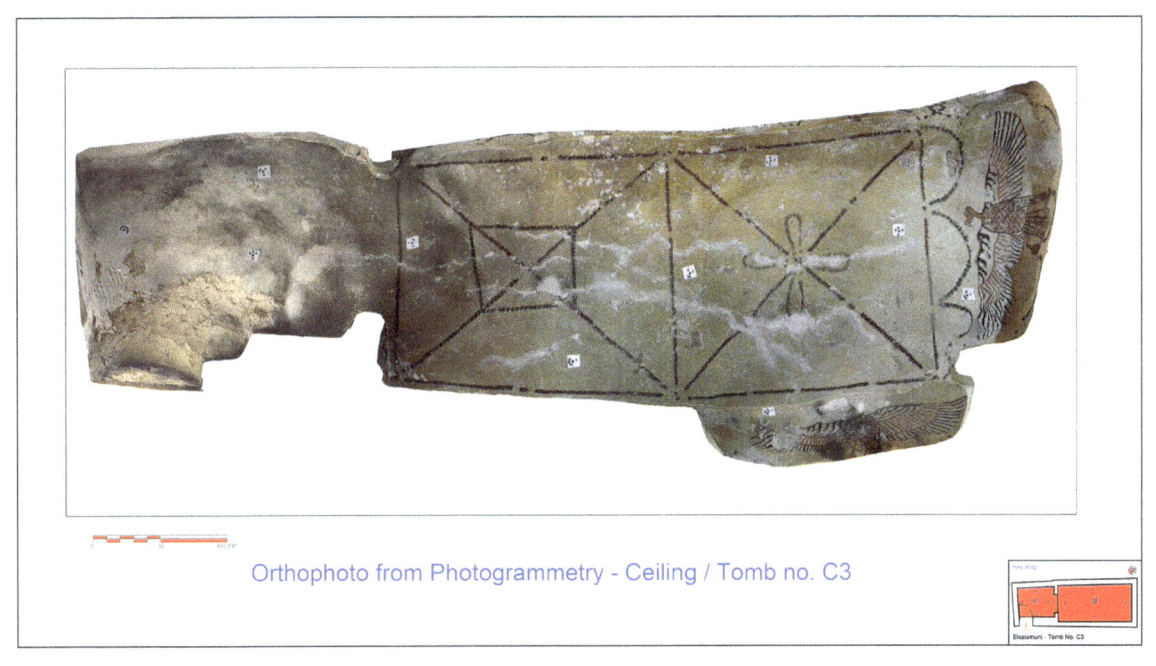

Figure 5.24c. A facsimile of the ceilings of tomb C3 ante and burial chambers.

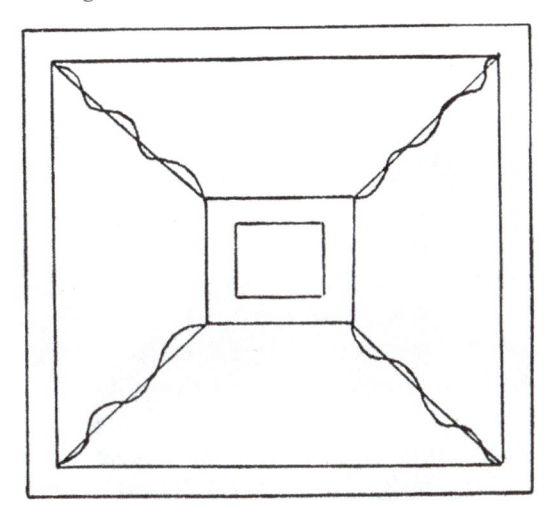

Figure 5.25. The geometrical squares which cover the ceiling of the so-called 'Tomb 1913 of von Bissing'.

Figure 5.26. The floor of tomb C3.

6
Conclusion

Akhmim still keeps many of its secrets. Researchers are only beginning to understand this important Egyptian-Hellenistic city, with its layout and civil buildings. An effort is thus underway to provide a more complete picture of the city and its inhabitants, religions, and customs. While researchers have uncovered an abundance of evidence for the religious cults and beliefs at Akhmim during the Graeco-Roman Period, very little is known about its main necropoleis during this time. Akhmim is a city of polytheism, where a special triad of deities was known to have existed, as well as various cults that were transferred from the adjacent cities of Ptolemais and Abydos to Panopolis. Local cults are known to have existed alongside the worship of Greek deities in this culturally rich hub.

With this book, the author tries to fill the gaps in the information available about Akhmim during the Graeco-Roman Period. There is currently a major lack of documentation for the urban architectural layout of Panopolis. During the Graeco-Roman Period, Hellenism was an important administrative and cultural feature of Panopolis, and the citizens of Panopolis expressed their Greek status in multiple ways, cultivating a new and multi-cultural urban identity. There is also insufficient information about the history of the temple(s) of Min from the early second century to the Early Christian Period. Furthermore, the necropoleis of Akhmim from the Graeco-Roman Period still need to be explored, and their funerary art and burial customs studied. This book constitutes the first in-depth study of the neglected and unknown necropolis of El-Salamuni.

In order to try to achieve a comprehensive picture of ancient Akhmim, it was necessary to remove the modern archaeological hill on top of which people have built their homes. Much of ancient Panopolis is still completely covered by earth, therefore making it difficult to study the earlier phases of its occupation. However, exploring the Akhmimic cemeteries is an essential step towards helping scholars understand the religious and burial customs of Akhmim over many periods of ancient history. It will also help scholars determine the chronology, topography, and architecture of each necropolis.

The El-Salamuni necropolis still lacks a clear topographical and archaeological survey to record all of its tombs. This is especially important for the tombs which are still without doors. An intended future survey of the area aims to define the locations of the tombs according to the mountain registers and according to their periods. Moreover, the intended survey aims to define the locations of the hewn entrances of suspected hidden and unexplored tombs, which are widely spread over the mountain's terraces. The survey, with its map, will be an important guideline for further excavations and investigations of the site, and will offer scholars a more precise historical typology of the tombs in regards to its architectural layouts.

The team additionally intends to carry out a 'first aid' process in the El-Salamuni tombs. This will be done by cleaning them from debris and rubbish. Cleaning the tombs will enable the project to measure the tombs' exact architectural dimensions, which are required for determining their layouts. Moreover, removing the debris may reveal new hidden funerary objects in the tombs, and even new tombs. The discovery of new tombs at the site would allow the team to update information about the local tombs, including their architectural typologies and related historical phases. For example, although Kuhlmann claims the Ptolemaic tombs at El-Salamuni are mainly shaft tombs, the newly discovered façade tomb B7 is also a Ptolemaic tomb, and its hieroglyphic texts can be precisely dated to the Ptolemaic Period.

The use of El-Salamuni Mountain as the main necropolis of Akhmim varied according to the mountain's importance as a quarry over different periods of time. The existence of the sanctuary of Min on the uppermost terrace of the mountain also impacted the use of the necropolis. El-Salamuni flourished as the main necropolis from the second century BC until the late third century AD, and its tombs were used as shelters during the Coptic persecution. Ever since the Old Kingdom, both the mountains of El-Hawawish and El-Salamuni have produced fine, white limestone of good quality. The cult of Min, the 'Lord of Quarries', was more prominent in El-Hawawish than in El-Salamuni. The local community, and not just the elite, were buried in El-Salamuni, while the elite tended to prefer El-Hawawish. During the Old Kingdom, the necropolis of El-Salamuni was used to a lesser extent than that of El-Hawawish B.

During the New Kingdom, a large quarry was opened in El-Salamuni, and King Ay and his wife Tiye took a special interest in the mountain, building a rock shrine of Min for the quarry workers who venerated the god in order to receive protection and help. In connection to this, the priests of Min were charged with supervising the burial and funerary affairs in the necropolis. It is clear that the mountain was widely used during the New Kingdom and onwards. Many New Kingdom and Late Period undecorated shaft tombs are documented by Kuhlmann. Unfortunately, during the author's visit to the site, all of the shafts were covered with sand. El-Hawawish A contains many tombs of the same periods, but because of the lack of excavations in both necropoleis, it is unclear which tombs were the most visited and distinguished of each period. The highly architectural and artistic design of the New Kingdom tombs in El-Salamuni highlights the high statues of the tomb owners. This suggest that El-Salamuni may have been a main necropolis for the area in the New Kingdom. On the other hand, the Late Period painted façade tombs in El-Hawawish A are more complete and decorated than the undecorated shaft tombs in El-Salamuni, suggesting the importance of El-Hawawish during this time.

From the Late Period until the Early Ptolemaic Period, the necropolis of El-Salamuni was used on a small scale. Most of the elite, including high-status officials, were buried in El-Hawawish. This is well-documented by the thousands of objects unearthed from the necropolis that date to this period. However, ever since the time of Philadelphus and the increased use of the El-Salamuni temple of Min, El-Salamuni Mountain became more utilized than that of El-Hawawish A. It became the main necropolis of Akhmim, and the elite were buried there until the Late Roman Period. Burials in El-Salamuni continued until the Late Roman Period. Meanwhile, during a contemporary time, local people were buried in plain shallow graves in the nearby necropolis of El-Hawawish A. It was not until the Coptic Period that El-Hawawish A recovered its value as a main necropolis of Panopolis. This was partially marked by the numerous silk textiles found in the necropolis.

The tombs of El-Salamuni are mostly family tombs, but there are a few cases of private tombs which contain only one burial niche. Family tombs are suggested by the existence of two or three burial niches in the burial chamber, in combination with two to four shallow pits in the antechamber. However, in the Late Roman Period, many tombs were also used as mass tombs, and could even be public. Von Bissing and Schmidt recognise some of these mass tombs when they write that they found a mass of mummies heaped on a tomb's bench. The local villagers confirmed this information.

As for the bodies themselves, mummification was the standard burial practice. Inhumation was used on a small scale in the necropoleis. In El-Hawawish A, shallow inhumation trenches are always found inside façade tombs, rather than as separate graves. The trenches are mainly found in the antechamber of the tombs. However, three shallow pits have also been recorded on the lower terrace of the most northern side of the mountain. Only two Greek *loculi* have been discovered; they are located in a tomb on the northern section of the mountain. Mummification remained the standard practice for the Roman tombs.

Mummification had typically been an elite practice in El-Salamuni. However, use of the practice was not limited Egyptians. The practice of mummification is certainly not an indication of the ethnicity of the patrons of these tombs, especially since the practice was adopted by so many members of the non-indigenous communities. On the other hand, cremation is often understood as a stronger signal for Greek ethnic traits. Inhumation was the most popular and cheapest rite. In El-Salamuni, a mix of cremations and inhumations are widely found together, appearing alongside each other in the same tomb. These are most likely family graves.

It is a very likely that the El-Salamuni necropolis contains the tombs of the famous Panopolite figures and priests whose names are inscribed on stelae, coffins, and funerary papyri of the Late Ptolemaic and Roman Periods. The high priest Hormaachreu, who constructed a rock-cut temple above his grave, is buried in El-Salamuni necropolis under the full patronage of his god Min. Furthermore, a Demotic text found in El-Salamuni tomb C5 mentions that the female patron of this tomb is 'Senekhebis, daughter of Tatriphis'. Tatriphis is the owner of P. Louvre E 10607, which contains a copy of the liturgy of the Opening the Mouth ceremony[1]. The same text was also given to the priestess Tatriphis, the owner of the P. MacGregor. Furthermore, the Demotic text in tomb F2 refers to its owner as 'Senobastis, daughter of Petemins'. Peteminis could be the father of Horos, the owner of the Demotic pBM 10507[2].

It is noteworthy to mention that the burials of the Old Kingdom in El-Salamuni were first dug into the northern section of the mountain, beyond the Old Kingdom shrine(?) of Min. Min was the chief god of the necropolis, and the protector of the quarry workers. Later, King Ay erected his temple there. The cemetery flourished during the Late Ptolemaic Period and lasted until the late third century AD. Though no Coptic altars, figures of saints, or crosses have been documented for the necropolis, it is highly likely that the tombs were used as shelters during the Coptic Period. Many Coptic vessels were found, as well as a pair of Coptic figures (in tomb F2).

El-Salamuni contains many special characteristics of funerary art and burial customs that are not found elsewhere in Egypt. While the El-Salamuni tombs, with their lack of texts, contain a richer range of Egyptian than classical decorative details, they are interwoven with narrative elements in a classical style. This speaks to cross-cultural contact and mixing that was happening at this site. Here, the religious function of the tomb is expressed via traditional Egyptian iconography, executed in a conventional Egyptian style. However, the Egyptian motifs and gods often seem poorly proportioned, which may indicate a Hellenistic Roman influence, especially in the use of foreshortening and the portrayal of a generally Hellenistic Roman garment. The deceased are often

---

[1] M. Smith, *New Middle Egyptian Texts in the Demotic Script*, Sesto Congresso Internazionale di Egittologia, Atti II (Turin 1993), 4.; id., *Traversing Eternity*, text 16.
[2] It is dated paleographically to the second half of the first century BC. It had been purchased by Budge at Akhmim, Smith, 'Budge at Akhmim, January 1896', in C. Eyre et al.(eds.), *The Unbroken Reed*, 293–303.; id., 'Aspects of the Preservation', in A. Egberts et al. (eds.), *Perspectives on Panopolis*, 233–47.

depicted in Roman clothing, which is voluminously draped, exemplifying the tombs' hybrid style. The interaction, mixture, and, in some cases, fusion of Egyptian and Hellenistic religious beliefs and burial customs speaks to the vibrancy and distinctive character of religious life in Panopolis during the Graeco-Roman Period.

The astronomical zodiacs are arguably the most distinctive feature of El-Salamuni. The Priests of Akhmim practiced wisdom literature and astronomy. Originally, astronomical ceilings were the domain of temples and royal tombs, but a small group of funerary zodiacs demonstrate their privatisation. This both ensured an eternal cycle of rebirth for the patron, and provides evidence of the patron's elite status.

In El-Salamuni, the familiarity with both Egyptian and Greek conceptions of the hereafter was well represented by the painter, who provided a common or shared point of reference between different cultures. The level of 'Greekness' and/or 'Egyptianness', as well as the (supposed) ethnicity of the deceased, cannot be easily defined. After all, these terms were more of a fluid cultural definition than a strict genetic one. Thus, 'cultural identity' is a more useful term than 'ethnicity' for discussing self-presentation in the tombs; being Greek or Roman was largely a cultural designation that could be earned. The interaction of people of the Egyptian and Hellenistic cultures seems to have existed throughout Panopolis, and was accompanied by changes to the funerary and religious practices in the city over time. The dual style is invariably documented in the El-Salamuni tombs. While a large, elite, classical figure was the popular choice for depicting the deceased, the Egyptian mummification practice was still highly appreciated. It was more common than Greek practices such as inhumation and cremation.

Classical culture was a part of education for the elite men of Panopolis. During the Graeco-Roman Period, a large urban community lived in Akhmim, including great numbers of Greeks and Romans. The Akhmimic pantheon was thus rich and varied, with Egyptian divinities being worshipped alongside Greek ones. It is possible that the Eleusinian Mysteries were celebrated in Akhmim; many sanctuaries (*hiera*) are known to have existed in Panopolis but are not yet located. These include sanctuaries to Persephone, Hermes, Agathos Daimon, and Isis, who held great importance in El-Salamuni, as discussed by Venit. In the late third century AD, a private school of philosophy was opened in Panopolis. Perhaps there was also once a sanctuary to Persephone that would have been housed in the *diatribe* ('class rooms') of Panodoros in Panopolis. Shenoute gives a detailed description of the statues that he found and destroyed in the houses of Akhmim, including those of Kronos, Hecate, Zeus, and other Greek ('pagan') idols). Though Emmel suggests that these statues may have been simply regarded as *objets d'art* for decoration[3],

the author believes that they were actually used for cultic purposes.

Decorated tombs in a mixed Egyptian-Hellenistic style are more numerous along El-Salamuni's east bank than in the Athribis necropolis of the Panopolite nome's west bank. The El-Salamuni tombs seem to feature a higher degree of 'Hellenisation'. The so-called 'tomb of von Bissing' of 1897 and tomb C3 both combine an Egyptian and Hellenistic visual language, reflecting the (at minimum) bilingualism of certain local scribes and artists. Both tombs C1 and C3 date to the Roman period, although they have some differences in their architecture and funerary themes. Both are tombs with two chambers, but while tomb C1 has three niches, tomb C3 has only two. In both tombs, the painters left large areas unpainted; the ceiling of the burial chamber in tomb C1 is unpainted, and the lower registers of the antechamber of tomb C3 are also undecorated. This could be due to the fact that the tombs were furnished quickly, in order to be ready for the burial of the deceased. It may also be that the cost of the burial was too high to pay for a full painting of the tomb.

Common scenes in tombs C1 and C3 include the Court of Judgement (with the special appearance of silhouettes), the Nut-goddess tree, and the daemonic Nehebkau. Scenes which are exclusively found in tomb C1 include the following: the Going Out of Min festival, an erotic scene, an unusual mummification scene, a daemonic procession, male and female processions, vignette 17 of the Book of the Dead, scenes of the deceased in classical clothing, and circular zodiacs in a Greek style. Tomb C3 is distinguishable by the use of *orthostat* panels, and the only known appearance of a musical scene taking place before Osiris in tombs of the Graeco-Roman Period. The classical festoons and the geometrical decorations on the ceiling of the tomb are also noteworthy.

Unfortunately, tomb C3 has no known inscriptions. However, tomb C1 features three short hieroglyphic texts. These texts use a common Akhmimic formula which is addressed to Osiris and which lacks any reference to the name of the deceased. The patron of tomb C1 is a male, while a female was buried in tomb C3. Both tombs emphasise the high social status of their patrons. The wealthy aspects of the tombs include the use of the *opus isodomus/ opus quadratum* decoration style and the inclusion of faience tiles, such as in the burial chamber of tomb C3. Likewise, the use of a circular zodiac is indicative of elite status in the private tombs of El-Salamuni. Both tombs also display the typical main moments in the journey to the beneficent afterlife and the celestial sphere. The existence of burial niches in the tombs confirms that the deceased were mummified. The tomb owners were most likely Hellenised Egyptians who were both acquainted with elements of the Hellenistic culture and loyal to local Egyptian funerary traditions.

As gods of the dead, Osiris and Osiris-Sokar were prominent in the pantheon of the Panopolite nome, and the

---

[3] Emmel. 'Shenoute of Atripe', in J. Hahn et al. (eds.), *From Temple to Church*, 171–72.; id., 'Shenute and Panopolis', in A. Egberts et al. (eds.), *Perspectives on Panopolis*, 99–102.

mummified deceased were believed to become Osiris in the tombs of El-Salamuni. The solar-Osirian cycle is well-attested in El-Salamuni through the use of the celestial zodiac, the depiction of Horus as the Lord of the Court of Judgement, and images of the transfiguration of the deceased. The deceased hoped that his or her *ba* would become associated with the solar-Osirian cycle. The daily separation and nightly reunion of the *ba* and the corpse was integral to Egyptian afterlife conceptions, and remained so, even with the increased popularization of a Greek and Roman pantheon in the region.

Bibliography

Abbas. E, *The Lake of Knives and the Lake of Fire, Studies in the Topography of Passage in Ancient Egyptian Religious Literature*, BAR Publishing 2144 (Oxford 2010).

Abdalla. A, *Graeco-Roman Funerary Stelae from Upper Egypt* (Liverpool 1992).

Abdel Nasser. G, Baumann. S, and Leitz. C, 'Une Nouvelle Chapelle Pour Atoum à Akhmîm', *Akhmîm, un tour d'horizon*, Égypte, *Afrique & Orient* 96 (2020), 15–26.

Abdel Nasser. G, Baumann. S, and Leitz. C, 'A Newly Discovered Edifice of Atum in Akhmim, Part of the Necropolis of the Primeval Gods?', *ENiM* 8 (2015), 187–221.

Abdel Nasser. G, Baumann. S, and Leitz. C, 'A New Doorway for Atum in Akhmim', *EA* 47 (2015), 3–6.

Abdel Nasser. G, 'A New Discovery from the Ptolemaic Period in El-Hawawish', *GM* 92 (1986), 7–8.

Abdelhalim. A, 'Snakes with Human Arms and Legs in Ancient Egyptian Books of the Afterlife', *ASAE* 88 (2015), 291-300.

Abdelhalim. A, 'A Lunette Stela of Pasenedjemibnash in the Cairo Museum, CG 22151', *BIFAO* 114.1, (2014), 1–18.

Abd El-Ghani. M, 'The Role of Ptolemais in Upper-Egypt Outside its Frontiers', in I. Andorlini (ed.), *Atti del XXII Congresso Internazionale di Papirologia. Florence, 23–29 agosto 1998, I, Istituto papirologico 'G. Vitelli'* (Florence 2001),17–33.

Abdelwahed. Y, *Egyptian Cultural Identity in the Architecture of Roman Egypt (30 BC–AD 325)*, Archaeopress (BAR Publishing) 6 (Oxford 2015).

Abel-Wilmanns. B, *Die Erzählaufbau der Dionysiaka des Nonnos von Panopoli* (Frankfurt am Main 1977).

Abell. W, *Representation and Form, A Study of Aesthetic Values in Representational Art* (Connecticut 1971).

Abouelata. M, and M. Hossain, 'Continuity of Themes Depicted on Coffin Lids from the Third Intermediate Period to Graeco-Roman Egypt', in A. Amenta and H. Guichard (eds.), *Proceedings of 1st Vatican Coffin Conference, 19–22 June 2013, A cura di Alessia Amenta e Hélène Guichard* (Vatican 2017), 21–30.

Abry. J, *Les Tablettes Astrologiques de Grand (Vosges) et L'Astrologie en Gaule Romaine, Actes de la Table-Ronde du 18 mars 1992 organisée au Centre d'Etudes Romaines et Gallo-Romaines de l'Université Lyon III* (Lyon 1993).

Abu Stet. D, 'New Insights into the Significance of Exotic Plants & Animals in Ancient Egypt', in A. Maravelia and N. Guilhou (eds.), *Environment and Religion in Ancient and Coptic Egypt: Sensing the Cosmos Through the Eyes of the Divine, Proceedings of the 1st Egyptological conference of the Hellenic Institute of Egyptology, Co-Organised with the Writing & Scripts Centre of the Bibliotheca Alexandrina and the Institute of Coptic Studies (University of Alexandria), at the People's University of Athens, Under the High Auspices of His Eminence Mgr Damianos, Archbishop of Sinai; Athens, Wednesday 1st, Thursday 2nd Friday 3rd February 201*, Archaeopress (BAR Publishing) 30 (Oxford 2020), 15–30.

Adriani. A, *Repertorio d'Arte dell 'Egitto Greco-Romano C I–II* (Palermo 1963).

Adriani. A, 'Ipogeo dipinto della Via Tigrain Pascia', *BSRAA* 41 (1956).

Alföld. A, *A Festival of Isis in Rome Under the Christian Emperors of the IVth Century* (Budapest 1937).

Allen. T, 'The Book of the Dead or Going Forth by Day, Ideas of the Ancient Egyptians Concerning the Hereafter as Expressed in their Own Terms', *SAOC* 37 (Chicago 1974).

Alrt. C, 'Deine Seele Möge Leben für immer und Ewig, Die Demotischen Mumienschilder im British Museum' *StudDem* 10 (Leuven 2011).

Alston. R, 'Urbanism and the Urban Community in Roman Egypt', *JEA* 83 (1997), 161–204.

Altenmülle. H,' Götter, apotropäische', *LÄ II*, cols. 635–40.

Altmann-Wendlig. V, 'Of Min and Moon: Cosmological Concepts in the Temple of Athribis (Upper Egypt)', in G. Rosati and M. Guidotti (eds.), *Proceedings of the XI International Congress of Egyptologists, Florence Egyptian Museum, Florence, 23–30 August 2015* (Oxford 2017), 7–13.

Altmann-Wendling. V, 'Shapeshifter Knowledge of the Moon in Graeco-Roman Egypt', in J. Althoff, D. Berrens, and T. Pommerening (eds.), *Construction and Transfer of Knowledge about Man and Nature in Antiquity and the Middle Ages* (Bielefeld 2019), 213–52.

Altmann-Wendling. V, 'Mond Symbolik, Mond Wissen: lunare Konzepte in den ägyptischen Tempeln griechisch-römischer Zeit, II', *SSR* 22 (Wiesbaden 2018).

Amelineau. E, *La géographie de l'Égypte à l'époque copte* (Paris 1893).

Amelineau. E, œuvres *de Schenoudi*, I (Paris 1907–14).

Amer. H, *Astronomical Representation of Egyptian Goddesses in Tombs and Temples from the New Kingdom to the End of Graeco-Roman Period, An Archaeological Religious Study, Alexandria University* (Alexandria 2021).

Amigues. S, 'Sur le perséa d'Égypte', in *Hommages à Francois Daumas* I (Montpellier 1986).

Ammon. D, *Crafts of Egypt* (Cairo 1999).

Arlt. C, *Deine Seele möge leben für immer und ewig: Die Mumienschilder im British Museum* (Leuven 2011).

Arnold. D, *Temples of the Last Pharaohs* (New York, Oxford 1999).

Arnold. D, *Die Temple Ägyptens, Götterwohnungen, Kultstätten, Baudenkmäler* (Zürich 1992).

Arnst. C, 'Vernetzung Zur Symbolik des Mumiennetzes', in M. Fitzenreiter (ed.), *Die ägyptische Mumie, ein Phänomen der Kulturgeschichte, Beiträge zum Workshop am 25. und 26. April 1998, Humboldt Universität zu Berlin, Seminar für Sudanarchäologie und Ägyptologie I* (Berlin 1998), 79–94.

Arslan. E, *Iside, Ilmitoilmistero la Magia, Palazzo Reale* 22 (Milan 1977).

Assmann. J, *Altägyptische Totenliturgien, I: Totenliturgien in den Sargtexten des Mittleren Reiches. Supplemente zu den Schriften der Heidelberger Akademie der Wissenschaften, Philosophisch-Historische Klasse 14* (Heidelberg 2002).

Assmann. J, 'Primat und Transzenden, Structure und Genese der ägyptischen Vorstellung eines ' höchsten Wesens"', in W. Westendorf (ed.), *Aspekte der spätägyptischen Religion*, *GOF* 9 (Wiesbaden 1979), 7–42.

Aubert. M and Cortopassi. R, *Portraits funéraires de l'Égypte romaine, Tome I, masques en stuc. Paris:* Réunion des musées nationaux (Paris 2004).

Aufrère. S, 'KRONOS, un crocodile justicier des marécages de la rive occidentale du Panopolite au temps de Chénouté?', in S. Aufrère et al. (eds.), *Encyclopédie religieuse de l'Univers végétal, Croyances phytoreligieuses de l'Égypte ancienne (ERUV III)*, *OrMonsp* 15 (Montpellier 2005), 77–93.

Aufrère. S, 'Démons vus par les premiers chrétiens', in M. Rassart-Debergh (ed.), Études coptes V, *Sixième journée d'études, Limoges 18–20 juin 1993 et Sixième journée d'études, Neuchâtel 18–20 mai 1995*, *CBC* 10 (Leuven 1998), 63–92.

Aufrére. S, *Collections égyptiennes, Collections des Musées départementaux de Seine-Maritime III* (Rouen 1987).

Aufrère. S, 'Études de lexicologie et d'histoire naturelle, IV–VI', *BIFAO* 84 (1984), 1–21.

Awad. F, 'The Development of Burial Types at Tuna El–Gebel During the Graeco–Roman Era', in M. Flossmann-Schütze, F. Hoffmann, and A. Schütze (eds.), *Tuna El-Gebel- eine ferne Welt, Tagungsband zur Konferenz der Graduade School 'Distant Worlds' vom 16. bis 19.1.2014* (München 2020), 100–09.

Awadalla. A, 'Une stèle cintrée de Ns-Mnw Caire CG 22053', *SAK* 25 (1998), 1–5.

Abdelwahed. R, 'Reflections on the Tree Im3/ I3m in Ancient Egypt', in A. Maravelia and N. Guilhou (eds.), *Environment and Religion in Ancient and Coptic Egypt, Sensing the Cosmos Through the Eyes of the Divine, Archaeopress Egyptology (BAR Publishing)* 30 (Oxford 2020), 3–14.

Bács. T, 'Amun-Re-Harakhti in the Late Ramesside Royal Tombs', in U. Luft (ed.), *The Intellectual Heritage of Egypt, Studies Presented to László Kákosy on the Occasion of His 60th Birthday* (Budapest 1992), 43–53.

Baqué-Manzano. L, 'Min-Osiris, Min-Horus: a propósito de un relieve del templo de Hibis en el oasis de El Jarga', in J. Autuori and A. Álvarez (eds.), *Estudios dedicados al Prof. Jesús López, Avla Aegyptiaca: Stvdia* 2 (Barcelona 2001), 35–49.

Baedecker. P and Reddy. M, 'The Erosion of Carbonate Stone by Acid Rain', *Journal of Chemical Education* 70 no. 2, (1993), 104–08.

Baedeker. K, Égypte, *Manuel du Voyageur* (Leipzig 1891).

Bagnall. R and Rathbone. D, *Egypt from Alexander to the Copts, An Archaeological and Historical Guide* (London 2004).

Bagnall. R, 'Later Roman Egypt, Society, Religion, Economy, and Administration', *Variorum Collected Studies* 758 (Burlington 2003).

Bagnall. R, 'Cults and Names of Ptolemais in Upper Egypt', in W. Clarysse, A. Schoors, and H. Willems (eds.), *Egyptian Religion, The Last Thousand Years, II. Studies Dedicated to the Memory of Jan Quaegebeur*, *OLA* 85 (Leuven 1998), 1093–101.

Bagnall. R, *The Census Register P. Oxy. 984, The Reverse of Pindar's Paeans*, *Pap. Brux.* 29 (Brussels 1997).

Bagnall. R, *Egypt in Late Antiquity*, (Princeton 1993).

Baillet. J, *Le papyrus mathématique d'Akhmîm*, *MMFAC IX.1* (Paris 1892).

Baines. J, 'Temples as Symbols, Guarantors and Participants in Egyptian Civilisation', in S. Quirke (ed.), *The Temple in Ancient Egypt. New Discoveries and Recent Research* (London 1997).

Baines. J, 'Society, Morality, and Religious Practice', in B. Shafer et al. (eds.), *Religion in Ancient Egypt, Gods, Myths, and Personal Practice* (Ithaca, London 1991), 123–200.

Bakowska-Czerner. G, and Czerner. R, 'Marina el-Alamein as an Example of Painting Decoration of Main Spaces of Hellenistic-Roman Houses in Egypt', *Arts* 11 (2022), 1–21.

Bakry. H, 'A Statue of Pedeamun-Nebnesuttaui', *ASAE* 60 (1968), 17–25.

Bandinelli. B, *Rome, the Centre of Power, 500 BC to 200 AD* (New York 1970).

Barakat. A, 'Notes of the Ancient Akhmim', *ASAE* 66 (1987), 155–59.

Barguet. P, 'Le papyrus N. 3176 (S), du musée du Louvre', *BiEtud* 37 (Cairo 1962).

Barrett. C, *Egyptianizing Figurines from Delos, A Study of the Hellenistic Religion* (Leiden, Boston 2011).

Barton. T, *Ancient Astrology* (London, New York 1994).

Bassem. G et al., 'Wall Paintings in a Roman House at Ancient Kysis, Kharga Oasis', *BIFAO* 113 (2013), 157–82.

Basilus. A, 'Eine Bislang Unpublizierte Priester Statuette aus Dem Ptolemäischen Panopolis', in A. Egberts, B. Muhs, and J. Van Der Vliet (eds.), *Perspectives on Panopolis, an Egyptian Town from Alexander the Great to the Arab Conquest; Acts from an International Symposium, Held in Leiden on 16, 17 and 18 December 1998*, P.L. Bat. 31 (Leiden 2002), 29–43.

Bataille. A, 'Les Memnonia', *RAPH* 23 (Cairo 1952).

Baum. N, *Arbres et Arbustes de l'Egypte Ancienne* (Leuven 1988).

Bayer-Niemeier. E et al., Ägyptische Bildwerke, Band III: Skulptur, Malerei, Papyri und Särge. Liebieghaus-Museum Alter Plastik, Frankfurt am Main, Wissenschaftliche Kataloge (Gutenberg 1993).

Beaucamp. J, *Le statut de la femme à Byzance (4e-7e siècle), II. Les pratiques sociales*, Travaux et Mémoires du Centre de Recherche d'Histoire et Civilisation de Byzance, Monographies 6 (Paris 1992).

Bell. D, 'Besa: The Life of Shenoute', *CSS* 73 (Kalamazoo 1983).

Bellucio. A, 'Le pianta del dio Min e la suo funzione sul piano mitico–rituale', *DE* 31 (1995), 15–34.

Bergmann. M, 'Stile und Ikonographien im kaiserzeitlichen Ägypten', in K. Lembke et al. (eds.), *Tradition and Transformation: Egypt Under Roman Rule, Proceedings of the International Conference, Hildesheim, Roemer and Pelizaeus Museum, 3–6 July 2008* (Leiden 2010), 1–36.

Berman. L, *Catalogue of Egyptian Art, the Cleveland Museum of Art* (Cleveland 1999).

Bernand. A, 'Pan du désert et ses adorateurs', in H. Maehler and V. Strocka (eds.), *Das ptolemäische Ägypten, Akten des internationalen Symposions 27–29. September 1976 in Berlin* (Mainz 1978), 161–64.

Bernand. A, *Pan du désert* (Leiden 1977).

Bernand. A, *De Koptos à Kosseir* (Leiden 1972).

Bernand. E, *Inscriptions métriques de l'Egypte gréco-romaine, recherches sur la poésie épigrammatique des Grecs en Égypte*, Annales littéraires de l'Université de Besançon 98 (Paris 1969).

Bickel. S, *La Cosmogonie égyptienne avant le Nouvel Empire*, OBO 134 (Freiburg 1994), 123–67.

Bilabel. F, 'Der Gott Kolanthes', *AfP* 8 (1927), 62.

Billing. N, 'You Are Not Alone: The Conceptual Background of Nut as the Eternal Abode in Text and Iconography', in A. Maravelia and N. Guilhou (eds.), *Environment and Religion in Ancient and Coptic Egypt: Sensing the Cosmos Through the Eyes of the Divine*, Archaeopress (BAR Publishing) 30 (Oxford 2020), 69–84.

Billing. N, 'Nut, The Goddess of Life in Text and Iconography', *Uppsala Studies in Egyptology* 5 (Uppsala 2003).

Binachi. R, 'Not the Isis Knot', *BES* 2 (1980), 9–31.

Bleeker. C, *Hathor and Thoth, Two Key Figures of the Ancient Egyptian Religion* (Leiden 1973).

Bleeker. C, *Die Geburt eines Gottes: eine Studie über den ägyptischen Gott Min und sein Fest*, Studies in the History of Religions, Supplement to Numen (Leiden 1956).

Bommas. M, 'Situlae and the Offering of Water in the Divine Funerary Cult, a New Approach to the Ritual of Djeme', in A. Amenta, M. Luiselli, and M. Sordi (eds.), *L'acqua nell'antico Egitto: vita, rigenerazione, incantesimo, medicamento; Proceedings of the First International Conference for Young Egyptologists, Italy, Chianciano Terme, October 15–18, 2003* (Roma 2005), 257–72.

Bommas. M, 'Schrein unter: Gebel es-Silsilah im Neuen Reich', in G. Heike, E. Hofmann, and M. Bommas (eds.), *Grab und Totenkult im alten Ägypten, Festschrift Jan Assmann* (München 2003), 88–103.

Bonnet. H, 'Apis', *LdÄR* (Hamburg, 2000).

Bonnet. H, 'Panopolis', *RÄRG* (Berlin 1952), 580.

Borg. B, *Mumienporträts, Chronologie und kultureller Kontext* (Mainz 1996).

Borkowski. Z, 'Local Cults and Resistance to Christianity', *JJP* 20 (1990), 25–30.

Borkowski. Z, *Une description topographique des immeubles à Panopolis (= SB XVI 16000)*, (Warsaw 1975).

Bourguet. P and Gabolde. L, 'Le temple de Deir al-Médîna', *MIFAO* 121 (Cairo 2002).

Bouriant. U, 'Notes de voyage', *RecTrav* 11 (1889), 140–41, 145–49.

Bouriant. U, 'Rapport au ministère de l'Instruction Publique sur une mission dans la Haute-Egypte (1884–1885)', *MMFAC* 1.3 (Paris 1887).

Bouriant. U, 'Petits monuments et petits textes recueillis en Égypte', *Rec. Trav.* 8 (1886), 163–64.

Bouriant. U, 'Les Papyrus d'Akhmim', *MMFAC* 1.2 (1885).

Bourriau. J and Millard. A, 'The Excavation of Sawâma in 1914 by G.A. Wainwright and T. Whittemore', *JEA* 57 (1971), 28–57.

Bowersock. G, *Selected Papers on Late Antiquity* (Bari 2000).

Bowersock. G, 'Dionysius as an Epic Hero', in N. Hopkison (ed.), *Studies in the Dionysiaca of Nonnus*, (Cambridge 1994), 156–66.

Bowersock. G, *Hellenism in Late Antiquity* (Cambridge 1990).

Bowman. A, 'Urbanization in Roman Egypt', in E. Fentress (ed.), *Romanization and the City: Creation, Transformations and Failures*, *JRA Suppl.* 38 (2000), 173–87.

Bowman. A and Rathbone. D, 'Cities and Administration in Roman Egypt', *JRS* 8 (1992), 107–27.

Bowman. A, 'Public Buildings in Roman Egypt' *JRS* 5 (1992), 495–503.

Bowman. A, 'Landholding in the Hermopolite Nome in the Fourth Century AD', *JRS* 75 (1986), 137–63.

Boyaval. B, *Corpus des étiquettes de momies grecques, Publications de l'Université de Lille III. Série 'Etudes archéologiques, Villeneuve d'Asq* (Lille 1976).

Boylan. P, *Thoth, The Hermes of Egypt* (London 1922).

Brashear. W et al., *The Chester Beatty Codex Ac. 1390. Mathematical School Exercises in Greek and John 10:8–13:38 in Sub-Achmimic* (*Chester Beatty Monographs 13*), (Leuven, Paris 1990).

Braunert. H, *Die Binnenwanderung Studien zur Sozial Geschichte Ägzptens in der Ptolemäer-und Kaiserzeit, Bonner Historische Forschungen* 26 (Bonn 1964).

Brech. R, *Spätägyptische Särge aus Achmim, Eine typologische und chronologische Studie* (Gladbeck 2008).

Bredford. D, *The Ancient Gods Speak, A Guide to The Egyptian Religion* (Oxford 2002).

Bremmer. J, 'Aëtius, Arius Didymus and the Transmission of Doxograph', *Mnemosyne* 51(1998), 154–60.

Bresciani. E, 'Un insolita figura di'concubina in terracotta, la suonatrice di tamburo', in P. Buzi, D. Picchi and M. Zecchi (eds.), *Aegyptiaca et Captica. Studi in onro di Sergio Pernigotti, BAR Publishing* 2264 (Oxford 2011), 27–32.

Bresciani. E, *Kom Madi 1977 e 1978 Le pitture murali del centafo di Alessandro Magno* (Pisa 1980).

Brewer. D, 'Shadow', in D. Redford (ed.), *The Oxford Encyclopedia of Ancient Egypt, III* (Oxford 2001).

Brokvarski. E, *Naga ed-Der in the First Intermediate Period* (Boston 2018).

Brunner-Traut. E, Brunner. H, and Zick-Nissen. J, *Osiris, Kreuz und Halbmond, Die Drei Religionen Ägyptens* (Mainz 1984).

Brunner-Traut. E, *Gelebte Mythen, Beiträge zum altägyptischen Mythos* (Darmstadt 1981).

Bruwier. M, 'Akhmîm antique', in M. Jeanne Paule and M. Bruwier (eds.), *Akhmîm, au fil des femmes, broderies et tissages de Haute-Egypte, 4000 ans d'art textile, MUMAQ* (Mariemont 2022), 12–16.

Bruwier. M and Mekis.T, 'Diversity of the Akhmimic Funerary Art in the 4th-3rd Centuries BC, A Case Study on a Priestly Family, and a Study on Canopic Chests of Akhmim in the Graeco-Roman Period: A Survey in Antiquity Collections', in M. Mosher (ed.), *The Book of the Dead, Saite through Ptolemaic Periods: Essays on Books of the Dead and Related Materials, SPBD Studies* (Prescott 2019).

Bucher. P, 'Les textes des tombes de Thoutmosis III et d'Aménophis II', *MIFAO* 60 (Cairo 1932).

Buck. C and Petersen. W, *Reverse Index of Greek Nouns and Adjectives* (Chicago 1945).

Budge. W, *The Egyptian Religion of Resurrection Osiris, I* (New York 1961).

Budge. E, *By Nile and Tigris, A Narrative of Journeys in Egypt and Mesopotamia on Behalf of the British Museum between the Years 1886 and 1913, I–II* (London 1920).

Budge. A, *A Guide to the Egyptian Galleries* (*Sculptures*) (London 1909).

Budge. W, *Book of the Dead, the Chapters of Coming Forth by the Day, the Egyptian Text According to the Theban Recension in Hieroglyphic, Ed. From Numerous Papyri* (London 1909).

Budge. W, *A Catalogue of the Egyptian Collection in the Fitzwilliam Museum* (Cambridge 1893).

Budge. E, *The Mummy, A Handbook of Egyptian Funerary Archaeology* (New York 1892).

Budka. J, 'Neues zu den Nutzungsphasen des Monumentalgrabes von Anch-Hor, Oberstthofmeister der Gottesgemahlin Nitokris (TT 414)', Ägypten und Levante 18 (2008), 62–85.

Buhl. M, 'The Goddess of The Egyptian Tree Cult', *JNES* 6, no. 2 (1947), 80–97.

Bulté. J, *Talismans Egyptiens d'Heureuse Maternité* (Paris 1991).

Cameron. A, 'The Empress and the Poet, Paganism and Politics at the Court of Theodosius II', *YCS* 27 (1984), 270–79.

Cancik. H and Schneider. H, *Der Neue Pauly Enzyklopädie der Antike, Band 6* (Stuttgart 1999).

Caneva. S, 'The Persea Tree from Alexander to Late Antiquity, a Contribution to the Cultural and Social History of Greco-Roman Egypt', *AncSoc* 46 (2016), 39–66.

Cannata. M, *Three Hundred Years of Death, the Egyptian Funerary Industry in the Ptolemaic Period, Culture and History of the Ancient Near East 10* (Leiden, Boston 2020).

Cannata. M, 'Funerary Artists, the Textual Evidence', in C. Riggs (ed.), *The Oxford Handbook of Roman Egypt* (Oxford 2012), 597–612.

Cannata. M, 'God's Seal-Bearer, Lector-Priests and Choachytes, Who's Who at Memphis and Hawara', in G. Widmer and D. Devauchelle (eds.), *Actes du IXe Congrès International des Études Démotiques, Paris, 31 août– 3 septembre 2005, IFAO, BdE* 147 (Cairo 2009), 57–67.

Capart. J, *Travels in Egypt (December 1880 to May 1891, Letters of Charles Edwin Wilbour)* (Brooklyn 1936).

Cartron. G, *L'architecture et les Pratiques funéraires dans L'Égypte romaine*, BAR Publishing 2298.2 (Oxford 2012).

Castiglione. L, 'Dualité du style dans l'art sépulcral égyptien à l'époque romaine', *AAASH* 9 (Budapest 1961).

Casanova. P, 'Qulques legends astronomiques arabes considérées dans leurs rapports avec la mythologie Egyptienne', *BIFAO* 2 (1902), 1–39.

Casson. L, 'Documentary Evidence for Greco-Roman Shipbuilding (P. Flor. I 69)', *BASP* 27 (1990), 15–19.

Castiglione. L, 'Hérodote II 91', in *Mélanges offerts à K. Michalowski* (Warsaw 1966), 41–49.

Cauville. S, *Osiris aux sources du Nil* (Leuven 2021).

Cauville. S, 'Le Pronaos d'Edfou : une voute étoilée', *RdÉ* 62 (2011), 41–55.

Cauville. S, *Le temple de Dendara, Les chapelles osiriennes*, I, *Transcription et traduction, BiEtud* 117, IFAO (Cairo 1997).

Cenival. F, *Les associations religieuses en Égypte d'après les documents démotiques*, *BdE* 46, IFAO (Cairo 1972).

Chassinat. E, 'Le Mammisi d'Edfou', *MIFAO* 16 (Cairo 1910).

Chauveau. M, 'Rive droite, rive gauche, Le nome panopolite au IIe et IIIe siècles de notre ère', in A. Egberts et al. (eds.), *Perspectives on Panopolis, An Egyptian Town from Alexander the Great to the Arab Conquest* (Leiden 2002), 45–54.

Chauveau. M, 'Autour des étiquettes de momies de la Bibliothèque nationale de Vienne', *BIFAO* 92 (1992), 101–09.

Chauveau. M, 'Les étiquettes de momies de la 'Ny Carlsberg Glyptotek' [Ét. Carlsberg 1–17]', *BIFAO* 91 (1991), 38–45.

Chauveau. M, *Les Etiquettes de momies démotiques et bilingues du Musée du Louvre provenant de la nécropole de Triphion*, unpublished PhD thesis, University of Paris III (Paris 1987).

Chauveau. M, 'Les cultes d'Edfa à l'époque romaine', *RdÉ* 37 (1986), 31–43.

Cherpion. N, Corteggiani. J, and Gout. J, 'Le Tombeau de petosiris a Touna El-Gebel, Relevé Photographique', *BiGen* 27, IFAO (Cairo 2007).

Claude. M, 'Du bloc au temple : nouvelles perspectives sur une architrave monumentale du temple de Min d'Akhmîm', *Dialogues d'histoire ancienne, 2022, Chronique des Travaux en Égypte Chronique 2022*, 48 (1), 345-364.

Claude. M, 'À propos de la relecture d'un anthroponyme à la lumière des inscriptions d'une chapelle d'Atoum récemment découverte à Akhmîm', *RdÉ* 68 (2017-2018), 217-221.

Claude. M, 'Nakhtmin, High Priest of Min and Isis in Akhmim and Overseer of Works for Ay, His Career, His Tomb, and Ay's Memorial Temple', *MDAIK* 76/77 (2021/2022), 63–82.

Claude. M, 'Le prêtres d'Akhmim de L'Ancien Empire a L'épogue romaine', *Akhmîm, une tour d'horizon, Égypte, Afrique & Orient* 96 (2020), 27–34.

Claude. M, *La IXe province de Haute-Égypte (Akhmîm), organisation cultuelle et topographie religieuse. De l'Ancien Empire à l'époque romaine*, unpublished PhD thesis, Paul-Valéry Montpellier 3 (Montpellier 2017).

Clerc. G and Leclant. J, *Lexicon Iconographicum Mythologiae Classicae LIMC* VI (Zürich 1981–99).

Clerc. G, 'Isis-Sothis dans le monde Romaine', in M. de Boer and T. Eldridge (eds.), *Hommages à M.J. Vermaseren, recueil d'études offert par les auteurs de la série Études préliminaires aux religions orientales dans l'empire romain à Maarten J. Vermaseren à l'occasion de son soixantième anniversaire le 7 Avril 1978 1, 247–281. Leiden, I, EPRO* 68 (Leiden 1978), 247–81.

Clère. J, 'Le Papyrus de Nesmin, Un Livre des Morts hiéroglyphique de l'époque ptolémaïque', *BiGen* 10 (Cairo 1987).

Colin. F, 'Onomastique et société. Problèmes et methods à la lumière des documents de l'Égypte hellénistique et romaine', in M. Dondin-Payre and M. Th. Raepsatcharlier (eds.), *Noms. Identités culturelles et romanisation sous le haut-empire* (Brussels 2001).

Collection Omar Pacha Sultan 1929 = ANONYMI, *Collection de feu Omar Pacha Sultan, Catalogue déscriptif, I. Art égyptien,* II. *Art musulman* (Paris 1920).

Coquin. R, Martin. M, and Sheila. M, 'Dayr Anba Bakhum', in A. Atiya (ed.), *CoptEnc* II (1991), 730–31.

Corcoran. L, 'They Leave Behind Them Portraits of Their Wealth, Not Themselves': Aspects of Self-Presentation in the Dress of the Deceased in Mummy Portraits and Portrait Mummies from Roman Egypt', in A. J. Batten, K. Olson (eds.), *Dress in Mediterranean Antiquity: Greeks, Romans, Jews, Christians* (London 2021), 137–58.

Corcoran. L, 'Mysticism and the Mummy Portraits', in M. Bierbrier (ed.), *Portraits and Masks, Burial Customs in Roman Egypt* (London 1997), 45–58.

Corcoran. L, 'Portrait Mummies from Roman Egypt, (I–IV Centuries AD), with a Catalog of Portrait Mummies in Egyptian Museums', *SAOC* 56 (Chicago 1995).

Cortopassi. R, 'Tissus de la cité égyptienne d'Akhmîm au musée de l'Homme', *La revue du Louvre et des musées de France* 3 (2001), 29–37.

Cozzolini. C, 'Recent discoveries in Campania', in R. Pirelli (ed.), *Egyptological Studies for Claudio Barrocas, Serie Egittologica 1, Istituto Universitario Orientale* (Naples 1999), 21–36.

Crevatin. F, 'Briciole epigrapfiche', *Rivista degli studi orientali* 85 (2012),155–59.

Crevatin. F, 'Una Nuova stele da Akhmim', *Quaderni Digitali* 3 (2005), 1–2.

Cribiore. R, *Writing, Teachers, and Students in Graeco-Roman Egypt, Am. Stud. Pap.* 36 (Atlanta 1996).

Criscuolo. L, 'A Textual Survey of Greek Inscriptions from Panopolis and The Panopolite', in A. Egberts et al. (ed.), *Perspectives on Panopolis, An Egyptian Town from Alexander the Great to the Arab Conquest* (Leiden 2002), 55–69.

Criscolo. L, 'Nuove riflessioni sul monumento di Ptolemaios Agrios a Panopolis', in G. Paci and L. Gasperini (eds.), *Epigraphai. Miscellanea Epigrafica in onore di Lidio Gasperini 1* (Tivoli 2000), 275–90.

Crum. W, *Catalogue of the Coptic Monuments in the British Museum* (London 1905).

Cumont. F, *L'Egypte des Astrologues* (Brussels 1973).

Cuvigny. H, 'Le Crepuscule d'un Dieu, le Declin du Culte de Pan dans le Desert Oriental', *BIFAO* 97 (1997), 139–47.

Darnell. J and Darnell. C, *The Ancient Egyptian Netherworld Books* (Atlanta 2018).

Darnell. J, *The Enigmatic Netherworld Books of the Solar Osirian Unity, Cryptographic Compositions in the Tombs of Tutankhamun, Ramesses VI and Ramesses IX, OBO* 198 (Göttingen 2004).

Dautant. A et al., 'Creativity and Tradition in the Coffin of Padiamun (Liverpool 53.72): A Case-Study of 25th Dynasty Mortuary Practice', in K. Kóthay (ed.), *Proceedings of the International Conference Burial and Mortuary Practices in Late Period and Graeco-Roman Egypt, July 17 [th]–19th, Museum of Fine Arts-Budapest* (Budapest 2017), 179–95.

De Buck. A, *The Ancient Egyptian Coffin Texts I, Texts of Spells 1–75* (Chicago 1935).

Defossez. M, 'Les laitues de Min', *SAK* 12 (1985), 1–4.

De Meuleanere. H, 'Prophètes et danseurs panopolitains à la Basse Époque', *BIFAO* 88 (1988), 41–49.

De Meuleanere. H, 'Un prêtre d'Akhmim à Abydos', *CdÉ* 44 (1969), 214–21.

De Meulenaere. H, 'Pastophores et Gardiens des Portes', *CdÉ* 31 (1956), 299–302.

Depauw. M, 'Bilingual Greek-Demotic Documentary Papyri and Hellenization in Ptolemaic Egypt', in P. Van Nuffelen (ed.), *Faces of Hellenism, Studies in the History of Eastern Mediterranean, 4th Century B.C–5th Century A.D), StudHell* 48 (Leuven 2009), 113–46.

Depauw. M, 'A 'Second' Amuletic Passport for the Afterlife: P. Sydney Nicholson Museum 346 b', *SAK* 31 (2003), 93–99.

Depauw. M, 'The Late Funerary Material from Akhmim', in A. Egberts et al. (eds.), *Perspectives on Panopolis, An Egyptian Town from Alexander the Great to the Arab Conquest* (Leiden 2002), 71–81.

Derchain. P, *Le papyrus Salt 825 (B.M. 10051), rituel pour la conservation de la vie en Égypte, 2 vols. Mémoires de la classe des lettres, Académie Royale de Belgique, collection in–8, 2e série* 58 (Brussels 1965).

Derchain-Urtel. M, 'Epigrafische Anmerkungen zu den Stelen aus Achmim', in A. Egberts et al. (eds.), *Perspectives on Panopolis, An Egyptian Town from Alexander the Great to the Arab Conquest* (Leiden 2002), 83–93.

Derchain-Urtel, M, *Priester im Tempel. Die Rezeption der Theologie der Tempel von Edfu und Dendera in den Privatdokumenten aus ptolemaïscher Zeit*, GOF 4/19 (Wiesbaden 1989).

Derchain-Urtel. M, 'Thot at Akhmîm', *Hommages a Francois Dumas* (Montpellier 1986), 173–80.

Derda. T, *P. Bodmer I Recto: A Land List from the Upper Panopolite Nome in Upper Egypt (after AD 213/4), JJP* Suppl. 14 (Warsaw 2010).

Devauchelle. D, and Quaegebeur. J, 'Étiquettes de momies démotiques et bilingues de l'IFAO', *BIFAO* 81 suppl. (1981), 359–77.

De Wit. C, *Les inscriptions du temple d'Opet* à Karnak, *BiAeg* 11 (Brussels 1958).

Deyoung. G, 'Astronomy in Ancient Egypt', in H. Selin and S. Xiaochun (eds.), *Astronomy Across Cultures, The History of Non-Western Science* (New York 2000), 475–508.

Dieleman. J, *Priests, Tongues, and Rites, the London-Leiden Magical Manuscripts and Translation in Egyptian Ritual (100–300CE)* (Leiden 2005).

Dils. P, 'Stucco Heads of Crocodiles: A New Aspect of Crocodile Mummification', *Aegyptus* 70 (1990), 73–85.

Donohue. A, 'Pr–nfr', *JEA* 64 (1978), 143–48.

Doxey. D, 'Anubis', in D. Redford (ed.), *The Oxford Encyclopedia of Ancient Egypt I* (Oxford 2001), 97–98.

Doxiadis. E, *The Mysterious Fayum Portraits, Faces from Ancient Egypt* (London 1995).

Drewbear. M, *Le nome hermopolite, Toponymes et sites*, Am. Stud.Pap. 21 (Atlanta 1979).

Dunand. F, and Lichtenberg. R, *Oasis Egyptiennes, Les Iles de Bienheureux* (Arles 2008).

Durand. M, and Saragoza. F, 'Historique de la collection de textiles égyptiens du musée départemental des Antiquités', in *La trame de l'Histoire, Textiles pharaoniques, coptes et islamiques* (Roanne, Paris, 2002–2004), 11–12.

Durand. M, and Saragoza. F, Égypte: *la trame de l'Histoire, Textiles pharaoniques, coptes et islamiques, Sous la direction de Maximilien Durand et. (Catalogue d'exposition, Rouen, Musée des Antiquités, du 19 octobre 2002 au 20 janvier 2003)* (Paris 2002).

Dunand. F, and Lichtenberg. R, *Les mommies et la mort en Égypte* (Paris 1998).

Dunand. F, and Zivie-Coche. C, *Dieux et hommes en Égypte :3000 av. J.-C. 395 apr. J.-C. Anthropologie religieuse* (Paris 1991).

Dunand. F, *Religion populaire en Égypte romaine, Les terres cuites isiaques du Musée du Caire*, EPRO 76 (Leiden 1979).

Dunand. F, 'Une Plainte de Pastophoros', *CdÉ* 44 (1969), 301–12.

Dunbabin. K, *Mosaics of the Greek and Roman World* (Cambridge 1999).

Dunbabin. K, '*Sic erimus cuncit*: The Skeleton in Graeco-Roman Art', *JDAI* 101 (1986), 185–255.

DuQuesen. T, *At the Court of Osiris, Book of the Dead Spell 194, a Rare Egyptian Judgement Spell*, Oxfordshire Communications in Egyptology 4 (London 1994).

DuQuesne. T, 'The Osiris-Re Conjunction with Particular Reference to the Book of the Dead', in B. Backes, I. Munro, and S. Stöhr (eds.), *Totenbuch-Forschungen: gesammelte Beiträge des 2. Internationalen Totenbuch-Symposiums, Bonn, 25. bis 29. September 2005*, SAT 11 (Wiesbaden 2006), 25–30.

Edgar. M, *Graeco-Egyptian Coffins, Masks, and Portraits* (Cairo 1905).

Eingartner. J, *Isis und ihre Dienerinnen in der Kunst der römischen Kaiserzeit* (Leiden 1991).

El-Aguizy. O, 'The Priesthood of the Temple of 'Medinet-Habu' in the Ptolemaic Period Through the Demotic Texts' (published in Arabic), in N. Grimal et al. (eds.), *Hommages a Fayza Haikal*, BdE 138, IFAO (Cairo 2003), 4–15.

El Farag. R et al., 'Recent Archaeological Explorations at Athribis (ḥw.t Rpiit)', *MDAIK* 41 (1985), 1–8.

Elias. J, and Mekis. T, 'Prophet Registers of Min-Hor-Isis at Akhmim', *MDAIK* 76/77 (2020/2021), 83–112.

Elias. J, and Mekis. T, 'The Yellow-on-Black Coffin of the Oracle Scribe Hor in the Swansea Museum', *CdÉ* 91 (fasc. 182) (2016), 227–63.

Elias. J, and Lupton. C, 'Gods at All Hours: Saite Period Coffins of the 'Eleven-Eleven' Type', in R. Sousa (ed.), *Body, Cosmos and Eternity, New Research Trends in the Iconography and Symbolism of Ancient Egyptian Coffins*, Archaeopress (BAR Publishing) 3 (Oxford 2014), 125–34.

Elias. J, 'Akhmim', in R. Bagnal et al. (eds.), *Encyclopaedia of Ancient History* (Oxford 2013), 1–4.

Elias. J, 'Overview of Lininger A06697, an Akhmimic Mummy and Coffin at the University of Nebraska, Lincoln', *AMSC Research* 16–3, LLC Carlisle (Pennsylvania 2016), 1–20.

El-Khadragy. M, 'The shrine of the rock-cut chapel of Djefaihapi I at Asyut', GM 212 (2007), 41–62.

El-Leithy. H, 'Iconography and Function of Stelae and Coffins in Dynasties' 25–26, in J. Taylor and M. Vandenbeusch (eds.), *Ancient Egyptian Coffins, Crafts, Traditions, and Functionality*, British Museum Publications on Egypt and Sudan 4 (Leuven 2018), 61–76.

El-Masry. Y, 'The Ptolemaic Cemetery of Akhmim', *OLA* 194 (Leiden 2010), 173–84.

El-Masry. Y, 'Further Evidence of a Temple of Ramesses II at Akhmim', *MDAIK* 59 (2003), 283–88.

El-Masry. Y, 'Recent Explorations at the Ninth Nome of Upper Egypt', in Z. Hawass (ed.), *Egyptology at the Dawn of the Twenty-First Century, Proceedings of the Eighth International Congress of Egyptologists, Cairo, 2000, I. Archaeology* (Cairo, New York 2003), 331–38.

El-Masry. Y, 'Seven Seasons of Excavations in Akhmim', in C. Eyre (ed.), *Proceedings of the Seventh International Congress of Egyptologists, Cambridge, 3–9 September 1995*, OLA 82 (1998), 759–66.

El-Saddik. W, 'Garten darstellungen in Gräbern', in C. Tietze (ed.), *Ägyptische Gärten* (Weimer 2011), 90–100.

El-Sayed. R, 'Zur Erforschung des Oberägyptischen Athribis, Erste Ergebnisse aus der Projektarbeit in den Jahren 2003 bis 2006', *SOKAR* 13 (2016), 74–77.

El-Sayed. R, and El-Masry. Y, *Athribis I, General Site Survey 2003–2007, Archaeological & Conservation Studies, the Gate of Ptolemy IX, Architecture, and Inscriptions*, IFAO (Cairo 2012).

El-Sayed. R, 'The Temple of Min and Repit at Athribis', *EA* 32 (2008), 20–24.

Emerit. S, 'À propos de l'origine des interdits musicaux dans l'Égypte ancienne', *BIFAO* 102 (2002), 189–210.

Emerit. S, 'Trois Nouvelles harpes decouvertes a Thebes oust, Quel apport pour l'egyptologie?', in G. Rosati and M. Guidotti (eds.), *Proceedings of the XI International Congress of Egyptologists, Florence Egyptian Museum, Florence, 23–30 August 2015* (Oxford 2017), 192–97.

Emmel. S, 'Shenoute of Atripe and the Christian Destruction of Temples in Egypt: Rhetoric and Reality', in J. Hahn, S. Emmel, and U. Gotter (eds.), *From Temple to Church, Destruction and Renewal of Local Cultic Topography in Late Antiquity* (Leiden 2008), 161–99.

Emmel. S, and Römer. C, 'The Library of the White Monastery in Upper Egypt', in H. Froschauer and C. Römer (eds.), *Spätantike Bibliotheken, Leben und Leser in den frühen Klöstern Ägyptens, Nilus. Studien zur Kultur Ägyptens und des Vorderen Oriens* 14 (Wien 2008), 5–14.

Emmel. S, 'Shenute and Panopolis', in A. Egberts et al. (eds.), *Perspectives on Panopolis, An Egyptian Town from Alexander the Great to the Arab Conquest* (Leiden 2002) 99–102.

Emmel. S, 'Ithyphallic Gods and Undetected Ligatures, Pan is not 'Ours', He is Min (Rectification of a Misreading in a Work of Shenute)', *GM* 141 (1994), 43–46.

Empereur. J, and Nenna. M, *Necropolis 1, Tombes B1 B2, B3, B8, EtudAlex* 5, IFAO (Cairo 2001).

Fairbanks. A, *Athenian Lekyothi with Outline Drawing in Glaze Vanish on a White Ground*, (New York 1907).

Fakhry. A, *The Oasis of Egypt, Siwa Oasis, I* (Cairo 1973).

Fakhry. A, *The Egyptian Deserts, Siwa Oasis, Its History and Antiquities* (Cairo 1944).

Fathi. E, *Tell Edfa*, unpublished MA thesis, Higher Institute of Civilizations of the Ancient Near East, Zagazig University (Zagazig 2000).

Faulkner. R, *The Ancient Egyptian Book of the Dead* (New York 1972).

Faulkner. R, 'The Papyrus Bremner-Rhind', *BiAeg* III (Brussels 1933).

Feder. F, 'Ammon und seine Brüder, Eine ägyptische Familie aus Panopolis (Achmim) im 4. Jh. zwischen ägyptisch-hellenistischer Kultur und Christentum', in M. Fitzenreiter (ed.), *Genealogie, Realität und Fiktion von Identität, Workshop am 04. Und 05. Juni 2004 in Berlin*, IBAES 5 (London 2005), 103–08.

Flossmann. M, and Schütze. A, 'Ein Römerzeitliches Pyramidengrab und seine Ausstattung in Tuna El-Gebel, Ein Vorbericht zu den Grabungskampagnen 2007 und 2008', in K. Lembke, M. Minas-Nerpel, and S. Pfeiffer (eds.), *Tradition and Transformation, Egypt under Roman Rule, Proceedings of the International Conference, Hildesheim, Roemer- and Pelizaeus-Museum, 3–6 July 2008* (Leiden 2010), 79–110.

Fluck. C, 'Akhmim as a Source of Textiles', in G. Gabra and H. Takla (eds.), *Christianity and Monasticism in Upper Egypt I, Akhmim and Sohag* (Cairo 2008).

Foat. M, 'Shenuti, Discourse in the Presence of Heraklammon', *OLP* 24 (1993), 113–31.

Forrer. R, 'Antike Bucheinbände von Panopolis-Achmim', *Zeitschrift für Bücherfreunde* 8 (1904–05), 311–15.

Forrer. R, *Über Steinzeit-Hockergräber zu Achmim Naqada etc. in Oberägypten* (*Achmim-Studien 1*) (Strasbourg 1901).

Forrer. R, *Mein Besuch in El-Achmim. Reisebriefe aus Aegypten* (Strasbourg 1895).

Forrer, R, *Die frühchristlichen Alterthümer aus dem Gräberfelde von Achmim-Panopolis (nebst analogen unedirten Funden aus Köln etc.)* (Strasbourg 1893).

Forrer. R, *Die Gräber- und Textilfunde von Achmim-Panopolis* (Strasbourg 1891).

Fowden. G, *The Egyptian Hermes, A Historical Approach to the Late Pagan Mind* (Princeton 1986).

Frankfurter. D, 'Religious Practice and Piety', in C. Riggs (ed.), *The Oxford Handbook of Roman Egypt* (Oxford 2012), 319–36.

Frankfurter. D, 'Iconoclasm and Christianization in Late Antique Egypt: Christian Treatments of Space and Image', in J. Hahn et al. (eds.), *From Temple to Church, Destruction and Renewal of Local Cultic Topography in Late Antiquity*, EPRO 163 (Leiden 2008), 135–59.

Frankfurter. D, 'Illuminating the Cult of Kothos, The Panegryic on Macarius and Local Religion in Fifth-Century Egypt', in J. E. Goehring and J. Timbie (eds.), *The World of Early Egyptian Christianity: Language, Literature, and Social Context* (Washington 2007), 179–82.

Frankfurter. D, ''Things Unbefitting Christians': Violence and Christianization in Fifth-Century Panopolis', *Journal of Early Christian Studies* 8 (2000).

Fankfurter. D, *Religion in Roman Egypt, Assimilation and Resistance* (Princeton 1998).

Fukaya. M, *The Festivals of Opet, the Valley and the New Year, Their Socio-Religious Functions*, BAR Publishing 28 (Oxford 2019).

Garnsey. P, *Social Status and Legal Privilege in the Roman Empire* (Oxford 1970).

Gabolde. M, 'La Fin du Temple d'Akhmim', in M. Chauveau et al. (eds.), *Curiosité d'Égypte, entre quête de soi et découverte de l'autre, de l'Antiquité à l'époque contemporaine* (Geneva 2020), 75–104.

Gabolde. M, 'La fin du temple d'Akhmîm', *Akhmîm, un tour d'horizon*, Égypte, Afrique & Orient 96 (2020), 53–64.

Gabolde. M, 'Le Grand Texte de Nakht Min dans la Chapelle d'Ay à Al-Salamouni', *Akhmîm, une tour d'horizon*, Égypte, *Afrique & Orient* 96, (2020), 3–14.

Gabolde. M, 'Une interprétation alternative de la 'pesée du coeur' du Livre des Morts', Égypte, *Afrique & Orient* 43 (2006), 11–22.

Gabra. S, *Peintures à Fresques et Scènes Peintes À Hermoupolis-Ouest (Touna El Gebel)*, (Cairo 1954).

Gabra. S, *Rapport sur les Fouilles d'Hermoupolis Ouest (Touna El-Gebel) (Avec la collaboration of* Ét. Drioton, P. Perdrizet, and W. Waddell) (Cairo 1941).

Gardiner. A, *Ancient Egyptian Onomastica II* (London 1968).

Gardiner. A, 'Addendum to 'The Baptism of Pharaoh', *JEA* 36 (1950), 3–12.

Gardiner. A, 'The Supposed Athribis of Upper Egypt', *JEA* 31 (1945), 108–11.

Gardiner. A, 'The House of Life', *JEA* 24 (1938), 157–79.

Gascou. J and Worp. K, 'The Panopolitan Village Συνορία', *ZPE* 112 (1996), 163–64.

Gascou. J, 'Les codices documentaires égyptiens', in A. Blanchard (ed.), *Les débuts du codex, Bibliologia* 9 (Turnhout 1989), 71–101.

Gasse. A, *Les Sarcophages de la troisieme periode intermediatere du Museo Gregoriano Egizio*, (Vatican 1996).

Gauthier. H, *Les fêtes du dieu Min*, RAPH 2 (Cairo 1931).

Gauthier. H, *Le personnel du dieu Min*, RAPH 3 (Cairo 1931).

Gauthier. H, 'Nouvelles notes géographiques sur le nome Panopolite', *BIFAO* 10 (1912), 89–130.

Gauthier. H, 'Notes géographiques sur le nome Panopolite', *BIFAO* 4 (1905) 39–101.

Gauthier. H, 'La déesse Triphis', *BIFAO* 3 (1903), 65–181.

Geens. C, *Panopolis, a Nome Capital in Egypt in the Roman and Byzantine Period (ca. AD 200–600)*, PhD thesis (Leuven 2014).

Gemoll. W, *Griechisch Deutsches Schul-und Handwörterbuch* (Wien 1997).

Germer. R, 'Die Bedeutung des Lattichs als Pflanze des Min', *SAK* 8 (1980), 85–87.

Giovetti. P, and Picchi. D, *Egypt, Millenary Splendour, The Leiden Collection in Bologna* (Milan 2016).

Glanville. S, *The Instruction of 'Onchsheshonqy (British Museum Papyrus10508), Catalogue of Demotic Papyri in the British Museum 2* (London 1955).

Gogny-Ghesquier. G, 'Le Breton: un collectionneur passionné', Études Normandes 1 (2005), 54–70.

Gordon-Cumming. F, *Via Cornwall to Egypt* (London 1890).

Gourdiaan. K, 'Ethnical Strategies in Graeco-Roman Egypt', in P. Bilde (ed.), *Ethnicity in Hellenistic Egypt, Studies in Hellenistic Civilization* 3 (Arahus 1992), 76–795.

Goyon, J and Postel. L, *Fastueuse Égypte, catalogue d'exposition du Musée Calvet à Avignon, 25 juin-14 novembre 2011* (Avignon 2011).

Goyon. J, *Rituels funéraires de l'ancienne* égypte, *Litteratures anciennes du Proche-Orient* 4 (Paris 2000).

Goyon. J, 'Le papyrus d'Imouthès, Fils de Psintaês', *MMA* 35.9.21 (New York 1999).

Graefe. E, 'Über die Verabeitung von Pyramidentexten in den späten Tempeln', in U. Verhoeven and E. Graefe (eds.), *Religion und Philiosophe im alten Ägypten, Festgabe für Philippe Derchain*, OLA 39 (Leuven 1991).

Graindorge-Héreil. C, *Le dieu Sokar* à Thèbes au Nouvel Empire, *GOF* 4/28 (Wiesbaden 1994).

Grapow-Erman. H, *Die Bildlichen Ausdrücke des Aegyptischen* (Leipzig 1924).

Graves-Brown. C, *Daemons & Spirits in Ancient Egypt, Lives and Beliefs of the Ancient Egyptians* (Cardiff 2018).

Graves-Brown. C, 'Hathor, Nefer and Daughterhood in the New Kingdom Private Tombs', in H. Navratilova and R. Landgráfová (eds.), *Sex and the Golden Goddess II, The World of the Love Songs* (Prague 2015).

Graves-Brown. C, 'A Gazelle, a Lute Player and Bes, Three Ring Bezels from Amarna', in A. Dodson et al. (eds.), *A Good Scribe and an Exceeding Wise Man, Studies in Honour of W. Tait* (London 2014), 113–26.

Graves-Brown. C, *The Ideology of Flint in Dynastic Egypt'*, unpublished PhD thesis, UCL Institute of Archaeology (London 2011).

Grenier. J, *Anubis Alexandrin et Romain*, EPRO 57 (Leiden 1977).

Griffiths. J, *The Origin of Osiris and his Cult* (Leiden 1980).

Griffiths. J, 'Osiris and the Moon in Iconography', *JEA* 62 (1976).

Griffiths. J, *Apuleius of Madauros: the Isis-Book (Metamorphoses, Book XI)*, EPRO 39 (Leiden 1975).

Griffiths. G, 'Eight Funerary Paintings with Judgement Scenes in Swansea Wellcome Museum', *JEA* 68 (1982), 228–52.

Grimm. G,'Tuna El-Gebel 1913–1973, eine Grabung des deutschen Architekten W. Honroth und neuere Untersuchungen in Hermopolis-West (Tanis Superior)', *MDAIK* 31 (1975), 221–36.

Grimm. G, *Die römischen Mumienmasken aus Ägypten* (Wiesbaden 1974).

Grumach. I, *Untersuchungen zur Lebenslehre des Amenope*, Münchener ägyptologische

Studien 23 (München, Berlin 1972).

Guéraud. O, 'Le monument d'Agrios au Musée de Caire', *ASAE* 39 (1939), 279–303.

Guerber. H, *Greece and Rome: Myths and Legends* (London 1996).

Guéraud. O, 'Notes gréco-romaines', *ASAE* 35 (1935), 1–3.

Guillaumont. A, 'Anachoresis', in A. Attiya (ed.) *CoptEnc* 1 (New York 1991), 119-20.

Guimier-Sorbets. A, Pelle. A, and Seif El-Din. M, *Resurrection in Alexandria, the Painted Greco-Roman Tombs of Kom al-Shuqafa.*, ARCE (Cairo 2017).

Guimier-Sorbets. A, 'Le Jardin pour l'au-delà de bienheureux, Archéologie des jardins, analyse des espaces et méthodes d'approche', *Arceologie et histoire romaine* 26 (2014), 151–60.

Guimier-Sorbets. A, and Seif El-Din. M, 'Life after Death, an Original Form of Bilingual Iconography in the Necropolis of Kawm al-Shuqafa', in A. Hirst and M. Silk (eds.), *Alexandria, Real and Imagined* (Alexandria 2004), 133–41.

Guimier-Sorbets. A, and Seif El-Din. M, 'Les Deux tombes de Perséphone dans la necropole de Kom al-Shuqafa', *BCH* 121/I (1997), 355–410.

Guimier-Sorbets. A, 'L'architecture et décor funéraire, de la Grec en Égypt', in C. Müller and F. Prost (eds.), *Identités et cultures de la monde méditerranéen antique, Mélanges Fr. Croissant* (Paris 2002), 159–80.

Hagedron. D, 'Papyri aus Panopolis in der Kölner Sammlung', in D. Samuel (ed.), *Proceedings of the Twelfth International Congress of Papyrology, Am. Stud.Pap.* 7 (Toronto 1970), 207–11.

Hahn. J, *Gewalt und religiöser Konflikt, Studien zu den Auseinandersetzungen zwischen Christen, Heiden und Juden im Osten des römischen Reiches von Konstantin bis Theodosius II, Klio, Beiträge zur alten Geschichte, Beihefte N.F.* 8 (Berlin 2004).

Hall. H, 'Greek Mummy-Labels in the British Museum', *PSBA* 27 (1905), 13–20, 48–56, 83–91, 115–22, 159–65.

Hallum. B, *Zosimus Arabus, the Reception of Zosimus of Panopolis in the Arabic/ Islamic World*, PhD of Combined Historical Studies, Warburg Institute (London 2010).

Hanna. M, 'Documenting Looting Activities in Post-2011 Egypt', *Countering Illicit Traffic in Cultural Goods. The Global Challenge of Protecting the World's Heritage* (Paris 2015), 47–63.

Hani. J, *La Religion Egyptienne dans La Pensee de Plutarque* (Paris 1976).

Harith. A, Khattab. S, and Al-Mukhtar. M, 'The Effect of Biodeterioration by Bird Droppings on the Degradation of Stone Built', in *Engineering Geology for Society and Territory* 8, Springer (2015), 515–20.

Hawass. Z, 'Recent Discoveries at Akhmim', *KMT* 16/1 (2005), 18–23.

Helck. W, *Die altägyptische Gaue* (Wiesbaden 1974).

Herbin. F, *Le Livre de Parcourir l'éternité*, OLA 58 (Leuven 1994).

Hodjash. S, and Berlev. O, *The Egyptian Reliefs and Stelae in the Pushkin Museum of Fine Arts* (Moscow, Leningrad 1982).

Hoffmann. F, and Quack. J, '*Pastophoros*', in A. Dodson, J. Johnston, and W. Monkhouse (eds.), *A Good Scribe and an Exceedingly Wise Man: Studies in Honour of W. J. Tait*, GHP 21 (London 2014) 127–55.

Hoffmann. F, and Quack. J, *Anthologie der demotischen Literatur* (Berlin 2007).

Hoffmann. F, 'Seilflechter in der Unterwelt', *ZPE* 100 (1994), 339–46.

Hollis. A, 'Some Allusions to Earlier Hellenistic Poetry in Nonnus', *CQ* 26 (1976), 142–50.

Hooft. P, *Pharaonic and Early Medieval Egyptian Textiles* (Leiden 1994).

Holst-Warhaft. G, *Dangerous Voices: Women's Laments and Greek Literature* (Routledge 1992).

Hollios. S, *Five Egyptian Goddesses, Their Possible Beginnings, Actions, and Relationships in the Third Millennium BCE*, Bloomsbury Egyptology (London 2020).

Hornung. E, 'Exploring the Beyond', transl. by D. Roscoe, in E. Hornung and B. Bryan (eds.), *The Quest for Immortality, Treasures of Ancient Egypt* (Washington 2002).

Hornung. E, *The Ancient Egyptian Books of the Afterlife* (Ithaca 1999).

Hornung. E, *Das Buch von den Pforten des Jenseits, nach den Versionen des Neuen Reiches, Teil 2, Übersetzung und Kommentar*, Aegyptiaca Helvetica 8 (Genève 1984).

Hornung. E, *Altägyptische Hollenvorstellung* (Berlin 1968).

Hussein. A, *Le sanctuaire rupestre de Piyris à Ayn al-Labakha*, MIFAO 116, IFAO (Cairo 2000).

Husson. G, 'L'hospitalité dans les papyrus byzantins', in E. Kiessling and H. Rupprecht (eds.), *Akten des XIII. Internationalen Papyrologenkongresses, Marburg/ Lahn, 2.–6. August 1971, Münchener Beiträge zur Papyrusforschung und antiken Rechtsgeschichte* 66 (München 1974), 169–77.

Huxley. M, *The Signs of the Zodiac in the Art of the Near and Middle East Up to and Including the Early Islamic Period* (London 1985).

Ikram. S, *Divine Creatures, Animal Mummies in Ancient Egypt* (Cairo 2005).

Ikram. S and Dodson. A, *The Mummy in Ancient Egypt, Equipping the Dead for Eternity* (London 1998).

Illés. O, 'An Unusual Book of the Dead Manuscript from TT 32', *Acta Antiqua* (2006), 119–27.

Ismail. M, *Wallis Budge, Magic and Mummies in London and Cairo* (London 2021).

Jansen-Winkeln. K, 'Die Hildesheimer Stele der Chereunach', *MDAIK* 53 (1997), 91–100.

Janssen. J, *Das Johannes-Evangelium nach der Paraphrase des Nonnus Panopolitanus. Mit einem ausführlichen kritischen Apparat*, Texte und Untersuchungen 23/4 (Leipzig 1903).

Jécquier. G, *Considérations sur les religions égyptiennes* (Neuchâtel 1946).

Jorgensen. M, *Catalogue of Egypt III, Coffins, Mummy Adornments and Mummies from the Third Intermediate, Late, Ptolemaic, and the Roman Periods (1080 BC-AD 400)* (Copenhagen 2001).

Jorgensen. L, 'Calvi and Non–Calvi, Definition of Various Bands on Roman Textile', in C. Alfaro Giner et al., *Textiles y tintes en la ciudad antiqua, actas del III Symposium international sobre textiles y tintes del Mediterraneo en el mundo antiguo, Naples, 13 al 15 de noviembre, 2008*, CNRS–EFR (Valencia 2011), 75–81.

Joyce. H, *The Decoration of Walls, Ceilings, and Floors in Italy in the Second and Third Centuries A.D*, Ph.D thesis, Archaeologica 17 (Roma 1981).

Junker. H, *Die Onourislegende, Die Stundenwachen in den Osirismysterien, Das Götterdekret über das Abaton* (Wien 1917).

Kahl. J, Sbriglio. A, Del Vesco. P, and Trapani. M, *Asyut the Excavations of the Italian Archaeological Mission (1906–1913)* (Modena 2019), 7–38.

Kákosy. L, 'Probleme der Religion in römerzeitlichen Ägypten', *ANRW* II 18.5 (Berlin, New York 1995), 2894–3049.

Kamal. A, *Tables d'offrandes, Catalogue général des antiquités égyptiennes du Musée du Caire*, IFAO (Cairo 1909).

Kamal. A, *Catalogue général des antiquités égyptiennes du Musée du Caire Nos 22001–208, Stèles ptolémaiques et romaines*, 2 vols. (Cairo 1904–05).

Kanawati. N, 'The Watchers/ Dependents of Min of Akhmim in the Old Kingdom', in Z. Hawass and J. Richards (eds.), *The Archaeology and Art of Ancient Egypt, Essays in Honor of David B. O'Connor*, CASAE 36 II (Cairo 2007).

Kanawati. N, *Sohag in Upper Egypt, A Glorious History*, Prism Archaeological Series 4 (Giza 1990).

Kanawati. N, *The Rock Tombs of El-Hawawish, the Cemetery of Akhmim*, 10 vols. (Sydney 1980–1992).

Kaper. O, 'Bès et Toutou, comparer les dieux égyptiens, Bès, une puissante figure divine (seconde partie) Égypte', *Afrique & Orient* 100 (2020), 27–34.

Kaplan. I, *Grabmalerei und Grabreliefs der Römerzeit, Wedisel Wirkungen Zwishen der Ägyptischen und Griechisch-Alexandrinischen Kunst*, BzÄ 16 (Wien 1999).

Kaplony-Heckel. U, *Ägyptische Handschriften III (Verzeichnis der orientalischen Handschriften in Deutschland)* 19 (Stuttgart 1986).

Karig. J, 'Achmim', *LÄ* I (1975), 54–55.

Kater-Sibbes. G, and Vermasseren. M, *Apis, I, The Monuments of the Hellenistic-Roman Period from Egypt* (Leiden 1975).

Kees. H, 'Der Götterglaube im alten Ägypten, Mitteilungen der vorderasiatischaegyptischen Gesellschaft', *EV* 45 (Leipzig 1941).

Kees. H, 'Die Schlangensteine und Ihre Beziehungen zu den Reich Sceiligtumern', *ZÄS* 57 (1922), 120–36.

Kees. H, 'Das Felsheiligtum des Min bei Achmim', *Rec. Trav* 36 (1914), 51–56.

Keimer. L, 'Die Pflanze des Gottes Min', *ZÄS* 59 (1924), 140–43.

Keller. M, 'Expressing, Communicating, Sharing, and Representing Grief and Sorrow with Organised Sound (Musings in Eight Short Sentences)', in P. Pickering et al. (eds.), *Humanities Research: One Common Thread the Musical World of Lament* 19 (Canberra 2013), 3–14.

Kessler. D, and Patrick. B, *Ägyptens letzte Pyramide: das Grab des Seuta(s) in Tuna El-Gebel*, (München 2008).

Kessler. D, *Die Heiligen Tiere und der König, Teil 1, Beiträge zu Organisation, Kult und Theolgie der Spätzeitlichen Tierfriedhöfe*, ÄAT 16 (Wiesbaden 1989).

Khaksar. S, 'Bès et les musiciens aux jambes arquées du médio–élamite', Bès, une puissante figure divine (*seconde partie*), Égypte, *Afrique & Orient* 100 (2020), 35–46.

Kibry. C, and Monkhouse. W, 'Filling the Gaps at Gebel El-Haridi', *EA* 14 (1999), 10–12.

Kibery. C, and Orell. S, 'From Cave to Monastery, Transformations at the Nome Frontier of Gebel El-Haridi in Upper Egypt', in R. Mathisen and H. Sivan (eds.), *Shifting Frontiers in Late Antiquity, Papers from the First Interdisciplinary Conference on Late Antiquity, the University of Kansas, March 1995* (Aldershot 1996), 201–14.

Kirby. C, and Ikram. S, 'Haridi's High Society', *JEA* 4 (1994), 32–33.

Kirby. C, 'Preliminary Report of the First Season of Work at Gebel El-Haridi 1991–1992', *JEA* 78 (1992), 19–27.

Kischkewitz. H, Gremer. R, and Lünig. M, *Berliner Mummiengeschichten, Ergebnisse eines multidisziplinären Forschungsprojektes Gebundene Ausgabe- 13. Oktober* (Berlin 2009).

Klales. A, *Computed Tomography: Analysis and Reconstruction of Ancient Egyptians Originating from the Akhmim Region of Egypt, A Biocultural Perspective*, Ph.D. Thesis, University of Manitoba (Winnipeg 2014).

Klemm. R, and Klemm. D, *Steine und Steinbrüche im alten Ägypten* (Berlin 1993).

Klos. H, 'Griechische Mumientäfelchen der Papyrussammlung der Österreichische Nationalbibliothek', *CdÉ* 27 (1952), 281–89.

Klotz. D, 'The Lecherous Pseudo-Anubis of Josephus and the 'Tomb of 1897' at Akhmim', in A. Gasse, F. Servajean, and C. Thiers (eds.), *Et in Ægypto et ad Ægyptum, Recueil d'études dédiées à Jean-Claude Grenier*, *CENiM* 5/II (Montpellier 2012), 383–96.

Kockelmann. H, 'Die Götting Nut und der Ba-Vogel', *BIFAO* 118 (2018), 225–31.

Kockelmann. H, *Untersuchungen zu den späten Totenbuch. Handschriften auf Mumienbinden, I: Die Mumienbinden und Leinenamulette des memphitischen Priesters Hor, Band II: Handbuch zu den Mumienbinden und Leinenamuletten*, *SAT* 12 (Wiesbaden 2008).

Kockelmann. H, *Praising the Goddess, A Comparative Annotated Re–Edition of Six Demotic Hymns and Praises Addressed to Isis* (New York 2008).

Koefoed-Petersen. O, *Catalogue des Sarcophages et Cercueils Egyptiens* (Copenhague 1951).

Koemoth. P, *Osiris et les Arbres, Contribution à l'étude des Arbres sacrés de l'Égypte ancienne*, *AegLeod* 3 (Liège 1994).

Koemoth. P, 'Le rite de redresser Osiris', in J. Quaegebeur (ed.), *Ritual and Sacrifice in the Near East, Proceedings of the International Conference Organised by the Katholieke Universiteit Leuven from 17th to 20th of April 1991*, *OLA* 55 (Leuven 1993), 157–74.

Kosciuk. J, 'The Architectural Record, General Description of the Individual Areas of the Town and their Monuments', in R. El-Sayed and Y. El-Masry (eds.), *Athribis I, General Site Survey 2003–2007, Archaeological & Conservation Studies, the Gate of Ptolemy IX, Architecture and Inscriptions*, IFAO (Cairo 2012).

Krebs. F, 'Griechische Mumienetikette aus Ägypten', *ZÄS* 32 (1894), 36–51.

Krupp. K, *In Search of ancient astronomies* (New York 1977).

Kucharek. A, 'Mourning and Lamentation on Coffins', in: J. Taylor and M. Vandenbeusch (eds.), *Ancient Egyptian Coffins, Craft Traditions, and Functionality* (Leuven 2018).

Kucharek. A, *Altägyptische Totenliturgien, Die Klagelieder von Isis und Nephtys in Texten der Griechisch-Römischen Zeit, IV* (Heidelberg 2010).

Kuhlmann. K, *Materialien zur Archaologie und Geschichte des Raumes von Achmim*, *SDAIK* 11 (Mainz 1983).

Kuhlmann. K, 'Archäologische Forschungen im Raum von Achmim', *MDAIK* 38 (1982), 347–54.

Kuhlmann. K, 'Ptolemaios- Queen of Nectanebo I, Notes on the Inscription of an Unknown Princess of the XXXth Dynasty', *MDAIK* 37 (1981), 276–79.

Kuhlmann. K, 'Der Felstemple des Eje bei Achmim', *MDAIK* 35 (1979), 165–88.

Kurth. D, *Materialien zum Toten glauben im römerzeitlichen Ägypten* (Hützel 2010).

Kurth. D, *Der Sarg de Teüris, Eine Studie zum Totenglauben im römerzeitlichen Ägypten*, *AegTrev* 6 (Mainz 1990).

Kurtz. D, and Boardman. J, *Greek Burial Customs*, Cornell University Press (Ithaca 1971).

Lacau. P, 'Textes coptes en dialectes akhmimique et sahidique', *BIFAO* 8 (1993), 43–109.

L'Hôte. N, *Lettres écrites d'Égypte en 1838 et 1839, contenant des observations sur divers monuments Égyptiens nouvellement explores et dessinés* (Paris 1840).

Lappe. G, *Die Vignette zu Spruch 15 auf Totenpapyri des Neuen Reiches* (Basel 2015).

Lapp. G, *the Papyrus of Nu (BM EA 10477), Catalogue of the Books of the Dead in the British Museum, I* (London 1997).

Legrain. G, 'Les carrières antiques de Ptolémais', *MMFAC* 8/3 (1894), 372–79.

Leipoldt. J, *Schenute von Atripe und die Entstehung des national-ägyptischen Christentum, Texte und Untersuchungen zur Geschichte der altchristlichen Literatur 25.1* (Leipzig 1903).

Leipoldt. J, *Sinuthii Archimandritae Vita et Opera Omnia 3*, *CSCO* 42 (Paris 1908).

Leitz. C, 'Ein Hymnus an den Kindgott Kolanthes in Athribis', in S. Lippert, M. Schentuleit, and M. Stadler (eds.), *Sapientia Felicitas. Festschrift für Günter Vittmann zu seinem 64. Geburtstag am 29. Februar 2016*, CENiM 14 (Montpellier 2016), 325–41.

Leitz. C et al., 'Die Inschriften des Torbaus Ptolemaios IX', in R. El-Sayed and Y. El-Masry (eds.), *Athribis I, General Site Survey 2003–2007, Archaeologial and Conservation Studies. The Gate of Ptolemy IX. Architecture and Inscriptions*, IFAO (Cairo 2012).

Leitz. C, Mendel. D, and El-Masri. Y, *Athribis 2, Der Tempel Ptolemaios XII, die Inschriften und Reliefs der Opfersäle, des Umgangs und der Sanktuarraüme* (Cairo 2010).

Leitz. C, 'Le temple de Ptolemée XII à Athribis- un temple pour Min(-Re) ou pour Repit', *BSFE* 172 (2008), 32–52.

Leitz. C, 'Le temple d'Athribis en Haute Égypte', *Annuaire de l'Ecole pratiqu des hautes études, Section des sciences religieuses* 115 (2006–07), 85–91.

Leitz. C, 'Die Sternbilder auf dem rechteckigen und runden Tierkreis von Dendara', *SAK* 34 (2006), 28–89.

Leitz. C, *Lexikon der ägyptischen Götter und Götterbezeichnungen, II* (Leuven 2002).

Lembke. K, 'Neferu- aesthesis- pulchritude, zum Wandel des Schönheitsbegriffs im ptolmemäisch-römischen Ägypten am Beispiel der Petosiris-Nekropole von Tuna El-Gebel', in M. Flossmann-Schütze, F. Hoffmann, and A.Schütze (eds.), *Tuna El-Gebel, Eine ferne Welt, Tagungsband zur Konferenz der Graduate School "Distant Worlds" vom 16. Bis 19.1.2014 in München, Tuna el-Gebel 8* (2020), 131–44.

Lembke. K, "A Beautiful Burial' at Tuna El-Gebel, Burial Customs and Commemorative Culture from the Ptolemies to the Romans', in M. Nenna, S. Huber, and W. Van Andriga (eds.), *Constituer la tombe, honorer les défunts en Mediterranée antique, EtudAlex46*, Alexandria: CEAlex (Alexandria 2018), 141–62.

Lembke. K, 'Terenuthis and Elsewhere, the Archaeology of Eating, Drinking and Dying in Ptolemaic and Roman Egypt', in D. Robinson and A. Wilson (eds.), *Alexandria and the North–Western Delta, Joint Conference Proceedings of Alexandria, City and Harbour (Oxford 2004) and the Trade and Topography of Egypt's North-West Delta (Berlin 2006), Oxford Centre for Maritime Archaeology Monographs* (Oxford 2010), 259–67.

Lembke. K, 'The Petosiris-Necropolis of Tuna El-Gebel', in K. Lembke, M. Minas-Nerpel and S. Pfeiffer (eds.), *Tradition and Transformation in Egypt Under Roman Rule, Proceedings of the International Conference, Hildesheim, Roemer- and Pelizaeus-Museum, 3–6 July 2008* (Leiden 2010), 255–63.

Lepsius. R, *Denkmäler aus Aegypten und Aethiopien, Text II: Mittelaegyptien mit dem Faijum* (Leipzig 1904).

Lepsius. R, *Briefe aus Aegypten, Aethiopien und der Halbinsel des Sinai: geschrieben in den Jahren 1842–1845 während der auf Befehl Sr. Maj. des Königs Friedrich Wilhelm IV von Preußen ausgeführten wissenschaftlichen Expedition-Berlin* (Berlin 1852).

Lesko. B, *The Great Goddess of Egypt* (Norman 1999).

Lesquier. J, *L'armée romaine d'Égypte d'Auguste à Dioclétien*, MIFAO 41 (Cairo 1918).

Lewis. S, *Early Coptic Textiles* (Stanford 1969).

Lewuillon-Blume. M, 'P. Giessen inv. 263', *CdÉ* 52 (1978), 118–22.

Lexa. F, *Papyrus Insinger, Les enseignements d'un scribe égyptien du premier siècle après J.C., I–II* (Paris 1926).

Lichtheim. M, *Ancient Egyptian Literature, A Book of Readings, The Late Period, III* (Berkeley, Los Angeles, London 1980).

Lichtheim. M, 'Situla n. 11395 and Some Remarks on Egyptian Situlae', *JNES* 6 (1947), 169–79.

Lichtheim. M, 'The Songs of the Harpers', *JNES* 4 (1945), 178–212.

Liddell. H, and Scott. R, *Greek-English Lexicon* (Oxford 1925).

Liebeschuetz. W, 'The Use of Pagan Mythology in the Christian Empire with Particular Reference to the Dionysiaca of Nonnus', in P. Allen and E. Jeefreys (eds.), *The Sixth Century, End or Beginning?, Byzantina Australiensia* 10 (Brisbane 1996), 75–91.

Lindsay. J, *The Origins of Alchemy in Graeco–Roman Egypt* (New York 1970).

Lindsay. J, *Men and Gods on the Roman Nile* (London 1968).

Ling. R, *Roman Painting* (Cambridge 1991).

Lippert. S, 'Ostraca, Graffiti, and Dipinti from Athribis in Upper Egypt', in M. Depauw and Y. Broux (eds.), *Acts of the 10th International Conference for Demotic Studies, Leuven, 26–30 August 2008*, OLA 23 (Leuven 2014), 145–53.

Liptay. É, 'Between Heaven and Earth, II/1, the Iconography of a 21st Dynasty Funerary Papyrus (Inv. No. 51.2547)', *BMH* 104 (2006), 35–61, 161–84.

Liptay. É, 'The Wooden Inner Coffin of Takhenemet in the Czartoryski Museum', *Studies in Ancient Art and Civilization* 13 (Krakow 2009), 83–117.

Litinas. N, 'Hierakapollon, the Title of Panos Polis and the Names in Apollon', *AncSoc* 37 (2007), 97–106.

Lloyd. A, 'Herodotus on Egyptian Buildings, a Test Case,' in A. Powell (ed.), *The Greek World* (London, New York 1995).

Lloyd. A, *Herodotus Book II, Commentary 1–98*, EPRO 43 (Leiden 1976), 367–70.

Lloyd, A, 'Perseus and Chemmis (Herodotus, II, 91)', *JHS* 89 (1969), 79–86.

Lucarelli. R, 'Daemons in the Book of the Dead', in B. Backes, I. Munro, and S. Stöhr (eds.), *Totenbuch-Forschungen. Gesammelte Beiträge des 2. Internationalen Totenbuch-Symposiums. Bonn, 25. bis 29 September 2005*, SAT 11 (Wiesbaden 2006), 203–12.

Lucarelli. R, 'Death, Gods, Daemons of the Book of the Dead', in F. Scalf (ed.), *Book of the Dead, Becoming God in Ancient Egypt,* Oriental Institut Museum 39 (Chicago 2017), 127–38.

Lucarelli. R, 'The Inhabitants of the Fourteenth Hill of Spell 149 of the Book of the Dead', in L. Morenz and A. El Hawary (eds.), *Weitergabe, Festschrift für Ägyptologin Ursula Rössler Köhler zum 65. Geburtstag, GOF IV, Reihe, Ägypten* 53 (Wiesbaden 2015), 275–91.

Lucarelli. R, 'The So-called Vignette of Spell 182 of the Book of the Dead', in R. Lucarelli, M. Müller-Roth, and A. Wüthrich (eds.), *Herausgehen am Tage, Gesammelte Schriften zum altägyptischen Totenbuch*, SAT 17 (Wiesbaden 2012), 79–91.

Lucarelli. R, 'Demonology During the Late Pharaonic and Greco-Roman Periods in Egypt', *JANER* 11/2 (2011), 109–25.

Lucarelli. R, 'The Guardian-Demons of the Book of the Dead', *BMSAES* 15 (2010), 85–102.

Luckaszewicz. A, *Les édifices publics dans les villes de l'Égypte romaine, Problèmes administratifs et financiers* (Warsaw 1986).

Lüddeckens. E, Thissen. H, and Brunsch. W, *Demotisches Namenbuch* (Wiesbaden 1993).

Lurker. M, *The Gods and Symbols of Ancient Egypt, An Illustrated Dictionary* (London 1980).

Lüscher. B, *Die Totenbuch Handschrift pBerlin 10477 aus Achmim, mit Photographien des verwandten pHildesheim 5248, HAT* 6 (Wiesbaden 2000).

Majcherek. G, "Crumbs from the Table', Archaeological Remains of Hellenistic Alexandria', in C. Zerefos and M. Vardinoyannis (eds.), *Hellenistic Alexandria: Celebrating 24 Centuries: Papers Presented at the Conference Held on December 13–15 2017 at the Acropolis Museum, Athens*, Archaeopress Archaeology (BAR Publishing) (Oxford 2018), 71–85.

Malaise. M, 'Le persea, l'olivier, le lierre et la palme dans la religion égyptienne tardive', in T. Duquesne (ed.), *Hermes Aegyptiacus, Egyptological Studies for B.H. Stricker on His 85th Birthday, DE* special no. 2 (Oxford 1996), 131–44.

Malinine. M, 'Taxes funéraires égyptiennes à l'époque Gréco-Romaine', in M. Mariette (ed.), *BdE* 32, IFAO (Cairo 1961), 137–68.

Manassa. C, *The Late Egyptian Underworld, Sarcophagi and Related Texts from the Nectanebid Period. Part 1: Sarcophagi and Texts, ÄAT* 72 (Wiesbaden 2007), 114–17.

Manassa. C, 'The Judgement Hall of Osiris in the Book of Gates', *RdE* 57 (2006), 109–42.

Manniche. L, *Music and Musicians in Ancient Egypt* (London 1991(.

Manniche. L, *Sexual Life in Ancient Egypt* (New York 1987).

Mannische. L, *Ancient Egyptian Musical Instruments*, MÄS 34 (Berlin 1975).

Marlar. M, 'Sex as a Votive Offering at the Osiris Temple,' in Z. Hawaas and J. Richards (eds), *The Archaeology and Art of Ancient Egypt, Essays in Honor of David O'Connor, Annales du Service des Antiquites de L'Egypte, Cahier* 36.II (Cairo 2007), 111–20.

Martin. A, and Primavesi. O, *L'Empédocle de Strasbourg (P. Strasb. gr. inv. 1665–1666)*, (Berlin, Strasbourg 1999).

Martin. C, and Kim. R, 'Put My Funerary Papyrus in My Mummy, Please', *JEA* 92 (2006), 270–74.

Martin. G, "Erotic' Figurines, The Cairo Museum Material', *GM* 96 (1987), 71–84.

Martin. V, 'Relevé topographique des immeubles d'une métropole', *Recherches de Papyrologie* 2 (1962), 37–73.

Martini. W, *Sachwörterbuch der Klassischen Archäologie* (Stuttgart 2003).

Massiera. M, *Les divinités ophidiennes Nâou, Néhebkaou et le fonctionnement des kaou d'après les premiers corpus funéraires de l'Égypte ancienne*, Thèse de Doctorat Montpellier 3, (Montpellier 2013).

Maspero. G, *Etudes de mythologie et d'archéologie égyptiennes, BE* 1 (Paris 1893), 214–15.

Maspero. G, 'Rapport à l'institut Égyptien sur les fouilles et travaux exécutés en Égypt, pendant l'hiver de 1885–1886', *BIE* 7 (Cairo 1887), 210–23.

Maspero. G, Sur Les fouilles exécutés en Égypte de 1881 à 1885, *BIE* 6 (Cairo 1886b), 84–90.

Maspero. G, 'Trois années de fouilles', *BIE* 5 (Paris 1886a), 69–91.

Maxfield. V, 'Stone Quarrying in the Eastern Desert with Particular Reference to Mons Claudianus and Mons Porphyrites', in J. Mattinglyand and J. Salmon (eds.), *Economies Beyond Agriculture in the Classical World, Leicester-Nottingham Studies in Ancient Society* 9 (London, New York 2001), 143–70.

Mayassis. S, *Le Livre des Morts de L'Egypte Ancienne est un Livre d'initiation* (Athens 1955).

Meyer. B, "Gymnase' et 'Thermes' dans l'Égypte romaine et byzantine', in B. Kramer, W. Luppe, H. Maehler, and G. Poethke (eds.), *Akten des 21. Internationalen Papyrologenkongresses, Berlin, 13.–19.8. 1995, AfP* 3.II (Leipzig 1997), 691–95.

Mcging. B, 'Lease of a Linen-weaving Workshop in Panopolis', *ZPE* 82 (1990), 115–21.

McNally. S, and Schrunk. I, *Excavations in Akhmim, Egypt, Continuity and Change in City Life from Late Antiquity to the Present, First Report*, BAR Publishing 590 (Oxford 1993).

Meinardus. O, 'Bir al-'Ain, eine volkstümliche Kultstätte bei Akhmim', *OstkStud* 34 (1985), 183–86.

Mekis. T, 'Données nouvelles sur les hypocéphales', *Kút* 7/2 (2008), 38–40.

Merkelbach. R, *Isis Regina-Zeus Serapis, Die Griechisch-Ägyptische Religion nach den Quellen Dargestellt* (Stuttgart, Leipzig 2001), 82–94.

Merkelbach. R, 'Der Eid der Isismysten', *ZPE* 1 (1967), 55–73.

Mertens. M, 'Alchemy, Hermetism and Gnosticism at Panopolis c. 300 A.D: The Evidence of Zosimus', in A. Egberts et al. (eds.), *Perspectives on Panopolis* (Leiden 2002),165–75.

Mertens. M, *Les alchimistes grecs. Tome IV, 1re partie, Zosime de Panopolis. Mémoires authentiques*, Collection des Universités de France (Paris 1995).

Meulenaere. H, *Compte-rendu sur Mosher, M. Jr.- The Papyrus of Hor*, Bibliotheca Orientalis 59, no. 5–6 (London 2002), 491–93.

Meulenaere. H, 'Le clergé abydénien d'Osiris à la Basse Époque', *OLP* 6/7 (1975/1976), 133–51.

Meurice. C, *Jean Clédat en Égypte et en Nubie (1900–1914)*, BdE 158, IFAO (Cairo 2014).

Middleton-Jones. H, *The Akhmim Project, the Analytical Catalogue of Material from the Late Period Cemeteries of Akhmim in Upper Egypt*, MPHIL thesis, Swansea University (Swansea 1997).

Milde. H, *The Vignettes in the Book of the Dead of Neferrenpet*, EU 7 (Leiden 1991).

Millard. D, 'St. Christopher and the Lunar Disc of Anubis', *JEA* 73 (1987), 237–38.

Milne. J, 'Greek Inscriptions from Egypt', *JHS* 21 (1901), 286–90.

Milne. J, *Greek Inscriptions, Catalogue Général des Antiquités Égyptiennes du Musée de Caire, Nos 9201–400, 26001–123, 33001–37* (Oxford 1905).

Minas-Nerpel. M, 'Egyptian Temples', in C. Riggs (ed.), *The Oxford Handbook of Roman Egypt* (Oxford 2012), 362–80.

Minas-Nerpel. M, *Der Gott Chepri, untersuchungen zu Schriftzeugnissen und ikonographischen Quellen vom Alten Reich bis in griechisch-römische Zeit*, OLA 154 (Leuven 2006).

Michalowski. K, *The Art of Ancient Egypt* (London 1969).

Mielsch. H, *Römische Wandmalerei* (Darmstadt 2001).

Möller. G, *Mumienschilder, Demotische Texte aus den Königlichen Museen zu Berlin I* (Leipzig 1913).

Montserrat. D, 'Death and Funerals in the Roman Fayum', in M. Bierbrier (ed.), *Portraits and Masks, Burial Customs in Roman Egypt*, British Museum Press (London 1997), 33–44.

Montserrat. D, *Sex and Society in Graeco-Roman Egypt* (London 1996).

Montserrat. D, 'The Representation of Young Males in Fayum Portraits', *JEA* 79 (1993), 215–25.

Montserrat. D, 'The Kline of Anubis', *JEA* 78 (1992), 301–07.

Morenz. S, 'Anubis mit dem Schlüssel', in E. Blumenthal, S. Hermann, and A. Onasch (eds.), *Religion und Geschichte des alten Ägypten* (Köln 1975), 510–20.

Morkot. R, 'The Darb El-Arbain, the Kharga Oasis and its Forts', in D. Bailey (ed.), *Archaeological Research in Roman Egypt. The Proceedings of the Seventeenth Classical Colloquium of the Department of Greek and Roman Antiquities, British Museum*, JRA. Supplementary Series 19 (Ann Arbor 1996), 82–94.

Morris. I, *Death-Ritual and Social Structure in Classical Antiquity* (Cambridge 1992).

Mosher. M, *The Papyrus of Hor (BM EA 10479), with Papyrus McGregor, Late Period Tradition at Akhmim, Catalogue of the Books of the Dead in the British Museum II*, The British Museum Press (London 2001).

Moussa. A, 'A Seated Statue of nHb-kA.w from Heliopolis', in Hommage J. Leclant, BdE 106/1 (1994), 479-483.

Munro. I, 'The Significance of the Book of the Dead Vignettes', in F. Scalf (ed.), *Book of the Dead: Becoming God in Ancient Egypt*, Oriental Institut Museum 39 (Chicago 2017), 49–66.

Munro. P, *Die spätägyptischen Totenstelen*, 2 vols. ÄF 25 (Glückstadt 1973).

Nagel. S, *Isis im Römischen Reich, Teil I, Die Göttin im griechisch-römischen Ägypten*, Philippika 109 (Wiesbaden 2019).

Naville. E, *The Temple of Deir El-Bahari II* (London 1896).

Navrátilová. H, and Landgráfová. R, *Sex and the Golden Goddess II, World of the Love Songs* (Prague 2015).

Neugebauer. O, and Parker. R, *Nagᶜ Hammad A, B, Egyptian Astronomical Texts III, Decans, Planets, Constellations and Zodiacs* (London 1969).

Newberry. P, 'The Inscribed Tombs of Akhmim', *AAA* 4 (Liverpool 1912), 99–120.

Norris. P, 'Lettuce as an Offering to Mnw (MIN)', in A. Maravelia and N. Guilhou (eds.), *Environment and Religion in Ancient and Coptic Egypt, Sensing the Cosmos Through the Eyes of the Divine*, Archaeopress (BAR Publishing) 30 (Oxford 2020) 317–29.

Nifosi. A, *Becoming a Woman and Mother in Graeco-Roman Egypt, Women's Bodies, Society and Domestic Space* (Routledge 2019).

Niwinski. A, *Sarcofagi della XXI dinastia (CGT 10101–10122), Catalogo del Museo Egizio di Torino* (Turin 2009).

Niwiński. A, 'The Solar-Osirian Unity as a Principle of the Theology of the "State of Amun" in Thebes in the 21st Dynasty', *JEOL* 30 (1989), 89–106.

Niwiński. A, 'Review: Mosher Jr., Malcolm 2001, The Papyrus of Hor (BM EA 10479), with Papyrus McGregor: Late Period Tradition at Akhmim (Catalogue of the Books of the Dead in the British Museum 2, British Museum Press', *JEA* 90 (reviews supplement) (London), 49–50.

Nordh. K, *Aspects of Ancient Egyptian Curses and Blessings, Conceptual Background and Transmission, Uppsala studies in Mediterranean and Near Eastern Civilization* 26 (Stockholm 1996).

Nuzzolo. C, 'Tradition and Transformation: Retracing Ptah-Sokar-Osiris Figures from Akhmim in Museums and Private Collections', in T. Gillen (ed.), *(Re)productive Traditions in Ancient Egypt: Proceedings of the Conference Held at the University of Liège, 6th–8th February 2013* (Liège 2017), 445–74.

Nuzzolo. C, 'Two Ptah-Sokar-Osiris Figures from Akhmim in the Egyptian Collection of the Museum of Fine Arts', *BMH* 119 (Budapest 2014), 13–41.

Ockinga. B, *A Tomb from the Reign of Tutankhamun at Akhmim*, *ACER* 10 (Warminster 1997).

Ockinga. B, 'The Tomb of Sennedjem at Awllad Azzaz (Sohag)', *BACE* 2 (1991), 81–89.

Olette-Pelletier, J, « Le dieu Min "protecteur de la lune" : aspects et rôles lunaires du dieu de la fertilité », *ÉAO - Supplément au numéro* 72 (n° 2) (2014), 9–16.

Omar. N, 'The God Nehebkau in Heliopolis', *Abgadiyat* 7 (2012), 32–38.

Omran, W, 'The Deceased in El-Salamuni Necropolis: Following Osiris in Classical Gesture', *MDAIK* 79 (forthcoming, 2023).

Omran, W, 'Berg der Toten-Die Felsgräber von El-Salamuni', *SOKAR* 41 (forthcoming, 2023).

Omran. W, Okasha. A, and Abu-Gebel. A, 'Resurrection in Panopolis; Graeco-Roman Period at the El-Salamuni Necropolis', *EA* 59 (2021), 16–19.

Omran. W, 'The Deceased is Breathing', *GM* 263, no. 2 (2021), 173–80.

Omran. W, 'Tithoes in El-Salamuni Necropolis', *GM* 261 (2020), 157–64.

Omran. W, 'Virtuous or Wicked: New Occurrences and Perspectives on the Black Silhouette in Graeco-Roman Egypt', *JARCE* 56 (2020), 143–67.

Omran. W, 'Petosiris in his Tomb at Dachla, Venerating the Deceased in Roman Egypt', *Journal of Association of Arab Universities for Tourism and Hospitality*, 19, no.3, Suez Canal University (2020), 97–112.

Omran. W, 'Transporting the Deceased by the Wheeled Cart in the Greco–Roman Tombs', *Journal of the Association of Arab Universities for Tourism and Hospitality*, 17, no. 2, Suez Canal University (2019), 40–42.

Omran. W, 'The Egyptian and the Hellenistic Characteristics of the Asklepieion', *Journal of Faculty of Tourism and Hotels*, 8, no. 2, Fayoum University (2014), 70–112.

Osing. J, *Denkmäler der Oase Dachla, aus dem Nachlass von A. Fakhry*, *AV* 28 (Mainz 1982).

Otto. E, 'Beiträge zur Geschichte in Agypten', *UGÄA* 13 (Leipzig 1938), 436–52.

Pestman. P, 'Der demotische Text der Mumientäfelchen aus Amsterdam', *OMRO* 46 (1965), 44–51.

Pagenstecher. R, *Nekropolis, Untersuchungen über Gesalt und Entwicklung der alexanderischen Grabenlagen und ihrer Malerien* (Leipzig 1919).

Padró. J, 'Recent Archaeological Work', in A. Bowman et al. (eds.), *Oxyrhynchus, A City and Its Texts, Graeco-Roman Memoirs* 93, EES (London 2007), 129–38.

Papaconstantinou. A, *Le culte des saints en égypte des byzantins aux abbassides, L'apport des inscriptions et des papyrus grecs et coptes* (Paris 2001).

Parker. R, *A Saite Oracle Papyrus from Thebes in the Brooklyn Museum, Papyrus Brooklyn 47.218.3*, *BEStud* IV (Brown 1962).

Parkinson. R, *The Tale of the Eloquent Peasant* (Oxford 1991).

Parlasca. K, and Seemann. H, *Augenblicke: Mumienporträtsund ägyptische Grabkunst aus römischer Zeit* (Munich 1999).

Parlasca. K, 'Bemerkungen zum ägyptischen Gräberwesen der griechisch-römischen Zeit', in Ägypten, Dauer und Wandel, Symposium anlässlich des *75 jährigen Bestehens des DAI Kairo am 10. Und 11. Oktober 1982*, *SDAIK* 18 (Mainz 1985), 97–103.

Parlasca. K, *Repertorio d'arte dell'Egitto greco-romano BI, BII, B III* (Rome 1969, 1977, 1980).

Parlasca. K, 'Osiris und Osirisglaube in der Kaiserzeit', in D. Françoise and P. Lévêque (eds.), *Les syncrétismes dans les religions grecque et romaine, Colloque de Strasbourg, 9–11 juin 1971* (Paris 1973), 95–102.

Parlasca. K, *Mumienporträts und verwandte Denkmäler* (Wiesbaden 1966).

Partie. S, 'Le Papyrus de Neferoubenef (Louvre III 93)', *BDE* 43, IFAO (Cairo 1968).

Pelletier. A, 'Note sur les mots ΔΙΑΤΡΙΒΗ, ΊΕΡΟΝ, ΔΙΑΘΗΣΙΣ dans P. Gen. inv. 108', *RechPap* 4 (1967), 175–86.

Pergo. E, 'Between Religion and Consumption: Culinary and Drinking Equipment in Venetic Ritual Practice (ca. 725 BCE-CE 25)', in A. Smith and M. Bergeron (eds.), *Pallas, Revue d'Etudes Antiques, the Gods of Small Things* (Toulouse 2011), 235–68.

Pernigotti. S, 'La Magia copta, I testi', *ANRW* II.18.5 (1995), 3685–730.

Pestman. P, *The Archive of the Theban Choachytes (Second Century BC)* (Leuven 1993).

Pestman. P, *Recueil des textes démotiques et bilingues I* (Leiden 1977).

Pestman. P, 'Two Mummy-Labels in the Museum of Antiquities at Leiden', *OMRO* 44 (1963) 24–26.

Petrie. F, *Seventy Years in Archaeology* (New York 1932).

Petrie. F, *Athribis*, BRSA 14 (London 1908).

Piankoff. A, 'The Osireion of Seti I at Abydos during the Graeco-Roman Period and the Christian Occupation', *BSAC* 15 (1958–60), 125–49.

Piankoff. A, and Rambova. N, *Mythological Papyri* (New York 1957).

Piankoff. A, 'Le Livre des Quererts', *BIFAO* 42 (1944), 1–62.

Piccione. P, 'The Gaming Episode in the Tale of Setne, Khamwas as a Religious Metaphor', in D. Silverman. (ed.), *For His Ka, Essays Offered in Memory of Klaus Baer*, SAOC 55 (Chicago 1994), 197–204.

Pillinger. R, 'Die Textilkunst der frühen Christen gezeigt am Beispiel der Funde aus Ägypten', in H. Harrauer and R. Pintaudi (eds.), *Gedenkschrift Ulrike Horak (P. Horak) 2 (Pap. Flor. XXXIV)* (Florence 2004), 429–35.

E. Pfuhl, *Masterpieces of Greek Drawing and Paintings* (New York 1979).

Pococke. R, *A Description of the East and Other Countries, I, Observations on Egypt* (London 1743).

Pool. R, *Catalogue of Coins of Alexandria and Its Nomes* (London 1892).

Preisendemz. K, *Papyri Graecae Magicae, Die Griechischen Zauber Papyri, I–II* (Leipzig 1928).

Pries. A, *Die Stundenwachen im Osiriskult, eine Studie zur Tradition und späten Rezeption von Ritualen im Alten Ägypten*, 2 vols., SSR 2 (Wiesbaden 2011).

Priskin.G, 'The Astral Myth of Osiris: The Decans of Taurus and Libra', *ENiM* 9 (2016), 79–111.

Priskin. G, 'Coffin Texts Spell 155 On the Moon', *BEJ* 1 (2013), 25–63.

Quack. J, ' Neue Fragmente der einleitung Erzählung der Lehre des Chascheschonqi', *Enchoria* 36 (2018/2019), 129–43.

Quack. J, 'Egypt as an Astronomical-Astrological Centre Between Mesopotamia, Greece, and India', in D. Brown (ed.), *The Interactions of Ancient Astral Science* (Bremen 2018), 69–123.

Quack. J, 'The So-called Pantheos on Polimorphic Deities in Late Egyptian Religion', *Egyptus et Pannonia* 3 (2006) 175–86.

Quaegebeur. J, and Cherpion. N, *La Naine et le Bouquetin, Ou L'Énigme de la Barque en Albâtre de Toutankhamon* (Leuven 1999).

Quaegebeur. J, 'P. Brux Dem. E. 8258 une lettre de recommandation pour l'au-delà', in S. Israelit-Groll (ed.), *Studies in Egyptology Presented to Miriam Lichtheim.II* (Jerusalem 1990), 776–95.

Quaegebeur. J, 'Thoth-Thot-Hermès, le dieu le plus grand', *Hommages à François Daumas II* (Montpellier 1986), 525–44.

Quaegebeur. J, 'Mummy Labels, An Orientation', *P.L. Bat.* 19 (1978), 232–359.

Quaegebeur. J, *Le dieu égyptien Shaï dans la religion et l'onomastique*, OLA 2 (Leuven 1975).

Quaegebeur. J, 'A propos de Teilouteilou, nom magique et de Têroutêrou, nom de femme', *Enchoria* 4 (1974), 19–29.

Quirke. S, 'Judgement of the Dead', in D. Redford (ed.), *The Oxford Encyclopedia of Ancient Egypt II* (Oxford 2001).

Quirke. S, *Going Out in Daylight, Prt m ḥrw, the Ancient Egyptian Book of the Dead, Translation, Sources, Meaning*, GHP Egyptology 20 (London 2013).

Quirke. S, *The Cult of Ra, Sun-Worship in Ancient Egypt* (London 2001).

Ragheb. A, 'Situla: Pelizaeus-Museum Inv. no. 4592, Roemer- und Pelizaeus-Museum, Hildesheim', *GM* 219 (2008), 73–78.

Ramadan. W, 'Was There a Chapel of Nehebkaw in Heliopolis?', *GM* 110 (1989) 55-63.

Reddè. M, 'Sites militaires romains de l'Oasis de Kharga', *BIFAO* 99 (1999), 377–96.

Refai. H, 'Hathor als Gleichzeitig West- und Baumgöttin', in E. Czerny et al. (eds.), *Timelines, Studies in Honour of Manfred Bietak*, OLA 149, no. I (Leuven 2006), 287–90.

Refai. H, 'Die Göttin des Westens in den Thebanischen Gräbern der Neun Reiches, Darstellung, Bedeutung und Funktion', *ADAIK* 12 (1996), 93–97.

Régen. I, 'Ombres, Une iconographie singulière du mort sur des « linceuls » d'époque romaine provenant de Saqqâra,' in A. Gasse, F. Servajean, and C. Thiers (eds.), *Et in Ægypto et ad Ægyptum, Recueil d'études dédiées à Jean-Claude Grenier*, CENiM 5 (Montpellier 2012), 603–47.

Rehm. R, *Marriage to Death, the Conflation of Wedding and Funeral Rituals in Greek Tragedy* (Princeton 1994).

Reisner. G, 'The Tomb of Hepzefa, Nomarch of Siût', *JEA* 5/2 (1918), 79–98.

Rémondon. R, 'L'Égypte et la suprême résistance au christianisme (Ve-VIIe siècles)', *BIFAO* 51 (1955), 63–78.

Renner-Volbach. D, *Diesogenannten Koptischen Textilien im Museum Andreasstift der Stadt* (Wiesbaden 2002).

Reynolds. J, *Discourses on Art* (New Haven, London 1997).

Riggs. C, *Unwrapping Ancient Egypt* (London, New York 2014).

Riggs. C, *The Beautiful Burial in Roman Egypt, Art, Identity and Funerary Religion* (Oxford 2005).

Riggs. C, and Stadler. M, 'A Roman Shroud and its Demotic Inscriptions in the Museum of Fine Arts', *JARCE* 40 (2003), 69–87.

Riggs. C, 'Facing the Dead: Recent Research on the Funerary Art of Ptolemaic and Roman Egypt', *AJA* 106 (2002), 85–101.

Riggs. C, 'Roman Period Mummy Masks from Deir El-Bahri', *JEA* 86 (2000), 121–44.

Riggs. C, *Art and Identity in the Egyptian Funerary Tradition, c. 100 BC to AD 300*, unpublished PhD thesis (Oxford 2001).

Ritner. R, *The Mechanics of Ancient Egyptian Magical Practice* (Chicago 1997).

Ritner. R, 'Anubis and the Lunar Disc', *JEA* 71 (1985), 149–55.

Robinson. J, 'The First Christian Monastic Library', in W. Godlewski (ed.), *Coptic Studies, Acts of the Third International Congress of Coptic Studies, Warsaw, 20–25 August, 1984*, (Warsaw 1990), 371–78.

Robins. G, 'Hair and the Construction of Identity in Ancient Egypt, c. 1480–1350 BC', *JARCE* 36 (1999), 55–69.

Robinson. J, *The Pachomian Monastic Library at the Chester Beatty Library and the Bibliothèque Bodmer (The Institute for Antiquity and Christianity, Occasional Paper 19)* (Claremont 1990).

Roeten. L, *Loaves, Beds, Plants and Osiris, Considerations About the Emergence of the Cult of Osiris* (Oxford 2018).

Rogers. B, and Rathbone. D, *Egypt from Alexander to the Copts* (London 2004).

Römer. C, 'Das Werden zu Osiris im römischen Ägypten', *ARG* 2 (2000), 141–61.

Rondot. V, *Derniers visages des dieux d'Égypte, iconographies, panthéons et cultes dans le Fayoum hellénisé des IIe-IIIe siècles de notre ère, Passé présent* (Paris 2013).

Rondot. V, 'L'Empereur et le petit prince, les deux colosses d'Argo, iconographie, symbolique et datation', in V. Rondot, F. Alpi, and F. Villeneuve (eds.), *La pioche et la plume, autour du Soudan, du Liban et de la Jordanie, Hommages archéologiques à Patrice Lenoble* (Paris 2011), 413–40.

Rostovtzeff. M, 'Ancient Decorative Wall-Painting', *JHS* 39 (1919), 147–48.

Rostovtzeff. M, *Anticnaja dekorativnaja zivopis na juge Rossi I* (St Petersburg 1914).

Rowe. A, *Excavations of the Graeco-Roman Museum of Kom El-Shukafa During the Season* 1941–42, *BSRAA* 35, (1942).

Rowlandson. J, *Landowners and Tenants in Roman Egypt: The Social Relations of Agriculture in the Oxyrhynchite Nome* (Oxford 1996).

Rubensohn. O, 'Archäologische Funde im Jahre 1905', *AA* 21 (1906), col. 130–31.

Rutschowscaya. M, *Tissues coptes* (Paris 1990).

Ryhiner. M, *L'offrande du Lotus dans les temples égyptiens de l'époque tardive, Rites égyptiens* 6 (Brussels 1986).

Saint-Génis. M, 'Notice sur les restes de l'ancienne ville de Chemmis ou Panopolis, aujourd'hui Akhmim, et sur les environs', in C. Panckoucke (ed.), *Description de L'Egypte, ou Recueil des Observations et des Recherches qui été faites en Égypte pendant L'Expédition de L'Armée Française II* (Paris 1821), 43–65.

Saleh. M, 'Das Totenbuch in den thebanischen Beamtengrabern des Neuen Reiches. Texte und Vignetten', *AV* 46 (Mainz 1984).

Saragoza. F, and Georges-Zimmermann. P, 'Doublement éternel Quand les Égyptiens inhumaient leurs morts deux fois', *ENiM* 7 (2014), 61–78.

Savvopoulos. K, *Alexandrea in Aegypto, The Role of the Egyptian Tradition in the Hellenistic and Roman Periods, Ideology, Culture, Identity, and Public Life*, PhD thesis, University of Leiden (Leiden 2011).

Sauneron. S, *Villes et légendes, Bibliothèque d'études* 90 (Cairo 1983), 71–77.

Sauneron. S, and Vercouter. J, 'Persee, Dieu du Khemmis', *RdÉ* 14 (1962), 53–57.

Sauneron. S, 'Le Temple d'Akhmim describe par Ibn-Gobair', *BIFAO* 51(1952), 123–35.

Sauneron. S, 'Notes Géographiques sur le Nome Panopolite', *BIFAO* 4 (1905), 39–101.

Schäfer. H, *Kunstgeschichte in Bildern, I, Das Alterum* (Leipzig 1913).

Scharff. A, 'Ein Denkstein der Römischen Kaiserzeit aus Achmim', *ZÄS* 62 (1927), 86–107.

Schiaparelli. E, 'Chemmis (Akhmim) et la Sua Antica Necropolis', in Études archéologiques, linguistiques et historiques dédiées à Mr. Le Dr. C. *Leemans à l'occasion du cinquantième anniversaire de sa nomination aux fonctions de Directeur du Musée archéologique des Pays-Bas* (Leiden 1885), 85–88.

Schmidt. C, 'Ein Griechisches Mumienetikett aus Achmim', *ZÄS* 34 (1896), 80–81.

Schönbron. H, *Die Pastophoren im Kult der ägyptischen Götter, Beiträge zur klassischen Philologie* 80 (Meisenheim 1976).

Schönbauer. E, 'Die rechtliche Stellung der Metropoleis im römischen Ägypten', *Epigraphica* 11 (1949), 115–46.

Schoske. S, and Wildung. D, *Gott und Götter im alten Ägypten* (Mainz 1992).

Schott. S, *Das schöne Fest vom Wüstentale, Festbräuche einer Totenstadt* (Wiesbaden 1952).

Schott. S, 'Das blutrünstige Keltergerät', *ZÄS* 74 (1938), 88–93.

Schreiber. T, *Expedition Ernst Sieglin, Ausgrabungen in Alexandria, Die Nekropole von Kom–esc-schukafa* (Leipzig 1908).

Schrenk. S, 'Spätrömisch-frühislamische Textilien aus Ägypten', in S. Emmel, M. Klause, and S. Richter (eds.), *Ägypten und Nubien in spätantiker und christlicher Zeit. Akten des 6. Internationalen Koptologenkongresses Münster, 20.–26. Juli 1996. 1. Materielle Kultur, Kunst und religiöses Leben, Sprachen und Kulturen des christlichen Orients* 4 (Wiesbaden 1998), 339–78.

Schubart. W, 'Metrische Inschrift aus Ägypten', *AfP* 2 (1903), 94–95.

Schweitzer. A, 'L'évolution stylistique et iconographique des parures de cartonnage d'Akhmim du début de l'époque ptolémaïque à l'époque romaine', *BIFAO* 62 (1964), 325–52.

Seeber. C, 'Untersuchungen zur Darstellung des Totengerichts im Alten Ägypten', *MÄS* 35 (München, Berlin 1976).

Shaw. M, 'Ceiling Patterns from the Tomb of Hepzefa', AJA 74/1 (1970), 25–30.

Shawn. I, and Nicholson. P, *British Museum Dictionary of Ancient Egypt* (Cairo 2001).

Shorter. A, 'The God Nehebkau', *JEA* 21(1935), 41–48.

Sijpesteijn. P, 'Fourteen Ostraca from a Private Collection', *ZPE* 14 (1974), 229–39.

Sijpesteijn. P, 'Eine Sammlung von Mumientäfelchen im Allard Pierson Museum zu Amsterdam', *OMRO* 46 (1965), 34–43.

Skeat. K, *P. Panop. Beatty, Papyri from Panopolis in the Chester Beatty Library*, Proceedings of the IX International Congress of Papyrology, Oslo, 19th-22nd August 1958 (Oslo 1961), 194–99.

Smith. M, *Following Osiris, Perspectives on the Osirian Afterlife from Four Millennia* (Oxford 2017).

Smith. M, 'Bodl. Ms. Egypt. A.3 (P) and the Interface between Temple Cult and the Cult of The Dead,' in: *Ägyptische Rituale der griechisch-römischen Zeit, Heraugegben von Joachim Friedrich Quack, Orientalische Religionen in der Antike* 6 (Tübingen 2014), 145–55.

Smith. M, 'New References to the Deceased as Wsir n NN from the Third Intermediate Period and the Earliest Reference to a Deceased Woman as Ḥ.t– Ḥr NN', *RdÉ* 63 (2012), 187–96.

Smith. M, *Traversing the Afterlife, Texts for the Afterlife from Ptolemaic and Roman Egypt* (Oxford 2009).

Smith. M, *Papyrus Harkness (MMA 31.9.7)* (Oxford 2005).

Smith. M, 'Aspects of the Preservation and Transmission of Indigenous Religious Traditions in Akhmim and its Environs During the Graeco-Roman Period', in A. Egberts et al. (eds.), *Perspectives on Panopolis, An Egyptian Town from Alexander the Great to the Arab Conquest* (Leiden 2002), 233–47.

Smith. M, 'Dating Anthropoid Mummy Cases from Akhmim, the Evidence of the Demotic Inscriptions', in M. Bierbrier (ed.), *Portraits and Mummies, Burial Customs in Roman Egypt* (London 1997), 66–71.

Smith. M, 'Budge at Akhmim, January 1869', in C. Eyre, A. Leahy, and L. Leahy (eds.), *The Unbroken Reed, Studies in the Culture and Heritage of Ancient Egypt in Honour of A. F. Shore* (London 1994), 293–303.

Smith. M, *The Liturgy of Opening the Mouth for Breathing* (Oxford 1993).

Smith. M, 'New Middle Egyptian Texts in the Demotic Script,' *Sesto Congresso Internazionale di Egittologia* 2 (Turin 1993), 491–95.

Smith. M, 'A Demotic Formula of Intercession for the Deceased', *Enchoria* 19–20 (1992–1993), 131–54.

Smith. M, *The Mortuary Texts of Papyrus BM 10507, Catalogue of Demotic Papyri in the British Museum III* (London 1987).

Smith. M, 'Demotischer Mythos vom Sonnen-auge', *LÄ* V (1984), 1082–87.

Sonnini. C, *Voyage dans la Haute et Basse Égypte, fait par ordre de l'ancient gouvernement, III* (Paris 1880).

Spencer. P, 'Dance in Ancient Egypt', *NEA* 66 no.3 (2003), 96–102.

Spiegelberg. W, 'Miszellen, Der Gott Kolanthes', *ZÄS* 58 (1923), 155–56.

Spiegelberg. W, *Der ägyptische Mythus vom Sonnenauge (der Papyrus der Tierfabeln- „Kufi"). Nach dem Leidener demotischen Papyrus I 384* (Strasbourg 1917).

Spielgerberg. W, *Der Sagenkreis des Königs Petubastis* (Leipzig 1910).

Spiegelberg. W, *CGC: Die demotischen Inschriften* (Leipzig 1904).

Spiegelberg. W, Ägyptische und Griechische Eigennamen aus Mumienetiketten *der römischen Kaiserzeit auf Grund von grossenteils unveröffentlichen Material* (Leipzig 1901).

Stadler. M, 'Funerary Religion: The Final Phase of Egyptian Religion', in C. Riggs (ed.), *The*

Oxford Handbook of Roman Egypt (Oxford 2012), 383–98.

Stadler. M, 'The Funerary Texts of Papyrus Turin N. 766, A Demotic Book of Breathing (Part II)1 D. The Theban Context of Papyrus Turin N. 766', *Enchoria* 26 (2000), 110–24.

Stambaugh. J, Sarapis under the early Ptolemies, *EPRO* 25 (Leiden 1972).

Stewart. H, *Mummy Cases and Inscribed Funerary Cones in the Petrie Collection* (Warminster 1976).

Strasser. J, 'Les Olympia d'Alexandrie et le pancratiaste M. Aur .Asklèpiadès', *BCH* 128–29 (2004–05), 421–68.

Tacom. L, *Fragile Hierarchies, the Urban Elites of Third-Century Roman Egypt*, Mnemosyne Supplements 271 (Leiden 2006).

Tallet. G, 'Fragments d'El-Deir (Oasis de Kharga) au tournant de notre ère- À propos de Carl Schmidt et de William Hornblower', in G. Tallet and C. Zivie-Coche (eds.), *Le myrte et la rose, Mélanges offerts à Françoise Dunand par ses élèves*, Cahiers Égypte Nilotique et Méditerranéenne 9 (Montpellier 2014), 385–412.

Tallet. G, 'Isis, the Crocodiles, and the Mysteries of the Nile Flood: Interpreting a Scene from Roman Egypt Exhibited in the Egyptian Museum in Cairo (SE 30001)', in C. Scibona and A. Mastrocinque (eds.), *Demeter, Aphrodite, Isis, and Cybele: Studies in the Greek and Roman Religion in Honour of Giulia Sfameni Gasparro* (Stuttgart 2012), 137–60.

Tarasenko. M, 'Gliedervergottung Texts and Theogonic Ideas in Ancient Egypt', in A. Maravellia and N. Guilhou (eds.), *Environment and Religion in Ancient and Coptic Egypt, Sensing the Cosmos Through the Eyes of the Divine, Archaeopress Egyptology (BAR Publishing)* 30 (London 2020), 431–42.

Tarasenko. M, 'Images of Papyrus Rolls in Vignettes of the Book of the Dead', in K. Kóthay (ed.), *Burial and Mortuary Practices in Late Period and Graeco-Roman Egypt, Proceedings of the International Conference Held at the Museum of Fine Arts, Budapest, 17–19 July 2014* (Budapest 2017), 71–82.

Tarasenko. M, 'Mythological Allusions Connected with Cosmogony in BD 17', in B. Backes, I. Munro, and S. Stöhr (eds.), *Totenbuch-Forschungen: gesammelte Beiträge des 2. Internationalen Totenbuch-Symposiums, Bonn, 25. bis 29. September 2005, Studien zum Altägyptischen Totenbuch* (Wiesbaden 2006), 342–43.

Taylor. H, *Death and the Afterlife in Ancient Egypt* (London 2001).

Taylor. J, *Journey Through the Afterlife. Ancient Egyptian Book of the Dead* (London 2010).

Teeter. E, *Religion and Ritual in Ancient Egypt* (Cambridge 2011).

Thiers. C, 'Les jardins de temple aux époques tardives', in S. Aufrère (ed.), *Encyclopédie religieuse de l'Univers végétal, Croyances phytoreligieuses de l'Égypte ancienne, I* (Montpellier 1999), 107–20.

Thissen. H, 'Achmim und die Demotische Literature', in A. Egberts et al. (eds.), *Perspectives on Panopolis, An Egyptian Town from Alexander the Great to the Arab Conquest* (Leiden 2002), 249–60.

Thissen. H, 'Zur Begegnung von Christentum und Heiden, Schenute und Gessios', *Enchoria* 19–20 (1992–93), 155–64.

Thissen. H, ,'Der Verkommene Harfenspieler, Eine altägyptische Invektive (P. Wien KM 3877)', *Dem. Stud.* 11 (Sommerhausen 1992).

Thissen. H, 'Die Lehre des Anchscheschonqi (P.BM 10508)', *Papyrologische Texte und Abhandlungen* 32 (Bonn 1984).

Thomas. J, 'Chronological Notes on Documentary Papyri', *ZPE* 6 (1970), 177–80.

Thompson. E, *A Study of the Architecture of the Cemetery of El-Hawawish at Akhmim in Upper Egypt in the Old Kingdom*, MA thesis, Macquarie University (Sydney 2001).

Tiano. P, 'Biodegradation of Cultural Heritage, Decay Mechanisms and Control Methods', in *Proceedings of the ARIADNE Workshop* (Florence 2002), 7–12.

Timm. S, *Das Christlich-Koptische Ägypten in arabischer Zeit, Teil A-Z* (Wiesbaden 1992).

Tkacyow. B, 'An Imitation of Opus Alexandrinum in Wall Paintings? Two Wall Paintings from Kom El–Dikka (Alexandria)', *RecTrav* 17 (1995), 324–25.

Töpfer. S, 'Theory and Practice/Text and Mummies, The Instructions of the 'Embalming Ritual' in the Light of Archaeological Evidence', in K. Kóthay (ed.), *Burial and Mortuary Practices in Late Period and Graeco–Roman Egypt, Proceedings of the International Conference Held at the Museum of Fine Arts, Budapest, 17–19 July 2014* (Budapest 2017), 23–34.

Treu. K, 'Christliche Papyri XIV', *AFP* 35 (1989), 107–16.

Tricocohe. A, *L'eau dans les espaces et les pratiques funéraires d'Alexandrie aux époques grecque et romaine (IVe siècle av. J.-C.-IIIe siècle ap. J.-C.)*, BAR Publishing 1919 (Oxford 2009).

Trombley. F, *Hellenic Religion and Christianization C. 370–529* (Leiden, New York, Köln 1993–94).

Toynbee. J, *Death and Burial in the Roman World* (Baltimore 1971).

Valdesogo. M, *Hair and Death in Ancient Egypt, Mourning Rites in the Pharaonic Period* (Zandvoort 2019).

Valloggia. M, 'This sur la route des Oasis', *BIFAO* 81 suppl. (1981), 185–90.

Van der Vliet. J, 'Preface', in A. Eegberts et al. (eds.), *Perspectives in Panopolis, An Egyptian Town from Alexander the Great to the Arab Conquest XI* (Leiden 2002), xi–ii.

Van der Vliet. J, 'Spätantikes Heidentum in Ägypten im Spiegel der koptischen Literatur', in D. Willers (ed.), *Begegnung von Heidentum und Christentum im spätantiken Ägypten ,Riggisberger Berichte* 1 (Riggisberg 1993), 99–130.

Van Haarlem. W, *Corpus Antiquitatum Aegyptiacarum, Allard Pierson Museum, Amsterdam, IV, Sarcophagi and Related Objects* (Hildesheim 1998), 78–80.

Van Rengen. W, 'Panopolis', in *The Oxford Encyclopedia of Ancient History* (Oxford 2013), 5028–30.

Van Minnen. P, 'The Letter (and Other Papers) of Ammon, Panopolis in the Fourth Century AD', in *Perspectives in Panopolis, An Egyptian Town from Alexander the Great to the Arab Conquest* (Leiden 2002), 177–99.

Van Regen. W, 'A New Paneion at Mons Porphyrites', *CdÉ* 70 (1995), 240–45.

Van Regen. W, 'Les Jeux de Panopolis', *CdÉ* 46 (1971),136–41.

Van Walsem. R, 'The Coffin of Djedmonthuiufankh in the National Museum of Antiquities at Leiden', *DE* 43 (1997), 55–56.

Van Walsem. R, *The Coffin of Djedmonthiufankh in the National Museum of Antiquities of Leiden, I: Technical and Iconographic/ Iconological Aspects, II, Tables, Graphs etc.* (Leiden 1997).

Vandier. J, *Le Papyrus Jumilhac* (Paris 1961).

Vandier d'Abbadie. J, *Nestor l'Hot (1804–1842), Choix de documents conservés à la Bibliotheque National et aux Archives du Musée du Louvre, DMOA* 11 (Leiden 1963).

Vandorpe. K, 'Les villages des ibis dans la toponymie tardive', *Enchoria* 18 (1991),115–22.

Vandorpe. K, *Egyptische geografische elementen in Griekse transcriptie,* unpublished M.A. thesis, K.U. Leuven (Leuven 1988).

Veisse. A, 'Les 'révoltes égyptiennes', Recherches sur les troubles intérieurs en Égypte du règne de Ptolémée III à la conquête romaine', *StudHell* 41 (Leuven, Paris 2004).

Velazquez. F, El dios Bes: aspectos iconográficos en el ámbito fenicio-púnico con especial referencia a la Península Ibérica e Ibiza, Tomo I (Madrid 2001).

Venit. M, *Visualizing the Afterlife in the Tombs of the Graeco-Roman Period* (Cambridge 2016).

Venit. M, 'Alexandria', in C. Riggs (ed.), *The Oxford Handbook of Roman Egypt* (Oxford 2012), 103–21.

Venit. M, 'Referencing Isis in Tombs of Graeco-Roman Egypt, Tradition and Innovation', in L. Bricault and M. Versylus (eds.), *Isis on the Nile, Egyptian Gods in Hellenistic and Roman Egypt, Proceedings of the IVth International Conference of Isis Studies, Liège, November 27–29 2008, EPRO* 171 (Leiden 2010), 89–119.

Venit. M, 'Ancient Egyptomania, The Uses of Egypt in Graeco-Roman Alexandria', in E. Ehrenberg (ed.), *Leaving No Stones Unturned: Essays on the Ancient Near East and Egypt in Honor of Donald P. Hansen* (Winona Lake 2002), 261–78.

Venit. M, *Monumental Tombs of Ancient Alexandria, the Theatre of the Dead* (Cambridge 2002).

Venit. M 'The Stagni Painted Tomb, Cultural Interchange and Gender Difference in Roman Alexandria', *AJA* 103/4 (1999), 631-69.

Venit. M, 'The Tomb from Tigrain, Pasha Street and the Iconography of Death in Roman Alexandria', *AJA* 101/4 (1997), 701–29.

Vermasern. M, *Etudes Préliminaires aux Religions Orientales dans L'Empire Romain* (Leiden 1925).

Vercoutter. J, *The Search for Ancient Egypt* (New York 1992).

Vermeule. S, 'Aspects of Death in Early Greek Art and Poetry', *Sather Classical Lectures* 46 (London 1979).

Vittmann. G, 'Tradition und Neuerung in der demotischen Literatur', *ZÄS* 125 (1998), 62–77.

Vleeming. S, 'A Priestly Letter of Recommendation (P. CtYBR inv. 4628)', in R. Jasnow and G. Widmer (eds.), *Illuminating Osiris, Egyptological Studies in Honor of Mark Smith* (Atlanta 2017), 375–78.

Vleeming. S, 'Demotic Graffiti and Other Short Texts Gathered from Many Publications, Short Texts III 1201–2350', *StudDem* 8, 9, 12 (Leuven 2008, 2011, 2015).

Vleeming. S, *The Berichtungsliste of Demotic Documents in A. D. 2007* (Brauneberg 2008).

Vleeming. S, 'The Office of a Choachyte in the Theban Area', in S. Vleeming (ed.), *Hundred-Gated Thebes, Acts of a Colloquium on Thebes and the Theban Area in the Graeco-Roman Period, P.L. Bat.* 27 (Leiden 1995), 241–55.

Von Bissing. F, 'Zu den griechish-ägyptischen Darstellungen', in *Expedition von Sieglin, Die Nekropole von Kom-esch-Shukafa* (Leipzig 1908).

Von Bissing. F, 'Tombeaux d'Époque Romaine a Akhmim, Lettre ouverte au Dr Étienne Drioton', *ASAE* 50 (1950), 547–84.

Von Bissing. F, 'Aus Römischen Gräbern zu Achmim (Panopolis) in Oberägypten', *JDAI* 61/62 (1946/1947), 1–16.

Von Bissing, *La catacombe nouvellement découverte de Kom el Chougafa (Les bas-reliefs de Kom el Chougafa) (Drawings by E. Gillieron)*, Société archéologique d'Alexandrie (Munich 1901).

Von Bomhard. A, *The Egyptian Calendar, A Work for Eternity* (London 1999).

Von Gonzenbach. V, *Unterschunungen zu den knabenweihen im Isiskult der römischen Kaiserzeit, Antiquitas I; Abhandlungen zur alter Geschichte* (Bonn 1957).

Von Känel. F, 'Les prêtres-ouâb de Sekhmet et les conjurateurs de Serket, Bibliothèque de l'Ecole des hautes études', *Sciences religieuses* 87 (Paris 1984).

Von Lieven. A, 'Of Choachytes and Saints, Demotic Documentary Texts as Sources for Religious Practices,' in R. Jasnow and G. Widmer (eds.), *Illuminating Osiris, Egyptological Studies in Honor of Mark Smith* (Atlanta 2017).

Wagner. G, 'Bandelettes de momies et linges funéraire inscrits en grec', in J. Vercoutter (ed.), *Livre du centenaire. 1880–1980*, MIFAO 104 (Cairo 1980), 329–38.

Wagner. G, 'Les Oasis d'Egypte', *Bibliothèque d'Etude* 100 (Cairo 1987).

Wagner. G, 'Étiquettes de momies grecques de l'IFAO', *BIFAO* 74 (1974), 45–61.

Wainwright. G, 'Orion and the Great Star', *JEA* 22 (1936), 45–46.

Wainwright. G, 'Some Celestial Associations of Min', *JEA* 21 (1935), 152–70.

Walker. S, and Montserrat. D, 'A Journey to the Next World: The Shroud of a Youth from Roman Egypt', *Apollo* 148, no. 437 (1998), 15–19.

Walker. S, and Bierbrier. M, *Ancient Faces, Mummy Portraits from Roman Egypt A Catalogue of Roman Portraits in the British Museum IV* (London 1997).

Wallert. I, ,'Die Palmen in alten Ägypten. Eine Untersuchung ihrer praktischen, symbolischen und religiösen Bedeutung', *MÄS* 1 (Berlin, 1962).

Wallin. P, *Celestial Cycles, Astronomical Concepts of Regeneration in the Ancient Egyptian Coffin Texts*, USE I (Uppsala 2002).

Walters. W, *Attic Grave Reliefs that Represent Women in the Dress of Isis, Hesperia Supplement XXII* (Princeton 1988).

Ward. B, *The Sayings of the Desert Fathers. The Alphabetical Collection* (Kalamazoo 1984).

Watterson. B, *The Gods of Egypt* (London 1984).

Weber. W, *Die Ägyptische-Griechischen Terrakoten* (Berlin 1914).

Welles. B, 'The Garden of Ptolemagrios at Panopolis', *TAPA* 77 (1946), 192–206.

Whitehorne. J, 'The Pagan Cults of Roman Oxyrhynchus', *ANRW* II.18.5 (1995), 3050–91.

Whittemore. T, 'The Sawama Cemeteries', *JEA* 1 (1994), 246–47.

Whitehouse. H, 'Roman in Life, Egyptian in Death, The Painted Tomb of Petosiris in the Dakhla Oasis', in O. Kaper (ed.), *Life on the Fringe, Living in the Southern Egyptian Desert During the Roman and Early Byzantine Periods, Proceedings of a Colloquium Held on the Occasion of the 25th Anniversary of the Netherlands Institute for Archaeology and Arabic Studies in Cairo 9–12 December 1996* (Leiden 1998), 253–70.

Wiedemann. A, 'Der Apis als Totenträger', *OLZ* 20 (Leipzig 1917), 298–303.

Wiese. A, and Brodbeck. A, *Tutankhamun. Das goldene Jenseits. Grabschätze aus dem Tal der Könige* (München, 2004).

Wilcken. U, 'Die Achmîm-Papyri in der Bibliothèque Nationale de Paris', in *Sitzungsber. Kgl. Preus. Akad.* (1887), 807–20.

Wilcken. U, 'Kaiserliche Tempelverwaltung in Aegypten', *Hermes* 23 (1888), 592–606.

Wild. R, *Water in the Cultic Worship of Isis and Serapis*, EPRO 87 (Leiden 1981).

Wilhelm. A, *Die Gedichte des Ptolemagrios aus Panopolis* (Wien 1948).

Wilkinson. T, *The Complete Gods and Goddesses of Ancient Egypt* (New York 2003).

Wilkinson. J, *Manners and Costumes of the Ancient Egyptians II* (London 1843).

Willeitne. J, 'Tomb and Burial Customs After Alexander the Great,' in R. Schulz and M. Seidel (eds.), *Egypt the World of the Pharaohs* (Köln 2004), 313–21.

Willems. H, and Clarysse. W, *Les Empereurs du Nil, à la mémoire de Jan Quaegebeur* (Leuven 2000).

Willems. H, and Clarysse. W, *Keizers aan de Nijl* (Leuven 1999).

Willems. H, 'Anubis as a Judge', in W. Clarysse, A. Schoors, and H. Willems (eds.), *Egyptian Religion, the Last Thousand Years, Studies Dedicated to the Memory of Jan Quaegebeur*, OLA 84.II (Leuven 1998), 719–43.

Willis. W, and Maresch. K, *The Archive of Ammon Scholasticus of Panopolis (P. Ammon), The Legacy of Harpocration, Texts from the Collections of Duke University and the Universität zu Köln*, PC 26/1 (Köln 1997).

Willis. W, 'The Letter of Ammon of Panopolis to His Mother', in *Actes du XVe Congrès international de papyrologie, Bruxelles-Louvain, 29 août- 3 septembre 1977. II. Pap.Brux*. 17 (Brussels 1979), 98–115.

Willis. W, 'Two Literary Papyri in an Archive from Panopolis', *ICS* 3 (1978), 140–53.

Winkler. A, 'Stellar Scientists: The Egyptian Temple Astrologers', *JNES* 8 (2021), 91–145.

Winkler. A, and Zellmann-Rohrer. M, 'Zodiacs and Monuments: An Early Pictorial 'Horoscope' from Egypt', *JHA* 54 (forthcoming, 2023).

Wipszycka. E, *L'industrie textile* (Krakow 1965).

Witt. R, *Isis in the Graeco-Roman World* (London 1971).

Worp. K, 'Localisation d'un camp de l'armée romaine à Psinabla', *Eirene* 52 (2016), 271–76.

Wreszinski. W, *Von Kairo bis Wadi Halfa* (Leipzig 1927).

Wreszinki. W, *Der Grosse medizinische Papyrus des Berliner Museums* (Leipzig 1909).

Xanthaki-Karamanou. G, 'Hellenistic Drama and Alexandrian Culture', in C. Zerefos and M. Vardinoyannis (eds.), *Hellenistic Alexandria: Celebrating 24 Centuries: Papers Presented at the Conference Held on December 13-15 2017 at the Acropolis Museum, Athens, Archaeopress (BAR Publishing)* (Oxford 2018), 139–47.

Youtie. H, 'P.Gen. inv. 108= SB VIII 9902', *ZPE* 7 (1971), 170–71.

Yoyotte. J, 'Une épithète de Min comme explorateur des régions orientales', *RdÉ* 9 (1952), 125–37.

Žabkar. L, 'A Study of the BA Concept in Ancient Egyptian Texts', *SAOC* 34 (Chicago 1968).

Zandee. J, 'A Site of Conflict between Horus and Seth', in P. Prior (ed.), *Exorbe Religionum Studia Geo widengren* (Leiden 1972), 32–38.

Zandee. J, *Death as an Enemy According to Ancient Egyptian Conceptions, Studies in the History of Religions* V (Leiden 1960).

Zauzich. K, 'Einige unerkannte Ortsnamen', *Enchoria* 15 (1987), 169–70.

Zauzich. K, 'Drei demotisch-koptische Ortsnamen aus der Gegend von Achmim', *Enchoria* 11 (1982), 117–18.

Zauzich. K, 'Verteidigung eines Mumienschildes', *ZÄS* 114 (1987), 95–100.

Zingarelli. A, 'Some Considerations About the Water Offered (Poured) by the Tree-Goddess at TT49', in *L'Acqua Nell'Antico Egitto, Vita, Rigenerazione, Incantesimo, Medicamento, Proceedings of the First International Conference for Young Egyptologists, Italy, Chianciano Terme, October 15–18, 2003* (Rome 2005), 381–88.

Milton Keynes UK
Ingram Content Group UK Ltd.
UKHW050941080823
426501UK00006B/21